MW00991911

THE 4TH MARINE BRIGADE
AT BELLEAU WOOD
AND SOISSONS

THE 4TH MARINE BRIGADE AT BELLEAU WOOD AND SOISSONS

History and Battlefield Guide

J. Michael Miller

Foreword by Lt. Gen. Richard P. Mills, USMC (Ret.)

University Press of Kansas

Published by the University Press of Kansas (Lawrence, Kansas 66045),
which was organized by the Kansas Board of Regents and is operated
and funded by Emporia State University, Fort Hays State University,
Kansas State University, Pittsburg State University, the University of
Kansas, and Wichita State University

Library of Congress Cataloging-in-Publication Data

Names: Miller, J. Michael, author.
Title: The 4th Marine Brigade at Belleau Wood and Soissons / J. Michael Miller ;
foreword by Lieutenant General Richard P. Mills, USMC (Ret.)
Description: [Lawrence] : [University Press of Kansas], [2020] |
Includes bibliographical references and index.
Identifiers: LCCN 2019045401
ISBN 9780700629565 (cloth)
ISBN 9780700629572 (paperback)
ISBN 9780700629589 (epub)
Subjects: LCSH: Belleau Wood, Battle of, France, 1918. | Soissons, Battle of,
France, 1918. | United States. Marine Corps. Marine Brigade, 4th. | World War,
1914–1918—Regimental histories—United States.
Classification: LCC D545.B4 M55 2020 | DDC 940.4/34—dc23
LC record available at https://lccn.loc.gov/2019045401.

British Library Cataloguing-in-Publication Data is available.

Printed in the United States of America

10 9 8 7 6 5 4 3 2 1

The paper used in this publication is recycled and contains 30 percent
postconsumer waste. It is acid free and meets the minimum
requirements of the American National Standard for Permanence of
Paper for Printed Library Materials Z39.48-1992.

CONTENTS

ILLUSTRATIONS

Photographs

Maps

Charts

FOREWORD

The experience in France during the First World War was a watershed event in the history of the United States Marine Corps. The Corps was a minor adjunct to the American military in 1918, but its involvement in the war changed that forevermore. The experience in France in 1918 altered the public persona of the US Marines, and it educated the generation of Marine Corps leaders who would win the Pacific campaign during the Second World War. The ripple-down effect through the years had a significant impact on the Marine Corps' character and attitude. As a result, the Corps became known as the "First to Fight" and the "Devil Dogs." One can argue that today's Marine Corps, with its brilliant record of success in World War II, Korea, Vietnam, Iraq, and Afghanistan, owes its existence to a commandant who demanded that the US Marines go to France and to a group of Marines who, once there, fought and sacrificed to prove they belonged on a modern battlefield.

The Marine Corps had done little during the American Civil War, and its role as a colonial constabulary and naval landing force in the late 1800s did little to embellish its reputation or gain support in Congress. Even the Marines' role as a brigade landing force during the Spanish-American War was considered an ad hoc mission hastily organized and executed. Their traditional assignment as an auxiliary to the US Navy did nothing to prepare them to fight a modern war on land against a first-rate enemy. Indeed, except during the Spanish-American War, the Marine Corps seldom operated at even the regimental level, let alone in larger, more complex formations. Its headquarters, training commands, and troop units were scattered along the East Coast of the United States and at navy facilities around the globe. Although newspaperman William Randolph Hearst had popularized the phrase "The Marines have landed and the situation is well in hand," the Corps' role in major operations in the event of war was in question.

But it took just a few days to change all that. A few hot days in June 1918 on the outskirts of Paris showed that perhaps the strongest fighting force up to that time, the Imperial German Army, could be stopped dead in its tracks during its last desperate attempt to capture the French capital and win the war. As the Allied front crumpled, it was the Marines of the 4th Brigade, finally freed from rear-area duties, who made a stand, fought the Battle of Belleau Wood, and changed history. Marines by the name of Lejeune, Cates,

Shepard, and Daly took their place on the world stage and would lead the Marine Corps to victory in 1918 and for years afterward.

Contrary to popular belief, Belleau Wood was not the end of the fight for the Marines of the 4th Brigade. They would go on to participate in the entire Soissons campaign and continue to distinguish themselves, and suffer casualties, until their final occupation duty on the Rhine and the end of the war.

While the US Army's contributions to the Battle of Belleau Wood and the Soissons campaign cannot be forgotten, Professor Miller's book concentrates on the story of the US Marine Corps. He examines the Corps' preparation as it readied for war and its initial contributions to the fighting. He discusses the senior leadership's determination to have the Marines involved in any fight the United States waged and tells the story of the courage and gallantry of individual Marines once they became engaged. In a larger sense, Professor Miller looks at an America fresh on the international stage, ready to flex its military muscle in defense of friends and allies. It is a scenario that has played out in many places since then. The United States is often slow to commit its young men and women to a fight, but once it does, no matter how grim the conditions, it is determined to win. An officer of the 4th Brigade may have summed up the American character best when he told a French officer urging withdrawal: "Retreat, hell! We just got here."

Lt. Gen. Richard P. Mills, USMC (Ret.)

PREFACE

Chaque objet possede une ame. (Every object possesses a soul.)

A few momentous decisions shape the course of every career. The first one I made occurred in 1983, when I was a very young curator of personal papers for the US Marine Corps. After considerable thought, I decided that my first major initiative would be to reach out to the fast-disappearing Marine Corps veterans of World War I. I searched the country for these men and women who were, at that time, in their golden years. I succeeded far beyond my expectations, reaching more than fifty veterans over the next ten years. I found them scattered across the country, each with his or her own story to tell. They donated their letters, diaries, photographs, memoirs, and artifacts, such as pieces of their own uniforms and other gear. A few contributed some ghostly artifacts of battle, such as German potato-masher grenades and scarred enemy helmets. The best moments we shared occurred during our interviews, when I was able to ask them about their service. I came to know them well, and they provided my first real moments of historical clarity. The battles I had read about were real events fought by real people who still cried about their lost comrades and still laughed at the same jokes told so long ago on the battlefields of Europe.

I count myself lucky to have known these Marines. Few other Americans have had the privilege of talking with veterans of World War I. They shaped my more-than-three-decade career in Marine Corps history. Everything I did during that career focused on one major point: preserve their history so that other Americans will know them as I do.

Many Marines of the Great War era went to France and are so recognized in history. Many others did not, and their stories reflect their duty in Cuba, Haiti, and the Dominican Republic. Others sat in Texas, watching over the Mexican oil fields. Perhaps the most bitter Marines were those of the 5th Brigade, who arrived in France too late to get into the fight. The three female Marines I met were all superb women, bursting with pride when they spoke of their service. Most of the combat Marines broke down in tears during our interviews, still mourning their friends lost in the wheat fields of Belleau Wood. Two of the Marines were over 100 years of age and passed away only months after I talked with them. But they were still proud of their service, one gripping my hand until it hurt as he sang every word of the Marine Hymn.

After one interview, the veteran's wife called to thank me for helping him get over his nightmares of France. He was able to sleep quietly for the first time in their marriage after releasing himself from the terrors of combat. He had been eviscerated by shrapnel and placed in a line of men waiting to die, while nearby, another line of wounded was waiting to be treated. He crawled off his stretcher and joined the line of men who had a chance to survive their wounds. He lived, but his identification tags were left behind in the line of dying men, and as a result, his family received a telegram informing them of his death. Only a letter from him ended their mourning, which turned to joy.

My determination not to let these stories be forgotten resulted in this book, the first in a series of histories I intend to write in my retirement. I made that pledge years ago, and now readers will know these individuals as I do. They will not be forgotten.

ACKNOWLEDGMENTS

As any author will gladly admit, the essential process of writing a book requires a cast of many, including family, friends, archivists, librarians, curators, and historians. A full list of everyone who provided support would require volumes. Conspicuous among those allies are the many archivists whose collections formed the backbone of this work. These hardworking professionals selflessly shared their accumulated knowledge to make this work possible and offered encouragement after long days spent in their reading rooms. Trevor K. Plante and Timothy K. Nenninger of the National Archives deserve prominent mention for their tireless assistance and friendship, which extend over many years.

Without question, the staff of the Marine Corps History Division in Quantico, Virginia, proved invaluable. Dr. James A. Ginther Jr. traveled the tangled roads of inquiry with me during the years of research and writing, fulfilling last-minute requests for information from across the Atlantic as well as from the nearby archives reading room. His camaraderie and support were incomparable. The staff of the Reference Section and Oral History Section of the History Division, along with the staff of the Alfred M. Gray Research Center Library, expertly responded to even my seemingly inexplicable requests for information with smiles and support.

Equally valuable was the staff at the Army History and Education Center in Carlisle, Pennsylvania. The years that passed during the formation of this book also saw the passing of Richard J. "Dick" Sommers, a lifelong friend who provided incalculable professional inspiration that greatly influenced my view of military history the way it should be written. Everyone on the staff at Carlisle assisted me during my seemingly endless string of research visits. Prominent among them were Melissa K. Wiford and Jessica J. Sheets, who tirelessly supported this endeavor with the treasures of their collection but also with their sincere camaraderie in striving for the best in our professional ventures.

The Service Historique de la Défense (SHD) in the Château de Vincennes in Paris is one of the most prominent military archives in the world and ably supported the work of this American historian. Alexandre Sheldon-Duplaix remained a steadfast ally throughout the years of research for this book, renewing the American and French alliance of 1918. The French perspective of American battles is essential to understanding the events of 1918, and the staff of the SHD generously supported my endeavors. The fruits of this research will no doubt illuminate future volumes of World War I Marine history. Guillaume Ange and his colleagues at the Agence d'images de la Défense proved invaluable; their encyclopedic knowledge of their photograph collection allowed the images in this work to be published in book form for the first time.

Jonathan Casey of the National World War I Museum and Memorial in Kansas City provided stalwart support during the writing of this work, as did Desiree Butterfield-Nagy at the Special Collections, Raymond H. Fogler Library, University of Maine. James Zobel of the MacArthur Memorial in Norfolk, Virginia, shared his professional camaraderie and encyclopedic knowledge of the Rainbow Division, while the entire staff of the Manuscript Division of the Library of Congress expertly responded to even my most peculiar requests. Dr. Carol Reardon deserves a special thank-you for her friendship as well as expert advice over many years.

Many more historians and archivists and librarians across the country helped this relentless, single-minded researcher, and there are too many to list individually. But they should know that their professional dedication helped this work give voice to so many persons from the past, allowing these soldiers, sailors, and Marines to have their stories told and not be forgotten. Thank you.

Mention must be made of the Marines who guided me in my apprenticeship in Marine Corps history. Commandant General Wallace M. Greene Jr. took an interest in the career of this young archivist beginning in 1983, spending many hours relating his own experiences and at the same time providing insight into the complicated ethos of the Marine Corps. Major General John P. Condon did the same, including his invaluable observations about Marine Corps aviation. World War II–era Marines George C. "Mac" MacGillivray, James Leon, and Carl M. "Bud" DeVere Sr. became lifelong friends, and their accounts of Japanese banzai charges on Guadalcanal, the battleship shelling of Henderson Field, the piloting of Corsairs against Japanese fighters on Okinawa, and the shoot-down of Yamamoto will be remembered forever. A special thanks goes to Brigadier General Edwin H. Simmons, who imparted his devotion to excellence early in my career. All but one of these men are now gone, but never forgotten.

The mountain of research required for this book was made possible by the Marine Corps University Foundation (MCUF) in Quantico, Virginia. My sincere gratitude goes out to Lieutenant General Richard P. Mills, USMC (Ret.), and his staff; they met every challenge that came their way during my work, from ensuring that French photographs found their way into these pages to facilitating my travel to such diverse places as Willacoohie, Georgia, and Fort McKinley, Maine. Colonel Jon Sachrison, USMC (Ret.), fulfilled every obscure request with flying colors, and Kimberly Niero in many ways proved to be my kindred spirit in the trenches. She smiled at every challenge I offered up, rendering order into the chaos of research and writing. Most of all, the support the MCUF provides to Marines on a daily basis was a constant reminder that they were the focus of this project.

Steve Stanley and Michael Beard proved superb mapmakers and chart builders. These pieces of the historian's puzzle are invaluable to understanding what happened in the summer of 1918. Both Steve and Michael answered my calls with a telepathic understanding of my thoughts and turned them into exactly what was needed. Many thanks to both of these gentlemen for their kindness and expert professional abilities.

My sincerest thanks and a round of applause to the staff of the University Press of Kansas. Hannah Coleman, editorial assistant, checked all the unique photographs and maps that make this book come alive. Kelly Jacques, production manager, helped me navigate the early stages of map preparation. Karl Janssen, art director, designed the superb cover for this work. Colin Tripp, production editor, guided this work through the editing and production process with expert precision. You all made this book a joy to complete. A special thanks goes out to editor in chief Joyce Harrison. Every author should have an editor like Joyce. Her skilled guidance during the writing of this book proved essential, as was her empathy for the Marines and soldiers described within these pages.

If there is one shining light among all those who contributed to this work, Sarah Holcomb deserves that star. Words cannot describe the many ways she contributed to this work, but her most important influence was the constant belief that this book (and those that will follow) is an essential chronicle of Marine Corps history and that I should be the one to write it. Although writing is sometimes glamorized in the media, the actual work is essentially a solitary exercise. But whenever I struck a wall in writing this narrative, Sarah provided the inspiration to overcome every obstacle. The long transatlantic flights we took were memorable, as were the idiosyncrasies of the cars we drove. Walking the pristine battlefields detailed in this work provided immeasurable insights into the Marines of 1918. The experience of visiting the cemeteries, fields, and forests and the hallowed halls of the Château de Vincennes provided inspiration that is reflected on every page of this book.

Every historian should be lucky enough to have friends like Bill and Marion Harris, Steve and Hannah Burns, Kurt Salziger, Tom and Karren Darone, and the late Al Ellis to accompany them on their writing journeys. Their kind support proved incomparable, no matter how far away my ramblings took me.

Most of all, my family bore the brunt of my peculiar immersive writing style. This work absolutely depended on their love, which fortified me in the early-morning hours and is reflected in every word written on every page. My twins most likely never informed their spouses of their father's eccentricities, but they soon discovered them on their own. Cody and Heather Miller of Boone, North Carolina, and Kalee and Corey Long of Fairfax, Virginia, formed my support team, bringing me back from 1918 as needed, and their children, Harper, Jake, and Beckett, provided the motivation to ensure that future generations will remember the sacrifices of the past.

Ultimately, my thanks go out to my wife, Debbie. She endured my travel and walked too many battlefields with me, helping with every phase of this work. Supporting a spouse who mentally travels to the past on a daily basis was not part of our wedding vows, but she adeptly made my work possible with her constant love and encouragement throughout this journey. This work is an inspirational reflection of her strength and commitment, which together made this book possible.

Introduction

THE PRESENCE OF A MARINE CORPS BRIGADE as part of the American Expeditionary Force (AEF) required a timely series of "miracles." The efforts of Major General Commandant George Barnett to send Marines to France met with initial refusal and then recurring rebuffs from the War Department and the US commander in France, General John J. Pershing. After the personal intervention of President Woodrow Wilson, three battalions constituting a Marine regiment were allowed to go to France with the first contingent of the US Army's 1st Division. However, this regiment did not yet exist; it had to be created. Colonel John A. Lejeune, the assistant commandant, received the assignment to establish this unit, known as the 5th Regiment, in time to join the army expedition. The time-honored Marine tradition of quickly forming expeditionary units from small, scattered detachments would be severely tested.

The cyclone of "miracles" originated at Marine Corps headquarters in Washington, DC, and then centered at the Philadelphia Navy Yard, well known as the source of many Marine Corps expeditions and, most importantly, the recent home of the Marine Advanced Base Force. A flood of orders emanating from Colonel Lejeune instantly generated a flurry of activity in Philadelphia as well as in Marine Corps detachments in navy yards along the East Coast of the United States, in the Caribbean, and in the Atlantic Fleet. Each commander from colonel to captain was accustomed to the cadence of rapid deployments, but this time, the United States' entrance into a world war added a spark of electricity to each moment of preparation.

The genesis of Major Julius S. Turrill's 1st Battalion began at the Marine Barracks in the Portsmouth, Virginia, Navy Yard. Marines from the various battleships of the Atlantic Fleet assembled there to form expeditionary companies. The detachment from the USS *New Hampshire* under Second Lieutenant George W. Hamilton merged into the 49th Company, which was already assigned to the navy yard. Marines from the USS *Louisiana* came ashore to create the 66th Company, and detachments from the USS *Alabama* and USS *Nebraska* combined to establish the 67th Company. The arrival of the 15th Company from the Marine Barracks in the Pensacola Navy Yard completed the battalion's four-company organization.

On May 25, 1917, Turrill's battalion moved by ship up the Potomac River to the newly acquired training base at Quantico, Virginia. Once they were ashore, Turrill's men found no trace of a military presence except for a string of tents occupied by a detachment of Marines in quarantine. The 49th Company later proudly claimed the dubious honor of erecting the second row of tents on what would eventually become a vital base. The 66th Company did little better. "We had to chase cows out of the field," recollected Private Albert Powis, "before we could put up our pyramid tents."[1]

Although a "beachhead" had now been established at Quantico, Philadelphia remained the most advantageous place to assemble the remaining 2nd and 3rd Battalions. Under the original plan, the nucleus of each battalion would comprise seasoned veterans drawn from deployments in Haiti and the Dominican Republic; the units would then be filled out with an influx of new recruits graduating from training. However, that plan was quickly altered.

Major Frederic M. Wise was already stationed at the Philadelphia Navy Yard when war was declared. After reading in the newspapers that a new Marine Corps regiment was being established for duty in France, Wise decided to go to headquarters and seek a command in the new unit. As a veteran of the Boxer Rebellion, the Philippine Insurrection, Cuba, Vera Cruz, Haiti, the Dominican Republic, and other Marine Corps expeditions, Wise found that the idea of a new war brought out his fighting spirit. He would not be denied a place in the new regiment, even though he had just returned from the Caribbean on Christmas Day 1916 and was a newlywed, having married his wife, Ethel, on May 5.

Before Wise could take action, his telephone rang, and Colonel Lejeune was on the other end of the line. Lejeune informed Wise that he had been selected to command one of the new battalions of the 5th Marines, if he agreed to accept the position. "It isn't your turn for foreign duty, as you have just got back from a tour," Lejeune told him, "but we want you to go. Do you object?" Wise spoke without hesitation. "You give me a plank for a transport," he replied, "and I'll go." Lejeune then informed Wise that Colonel Charles A. Doyen would command the regiment, with Lieutenant Colonel Logan Feland serving as the executive officer. Both men were old comrades of Wise's from many previous campaigns. Years later, Wise would state in his memoirs, "Mrs. Wise was just as pleased as I was."[2]

With the Marines from the Caribbean deployments now at the navy yard, Wise and Major Charles T. Wescott began the process of weeding out the veterans who were unfit. This proved to be a difficult task. "I went around to the company commanders," Wise wrote, "and told them we didn't want a man who had the slightest thing wrong with him." This soon created a storm among the rejected noncommissioned officers, who approached Wise with a vengeance. He was inflexible. "I told them they were too old," he remembered, "that they couldn't stand the gaff in France; that it was a young man's game."[3]

Each of the four companies was reduced to approximately forty veterans. Wise then brought the companies up to their proper strength with an influx of about 200 young recruits. These fledgling Marines arrived directly from the farms, small towns, and great cities of America—educated young men from upper-class families and rough sharpers from the mean streets. They were all bound by one theme: a desire to serve their country, even if that meant sacrificing their lives. "From all of which and a dash of good luck, perhaps, we caught something of an undying spirit," Captain Joseph D. Murray commented after the war, "though plenty of us did die."[4]

Captain Murray, commander of the 43rd Company, was facing the complete reformation of his company in less than two weeks. He was assisted by two second lieutenants fresh from the Virginia Military Institute (VMI): Benjamin Goodman and Charles Nash. Ben Goodman was a star football player from Hampton, Virginia, who had served as president of the Monogram Club. Charley Nash hailed from Alderson, West Virginia, and had been the captain of Company C, Corps of Cadets. Both had graduated from VMI on May 2 and then passed the Marine Corps examination. With less than a month of experience, Goodman and Nash had much to learn to prepare their Marines for combat.[5]

Given the inexperience of his lieutenants, Murray relied heavily on Gunner Charley Dunbeck, a grizzled veteran of many campaigns who was normally quiet and reserved. Dunbeck immediately recognized the challenge before him and took charge of the newly enlisted officers and men, becoming the backbone of the company. First Sergeant James Gallivan, an old salt of mythical proportions, worked in tandem with Dunbeck to square away the company. Major Wise, who already knew Gallivan, advised Murray to leave the older man behind, noting that although "he was too old for the rigors of war . . . he would make an excellent drill-master for the hordes of recruits, volunteers all, pouring in hourly."[6]

By some means, Gallivan learned of the "plot" to keep him out of the war. The thought of being left behind sent him into a rage, and he first blindsided Captain Murray. "He was in a more agitated state than I'd have believed possible in such a staunch oldtimer," Murray remembered. He advised Gallivan to see Wise in person and argue his case. The tough Irishman bided his time and then ambushed Wise as he walked across the yard, stating, "I hear, sor, that you're not goin' t' take me t' France." Wise countered simply, "That's right." Gallivan respectfully replied, "There's room in France for both av us, sor." As a veteran commander of many campaigns, Wise instinctively knew that he would need this man in combat and conceded victory to the Irishman. Captain Murray knew the results of the encounter as soon as Gallivan returned, evidenced by the wide grin on the sergeant's face. "He was a persuasive old harp," Murray recollected, "and really in better shape physically than half of the youngsters in the company." As Wise would later write in his memoir, "It was one of the best decisions I ever made."[7]

Each veteran infantry company was filled to war strength with fresh recruits from Parris Island and the Philadelphia Navy Yard. The few remaining veterans of Mexico, Cuba, Haiti, China, and elsewhere banded together to teach the new "boots" the ways of the Marine Corps. Most of the companies developed their own style, polished by the individuality of their officers and senior enlisted men. The mascot of the 43rd Company was a coati that Captain Murray had acquired from a young lady in Vera Cruz during the landing there in 1914. The Marines of 43rd Company called the animal "Jimmy" and identified him as a "honey bear," as no one could figure out his actual species. Jimmy was already a veteran and served as a source of pride for every man in the company. The young coati accepted all Marines as shipmates, no matter how recent their enlistment date.[8]

Once the eight companies were formed, the Marines embarked on a frenzy of focused activity. Almost every man had something to first learn and then master, particularly in terms of rank and responsibility. Major Wise commented with wonder as he watched his new leaders: "non-coms putting recruits, who had never worn a uniform before, through their first drill; new non-coms up from the ranks with their first chevrons; old non-coms with their first commissions; lieutenants suddenly made captains years before they expected it."[9] All of them knew that there was little time before they would be ordered to begin the journey overseas.

The fundamental fighting unit in the Marine Brigade was the rifle company. Although there were many similarities with the prewar organization of US Army companies, there were a number of differences in similar Marine Corps organizations, including the fundamental designation of companies. In the early months of 1914 all Marine companies were numbered to assist in the rapid composition of expeditionary forces while retaining some sense of stable organization from one deployment to the next. The numbered company system was carried over to France with every Marine Corps unit.

However, the Marine Corps conformed to the US Army table of organization and command structure as part of the agreement that allowed Marines to participate in the American Expeditionary Force. The army tables of organization required 256-man companies, each commanded by a captain. Four companies formed a 1,024-man army or Marine battalion, led by a major. A 3,806-man regiment consisted of three battalions commanded by a colonel. Supply and headquarters companies were attached to the regimental command, along with a machine gun company. Two regiments formed an entire brigade, amounting to 8,417 men under the command of a brigadier general. The brigade also included expanded support units, such as medical and ordnance units, and a four-company machine gun battalion.[10]

For example, the 74th, 75th, 76th, and 95th Companies belonged to the 1st Battalion, 6th Marines; each company had 6 officers and at least 256 enlisted men. A captain led each company, supported by a first lieutenant executive officer, first sergeant, supply sergeant, mess sergeant, sergeant, and four runners. Each company was divided into four platoons; in the 74th Company, two were commanded by a first lieutenant, and two by a second lieutenant. Each officer utilized a sergeant as his second in command. Each platoon of the 74th Company was divided into four sections of varying size and composition, as follows:[11]

1st Section: corporal, twelve men (hand grenades)
2nd Section: corporal, nine men (rifle grenades)
3rd Section: sergeant, seventeen men (riflemen)
4th Section: sergeant, fifteen men (automatic riflemen)

Companies were seldom at full strength. Providing the large number of lieutenants required to staff these companies proved to be a constant source of frustration for the rapidly expanding Marine Corps of 1917. When war was declared, only 511 Marine Corps officers were on active duty, supported by 43 reserve officers. Of this number, only 193 were first or second lieutenants. A full-strength brigade required at least 38 captains and 179 first and second lieutenants. To meet this challenge, the Marine Corps pulled together 761 new officer candidates from April through October 1917, including graduates and former graduates from the US Naval Academy, warrant officers, paymaster clerks, and noncommissioned officers. However, the largest contingent of officer candidates, numbering 284, were graduates of military schools such as the Virginia Military Institute, Norwich Academy, Texas A&M, Virginia Polytechnical Institute, and Culver Military Academy. Another 136 civilian candidates were found who either possessed some type of military training or passed a competitive examination on July 10, 1917. Many of these men were from the great universities across the nation and were champion athletes.[12]

The task of expanding the Marine Corps' enlisted ranks proved just as difficult. With a prewar enlisted strength of 13,725, obtaining and training the 8,417 Marines required for a brigade in France would have been a lengthy process—taking months the Marine Corps could not afford. Massive numbers of men enlisted in the first days of the war, which seemed encouraging. The Marine Corps received 14,607 applications by April 30, 1917, and another 15,498 the following month. However, most of these men were deemed physically unfit for service by navy medical officers. Only 2,864 men became Marines in April and another 5,295 in May—an alarming 27 percent acceptance rate.[13]

The fledgling base in Quantico, Virginia, quickly replaced Philadelphia as the primary assembly area for Marine Corps units during World War I. Living conditions were spartan for much of 1917, as civilian construction crews poured into the town to build the many facilities necessary to accommodate the Marines arriving from recruit depots at Mare Island, California, and Parris Island, South Carolina. The influx of recruits and laborers resulted in an invasion of prostitutes, who arrived on the trains that conveniently ran directly through the base. These women set up shop in town and began a prosperous trade, particularly on payday weekends. This activity came to the attention of the post adjutant, Captain William T. Hoadley, who ordered First Lieutenant William B. Worton to gather up all the women from the "houses of ill repute," escort them to the train station, and issue each lady a one-way ticket out of town. Worton wisely waited until after the weekend, noting, "If we'd gone in there Saturday, we'd [have] had a row with the construction workers, had to fight them." As the hundred or so women were assembled on the platform, it soon became apparent that at least some of the Marines assigned to run them out of town were not happy with this turn of events. Two veteran sergeants leading the procession "whispered something to one girl," Worton recalled, and "as the train rolled in, about six of them came over and kissed me goodbye, 'Goodbye sweetheart,' [they said] and they all waved, and so forth, to me." Though properly embarrassed, Worton retained his composure but recollected later, "God, I was mad as Hell!" Captain Hoadley further irritated the disconcerted lieutenant when he taunted, "I understand you gave them a grand send off, young man . . . somebody told me they were kissing you right and left. You been running down there and looking those girls over every night?"[14]

Marine headquarters in Washington, DC, initially furnished veteran leadership for regimental headquarters and commanders for infantry and supply companies. However, as many as 95 percent of the privates assigned to these companies were recruits just out of boot camp and junior officers fresh from camps of instruction at Mare Island, Parris Island, and the Marine Corps rifle range in Winthrop, Maryland.[15]

On June 4, 1917, General Barnett issued Marine Corps Order 25, which stated: "Owing to the fact that there are already on file so very many more applications of civilians for appointment as second lieutenants than there are vacancies to be filled, it has become necessary to discontinue the consideration of any additional applications for either regular or temporary appointments." Instead, "practically all vacancies during the war will be filled by the appointment of meritorious noncommissioned officers who distinguish themselves in active service."[16] This fateful order altered the influx of officer candidates from across the United States and slowed the training of officers for the Marine Brigade in France. The first class of officers under Order 25 did not graduate until April 1918. The ensuing shortfall eventually resulted in army officers commanding Marine platoons in 1918.

Two months after the United States entered the war in April 1917, the first convoy carrying the initial American combat units sailed to join the Allied forces in France, arriving in Saint-Nazaire on June 26. The men of the newly formed 5th Marine Regiment were among the first Americans to go ashore. Barnett's immediate mission, however, was to send another regiment to France to join the 5th Marines. Together, the two regiments and a supporting machine gun battalion would form the Marine Brigade. Without the apparent knowledge of the US Army, Secretary of the Navy Josephus Daniels wrote to President Wilson on August 4, 1917, and requested that an additional regiment of Marines be formed and sent to France to be brigaded with the 5th Marines. The president approved the request the same day. Daniels then ordered Barnett to organize the 6th Marine Regiment for service with the army in France.

Pershing opposed any additional Marines in France, asserting that an extra regiment would unhinge the 1st Division's organization of four regiments per division. "Its uniform, certain features of supply, inability to meet hospital expenses, and this odd replacement organization do not assimilate with Army organization. . . . If Marines can be spared from the customary duties for which maintained," Pershing wrote at the end of August, "it is believed that their force thus surplus should become part of the army and that no more Marines be sent to France."[17] On September 17 Brigadier General Henry P. McCain, adjutant general of the army, informed Pershing that "the President has directed an additional regiment (the Sixth) to be sent and it is now impossible to change the arrangements . . . you will form a brigade and become part of the Second Division." McCain ended the telegram with an ominous message: "About one thousand two hundred of the Sixth Marine Regiment sails today."[18]

The actual departure occurred on September 23, 1917. Major John A. Hughes's 1st Battalion, with 27 officers and 1,046 Marines, became the first unit of the 6th Marines to depart for France, followed the next month by Colonel Albertus W. Catlin and his regimental headquarters detachment. Despite his own orders, Pershing sent a cablegram to his chief of artillery,

Major General Peyton C. March, on the same day, informing him that a "complete Infantry Brigade Marine Corps organized according to Army Tables of Organization will be sent to you to be used as you see fit. They are not to be assigned to a division or other organization."[19] The War Department authorized the formation of the 2nd Division on September 20, 1917, three days after McCain's cablegram and three days before Pershing's communication with March.

Despite the opposition within the War Department and at the headquarters of the American Expeditionary Force, Catlin's arrival caused Pershing to officially create the 4th Marine Brigade on October 23. By the end of the year, two regiments of Marines supported by a machine gun battalion and other units totaled 197 officers and 6,976 men. Despite all odds, the Marine Brigade was now operational.[20]

In October 1917 the entire 2nd Division came into being in Bourmont, France, with an authorized strength of 991 officers and 27,114 men. It earned the unusual distinction of being the only division of the American Expeditionary Force to be formed overseas. The 2nd Division conformed to the organizational structure of every other American infantry division: two infantry brigades of two regiments each, an artillery brigade of three regiments, an engineer regiment, attached machine gun battalions, and divisional support troops. The new American divisional structure was large for this period of the war, being about twice the size of British and French divisions. However, the elements of the 2nd Division remained scattered; it was not until January 1918 that all the army and Marine units were assembled and started training together.[21] Pershing could not prevent the Marines from reaching France, but he could disperse the 5th and 6th Marines along the army's line of supply and assign them to other rear-area duties in accordance with March's wishes. The two Marine regiments and machine gun battalion failed essential training as a brigade and then as part of the 2nd Division; to make matters worse, they were wedged in a rear-area mission with no potential end. With only complete divisions being sent to France, there was little chance of the Marines being assigned to a new unit.

On November 10, 1917, General Pershing shared his thoughts about Marines with General Barnett. Although acknowledging their "excellent standing with their brothers of the army and their general good conduct," Pershing stated that the absence of "transportation and equipment" limited their use to maintaining the American line of supply in France, providing security for ports of entry, and performing other necessary labor such as unloading ships and working on construction projects. He described these duties as "highly complementary to both officers and men, and was so intended."[22] At the same time, Pershing guaranteed Barnett that once adequate army units had arrived to replace the Marines, they would all be returned to the 4th Brigade to join the 2nd Division. For now, Marines would continue to perform guard duty across France and England, unload ships, and form working parties of 200 men assigned to build an outsized dam near Bordeaux and construct docks at nearby Bassens.

The new year brought resolution for the Marines in France. On January 16, 1918, the War Department informed Barnett that the "Marine Brigade now forming part of the Second Division [will be] designated Fourth Brigade Marine Corps from [the] fifteenth instant."[23] The scattered elements of Major General Omar Bundy's division came together in the 3rd Training Area, centered in Bourmont. The last major element of the brigade, Major Thomas Holcomb's 2nd Battalion, 6th Marines, received long-awaited orders to depart Quantico by train for the Philadelphia Navy Yard, where their transport to France awaited.

On January 18, the night before their departure, an assemblage of 2nd Battalion officers gathered in the officer-of-the-day quarters by the town's railroad station to celebrate their departure. Led by Captains Donald F. Duncan of the 96th Company and Robert E. Messersmith of the 78th Company, the group engaged in an alcohol-fueled farewell of epic proportions. In theory, First Lieutenant Charles I. Murray was the ringleader of the merriment, but other lieutenants of the battalion added to the drunken celebration, including future commandant Clifton B. Cates and eventual lieutenant general Graves B. Erskine.

The sergeant of the guard tolerated the merrymaking until he heard gunshots. He then woke the officer of the day, the ever-present Lieutenant Worton, and declared, "The officers are shooting themselves down there." Worton refused to believe the sergeant until he walked outside his quarters and heard the echoes of gunfire across the post. He mounted his horse and rode down to the train station with the sergeant to investigate. Worton ordered the sergeant to wait outside while he entered the building. "I didn't know what in the hell I'd find in there," he later remembered, but thankfully, he discovered that the group was just "hollering and singing, [and] I knew they were all drunk . . . swacked to the gills." The explosions were the result of dropping .45-caliber rounds into a fully operational potbellied stove, which was sturdy enough prevent any bullets from escaping into the room. "Gentlemen," Worton warned, "this must stop." The Marines responded by seizing Worton from behind and tying his hands. He recalled that they "poured liquor down my throat and, god damn it, they were going to get me in on the party, whether I liked it or not."[24]

When Worton failed to exit the building, the duty sergeant intervened, causing the frivolity to come to a crashing halt. As Worton recalled, "They got kind of scared of him." Worton was released, and he allowed the party to continue, but without expending any more ammunition. However, Worton exacted his revenge at 4:00 the next morning when he woke the revelers and announced a 5:30 a.m. formation and their departure for Philadelphia, where a transport awaited. The hung-over Marines "had terrible heads" and fired back, "Oh for God's sake, use your head, let's delay it, what the hell do we care?" He replied, "Well, you damn well had better get going," turning the tables on his former "captors." He fondly related the incident in later years, confiding that "the boys used to play in those days."[25]

The battalion was formed without further incident, with packs on every back and in full marching order, all under the gaze of Major Holcomb. According to Lieutenant James McBrayer Sellers of the 78th Company, the major "was exceedingly anxious for us to make our departure a model of orderliness and precision." The battalion marched the short distance to the train station in darkness, the way ahead lit only by the stars and the dim light of streetlamps. A frigid group of bandsmen met the battalion by the tracks, playing some jaunty tunes. "The men didn't need much cheering up however," Sellers remembered. "They were all very much elated at the prospect of leaving." Within minutes, the entire battalion was aboard the train bound for Philadelphia. Sellers sent one last letter to his father as he departed Quantico. "Now I do not want you and Mother to worry about me in the least," he wrote, "with the memory of you and Mother and your prayers behind me, I feel absolutely safe."[26] Almost every Marine on that train would be either killed or wounded in the coming months, with many receiving awards for valor.

Major Holcomb's battalion arrived in France on February 5, 1918, completing the formation of the Marine Brigade. Although February 10, 1918, is formally remembered as the day the Marine Brigade finally came together, the 67th Company served in England until March 7.[27]

The Marines, soldiers, and sailors trained in the frozen mud and snow during January and February. Thankfully, the Marines ended their training on March 13, 1918, as the 2nd Division became part of the French X Corps for the Americans' first exposure to combat. They entered a quiet sector of the western front at Sommedieue, southeast of Verdun.

On April 1, 1918, Private Emil H. Gehrke of the 82nd Company became the first Marine killed in action. He died as a result of a shell "fragment passing through his chest from behind."[28] The twenty-two-year-old Marine was a native of Arbor Vitae, Wisconsin, and had been in the service for eleven months when he died. Gehrke was a member of a working party in a wood behind the main line of trenches when a barrage struck their position, badly wounding three men.[29] On April 6 Commandant Barnett sent his first Marine Corps casualty telegram of the war, informing Gehrke's parents, six brothers, and three sisters of their loss. Both parents were natives of Germany who had come to the United States in the 1880s, settling in a German American community in Wisconsin. Private Gehrke was initially buried in a French military cemetery but was eventually returned home, where he now rests in his family cemetery.[30] Private Harry R. Williams became the second Marine casualty, dying of his wounds the following day from the same shelling.

On April 15 Major General Bundy recommended that Brigadier General Doyen be promoted to the rank of major general, qualifying him to rise to divisional command within the American Expeditionary Force. Such a promotion would create an opening for a new commander of the Marine Brigade, and there was no Marine brigadier general in France to step into that slot. On April 29, however, Pershing informed the army adjutant general at the War Department that Doyen had to return to the United States, based on the results of a medical board review. Pershing ordered that his chief of staff, Brigadier General James G. Harbord, be detached from headquarters to command the Marine Brigade. Harbord immediately attempted to extinguish any hard feelings on Doyen's part, writing a personal letter on April 30 to recognize Doyen's professional handling of the brigade and asking for his assistance in "reconciling" the brigade officers to the change in command, noting that following Doyen would necessarily be a difficult assignment.

Pershing then officially informed Secretary of the Army Newton Baker of his orders concerning Doyen. Pershing told Baker that if any additional Marine brigadier general were sent to France, he would have to serve in a unit "not actively engaged in the line."[31] Pershing also sent a telegram to Barnett, informing him of the change and of Bundy's recommendation. Pershing closed by expressing his "regret that General Doyen's physical condition prevents a recommendation for his promotion to Major General, to which he might otherwise be entitled."[32] Baker immediately informed Secretary of the Navy Daniels and requested comment from Commandant Barnett. Barnett later wrote that he was "extremely sorry indeed that we had no Marine General in France for that duty. But when I learned that a man such as General Harbord, whom General Pershing considered one of his best officers," would command the brigade, "I was more than happy."[33]

Consequently, Doyen was ordered to return home, where he took command of the burgeoning base at Quantico. Doyen bitterly opposed his removal, but to no avail. "Your command is considered one of the best in France," Pershing wrote, "and I have nothing but praise for the service you have rendered to this command."[34] The news initially caused some uncertainty within Marine Corps ranks, but the choice of Doyen's replacement smoothed over any discontent.

Harbord, a veteran army officer, began his relationship with the Marine Brigade on May 6, eager to learn the curious eccentricities of the Marine Corps. On the ride to brigade headquarters to assume command, Harbord admitted, "I confess to having had a few misgivings." As anyone in the regular service knew, Harbord's temporary rank of brigadier general was known as "Mex rank," referring to the difference between the Mexican silver dollar and the US gold dollar. Harbord held the regular rank of lieutenant colonel and was therefore outranked by both his regimental commanders, who were full colonels of long standing.[35]

After the formalities of the change-of-command ceremony, the two regimental commanders personally welcomed Harbord. Colonel Wendell C. "Buck" Neville, commanding the 5th Marines, remarked, "the motto of the Marines is 'Semper fidelis' and that [meant] I could depend on them." An 1890 graduate of the US Naval Academy, Neville received his baptism of fire at Guantanamo Bay during the Spanish-American War, resulting in a brevet medal and the rank of captain for his bravery under fire. Neville's combat career continued with duty during the Philippine Insurrection and the Boxer Rebellion in China. One of his subordinates recalled Neville as a "wild Indian, violent tempered, and yet kind hearted."[36] He served various tours of duty in Cuba, Nicaragua, Panama, and Hawaii before going ashore at Vera Cruz in 1914, where he received the Medal of Honor. Few Marines had seen as much combat as Buck Neville.

Colonel Albertus Catlin, commanding the 6th Marines, had been Harbord's classmate at the Army War College in 1917 and was considered "a good man."[37] Born in Gowanda, New York, Catlin had also been Neville's classmate at the Naval Academy, where he captained the football team. Catlin saw his first combat as commander of the Marine detachment on the USS *Maine* when it was destroyed in Havana harbor. He was rapidly promoted, reaching the rank of major in 1905. Like Neville, he served at Vera Cruz in 1914, where he too was awarded the Medal of Honor. Catlin entered the Army War College at Fort Leavenworth in 1916, where he first met Harbord. Upon his graduation in May 1917, he took command of the newly formed 6th Marines and led them to the war in France.[38]

Diplomacy proved to be Harbord's biggest challenge during the first few weeks of command. "The marines are a proud organization," a national publication wrote about the transition, "and they no more consider themselves a part of the regular army than they consider themselves a part of the forest service." The same article acknowledged friction with the army, whose soldiers felt that there should be only one infantry presence in the war. The audacity of the Marines was well known, and they "do not hesitate to inform the world on all occasions that they are [Marines]."[39] Harbord was able to overcome the initial mistrust, and within a week he was considered a "Marine" by his men.

After several months of low-level but costly trench warfare, the division came off the line on May 13 to begin more ominous training for open warfare. It became part of the French Group of Armies of the Reserve and was encamped at Chaumont-en-Vexin, a quiet area northwest of Paris.[40] Rumblings among the army officers of the division soon fomented rumors that Harbord had forsaken the army, and there were suggestions that he should transfer his commission to the Marine Corps. A return to the front would dampen this camp chatter, where Harbord and his Marines would be tested in the fury of combat.

On May 27 German general Erich Friedrich Wilhelm Ludendorff launched Operation Blücher, a fifteen-division assault supported by the greatest German artillery barrage of the war. The attack overwhelmed a quiet area of the front held by four British divisions, each of which had been battered during the recent battles to the north. The assault proved to be one of the most successful by either side during the entire war, penetrating thirty miles into the French countryside in five days.[41]

More than 50,000 Allied soldiers were captured as the Germans cut the vital Paris-Reims road and threatened to cross the Marne River. Even Paris was threatened by the German tidal wave, causing near panic in all the Allied nations. This crisis renewed the call for American forces to help halt the German advance. Pershing agreed to fulfill the request. Orders were quickly dispatched to the 2nd Division to join the French army's fight to halt the German offensive.[42]

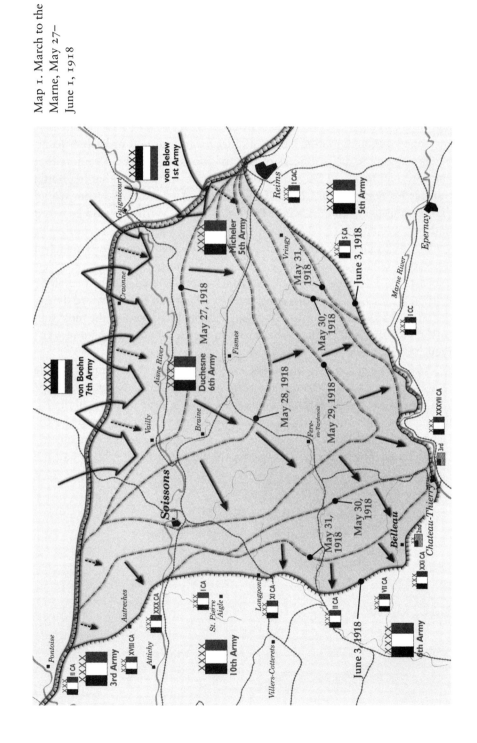

Map 1. March to the Marne, May 27–June 1, 1918

I

May 31–June 1, 1918—Movement to the Marne
"I Could Feel the Warm Drop of His Tears on My Hand"

MAY 30, 1918, was a day of rest for the 26,678 officers and men of the American Expeditionary Force's 2nd Division. The Americans were still in training in the Courcelles, Les Gisors, and Mantagny-en-Vexin area northwest of Paris as part of the French Group of Armies of the Reserve, but they were given time off for the Decoration Day holiday. A return to combat would be only a few days in their future, so the men of the 4th Marine Brigade, 2nd Division, enjoyed the break. After breakfast, the 6th Marines marched to its headquarters at Serans Cerau, without the usual packs and sidearms. "I enjoyed that hike," remembered Corporal Havelock D. Nelson. "The cooling night air had not yet been dispelled from the rising sun and our shoulders and arms were free from the weight of the usual pack."[1] Marines from the regiment's 95th Company squared off with a group from 6th Marine headquarters in a furious baseball game that ended in a 12 to 7 victory for 95th Company.[2]

As the Marines and soldiers dispersed after the game, roving messengers met them with orders for every Marine to return to his company. Excitement and rumor permeated the bivouac areas. Captain Messersmith, commanding the 78th Company, remembered, "The air was so charged that one actually felt that a moment of monumental importance was approaching."[3] The brigade expected a move to Beauvais. Messersmith was experienced and sensed that there would be a change in the order before it arrived, however. Even French civilians came to the camps to share the rumors of movement they had heard in town. At 5:00 p.m. a French staff officer arrived at division headquarters with a new order. The 2nd Division would be transported by French camions (trucks) at 5:00 the next morning. Instead of going to Beauvais, the Americans were ordered to the area around Meaux, directly in the path of the latest German offensive and approximately fifty-six miles from the present 2nd Division camp. Army colonel Preston Brown, the division's new chief of staff, called his headquarters staff together and informed them that the Germans had broken through north of Château-Thierry. A new transportation plan was needed immediately.[4]

Within the camps of the 5th Marine Regiment, many commanders prepared to move before they had definite orders. The men of the 1st Battalion reacted in different ways. After waiting hours with a full pack for the order to move, Private Onnie Cordes of the 17th Company sought the comfort of a nearby haystack and fell fast asleep. He awoke at 12:30 a.m. to find that the galley had served a hot meal at midnight. The hungry Cordes shook the loose straw from his uniform and ran over to get his fair share, but unfortunately, he was too late. The cooks had finished with the serving line and dumped the leftover portions of the appetizing feast of beans, applesauce, and coffee into one large pot. "I jammed my mess pan far down and filled it up," Cordes recalled. "I was nearly starved and at the same time I thought it might be the last chow we would get for some time. I was not mistaken about this."[5]

The men of the 95th Company had just eaten their evening meal when the order came: "Roll up and stand by to move, thirty minutes to get out."[6] At the appointed time, a river of Marines descended a ladder from the hayloft where most of the company was quartered, and they assembled in company formation. The order to "stand by" seemed to become more long term by the minute, and the company was finally allowed to stack arms and sleep by the roadside, although they were without their previous soft beds of hay. The Marines' efforts to sleep met with varied success. "The cool night air did not encourage them," wrote Private W. R. Jackson, "and orders had been given not to unroll packs. Others were grouped about smoky fires talking of possible plans for the future."[7]

The bleary-eyed Marines began loading the newly arrived camions at 5:00 a.m. At last, order appeared out of chaos. The column of waiting vehicles stretched almost 2,800 yards, one after the other. The men of the 6th Marines were concentrated about five miles to the south at the French town of Serans, where similar transport awaited them. Private Albert Powis of the 66th Company noticed that the drivers of the camions were from Indochina, or modern-day Vietnam. Two of them were assigned to each truck, so they could alternate the driving. "The drivers were short men," Powis recalled, "and their talk was sing song."[8] In less than fifty years, the descendants of both the Marines and the Vietnamese might be fighting on the opposite side of the world in South Vietnam. For now, both were on the same side, comrades in arms. "It was a cool clear morning," remembered one Marine, "and despite the men having had no breakfast, everyone was in good spirits." In a few moments, the company entered the town of Gizors, where both men and women lined the streets to watch as the long line of vehicles passed by. Men at an automobile repair station shouted over the noise to ask where the Marines were going. They answered simply, "To the front!"[9]

At first, the Marines enjoyed the ride, "but in a couple of hours, we had different ideas," remembered Second Lieutenant Elliot D. Cooke, serving in the 18th Company. He was one of many army officers assigned to each company of the Marine Brigade to satisfy the shortage of Marine second lieutenants. Cooke had been born on Staten Island, New York, in 1891 and served as an enlisted man until becoming an officer in 1917. "The board seats were hard and narrow," Cooke noted. "The wheels of the truck had solid rubber tires and our vertebrae were constantly jerked and jarred like a string of boxcars behind a switch engine. But the dust was worst of all." Choking clouds of dirt and grime poured into the trucks through cracks in the floorboards as the vehicles seemed to bounce over every hole in the road. Some Marines tried wearing their gas masks to fight the dust but decided that "air with dirt was better than no air at all."[10]

The faces of the men of the 55th Company were soon coated with layers of the ever-present dust, which had the consistency of a "yellow powder-like substance." At the town of Pontoise, the trucks carrying the company halted. The high-spirited Marines jumped out to stretch and converse with nearby civilians. Within minutes, the men leaped back aboard the camions, "shouting greetings to every mademoiselle," and pulled away again.[11] Immediately, the men noticed that they were no longer heading for Paris. Instead, the column proceeded east, toward the front.

Upon arrival at the city of Meaux, the 2nd Division came under control of General Denis Auguste Duchêne's French 6th Army. The French general and his men were fighting well, but the German offensive continued to roll forward, threatening the Paris-Metz road and Château-Thierry on the Marne River, as well as extending west to Soissons. When the American column began to move again, the Marines noticed a change in the countryside. Civilian refugees, both young and old, were streaming down the roads. The sight shocked the Marines. "Where were they going? What were they going to do?" the men asked one another. "Tired, hungry, and saddened by the loss of their homes," recalled one Marine, these civilians "walked despondently behind the wagons bearing all the earthly possessions they had somehow managed to get together." The sight of young children and babies who "slept the sleep of the exhausted on top of the furniture" infuriated the Marines, as did the few women who called out and "urged us to show no mercy on the Huns."[12]

First Lieutenant Raymond E. Knapp of the 47th Company, 3rd Battalion,

5th Marines, wrote that the sight of so much misery sobered the Marines, and they felt "a determination to blot from the earth the nation that was wreaking this destitution." As the line of camions halted in the road, waiting for a bridge to clear, Knapp felt a hand reach inside the cab of the truck and cover his own hand. The surprised Marine turned to look into the eyes of a battered old man, "full of all the miseries the world has known." When the elderly Frenchman learned that Knapp was an American, he stepped up on the running board of the truck and kissed the Marine on the cheek. Knapp later wrote, "I could feel the warm drop of his tears on my hand." Then the Frenchman's wife came up and pulled him from the vehicle. As the couple walked away, the woman indicated that the old man was blind. "I could still feel the drop of tears on my hand, this time my own," wrote Knapp. "I knew then what our being there meant to these people."[13]

After a fitful night's sleep, the 2nd Division moved again toward the front, with most of the 6th Marines in camions and most of the 5th Marines on foot. "Kitchens were lost, the band was lost. Hq was lost and we were lost," noted one man in the 55th Company, "but at least we marched, after the fashion of the Marines when in doubt, toward the sound of the enemy's guns."[14] As the sun rose in the sky, "the going got tough," remembered one participant. "Canteens were empty. . . . 'Take the lead out of your pants' growled the noncoms. . . . Dirt, heat, thirst, and hunger."[15] Private Powis of the 66th Company noted, "This march was the first time I ever went to sleep while walking. I would wander off the road and start on the slant for the ditch." That, the exhausted Marine recalled, "would wake me up and I would get back into ranks."[16]

Despite their pain and fatigue, the Marines never lost their sense of humor. A bomb fragment wounded Lieutenant Cooke during a German aircraft raid. The shrapnel struck the unfortunate lieutenant in the seat of his pants but left him little the worse for wear, except for the loss of "a few inches of hide." Word of the wound passed quickly through the company, and when the Marines began to march, they sang their old favorite, "the parly voos song," with a new verse that began, "The lieutenant, he saw an airplane pass." Then the lyrics described in detail where the shrapnel had found its mark.[17]

As the Marines listened to the fighting in the distance, the French line to their front suffered a traumatic blow. With the sounds of battle drawing nearer, Brigadier General Harbord received orders to move to the front line in support of the embattled French soldiers defending the direct road to Paris. The 9th Infantry and the 6th Marines led the advance on June 1, taking position in the fields northwest of Château-Thierry, forming a second line behind the French. Harbord took stock of his new position and made

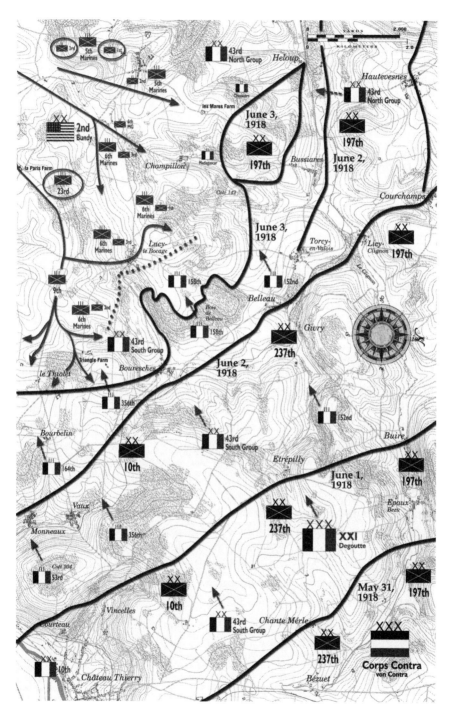

Map 2. Opening battle, May 30–June 3, 1918

sure his flanks were secure. Although the 9th Infantry was holding his right flank on the Paris road, no one seemed to be holding the left past the 6th Marines toward Hill 142. At 4:00 p.m. he ordered Major Edward B. Cole to move his 6th Machine Gun Battalion forward to bolster the two battalions already digging in. Although forming a second line of defense behind the French, losses accumulated primarily due to German artillery.

Only Major Thomas Holcomb, commanding the 2nd Battalion, 6th Marines, actually directly faced German forces. They returned just as night was falling, carrying heavy bandoliers of ammunition on poles. Unseen German observers allowed the Marines to reach the middle of an open field, just half a mile from the cover of Triangle Farm. Without warning, merciless airbursts bracketed the ammunition party. The headquarters and reserve Marines of the 2nd Battalion watched helplessly as the Germans walked shells over the Marines in the open field, who staggered under their heavy loads. "We could see those who were wounded or killed lying amidst the smoke of the shells," recalled Sergeant Don V. Paradis, a headquarters runner, "but were powerless to help them or retaliate in any way."[18] After the shelling ended, corpsmen retrieved the wounded, and others brought in the ammunition. The loss of men due to inexperience proved to be a lesson about the effectiveness of German artillery.

The Marines of the 4th Brigade knew little of the bigger picture around them, but they sensed the importance of stopping the German advance. At the highest levels of the Allied command, however, concern about the future of the German offensive seemed to border on panic. General John J. Pershing, commander of the American Expeditionary Force, was very blunt in his assessment of the war. The moment had arrived to alert America that a critical juncture was at hand. "It should be most fully realized at home that the time has come for us [the United States] to take up the brunt of the war," he confided to Secretary of War Baker, "and that France and England are not going to be able to keep their armies at present strength very much longer."[19] The only question yet to be answered was how well the inexperienced Americans would fare against the veteran German army. The Marines, sailors, and soldiers of the 4th Marine Brigade stood ready to provide that answer in the fields in and around Belleau Wood.

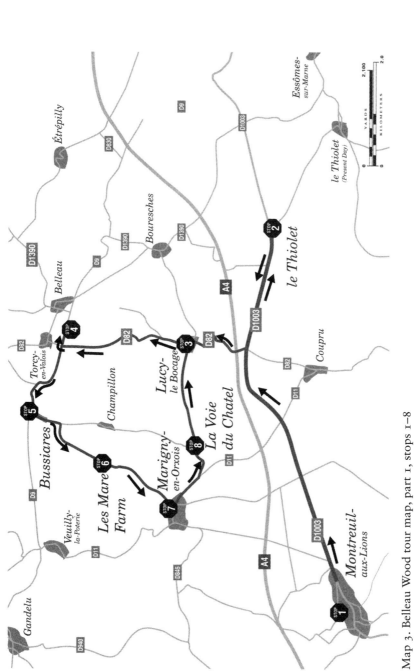

Map 3. Belleau Wood tour map, part 1, stops 1–8

Belleau Wood Tour

Stop 1. *Montreuil-aux-Lions,* 49°01′18.8″N 3°11′41.0″E

The 4th Marine Brigade concentrated here on June 1, 1918, with the lucky 6th Marines traveling by camion and two battalions of the 5th Marines on foot. Brigadier General Harbord maintained his headquarters in his parked car here, where he received orders to deploy forward to the main line of battle. Harbord dumped rations from a nearby truck convoy, loaded up Major Holcomb's battalion, and moved up the Paris road past the present British Cemetery to battle. Red Cross workers tossed doughnuts to the hungry Marines on the trucks.

Captain Messersmith of the 78th Company was astounded when his orderly appeared with "a meal fit for a king," gathered from the town's abandoned houses and gardens.[1] Other Marines were not as lucky. "The first thing we did," remembered Private Chester Lancaster, "was dove into the wine cellars but all we found was cider."[2] Second Lieutenant Clifton Cates was more fortunate, writing to his mother in Tennessee that "most everyone got something to eat . . . a lot of wine cellars were also located."[3]

Stop 2. *Le Thiolet, 2nd Division Boulder,* 49°02′22.8″N 3°18′55.9″E

Leave Montreuil-aux-Lions and proceed east on D 1003 for 9.6 kilometers. Just after passing Le Thiolet, turn right on Rue du Thiolet and stop at the 2nd Division boulder immediately on your left.

On June 1 the 2nd Division took up its position to block the German advance down the Paris road to your left. Holcomb's battalion moved to the left of the road, while the army's 9th Infantry went to the right, extending south to the Marne River. For the next two days, German artillery punished the Marines and drove the French defenders back toward the position here.

On June 3 the men of the Marine battalion had an opportunity to repay the enemy for their suffering. The German 1st Battalion, 6th Grenadier Regiment, attacked Holcomb's position, advancing toward you (as you face left) over the fields. The marksmanship of Holcomb's Marines quickly proved devastating. Private Thaddeus S. Allen of the 78th Company remembered, "One looked at them [the Germans] with almost a friendly interest. No

Mairie (town hall) of Montreuil-aux-Lions. (Marine Corps Archives, Quantico, VA)

particular hate or fear. And yet there was a queer sensation along the spine, and the scalp seemed to itch from the tug of the hair at the roots. The fingers bit into the rifle."[4] The Germans made repeated attempts to advance on the American positions, with little positive result; in fact, they suffered many casualties. "At three hundred yards, it was like being on the rifle range," Corporal Glen G. Hill remembered. "Any German that came out was almost surely a dead one before he could get back to the woods."[5]

Stop 3. Lucy-le-Bocage, 2nd Division Boulder, 49°03'25.2"N 3°16'47.0"E

Once you have completed your examination of the terrain, return to the D 1003, turn left, and head west toward Montreuil-aux-Lions. After 2.9 kilometers, turn right on Rue de Torcy and proceed 1.7 kilometers to Lucy-le-Bocage. Stop at the town square, where you will see the 2nd Division boulder.

You are standing in the heart of the 4th Marine Brigade's line for almost the entire battle. The town served as a supply and medical base, which attracted incessant German artillery fire that caused heavy damage. From here, you can check your map to see the Marines' line extending to your right to the Paris road and to your left to Hill 142. Almost every participant

Lucy-le-Bocage, June 13, 1918. (© Emmanuel MAS/ECPAD/Defense)

remembered this small town as a focal point of his experiences during the battle. Major Shearer's 1st Battalion, 6th Marines, initially occupied the town on June 1. The only excitement occurred when an argument over bottles of wine sparked a fistfight between two Marines.

The military occupants of the town initially seemed to be several French hospital corpsmen, who greeted the Marines with the insightful news that Paris would fall in eight days. The Marines of the 95th Company asked how long until the town of Lucy would fall. "Trois Jours [three days]," cheerfully replied one of the Frenchmen, "with the certainty one feels that day follows night."[6] The 74th Company of Shearer's battalion occupied the town itself, which was deserted of civilians except for an old man and woman who stubbornly refused to leave their home, no matter the consequences.

As the French units withdrew from the front, the batteries of the 17th Field Artillery Regiment moved down the Paris road from Montreuil-aux-Lions in darkness, hidden from the ever-vigilant German artillery observers. Unfortunately, the soldier leading the column became disoriented in the dark, and the guns, caissons, and supporting wagons moved less than a mile from the front line before being warned of the danger. Once it was properly positioned, the regiment opened a harassing fire on the German rear lines, announcing for the first time the presence of the American artillery.[7]

2

June 3, 1918—Digging In
"When One Hits You Direct, You Are Just Saving Someone from Digging a Grave"

AS THE DAY PROGRESSED, GENERAL CAMILLE MICHEL, commanding the French 43rd Division, witnessed the true condition of his command and realized the inevitability of a French retreat. However, he was still unsure of the units in his line of battle. Michel informed Colonel Paul B. Malone of the 23rd Infantry that he expected a "continuous American line in rear of the French line."[1] In reality, some units of the 2nd Division were directly facing the Germans, such as the 23rd Infantry holding the left of the French 3rd Battalion, 133rd Infantry, and Holcomb's 6th Marine battalion in the fields north of the Paris road. Malone appealed to the 2nd Division commander, Major General Bundy, for clarification, explaining that his soldiers and the Marines would have to extend their lines together to establish contact. He received no immediate answer.

Malone was experienced in command relationships and in both the theory and actual practice of combat. A native of New York City, he had attended college close to home at the Military Academy at West Point. Upon graduation in 1894, Malone first went to the Western Territory and then was stationed at Forts Niagara and Porter near Buffalo, New York. In 1898 he went to Cuba as a staff officer, where he made a name for himself delivering dispatches under fire during the Battle of San Juan Hill. A tour of duty in the Philippines came next, resulting in even more distinction. He was an honor graduate of the Army School of the Line in 1909 and graduated from the Army Staff College the following year. Service in Cuba followed, along with duty on the Mexican border. Malone also went back to West Point as a chemistry instructor; teaching may have been his second preferred profession, after the army.[2]

Malone was a man of many talents but was best known among the general public for a series of children's books about life at West Point. Malone went to France in July 1917 as a member of the Operations Section and then served as chief of the Training Section, General Headquarters Staff. His competence resulted in command of the 23rd Infantry as part of the stand-up of the 2nd Division. At the time, he was one of only six regimental commanders in the American Expeditionary Force.[3]

Harbord too was dissatisfied with the information coming back to him about the 5th Marines' positions. Captain Holland M. Smith sent a message to Colonel Neville, requesting a return runner with a response containing the regimental battle line identified by companies; then he sent another message, relaying General Michel's concern about the gap between the Marines and soldiers of the 23rd Infantry. Harbord ordered Neville to "report if he was elbow to elbow with people on the right and left of you."[4]

At the same time, no one was certain where the 5th and 6th Marines were linked, even after a considerable portion of the day had been spent trying to establish this vital information. This uncertainty was particularly dangerous given reports that the French were rapidly losing their grip on the battlefield. Both Major Wise, commanding the 2nd Battalion, 5th Marines, and Major Maurice E. Shearer, commanding the 1st Battalion, 6th Marines, would soon face the German onslaught head-on. The undefended gaps in the Allied line were just the thing the enemy was superb at exploiting. At 3:30 p.m. Harbord sent a terse message to Colonel Catlin, stating, "Send a reliable officer to [Hill] 142 find out if Shearer left rests there and report to me as soon as possible."[5]

Despite every effort to close the fissure between the two Marine regiments, the key vulnerability for the 4th Marine Brigade remained the gap between Wise and Shearer. A spat ensued between the two regiments, as both claimed to be holding Hill 142 but admitted there was no actual contact between them. The executive officer of the 5th Marines, Lieutenant Colonel Logan Feland, set off to settle the matter personally. At 1:30 p.m. he determined that Shearer's battalion was at least 1,000 meters southeast of Wise's line. At long last, the problem was clear: each battalion was mistaking the actual location of Hill 142. The 5th Marines correctly believed that their right lay on Hill 142, but the 6th Marines thought that forward sections of Hill 169 were extensions of Hill 142 and had halted their line there.[6]

As the Marine commanders struggled to harden their established positions, the linkup between the 5th and 6th Marines finally occurred at 2:15 p.m. Two platoons of the 95th Company reached Captain Lloyd W. Williams's 51st Company defending Hill 142. Williams reported the arrival of Shearer's men but also noted that all the French infantry had now departed. The two platoons could not fill the breach alone, so Williams requested that more Marines "be ordered to fill the gap at once."[7]

Captain Williams was one of the best officers in the battalion. A native of the fox-hunting country of Virginia, Williams graduated from Virginia Tech in 1907 as a company cadet captain. At Virginia Tech, he had been a member of the Athletic Association, president of the Mechanical Engineering Club, and secretary of the senior class. Williams became a Marine officer in 1910.

Following a year of sea duty aboard the USS *Mississippi,* Williams served in Panama, Nicaragua, Guam, and Cuba and was commissioned captain in 1916. He assumed command of the 51st Company in 1917, bringing it to France the same year. Williams proved to be as tough as his record. The Saturday night before the battle, he attended a dinner with nine of his fellow officers and three navy surgeons—a total of thirteen participants. Someone commented about the bad luck due to the number of men present. Williams announced, "It would be a bum war if somebody didn't get bumped off."[8] Six of the thirteen would be killed or wounded within the next five weeks. Williams was just two days short of his thirty-first birthday, with a daughter at home he had yet to see.[9]

Even as the various headquarters of the 4th Marine Brigade recognized the vulnerabilities of their position, German attacks achieved good fortune against the French in the small woods north of Wise's position. At 2:15 p.m. on June 3, all French units were reported withdrawn from the right of the 51st Company, which held the battalion's right, leaving a gap near Hill 142. Shortly thereafter, a French major from the neighboring Chasseur Battalion arrived at 51st Company's headquarters. The French officer approached the second in command, Captain William O. Corbin, took out his memo pad, and wrote in English, "Retreat, the Germans are coming!" When Captain Williams saw the message, he exploded: "Retreat, Hell! We have orders to stay and hold at any cost, and that's what we'll do."[10] Williams then sent a field message to Major Wise, informing him of the incident. "The French Major gave Capt. Corbin written orders to fall back," Williams wrote. "I have countermanded the order—kindly see that the French do not shorten their artillery range."[11] Wise himself became enraged at the French order and expanded on Williams's words. Wise "naturally knew more about 'cussing' than Captain Williams," as he had eleven years more experience in the art of Marine Corps swearing.[12] Little did Williams know that his fateful words would become immortal to all Marines and permanently embedded in American history.

At the same time, the ongoing irritation of the Hill 142 gap refused to go away. Evidently, the opening between the 5th and 6th Marines proved too wide for Captain Dwight F. Smith's 82nd Company to fill alone. At 4:00 p.m. Brigadier General Harbord dispatched a message to Colonel Catlin authorizing the use of the rest of Major Berton W. "Ma" Sibley's 3rd Battalion, 6th Marines, still in reserve. As darkness neared, Neville personally instructed Sibley to take command of the Hill 142 area and fill the gap. As darkness fell, a second company of Sibley's battalion moved to permanently plug the gap on Hill 142. After meeting with Captain Smith, Sibley adjusted the 82nd Company's lines.[13]

The 83rd Company moved to the left of Smith's men, while one platoon of the 73rd Machine Gun Company, commanded by First Lieutenant Evans S. Spalding, stationed itself in positions with good fields of fire along the line. Marines of the 3rd Battalion, 6th Marine headquarters, also supported the line. Shearer's 1st Battalion again pushed to the left to meet Sibley's men. The tired Marines dug their fighting holes in the darkness, extending the line almost 1,000 yards to the right of Hill 142, and by 9:00 p.m., the area was secure.[14]

No such problems existed between Major Thomas Holcomb and the US Army's 3rd Brigade south of the Paris road. Major Edward Cole even offered the assistance of the gunners of his 6th Machine Gun Battalion to the lieutenant holding the position next to the Marines. Cole placed two of his machine guns behind the juncture of the two units to ensure that the bond would be unbreakable.[15]

However, another threat emerged near the Paris road. Captain Louis R. de Roode, commanding the right group of the 6th Machine Gun Battalion, reported that the Germans were massing around Bouresches. Captain de Roode had joined the Marine Corps after graduating from the US Naval Academy in 1915, where he was class president, played starting tackle on the football team, and rowed crew. His senior yearbook noted, "He is in a nutshell: a genial companion, an admirable mixer, a talented musician, an able athlete, and, above all, a real friend."[16] Captain de Roode's two companies of machine gunners now supported Holcomb's battalion, extending all the way to the Paris road.

Chief of Staff Brown informed Brigadier General Harbord that, based on French 21st Corps' intelligence, a German division would soon attack down the Paris road. French general Jean-Marie Degoutte, commander of the 21st Corps, also wanted Sibley to move in support of Holcomb. In truth, the battered German 10th Division on the road had no plans for an attack, but just the suspicion of such an attack forced Catlin to deploy his reserve.[17] Another German assault did hit the Allied right beyond Holcomb's position, but when the Germans found that the Americans of the 3rd Brigade were still defending the line in strength, they withdrew.

Unaware of the tension at the various levels of Allied headquarters, the Marines of the 4th Brigade were becoming used to the German shelling and had become resigned to digging field trenches and foxholes as if their lives depended on them—which they did. Marines had a healthy respect for the accuracy of the enemy shells, and Private Arthur Clifford of the 23rd Machine Gun Company, 6th Machine Gun Battalion, wrote, "When one hits you direct, you are just saving someone from digging a grave."[18] The German artillery spotters managed to locate the headquarters of First Lieutenant

Jack S. Hart's machine gun section. Shells smashed into the small, square wood, wounding Sergeant Chris M. Bond in the leg and killing the Marines' newfound milk cow.[19]

The French suffered heavy casualties as well. Despite a tenacious struggle along the Clignon Creek valley, signs of an unavoidable withdrawal were mounting for the French commanders. At 3:08 p.m. General Michel sent a message to Colonel Neville, instructing him to reach out and locate the 23rd Infantry flank on his left and to make certain that "you are elbow to elbow with people on the right and left of you."[20] At 4:00 p.m. General Degoutte issued Order 72, which established the relief of General Michel's 43rd Division by General Bundy's American 2nd Division after nightfall. He expected both division commanders to complete the transfer by 8:00 a.m. on June 4. Only the French machine guns and artillery would remain in place to support the Americans, but the machine gunners would depart in twenty-four hours. No matter what might happen on the battlefield on June 3, the Americans would hold the front the following day.[21]

Every sign pointed to battle for the Marine Brigade before relief arrived. Neville expected the Germans to reach Wise's battalion at any moment, irrespective of orders from headquarters. At 5:30 p.m. he instructed Wise to expect a German attack on the Bois de Veuilly and noted that the French will "dribble" back through his lines during the night, "no matter if the attack is made or not." He then chided Wise by saying, "You *must* send me more information. Everything will be reported at once."[22]

When Neville's message reached headquarters of the 2nd Battalion, 5th Marines, Major Wise was in the field with his two left companies, ensuring that the left flank was secure after all the attention given to Hill 142 on his right. The somewhat shaken senior officer "reported at once" that nothing had been heard from the companies after his departure, but the French 12th Madagascar Battalion had moved past them toward Champillon and then come back, informing the Marines that they were headed "to the left."[23] Wise's dispatch went back to headquarters within a minute of the arrival of Neville's message.

At 5:00 p.m. Colonel Dusange ordered the 12th Madagascar Battalion to fall back to the American lines when the German attack proved overwhelming. Despite their best efforts to hold back the German assault, the battalion withdrew to Wise's Marines at Les Mares Farm to await further orders. In six days of fighting, the battalion lost 46 men killed in action, 298 wounded in action, and 220 missing in action, totaling 564 casualties. The battalion had almost ceased to exist, just one example of the casualties suffered by the beleaguered French units fighting desperately in front of the Marines.[24]

As the French line fragmented through the 2nd Division's positions, each American commander worried about his flanks being left dangling in the air for a German attack. At 6:30 p.m. Colonel Malone sent another message to General Bundy, again questioning the order to link up with the Marines to his right. He reported that a gap still existed in the American lines, between his regiment on the front line and Wise's 2nd Battalion, 5th Marines, in the second line at Les Mares Farm. The only way to reach the Marines would be to commit his reserve, leaving him with no support in the event of a German assault. Again, Malone asked for guidance from 2nd Division headquarters. He remarked as an afterthought, "Very Quiet on Front."[25] This calm was unusual, and it was the calm before the storm. Both sides supplied their forces and made ready for the next attack.

Although the French turned over their front to the Americans in a matter of hours, they refused to depart without punishing the Germans as much as possible. After driving back two German attacks, the French 152nd Infantry began a long-awaited counterattack at 6:15 p.m., driving north along Hill 142 and into the St. Martins Woods, intersecting the Torcy road. But the French were soon repulsed by the German defenders in a bloody battle. Unfortunately, one of the supporting units, the French 1st Battalion, 133rd Infantry, underwent thirty minutes of a 75mm artillery barrage when the supporting artillery fired short. After some initial gains, the French 152nd Regiment took heavy losses due to flanking fire from the German 461st Regiment's machine guns located in Belleau Wood and could advance no further. The French 158th Regiment was also stopped in Belleau Wood, again by the flanking fire of machine guns from Hill 189. The French paid dearly for the captured ground. The 152nd Regiment alone lost 14 officers and 618 men, including 166 taken prisoner.[26]

The Germans were frustrated by the tenacity of the French defense. When informed of the lack of success, Major General Richard von Conta, commanding the IV Reserve Corps, renewed his order to advance, stating, "The line Veuilly–Marigny must be taken under all circumstances." The German 197th Division then issued orders for a reinforced assault on Hill 165. The German 26th Jäger Battalion joined the fight, ready to move forward on the left of the road to Marigny while the German 2nd Battalion, 273rd Regiment, moved right of the road. The 273rd Regiment's battered 1st Battalion moved to the right of the Jäger battalion, protected by the 3rd Battalion, which was securing the line's extreme right. Even as the Germans moved into attack positions, the assault was postponed because the front-line units had to be resupplied with ammunition.

Although the Germans had ordered a pause in their attacks, some units attempted to capture terrain that would facilitate their next advance. German artillery continued to concentrate on Marigny, sending the roofs of houses flying into the air and wrecking the town's church. By evening, the entire village seemed to be in flames. By late afternoon, the remaining French infantry had pulled back through the 55th Company's lines at Les Mares Farm without notice. The soldiers fell back under intense shelling, indicating that the Germans would renew the attack shortly. The ever-vigilant Captain John Blanchfield ordered his 3rd Platoon to run forward and occupy the abandoned positions. "Leaping out of their foxholes with rifles, belts and bayonets and extra ammunition," one Marine recalled, "the men proceeded on the double for the new position."[27] The excited French infantrymen mistook the Marines for the enemy and opened fire on them, wounding a corporal before the confusion could be unraveled. German fire also raked the 18th Company's positions in the Bois de Veuilly, causing light casualties.

A German artillery barrage ranged over the area occupied by the 2nd Battalion, 5th Marines, and the German 26th Jäger Battalion prepared to attack Hill 169. Lieutenant Lemuel C. Shepherd Jr. of the 55th Company awaited the enemy's advance. "Lem" Shepherd was the son of a prominent Norfolk, Virginia, doctor. After a local grade-school education, he attended the Virginia Military Institute with several of his friends. He played four years of football and ran track for two years. "Occasionally he studies," his 1917 yearbook stated, "and in honor of the occasion assumes remarkable poses to keep himself awake." Shepherd later remembered, "I wasn't particularly military," and he did not distinguish himself as a leader at VMI. He rose above the rank of private once during his four years there, only to be demoted due to an unfortunate "fire cracker incident." However, Shepherd wanted to be one of the first to fight the Germans. On April 11, 1917, he became a Marine second lieutenant.[28] The Marine Corps transformed Shepherd into a leader of men. "With me, it's like playing a game," he wrote from the trenches in April. "A man wants to be in on it . . . it's the same old VMI fighting spirit that makes them turn out such good teams . . . a man that misses this war misses the greatest thing of the age." An important part of Shepherd's leadership style was his instant affinity with his men. He wrote that an "officer especially must show bravery and confidence because your men notice your being timid quicker than anything else. . . . It's a great game I tell you."[29] Shepherd would eventually become the twentieth commandant of the Marine Corps in 1952.

Shepherd anticipated the German attack and posted two squads to a forward position on a knoll ahead of the main line to observe any advance, with instructions that the fourteen Marines should withdraw to the safety of the main line if there were any serious attack. As the German shelling continued, Shepherd became concerned for the Marines and told Captain

Blanchfield, "I am worried about that outpost. I sent them out there and I think I ought to check them." The captain agreed, and Shepherd went forward with his runner, Private Pat Martin. Shepherd immediately questioned the wisdom of his decision as shells burst around him. "If we get through this," he told Private Martin, "we're really going to be lucky." In the midst of an overwhelming barrage, a shell landed ten feet in front of Shepherd, digging itself into the ground. "I just stood there, waiting for the shell to go off," he remembered. "Thank God it was a dud."[30] The two Marines arrived at the outpost without a scratch and found the two squads firing at the advancing German infantrymen only several hundred yards away. Shepherd took cover behind a small tree on the knoll and directed the Marines' rifle fire against the advancing Germans. Just then, a burst of German machine gun fire struck the knoll, sending several rounds into the tree trunk and one into Shepherd's neck, spinning him completely around. The bullet made a small furrow in the lieutenant's flesh, close to the jugular vein. "I was a lucky beggar," Shepherd wrote to his mother, "as half an inch would have finished me. . . . [We] mowed a bunch of them down."[31]

The German 26th Jäger Battalion began the main attack, and in half an hour the Germans were only fifty yards from the Marines' line, but they could advance no further. The Germans tried to move through a wheat field around the left of a farmhouse, but the vigilant Marines of the 3rd Platoon drove them back. The German commanders halted the attack and gave the order to hold the line. The Marines had been tested and were resolved to hold their position.[32] The outpost held until nightfall, when the 26th Jäger Battalion retired. At 7:30 p.m. the Marines fell back to the main line, where Lieutenant Shepherd bandaged his neck and remained with his company. The nearest German had fallen a hundred yards from the Marines' line.[33]

Elsewhere along the front line, news of the Marines' takeover of the front from the French was met with some skepticism. First Lieutenant Robert W. Blake, assistant commander of the 17th Company, recalled, "We relieved no one. We saw only two French Soldiers wandering to the rear."[34]

By 6:15 p.m., the German 237th Division prepared to renew its attack by suppressing the deadly machine gun nests on Hill 142 with artillery; then, following the barrage, it planned an assault to capture the hill, allowing it to advance down the Torcy road. However, reports from the German 1st Battalion, 462nd Regiment, which was attacking south of Torcy, indicated that its assault had been a disaster. Second Lieutenant Mollman reported that the "combined 2nd and 3rd Companies have suffered overwhelming losses, one might say they had been completely annihilated." The rest of the unit was similarly hit, and Mollman admitted that he was able to hold his own company of twenty men together "only by force."[35]

The major problem for the German battalion continued to be a lack of support from Captain Block's 3rd Battalion, 460th Infantry, which remained stationary, allowing the French defenders to focus on the German 1st Battalion. Earlier in the afternoon, the German 9th Company, 460th Infantry, had captured the small wood at the north end of Hill 142 but could advance no further until Block's men moved. During the attack, Block disappeared from the battlefield, leaving his men immobile as they awaited his return. However, the failure of both senior and junior commanders to take action when the unit commander was missing for hours was evidence of the exhaustion of the German leadership.

The 237th Division's attack orders were dispatched at 10:30 a.m. and again at 1:35 p.m. By the time the orders finally reached the German 3rd Battalion, 460th Infantry, at 6:18 p.m., it was too late to participate in the battle. Adding to the misery, Block's battalion had finished its last meal on the morning of June 2 and its only "iron" rations the night before. The exhausted men remained in place, hungry and tired, as the battle swirled around them and misplaced shells from their own cannon struck overhead.[36]

At the same time, the commander of the German 462nd Regiment had heard nothing from Block and assumed that he was dead, leaving the battalion leaderless. Something had to be done to renew the attack on the front line. Obviously, more men were needed to overcome the Allied defenses in the woods along the road to Lucy. Reinforcements were ordered to continue the advance. The reserve assault companies would move into the line, supported by the remnants of the German 3rd Battalion, 460th Infantry, and 1st Battalion, 462nd Infantry. However, these reinforcements would have to move forward from reserve positions, thereby delaying the attack.[37]

Although the fight had been fierce before, the struggle for the woods now reached a new intensity as the Germans and French grappled with each other in hand-to-hand combat within the tree line. The French battalion commander issued the order to withdraw, but the fight continued to rage in the undergrowth as the poilus were simply unwilling to give up their position, which had already claimed the lives of so many comrades. "Captain Garnier is surrounded in the midst of his *chasseurs*," the battalion journal recorded, and "Lt. Benecq falls in single combat. Lt. Bekeart claims not to have killed enough Boches and refuses to abandon his machine guns." Finally, unable to hold their positions, the remnants of the battalion withdrew toward the safety of Les Mares Farm. "The retreat is extremely painful," the journal continued. "Not only are the woods surrounded, but it [is] under fire by machine guns from three sides . . . and by [an] artillery barrage."[38]

Withdrawing from the confused battle in the tangle of underbrush and trees resulted in many casualties. Seventy-five men were unaccounted for, killed, wounded, or captured. The surviving chasseurs found their way to back to Marigny, but German shells refused to allow them to rest, killing two and wounding twelve more Frenchmen. During the past five days of fighting, the battalion had suffered 284 casualties, or a 76 percent loss. After two hours of rest, the surviving seven officers and eighty-two men of the French 1st Chasseur Battalion trudged back up the road in support of the American Marines at Les Mares Farm, ready to continue the battle.[39]

Within twenty minutes of the 1st Chasseurs' withdrawal, the neighboring French 2nd Battalion, 133rd Infantry, also withdrew, trying to avoid capture. Unfortunately, the enemy had nearly surrounded the unit. The resulting melee caused staggering casualties on both sides. Commandant Boulmer, commanding the battalion, was captured, along with two of his lieutenants. His regiment's losses, concentrated in the 2nd Battalion, were five killed in action, sixty-eight wounded in action, and eighty-seven missing in the woods. The remainder of Boulmer's men rallied in Marigny, where they spent the night. Their opponents, the German 273rd Infantry, lost sixteen dead and seventy wounded during the fight, while capturing five light machine guns and sixty prisoners. The commander of the 1st Battalion, Major Boehm, was wounded as well.[40]

At last, the Germans captured both Triangle and Rectangle Woods. With that objective taken, the attack stalled. The exhausted German infantry could move no further. The situation was similar along the front of the German 273rd Division at Hill 142, St. Martins Woods, and Belleau Wood. At 9:00 p.m. the German 461st Infantry reported that the only bright spot on that portion of the line remained the occupation of all portions of Belleau Wood. At the same time, the regiment reported that no further advance could be made on Lucy-le-Bocage due to the strong flanking Marine position at Triangle Farm. The German 462nd Regiment reported another disappointment: Hill 142 could not be attacked before dark, so no progress could be made there until morning. The movement of the German 237th Division came to a halt after gaining little ground.[41]

Finally, the "lost" Captain Block reappeared, but only after his company commanders had been ordered to report to Captain Schlem, commander of the German 2nd Battalion, 462nd Infantry, who would now lead the 3rd Battalion as well. "To clear matters up," Block recorded, "I [will] go at once with my adjutant to the west exit of Torcy."[42] When Block arrived, the surprised Captain Schlem informed headquarters that the battalion commander had risen from the grave. After some minutes of consultation with regimental headquarters, Block explained that he had been unable to send any messages due to the German artillery constantly firing short rounds and the French aircraft strafing his position, sometimes only ten meters from the ground.[43]

In the end, Block was allowed to keep his command and hold his men in a reserve position. This episode involving the 3rd Battalion illustrated the breakdown of the German offensive. Ironically, the French units' withdrawal from Hill 142 had alerted Captain Block and his men that the key piece of terrain above them was now unoccupied. At 10:50 p.m. a company of the battalion took possession of the north end of already captured Hill 142 without the loss of a single soldier. Despite all the mistakes of the day, Block had "achieved" his objective. His experience typified the buildup of exhaustion as the German soldiers attacked constantly without rest. Judging from the results of the past two days, the German leadership at the battalion and regimental levels was becoming numb to the requirements of the battlefield.[44]

Like the French, the German soldiers used voluminous amounts of ammunition when driving up the hills. During the interval between attacks, German artillery pounded the ground from the Triangle Wood to Hill 142, with limited success. There was still no contact with the German 460th Regiment, 237th Division, coming from Torcy, so most of the Allied fire could concentrate on the lead elements of the German 197th Division. The attack was halted, with orders to begin again at 7:30 p.m., preceded by a fifteen-minute artillery barrage.[45]

Promptly at 7:15 p.m., German artillery battered the hill for fifteen minutes to soften the French defenses. The attack was set into motion at exactly 7:30 p.m., again into the face of fierce resistance. The Germans used their 2nd Battalion to clear Hill 142 and secure the flank there. "The main resistance is found in the enemy artillery, the effectiveness [of] which was not neutralized," the Germans noted, "and in the machine gun nests on [Hill] 165 and in the ravines in the vicinity of Les Mare Fme."[46] Two attempts to drive the French from the woods by the German 273rd Regiment and 26th Jäger Battalion failed; the Germans were pinned down on the north edge of the hill, unable to advance. A new French counterattack was also repulsed by German artillery.

By 7:55 p.m., the lead German skirmishers found a weakness in the French defense. They led the German 26th Jäger Battalion forward from the Bussaires Calvaire while the French were fighting desperately on the other side of the woods, oblivious to the danger behind them. The German infantry moved up shallow ravines on the front slopes of Hill 165, overrunning a single line of French defenders. They then progressed around the front side of the hill, defiladed from the machine guns on top of the hill, and reached the eastern boundaries of Triangle and Rectangle Woods. The appearance of the enemy infantry caught the French 1st Chasseur Battalion by surprise, as most of the French defenders' attention was focused on attacks by the German 1st Battalion, 273rd Infantry, on the opposite side of the woods. The Germans poured into the trees behind the French 1st Chasseur Battalion while a frontal assault was launched at the same time to hold the French defenders in place.[47]

At 10:20 p.m. the German IV Corps' attack was officially ordered to halt, even though the serious fighting was already long over. In turn, 237th Division headquarters received a telephone call from the IV Corps commander himself, ordering the attack to stop. In addition, the plans for a follow-up assault at dawn on Hill 142 had to be abandoned. "The attack on June 4 will not be continued," Major General von Conta ordered. "The positions just captured will be held. Further orders would follow."[48] The men of the German 273rd Regiment held their position on the ground at the farthest point of the advance, eighty meters short of Les Mares Farm, where they paused to rest for the night. Better news came from the German 28th Ersatz Regiment, which reported the only real success of the day: the capture of Veuilly by the 7th Company, 1st Battalion, at 10:30 p.m. In fact, the village was only lightly held. Encouraged by their initial success, the Germans moved southeast to Hill 123, where they took hold. A counterattack by the French 133rd Infantry recaptured the hill, and all initiatives toward the Veuilly Woods were repulsed by Wise's battalion and the army's 23rd Infantry.[49]

At 10:46 p.m. the German 197th Division suspended its attack as ordered, with the 273rd Regiment holding its positions and establishing liaison with the neighboring 237th Division on Hill 142. The order confirmed what the German infantry on the front line already knew: the attacks could not go on as planned. The daily loss of men, combined with the strengthening will of the Allied defenders, was proving too great an obstacle for von Conta's men. Accordingly, the new order was to hold the newly won woods against any counterattacks, but there would be no further advance the following day. In addition, the machine guns were deployed in a defense in depth, and covered artillery fire was arranged. In all, the German 197th Division suffered more than 200 casualties during the day's fighting, most within the three battalions that captured Hill 165 and Triangle and Rectangle Woods.[50]

The Americans had no idea of the state of affairs on the German side of the line. With the sight, sound, and fury of advancing German infantry coming nearer, Colonel Malone became alarmed at the possibility of a French withdrawal from Hill 169. A German breakthrough would isolate the Marines at Les Mares Farm from the 23rd Infantry, leaving a hole in the untested American line of defense for the enemy to exploit. At 8:30 p.m. the 2nd Battalion, 23rd Infantry, at last made contact with the 2nd Battalion, 5th Marines, but reported a 300-yard gap between their units.[51]

At 8:00 p.m. 2nd Division headquarters issued Field Order 7, specifying that the Paris road–Lucy-le-Bocage–Les Mares Farm sector of the line would be under American control—specifically, under the orders of the 2nd Division commander, Major General Omar Bundy—the following morning at 8:00. The order included the French units still holding in front of the Americans. The only French units remaining in support of the Americans after their withdrawal would be the French artillery, Aviation Squadron Escadrille 27, Balloon Squadron 21, and the dismounted cavalry on the 9th Infantry's right. The ground would soon belong to the American 2nd Division.[52]

The transition of the French lines was already under way. Enemy activity during the night was limited to a German barrage at 2:25 a.m. in the area where Wise's battalion joined the right flank of the 23rd Infantry, but no infantry attack followed. At 3:30 a.m. Captain John F. Burnes's 74th Company, 1st Battalion, 6th Marines, moved into the positions held by the French units in front of them. The French machine gunners remained with the Marines, as ordered. At 4:00 a.m. on June 4, the few French troops on the line withdrew through the 4th Brigade's line. The line was now truly Marine. Little ceremony marked the event, and for the most part, the morning remained quiet, although this was soon broken by artillery and machine gun fire.[53]

After the tremendous victories of the past week, German general von Conta and his senior officers viewed June 3 as a great disappointment. Even the planning of the attacks demonstrated the weakening of the German divisions. In contrast to the crushing attacks of June 1 and 2, only half of the German 197th and 237th Divisions attacked on June 3, and both failed to reach their stated objectives of Lucy and Marigny. In fact, a major portion of the 237th Division's attack collapsed when one battalion became isolated and refused to advance. Despite the uneven day, the 237th Division suffered 252 casualties. As darkness fell, the French artillery fire lessened, and the German field kitchens were able to get food to the front lines. According to the war diary of the German 2nd Battalion, 462nd Infantry, "The food is good and ample."[54] The order to halt and dig in was a wise one. The men needed time to rest and refit.[55]

Food raised the spirits of men on both sides of the battle. Morale in the 4th Marine Brigade's line companies improved when trucks arrived with rations of bread, cold bacon, and tinned beef. The Reverend Lynn T. White of the YMCA was assigned to the 5th Marines and immediately struck up an affinity with the men of the regiment. "I enjoy very much marching with the men," he wrote in a letter home. "It gives one a feeling of real comradeship not obtainable in any other way."[56] White appeared at Les Mares Farm dragging a sack of food for the hungry Marines. He crawled out to the

Marines' positions one by one, avoiding the German bullets and shells to distribute cigarettes, "chocolates and delicacies," all crammed into his pockets.[57] White later assisted with the removal of wounded Marines, under fire. Colonel Neville recognized his courage and requested that White be assigned to the regiment permanently; he also endorsed the minister for a decoration. White, from the First Presbyterian Church in San Rafael, California, would eventually receive the Croix de Guerre for his bravery in supporting the 5th Marines.[58]

The Marines continued to dig trenches and foxholes along the line until every man had an adequate emplacement for protection. Second Lieutenant David Kipness led a patrol from Captain Frank M. Whitehead's Headquarters Company, 5th Marines, into the nearby tree line, where he heard Germans preparing to raid the Marines' lines. The patrol dispersed the enemy and collected the shoulder insignia from enemy casualties for examination by battalion headquarters. Kipness, born in Moscow, Russia, in 1882, had immigrated to the United States in 1901. He enlisted in the Marine Corps in 1904 and, like Whitehead, became an officer after many years of enlisted service. Private Kipness served on the 1904 Panama expedition, with subsequent expeditionary deployments to Haiti in 1912 and 1916, a signal assignment in Vera Cruz in 1914, duty aboard the battleship USS *Mississippi* and at recruiting stations, and Marine Barracks. In the midst of his deployments, Kipness disavowed allegiance to Czar Nicolas II of Russia and became an American citizen in 1912. Once the United States entered World War I, he went to France in 1917 as a first sergeant with Headquarters Company, 5th Marines. He achieved the lofty rank of Marine gunner in November 1917, served as the company intelligence officer, and became a second lieutenant in May of the following year. He survived the war but was hospitalized with shell shock in 1919. Kipness died of natural causes in 1970 during a return visit to France.[59]

As the day ended, Harbord was pleased with the performance of his brigade. Most importantly, Sibley's two companies had provided the answer to the aggravating situation on Hill 142 when both Captain Smith and Captain Williams refused to retreat with the French units. Smith confidently reported at 8:20 p.m. that the enemy had yet to attack his position and that his 82nd Company had completely filled the area from which the French infantry had withdrawn. He reported, "Situation much better than I thought at first," and he noted that not all the French units had withdrawn that day.[60] Smith was able to locate the Allied troops but stressed the urgent need for machine guns to hold his line. By 9:40 p.m., 956 bandoliers of rifle ammunition and 10,000 light machine gun rounds were being delivered by runners to the 82nd and 83rd Companies, to be used in the fight expected in the morning.[61]

French units were seen passing south from Torcy through the positions of Major Shearer's 1st Battalion, 6th Marines, on the Lucy–Torcy road. After nightfall, all French units that were still holding anywhere along the 4th Brigade's line would retire, passing the line to the Americans at last. Casualties on June 3 had been light but were rising daily, with the brigade losing 164 officers and men.[62]

As the battle began to dissipate in his front, Brigadier General Harbord reflected on the events of the day. He had received orders from General Degoutte to center his defenses on the town of Lucy, but as Harbord wrote, "Our line runs now just in front of Lucy and is entrenched, so I did not think further action necessary." Most of the brigade's casualties were the result of enemy artillery fire, which ranged from Marigny to the Paris road. Despite their losses, the Americans continued to provide easy targets for the enemy artillery spotters by bunching up near road crossings and other significant positions, notwithstanding the warnings by the French. Harbord regretfully admitted, "This is a practice which I have found great difficulty in repressing in the vicinity of my headquarters."[63]

The German shells continued to land on the 96th Company's line. A Marine from Texas, appropriately nicknamed "Tex," decided to leave his foxhole after a German shelling and take possession of a large crater left by the barrage. Tex had just arrived in his new hole when another shell hit on the edge of the crater, sending the Marine into the air and over the heads of his comrades. At first, his friends thought Tex had joined the "aviation, and was going to Heaven," but when the dust from the explosion cleared, Tex was sitting on the ground, cursing. He looked over to the nearest dugout and cried, "Can you imagine those Dutchmen sniping at me with an eight inch gun?"[64]

Harbord believed in retaliating for the artillery punishment suffered by his 4th Marine Brigade that day and sought to inflict the same on the Germans. The newly arrived heavy cannon of the American 12th Field Artillery provided just the right response. "I am strongly of the opinion that our 155's should be industriously employed all night on the back areas and cross roads of rout[e]s approaching our front," he wrote. "The Germans are probably moving on all these important roads every night and the French artillery from motives of economy in ammunition are not registering on these points."[65]

As the day's fighting ended along the entire front, General Ferdinand Foch, supreme commander of the Allied armies, was encouraged by the reports arriving at his headquarters. In addition to the offensive against the French 21st Corps, the Germans initiated new attacks in their ongoing attempt to widen their salient west of Soissons. Two brutal new assaults struck the French 1st Army Corps north of the Aisne River, but the lines held after a fierce hand-to-hand struggle. The strongest enemy attacks, however, focused south of the river at La Croix-de-Fer and Missy-aux-Bois. A crushing artillery bombardment began at 6:00 a.m., followed by the inevitable German infantry. Taking advantage of several ravines that allowed covered access to the French line, the Germans infiltrated into French positions and drove the poilus back.

The enemy also exploited the juncture between two infantry divisions by breaking through to La Raperie and the Crucifix, forcing the entire line to reform back to the Pernant–ancien Château crest. Far more serious was the situation in the Montaigu region, where significant German breaches caused conditions to become grave. The commander of the French 170th Division was found lacking, and the unit was assigned to the command of the French 162nd Division. "Losses are not known but they are severe," the French 1st Corps report concluded. "The troops who have fought foot by foot with extreme courage are very tired."[66]

Violent battles continued on the Soissons front as the Germans persisted in their struggle to expand their salient to the west. The German commanders unleashed fresh divisions to attack the area between the Villers-Cotterets woods and the Aisne. Most of the fighting occurred between Faverolles and Mosloy and in the village of Veuilly-la-Poterie, which was taken by the Germans late in the day. Now, the inevitable French counterattacks could be depended on to either slow the enemy advance or drive the enemy back from their newly won ground and exhaust the German reserves. The French 30th Corps' defense in depth countered the Germans' assault tactics.[67]

Farther south, June 3 proved to be a memorable day for the French 6th Army. After so many days of retreat, the German advance had now been stalled. The 6th Army's war diary proudly proclaimed that the Germans have "launched violent attacks on a number of points . . . and on the Belleau–Bussaires front where very lively fighting has taken place all day long without any appreciable gain by the enemy. In sum, the troops have held their own against the enemy everywhere, inflicting heavy losses via numerous offensive reverses and, at the end of the day, our entire front remains intact."[68] For the first time since the beginning of the offensive on May 27, the beleaguered French army had stopped the Germans.

With the final German advance stalled, the French and American commanders planned for the relief of the battered French 43rd and 164th Divisions and the assorted units attached to General Michel's and General Leon Gaucher's commands. The fresh 167th Division, commanded by General Schmidt, would arrive and take over the sector held by scattered French units, Wise's 2nd Battalion of the 5th Marines, and Malone's 23rd Infantry on the night of June 4. Their line would begin at the creek flowing from Champillon to the east of Bussaires.[69]

For the moment, Degoutte could breathe easier about the situation on the French 21st Corps' front, but there was no rest for the weary general. Only by the greatest efforts at every level of command had disaster been averted over the past few days, and the arrival of the American 2nd Division now allowed Degoutte to pull back and rest his tired divisions. The appearance of the fresh French 167th Division provided additional fighting power. At 8:00 p.m. Degoutte ordered General Schmidt to push the French 174th and 409th Regiments close to the remnants of the French 43rd Division, in preparation for taking over the front the following day. These new units would completely close the gaps to the left of the 21st Corps while the fresh 3rd American Brigade held the ground south of the Paris road with a firm grip. The Marine Brigade defended the center of the line with enough time to prepare its positions for a renewal of the German attacks.

The French success was not without cost. The French 43rd Division alone had suffered 2,600 casualties since the beginning of the fight. On June 2, 384 wounded from the French 149th Regiment, 1st Chasseur Battalion, and 152nd Regiment were treated at the French 21st Corps hospital at Montreuil-aux-Lions. On the following day, 392 more wounded were brought to the hospital. Of these, 99 were members of the French 43rd Division and 119 were from the French 152nd Regiment, injured in the counterattacks around Belleau Wood.[70]

Interestingly, General Duchene issued an order that must have infuriated his subordinate commanders. "It is recognized that during the week that has just ended," he wrote, "combat units have not made enough of an effort to reinforce positions held by digging trenches and building defenses to the terrain." Such a comment illustrated a lack of understanding about the nature of the open, fluid combat the 6th Army had just engaged in. "At this time when more than ever before all battle forces must become embedded in the terrain for which they are responsible," the order continued, "it is essential to resist this tendency. I require that all units, whether on the line or in reserve, immediately dig in so as to reduce their vulnerability and to increase their ability to resist." Now that the lines of battle were becoming more stable, such instructions made more sense, but Duchene ended with this callous remark: "I will not accept that commanders at all levels use the excuse of troop fatigue to avoid this critically important work. I count on each man's sense of duty."[71] For the men who had just endured the hell of combat, fighting every day for their survival, and had finally succeeded in stopping the German advance, such an order was almost an insult. Perhaps the intent was correct, but the tone of the dispatch could not have endeared the 6th Army commander to his men.

Another unexpected blow came at 9:30 p.m., when General Duchene placed a telephone call to Degoutte's headquarters. The words exchanged between the two were brief but to the point. "I expect that you will retake the terrain you have lost," Duchene ordered. "With the 167th I.D. [Infantry Division] at your command, you do not want for resources and a division entering the front should make itself and its fresh troops felt by advancing." Degoutte's reply was not recorded, but such a conversation reflected the 6th Army commander's inability to understand the true conditions on 21st Corps' front. If anything, the attempted counterattack during the day proved that Degoutte's men were some days away from an effective effort to regain lost ground. For the moment, any counterattack would have to wait.[72]

The Americans of the 2nd Division had no idea of the drama unfolding at higher headquarters. Instead, they concentrated on the logistical and tactical matters they could control in their own sector of the defense line. For the first time, US Marine and Army casualties began to flow back in significant numbers from the forward aid stations. In all, ninety Americans were wounded on June 3 and were evacuated to Meaux. The Americans were now in the fight and would soon be further tested.[73]

The Marine Brigade focused on the turnover of the front line during the night. Harbord ordered Major Holcomb to send forward enough men to support the French line just ahead of his own defenses, covering the French flank and stabilizing the line of defense to the right. At 9:45 p.m. he instructed his commanders that the positions now occupied by the Marines were the line to be held by the brigade, but he wanted any local terrain advantage to be utilized before the French withdrew at 4:00 a.m. on June 4. Harbord ordered that "any strongpoints in the French line in front of ours be occupied by detachments when the French retire."[74] Only one company of Major Benjamin S. Berry's 3rd Battalion, 5th Marines, was not engaged.

Far from the confused fighting around Belleau Wood, promising news about the day's battle reached French Army Group North headquarters. Reports from the 5th Army at Reims confirmed that the Germans had apparently given up any further attacks on that side of the salient, while the 6th Army reported that all the German bridgeheads south of the Marne had now been eliminated and the Marne River sector was quiet. In fact, the 38th Corps' intelligence summaries for that sector confirmed that the Germans were at least temporarily halting their attacks. Aerial reconnaissance revealed strong enemy forces stretching from Hill 204 through Château-

Thierry, but in a message to French 6th Army headquarters, the corps plainly reported, "The enemy does not appear to have offensive intentions."[75]

However, the tangled German attacks and French counterattacks in the Belleau area proved inconclusive. The day's fighting gave little advantage to either side, but standing toe to toe with the Germans resulted in an uptick in French and American morale that proved decisive. "In sum, our troops stood up to the enemy everywhere," the daily report proudly noted, "inflicting numerous losses by a number of counter offensives, and at the end of the day our front remained intact."[76] At long last, the relentless tide of the German offensive seemed to have crested and had now come to an apparent stop.

The Reserve Army Group's assessment of the day's progress was also somewhat favorable. Although recognizing the potential of a two-pronged German advance on the Nouvron-Vingre plateau and the Villers-Cotterets woods, it admitted that the "considerable slow down of the German advance south of the Aisne caused by the increasingly offensive intervention by our reserves could induce the Germans to unleash a new offensive soon."[77] This concern was focused on the area now weakened by the transfer of Allied reserves to deal with current threats: the north side of the Oisne River at Montdider. The major worry was that the Germans might break through the now depleted lines of the French 3rd Army and outflank the entire Allied line from the Oisne to the Marne River, cutting the Paris road from behind. Such an attack could also allow the Germans to approach Paris from the north. These concerns certainly gave more credit to General Erich Ludendorff and the capabilities of the German army than they deserved, but they illustrate the state of mind at French headquarters after the three recent enemy offensives. The crowning German blow seemed inevitable in the early days of June.[78]

The same sentiments reached far into the Allied High Command. Despite the apparent stabilization of the front line, the feeling at Allied headquarters was still one of nervousness. The German pause only foretold an eventual renewal of the attacks. Pershing informed Washington of the excellent stand by the American divisions, especially the fighting done by the 2nd Division. He was not as optimistic in reporting on his meetings with the Allied commanders. Pershing's message began with the ominous words: "Consider military situation very grave. The French line gave way before what was thought to be a secondary attack." He stated, "The attitude of the Supreme War Council which has been in session since Saturday is one of depression."[79] The French and British leaders pleaded that more American troops be sent to France, even if they were barely trained. Pershing noted that combat-ready infantry would be exhausted by mid-July, and he refused to send over "raw" formations until they had received the proper training. The Allied forces at hand would simply have to hold the Germans until the new formations arrived.

Far away from the battlefield, Ludendorff paused his German IV Corps' offensive down the Paris road and confidently assessed the battle. "Our troops remained masters of the situation both in attack and defense," he wrote. "They proved themselves superior to both the English and the French."[80] Assessing the heavy casualties suffered during the previous four days, and with strong resistance now being met, von Conta ordered his 197th and 237th Divisions to join the 10th Division and remain temporarily on the defensive. Under these orders, IV Corps' mission was still to defend 7th Army's flank during the continued offensive to the north. Von Conta also prepared a new offensive to begin after June 7 to gain better ground closer to the Paris road. The German commander was concerned that his men might lose their fighting spirit, so he issued an order on June 4 stating, "We are the victors and will remain of the offensive. The enemy is defeated and the high command will utilize this great success to the fullest extent."[81]

3

June 4, 1918—First Contact
"Those Germans Just Melted Away"

DURING THE NIGHT OF JUNE 3–4, 1918, a Marine patrol advanced north from the Hill 142 area, sent out by Major Sibley commanding the 3rd Battalion, 6th Marines. First Lieutenant Ralph W. Marshall, the battalion intelligence officer, led the patrol with the mission of finding out whether the Germans would renew their attack on the morning of June 4. Accompanied by Corporal J. E. Rendinell and Private Moore, the young lieutenant crawled down the ravine toward Bussaires and Torcy. Before they could go any further, they discovered a mass of German soldiers on the ground in front of them, "looking like they were going to attack and were just waiting for orders." The three Marines turned silently and inched their way back toward friendly lines. As they moved stealthily through the farm fields, Marshall and his two companions were surprised to discover a German patrol returning from scouting the American position. The Marines attacked the unsuspecting enemy, using only bayonets and trench knives to avoid detection. "They never got back to their lines," Corporal Rendinell later wrote. "We killed them all in hand to hand fighting."[1]

At 3:00 a.m. the last Marine unit reached the field: the 73rd Machine Gun Company, 6th Marines. After learning that there were not enough trucks to transport the company with the rest of the regiment, the men had started marching at midnight on May 31. "That hike is pretty much a blur," wrote Private Einar A. Wahl. "I hope I will never have to do one like it again . . . it was just tramp, tramp, tramp."[2] On the evening of June 3, camions finally arrived to complete the movement, much to the delight of the weary machine gunners. Wahl remarked, "Did those trucks look good to us! Tired out beyond description, we didn't care where we were or where we were going, just so we could ride."[3] The Marines were deposited in Montreuil-aux-Lions and were allowed to sleep after their long journey.

The transition of the French lines was already in progress. At 3:30 a.m. on June 4 Captain John F. Burnes's 74th Company took over positions held by French units. Only the French machine gunners remained behind with the Marines. At 4:00 a.m. the few French troops remaining on the line withdrew through the 4th Brigade's line.[4] General Degoutte also released the

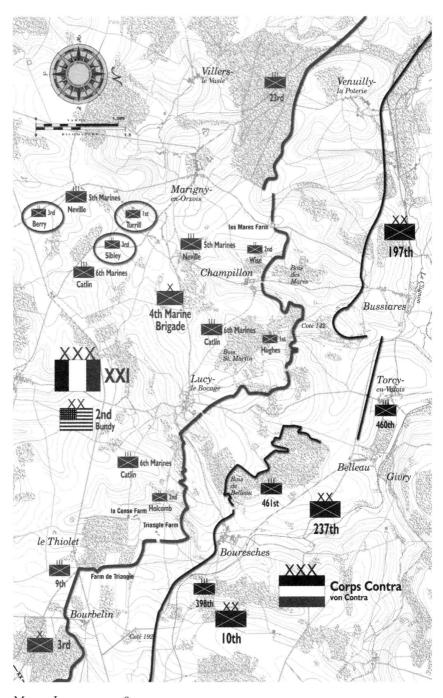

Map 4. June 4–5, 1918

two 5th Marine battalions that were theoretically still under his control, as well as the one battalion of the 9th Infantry held in French 21st Corps' reserve. Major General Omar Bundy's American 2nd Division now had all the assets it needed to assume the front-line positions. At 8:00 a.m. Bundy officially took command of the front from General Michel of the French 43rd Division.[5]

Now that they were responsible for the front-line defense, the Marine commanders reexamined their positions for weakness. Colonel Neville anticipated a renewal of the attack on the high ground at Les Mares Farm held by Wise's battalion. He had advanced Major Julius S. "Ole Jule" Turrill's 1st Battalion to support Wise the previous evening, and now he moved the battalion forward to replace the French infantry withdrawing from the Bois de Veuilly. Turrill placed the 17th and 66th Companies on the north edge of the woods and attached them to Wise's command, while the 67th and 49th remained in reserve in the ravine between the trees and the town of Marigny.

At Hill 142, Major Sibley received word that the French battalion in his front had withdrawn at 4:30 a.m. "Well, I can't help that," he calmly replied to the news. "Let them go through. We have no orders to retreat."[6] Sibley dispatched the platoon of Second Lieutenant Louis F. "Louie" Timmerman Jr., of the 83rd Company, forward several hundred yards into a wheat field to hold the trenches formerly held by the French infantry. In turn, Sibley sent two scouts to Lucy to find out who and what were on his flank. As the two Marines entered the village, a shell smashed into a wall only yards away. The explosion knocked down Lieutenant Marshall and sent Corporal Rendinell flying into a passing French soldier, propelling the surprised Frenchman ten feet down the street. The two Marines stood up and shook the dirt and dust from their uniforms. "You don't need to worry no more," Marshall alleged. "You wrote home and told your mother the Germans did not make the shell with your address on it, didn't you?" Rendinell responded, "Yes, but they sure are knocking next door."[7]

Sibley then personally examined his flanks, tying off with Wise on his left and Shearer on his right. He conferred with Shearer about the proper defense of the area, and for the first time he understood with certainty the 6th Marines' line up to Lucy-le-Bocage. Sibley still had only two companies under his direct command, along with a platoon of the 73rd Machine Gun Company and the battalion headquarters detachment. The 84th Company remained behind as regimental reserve, and the 97th Company was still part of Holcomb's defenses at Triangle Farm.[8]

The positions were intended to be temporary, as the French would continue to take over the line to the east toward Hill 142 on the night of June 5–6. This movement would allow Sibley to remove his two companies of the 3rd Battalion, 6th Marines, from Hill 142 and consolidate his battalion in the woods north of Lucy and Hill 142. Neville made certain that Wise's battalion was in close contact with Turrill, who in turn connected with Malone's 23rd Infantry by extending a platoon of the 66th Company to its trench line.[9]

As Turrill's battalion moved forward, random French soldiers came through the Marine line calling out, "Allez! Allez! Boche! Beaucoup Boche! Allez!" Private Cordes of the 17th Company summed up the Marines' impression when he stated, "We did not go to France to run back, so we just kept going."[10] Daylight brought the ever-present German artillery, which welcomed the company to the front. The Marines had little shelter, so they flattened on the ground when the shells began to explode. "I heard a scream at the same time and looked up," recalled Private Wahl. A shell had struck a nearby hole where two Marines had taken refuge. "Several of us rushed over to the spot and pulled them out. They were horribly cut up, but not dead. A horse tied to a tree about five feet away was killed instantly. I think it was the poor animal that screamed."[11] Enemy shells also pounded the 66th Company, causing the first two casualties of the fight; Sergeant Cleo B. Davis and Private Stanley D. Carpenter both suffered shrapnel wounds. Carpenter survived rumors of his death, but Davis died of his injuries.

A native of Bowling Green, Kentucky, "Bud" Davis enlisted in the Marine Corps in 1915 and soon shipped out aboard the battleship USS *Connecticut*, beginning a tour of sea duty with the Atlantic Fleet. With the advent of World War I, Davis went ashore and joined the 66th Company; he was one of the first Marines to go to France in 1917. He was promoted to sergeant on June 1 the following year and died only five days after receiving his new stripes. His mother Mattie received a letter from her son a week before she learned of his death. "I had a very pleasant dream the other night," Davis wrote. "I dreamed I was sent back to the good old United States Battleship Connecticut, and from there home, when I arrived at the depot, you and dad were there to meet me. But I awakened only to find myself in dreamland, dreaming of loved ones at home. But never mind, that dream and lots more will come true some day."[12] Davis did return home in 1921 and was buried in the Fairview Cemetery in Bowling Green. More than 2,000 people attended the funeral, including his friend Sergeant George W. Nolan of the 66th Company, who lost his leg at Soissons.[13]

Brigadier General Harbord expected the German attacks to resume at daybreak, and he was surprised when the morning began more quietly than usual. He took advantage of the lull to request clarification of the orders establishing the brigade's positions for the day. At 7:45 a.m. Harbord sent a message to division headquarters stating that the 3rd Battalion, 5th Marines, would be released from the French 21st Corps' reserve once the army's 1st Battalion, 9th Infantry, took its place. The order was confirmed, and once the army arrived, Harbord ordered the battalion to support his left, the connection between Wise's battalion and the 23rd Infantry. Major Berry's 3rd Battalion took a position just southwest of Marigny, again in support of Wise, and Turrill's men posted on the front lines at Les Mares Farm and the Bois de Veuilly. The 5th Marines was now intact, ready to fight as a cohesive unit.[14]

Harbord also took the opportunity to relocate his headquarters from the Issonge Farm to La Loge Farm, a short distance to the south. The Issonge Farm had become too conspicuous a target due to a bright red roof and the constant traffic along the nearby road and in and out of the farmhouse itself. The Germans had shelled the building several times, resulting in human casualties and dead horses. When General Michel, headquartered at La Loge, began to move his French 43rd Division to a reserve position, Harbord took advantage of the opportunity and moved in. As Michel bade farewell to Harbord, he affirmed his appreciation of the conduct of the 4th Marine Brigade.

The small farm's location proved perfect for the new command post, sitting only 300 yards north of the Paris road. Colonel Manus MacCloskey, commanding the 12th Field Artillery, and his staff shared the house with the Marines. Many of the young artillerists had been members of the Yale University Banjo Club before the war. Along with an artillery officer with a violin and a guitar-playing Marine, First Lieutenant Fielding S. Robinson, these American musicians played lively tunes almost every night. Robinson came to the Marine Corps from the Virginia Military Institute, having graduated on May 3, 1917, with a degree in chemistry. Sixteen days later, Robinson reported to Parris Island. The Norfolk, Virginia, native served as a platoon leader with the 67th Company before joining Harbord at brigade headquarters in May 1918.[15]

As darkness approached, the 2nd Field Artillery Brigade began carrying out a plan to announce to the Germans that the American artillery had arrived. In the first phase, starting at 9:30 p.m., two battalions of the 12th Artillery Regiment and two from the 15th Artillery Regiment would begin a brutal concentration of fire on a single crossroad behind the German lines, crushing it with five rounds per gun per minute for five minutes. After the first shelling, a second raking barrage would occur, this time three rounds per minute for five minutes and focused on the roads leading away from the target intersection, with the intention of eliminating any enemy soldiers and vehicles that had escaped the initial shelling. This continued six times during the night at random intervals, finally ending just before 3:00 a.m.[16]

As the French troops fell back through Wise's 2nd Battalion, 5th Marines,

5th Marine Regiment
Belleau Wood June 1918
Col. Wendell C. Neville

Casualties during the battle drastically altered the battalion command structure.

Headquarters Company
Capt. Alphonse DeCarre

Supply Company
Maj. Bennett Puryear, Jr.

8th Machine Gun Company
Capt. John H. Fay

1st Battalion
Maj. Julius S. Turrill

17th Company (A)
Capt. Roswell Winans

49th Company (B)
Capt. George W. Hamilton

66th Company (C)
Capt. Raymond F. Dirkson

67th Company (D)
1st Lt. Orlando C. Crowther

2nd Battalion
Maj. Frederic M. Wise

18th Company (E)
Capt. Lester S. Wass

43rd Company (F)
Capt. Joseph D. Murray

51st Company (G)
Capt. Lloyd W. Williams

55th Company (H)
Capt. John Blanchfield

3rd Battalion
Maj. Benjamin S. Berry

16th Company (I)
Capt. Robert Yowell

20th Company (K)
Capt. Richard N. Platt

45th Company (L)
Capt. Peter Conachy

47th Company (M)
Capt. Phillip T. Case

Chart 1. 5th Marine Regiment, Belleau Wood

the Germans were still focused on taking the heights at Les Mares Farm. The Jäger battalions ordered a heavy assault following the French withdrawal to see whether the Americans would hold. Well aware of their good fortune, the remaining French units lost little time withdrawing before the advent of the storm. A battalion of French colonial troops withdrew in panic through Wise's left company, with only a few of the Allied soldiers still in possession of their weapons. "For a time," read the battalion's report of operations, "it was rather embarrassing for the new line established."[17] The Marines were resupplied with ammunition but were more concerned about the lack of food. When rations arrived that morning from headquarters, the Marines were "ravenous" and ate the hardtack and "Willie" with a vengeance, washing it down with stagnant water from nearby wells.[18]

Although threatened by the German advance, the hungry Marines of the 55th Company had not had a hot meal since May 30 and were forced to forage on the surrounding farms. The platoon at Les Mares Farm was lucky, surviving on chickens and rabbits left behind when the owners fled to safety. Others who were not so fortunate were left to their own devices. Corporal William R. Sempf took matters into his own hands upon observing a stray calf between the lines. One shot took care of the calf, and several small fires later, sizzling steaks were served to his platoon.[19]

As the aroma of steak wafted along the front, the Marines remained quiet, awaiting the enemy's next move. Wise ordered his company commanders to allow any German advance to approach close to the Marines' line before opening fire. "We could stop them with the rifles," Wise wrote. "I was certain."[20] While the Marines waited, the stubborn German 26th Jäger Battalion again decided to attack and take Les Mares Farm with a surprise assault. At 2:00 p.m. reports of a German advance reached Wise's battalion. The German 1st and 2nd Battalions, 237th Infantry Regiment, 197th Infantry Division, supported the attack.

Captain Blanchfield shifted a portion of his 55th Company forward to fill the gap between the farm buildings and the 43rd Company in the trees to the left. As his Marines filed by, Blanchfield, his blood up, shouted in his Irish brogue, "The devils are coming on, you have been waiting for them for a year; now go get them."[21] At first, the Marines could see only distant Allied shell bursts to identify the German advance. The Allied artillery slowly followed the German advance until, at a range of a thousand yards, individual soldiers in field gray could be seen.

At the report of enemy movement, Wise ran forward to observe. The Germans approached in four or five lines, each spaced with six or seven steps between soldiers. "Now and then a shell would get one of them," remembered Private Paul Bonner of the 55th Company, "but the rest kept coming." As the Germans came nearer, the shelling stopped, and the only sound was the order to "hold your fire," along with the "choice collection of profanity that belongs to the Marines."[22] Lieutenant Shepherd watched the German advance and called for a renewed artillery barrage to the left of Les Mares Farm, where the ground was open. The Marines had been warned about the dollar cost of every artillery barrage, but Shepherd decided they really needed the artillery fire in this situation. Soon the shells burst over and among the German soldiers.

As the Germans approached nearer, the Marines could see their helmets and fixed bayonets, but they still held their fire. The Germans entered a sweeping field of wheat, waist high. When the lines reached a distance of 100 yards, the Marines opened fire with their Springfield rifles, and the German front line disappeared. The second line ran forward firing, but the Marines' rifle fire ripped the German line to shreds. "Those Germans just melted away," one Marine recalled. "Whole columns went down and the others scattered to the right and left . . . there was not an answering shot."[23]

Blanchfield's Marines fired from the farm buildings at Le Mares Farm. The captain later wrote, "It was here that the months of training the Marines had been through, helped them."[24] The Marines scattered to "positions in windows and doorways of the farm buildings and at breaches made by shells in the wall that surrounded the farm."[25] Other men took advantage of the many shell holes around the farm and used them as firing positions. An enemy bullet struck Second Lieutenant Arthur Tilghman, US Army, commanding the 3rd Platoon. The round initially smashed into Tilghman's forearm and then ricocheted further up his arm, forcing his evacuation by stretcher to a French medical unit in the rear. As Tilghman was being carried to the rear, a German gas shell burst, the noxious fumes causing more damage than his original wound. This was the second time the unlucky army officer had been gassed, the first incident occurring on April 14, 1918.[26]

Gunnery Sergeant Herman "Babe" Tharau repeatedly walked the 55th Company's lines, calling out the range of the German attackers with complete disregard for his own safety. Tharau was an old-time Marine from Buffalo, New York. He had enlisted as a private in 1914 at the age of thirty-six. Every one of his men believed the gunny had actually enlisted much earlier under a different name, for reasons known only to Tharau, and had served in China and the Philippines. He joined the 55th Company before the war, when it was aboard the USS *Maine*. At well over six feet tall and weighing more than 200 pounds, he was a physically imposing leader. The nickname "Babe" came from his resemblance to the legendary ox of Paul Bunyan. Babe was an inspiration to every Marine who knew him. When bullets tore the pack on his back into pieces, Private Frank Barczykowski remembered the gunny shouting, "Hell, if they can't hit me, they'll never be able to hit you!"[27] Lieutenant Shepherd ordered Babe, who was one of the best shots in the company, to climb to the top of a nearby haystack to deliver more effective fire on the German advance. Within seconds, the surviving Germans broke for the rear in confusion. Although the artillery slowed the German advance, Marine rifle fire halted the German assault. Major Frank Evans observed the attack from 6th Marine headquarters and later wrote in admiration of the Germans, "It seemed perfect suicide for them to try [to break the Marine Line]. You couldn't begrudge a tribute to their pluck at that!"[28]

When Lieutenant Shepherd ran to check the right of the line, he found a gap between his men and the next company. He had mistakenly assigned a French colonial platoon to fill the gap, but there was no sign of the Allied troops. Suddenly, rifle fire erupted several hundred yards to the rear, where a French platoon had withdrawn through Marine lines. For several minutes, Shepherd and his runner, Private Harry W. Califf, dodged both German and French bullets, taking cover on alternate sides of a nearby tree. The French left the field after several volleys, one of which wounded Private Califf.[29]

Not every Marine was a crack shot. One frustrated Marine rifleman sighted a German in the wheat fields but could not seem to hit him. Enraged, the Marine charged forward, chased the German down, and killed him with his bayonet. Marine snipers of the 55th Company were placed on haystacks where they could look down into the wheat fields, and they reported movement there. Corporal Francis J. Dockx volunteered to lead a patrol and took three Marines forward into the wheat. After moving fifty yards, Dockx and his men encountered a thirty-five-man German patrol from the 1st Company, 26th Jäger Battalion, searching for a weakness in the Marine line. A quick exchange of gunfire and German hand grenades alerted Sergeant David L. Buford that the Marines were outnumbered. Buford led two Marines to Dockx's position, where they found the Marine patrol holding its own against the Germans.[30] Now facing Marine reinforcements, the Germans broke off the attack. Buford positioned himself on their line of retreat and killed seven Germans as they withdrew. At last, only a German machine gun remained behind and showed no signs of giving up the fight. Corporal Dockx and his men rushed the gun and captured the German crew. Sadly, Dockx and one other Marine were killed in the final charge. In the course of a few short minutes, twelve Germans were killed, seven by Sergeant Buford alone. Only five Germans returned to their line.[31] Two Germans were sent to the rear to be interrogated by the division—a badly wounded corporal and a private wearing French artillery breeches.[32]

On the 18th Company's front, the Germans did not press the attack. Not a single German could be seen in the open fields ahead of the positions, and the attack settled down to an exchange of machine gun fire, which soon dissipated. The Germans made no further attack but continued to send aircraft over the American lines, and artillery tested the Americans with shrapnel and high-explosive rounds. The two sides sparred with artillery, firing at every observed movement. At times, the German shell fire proved terrific, but the Marine line held steady.

On Hill 142, the 95th Company once again extended to the left to contact the 5th Marines. The French had suffered heavily in defending the hill over the past few days. One Marine noted that bodies of the French defenders seemed to be everywhere. The Marines were shocked by the horrors of war; for many, it was their first combat experience. Three French poilus lay in a dugout, all killed by a German shell burst. One man's headless body lay against the side of the hole, while the two others had been ripped apart by shell fragments. Once they got over the initial shock, the Marines carefully buried the dead Frenchmen.[33]

Once the 95th Company was in place, Captain Oscar R. Cauldwell ordered details to visit Lucy and return with food for his Marines. The men returned with rations of hardtack and corned beef, or "monkey meat." One Marine remembered that "when dipped in coffee [the hardtack] attained a mushy softness almost instantly. Without this immersion, it had the physical characteristic of a brick." The beef was not a favorite among the Marines either. "Had water not been so scarce this meat would have done very well as a substitute for something to eat, but it was as salty as brine," remembered Private Jackson. "When a fellow ate this monkey meat, he was ravenously thirsty."[34]

Eventually, the 95th Company was relieved and moved back to the woods that formed a salient in the 4th Brigade's line. To the right, the battalion line bent back toward Lucy. On the left, Marines extended toward Hill 142 and Les Mares Farm. This position received a great deal of attention from the Germans, who fiercely pounded the area with artillery throughout the day. To add to the Marines' misery, enemy snipers also ranged in on the woods, taking shots at anyone who left cover. A sniper seriously wounded Captain Cauldwell through both hips, forcing his evacuation to Lucy. The Marines dug in deeper and stayed in their holes, sleeping as best they could under cover of the earth.[35]

The field kitchens of the 2nd Division had arrived by this time and prepared hot meals for every Marine, but these provisions did not always reach the front lines. The Marines of the 78th Company received only raw quarters of beef, coffee beans, and small portions of bread. Men of the 79th Company lured cows from nearby farms behind the lines so they could be milked. The Marines would then soften their hard loaves of French bread with milk to make a decent meal, or they would sprinkle the bread with sugar found on local farms.[36]

General Pershing himself visited the Marine Brigade to inspect the lines. During a pause for lunch at Meaux, Pershing was accosted by several zealous newspapermen requesting clearance to report on the American 2nd and 3d Divisions in the vicinity of Château-Thierry. Pershing tersely noted in his diary, "I gave permission." After meeting with Bundy, he proceeded to Marine headquarters and had a long talk with his former chief of staff. The sound of nearby artillery and machine guns punctuated the meeting. "There are some reports that General Bundy is not equal to his task," Pershing confided in his diary that evening. "Everyone speaks particularly well of the work of General Harbord. The division appears to be in excellent spirits."[37]

On the 6th Marines' front, German artillery and snipers ranged over the American line. An observant German artillery spotter identified La Cense Farm as Holcomb's command post and the 80th Company's reserve position. The men of the 80th Company initially considered themselves fortunate to be away from the front line. Then, without warning, German 150mm artillery pieces began pounding the farm buildings. One of the first shells passed through the roof of the main barn and exploded inside, wounding several Marines. "How I escaped the falling debris," remembered Private Hugo A. Meyer, "I couldn't understand, but can now—God was with me."[38] Lieutenant Thomas S. Whiting was next to Meyer and was horribly wounded by shrapnel. Other explosions inside the barn caused a wall to collapse. The falling stone crushed the foot of Sergeant Leo L. Liptac and wounded others. Amidst the smoke, dust, and confusion, an order was given to abandon the barn and run for the nearby woods. The Marines burst out the double doors of the barn and sprinted for the tree line "like a pack of sheep seeking questionable safety."[39]

Likewise, Holcomb ordered that his command post be abandoned and moved his headquarters to the nearby Bois de Clerembauts. Sergeant Don Paradis and the other battalion runners took shelter behind the wall of the horse barn, while the shells exploded around them. After a dozen shells, quiet was restored. Paradis ran across the courtyard and into the headquarters office to find Captain Parry Wilmer pacing the floor alone. Wilmer informed the sergeant that Major Holcomb had evacuated the buildings and was in the nearby woods, where the runners were ordered to report. "Why he didn't quit his pacing and come across the courtyard and tell us," remembered Paradis, "I'll never know."[40]

Paradis gathered his runners and moved quickly past the barn and across the farm lane toward the woods. As he sprinted, Paradis noticed several dead and wounded Marines lying beside the road. First Sergeant Frank L. Glick lay on his stomach, both legs taken off above the knees by shrapnel. The sergeant raised his head and smiled as Paradis ran by. The Marine runner gained the safety of the trees, where he found Major Holcomb with his staff and the remainder of the 80th Company under cover at the edge of the woods. Haunted by the smile of "Top" Glick, Paradis threw down his pack and rifle and shouted, "My God, who will go back and help those men?"[41]

First Lieutenant John G. Schneider Jr., Sergeant Major Charles A. Ingram, and Corporal Archibald Smith all volunteered to join Paradis. Luckily, the enemy shells were now bursting over the 79th Company's position at Triangle Farm. Paradis and his small of band of Marines sprinted back over the field, carrying shelter halves to transport the wounded. When they arrived at the farm, they found Glick dead, as were most of the other men along the road. Private Fred E. Lomax, however, was alive and lay on the right side of the road. A piece of shrapnel had broken his leg at the hip and left it twisted at a right angle to his body. Lomax tried again and again to stand up and repeatedly called for help. The four Marines knelt next to Lomax, and Paradis discerned that his face was gray—the color of shock. Paradis shouted, "Let's get Lomax out, he's alive." The four straightened the shattered leg and lifted the private onto a shelter half. Paradis realized that his hands were now covered in blood.

Predictably, a German artillery spotter was tracking the Marines on their errand of mercy. He patiently watched the Marines, and once they had picked up their wounded comrade, they presented an excellent target. As the men started to move clumsily, carrying their load, two German 75mm shells struck only twenty-five yards away. The Marines fell for cover, hugging the earth, and waited. Lieutenant Schneider was praying, "My God, my God, help us."[42] As if in answer to his prayer, the firing stopped, and the four Marines, who were unhurt, were finally able to carry Lomax to the safety of the woods.

Other wounded Marines were also recovered and brought into the woods. Lieutenant Julius C. Cogswell had been injured in the shelling but refused to leave his platoon. However, Lieutenant Thomas S. Whiting was more seriously wounded, as was Gunnery Sergeant Max Krauss. An ambulance soon arrived to carry the wounded Marines to the rear. Major Holcomb shook hands with Lieutenant Whiting as he was loaded into the vehicle, expressing his sorrow at losing the officer. Whiting replied, "I'll hurry back as soon as possible, Major."[43] Sadly, Whiting was disabled by his wounds and never returned to the company.

Holcomb ordered Paradis to go back to the farmhouse and return with the errant Second Lieutenant Charles H. Ulmer. The sergeant sprinted a second time to the farm, and as he walked through the yard searching for Ulmer, Paradis noticed a white earthen pitcher of milk, sitting undisturbed from the interrupted milking of one of the farm's cows. He carefully carried the pitcher back to the woods, hoping to give Private Lomax a drink. But when he arrived, Paradis learned that the young private had died from his wounds. Rather than see the milk go to waste, the sergeant shared it with Privates Ralph O. Sampson and Walter S. Duncan, both of whom were seriously wounded. Later in the evening, thirteen Marines of the 80th Company were buried side by side in a common trench. The company was not allowed to witness the burial due to the danger of German shells. "Old Man Fear joined us that day," remembered Paradis, "and remained with us, as far as I am concerned, every moment we were within range of German shell fire and rifle fire."[44] At 10:00 p.m. the 80th Company moved from the Bois de Clerembauts to the outskirts of Lucy, replacing the 75th Company, 1st Battalion, 6th Marines.[45]

Every evening, Colonel Catlin walked the line and told his Marines that "we were not to take a step backward but we could go as far as we wanted towards Berlin."[46] In a final straightening of the line, General Degoutte ordered the army's 23rd Infantry pulled out during the night and moved to reserve to the right of the division. The French 167th Division replaced the 23rd on the line, allowing Major Wise's battalion to go into a reserve position on the night of June 5. The move still meant that the Marines were holding the far left of the American defense line, with the intent of extending French control all the way to Hill 142 the following day.

With two new divisions now on the line and his battered units withdrawn, Degoutte sensed that the crisis on his front had passed. He ordered both units to begin to build a defense in depth, organizing command posts, supply lines, interlocking points of fire, and camouflage of rear areas to protect them from German artillery fire. Such efforts seemed a luxury after the uninterrupted bitter fighting of the past week, and Degoutte wasted little time in planning a counterattack. "The end to be obtained," he ordered, "is the establishment of a defensive system, capable of meeting the requirements of stabilization on the present line, or preferably farther forward."[47]

The 2nd Division commanders welcomed the lack of activity during the day, which gave them time to solidify their defenses. Brigadier General Harbord could not explain the absence of German attacks. The violent morning battle at Les Mares Farm was the only real challenge to the Marines' lines. Knowing that the following day could be much different, he sought intelligence that would allow him to prepare a better defense for tomorrow. Rather than waiting for the Germans to reveal their intent, Harbord ordered small patrols to push forward under darkness and locate the German positions.[48]

After dark, members of the 97th Company were selected to resupply Holcomb's position at Triangle Farm with rifle ammunition. By now, the Marines had learned enough about the accuracy of German artillery to resupply at night. Still, the task was dangerous, particularly if enemy aircraft appeared. The German planes would drop flares wherever they located movement and follow up with the ever-present shells. The Marines loaded themselves up with as many bandoliers of ammunition as they could carry over their shoulders and set off for the front line. As the men walked from the trees into the wheat field beyond, they heard German observation aircraft overhead. The Marines moved forward quickly, trying to stay with their guide as well as watch for the sparks of flares. Moments later, a flare popped open, and "the wheat field for seventy five yards on all sides of us was as brilliantly illuminated as if it were noon." The Marines stood still, not moving until the flare had burned out. Each man thought, "How could the enemy observer fail to pick us out?" The German aircraft circled the field but could not find the column in the shadows. As soon as one flare burned out, the Marines sprinted forward until the next one popped into the air. Each flare lasted only a minute, but it "seemed to be three times that long."[49] At long last, the column reached the front and delivered the much-needed ammunition without the loss of a single Marine.

The same scene was occurring all along the line, with varying degrees of success, but day after day, the brigade of Marines was proving adept at learning the art of war. Indeed, the total number of casualties from the relentless German artillery and infantry attacks was thirty-five Marines killed and wounded on June 4. The final indignity of the day occurred after dark when a German shell set ablaze the outhouse of Les Mares Farm, which some of the 55th Company had fortified. The flames destroyed the structure, signaling the end of the Marines' last civilized comfort.[50]

The French headquarters of Army Group North noticed the ongoing changes in activity along the front lines. The French 4th Army reported, "Calm on the entire front."[51] The French 5th Army reported the same, with only artillery fire and German aviation disturbing the stillness of the day. The French 6th Army continued to bear the brunt of the fighting, with local attacks at Veuilly and Les Mares Farm and ferocious fighting on the Aisne River front. Despite the intensity of the German attacks, the 6th Army held the line, even recapturing La Loge-aux-Boeufs. The momentum of the German offensive seemed to have reached high tide. The following days would reveal whether the Germans' halt had merely been a pause before renewing their attacks.

4

June 5–6, 1918
"Would the Lieutenant Like Some Cow Stew, Sir?"

JUNE 5 BEGAN MUCH THE SAME AS THE DAY BEFORE. The frustration of undergoing several days of German sniping, shelling, and local attacks wore heavily on the 4th Marine Brigade, particularly because of the resulting casualties. Private Leo Freel of the 95th Company, 1st Battalion, 6th Marines, noted in his diary that he was "Hungry, Tired and Disgusted." He left his foxhole to get water but was ordered back into his burrow due to the heavy shelling of the company's position. Freel could now add "thirsty" to his list of complaints. He made the only improvement to his situation that was possible: burying more of the dead Frenchmen who were now creating a horrible stench throughout the woods. At some point during the day, Freel was finally able to take a shot using the sniper rifle of Private Roy H. Myers. Freel recorded in his diary, "Shot Myers rifle at Fritz, got him." He then noted with some satisfaction, "a shell finished him in little pieces."[1]

Despite the relative "quiet" of daily shelling and sniping, the Germans showed every sign of preparing to renew their attack. At least eighty-nine enemy aircraft flew over the 2nd Division lines (two were shot down), along with four observation balloons overlooking the Marines' positions. Enemy artillery continued to hit at any observed American movement. The Germans also launched a gas attack on the town of Lucy-le-Bocage at 6:00 p.m.

With the Allied lines beginning to stabilize in the Belleau sector, General Degoutte saw immediate danger in the Germans' terrain advantage. The latest enemy penetration south of the Clignon Creek was a perfect place to launch further attacks to batter the Allied lines. The rolling hills, valleys, and small bands of woods could conceal any number of German troops in preparation for an assault. At the same time, the present German positions allowed artillery to rain shells on the Allies. Degoutte's solution was a series of local counterattacks to seize commanding terrain and push the German advance back to the Clignon Creek. On June 5 Degoutte ordered his 167th Division to assault the ground south of Champillon at first light the following morning. The attack would be coordinated with the American 2nd

Division on the right, which would engage in a supporting attack to secure the French right flank.[2]

Following seizure of the high ground overlooking the Clignon Creek, and "as soon as possible after the execution of the first operation," the 2nd Division was to capture the Bois de Belleau and the high ground overlooking the towns of Belleau and Torcy. This attack would firmly establish the Allied line along the river, putting the Germans at a great disadvantage. The French set the time for the initial attack as 3:45 a.m. on June 6.[3]

Chief of Staff Brown alerted the 2nd Division and ordered the 4th Marine Brigade and division artillery to join the attack, on the right of the French 167th Division. Brown spoke to Harbord at 3:00 p.m. and pointed out that the Marines' objective was Champillon Heights, overlooking the town of Bussaires on the Clignon Creek, known as Hill 142. Artillery would fire a barrage thirty minutes before the attack, and then the Marines would move, attacking by infiltration, not waves. The brigade commander and his staff planned the attack in the "dingy" wine cellar of La Loge Farm, "surrounded by maps and telephones."[4]

At 10:25 p.m. Harbord issued Field Order 1, formally assigning the attack to Turrill's 1st Battalion and Berry's 3rd Battalion, both from Colonel Neville's 5th Marines. These two battalions were alerted that day to move forward and get into position after dark, relieving Major Sibley's and Major Shearer's battalions of the 6th Marines already in line. Although fresh troops would be best in the attack, moving them into position after dark to avoid tipping off the enemy was a time-consuming enterprise at best. The unit leaders would have no time to examine the ground before the assault, and Turrill's battalion could not start moving until it was relieved by the French. Wise's 2nd Battalion, 5th Marines, would be replaced that same night by the French 116th Infantry and would go into reserve for the planned attack.[5]

Essential to the success of the attack was Sibley's relief by Turrill before dawn. Beforehand, Sibley inspected his entire front line, ordering his men to "hold what you got." "Ma" Sibley had learned one important lesson: his men were becoming used to death. In some places, they used the bodies of dead Marines as breastworks. Sibley found one spot where several bodies had been spread, mutilated by artillery. Shocked by the scene, Sibley went to the nearest Marine and ordered the men buried. "Major, they were buried once, sir," the man allowed, "but the German artillery blowed them out again."[6]

A storm in the form of Major John A. Hughes arrived at 6th Marine headquarters that afternoon. In January 1918 Hughes had been ordered to leave the 6th Marines and report to the Army School at Langres for temporary duty as an instructor. A gifted tactician, the veteran Hughes rose to command the Infantry Specialist School on May 1, but the assignment sidelined him from his beloved 1st Battalion, 6th Marines. He suspected the teaching assignment was the result of a festering wound he had suffered in 1916, inflicted by a bullet from a Dominican insurgent's .45-caliber pistol. When Hughes learned that the Marines were entering the fray at Belleau Wood, he badgered the doctors into filing a medical report indicating his fitness for combat duty. Hughes, a Medal of Honor recipient from his service in Vera Cruz in 1914, was known to his men as a "tough hombre."[7] Colonel Catlin had little choice, so he pulled Shearer back to headquarters and restored Hughes to command of his former battalion.[8]

Hughes became visibly upset by the formation of the front line and spent the day reconnoitering his battalion's positions. "This front line is in a hell of a mess," Hughes told his staff. "I can't make head or tails of it."[9] Hughes and Catlin went to the front line near Hill 142 and inspected the line extending to the right. Hughes also met with scouts who had prepared a rough sketch map of the front lines. He found the position of the battalion unsatisfactory. The entire line was under German observation, and he recommended that Catlin withdraw the battalion to a more defensible ridge in the rear. Catlin approved the request, and the withdrawal was scheduled to take place that night. Hughes reported that, except by moving back, "Nothing could be done to rectify the position."[10]

However, the arrival of attack orders from the brigade changed everything. Hughes would be relieved at dusk, and Berry's 3rd Battalion would hold the line. At sunset, Berry met with Hughes to prepare for the relief. Sergeant Gerald Thomas remembered the conversation that took place between the two men at about 8:30 p.m. Berry explained to Hughes, "Deadoe, I'm going to relieve you tonight, and we are going to attack tomorrow morning." Hughes was astounded. "Berry, you are a goddamned fool," he exploded. "I don't believe a word you say." Berry could only respond, "Well, we are."[11]

At dusk, First Lieutenant Jonas Platt reported to the 49th Company, 1st Battalion, 5th Marines, as a replacement officer. Captain Hamilton assigned him to command a rifle platoon and warned him of the coming assault. "Captain Hamilton's company had holes in it that must be corked," remembered Platt. "I was to be one of the corks." Platt had only hours to become familiar with his new command before the attack. He never forgot the first sight of his Marines. "Here and there the men lay on the ground, with their muddy feet sticking out beneath salmon pink coverlets, baby blue satin quilts, even lace curtains they had taken from the ruined chateau." An occasional German shell passed overhead, causing one of the Marines to call out, "Aw, say Fritz, pipe down! Cut it out! Can't you let a fellow sleep!"[12] Satisfied that his complaint had been registered, the Marine pulled his borrowed blankets up to his neck, wiggled his feet, and fell back asleep.

Lieutenant Platt's first test of command came when the soft sound of a mooing cow penetrated the Marines' position. Platt noticed that within seconds, "where there [had been] lumps of humanity under various silk coverlets, there was now nothingness." Two rifle shots came through the trees, and then "four wide eyed mess sergeants, one with his baby-blue coverlet dragging behind him where it caught on a belt hook, galloped past, dragging out their bayonets as they dived into the woods." Platt followed the sergeants but was intercepted by "the most innocent looking Marine I ever saw," he recalled, who saluted and reported a cow killed by German artillery. The company was now preparing the carcass for an evening meal in the nearby château, and the Marine asked politely, "Would the lieutenant like some cow stew, sir?" Platt thought a moment and realized that some of his men would likely die in the morning attack, now only hours away. "I grinned and nodded," Platt later wrote, "and the blandlike, innocent Marine hurried away to assist with the barbecue. . . . I never realized that cow could cook so quickly." The smell of the feast attracted Marines from every nearby command, and a German shell that burst nearby delayed the meal by only five minutes. One sergeant was half buried by debris, and another Marine was blown out a window. Both of them were dusted off, "and the pot boiled on."[13]

The smell of the stew also attracted a band of French machine gunners passing to the front to relieve the battalion. "Bon chance," the French called out, to which the Marines replied, "Same t' you and many of them . . . and say frogs, old chaps, you hold that line until we stow away this chow, will yer?" The French cheerfully answered, "Ah, oui, M'sieurs. Dejeuner, n'est pas?" First Lieutenant Clarence "Seaweed" Ball, an old friend of Platt's, also stopped by when he smelled the stew. "Is she done?" he asked Platt eagerly. When told that the feast was ready, Ball picked up two nearby buckets and said, "Then gimme!" As he prepared to carry the stew back to his platoon, German artillery began to shell the position. Lieutenant Ball ran forward, dodging the shell bursts, while trying not to spill the stew. Platt thought he looked like "a performer on a tight rope" and called after him to be careful. The last the Marines heard from Ball was when he called over his shoulder, "You said it." Two hours later, a dispatch rider on a battered motorcycle pulled up to Platt and handed him a folded message that read, "Never spilled a drop. Ball."[14]

The 49th Company's late dinner signaled the unraveling of the attack orders. The 1st Battalion commander, Major Turrill, expected to be relieved by the French at 9:00 p.m., allowing the battalion to move into position and relieve Sibley, but no French units arrived at the appointed time. Neville's written attack orders reached Turrill at about 12:45 a.m., only three hours prior to the attack, but there was still no sign from the French.

Lieutenant Colonel Feland, second in command of the 5th Marines, joined Turrill in his headquarters. Feland directed Turrill to bring the two nearby company commanders to the musty, damp powerhouse. When they arrived, the officers looked over a map of Hill 142, while Feland gave direct orders to Turrill to push his two lead companies forward to the jump-off point and capture the hill, then halt at a road just north of the hill. However, Turrill could not move his entire battalion until the French arrived. Two of Turrill's companies, the 17th and 66th, were holding the front line and could not move until relieved. The other two companies, the 67th and 49th, lay in reserve at Marigny and could march immediately. By necessity, the battalion would have to move in two separate columns and initially fight without immediate reserves.[15]

After receiving the order to move, Captain Hamilton passed the word for his 49th Company to form up and move out. Most of the Marines had gotten little sleep between the impromptu barbecue and the rumors of Germans infiltrating the lines. In the bleak darkness, the tired Marines of the 67th and 49th Companies assembled at Marigny and then moved steadily toward Hill 142, covering the mile distance at a plodding pace. Each Marine placed as many ammunition belts over his shoulders as he could carry, causing Lieutenant Platt to remark that they "looked like a bunch a Mexican revolutionaries."[16] It was 3:30 a.m. when Hamilton assembled his 49th Company on the line of departure, fifteen minutes before the expected attack. Just then, the French infantry relieved the other half of Turrill's battalion back in its front-line positions. The appearance of the French startled the men of the 17th Company. "I am not wanting to discredit the French soldiers, or to say they were cowards," Private Cordes wrote later, "but I must say these old Veterans were scared to death."[17]

As the Marines moved into position, the US Army's 12th Field Artillery Regiment opened fire on the German positions, hitting the enemy defenses on Hill 142 and the crossroads behind their lines. The harassing shelling continued intermittently during the night, causing the Germans to return fire, wounding five soldiers in Battery C with shrapnel.[18]

Opposing the Marines was the German 3rd Battalion, 460th Infantry Regiment. The approximately 175 men of Second Lieutenant Wessberge's 9th Company waited directly in the path of the attack. Alerted by the artillery fire, Wessberge's company was awake and ready for an impending infantry assault. Two other German companies, the 10th and 11th, supported Wessberge's line in a square patch of woods on his east flank, with the 12th Company in

The Germans' first line of defense in the trees, as viewed from the jump-off positions of the 1st Battalion, 5th Marines. This photograph was taken after the battle. (Marine Corps Archives, Quantico, VA)

reserve. Artillery supporting fire was registered, awaiting the signal of flares. The Germans were prepared and waiting for Turrill's Marines.[19]

At the appointed time, 3:45 a.m., Turrill inspected his forward positions and found much confusion among the attacking units. Of the two machine gun companies assigned to support the attack, one had yet to arrive, and the other was just moving into place after being relieved behind schedule and getting lost on the march. Only Captain Hamilton's 240 Marines of the 49th Company on the right and First Lieutenant Orlando C. Crowther's 246 Marines of the 67th Company on the left were in line for the attack. The attack force thus contained almost 500 Marines in total—only one-third of its planned strength. Nearby in support, Sibley's 3rd Battalion, 6th Marines, would stay in line until the attack began and then withdraw and prepare to attack Belleau Wood.

Turrill waited for signs of the French attack but could not see or hear anything from the left. Although the designated time for the assault had arrived, Turrill remained uncertain about giving the actual order to launch the attack without additional support.

The two companies of Marines felt no such hesitation. On the left, Lieutenant Crowther prepared his 67th Company for the fight. Crowther and First Sergeant Daniel A. "Pop" Hunter established the assault formation, preparing the young Marines to cross the wheat fields ahead. Private Jo-

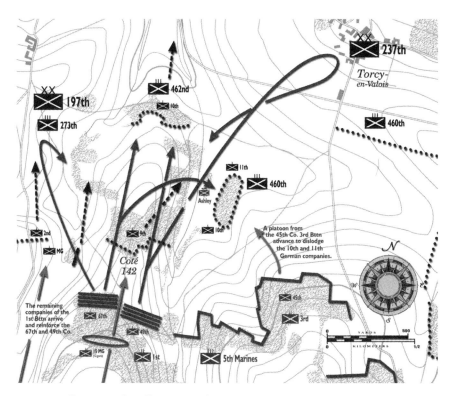

Map 5. Belleau Wood, Hill 142 (attack), June 6, 1918

seph Feingold recalled, "With a cigarette in each mouth, a grim handshake with our bunkies, and a smile of grim feeling of what we were going after," the company was ready.[20] Hunter calmly stepped into the wheat field and looked left and right, making certain that his company was in position. Once he was satisfied, the sergeant blew his whistle to announce the attack, and the company watched as "his cane swung overhead and forward, pointing toward the first objective."[21]

The Marines of the 67th Company moved forward swiftly, running toward the Germans in the far tree line. While Hunter examined his line, one of the 67th Company's platoon leaders, Lieutenant Tom Ashley, held his watch and counted the seconds as the time of the attack approached. His men had their eyes fixed on the lieutenant, who seemed full of self-assurance. American shells were roaring overhead, and German artillery replied with a vengeance, "but Tom stood there calmly and confidently, at times looking out ahead as though trying to see through the morning half-light which hid the enemy." Promptly at 3:45 a.m., Ashley called out, "Over you go, and every man sprang from the trench to follow him."[22]

At 3:50 a.m. Hamilton grew tired of waiting for the order to attack and took matters into his own hands. "I started things myself," Hamilton wrote later, "and we were off."[23] The captain ordered the first wave of Marines to move across an open field of wheat toward a small woods 300 yards away. The lead waves of both companies were twenty-five yards from their starting points within seconds.[24]

Turrill learned that the attack was under way only after observing the initial platoons moving into open ground. The battalion commander now had to make a fateful decision. Should he try to postpone the attack, waiting until his full force was on the field, or should he let the attack continue with the men he had available, trusting that the rest of his battalion would arrive soon? If he stopped the attack, the French on his left might be bloodied due to flank fire. Without delay, Turrill ordered the first line to continue the assault, but the order was unnecessary. The waves of Marines quickly moved forward into the wheat field with fixed bayonets, "barely visible in the morning mist."[25]

From the low ground to the right, Captain Peter T. Conachy and his 45th Company observed the advance, awestruck by the sight of the Marines' attack. Enlisting as a private in 1904 after emigrating from Ireland, Conachy had served in Cuba, the Philippines, Japan, and China during the revolution of 1911, as well as extended tours of duty aboard ships. The veteran captain was not easily impressed, but he later recollected that "the prettiest sight of his life was to see them [the Marines] on his left in four waves, walking toward their objective with their bayonets gleaming in the bright sunlight."[26]

The trees were held by the advance German picket line commanded by Second Lieutenant Bezon's 1st Platoon, 9th Company, supported by three light machine guns. Bezon knew that once the Allied artillery fire ceased, the enemy would attack, and he was ready. When the shells stopped falling, Bezon heard a whistle from the Marine tree line, followed by a second whistle. Bezon then saw the first wave of Marines charge into the wheat field. He immediately fired three red flares for artillery support, while his machine guns tore into the Marines, turning the attackers into "disordered masses."[27] Struck by machine gun rounds, the 67th Company's first casualty went down in the wheat. Another Marine yelled to Pop Hunter that the man was hurt. The tough sergeant replied with the wisdom of many years of Marine Corps service: "C'mon goddammit! He ain't the last man who's gonna be hit today."[28] Hunter himself, a forty-two-year-old native of Baltimore, Maryland, would die of wounds inflicted during the attack.

The German machine gun fire stunned the Marines, causing Hamilton to write later that there were "more machine guns than I ever had heard before."[29] The captain knew he had to get his men moving forward. He ran along the line, urging each man to stand and rush the woods. The 49th Company sprinted forward through the wheat in small groups, trying to avoid the killing fire. The German machine gun in the center of the woods jammed just at that moment, providing a few fateful moments for the Marines to run forward facing only rifle fire.

On the left, Lieutenant Ashley led his 1st Platoon into the wheat field until it started taking fire from the woods down the hill to his right. The trees were occupied by a German machine gun that raked the Marine line. Without a moment's hesitation, Ashley turned his men toward the German position. "Tom was known for his thoroughness," a classmate wrote. "He lived well, studied well, and fought well."[30] The lieutenant and his men crawled through the wheat until they were close to the edge of the tree line. With a shout of "Come on, follow me," he jumped up and charged the German machine guns. The enemy fled, and Ashley pressed forward through the trees.[31]

Inside the woods, Bezon saw his center machine gun jam and could hear only one other gun firing. The promised artillery support had yet to arrive, adding to his predicament. To his front, the Marines had now advanced to within twenty feet of the tree line. With his position crumbling around him, Bezon quickly determined that "resistance on our part was useless," and he ordered the men around him to withdraw. Most of the German platoon ran back through the woods in relatively good order, racing for the safety of the main line of resistance. Others never received the order and remained behind, still fighting. The retreating Germans broke from the woods and into another wheat field, trying to reach the main German line in the woods beyond. The unlucky Germans were mistaken for Americans and were hit by machine gun fire from their own line, throwing Bezon and his men into extreme disorder. Only with great difficulty did the survivors of the platoon rejoin their company, as the battle in the woods raged on.[32]

Hamilton's 49th Company and Ashley's platoon of the 67th Company were close behind Bezon. After the Marines broke into the tree line, the situation improved and they were able to repay the Germans for their losses in the wheat field. Sergeant Becker of the German 9th Company kept his last machine gun in action until all its ammunition was expended. He then held the Marines back with hand grenades while Private Joseph Brandt ran to safety, taking the machine gun with him. The Americans were so close that Becker ordered Brandt to remove the bolt from the gun to prevent any chance of its use if it were captured. The sergeant then broke for safety and ran through the trees surrounded by cries of the Marine "hurrah" as he battled his way back into German lines.[33]

Lieutenant Platt was trying to gather his platoon in the woods when he heard a machine gun firing just ahead. He crawled forward and discovered ten Marines of his platoon firing a captured machine gun into the trees. "Come back here," he yelled, to which one of the Marines replied, "Jimmy! It's the Loot! Cut it." The men disabled the gun, looking "like schoolboys caught at hooky." After being rebuked for getting ahead of the lines, one of the Marines innocently explained, "You see, sir, we were shore headed for Germany, weren't we now?" Other Marines of the platoon moved ahead in small groups, shooting down three snipers from the trees overhead and then arguing over who was entitled to souvenirs from the bodies. The most prized items were Iron Cross medals and belt buckles. Less lucky Marines had to settle for uniform buttons.[34]

Some of the Germans in the woods surrendered, and Hamilton "snatched an iron cross ribbon from the first officer I got." The woods remained a mass of confusion, but Hamilton pushed his men forward into the next wheat field, which was full of red poppies, adding a bit of color to the early-morning scene. The poppies proved a bad omen as the 49th and 67th Companies ran directly into the main German defense and "caught hell," remembered Hamilton.[35] Reinforcements arrived when Ashley and what was left of his platoon came out of the trees, joining Crowther and the rest of the company.[36]

The blazing German defense forced the Marines to hesitate and go to ground, hidden by the wheat. The main body of Lieutenant Wessberge's 9th Company defended the second woods with a platoon of two machine guns from the 3rd Machine Gun Company under Corporal Grosse-Bohle on the left. The machine guns laced the wheat field with a withering hail of bullets, but still the Marines attacked, crawling forward until they were close enough to rush the guns. In small groups, the 49th Company charged the woods with bayonets fixed, eager to kill the German gunners. As other Marines fell dead and wounded around him, Private John Kukoski found himself alone as he neared the tree line. Without hesitation, the private charged a machine gun with his bayonet fixed, capturing the crew and a German officer. Kukoski personally took the captured machine gun and his prisoners back to headquarters.

With many of the machine guns now out of operation, Marines of both companies flooded the second woods, ready to close with the German defenders. Lieutenant Platt led his platoon forward into the wheat field, taking command of not only the remnants of his own unit but also those of neighboring platoons. Platt seemed to lead a charmed life. He pushed forward until he was close to the tree line and then charged yet another German machine gun. The crew fled, leaving Platt in possession of the gun and a small piece of the enemy's defense line. When he halted and looked for his men, he found them pulling Iron Crosses and belt buckles from the "beaucoup" German casualties in the grove of trees.[37]

Lieutenant Crowther's 67th Company also moved forward, despite heavy machine gun fire from a ravine on the left, where Corporal Grosse-Bohle's two machine guns protected the German flank. Crowther was hit in the arm by one of the first bursts of machine gun fire but refused to stop for his wound to be treated. Instead, he pushed his company forward until it was only yards from the lead gun, where he ordered a halt. Even as the blood flowed from his arm, Crowther "walked up and down the line placing his men and instructing them in taking cover."[38] The Marine lieutenant almost dared the Germans to kill him. Marine rifle fire soon tore the machine gun crew apart, leaving only one man alive. The 67th Company rushed forward, capturing the gun. The Marines charged the position of the last heavy machine gun to the rear but were disappointed upon discovering that the crew had abandoned the weapon after firing all the available ammunition.

The fighting continued in brutal desperation for Marines and Germans alike. Resolved not to lose the woods, Lieutenant Wessberge ordered his company to fix bayonets, but the Marine "hurrah" signaled that Hamilton's men were already within the trees. The scrub was so thick that command and control was nonexistent on both sides, and each man battled on his own. "In the thick underbrush no orientation was possible," a German officer remembered. "We were entirely mixed in with the Americans." Wessberge was captured, and the rest of the company was soon annihilated. Only one German officer and a few men were able to make it out of the woods to safety.[39]

The capture of the Germans' main line slowed the American attack for only a few minutes as the surviving Marines paused to collect souvenirs. Soon the men of both companies pushed on, individually and in small groups, through the trees and yet another wheat field. They quickly encountered the German reserve on the crest of Hill 142—about 100 men of the 9th Company, 3rd Battalion, 462nd Regiment. This reserve company held the northern end of the woods and faced fierce combat with Hamilton's men. Again, the German machine guns took a fearful toll on the Marine attackers. "Men [were] dropping so fast," remembered Lieutenant Platt, "I couldn't count them."[40] Despite their losses, the Marines soon enveloped the Germans, surrounding the shallow dugouts at the edge of the woods and engaging in short, fierce hand-to-hand contests with bayoneted rifles. Second Lieutenant Emich, commanding the German 9th Company, gave the order, "No one gets through here."[41] The German officer died defending his position.

A German soldier sat wounded just outside the tree line in the open field, pinned under the bodies of two of his comrades. The German called over and over, "Kamerad, Kamerad," but the Marines were certain he was trying to lure them out into the open, where they would be cut down by machine gun fire. The thought enraged Private Walter H. Smith, who ran forward to bayonet the German. "Before I knew what I was doing," Smith later remembered, "and before I realized that everyone was shouting for me to get stay back I bobbed up . . . and got that Kamerad bird." Smith made it back to the tree line, but the German bullets "came so close I could almost feel their touch. . . . After that I thought I was bullet proof."[42]

The nature of the fierce struggle in the woods was reminiscent of the combat practiced by old-time Marines fighting in the Banana Wars in places like Coyotepe, Nicaragua, in 1912; Vera Cruz, Mexico, in 1914; and Cuba, Haiti, and the Dominican Republic from 1915 to 1917. "It was the same old fighting that the men had known," wrote Platt, and "no one can give a Marine pointers on that sort of thing."[43] Surrounded and surprised by the sudden appearance of the Americans, the survivors of the German 9th Company were soon killed or captured.

After only a few furious minutes, Hill 142 belonged to the relentless Marines led by Hamilton and Crowther, but the two companies had accomplished their objective at extreme cost, losing many officers and senior enlisted men and leaving the companies with a rapidly diminishing squad-level strength. The confused nature of the attack also caused friendly-fire casualties. At one point in the fight, as the men of the 49th Company advanced through the wheat fields shrouded by morning mist, they took fire from the 67th Company, advancing alongside them in the fog. Pharmacist Mate Third Class Algernon G. Brumbeloe ran back through the deadly field to find someone to stop the rifle and machine gun fire that was causing casualties in the 49th Company. The young corpsman from Danville, Virginia, encountered Major Turrill and told him about the friendly fire ahead. Duty done, Brumbeloe sprinted back to care for the Marines wounded in the exchange, bandaging their injuries and then dragging each man to safety. Brumbeloe was under constant fire from German snipers and machine guns, but miraculously, he survived that day without a wound. Brumbeloe's luck ran out the following day. A German sniper shot him in the knee as he searched the same field for dead to be buried and any wounded Marines who had been overlooked. Turrill recommended the corpsman for the Medal of Honor, but Brumbeloe received the Navy Cross instead.[44]

Although they had destroyed two German companies, Hamilton and Crowther were not ready to halt their attack. Ahead lay open ground sloping down to the village of Torcy. In the field lay a road, and an embankment alongside it offered an excellent line of defense. Hamilton ordered his lead platoon forward to occupy the position, knowing that the rest of his company would follow behind. Unknowingly, Hamilton's and Crowther's Marines had pierced the German front line and were now pushing forward against the German reserves in and around the village of Torcy. In a combination of small groups from both companies, the Marines attacked in all directions. Small bands of Marines pressed forward from Hill 142, fanning out from the northwest side of the hill all the way to the east side. The Marines ran forward with no real orders or organization, other than a burning desire to advance. "We just couldn't stop despite the orders of our leaders," recalled Private Walter H. Smith.[45]

As the Marines pressed into the open fields, withering machine gun fire struck them as the German front line and reserves turned and shifted their fire toward the attackers. The lead element was one of Hamilton's platoons. "What saved me from getting hit," Hamilton later wrote, "I don't know."[46] The platoon broke into two parts, unbeknownst to the captain. Most of the Marines turned left to take on the machine guns, while Hamilton pressed forward with an automatic rifle section, advancing 600 yards to the Torcy road.

The 320 men of the German 2nd Battalion, 462nd Infantry, lay in line just east of the 11th Company, south of the Torcy–Belleau road. The battalion commander observed the Marines sweeping down on his front and rear and moved his heavy machine gun company back to Torcy to secure the town. With the threat to his front halted, he then turned the 6th Company on his right flank to face the threat from Hill 142. Two German platoons counterattacked the Marines, blunting the advance and leaving many Marines dead and wounded. However, other small groups of Marines penetrated all the way to the town of Torcy. One Marine corporal sent word back with a wounded man that he and a companion had captured the town and needed reinforcements and ammunition. The two were never heard from again. In 1927 two bodies still clad in Marine uniforms were found in a small pit just outside a house at the south end of the town. Two German bodies lay in the pit as well.[47]

On the brow of Hill 142, Lieutenant Platt pulled together the remnants of his platoon and any other Marines he could find. He was surprised to discover Sergeant Hunter with twenty Marines from the 67th Company in his front. Platt questioned Hunter, asking who his commanding officer was. "Me," Hunter replied. "All the rest are deados." The sergeant then added, "We are going over," meaning that he and his small band of Marines intended to attack Torcy. Platt responded, "Why, man, the whole Boche army is over there." Hunter simply shrugged and said, "Well, my tactics are simple: go get them." Platt spent several minutes arguing with Hunter, trying to convince him to cancel his attack due to the German numbers. The lieutenant eventually extracted a promise from the stubborn sergeant that he would wait until Platt returned with orders from Hamilton. Hunter reluctantly promised, but Platt noted that every one of those words had to be "dragged from his lips." The Marines with Hunter were also disappointed, "looking about as pleased as a man who has bitten into a green persimmon."[48]

Second Lieutenant Winter's German 12th Company lay in reserve just south of Torcy. His men were on alert, and at 4:50 a.m. the Americans were reported to be moving down a depression in his front and also approaching to his rear. Winter ordered an immediate counterattack. Half of the company under First Lieutenant Vollmecke pushed forward toward the front of Hill 142, while Winter took the other half in a flanking attack to the west. Moments later, Captain Hamilton spotted the German units gathering for the counterattack. Flanked and outnumbered, Hamilton ordered the surviving Marines back up the hill. "I realized that I had gone too far," Hamilton wrote, and "it was a case of every man for himself."[49] The captain escaped only by crawling through a cold, wet, reed-choked drainage ditch. German machine gun bullets passed inches over his head, but he arrived safely back on the hill. Private Smith was running along the Torcy road with a band of Marines when a German jumped up from the roadside and wounded one of the 49th Company's sergeants in the wrist. "I got the German before he dropped back in the weeds," recalled Smith.[50] They too made it safely back to the hill.

Platt found Hamilton in a ravine on the front slope of Hill 142. The captain asked how many men remained with Platt. "A few from my outfit and twenty strays that I just found," he answered. "Fine," Hamilton replied. He smiled and said, "You've got a whole army. Consolidate 'em. We are going back." Platt was surprised, but Hamilton explained that his map was faulty and there were Germans on three sides of the position. "So, go to it," the captain ordered. "Get the men. Skate." Platt sprinted back to his men, who, upon hearing the order, thought the lieutenant was some sort of a coward. Just then, one of the Marines was hit in the back from fire up the hill. "That was enough," remembered Platt. "My reputation was saved. All those Marines wanted was something to fight and directions didn't count."[51] Platt's men went back up Hill 142.

Vollmecke's men advanced across the ravine and reached the base of the hill but were halted by the Marines' fire. On the flank, Winter pushed up the hill but was surrounded by more Marines, some of whom were still attacking down the hill while others were withdrawing to the crest. The action turned into a bloody free-for-all, with Marines and Germans swirling about in small groups through the wheat and the brush. Neither line remained intact. Still bleeding from his arm wound, Lieutenant Crowther asked for men to move the captured German machine guns to repel the counterattack. While placing the guns, Crowther fell, riddled by German machine gun fire. The Illinois farm boy would never return to his hometown on the prairie. Crowther was posthumously awarded the Navy Cross for his actions that morning.

German commander Winter died with his pistol in his hand, leading his men up the hill. Vollmecke was wounded by Marine fire. With no officer left standing, the remnants of the German 12th Company's counterattack withdrew across the ravine to their original positions.

Although taking heavy losses of their own, the 67th Company inflicted serious casualties on the enemy. In the melee, Private Dewey E. Shepherd led a small remnant of the company in the capture of fourteen German soldiers and several machine guns within a small stand of poplars beyond the hill. Without more men, the Marines could not safely escort their prisoners to the rear. Dodging German fire, Shepherd raced across two open fields to find help. Hamilton saw the private running in the open and sprinted forward to meet him and try to save the man's life. Both of them survived the encounter, and additional Marines went to help the few men remaining in the poplars. The young private was later awarded the Croix de Guerre for his bravery.[52]

As the scattered bands of Marines pulled back, Platt and Hamilton met again about halfway up the other side of Hill 142. They brought together the remnants of the 49th and 67th Companies. Hamilton gave Platt the choice of forming the men into a defensive line or taking on a German machine gun that had found its way up Hill 142. "I'll take the easy job," replied Platt. "I'll go after the gun." The lieutenant took only four men with him, and they soon found that the Germans had abandoned the machine gun as the Marines approached. Platt's men were curious about the weapon, and when one of them pulled a lever on the gun, it began to fire on its own, narrowly missing the lieutenant. "Turn that damn thing off," shouted Platt after hitting the ground. The man replied, "Can't sir, don't know how!"[53] The Marines held the gun down, allowing it to fire into the ground, until the ammunition belt had fed through the weapon.

Help soon arrived in the form of ten heavy machine guns. Captain Matt Kingman led his 15th Company, 6th Machine Gun Battalion, in support of the attack. The guns initially placed overhead fire on the German reserve positions and assembly points until they were called forward to bolster the line on Hill 142. The young captain was wounded during the movement, but his Marines kept going under heavy artillery and machine gun fire. Once in position, Privates Emanuel Smolik and Russell D. Smith returned fire with their French Hotchkiss machine gun until German bullets destroyed their weapon. Corporals Frank W. Dunham and John G. Dickson Jr. also maintained their position, despite the accurate enemy gunfire. The constant firing caused the company's ammunition supply to become dangerously low. Private William F. Hughes ran to the rear for more ammunition, mistakenly passing through German lines. While he was behind the enemy, Hughes spotted a German machine gun withdrawing under attack by the Marines from Hill 142. Hughes opened fire on the three Germans manning the gun, pinning them until the advancing Marines killed them.[54]

Back at the initial line of attack, Major Turrill waited anxiously for the last two companies of his battalion to arrive. Lieutenant Colonel Feland learned that the 8th Machine Gun Company and the 17th Company of Turrill's battalion had gotten lost en route to the jump-off position. Feland moved quickly and found the 8th Company as well as part of the 66th Company, not the 17th, as he had expected. The colonel led the Marines through the town of Champillon under heavy shell fire toward the darkness of Hill 142.[55]

The lead platoon of First Lieutenant Walter T. H. Galliford's 66th Company soon reported to Turrill. Galliford was new to the company, having been detached on June 1 from the 17th Company after both Captain Raymond F. Dirksen and First Lieutenant Robert C. Anthony became ill during the move to Montreuil-aux-Lions and were directed to the hospital. The 66th Company was in good hands under Galliford, a 1917 graduate of Texas A&M, where he studied mechanical engineering.

Turrill quickly sent the Marines forward, following the path of Hamilton's men. Turrill then set up a defensive position across the first wood line and expanded it as the rest of the 66th Company and the 8th Machine Gun Company arrived at about 4:30 a.m., led by Feland. The colonel then returned to Champillon to search for the missing 17th Company, the only unit yet to arrive.

Several Marines of the 66th Company passed the front line and ran forward, "giving the Marine yell." The men plunged over some wire entanglements and found some Germans still in their dugouts. The fight became a duel of bayonets and sidearms. "I quickly picked out a German captain as my man," remembered Private Charles J. Galloway. The captain stood before Galloway with a drawn pistol, but "he was not as quick on his trigger as I was with my bayonet . . . I made a lunge for him and got him right."[56] Galloway grabbed a pair of shoes strapped to his opponent's shoulder as the bleeding man fell to the ground. The surviving Marines ran back to the safety of their line. The 66th Company took position on the left, on the edge of the wood, with the Germans 500 yards away across a field of ripening wheat.

The enemy soon moved forward through the wheat in yet another coun-terattack. "We would aim and fire slowly," Private Powis recalled, "and large gaps would appear in their lines."[57] The initial attacks came within fifty yards of the Marine line before breaking. As the Germans turned to run, individual Marines charged forward with fixed bayonets to close with the enemy, only to be shot down. Officers shouted to the men to remain in their positions, and they needed little urging after watching their comrades fall. Powis discarded his French Chauchat light machine gun after it jammed and picked up a rifle from a dead Marine to continue the fight. The Germans attacked the 66th Company six separate times, always with the same result. The Marines used the Chauchat machines guns and some grenades, but "the main thing we used was the rifle," according to Powis.[58]

Four machine guns of the 8th Machine Gun Company moved up to bol-ster the position. Captain John H. Fay led his machine gunners forward, crawling through the wheat fields to position the guns. Fay was a former enlisted man, having joined the Marine Corps in 1899. He was on his fourth enlistment when he accepted a commission as a second lieutenant in 1917, becoming an officer at almost thirty-eight years of age. Fay commanded the company in October and was promoted to captain in November. Now he moved along the line "and encouraged his men by his utter indifference to danger."[59] Fay would eventually receive the Navy Cross for his bravery under fire.

At dawn, Captain Roswell Winans was finally relieved of his position by the French and took his 17th Company to join the attack. Unfortunately, Winans had little idea where the rest of the battalion was located. First Lieutenant William R. Matthews, intelligence officer for the 2nd Battalion, 5th Marines, was awakened by the voice of First Lieutenant Blake shouting, "All right 17th Company," as he deployed his platoon for an attack, though it had yet to move through Champillon, far from the German positions.[60] Captain Winans ordered his company into the line of battle on the nearby road amidst random German shell bursts and gave the order to double-time. At first, the men believed they were going into reserve, but soon rifle and machine gun bullets passed overhead, causing one Marine to remark, "Our only rest would be a 'Blighty' or a 'Trip West.'"[61]

Wounded Marines moving to the rear passed along information about friends to men in the company. One bloody Marine called out to Private Cordes, "I am sorry to say that our good old pal Bill Flaherty was lamped off." The news shocked Cordes. "Oh God!" he later wrote. "How that did unnerve me and set my blood boiling."[62] Cordes advanced with the company, vowing to exact revenge.

The ever-present Lieutenant Colonel Feland met Winans's column and led it directly to Hill 142 through Champillon. By 5:30 a.m., Winans had his 17th Company at the original attack line and was moving forward to reinforce the two lead companies. Feland joined Turrill at his command post and continued to provide leadership to the 1st Battalion.[63]

As the 17th Company advanced, Blake knew that the random German fire would soon become accurate, so he took several Marines to the right to search for a better route forward. Blake and his men moved up a ravine that was "filled with German dead" until he made contact with Captain Hamilton. Blake reported that he could bring the entire 17th Company forward over the same route under cover. Hamilton agreed, and Blake went back and led the company onward with virtually no losses.

Once in line, Winans placed his 17th Company on the right, overlooking a German strongpoint in a strange-looking rectangular wooded area.[64] The German 10th and 11th Companies, 3rd Battalion, 460th Infantry Regiment, held the woods, supported by the 12th Company in a smaller stand of trees to the north. Recognizing the critical nature of the terrain, these three German companies were determined to hold their position at all costs. They were reinforced by two platoons of the 3rd Machine Gun Company, adding firepower on each flank. Second Lieutenant Koch, commanding the 10th Company, watched the early-morning fight on Hill 142 with much interest. He initially believed the attackers were Englishmen, having yet to face any Americans. The "British" had obviously destroyed the battalion's 9th Company on the hill and, Koch thought, would soon come toward him. Koch placed his men in position on the edge of the woods facing the hill and waited. Moments later, he saw Marines charging across the wheat fields to reach the north side of the woods.[65]

These Marines were from the 67th Company, commanded by Second Lieutenant Thomas W. Ashley. Second Lieutenant James McB. Garvey found Ashley in the middle of a field wielding a German machine gun but unable to locate the mechanism to fire the weapon. Garvey asked Ashley if he knew where the other companies were. Ashley replied that "he did not know but said nothing about the experiences he had." The two officers spent several minutes trying to operate the machine gun, but to no avail. Garvey finally bade his fellow lieutenant good-bye and returned to his platoon. Ashley "decided to stay," Garvey later wrote, and "that was the last time I saw him."[66]

On Hill 142, the sight of the German counterattacks seemed to infuriate Ashley, and his anger inspired his men to drive the Germans back down the hill. There, in the midst of the battle, Ashley was at his best. He led his few remaining men into the ravine at the base of the hill and then into a wheat field, straight at the enemy. Armed with his captured machine gun, Ashley scattered the German advance, driving the Germans into the wheat field beyond.

Captain Winans with his 17th Company watched in amazement as the small band of Marines charged through the open wheat fields. The courage of the attackers inspired the men of the 17th Company, who wished to join the fight. Winans held them back, though, knowing that the effort was hopeless. "Our Captain ordered us to stay in the ravine," Private Cordes remembered. He watched the thin line of Marines sprint into the wheat field and later wrote, "It meant death to cross it but our boys went through."[67]

Ashley and his men pushed through the wheat toward the rectangular woods perched atop a commanding knoll that dominated the flank of Hill 142. Receiving heavy fire from the woods, Ashley placed his men in the cover of a small stand of trees just north of the woods. He then divided his command, sending part of his platoon in a charge for the tree line, striking the 10th Company from the west while he attacked from the north. Lieutenant Koch reacted swiftly, moving his German reserve platoon to the north edge of the woods and meeting the Marines there, who were only three feet from the tree line. The German riflemen cut down the charging Marines, leaving few survivors. Private Cordes of the 17th Company watched from Hill 142 as "nine out of every ten fell either killed or mortally wounded. Some few got to the next woods but never returned."[68]

Once the attack had been bloodily repulsed, Koch immediately called for support from the 11th Company. The German reserves arrived as the wounded Marines began to drag themselves back through the wheat. Before the Marines could regroup, the 11th Company's reserve platoon counterattacked out of the trees, hitting both the wheat field and Ashley's position in the stand of trees. Ashley and his men took up the challenge and stood their ground. The fighting was fierce, and according to Second Lieutenant Weitkunat, the German company's commander, "No prisoners were taken." The battle became a modern type of Wild West gunfight, with the two sides only yards away from each other. There was no cover for either side except for the waist-high wheat.

Marines of the 67th Company began to fall around him, but Ashley seemed to be "a superman," impervious to enemy bullets. Within minutes, Ashley was the only Marine left standing. Every man in his platoon lay in the wheat, either dead or wounded. At least one 1st Platoon Marine survived long enough to inflict serious damage on the German advance. His body was found in a shell hole with eighty empty cartridges around him and the rim of the crater pockmarked by German bullets. In the midst of such bedlam, Ashley's fighting spirit ruled the battlefield. Despite being alone, he continued to fire and "accounted for the enemy as fast as they appeared."[69]

Finally, inevitably, Lieutenant Ashley was struck down at point-blank range, desperately wounded. Bullets cut into his legs, hips, and stomach. The impact drove him backward to the ground, where he lay in shock, bleeding heavily. The bodies of three Marines surrounded him, a silent tribute to the ferocity of the battle. Determined to survive, Ashley dragged himself across the wheat field to the cover of a few trees. Within minutes, he died from loss of blood. In 1911 Ashley had presented Henry Ward Beecher's "The Message of Our Flag" at the commencement ceremony at Deerfield Academy: "You go to serve our country in the cause of liberty, and if you fall in that struggle, may some kind hand wrap about you the flag of your country, and may you die with its sacred touch upon you." Those prophetic words had come to pass. After the fight was over, members of the company searched unsuccessfully for Ashley's body on Hill 142. No bodies of the platoon could be found; nor were there any survivors of the final action to locate them in the rectangular woods.[70]

The German defenders were so impressed by the incredible bravery of the Marines that they gathered the fallen Americans and honored them by placing their bodies in line for later burial. The Germans searched the bodies but took nothing except food, reluctant to disturb the honored dead. When Marines captured the woods several days later, they found the bodies still in line, just as the enemy had left them. The exception was Tom Ashley. His body remained in the wheat he had fought so hard to capture. A Marine advance found the fallen lieutenant days later, close to his captured German machine gun.[71]

A new Marine advance came from Major Berry's 3rd Battalion, 5th Marines, from the southeast. Berry had been ordered to "advance my left flank to straighten out the line" with Turrill's advance on Hill 142, but not to advance as far as the German positions.[72] Berry's second in command, Captain Henry L. Larsen, arrived at Captain Conachy's 45th Company headquarters with orders to advance and support Turrill's right. Conachy and Larsen went to Lieutenant Edward B. Hope's platoon, located on the edge of the wheat field south of the now hotly contested rectangular woods. The lieutenant was instructed to take his men forward into the wheat but halt short of the German positions.

Hope quickly fielded his platoon in four assault waves. The lieutenant had little idea what was in front of him, but he and his men had watched the attack earlier that morning and wanted to support it. At 6:05 Captain Conachy launched two platoons of his 45th Company across the wheat field, striking at the rectangular woods and the open ground held by the two companies of the German 3rd Battalion, 460th Infantry. The Germans in the woods reacted quickly. The advance fell primarily on Lieutenant Weitkunat's 11th Company, which opened a blazing fire with light machine guns as soon

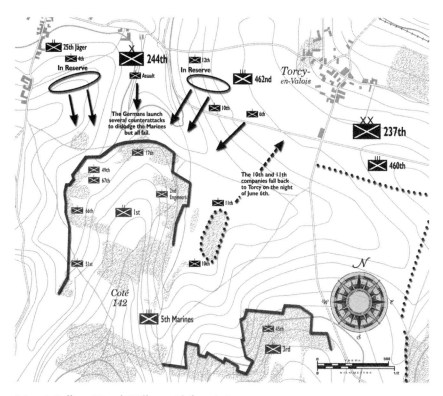

Map 6. Belleau Wood, Hill 142 (defense), June 6, 1918

as the first wave of Marines appeared in the wheat. Weitkunat later reported that the guns "fired excellently, no gun having to interrupt its activity for any length of time because of stoppages."[73]

Lieutenant Koch shifted all available men of the German 10th Company to join Weitkunat's 11th Company. The rapidity of the veteran German fire stunned the Marine advance. Another Marine platoon directly south of the tree line became pinned down immediately, but Hope's 1st Platoon advanced to a farm road only 200 yards short of the woods. One of the first bursts of machine gun fire struck Hope in the right knee. "I felt my legs suddenly knocked from under me," he later wrote to his father. "I guess I squirmed around on the ground like a chicken with it's [sic] head cut off but kept my mouth shut at least."[74] Lieutenant Hope continued to lead his men despite his injury, refusing treatment until all the other wounded men around him had been cared for. A Marine stemmed the flow of blood by stuffing one of Hope's puttees in the wound. Hope received the Navy Cross for his leadership in the attack.

The Marines could go no further and dug in. Evidence of the ferocity of the fight could still be witnessed in 1919, when an observer noted, "One could see today helmets, equipment, rifles etc., in a well defined row across the open space where some damaging fire hit the advancing lines."[75] Lieutenant Hope's platoon grimly held the farm lane alone, but they ran short of rifle ammunition as the morning battle continued. The Marines signaled for resupply, but Captain Conachy refused to order any Marine to traverse the fire-swept fields to reach the 1st Platoon, stating, "A live marine is better than a dead or wounded one any day."[76]

The enemy artillery sought out the newly arrived Marines on Hill 142 before they could entrench. Chains of explosions rained shrapnel over the company. "Lord! How those shells did kill and maim our boys," Private Cordes recalled. "It was worse than *hell!*" The Marines responded by remaining in the ravine and shooting down every German soldier in sight. "Here we could get a good shot at the Germans, and kept picking them off like flies . . . it was great sport," remembered Cordes. The former printer from St. Louis joined a group of riflemen who held an informal marksmanship competition. The deadly game began with a Marine calling out his mark and then offering the target to his comrades if the German did not fall at the first shot. The sport was ruined because "every time we shot, they fell."[77]

The Germans to the west joined in the attack to secure their line. The Marines opened fire on the German lines across the ravine held by the German 2nd Battalion, 273rd Reserve Infantry, 197th Infantry Division. The fire elicited a message to the German regimental headquarters, "stating that a counterattack against Hill 142 was imperative."[78] At 7:30 a.m. the 4th Company of the German 25th Jäger Battalion attacked the hill, trying to secure the 197th Division's flank. The Germans attacked up the ravine and pushed up the hill but were halted after a severe hand-grenade battle with the Marines. Despite their repulse, by 9:00 a.m., the Jägers had linked up with Sclemm's 3rd Battalion, 462nd Infantry, thus restoring the German front line at the base of the hill.

Other bands of Marines worked their way directly north, moving under cover of the creek ravine all the way to the east edge of Bussaires. However, the relentless German counterattacks forced the Marines to fall back to Hill 142. With the lines now stabilizing, the Marines began to measure the extent of their loss. The attacks carried out by the 67th and 49th Companies proved costly to the leadership of both units. All four officers of the 67th Company were killed or wounded, along with twenty sergeants and corporals. Marine Gunner Henry L. Hulbert and First Sergeant Pop Hunter were the only survivors of the 67th Company's senior leadership. Every other officer and staff noncommissioned officer was killed or wounded.[79]

Gunner Hulbert was one of the more colorful figures in a colorful unit.

Decorative tattoos of a dragoon, a frog, a snake, a spider web, an eagle, and several women adorned Hulbert's body, which must have thoroughly impressed the men of the 67th Company, almost as much as the Medal of Honor he received for his bravery in Samoa in 1899. In 1917 Hulbert served on the personal staff of Commandant Barnett at Marine Corps headquarters and was known as the "tall white-haired gunnery sergeant who kept guard at the door of the commandant at Washington."[80] When America went to war, Hulbert rejected all efforts to keep him at headquarters and insisted on going into combat with a line infantry company. At fifty-one years old, Hulbert was one of the oldest and most experienced Marines in the 4th Brigade.

Together, Hulbert and Hunter pulled the remnants of the 67th Company together and set up an adequate defense of Hill 142, moving around the position as if immune to enemy fire. Hunter inspired the Marines to repulse the German attack, but he was wounded three times and died sometime during the morning from a gunshot wound to the head; he was posthumously awarded the Navy Cross for his bravery. Despite the confusion of battle, Hunter's personal effects were recovered. One of his last requests was that his watch be returned to his wife, and Major Keller E. Rockey carried the watch with him until he returned the timepiece to Mrs. Ida May Hunter in 1919.[81]

By midmorning, Captain Hamilton and Lieutenant Platt were the only officers of the 49th Company left standing; all the others had been killed or wounded. All told, twenty-four of the company's sergeants and corporals had become casualties. However, scattered groups and individual Marines that had been separated from the company during the attack joined the position as the morning went on.[82]

Platt placed his men in the captured German foxholes and ordered them to stay under cover. The Marines protested and asked for orders to advance again, but Platt remained firm. Hamilton sent Platt into the trees below the hill to determine the location of the German advance. The lieutenant was surprised to find a lone Marine with a wounded foot smoking a cigarette and guarding three Germans roped to a tree. Platt questioned the man, who simply stated, "Couldn't walk sir. So I just thought I'd tie them up till somebody came up."[83] Platt ordered the three Germans to carry the injured Marine back to the Americans' position.

By 6:00 a.m., Turrill was consolidating his battalion's position and attempting to secure his flanks. The French had yet to come up on his left, and Berry's battalion was not supporting his right, leaving Turrill and his battalion like a spear stuck directly into the German position. He asked Feland for a reserve company to clear the ravine to his left and connect with

the French. The best news came in the form of two platoons from the army's
2nd Battalion, 2nd Engineer Regiment.

The quantity of gunfire increased as the engineers neared Hill 142, promising a heated fight ahead. German shells rained over First Lieutenant Russell
A. Warner and his army platoon of D Company as they neared the hill. Warner ordered his men under cover while he pushed ahead to find a protected
path to the Marines. "It was then I got shot, probably by a sniper," he later
wrote. "The bullet must have passed thru my gas mask, it cut a hole in the
edge of one of my dog tags, plowed through my left breast above the ribs
and . . . thru a note book I had in my left breast pocket." Warner staggered
back to his platoon and then collapsed, bleeding heavily from the chest. The
bullet broke several ribs and punctured a lung before exiting through Warner's leg, prevented from causing any further damage when it fragmented
his .45-caliber pistol. The young lieutenant lost consciousness from shock
and blood loss and awakened days later in a hospital bed to the sound of a
nurse asking, "Lt. do you want some cocoa?"[84]

Sergeant Jimmy Hughes took command of the platoon, linked up with
the Marines, and was promptly placed on Winans's right. The soldiers positioned themselves in the ravine at the base of the hill, bending low to escape
the ever-present snipers. The Marines and engineers began to dig trenches
on Hill 142, expecting an enemy counterattack.[85]

To their right, Second Lieutenant Blohm's Assault Company of the German 244th Brigade moved to the attack. The Germans used the heavy brush
on the hillside for concealment and actually climbed twenty yards up the hill
before running into the Marines' line of defense. Corporal Prentice S. Greer
and several other men of the 67th Company found themselves cut off from
the main Marine position and vulnerable to enemy fire. Greer "jumped to
the front yelling to the men to follow him," attacking the nearest Germans.
He took a German machine gun placement with his bayonet, capturing the
crew and driving back the supporting infantry. For his actions, Greer later
received a Navy Cross and a lieutenant's commission.[86]

The Germans continued to attack, tossing hand grenades into the Marines' position and trying to knock out an American machine gun. One of
the explosions kicked up a rock that struck Captain Hamilton behind the
ear, momentarily stunning him.[87] The Marines were surprised, as the grenades were the first sign that the Germans were so near. Hamilton and Gunnery Sergeant Charles F. Hoffman noticed twelve German soldiers crawling
toward them, armed with five light machine guns. They jumped to their feet
and charged the German advance. Hoffman bayoneted the German commander, withdrew his dripping blade, and then stabbed the next German,
killing him as well. Hamilton attacked with a bayoneted rifle, and the two

Marines fought hand to hand with the remaining Germans, who responded with rifle fire, bayonets, and hand grenades. The fight was over within moments, as the survivors of the German platoon abandoned their weapons and ran down the hill to safety. For this action, Hoffman was later awarded the Medal of Honor, the first Marine so honored in World War I.[88] Hamilton was nominated for the Medal of Honor as well, but his award was downgraded to a Distinguished Service Cross. "His deed, to my mind, satisfies the requirements for the award of a Medal of Honor," Commandant Lejeune wrote in 1923, "in that it was one of extraordinary heroism at the risk of his life on the field of battle and beyond the call of duty."[89]

In the 49th Company, one of the officers wounded in the initial assault was First Lieutenant Vernon L. Somers from the Eastern Shore of Virginia. By 10:00 a.m., "Apple" Somers was covered with blood from arm and leg wounds received during several hand-to-hand encounters to break the German line. He now moved about the hill, carrying a knife in one hand and a pistol in the other, trying to improve his Marines' position. Without warning, German machine gun bullets struck the lieutenant at close range, mortally wounding him. Stretcher bearers pulled Somers to safety and started to carry him to the rear, but Somers knew his wounds were fatal. He ordered the men to stop, saying, "Put me down, I am dying and want to die with the boys."[90] Members of his platoon left their positions to surround Somers. He ordered them back under cover, knowing he had no chance to survive. Somers's Marines ignored the order and stayed with their dying lieutenant. The Marines gathered close, giving Somers "aid and comfort . . . in his last moments." Somers then spoke his last words: "Stay with them, boys, and show them where you are from."[91] He lay back on the stretcher, put his hands behind his head, and "went to sleep, never to wake any more." Private Leonard D. Hall wrote home two weeks later, saying of the lieutenant, "Tell his mother and any of his people he was a boy to be proud of."[92]

Belleau Wood Tour

Stop 4. German Cemetery, 49°04'58.6"N 3°17'01.3"E

Leave Lucy-le-Bocage and continue north on the Route de Torcy, D 82, passing Belleau Wood to your right and the original Marine line to your left. After 3.2 kilometers, turn right onto the D 9. In 400 meters, you will see the German Cemetery on your right. Enter the small parking area at the cemetery.

There are 8,630 German soldiers buried here. Almost all were killed during the 1918 battles nearby. More than half that number rest in two mass graves.

Walk to the back wall of the cemetery, where you can gain a view looking south at the 4th Brigade's line of defense. You now have the perspective of the German defenders on June 6, holding Belleau Wood to your left and extending to Hill 142 on your right. The infamous rectangular woods can be seen at the base of the steep hillside. Just as you were in the center of the Marine line at Lucy-le-Bocage, here you are in the center of the German line, with the towns of Belleau and Torcy behind you on the slope to Clignon Creek. On June 6 you would have seen the battle for Hill 142 in the morning and the attack of the 45th Company, 3rd Battalion, 5th Marines, directly ahead, striking at Belleau Wood.

The officer leading the company, Lieutenant Thomas H. Miles, died in these fields, and almost half his Marines were killed or wounded. The company suffered heavy losses among its squad leaders. At least eighteen sergeants and corporals were killed or wounded, including First Sergeant William P. Higginson. The town of Buffalo, New York, was hard hit. Native sons Sergeant Franklyn L. Dost, Sergeant James J. Gibbons, and Private Frederick W. Florian Jr. were killed in the assault, leaving the town in mourning. Six Navy Crosses were awarded to members of the company who were killed while attacking in the wheat fields. Of the three platoons attacking the woods, only nine Marines were available for duty at nightfall.

Stop 5. Bussaires, 49°05'29.7"N 3°15'27.7"E

Before you leave the parking lot, look to your left down the D 9. Locate the spires of Torcy in the trees to your right and then the high ground of Hill

180 beyond the town; both were taken by the Germans before the Marines arrived. Hill 142 is the long ridge to your left. Turn left on the D 9 and proceed 2.4 kilometers to Bussaires. Turn right on the Rue du Moulin. Stop at the church on your left.

In the center of town, locate the monument to the local people who lost their lives in World War I. By the end of your driving tour, you will have seen many such memorials honoring the sacrifice of the French people during the war. This town was captured by the Germans on June 1 and held by them throughout the battle. During this stop, it is important to appreciate the terrain of the Clignon Creek valley, which is critical for understanding the German defense of the area and the resulting Marine attacks. This valley is in defilade to Marine observation, giving the Germans an easy route to supply and reinforce their positions on the high ground ahead of the three towns of Belleau, Torcy, and Bussaires. The Marine Brigade focused its combat on Belleau Wood and never captured these towns. They remained in German hands until the joint French 167th Division and 26th "Yankee" Division offensive in July 1918.

Stop 6. Les Mares Farm, 49°04'17.7"N 3°14'23.2"E

Retrace your route and proceed directly across the D 9 on the Rue du Lieutenant Peyroche, named after a French officer who was killed nearby in the July offensive. Leave Bussaires en route to the high ground occupied by the Marine Brigade. In 700 meters, you will come to an intersection with multiple farm roads. *Do not* take the road on your immediate right. Proceed on Rue du Lieutenant Peyroche, which leads up the hill to your right front. Proceed to the Les Mares Farm, 850 meters ahead. *This farm is private property. Please respect the property owners and pull off the road just short of the farm, allowing traffic to pass your vehicle.*

Major Wise's 2nd Battalion, 5th Marines, defended this area, holding the left of the 2nd Division's line. You can compare the terrain here with that of Major Holcomb on the opposite flank, holding the Paris road. The high ground here also allows you to see the German high ground beyond Clignon Creek, Hill 142 to your right, and Belleau Wood beyond. Notice the ravines cutting back into the Marine positions, offering the Germans avenues of approach to the American lines.

Just as the Marine lines were tested on the Paris road, the Germans attacked here on June 3, with similar results. Rather than using the ravines, the Germans advanced over the open wheat fields, taking the same route you have just driven. On June 4 the Germans attacked; as they approached, the Marines could see their helmets and fixed bayonets but held their fire. The Germans entered a sweeping field of wheat that was waist high. When the enemy lines reached a distance of 100 yards, the Marines opened fire with their Springfield rifles, and the Germans' front line disappeared. The second line ran forward firing, but the Marines' rifle fire ripped the German line to shreds. "Those Germans just melted away," one Marine recalled. "Whole columns went down and the others scattered to the right and left . . . there was not one answering shot."[1] Captain Blanchfield's 55th Company fired from the farm buildings at Les Mares Farm. The captain later wrote, "It was here that the months of training the Marines had been through, helped them."[2]

Stop 7. *Marigny-en-Orxois,* 49°03'36.7"N 3°13'35.5"E

Continue south down the road toward Marigny. In 1.4 kilometers, pause by the town cemetery on your left. Major Wise's 2nd Battalion headquarters was located here on June 6, on the back side of the cemetery wall, taking advantage of its protection from German artillery. Proceed 500 meters to the center of Marigny-en-Orxois, which was punished heavily by German artillery during the battle.

As Captain Robert W. "Bert" Voeth's 97th Company neared the tree line to the south, they noticed German artillery pounding the nearby town of Marigny into rubble. Each new shell burst covered the houses with rolling clouds of dust. "The enemy seemed to be very anxious to bring down the steeple of the church," remembered one Marine. And several direct hits set the steeple on fire.[3]

"Squads Right, Double Time! March!" shouted Captain Voeth, sending the column into the cover of the trees unharmed.[4] Each squad then started a small cooking fire to prepare its two cans of "Corned Willie" and three boxes of hardtack. A French artillery unit fired from the town, while a nearby band of Chasseurs Alpine passed out cider to the thirsty Marines.

Other more adventuresome Marines searched for food in Marigny. Most came back with empty pockets, except for Private Roberts, who appeared with an iron pot and was "literally grinning from ear to ear." The pot was filled with the "most luscious looking, golden brown, French fried potatoes any of us had ever seen." When asked where he had found such a miraculous feast, Roberts replied that he had liberated the pot from the French artillery mess when the gunners scattered during counterbattery fire.[5]

Stop 8. *La Voie du Chatel,* 49°03'14.3"N 3°14'30.5"E

Proceed 1.2 kilometers on the D 11 (Rue du Pre des Saules) east to La Voie du Chatel. Select a point where you can look back to Les Mares Farm. Park and then walk to any spot and view the battlefield from the Marine perspective.

You are following the steps of Major Berry's 3rd Battalion, 5th Marines. The leading files entered the small village, where French doctors had established an aid station. The Marines stared at the bloody Frenchmen, who gazed back with little interest. On the far side of town, a single French artillery piece fired round after round at the German advance. Berry's Marines marched past the Frenchmen to a reserve position in a nearby wood. Colonel Catlin set up the 6th Marine headquarters here on June 2 until June 5. He watched the repulse of the German attacks from this vantage point. The village was busting with excitement as runners raced back and forth with urgent messages from Marine battalion commanders and intelligence officers attempting to maintain contact with their Allies.

5

June 6, 1918—Berry's 3rd Battalion, 5th Marines
"It Is Uncertain Who Holds Bois de Belleau"

WORD OF THE SUCCESSFUL MARINE AND FRENCH ASSAULT on Hill 142 passed up the chain of command and reached General Degoutte. The apparent ease of the morning's advance caused Degoutte to expand the follow-up attack. He issued Supplementary Order 81, which put the second phase of the operation in motion: the attack on Belleau Wood and the high ground beyond. Assured by the morning's success, Degoutte ordered the capture of Belleau Wood that same evening. General Bundy, commanding the 2nd Division, would coordinate the attack. Brigadier General Harbord later remembered that there was no written order; he received only the direct oral communication from the French corps commander to advance his line.[1]

Most important, General Degoutte assured the Americans that there was no longer a significant German presence in Belleau Wood. Prior to June 6, however, daily intelligence reports had indicated that the Germans held the woods. A telephone message from 21st Corps to 2nd Division headquarters at 1:35 a.m. on June 3 reported that the Germans had captured Belleau Wood the previous evening. French aircraft from Squadron 27 provided constant reconnaissance of the German position. On June 3 German troops were observed within the woods, according to a message dropped to 2nd Division headquarters, and another pilot actually strafed some of the German infantry in the woods after they fired on his airplane. As late as June 5, a French pilot from Squadron 252 reported that he was taking fire from German detachments in the woods.[2]

The German 237th Division not only still occupied Belleau Wood; it had every intention of defending the ground against the attacking Marines. Alerted by the shattering of the 460th Regiment on Hill 142, the division's other two regiments were ready should the Americans continue their attack. The 462nd Regiment still held the ground from the rectangular woods to Belleau, while the 461st Regiment held Belleau proper.

After the capture of Hill 142 on the morning of June 6, Lieutenant Rene P. L. Hadrot of Squadron 252 dispatched a message that significantly altered the estimate of German positions. Written at 7:30 a.m., the report carried these fateful words: "It is uncertain who holds Bois de Belleau." At 2:00 p.m. another dispatch from the 21st Corps stated, "Information from the civil population and observation leads to the belief that elements of the enemy are located in Torcy, Belleau, La Grande Ferme De Torcy and on Hill 201."[3] No mention was made of any German occupation of Belleau Wood, and in fact, the main enemy line was believed to be behind the forest. Because of this flawed intelligence, the Marines would launch their attacks that afternoon into the well-prepared German defenses within the woods, studded with interlocking machine gun positions.

French intelligence informed Harbord that "there were no Germans in the wood, and had not been [there] except for a short trench in the northeast corner of it."[4] Although the Americans had held the line in the area since June 4, the 4th Brigade commander was largely unaware of the locations of the Germans posted opposite him. Little of his front-line commanders' knowledge of the situation reached Harbord. Based on the French information, Harbord ordered the brigade to attack Belleau Wood with "no artillery preparation, thinking thereby to take it by surprise or find it unoccupied."[5] When the assault began, the division artillery would place only interdiction and harassing fire in the zone of attack, with destructive fire on parts of Belleau Wood and the surrounding hills.[6]

The French intelligence estimate was contradicted by that of the 2nd Division. An American patrol went into Belleau Wood on the evening of June 4 and found the position occupied by Germans, but it estimated the enemy's strength as "unknown."[7] The division's intelligence report for June 5 stated that the German line ran west of Belleau Wood. The report for June 6 focused primarily on the Hill 142 area, ignoring Belleau Wood. Based on the success on Hill 142 and the French intelligence assessment, Harbord expected to be in possession of the heights beyond Belleau Wood by nightfall. General Bundy, the 2nd Division commander, agreed with the French estimate and directed the attack to begin at 5:00 p.m. This meant there would be no time to send new reconnaissance patrols into the woods or to consult front-line commanders. Harbord ordered his staff to prepare for the assault.[8]

At 2:05 p.m. the 4th Brigade commander and his staff drew up the order for the attack. Major Berry's 3rd Battalion, 5th Marines, would strike Belleau Wood proper and secure it for the follow-up attack. Major Sibley's 3rd Battalion, 6th Marines, would attack on Berry's right, taking the southern end of the woods. Major Holcomb's 2nd Battalion, 6th Marines, would attack on Sibley's right flank. The initial advance would be followed by an attack on the village of Bouresches to the southeast and attacks west and north to the high ground behind the woods (Hills 126 and 133), supported by the 1st Battalion, 5th Marines, and one company each from the 2nd and

3rd Battalions. Harbord's orders reflected the success of Turrill's morning battle for Hill 142. There seemed to be no reason to doubt that similar gains could be made in Belleau Wood.[9]

The order to attack arrived at Colonel Catlin's headquarters at 3:45 p.m., delivered by Second Lieutenant Richard N. Williams of Harbord's staff, riding a motorcycle. Catlin had only one hour to prepare for the three-battalion assault. He tried to reach Berry immediately but was unsuccessful, as no phone lines had been laid. He dispatched runners but could only hope that they would reach Berry in time. Catlin prepared Sibley's battalion to carry the assault into the woods, but after studying his orders, he questioned its chance of success. The terrain ahead presented the greatest problems. Berry's battalion had to cross 400 yards of green wheat before reaching the wood line, while Sibley faced primarily open fields. No Marine patrol had yet to penetrate the woods and test the German defenses. Undaunted, Catlin moved to Major Holcomb's headquarters and briefed Holcomb and Sibley there. Having done all he could, Catlin moved to Lucy to observe the attack. He had still not communicated with Berry or his men.[10]

In anticipation of casualties, a somber memorandum was issued to each battalion commander and the regimental chaplain, providing instructions for the burial of Marines killed in action. Each Marine had two identity disks: one would remain with the body, and the other would be attached to the grave marker "by whatever method can be observed." All burials would be made under the cover of darkness, or in daylight if the area was protected from German fire by terrain. In a final note, the regimental chaplain was instructed to "make an accurate record of these graves."[11] In the future, the Graves Registration Service would provide photographs of the grave sites to the next of kin after the bodies had been collected at designated cemeteries.

Meanwhile, Major Berry was celebrating his thirty-seventh birthday, which would be memorable. The choice of his battalion for the attack was a good one, as three of his companies were laced with prewar Marines. The 16th Company had combat experience in Haiti, and the 45th and 47th Companies had fought in the Dominican Republic. The 20th Company, however, was composed of many men from the University of Minnesota. The natural rivalry that existed between the veteran and rookie companies ended when a Minnesotan physically whipped a French instructor who had been abusing a fellow Marine. The old-time Marines "closed in to shake hands with every man of the 20th. The feud was over."[12]

As Berry's companies prepared for battle, a war correspondent came up behind the Marines' positions and noticed scraps of paper littering the ground.

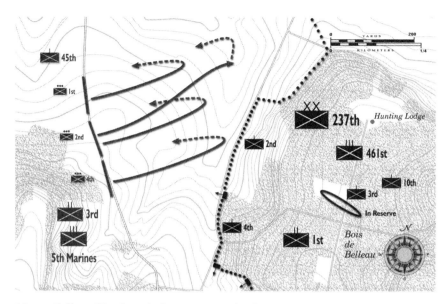

Map 7. Belleau Wood, 45th Company attacks, June 6, 1918

Curious, he picked up several bits of paper and found that they "were letters from American mothers and wives and sweethearts."[13]

By the time the 45th Company was in position, it was almost 6:00 p.m., long after the supporting artillery fire has ceased. Undaunted, the 45th Company pushed into the farm fields. Second Lieutenant Thomas H. Miles dashed ahead, leading his three platoons forward. Miles, a native of Philadelphia, had graduated from Princeton University in 1917, where he was best known as a track star and a member of Clio Hall and the Cap and Gown Club. Miles entered the steel business before receiving his diploma, only to leave and join the Marine Corps in May and then spend the summer in training at Quantico, Virginia. With his departure for the war imminent, Miles obtained leave from the Marine Corps and married Nancy H. Smyth on November 3, 1917. He left for France a little over a month later and joined his new unit in February 1918. Several days before the attack, Miles and his best friend in the company, First Lieutenant John F. Blanton, made a pact: if one of them should fall, the other would write a letter to his next of kin. Shortly after Miles entered the open field, a German shell scored a direct hit on the lieutenant. It was a poor omen for the start of the attack. After the battle, Blanton kept his word and wrote to Miles's widow, stating, "He was an excellent officer and I had grown to esteem him highly as one of my best friends. You have my heartfelt sympathy in your sorrow."[14] Miles would never see his daughter, who was born the following month.

German machine gun fire raked the 45th Company, which suffered horribly in the wheat. Seventy-three Marines were killed or wounded, and the rest of the company was pinned down in the fields. Battalion headquarters grimly noted, "Nine men only reported returned of the three platoons of the 45th that went over the top."[15]

Captain Richard N. Platt's 20th Company was next in line. Sergeant Merwin H. Silverthorn's platoon lay in the portion of the forest jutting out toward the Torcy–Lucy road; this was the nearest point to Belleau Wood, only 250 yards away. At 5:15 p.m. the lieutenant announced to the platoon, "We were supposed to attack at five o'clock, so we have to assemble."[16] The Marines moved quickly across the road and into a narrow band of trees, attempting to get as close to the German positions as possible. Each fifty-two-man platoon assumed a revised four-wave attack formation, as modified from the standard American two-wave assault. Again, the attack was very late, almost an hour behind the artillery barrage. The lead wave moved forward through the wheat fields "at a steady slow cadence," with rifles at high port; it was followed by the succeeding lines, separated by only about seventy-five yards. No shots were fired by either side initially, and the Marines believed that no one occupied the tree line. Directly ahead, silently awaiting the Marine advance, was the German 4th Company, 461st Infantry, supported by two heavy machine guns.

The 461st Regiment was commanded by Major Josef Bischoff, a veteran Prussian officer who had honed his craft in the small wars in Africa and was wounded in Namibia in 1904. He served on the Vosges front in 1914 and then supported the Turkish battles in Palestine and the Sinai peninsula, commanding the 1st Turkish Camel Regiment. Bischoff returned to Germany in 1917 with the formation of the 237th Division and fought in Russia throughout that year. Bischoff's varied combat experience proved invaluable in defending the tangled terrain of Belleau Wood.[17]

Bischoff tailored his defense based on the varied terrain features of Belleau Wood. The 20th Company advanced toward established kill zones laced with machine guns concealed in the tree line, ready to unleash interlocking fields of fire. The machine guns were expertly located to rake any attack from both front and flank. With little or no cover, the wheat fields would become fields of death. The veteran German gunners allowed the Marines to advance well into the wheat before firing, giving their enemy little chance of survival. With no opportunity to send forward scouts, the Marines had only seconds to recognize their dilemma before the bullets started to scream through their orderly lines of battle.

Before they started to advance, Sergeant Silverthorn and his best friend,

Sergeant Stephen G. Sherman, shook hands with each other, "happy and exultant in the fact that at last we were going over."[18] Like many of the men in their company, they had both been students at the University of Minnesota and had enlisted in the Marine Corps in April 1917. With bayonets fixed, the platoon charged into the wheat field, only 250 yards from Belleau Wood. Once the Americans had advanced deep into the field and reached the spot where the ground dropped into a shallow ravine, the German machine guns opened fire, spewing 250 to 500 rounds per minute. The bullets ripped into the Marine ranks, slaughtering most of the lead platoon. Within two minutes, Sergeant Sherman was killed by machine gun fire, "with his face toward the enemy and a smile on his face."[19] He received the Navy Cross for his "extraordinary heroism," serving as an example to his fellow Marines in their first combat offensive. The University of Minnesota continued to lose heavily in the attack. Engineering freshman Corporal Robert McC. Fischer led his men forward into the fields but was cut down by the intense fire. He was awarded the Navy Cross for inspiring his men to advance into the torrent of machine gun bullets. "He gave the supreme proof of that extraordinary heroism," his citation read, "which will serve as an example to hitherto untried troops."[20]

None of the Marines returned fire, as they had been ordered not to shoot until they had closed with the enemy. Within seconds, the platoon ceased to exist. Of the fifty-two members of the platoon who attacked out of the woods, only six reached the cover of a woodpile seventy-five yards away. The lieutenant looked back across the field and shouted, "Where the hell is my platoon? . . . I'm going back."[21]

The other platoons of the 20th Company attacked at the same time. Private Carl B. Mills remembered that he kept an eye on his officers as they checked their watches, and then his platoon moved forward toward Belleau Wood. "Everyone seemed to be in his place," Mills remembered. The platoon crossed the Lucy road, and then all "hell broke loose." A machine gun bullet tore into his right leg, knocking him to the ground. Before Mills could get his bearings, he heard the signal to advance. "I made one lunge and found myself on the ground again," he remembered. As he fell, he took another bullet in his left knee. "I began to see," mused Mills, "that this was no dream or kids stuff."[22]

In the wheat fields, the wounded men of the 20th Company remained under heavy German fire. Private Mills crawled to check on the other Marines lying around him, hoping he could help, but they were all dead. "The machine gun had done a thorough job," he noted. The private dragged himself to the road, where he and a few other survivors crawled back to their jumping-off point. German snipers tried to kill the wounded Marines as

Marine dead in the wheat fields on the edge of Belleau Wood. (Marine Corps
Archives, Quantico, VA)

they moved, but Mills lifted his helmet just enough to attract the sniper's
attention and then continued to crawl once the German had fired. Mills recalled later, "I would laugh at him when he missed." Eventually, the private
regained the original wood line, where he was rushed to company headquarters and questioned.[23]

Back in the fields, Sergeant Silverthorn remained behind the woodpile. He
was shaken by the destruction of his platoon and later said of his comrades,
"as they plunged on in that seething mass of Hell, they met their end like
true Americans."[24] Silverthorn began to work his way north along the slight
cover of the ravine until he reached the survivors of the next platoon in line,
now commanded by Gunnery Sergeant Harry Gay. The Marines took cover
in a small protected area of the ravine, where the machine guns could not
reach them.

Sergeant Gay attempted to resume the platoon wave attack, but the incoming fire caused him to abandon that maneuver and move forward by
short rushes. Gay was shot in the shoulder and began to bleed heavily. Silverthorn bandaged the sergeant's wound and found himself in command of
the survivors of the two platoons. He continued the advance, trying to cover
the remaining hundred yards to the woods with short sprints and then diving
for cover. Of the forty men in the combined platoon, only four were still un-

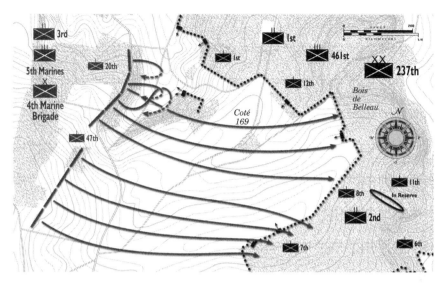

Map 8. Belleau Wood, 20th and 47th Companies attack, June 6, 1918

hurt. After the second rush, Silverthorn dove to the ground at the edge of a plowed field, grazed in the knee by a machine gun bullet that luckily did not strike bone. Now only Sergeant Silverthorn and Private Francis E. Green remained. The sergeant ordered Green to take his automatic rifle and run into the woods, leaving Silverthorn behind. Green charged forward and entered the tree line, the first man of the 20th Company to reach Belleau Wood.[25]

Silverthorn remained in the dirt field, protected by the furrows. He watched as the German machine guns repeatedly swept the field, cutting the red clover growing only an inch from his body. Silverthorn knew that to survive, he must reach the cover of the woods. The sergeant chose his moment and then struggled to make it across the plowed field into a stand of tall grass. From there, he crawled into Belleau Wood, where he remained alone until nightfall. The entire ordeal lasted two hours, with the Marines crossing only 200 yards under fire.[26]

The surviving men of the 20th Company hung on until nightfall, when they were able to fall back under cover of darkness and regroup. The remnants of two of the platoons shifted to the right and entered Belleau Wood to join the neighboring 47th Company, but they could advance no further. "In long rows and in places rolled in heaps," a German correspondent noted, "lay the dead Americans in front of Belleau Woods."[27] Approximately 247 Marines of the 20th Company had entered the farm fields in the attack. Almost half of them, 107 officers and men, became casualties. Nine Marines of the company received the Navy Cross posthumously for their heroism.[28]

Machine guns from the 23rd Company, 6th Machine Gun Battalion, moved forward to support the attack. Private Arthur Clifford was one of a twelve-man ammunition party that was also moving up to support the guns. Clifford and his group were ordered to follow the 3rd Battalion across an open field, where the "lead was flying around like hail." The Marines were under fire by machine guns and snipers every step of the way, but most of them reached the cover of scrub brush at the edge of the field "with a whole skin." Clifford found a Marine gun crew concealed there in the brush. While they remained hidden, two German shells struck nearby but failed to explode. The Marines hugged the ground, causing Clifford to remark later, "I guess we looked like pancakes but I assure you the feeling was as though we were looming up like mountains." Led by the gun crew, the Marines charged across the Lucy road one by one, still under fire. After the members of the gun crew had either "crossed or fallen," Clifford and his band of ammunition bearers made the same deadly sprint. "You could feel the burn of the bullets across your face; thousands of them," Clifford remembered, "and how anyone could live through it, I can't yet see."[29] Once they had crossed the road, the machine gunners moved toward the looming mass of Belleau Wood.

On the right, the 47th Company extended the attack across the fields. Just as it had for the other companies, the order to attack came late. Captain Philip T. Case returned from Berry's headquarters with "a handful of papers and a 14k smile on his puss." His officers strapped on their equipment as Case shouted, "Get your men out into positions as fast as you can, we attack at 5:00." The captain paused and looked at his watch, noting, "It is now 5:15."[30] Case took his company forward without the benefit of artillery or even the usual sound of a whistle. "There is no bugle call, no sword waving, no dramatic enunciation of catchy commands, no theatricalism," an observer noted. "It's just plain get up and go over."[31] The order to attack spread through the company like wildfire.

Private Gerald B. Clark later wrote to his parents and described the frantic few minutes they had to prepare. "I had many funny feelings in that five minutes, believe me," he related. "I can never describe them."[32] The men scrambled into the assault formation, just as they had practiced so many times before, with the 1st and 2nd Platoons in the first line and the 3rd and 4th Platoons forming the second line. The men of the company looked as though "they had been on the parade ground," recalled First Lieutenant Raymond E. Anthony.[33]

The Marines anxiously watched as the 20th Company moved forward, and then Captain Case ordered his 47th Company down the short slope to the Torcy road. Upon reaching the roadbed, Private Clark regained his composure. "After I got to the road I felt fine, and good for about ten Boches myself," Clark later wrote. "Up till then I would have felt better anywhere else."[34] The 47th Company crossed the road and entered a wheat field. Once again, the veteran German machine gunners allowed the Marines to move halfway across the open field before opening a withering fire on the 47th Company's 260 men. "I never felt so conspicuous in my life," wrote Corporal Victor M. Landreth.[35] "Machine gun fire cut like a scythe across our ranks," wrote First Lieutenant Raymond E. Knapp, "but we pressed on, spreading out in the wheat and taking the old formations we had used so many times in the cane fields of Santo Domingo."[36]

As the Marines moved closer to the trees, the inexorable German fire pushed them to the right, to the protruding corner of Belleau Wood. The leading Marine platoons plunged gratefully into the woods, where, as one Marine remembered, "we were more in our element of guerrilla warfare."[37] The 47th Company suffered only thirty casualties while crossing the fields, primarily due to its members' prior experience in the Caribbean. Luckily, the German defenders in that section of the woods had been ordered to hold only as a line of reconnaissance and to withdraw in the face of the American advance. The Marines pursued quickly, running through the thick brush and trees in an attempt to catch the Germans on the move.

Marines began to drop from enemy gunfire as they ran forward through the trees. The fighting was bitter and sometimes involved bayonets. "I guess we left someone every ten yards we went," recalled Corporal Landreth, but "we weren't taking any prisoners."[38] The Marines were encouraged by their rapid advance, until they came to a hundred-yard clearing in the woods. The trees had been felled but still lay on the ground so that the interlocking branches formed a natural obstacle. Paths could be seen through the tangled branches, so the Marines charged across, looking to keep pressure on the enemy. Instantly, machine gun fire dropped the leading Marines, their blood splattering the forest floor. The leading 47th Company platoons recoiled and then grouped to the right of the clearing. Private Clark remembered, "This was one hot place."[39] One bullet nipped his finger, searing out a divot of bloody flesh. Private J. Willard Stranahan, one Clark's close friends from the sands of Parris Island and the mud of Quantico, was not as lucky. A shrapnel fragment smashed into his face just above his right eye. Stranahan would be discharged to his home in Mt. Ayr, Iowa, with a replacement eye made from glass.[40]

The German defense was designed to form a deadly crossfire down the paths. First Sergeant Edmund T. Madsen and two of his Marines charged one of the machine guns in a "bull rush." The men of the company who witnessed Madsen's actions were taken aback by his boldness. Bullets tore

Marines in one of the many trails in Belleau Wood. Note the dense undergrowth, which caused so many casualties on both sides. (© Emmanuel MAS/ECPAD/ Defense)

into the sergeant, and he fell dead within three feet of the gun. For this act of bravery, Madsen was awarded the Navy Cross posthumously. His only next of kin was his mother, who lived in Denmark.[41]

There was little doubt that the Marines could advance no further until the machine guns were destroyed. Captain Case ordered four men to flank the guns. When the Germans were still firing fifteen minutes later, Case ordered six more Marines forward, but the machine gun fire continued unabated. "They fared no better than the first party," recalled one Marine. No word came from the detachments, and still the company could not advance. Lieutenant Knapp finally took ten Marines on a wider sweep of the guns, determined to break the German line. When they were only halfway around the German position, a new machine gun tore into the detachment. By the time Knapp got his men under cover, only three remained unhurt. The lieutenant crawled back through the brush with his sergeant to find out what had happened to the rest of his men. He located the bodies of his own Marines as well as those of the other two patrols. "All had been killed within the space of a few yards," remembered Knapp. "It was not a comfortable spot."[42]

The Americans peered through the woods, trying to locate the German machine guns, but they saw no sign of the weapons. Finally, the sergeant noticed the angle of the bullet scars on the trees. "Them suckers is in trees," whispered the sergeant as he lifted his rifle and fired. "I heard the banshee scream of a dying hun," Knapp recalled, "and then I saw him fall, tearing off limbs in his heavy descent until he stuck with a fleshy thud in a tree crotch about thirty feet off the ground." The German's helmet "struck the ground with the rattle of an empty bucket." Seventeen Marines lay under the tree, either killed or wounded. Knapp then returned to his two remaining men and brought them forward. The four Marines moved through the trees, spread out like "a bunch of Tennessee turkey hunters."[43] They silenced three more machine guns hidden in the trees and killed four snipers as well. Knapp sent word across the clearing that the way was open to advance, but now new guns opened fire on the Marines. "Every time anyone moved they opened up," Corporal Landreth wrote later, "and how them bullets did whisper."[44]

With dusk approaching, Captain Case worried that he had gone too far into the woods. Case and scattered groups of his company pressed through the woods to open ground, where they could see the railroad ahead, across the fields. Any further advance would require movement to secure the 20th Company's area. Fragments of two 20th Company platoons arrived to join Case, but even a weak German counterattack would have been able to force the Marines back. Case pulled his remaining men back into the woods, linking the scattered detachments of Marines for the night. Case's Marines dug foxholes or took captured German positions and prepared to hold their hard-won portion of Belleau Wood. Of the 260 men who had walked out into the wheat field, only 40 remained. Four Navy Crosses were awarded to members of the company for their actions during the attack.[45]

Unwilling to allow the Marines their foothold in the forest, the German defenders took advantage of the dense woods and worked their way around the Marines' position until they had encircled Case and his men. The 47th Company survivors were alone in the woods with no support to their left, as the 20th Company was no longer intact. Rather than allow the Germans to continue their movement unopposed, Second Lieutenant Joseph A. Synnott advanced his platoon to take on the enemy machine guns. The thirty-five-year-old lieutenant had been orphaned as a young boy, and he and his sister had been raised by an aunt in Montclair, New Jersey.[46] Synnott enlisted in the Marine Corps as a private in 1900, serving for the next seventeen years on battleships, at navy yards, and on deployments to Cuba, Nicaragua, the "Around the World" voyage of the Great White Fleet, Vera Cruz in 1914, and two tours in Panama. He came to France as a gunnery sergeant but later became an officer in command of a platoon of the 47th Company. Sensing

Navy corpsmen in a triage station in the shadows of Belleau Wood, June 13, 1918. (© Emmanuel MAS/ECPAD/Defense)

that he would soon see combat, Synnott dispatched a letter to his sister on June 4, advising her "to watch out for big fighting, as the Marines were ready to go into action at any time."[47]

True to his word, Synnott entered the fight with a vengeance. A few hours before the attack, he was struck in the neck by a fragment from an exploding shell. Despite the pain, Synnott refused to leave his men to seek medical treatment in the rear. He led his platoon in the assault, and they immediately encountered heavy machine gun fire. Synnott, who was focused on putting the offending machine gun out of action, plunged into the woods ahead of his Marines and collided with the German defenders.[48]

In the midst of the melee, two German soldiers attacked the lieutenant, and the three combatants engaged in a hand-to-hand struggle to the death. Private Adrian J. Michels rose from his position to help Synnott in the uneven fight. "Keep away," Synnott shouted. "Go back with the others."[49] Despite his lieutenant's warning, Michels did not hesitate to join the brawl. Together, the two Marines managed to gain the upper hand, until two rifle shots rang out. Both Synnott and Michels were killed instantly, their bodies collapsing to the forest floor.

Overcome with anger, the men of Synnott's platoon fired back, taking vengeance on the two Germans standing over the bodies of the fallen Marines. Both of the enemy soldiers slumped to the ground as well. The bodies of the four men lay tangled together where they had been fighting only seconds before. The sight was imprinted forever on the men of the 47th Company. Word of Synnott's death first reached his sister on July 8, when she read a newspaper listing of Marine casualties from Belleau Wood. The War Department confirmed his death three days later. Lieutenant Synnott received the Navy Cross for his bravery, and his body was eventually returned to his family for burial in Montclair, New Jersey.[50]

The body of Private Michels was lost in the confusion of the battle and was never recovered. The young student from Milwaukee had been only seventeen when he enlisted in 1917, and he had to obtain his mother's consent to go to Parris Island. The news of Michels's death deeply affected the people of Escanaba, his hometown on the upper peninsula of Michigan. "He worked for me and was just the sort of chap to go to the rescue of a man in danger," remembered James W. Bayley. "He had no fear and would fight to the finish for a friend."[51] Bayley placed a photograph of Michels in his storefront window to honor his former employee, and Michels's childhood friends wore gold stars to remember their chum. One of his classmates warmly recalled many years later, "We didn't get along so well because I was a couple of grades ahead of him and for weeks straight I had to whip him every day. But he never had enough and never quit."[52]

In 1920 Elsie M. Michels wrote to the army's Graves Registration Service to locate the grave of her son, as his grandfather wished to travel to France to visit it. The apologetic response informed her that "all efforts to locate your son's grave have proved futile."[53] In 1922, still hopeful that her son's remains would be found, Mrs. Michels contacted Marine Corps headquarters. "I am sorry to bother you," she wrote, "but would like to know about when he will be returned."[54] Again, the Marines could provide no definitive information about his burial site. In 1932 Mrs. Michels traveled with other Gold Star mothers and widows to the Aisne Marne Cemetery to visit the place where her son had died. Today, the Memorial Chapel still lists Michels as among the missing.[55]

The sustained combat in the forest clearly indicated that the 47th Company required support. Captain Case dispatched messengers to battalion headquarters, asking for reinforcements. Private James L. Clark carried a message back to Major Berry that read, "Help, we have been cut off. We're surrounded by Germans."[56] Clark was born and raised on a farm in Adams County, Ohio. After being orphaned at the age of nine, he was taken in by relatives. Eleven days after war was declared, Clark joined the Marine Corps, leaving home for the first time in his life to learn how to become a Marine at Parris Island, South Carolina. By the time Clark's classmates were receiving their high school diplomas, the Ohio farm boy was in France wearing the uniform of a Marine. Now, engaged in battle in the depths of Belleau Wood, Captain Case had chosen Clark to carry that important message because "he was small, tough and brave."[57] As Clark made his way through the woods, a shell burst overhead, sending a piece of shrapnel into his shoulder. Bloody and dazed, the wounded Marine still managed to crawl more than two kilometers to deliver his message to battalion headquarters. Clark then lost consciousness and was carried to an aid station, where he was treated for his wounds. Private Clark received the Navy Cross for his bravery.

Back on their starting line, Major Berry grew concerned over the fate of his battalion. He had seen the 47th Company enter Belleau Wood but could no longer see his other two companies. Berry feared that few of his men survived. The 16th Company remained in reserve, holding the battalion line, but it was stretched very thin. At 6:10 p.m. Berry sent a message to Colonel Neville, reporting that the remains of his battalion were now holding a line in the trees along the Torcy road; however, he was unsure if he could hold the line in the face of a counterattack. Berry then set out himself to locate his forward companies, before they could be isolated and counterattacked.

Berry moved into the wheat field with two staff members, ten runners, and two war correspondents who had requested permission to accompany him. All the Marines went forward with drawn pistols, searching the wheat fields and trees for German snipers. The party crossed the Lucy–Torcy road easily, passing the bodies of several recently fallen Marines as well as the remains of some French soldiers killed during the first days of the battle. Enemy machine guns covered the road, but the group was allowed to advance into the wheat field beyond. Now only a hundred yards from Belleau Wood, Berry took the lead, ordering the group to follow behind him in ten- to fifteen-yard intervals.[58]

The sound of the German machine guns became extremely loud, and bursts of bullets cut through the young wheat, kicking up clouds of dirt on impact. Suddenly, Berry looked to his left and saw silent German machine guns at the ready, waiting to cut the party to pieces once they had advanced too deep into the field to return to safety. He called back, "Get down everybody," and the Marines dived into the wheat. Berry's cry also alerted the German machine gunners that they had been spotted, and they opened fire with a vengeance. "It began to come hot and fast," remembered correspondent Floyd Gibbons. "Perfectly withering volleys of lead swept the tops of the oats just over us." One of the first volleys struck Berry in the left elbow and then tore through the muscles and nerves of his forearm until coming to a stop in the palm of his hand. The major grabbed his arm by the wrist and tried to get to his feet. "My hand's gone," he exclaimed, as he staggered forward. The rest of the party shouted for Berry to get down before he was killed, but Berry only shouted, "We've got to get out of here. . . . They'll start shelling this open field in a few minutes."[59]

Major Berry was only twenty yards from the edge of the trees, and Gibbons was the man closest to him. Gibbons told Berry to wait until he was able to crawl over to him, and then they would both run for the safety of the woods. Gibbons pushed himself forward through the dirt, trying to make as little motion in the wheat as possible. A bullet struck the correspondent in the left arm, passing through the biceps muscle. Gibbons kept crawling, using just his right arm, when a second bullet clipped his shoulder. Bleeding but undaunted, he continued to move forward. As he neared Berry, "it seemed everything in the world went white." A third bullet had struck the ground in front of Gibbons's face, bounced up into his left eye, and exited through his forehead and helmet, leaving the correspondent conscious but bleeding heavily from his face. Through his right eye, Gibbons watched as Berry ran the remaining twenty yards into the trees, miraculously unscathed. However, the major was now out of contact with the battalion and dangerously wounded. Several members of the 20th Company were in the brush, and they joined their wounded battalion commander.[60]

As Gibbons lay bleeding in the field, machine gun bullets passed inches over his head; it seemed that the Germans had "an inexhaustible supply of ammunition." A wounded Marine lay sprawled only twenty feet to his left. The injured man repeatedly tried to roll over on his back to ease his pain, but the movement only drew renewed German machine gun fire. The Marine was still wearing his pack, which raised his chest higher whenever he rolled over. "I could see the buttons fly from his tunic and one of the shoulder straps of the back pack part as the sprays of lead struck him," remembered Gibbons.[61] The wounded Americans could only lie still, wait for darkness, and hope to escape the deadly German bullets.

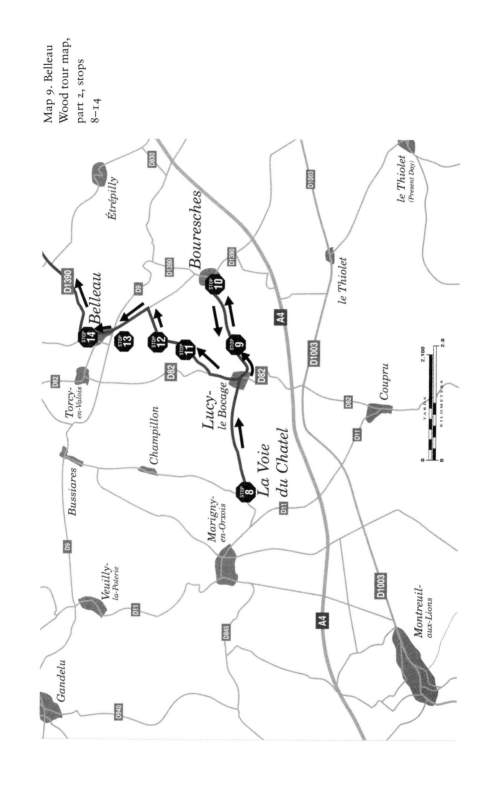

Map 9. Belleau
Wood tour map,
part 2, stops
8–14

Belleau Wood Tour

Stop 9. Wheat Field Attack, Belleau Wood Road,
49°04'04.5"N 3°17'20.9"E

Retrace your steps from the Route de Bouresches to Lucy-le-Bocage, and take the D 82 (Rue de Torcy) north to Belleau. Just north of town, at 2.8 kilometers, you can pause at the marker on your right commemorating the Marine burials after the battle. Proceed north for 210 meters and take the first hard paved road to the right toward the Belleau Wood memorial. As you drive, look at the fields to your right. This is where many of the Marine casualties occurred on June 6, primarily in the 20th and 47th Companies. After driving 850 meters, just past a small stand of trees on your right, park your car in a small pull-off on the right and face Belleau Wood.

The Marines who attacked in this area on June 6 crossed the road behind you, dropping to a ravine and then rising up to Belleau Wood. The left-hand platoons of the 20th Company advanced here, attacking directly toward the trees on the far crest of the ravine. As they moved into the ravine, German machine guns hidden in the woods to the left turned the terrain into a killing ground.

The Germans watched the Marines advance, noting that the Americans were "sportsman like, as if participating in a track meet, they came on the run."[1] Sergeant Luther W. Pilcher led his men forward. Miraculously, he was unhurt until a piece of shrapnel struck him just short of the woods. He crumpled in the field, crying and moaning from a stomach wound. Pilcher died shortly thereafter, alone in the field. He was posthumously awarded the Navy Cross for his bravery in leading the attack. An eventual calm settled over the field, with the few Marine survivors now huddled among the plowed furrows. After twenty minutes, German snipers began firing from the woods, picking off the wounded.[2]

Stop 10. Belleau Wood Monument,
49°04'23.0"N 3°17'26.7"E

Continue driving into Belleau Wood for 700 meters, where you will find the Belleau Wood memorial area. You can park your car here and get out to view the US Marine Corps monument and relics of the 1918 battle. This area of the battlefield was the last portion of Belleau Wood captured by the 4th Marine Brigade before declaring the woods secure. Walk the nearby trails into the woods to get a sense of battle in a heavily forested area and to view the shell holes and trench systems left behind. Make sure to take the back trail to the famed Hunting Lodge, one of the most iconic landmarks of the battle, which overlooks the Aisne Marne Cemetery, your next stop.

6

June 6, 1918—Sibley's 3rd Battalion, 6th Marines
"Come on You Bastards and Just Go. . . . What Do You Want to Do, Live Forever?"

AS BERRY'S MEN JUMPED OFF INTO THE WHEAT FIELDS, Major Sibley's 3rd Battalion, 6th Marines, also began its assault on Belleau Wood. Sibley was a tough, experienced commander with almost seventeen years of service in "every clime and place." He was known throughout the regiment as "Ma" Sibley because of the care and attention he gave the Marines of his unit. "He is a very amiable, amusing, exasperating, good soldier," First Lieutenant David Bellamy wrote of Sibley in 1917. "The big things he is always ready to handle in his wise experienced way."[1] Norwich University, Vermont's military school, proved to be a strong influence in the battalion. Major Sibley was a 1900 graduate of the school after serving as a corporal in the 1st Vermont Infantry during the Spanish-American War. Second Lieutenant Clinton I. Smallman, an officer in Captain Smith's 82nd Company, was also an alumnus of Norwich, class of 1914. Sibley took his battalion to France in October 1917 and trained his Marines in the cold snows of Bourmont, reminiscent of those in Vermont. On March 18, 1918, the battalion entered the line, and the real war began for Sibley.[2]

Turrill's battalion had replaced Sibley's battalion early on the morning of June 6, just minutes prior to the attack on Hill 142, allowing Sibley's men to move into the fields south of Lucy-le-Bocage and rest until afternoon. The exception was the 97th Company, which did not join the battalion until 5:00 p.m. Colonel Catlin called Sibley to Holcomb's headquarters late in the day and gave him the order to attack both Belleau Wood and along the road to Bouresches. Catlin later remembered, "It looked as though Sibley's Battalion would have to bear the brunt of the action."[3]

After being briefed by Catlin, Sibley assembled his company commanders to outline the order to attack. However, he could tell his four captains nothing about the terrain ahead or the German dispositions. Sibley pointed out the objectives on his map and then went over the plan of attack. There was no time for any reconnaissance. The 82nd and 84th Companies would

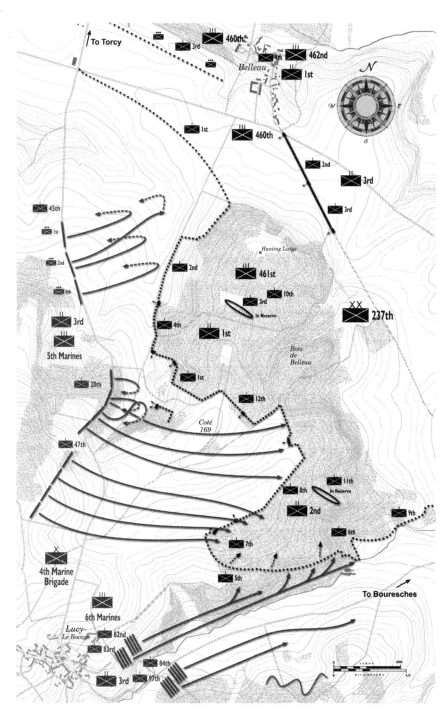

Map 10. Belleau Wood, attack of the 5th and 6th Marines, evening of June 6, 1918

6th Marine Regiment
Belleau Wood June 1918
Col. Albertus W. Catlin

Casualties during the battle drastically altered the battalion command structure.

Headquarters Company
Capt. Walter H. Zitz

Supply Company
Capt. Fred C. Patchen

8th Machine Gun Company
Capt. Roy C. Swink

1st Battalion
Maj. John A. Hughes

74th Company (A)
Capt. John F. Burnes

75th Company (B)
Capt. Edward C. Fuller

76th Company (C)
Capt. George A. Stowell

95th Company (D)
Capt. Oscar R. Cauldwell

2nd Battalion
Maj. Thomas Holcomb

78th Company (E)
Capt. Robert E. Messersmith

79th Company (F)
Capt. Randolph T. Zane

80th Company (G)
Capt. Bailey M. Coffenberg

96th Company (H)
Capt. Donald F. Duncan

3rd Battalion
Maj. Berton W. Sibley

82nd Company (I)
Capt. Dwight F. Smith

83rd Company (K)
Capt. Alfred H. Noble

84th Company (L)
Capt. Frederick W. Karstaedt

97th Company (M)
Capt. Robert W. Voeth

Chart 2. 6th Marine Regiment, Belleau Wood

form the first line of advance, moving along both sides of a ravine leading to Belleau Wood. Their objective was the Belleau rail station on the east side of Belleau Wood. The remaining two companies would follow behind the front line in supporting range, ready to move up if needed. Sibley ordered every company in the advance to use the same four-wave attack they had learned in training. The captains returned to their companies to ready their men for action.[4]

The formidable resistance met by the Marine Brigade on Hill 142 and in Belleau Wood was mounted primarily by the three regiments of the German

237th Division. Formed in January 1917, the 237th was rated a third-class division. Most of the men in the fields around Belleau Wood had been recruited from coal and ore mines around Saarbrücken, with a fair number from Alsace-Lorraine. The 460th and 462nd Regiments defended Hill 142 and the fields extending from the hill to Belleau Wood, while more than 1,100 veteran German infantrymen of the 461st Regiment lay in wait within the confines of the wood, ably commanded by Major Josef Bischoff.[5]

Captain Smith's 82nd Company led the attack. The young captain and his company had arrived in France in November 1917 and been assigned to build docks with the army engineers. In December Smith and his men rejoined the battalion and began training for combat. Smith now formed each of his four platoons into four waves as they waited in the wheat fields outside the town of Lucy. With little ceremony, the company fixed bayonets, advanced on the north side of the ravine, and ran into the projecting arm of Belleau Wood. A frightened, unarmed German soldier jumped up in the face of the Marine advance, raising his arms and shouting, "Kamerad!" Instantly, twelve Marines ran forward and bayoneted the German until "that man was full of holes," Sergeant Karl P. Spencer remembered. The company's "orders were to take no prisoners." In return, German machine gun and artillery fire tore into the Marine ranks with precision.[6]

"Our company formed the first wave," Sergeant David M. Vincent recalled, "and so suffered more than any of them. . . . We didn't have an officer left. . . . They went thru wheat fields that the machine guns made wave like water." Airbursts also took their toll on the Marines. "Big shells were bursting in the air, and every shell contains two hundred and fifty pieces of steel shrapnel," Vincent noted. "Other shells would throw up large columns of smoke and dirt, and would leave holes six feet wide and three feet deep." Men began to fall, but the 82nd Company never faltered. "It is not an easy thing to keep on going forward through all that," remembered Vincent, "and besides see your comrades, that you had drilled and trained with for over a year, fall at your side, dead and wounded."[7]

At first, Gunnery Sergeant Dana C. Lovejoy marveled at the beauty of the fields before him. Later, he described the "long level fields of yellow grain with scarlet poppies gently whispering to strange breezes" and the "brilliant sunshine—brilliant blue sky. Birds sing. Is this war?" He pressed through the wheat with bullets whining overhead. The pastoral scene vanished when the German machine gun bullets struck the Marines. "That mans [sic] face is like a mass of bloody rags. He should keep his hands away from it," Lovejoy thought. "Why can't someone make him stop screaming." Enemy shells burst over the company, sending deadly shrapnel into the advancing lines of Marines. Lovejoy and his platoon dropped to the ground, digging furiously to escape the German barrage. One nearby Marine went down. "There goes that boy. He's dead. A second ago alive, now dead," Lovejoy recalled. "Bullets still thump him. He does not jump as they thump him."[8]

Stopping in the field only gave the enemy machine gunners better targets. Casualties mounted as the Marines furiously dug with their bayonets. A bullet struck Lovejoy in the left buttock, and he hobbled to a nearby shell hole for cover. "Blood is running. My blood! It lies wet and red on the grass," he recollected. After a quick examination, Lovejoy bandaged his wound. Flies soon arrived in the shell hole, and the gunnery sergeant swatted at the pests until he was too weak to care about them. He eased himself down in the dirt, wishing for some water to combat the burning heat of the sun. "My leg throbs, throbs, throbs. Someone must bring me water," he thought. He took in his surroundings, noting the "quiet with the flies and the blood. . . . How blue the sky is!"[9]

Major Sibley was nearby to help Smith maintain the attack. Despite all efforts by the Marines, the initial line of interlocking machine guns could not be broken. "Until we got within hand grenade distance of them we didn't have a chance," remembered Corporal Austin R. Lowery, "but of course we got there in the end after several attempts and the loss of half our men."[10] The Marines faced an experienced German commander, Lieutenant Colonel Hans von Hartlieb. A cavalryman, he had begun the war as an officer of dragoons and served on both the eastern and western fronts. In 1917 he transferred from the cavalry to command an infantry battalion at Verdun, Champagne, Somme, and Argonne. On March 16 von Hartlieb assumed command of the German 1st Battalion, 461st Infantry, and then moved to the 2nd Battalion of the same regiment.

Inside the woods, Major Bischoff anticipated the Marine attack. The tree line reached out toward the Marines like the toe of a boot, making it indefensible. Instead of meeting the Americans on the edge of the woods, he ordered his men to make a fighting withdrawal, leading the Marines toward the Germans' main line of resistance deeper in the forest. The Germans constructed a killing ground there by felling trees and creating a tangled mat of branches to slow down the advance. This time, German machine gunners were placed in the trees, ready to massacre any movement with interlocking streams of bullets. A devil's den of boulders supported the German flank.

At 6:15 Bischoff ordered his advance German 5th Company to withdraw from the southwest extension of Belleau Wood into the field of fallen trees. The attack then fell primarily on the 5th, 6th, and 7th Companies of the 2nd Battalion, 461st Infantry. As the Marines entered the killing zone, Bischoff brought his 11th Company forward from reserve to bolster the line. The combination of interlocking heavy and light machine guns and *Minenwerfer* fire effectively halted the Americans' initial advance. Command and control of the 82nd Company was impossible, and the battle became a series of individual combat actions. Attacking the woods proved costly for the Americans. Corporal Lowery later wrote, "It seems that every one of the pals I had got bumped off."[11] Three officers and thirty-nine enlisted men were killed or wounded among the 231 men of the 82nd Company.[12]

Just outside the town of Lucy, Colonel Catlin watched Sibley's men as they advanced. He moved forward to a low trench along a line of brush by the Lucy–Torcy road, only 300 yards from Belleau Wood. Catlin watched the advance with pride. "My hands were clenched," he wrote later, "and all my muscles taut as I watched."[13] Through field glasses, he saw men fall, but still the line moved forward in silence, with only the commands of the officers and noncommissioned officers heard over the German fire. Captain Jean R. Tribot-Laspierre, the 6th Marines' French liaison officer, repeatedly urged Catlin to move to a safer position to watch the attack, but Catlin refused. As the first line of Marines reached the woods, a bullet ripped into the right side of Catlin's chest. "It felt exactly as though some one had struck me heavily with a sledge," Catlin remembered.[14] The force of the blow spun the colonel around and knocked him to the ground. When he tried to regain his feet, he discovered that he had no feeling on the right side of his body. The bullet had passed completely through, piercing his right lung, which soon filled with blood. Captain Tribot-Laspierre quickly pulled the colonel back to the safety of a slit trench. Conscious but unable to command, Catlin sent runners back to Lucy, calling forward his second in command, Lieutenant Colonel Harry Lee, to direct the attack.

Captain Tribot-Laspierre tried desperately to reach Neville to notify him of Catlin's wounds and pass on the colonel's plans and other information vital to the attack. German observers picked up his movement and called artillery fire on the French captain. A shell burst close by, stunning Tribot-Laspierre and causing him to breathe in noxious fumes. He managed to continue the search for Neville, even though every movement caused excruciating pain. At last, Tribot-Laspierre found Colonel Neville and briefed him on the problems encountered during the 6th Marines' attack, "although his injuries made every effort torture."[15] Almost as soon as he finished his report, the captain collapsed and was evacuated for medical treatment. The Frenchman survived his wounds and received the Distinguished Service Cross for his bravery.

Word of Catlin's wounding reached the aid station in Lucy, and a stretcher party was assembled to find the colonel and carry him to safety. Assistant surgeon Frederick R. Hook, US Navy, took command of the party, which included YMCA volunteer John H. Clifford. Hook and his men scrambled through the ditch along the road to Torcy under heavy enemy fire. They came upon navy regimental surgeon Lieutenant Commander Wrey G. Farwell and informed him of their mission. Farwell ordered Hook back to Lucy and then crawled forward into the field himself to find Catlin. Undeterred by Farwell's orders, Hook and his men followed him into the field, crawling on their stomachs under the sweep of German machine gun fire. When Hook's party reached a small trench, they found Catlin lying on his back and in great pain, although Farwell had given him an injection to ease his suffering. Catlin was little concerned about his wound. "I was merely annoyed," he later wrote, "at my inability to move and carry on."[16]

Meanwhile, Private John L. Tunnell, Headquarters Company, 6th Marines, had been instructed by Major Sibley to find Colonel Catlin, request more ammunition, and report the use of poison gas by the Germans. Tunnell found Catlin lying on his back in the trench, "blood streaming from a chest wound, calmly directing the activities of a machine gun crew . . . covering the advance." Machine gun bullets ripped the air around the trench. "Leaves would gently detach themselves from the bushes and float to the ground," remembered Tunnell. "Some unseen hand seemed to be mowing the grass." Despite the danger, Tunnell stood at attention and made his report until Catlin called out to him, "Down here, lad, quickly."[17]

Moments later, Lieutenant Colonel Lee arrived with several other officers to meet with Catlin and get his orders, but Catlin simply said, "No, just carry on and carry out the previously arranged plan." The colonel gave Lee his dispatch and map cases, which had been secured in an earthen bank in the open field. Catlin briefed Lee on the progress of the battle and then relinquished command of the 6th Marines. Lee left the trench and took control of the regiment. The doctor kept Catlin in the ditch until the situation stabilized, as aircraft, bullets, and artillery shells continued to pass overhead. Twice the group thought gas shells had hit nearby, and the weakened Catlin needed help adjusting his mask to cover his face. As Catlin continued to lose strength, Hook decided they had to get the colonel to Lucy-le-Bocage. Sergeant Sydney J. Colford Jr. commandeered an ambulance in the town, while Pharmacist Mate Third Class Oscar S. Goodwin, YMCA volunteer Clifford, and two Marines grasped Catlin's stretcher and began a series of rushes to get back to the road. Every twenty yards, the group would go to ground while bullets struck around them, at one point shattering the walking stick carried by Clifford. Eventually, they made it to the waiting automobile that would transport Catlin to a Paris hospital.

Clifford did not have to be on the battlefield. He was the pastor of the First Baptist Church in Tucson, Arizona, and had attached himself to the Marines the previous winter, despite an initial snub. "We don't want you

Marine command post, Belleau Wood, June 13, 1918. Note the officer wearing a raincoat on the left. (© Emmanuel MAS/ECPAD/Defense)

around here," a cantankerous member of the 5th Marines had told him. He doubted the minister would be physically capable of keeping up with the brigade and continued to test Clifford, saying, "The Marines don't want the Y.M.C.A. around here. You can go to hell as far as we are concerned." The minister replied, "Well, son, I expect I would be a lot warmer in hell than I am here now."[18] Clifford's quick retort won the Marines over, and the doctor of divinity became affectionately known as "Doc."

Meanwhile, the 82nd Company pressed forward into the thick underbrush. After several hundred yards, the company ran head-on into the main German line, based around the area of fallen trees, rocks, and boulders. "Our company, and especially our platoon, got into the worst nest there was to clean out," Corporal Lowery remembered.[19] The German machine guns drove the company to cover. Corporal Ben Cone and Private Andrew K. Axton tried to move forward, taking on one of the machine guns with automatic rifles in what they knew was an unequal battle. Both Cone and Axton were killed in their ill-fated attempt to break the German line, and both were awarded the Navy Cross for their bravery.[20]

One of the 82nd Company's platoon leaders was Second Lieutenant

Caldwell Colt "Robby" Robinson. A native of Hartford, Connecticut, Robinson came from a wealthy family: his father was president of Colt's Patent Fire-arms Manufacturing Company. The military life appealed to Robinson early on, and he graduated from the New York Military Academy in 1916. He then spent the summer after his graduation at the Plattsburg military camp. After a trip around the world, Robby followed a proud family tradition and attended Yale University. Among the family's many Yale men was the first graduate of Yale College and Robby's own father. Indeed, Robinson had been the class boy for his father's class of 1895. Activities during Robby's freshman year included wrestling and crew, and he was a member of the Delta Phi Fraternity and St. Elmo Society.[21]

With America at war, Robinson joined the Marine Corps as a reserve officer on July 5, 1917. He quickly adapted to military life and accepted a regular commission as a second lieutenant on September 13. He married Ruth A. Stone four days later. After a short honeymoon, Robby bade his new wife good-bye and sailed for France on October 25, 1917, as a member of the 82nd Company. Early in 1918 Robinson was gassed while training in a supposedly quiet sector. Much to his surprise, the ambulance that picked him up bore his father's name and class at Yale, one of several that had been presented in his father's memory.[22]

As the attack began, Lieutenant Robinson faced his first offensive combat. He told his platoon that "he wanted every man to go, but that he would lead them." True to his word, Robinson led his platoon through the dense woods and uphill into a rough clump of boulders where the Germans had placed their machine guns. Members of the platoon began to fall under the German fire. Without hesitation, Robinson charged directly at the enemy, and within seconds, he was riddled with machine gun bullets and died instantly. Inspired by their commander, the platoon continued the attack. For his bravery, Robinson was awarded the Navy Cross. Robinson would long live in the memory of his Marines. One of his men later testified, "Both the living and the dead consider it an honor to have been led by him." His class at Yale gave him the finest testimony by simply stating, "His life leaves us an example of all that is best in self-sacrifice, courage, and honor."[23]

In addition to the loss of Robinson, First Lieutenant Frederick I. Hicks, a former enlisted Marine from Brownsville, Texas, was rendered senseless from a shell burst, and Second Lieutenant Smallman was also wounded, leaving only two of the five company officers standing. Smallman was a native of Malden, Massachusetts, a town just outside of Boston. The German defenders easily picked Smallman out as an officer and concentrated their fire on him. A bullet pierced his leg, driving the lieutenant to the ground. The round shattered his right thigh, splintering the bone. The one-time mathematics instructor would survive the wound but would never return to combat.[24]

Just behind the 82nd Company were the lead waves of First Lieutenant Alfred H. Noble's 83rd Company. A native of Federalsburg, Maryland, Noble had attended St. John's College in Annapolis, which was a military school at the time. After being briefed by Major Sibley, Noble called his executive officer and platoon leaders together to inform them of the impending attack. The first target was Belleau Wood, followed by the town of Bouresches just beyond. Noble advanced his two lead platoons in a wave formation, with the two support platoons following in column. After allowing Captain Smith's company the proper interval, Lieutenant Noble started forward with his executive officer and a runner, walking among the company and encouraging his men. Noble's general understanding of the overall method of attack from his superior officers was to "go ahead and fight 'em and kill 'em, damn it! Straight ahead, what are you waiting for?"[25] The company followed close behind Smith, with one platoon commander later remarking on the sheer irony of going into battle in the midst of such beautiful countryside and on such "a clear lovely, sunny, warm day."[26]

Private Edward E. McCormack, who was serving as a runner to Second Lieutenant Louis Timmerman's platoon, witnessed the advance with Noble. "We loaded up with plenty of ammunition and got started," he wrote in a letter. "It was a grand sight to see the boys on their way. . . . They held their bayonets at high point and never once stopped."[27] Unlike the 82nd Company, the 83rd Company covered the 500 yards to the wood line with no casualties nor any sign of the enemy.

The 250 men of the 83rd Company bolstered the 82nd Company's attack, but the progress made by the Marines proved slight. The Germans fired at the sound of the 83rd Company's advance, cutting down the leading files. Noble had trouble keeping his platoons together, but each moved toward the sound of the firing ahead. As the individual platoons passed into the forest, the company's tight organization completely failed. "It was impossible once one got into the woods to see for more than a few yards in any direction," Timmerman recalled. "Once we got into the wood . . . it became a platoon leaders' battle."[28]

Noble's men could not see the machine guns in the woods. "We went in barehanded," Noble recalled, "and we got slaughtered."[29] The two remaining platoons forming the left of the company tried to attack through the trees but could not penetrate the interlocking machine gun fire. In addition, the entire company's line of battle failed to extend completely across the woods to join the efforts of the 47th Company, 5th Marines. As the attack moved deeper into the forest, the Germans' flanking fire became even more effective. The combined two left flank platoons of both companies faced left and attacked, but to no avail.

Second Lieutenant Richard W. "Dick" Murphy from Greensboro, Alabama, commanded one of the attack platoons. "Murphy was a great powerfully built man of about 6–2," remembered a fellow lieutenant, with "an extremely rugged frame . . . of complete steel muscle."[30] His father was a cattleman in Texas, the first to drive a herd of cattle by trail to Wyoming; both of his grandfathers had been Confederate officers in the Civil War. Murphy entered the Virginia Military Institute in 1911 but was dismissed for deserting two days before Christmas 1912. Murphy worked himself back from oblivion, graduating from Marion Military Institute and being reinstated to VMI in 1913. Murphy achieved the rank of first sergeant of his cadet company, but the following year he was dismissed again for striking an instructor and "gross excess demerits."[31]

The Marines of the 83rd Company moved to covered firing positions and then attempted to pick off the German machine gunners and deadly snipers. A bullet struck Private Earl T. Durbin in the shoulder and then passed down his arm. Just as Durbin raised his other arm to assess his wounds, a second sniper's bullet crushed that arm as well. Durbin desperately needed water but was unable to retrieve his half-full canteen. He waited hours for help, convinced that he would die before anyone arrived. Another wounded Marine finally reached Durbin's shell hole, gave him water, and helped him to an aid station. Only a short distance away, Private Peter P. Bymers personally killed six German soldiers from his position, inspiring his fellow Marines. Bymers was later awarded the Silver Star for his "remarkable courage and steadiness" during the fight.[32]

Now in the confined terrain of the trees and boulders of Belleau Wood, Murphy led his men forward with relentless force. "He was always hankering for a fight," remembered Lieutenant Timmerman.[33] Another Marine wrote, "When the orders to advance came, he would not turn back, and . . . the only thing that would stop him would be a bullet."[34] Lieutenant Murphy led his men directly into a German machine gun position that was holding up his platoon's advance. The fight raged with great fury, and each man was able to look his enemy full in the eye as he fired his weapon. Murphy took a position in front of his men and charged further into the woods. He was hit in the stomach by a full burst from a German machine gun. The impact knocked the lieutenant to the ground, where he lay bloody but still conscious. Murphy was pulled to the rear and carried to an aid station. That was the last the company saw of Dick Murphy. The young Alabaman died in the hospital the next day. His death was not initially reported to the company, which listed him as missing in action. Despite their impassioned pleas for information, friends and family received no word of his fate until June 17, when his grave was located near the field hospital. Murphy's great friend, Second Lieutenant William B. Moore, assumed the sad task of writing to his fiancée in New York. In Alabama, Murphy's bereaved mother received many telegrams, including one from his brother Matt, who wrote, "No mother had a braver or a more noble son or one that ever died a more glorious death than poor Dick."[35]

Gunnery Sergeant John Groff, assigned as the company's first sergeant, kept the platoon moving forward, despite one of his men being hit in the face by a bullet that sliced off his chin. Groff took eight men on a patrol into the woods and quickly ran into the main German position. He moved his Marines behind a pocket of boulders and crept behind the Germans, using rocks and underbrush as cover. Once in position, Groff ordered his men to attack. It was "a tangled, terrific meeting," one account reported. "The crackle of pistol and the cries of the wounded" rang out through the woods.[36] In the short, bloody struggle, five German machine guns and six prisoners were taken. One of the company's field musicians attempted to take revenge for the Marines' earlier losses by killing the prisoners, but he was stopped by Groff. The gunnery sergeant was wounded in the fight and was later awarded the Navy Cross for his actions. Groff would retire a brigadier general in 1946 after a lengthy and distinguished career. But the bloody images of dying Marines in Belleau Wood would haunt this extraordinary Marine forever.[37]

One of Groff's Marines taking part in the assault was twenty-eight-year-old Private Carl Williams, now entering his sixth month as a Marine. Before the war, Williams had lived a quiet life as a farmer and an employee in his father's cannery in Waynesville, a small town nestled in the mountains of western North Carolina. He eventually became a bank clerk and a well-liked and respected member of the community. One of eight children, Carl was fiercely patriotic and determined to fight for his country. His family was very upset when both he and his brother Thurman left North Carolina to join the Marine Corps in December 1917, but they were proud of the young men too.

Unlike his brother Thurman, Carl Williams never returned to the Great Smoky Mountains. Private James R. Scarbrough saw Williams fall just ahead of him and ran to his side. "I couldn't see where he was hit," Scarbrough later remembered, "but he didn't move."[38] Another fellow Marine, Private Edward A. Graham, reported that Williams fell after being hit directly in the chest by machine gun fire. "Poor old Carl got almost there before he went down not to get up," remembered Graham. "Carl was a real man and the best pal I ever had."[39]

Williams's family received news of his death, along with confirmation from Graham of his burial on the battlefield. Only his identification disks were recovered to comfort his family. However, the Department of the Navy maintained that Williams was still alive and well in the Marine Brigade. With the ongoing agony of not knowing his fate for certain, his family and friends requested confirmation of his death through their representative in Congress and the secretary of the navy. The Graves Registration Service was able to confirm Williams's death by contacting Graham, but he was not listed among the burial records of the Marines who died in the battle. "Carl's folks should be proud of him," Graham related, and they would be if they knew "of the wonderful fighting the Marines did that day."[40]

In May 1919 a memorial service was held for Williams at the Methodist church in Waynesville. The church was overflowing with friends and family. Carl's best friend from childhood spoke first, recalling their days as young boys together, followed by more platitudes for the fallen Marine. The service ended with the singing of a selection of Private Williams's favorite hymns. Today, he still rests in an unknown grave in France. Another large gravestone holds his place in the Green Hill Cemetery in Waynesville, North Carolina, nestled under the nearby mountain peaks.[41]

With most of the 83rd Company pinned down and scattered in the woods, the Germans counterattacked, capturing many of the wounded Marines who had taken cover in shell holes and behind boulders. Private Wayne C. Colahan and Private Eugene S. Schrautemeier, a former St. Louis bank clerk, had entered the battle as company runners and were now pinned down together in a shell hole, formerly an enemy machine gun position, just on the edge of the woods. A handful of other wounded Marines lay nearby, also unable to move. Sergeant Charles Fleming called out to Colahan and ordered him to withdraw to the rear. The private crawled over the edge of the hole and slowly moved into the wheat field, using one of the small furrows as a shield against the machine gun bullets ripping the air over his head.

Nearby, Private Jules A. Martin also moved to the rear, but he collapsed in the wheat from loss of blood near Schrautemeier's position. As Martin lay resting, he heard the distinct sound of a pistol shot, and Schrautemeier cried out in pain from his shell hole only thirty feet away. Several nearby Marines responded, warning him to "keep quiet and protect himself." He replied, "I can't, my uncle has got me." Whenever an 83rd Company Marine was hit, the inside joke was that an "uncle" had got him, referring to Schrautemeier's two uncles serving in the German army. Martin looked back and saw a German soldier standing over Schrautemeier, tracking the Marine as he crawled toward safety. The German fired a second round into the American, ending his life. More Germans came forward and captured Fleming, Colahan, and

Martin. At least eighteen Marines of the 83rd Company were taken captive on June 6. Private Schrautemeier's body was recovered after the war, and he was laid to rest in 1921.[42]

Noble's right rear platoon, under the command of Murphy's close friend "Louie" Timmerman, lost contact with the rest of the company and moved forward to the right, using the edge of the woods as a guide. Born in New York City, Timmerman came from a wealthy family, and his father was secretary of the Western Maryland Railroad. He prepared for college at Exeter Academy and entered Princeton University in 1915. Timmerman was interested in military life and attended the Plattsburg military training camp in 1916. While at Princeton, he tried out for the football team and was a member of the Cap and Gown Club. When war was declared, he interrupted his studies and enlisted in the Marine Corps on July 5, 1917. Timmerman joined the 83rd Company in August and was on a ship, on his way to France, in October of that year.[43]

As he moved into the woods, Timmerman heard heavy machine gun fire, but the further he advanced into the trees, the less firing he heard. He passed two American machine guns being set up in the tree line and assumed that he was still in the rear ranks of the assault, with at least a lead platoon and most of the 83rd Company ahead of him. In fact, his lone platoon was moving beyond the rest of 83rd Company and was now crossing the front of the Germans' main line of resistance. Timmerman was mistakenly concerned that he was not keeping up with his company and pressed his men forward. "I advanced at an extremely rapid pace," remembered the lieutenant, "even though there was thick underbrush and brambles—we just went through them."[44]

Unknown to Timmerman, he was leading just two squads of his platoon. The other two under Sergeant Morris D. Moore had peeled off to the left as they took fire from the German machine gun line. Moore was an old-time Marine, first enlisting in 1907; he left the Marine Corps in 1911 as a sergeant but, with the onset of war, quit his job at a shoe company and reenlisted in early 1917 as a private. He was promoted to recruiting sergeant on April Fools' Day and was transferred to the recruiting station in Omaha, Nebraska. Moore was reduced to the rank of private in August for an unspecified offense, and five days later he was on a train bound for the Marine Barracks at Quantico to join the newly formed 83rd Company. Moore regained his sergeant's rank in September 1917, but his Nebraska indiscretion eventually brought him to the tangled trees and underbrush of Belleau Wood.[45]

Sergeant Moore captured four German soldiers during the attack. As he ordered another Marine to take them to the rear, German machine guns sprayed the group, killing the prisoners and Moore. "Always of a witty and cheery disposition, he has many times kept up the lagging spirits of the men," Noble confided in a letter to his sister. "May God in his mercy help you and all others who must make losses for the sake of the country."[46] Moore was laid to rest in the family cemetery in Bennett, Missouri, in 1921.

Private James R. Scarbrough evaded the German machine gun in the melee, edging quietly through the mass of boulders and trees to gain a firing position on the German crew. He could hear them talking excitedly but could not determine their exact location. "All I could see of them was what you would see if you were hunting squirrels amongst the canopy," he remembered, "a flash of cover, a little movement in the brush, some light peeking out from behind them, but no shape or form."[47] Using one of the large boulders as cover, Scarbrough came in behind the Germans and slid down on their dugout. The surprised gun crew had no time to react. "One of them was fiddling with the gun, maybe reloading it," Scarbrough recalled, "and he turned to look at me with as much shock and surprise in his eyes as I had in mine." He shot the German in the chest and kicked another gunner in the face with his hobnailed boot as the soldier was pouring himself a drink. He then turned to the third German, who saved his life by shouting, "Kamerad! Kamerad!"[48] Scarbrough took a pistol off the dead German and escorted his two prisoners down a ravine to join the rest of his platoon. One of Scarbrough's lasting impressions from the encounter was the smell of peppermint schnapps wafting off one of his captives. The German had spilled the liquor, soaking his uniform, when his face had come into contact with the Marine's boot.

Timmerman and his twenty-eight Marines were the only unit of Sibley's two left flank companies still in the advance. Their movement through the woods had been so rapid that they overran the German outposts. "I practically stepped on two German enlisted men," Timmerman recalled. "Their position was under a piece of shrubbery or bush I walked right onto."[49] The lieutenant never paused, sending the prisoners to the rear with one guard. Suddenly, the two squads burst out into the open, overlooking the town of Bouresches. The Marines had swept through the southern end of Belleau Wood and emerged on the eastern edge of the forest, deep within the Germans' defense line. Timmerman now saw the town as his target, and it was only 400 yards away. However, there were no other Marines in sight—not the 82nd Company nor any of the other platoons of his own unit.

Before Timmerman could decide on his next course of action, Private Charles Henry appeared and shouted that "the woods were full of Germans behind us."[50] Although he believed the private, the lieutenant tried to downplay the danger, concerned that his men would lose their momentum. Private Henry was bleeding from a bullet wound and gestured toward a German

Marine fighting position, Belleau Wood. (© Emmanuel MAS/ECPAD/Defense)

machine gun position. The lieutenant sent the private to the rear, formed his men into a skirmish line, and advanced into the field. He halted his men behind a mound of earth after only fifty yards when he noticed a band of Marines taking cover in a thin sliver of trees further out in the field. Timmerman dispatched Corporal Edwin J. Larsen and Private Benjamin Wierman to learn the identity of the Marines in the trees. The two Marines double-timed into the field ahead as Timmerman and his men watched. They had run almost fifty yards, reaching the halfway point, when the German machine guns opened fire on them. Both fell to the ground as the "beet plants and dirt kicked up all around where they were hiding." The Marines watched as the bodies of the two men twitched with the impact of each shot. Both Wierman, a clerk from Lexington, Kentucky, and Larsen, from Manistee, Michigan, died in the middle of the field. "To see Corporal Larsen killed and his body riddled with bullets," Private Scarbrough recalled, "it was like losing a mentor. He was a man I had hoped to be like, and now he was dead, killed right in front of us."[51] The Germans then raked the thin line of woods, causing the leaves and foliage to rain down on the Marines sheltered there.

At that moment, Lieutenant Timmerman realized that he and his men were alone and were taking rounds from the woods behind them. German machine gun and rifle fire erupted from the tree line to end the debate. "A man to my immediate left was hit," remembered Timmerman, "groaning and dropping his head to the ground." Private Walter E. Swenson, an official spice taster from St. Louis, took a bullet through the forehead and died while kneeling against a mound of dirt. Swenson had recently written to his mother about combat and the possibility of his own death. He had predicted, "If I have to cash in I sure will take a few Huns with me."[52] Private McCormack wrote of Swenson's death in a letter to his own mother: "[He] was the only one killed out of our bunch from St Louis. I sure lost a good friend."[53] An official telegram reached Swenson's mother back in St. Louis later in June. Already a widow, she was devastated by the death of her only son. That same day, the postman walked up the steps to her door and said, "Here's a letter from the boy in France. I heard you had bad news this morning." Swenson's mother broke into tears, kissed the letter, and cried, "This is too much." She read the letter from her fallen son, which asked her to send chocolate bars and cigarettes, "if you can." Grief swept over her as she realized she "could never give him comfort again."[54]

Timmerman knew that if his Marines remained in the field any longer, they would all become casualties. The unarmed lieutenant leaped to his feet and "shouted to the platoon to follow me." The effect on his men was electric. "I'd never heard him angry before. I can't describe that yell, it was bloodthirsty you might say," recalled Private Scarbrough. "He didn't even form words, but we all knew exactly what we wanted and we all ran towards that nest hollering like demons. . . . It was the first time I saw us attack like a pack of wolves." Scarbrough was certain the lieutenant was "fixing to kill them with his bare hands for what the Germs had done to his men."[55] Timmerman raced the fifty yards back to the tree line unscathed and found himself standing over a German machine gun position. He immediately jumped into the ditch and "waded into the nearest [Germans] with my very heavy boots which were steel tipped." The frightened soldiers cowered under the lieutenant's blows, kneeling "on the ground and begging for mercy."[56]

Private Ira O. Arbuckle, a farmer from Missouri, leaped in after the lieutenant. Soon, seventeen German soldiers had surrendered to the Marines, along with two machine guns. The sudden appearance of the Marines' fixed bayonets frightened the Germans into submission. The Americans stripped off all the German soldiers' equipment, and Timmerman armed himself with two German Luger pistols. Just at that moment, Sergeant Groff appeared with three Marines from the leading platoon of the 83rd Company. Timmerman ordered Groff to escort the prisoners to the rear while he and his men focused on the original objective: the town of Bouresches. The lieutenant still believed that the 82nd Company would be attacking the town, and he would do the same.

Dutifully, the Marines charged back into the field, taking cover near the same dirt mound, now littered with Marine casualties. Just as before, German fire exploded from the town, along with a wave of bullets from the trees behind them and from a small hill just to the north. The fire devastated the Marine platoon. One round tore into Timmerman's face, knocking him to the ground. Dazed and bleeding, he looked around to see his Marines sinking to the ground, dead or wounded. Timmerman staggered to his feet and called for his men to follow him back to the safety of the tree line. Miraculously, the lieutenant made it back to the woods and the captured German position without being struck again. The rest of his platoon followed. Of the fifty-six men who began the assault that morning, only six were left standing.[57]

Though still bleeding from the face, the lieutenant remained full of fight. One of his men dressed Timmerman's wound, and the lieutenant ordered Sergeant Elmer I. Fadden to turn the captured machine guns against the inevitable German counterattack. As soon as he gave the order, he spotted a file of German soldiers moving through the trees toward the Marines' position. He ordered his six men to take cover, and they waited for the Germans to approach within forty yards of the American defenders. At that moment, he gave the order to fire, and the German advance disappeared. The seven Marines were now masters of one small section of Belleau Wood. Private Arbuckle had been seriously wounded during the intense fighting in the woods, but a German corpsman had found him and expertly bandaged his wounds. The Marine was grateful for the kindness of his enemy, until the man tried to take him prisoner. Arbuckle killed the German and then made his way back to Timmerman's position.[58]

Private Edward J. "Eddie" Steinmetz, a twenty-three-year-old machinist from Hamilton, Ohio, responded to the nation's call for marksmen. Steinmetz proved to be one of the most lethal Marines in the company. Eddie was born in 1895 in Alsace, then a part of Germany. His father brought the family to the United States in 1901 to avoid compulsory military service for his three sons, but they all enlisted in 1917 to defend their adopted country. Only one would return to Ohio alive.

Steinmetz had been temporarily blinded and deafened by poison gas in April, and he now looked forward to getting revenge on the enemy. He carefully inched his way into the brush and soon located the lair of two German snipers. "A wait; then there showed for just an instant the barrel of a rifle and the top of a head as the German sniper rose to aim," one account noted. "A flash came from the Marine's gun. His duty was half done." After that first shot, Steinmetz waited for his chance at the other sniper. After a long, draining pause, he caught a hint of the German, and "once more the rifle spoke, and the second German sniper had fallen."[59]

Private Scarbrough heard a scuffle in the brush near his position, followed by shouts and muted pistol shots. He ran into the woods to find Steinmetz standing over a dead German private, his pistol still smoking. "Are you hungry, Jim?" he asked with a smile. After the scathing combat of that evening, Scarbrough was puzzled by the question, until Steinmetz added, "I just made some swiss cheese," as he gestured to the body on the ground. Eddie Steinmetz would die from machine gun fire on June 22, and his brother Louis would be killed in action only a few miles away on July 21.[60]

With the immediate German threat now disposed of, Timmerman sent one of his men back with a message informing Major Sibley of his location. The sounds of battle continued to echo through the trees, but no enemy appeared. Suddenly, small groups of Marines from the 47th Company arrived in bands of two or three men. They had been separated from their company on the far side of the woods and had worked their way through the German front line until they reached the edge of the trees. More Marines joined Timmerman, numbering approximately forty men. As darkness approached, the lieutenant felt confident that he could hold his position. Timmerman received the Navy Cross for his actions on June 6, as did six other members of the 83rd Company.

Across the Lucy–Bouresches road, the two remaining companies of Major Sibley's battalion pressed forward. Captain Frederick W. Karstaedt's 84th Company, consisting of approximately 250 men, led the advance, followed by Captain Bert Voeth's 97th Company. Sibley had previously described Karstaedt as "calm, even tempered, active, and painstaking."[61] Now, the veteran of so many wars and conflicts led his company directly across the fields toward Bouresches with confidence. "All of the men seem to take things calmly and cool," he wrote of the 84th Company. "We expect to do some good work before we get through."[62] The attitude of Private Maynard Dunham was typical of the young Marines crossing the fields. He later remembered, "That's when we knew we were going to have to kill people, and we did."[63]

The advance was much more difficult for Karstaedt and Voeth than for the two companies on the left side of the road, for their only cover consisted of knee-deep fields of wheat. German artillery fire exploded in the lines, and machine gun fire erupted from the town of Bouresches. "I looked across the wheat field," a Marine scout remembered, and "there were our buddies still coming along through the machine-gun bullets. As fast as they would drop, another Marine would take his place."[64]

First Lieutenant C. Boyd Maynard led his platoon into the wheat field, inspiring every Marine he encountered. Maynard was born and raised in Colton, Washington, where he attended local schools and then entered Washington State University in 1913. He first studied pharmacy, but by his junior year he had changed his major to agriculture. When America entered the war in 1917, Maynard left school to join the Marine Corps. The life of a Marine appealed to Maynard, and after training at Mare Island, he was ordered to report to Quantico, where he rose to the rank of first lieutenant in the 84th Company; from there, he was bound for France. Knowing that he was heading for combat, Maynard asked his college sweetheart, Helen Layton, to marry him. She agreed, and Maynard's father brought Helen to the East Coast, where the young couple was married in New York City.[65]

Boyd Maynard was not supposed to be with his company at Belleau Wood. He was on leave in Paris after finishing an officer's course when he learned of his company's movement. Maynard left Paris to join his men, arriving only an hour before the assault. Attired in a new dress uniform and lacking a sidearm, a helmet, or any other equipment, he joined his platoon, ready for the attack. Captain Karstaedt urged him not to go, but Maynard insisted on leading his Marines into the wheat fields. He took a position in advance of their formation instead of his usual place behind and gave his Washington State University battle cheer, "Give them Hell, Boys! Give them Hell!"[66] Conspicuous in his new uniform, Maynard fell during the first few minutes of the attack, his body hit five times in the stomach and groin. The young lieutenant was alive but mortally wounded. The Marines of his platoon pushed beyond his broken body, determined to avenge their leader. Maynard died during the night, just as he reached an operating table at the 6th Marines' dressing station.

After the battle, Maynard was buried by his men, who showed their "esteem and love" by carving a crude cross for the head of his grave. The men wrote a simple epitaph on the cross: "Here lies Lieutenant Maynard, who gave his life today for other's tomorrows."[67] Maynard's wife and parents received the telegram at the family home in Colton informing them of his death. Chaplain Harris A. Darche of the 6th Marines sent a letter to Maynard's father, providing the details of his final days. "Mr. Maynard, your son was one of our best officers, and his loss was keenly felt," Darche wrote, "but like many Americans, he laid down his life for right and justice, and so we placed the crown of victory on his grave."[68]

Another 84th Company platoon leader was Second Lieutenant Allan C. Perkinson, a Virginia Military Institute graduate. He was awarded the brigade's first Croix de Guerre for his actions in April 1918. He wrote home expressing his concern about being decorated by the French division commander, noting, "I expect he, being a Frenchman, will kiss me . . . I wish he would send his daughter instead." Perkinson led his 3rd Platoon forward, having instilled in the men the concept that the attack was "straight football, one continuous series of line bucking." When the first Marine in the platoon fell, Perkinson picked up the man's rifle and led the assault with the bayonet. A bullet struck the rifle's trigger guard and was deflected up into his collar, taking off his collar clasps. Perkinson maintained that the bullet "changed my voice for about an hour, but never even scratched my throat."[69]

After the attack, only twenty-three of the platoon's forty-seven Marines would be left standing. Despite the losses, Perkinson took his men forward, advancing until they reached the end of the wheat field. A small knoll offered protection from enemy fire, but beyond that lay 300 yards of descending ground completely dominated by the machine guns in Bouresches. The 84th Company halted, still concealed in the wheat, and could advance no further. At least fifty Marines from the company were killed or wounded in the initial attack.

The 97th Company followed the 84th and began to take casualties only 200 yards from the jump-off point. The company advanced with only three platoons. Army Second Lieutenant Edward A. Kennedy's 4th Platoon had yet to join Voeth's company when the order came to advance; it had been detached from the company for duty at Triangle Farm. Second Lieutenant Alfred G. Skelton had only just arrived from training school when the order came to attack. Like Maynard, the young lieutenant went into combat with no weapon or helmet. Casualties would soon provide him with both.[70]

The Marines could see the town of Bouresches ahead. German artillery broke over the company, causing more casualties. The survivors crawled forward to the knoll overlooking the town. Captain Voeth walked among his men, followed by the company's mascot, a German shepherd dog belonging to Lieutenant Moore. The whine of the enemy bullets intrigued the dog, and it snapped at the falling wheat stalks as the bullets clipped them. As bullets struck the dirt near the captain, the dog ran to the impact points and furiously attempted to dig them up. Failing, the dog ran back to Voeth and leaped at the captain's hand. Ignoring the passing rounds, he told the dog in a commanding voice, "Down!" Then he told one of his corporals, "You'll never see what's going on with your nose stuck down in the mud."[71]

After inspecting the ground, Captain Voeth gave the order, "Ninety-Seventh Company, advance by rushes!" Although the 97th Company's 241 Marines advanced in the normal wave formation, they moved by rushes. The Marines raced fifteen yards until a whistle blast alerted them to go down and conceal themselves in the wheat. Another whistle brought the Marines to their feet for another rush. Word was sent down the lines to keep all bayonets down to prevent the flash of sunlight on metal from serving as markers for the German machine gunners. As the Marines advanced, Corporal William T. Scanlon admonished some of his squad not to advance too quickly and remarked, "We hold a perfect line."[72]

The Marines charged ahead, advancing thirty yards in two rushes before halting under the incessant machine gun fire. The company had no cover, and dead and wounded Marines fell on the open ground. The captain shouted out, "Automatic rifles to the left!" in an attempt to get covering fire from Belleau Wood. Two Marines ran forward but were cut down before reaching the trees. "Every now and then a machine gun hits in front of me and kicks dirt in my face and eyes," remembered Corporal Scanlon. As he lay there, Scanlon considered which part of his body to place toward the incoming rounds. He mused, "My right arm should not be sacrificed, as I use it the most. . . . Can I spare my legs. . . . Never to dance again. No, I can't let my legs go." A shell exploded nearby, scoring a direct hit on one of the Marines. "I can pick out his legs, arms, and body," Scanlon wrote. "My eyes seem fixed and follow the upward movement and watch the parts coming down. Bits fall on me."[73]

Although they were only 250 yards from the village of Bouresches, Voeth's company remained in the fields, unable to advance any further. The Marines hastily dug foxholes in the open ground, but the German fire continued unabated, and casualties mounted. At least fifty-six Marines of the 97th Company lay dead and wounded in the farm fields. Amid the carnage and confusion, Private Leon D. Huffstater of the 97th Company volunteered to carry the wounded to shelter, despite the deadly accurate enemy fire. The journey to the French killing fields had started for him in August 1917, when he entered a Marine Corps recruiting station and signed his enlistment papers. Huffstater was a native of Oswego, New York, and left his job as an engineer to become a "Soldier of the Sea." Parris Island proved to be a rude awakening for Huffstater, who struggled under the harsh discipline of the veteran drill instructors. However, once he joined the 97th Company in April 1918, he found his niche in the combat zone and became an exemplary Marine.[74]

Major Cole and his 6th Machine Gun Battalion worked to support the advance. However, command and control over the four machine gun companies was nearly impossible. Theoretically, each company was assigned to provide support to a single infantry battalion. However, in the days leading up to the attack, his battalion was spread across the front, and mingling of the companies was standard.[75]

The 23rd Company, supporting Berry's 3rd Battalion, 5th Marines, was able to lay down a preliminary barrage before the attack and another during

Southern portion of Belleau Wood, photographed by French aircraft on June 6, 1918. Note the variations in the cultivated fields crossed by the Marine battalions. (National Archives and Records Administration, College Park, MD)

the movement across the fields. However, because of the range and German concealment, the barrage could not suppress enemy machine gun fire. German shell fire proved more accurate. A shell burst behind Second Lieutenant Daniel W. Patterson, an army officer assigned to the company. Although he was not wounded by the explosion, shrapnel ripped into a number of Marines from his platoon. The violence of the blast and the sight of his men mauled and dying around him caused Patterson shell shock and memory loss. Two days would pass before the young lieutenant regained his senses.[76]

Lieutenant Harold D. "Soup" Campbell took his 23rd Company machine gun section forward and toward the right, in support of the 82nd Company. A native of Waterbury, Vermont, Campbell entered Norwich University in 1913, where his on-campus "escapades" were legendary. He also organized the school's first basketball team and was editor of the *Reveille*, the student newspaper. Campbell took to military life and attained the rank of first lieutenant by his senior year. In 1916 he saw his first field service on the Mexican border with the 1st Vermont Cavalry. The experience only solidified his desire for a career in the military. Campbell graduated with a degree in chemical engineering in 1917, but on the day war was declared, Campbell enlisted in the Marine Corps, believing that branch to be the best place to serve his country. He initially went to the Marine Barracks at Portsmouth, New Hampshire, and then to Parris Island, where he spent two months

6th Machine Gun Battalion
Belleau Wood June 1918
Maj. Edward B. Cole

Casualties during the battle drastically altered the battalion command structure.

15th Company
Capt. Matthew H. Kingman

23rd Company
Capt. John P. McCann

77th Company
Capt. Louis R. de Roode

81st Company
Capt. Alan M. Sumner

Chart 3. 6th Machine Gun Battalion, Belleau Wood

learning the ways of the Marine Corps. On June 4 Campbell joined the 23rd Company at Quantico, Virginia, and sailed for France ten days later.[77]

Less than three months after donning the uniform of a Marine lieutenant, Campbell stepped onto French soil with his company. "I would not have missed the chance," he wrote home, "to come across the pond with the first contingent."[78] He received training in field fortifications, explosives, signals, and gas at the army's I Corps School and remained with the 23rd Company when it became a machine gun unit. Campbell participated in winter training and then went into the trenches in the quiet sectors. Now he led his men forward in the attack on Belleau Wood. "It was a grand sight to look upon," Campbell remembered, "all those men, wave after wave going 'over the top' into the open fields and through the artillery and machine gun barrage."[79] The young lieutenant was momentarily staggered by a German machine gun bullet, but the wound was only a bruise. He continued forward in the attack.[80]

The cannon of the 12th Field Artillery continued to fire into the German lines, but the gunners were hampered by their lack of knowledge of the actual line of attack. Belleau Wood prevented any real reconnaissance from the air, so the artillerymen concentrated on the hills beyond the woods, which had been the original objective. German counterbattery fire proved ineffective, except when a single 150mm shell hit the artillery train, killing eighteen horses outright and wounding five more. The only human casualties were several teamsters who were "badly shaken up."[81]

The machine guns of the 23rd and 73rd Companies were assigned to support the attack. First Sergeant Daniel J. Daly of the 73rd Company, already a Marine Corps legend with two Medals of Honor, walked among the foxholes and said in his rich Irish brogue, "All right now, boys, you've got 50 seconds. . . . Now you have 40 seconds . . . you've got 30 seconds . . . and you've got 20 seconds." Daly continued to count down until there was only five seconds to go, and still no one was moving. This enraged the dour sergeant, who had seen combat from the Boxer Rebellion to Haiti. "Come on you bastards and just go!" Daly bawled. "What do you want to do, live forever?"[82]

Belleau Wood Tour

Stop 11. Attack of the 3rd Battalion, 6th Marines,
49°03'25.2"N 3°16'47.0"E

Proceed 3 kilometers to the 2nd Division boulder in Lucy-le-Bocage. Proceed on the Route de Bouresches for 650 meters. Pause after you leave the town as you pass over "Gob Gulley," the small creek where the 6th Marines' aid station was established. Continue until you arrive at the opening of the valley leading to Bouresches itself. You are now on the right flank of the 4th Marine Brigade's attack, following Major Sibley's movements on June 6.

Pause again to orient yourself to the terrain. There are no turnouts here, so be mindful of local traffic. You have now traversed the 4th Marine Brigade's entire line, from the left at Les Mares Farm to Major Holcomb's battalion holding the high ground to your right. Belleau Wood is to your left front, and the road ahead leads directly to Bouresches.

You are in the center of Major Sibley's advance. The June 6, 1918, attack of the 82nd and 83rd Companies took place on your left, and the high ground to your right is where the 84th and 97th Companies suffered tremendous casualties that day.

7

June 6, 1918—Evening
"Come on Down and Join the Party"

THE ADVANCE OF SIBLEY'S BATTALION GROUND to a halt, leaving Major Thomas Holcomb's battalion the last to assault Belleau Wood. Holcomb's relationship with his command was complex. Initially, many of the officers and men disliked Holcomb. According to one lieutenant, "We didn't think too much of him. We thought he was a little too uppity."[1] Holcomb was exacting in his treatment of the Marines in his battalion. Every day after drill, the major would hold school to instruct his new officers on the art of war. One day, he asked Second Lieutenant Cates of the 96th Company, "How many entrances should a dugout have?" Cates, having failed to study the manual, said, "Well, at least one." Holcomb replied with disgust, "That's a hell of a bright answer!"[2] Both men would eventually rise to become commandants of the Marine Corps.

In time, Holcomb's men would change their opinion, and the tough Marine major would be considered "a grand old man in every way." But on June 6 the Marines of the battalion were still withholding judgment of their commander.[3] Born in New Castle, Delaware, in 1879, Holcomb entered the Marine Corps in 1900 as a second lieutenant. His early assignments included sea duty with the North Atlantic Fleet and expeditionary duty in the Philippines. He spent the majority of his time before the First World War in China, serving with the Legation Guard and later as attaché on the staff of the American minister, where he learned to speak Chinese.

Only two of Holcomb's four companies were on the front line. The 23rd Infantry was moving across the Paris road to relieve part of the battalion's defensive area. The 78th Company still held the right around Triangle Farm, while the 79th Company extended the line toward Lucy-le-Bocage. The 80th Company moved with battalion headquarters to the woods near Maison Blanche, but a delay in the 96th Company's relief forced that unit to stay in reserve in the Bois de Clerembauts.[4]

Holcomb first learned of an impending attack at noon. He was called to regimental headquarters in the late afternoon and briefed by Colonel Catlin. Holcomb returned to his battalion at 4:30 p.m., after the assault battalions had already started to move into their attack positions. He briefed his company commanders about their mission in the coming attack, only half an hour away. The battalion's mission in the initial attack was simply to move and conform to Sibley's right as it advanced. One company would support the attack on Bouresches by passing south of the town, following the advance of Sibley's right flank units. Once Sibley had taken the initial objectives in Belleau Wood and Bouresches, Holcomb would order his battalion to Bouresches and assault the railroad on the high ground beyond it. The 78th Company would anchor the right of the Marine line and act as a pivot. Holcomb selected the 96th Company to lead the advance. It would move forward along the ravine from La Cense Farm. Once in position, the company would take the ground south of town, leaving the capture of Bouresches itself to Sibley's battalion. On the left, the 79th Company would support the 96th Company. The 80th Company, in reserve, was ordered to support, as necessary, Sibley's advance.[5]

The company commanders quickly returned to their units, recognizing that time was of the essence. Captain Randolph T. Zane ordered his 79th Company platoon commanders to report to his headquarters at "double time." The thirty-year-old from Philadelphia was known to his men as "a very fine, gentlemanly guy."[6] Zane had entered the Marine Corps in 1909, serving aboard the battleship USS *New Hampshire*, at the Portsmouth Naval Prison, and on expeditionary duty in Cuba. He married the daughter of the governor of California and became a distinguished member of society. In 1917 Zane was on duty in the Hawaiian Islands when he was called to Quantico to serve with the 6th Marines. He assumed command of the 79th Company in October 1917. Zane took the men to France in January 1918, along with their company mascot, a Virginia goat smuggled ashore inside a bandsman's drum. Now, Zane prepared to lead his men into battle.[7]

Zane placed a map on the ground and gathered his officers around it. By now, the young captain had earned the respect of his subordinate officers. "He had a tremendous brain," one later remembered; he was "a wonderful captain for a young officer to serve under."[8] The company would pivot on First Lieutenant Murray's platoon on the right. Second Lieutenant John A. West's 3rd Platoon on the left would follow Sibley's battalion by sweeping across the ravine to the edge of Belleau Wood and then turn and advance on Bouresches 500 yards behind the lead battalion. The 1st and 2nd Platoons would fill the gap between left and right.

The lieutenants ran back to their platoons and dispatched runners, alerting each squad leader to take his men forward to the attack positions. As the left flank company of the battalion, Zane's men would move first, as soon as Sibley's men cleared their front. First Lieutenant Wallace M. Leonard Jr., on loan from the US Army, commanded the 2nd Platoon. He was "a slim small man with a whisper of a mustache," remembered one member of his platoon. Leonard respected his men. "The more I see of my Marines the fonder I grow of them," he wrote to his father. "They are a cocky lot . . . proud as Lucifer, but their equipment always shines."[9] Born into a wealthy family residing in Newton, Massachusetts, Leonard attended Amherst College, where he starred as captain of the gymnastics team, editor of the school newspaper, and member of the Sphinx Club. After graduating in 1916, Leonard joined his father in the publishing business before joining the army. He was married on June 7, 1917, and entered the army officers' camp in Plattsburg, New York. In November of that year, Leonard received his commission as army first lieutenant.

Leonard returned to his platoon to find most of the Marines awakening from a hurried sleep after the exertion of the past several days on the line. The lieutenant passed the word to his men to "stand by to go over."[10] They would move at exactly 5:00 p.m., he informed them, and he would fire his .45-caliber pistol to signal the attack. However, much of the expected drama of this announcement was lacking because the men had already learned of the attack from a passing captain who, when asked why the hurry, curtly replied, "We make an attack at five o'clock."[11] Leonard ordered his men to discard all extra clothing and to carry only necessary equipment into the assault. The platoon moved forward to a small grove of trees to await the signal to attack. German machine gun fire searched for the Marines in the tree lines on the small hills facing Bouresches from the south, and shells burst around their position, directed by an observer in a balloon behind the town.[12]

A runner delivering a message to Leonard was shot through the arm as he turned to leave. A shell burst just behind the platoon, causing Corporal Glen G. Hill to crawl back and check for casualties; he was particularly concerned about his brother, Corporal Sidney B. Hill, who was serving in the same platoon. Both Marines had attended the University of Washington and were members of the same fraternity. Glen Hill was surprised to find his brother and several other men gathered in the crater caused by the shelling, eating French bread and the "black stringy Australian beef" known as "monkey meat." Hill was relieved, but also hungry, as the Marines had had nothing to eat during the day. "Come on down and join the party," shouted Sergeant Robert E. "Bobby" Barrett. "You might as well die on a full stomach."[13] Hill took a portion of the beef and bread and crawled back to his position.

The Marines of the 79th Company remained in the tree line and watched as the 84th and 97th Companies moved across their front from the left. "You could see the exploding shells and [hear] the incessant whine of the machine gun bullets," recalled Corporal Hill, "and the men dropped along

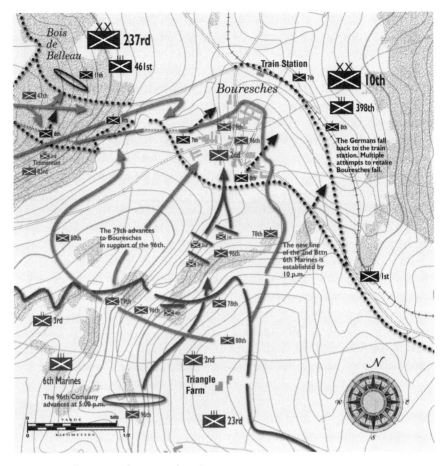

Map 11. Belleau Wood, Bouresches, June 6, 1918

the way."[14] With the Marines' advance stalled, Major Holcomb's objective of covering Sibley's right no longer mattered. He decided to alter the plan of battle, going forward immediately. Holcomb ordered Captain Duncan's 96th Company to make a direct attack on the town of Bouresches, supported on the left by the 79th Company.

The choice of the 96th Company was a good one. It had been pulled from the line at 8:00 a.m. and had spent the day resting. Most important, Captain Duncan was an experienced officer, having entered the Marine Corps in 1909 from his native state of Missouri, where his family had helped found the town of St. Joseph. Duncan graduated from Culver Military Academy, where he received the honorable nickname "Napoleon." His indoctrination into Marine expeditionary duty began one year later with service in Panama and later in Nicaragua. Duncan then served at both the Naval Prison in Portsmouth, New Hampshire, and the Naval Disciplinary Barracks in Puget Sound, Washington. He returned to the Pacific Fleet in 1914 as part of the 4th Marines stationed off the west coast of Mexico and was sent to Guam the following year. In August 1917 Duncan reported to Quantico, where he took command of the 96th Company.[15]

Now, amongst the shell bursts and machine gun fire, Duncan was in his element. His high school yearbook had described him with a quote: "So over violent, or over civil, that every man with him was God or Devil."[16] Under his leadership, the company became known as "a wild bunch of indians that didn't give a dam[n] for anything." Duncan assembled his officers at 4:45 p.m. and informed them of the attack order, providing them with what little information he had. The main attack would be made by the 1st, 2nd, and 3rd Platoons; the 4th Platoon would move in echelon to tie in with Sibley's battalion. The company then proceeded up a ravine to the jump-off point. The captain, dressed in his best uniform and smoking his straight-stem pipe, moved among his men, impressing them as "the coolest man on the field always giving orders and smiling all the time."[17] Duncan moved forward to lead the first two platoons and ordered First Lieutenant James F. Robertson to command the other two platoons.[18]

The attack seemed hopeless. The town bristled with machine guns and could be approached only through the surrounding wheat fields, which provided no cover. The Germans had already repulsed two companies of Sibley's battalion, but Duncan and his Marines seemed little troubled by the daunting task and anxiously awaited the order to attack. "I cannot describe the feeling one has while waiting for the word," remembered Private John T. Miller. "It seemed to me that the time would never come." Duncan broke the tension with a blast of his whistle. He pressed his men forward into the wheat field leading to the town, only 600 yards away. With the shriek of that whistle, Private Miller later wrote, "We were on our way."[19]

First Lieutenant George B. Lockhart's 1st Platoon broke into the open first, pushing ahead in its haste to take the objective, but Duncan calmly ran over and halted the platoon until the rest of the company caught up. A native of southwestern Virginia, Lockhart had graduated from the Virginia Military Institute in May 1917 and gone directly to Parris Island three weeks later. He was an original member of the 96th Company and Duncan's executive officer as well.[20]

Bullets passed in and around the Marines as they nervously awaited the order to advance. Sergeant Aloysius P. Sheridan, a former shoe salesman from Kansas City and a boyhood friend of Duncan's, jokingly asked if they would see much action. "Oh! yes, we will give and take," replied Duncan, "but be sure you take more than you give."[21] The captain watched his men advance, tapping his legs with his swagger stick. Once in line, the 232 men of the 96th Company moved forward through the wheat fields laced with red poppies, directly into the German gunfire. The Marines advanced in four perfect waves, causing Major Cole, commanding the supporting machine guns, to say later that the advance "was the most beautiful sight he had ever seen."[22]

Almost immediately, Captain Duncan went down, struck by a bullet in the stomach. He was the first man hit, only a minute into the assault. First Sergeant Joseph A. Sisler was quickly at his side, followed by Sergeant Sheridan. Regimental Dental Surgeon Junior Grade Weedon E. Osborne and a corpsman also ran over to assist the captain, and the four men carried Duncan to a small clump of trees out of the line of fire. The group placed the bleeding captain on the ground, only to have a German shell burst among them, killing everyone but Sheridan. The dazed and partially blinded sergeant picked himself up and surveyed the scene of destruction. Sadly, he could do nothing for the men, so he left to rejoin his platoon. Osborne, a practicing dentist in Salt Lake City, Utah, became the first naval officer to die in ground combat in World War I. He was posthumously awarded the Medal of Honor for heroism in the attack on Bouresches.[23]

With the death of their captain, the attack faltered, and the Marines were unsure what to do next. First Lieutenant Robertson knew that Sibley's men had halted, and his own supporting role must change if they were to capture Bouresches. After a pause of several minutes, Robertson jumped to his feet, motioned with his pistol to the 4th Platoon, and shouted, "Come on, let's go." With those words, the remnants of the company jumped up and charged the town. German machine gun fire burst from the village, raking the Marine lines. Cries of "I'm hit" and "Heine got me" were heard as men began to fall in the wheat. One Marine was struck by a bullet in the ankle and fell beside Private Miller, saying, "They won't even let me get started. When you get into the town, kill ten for me."[24] Miller made the promise and kept moving toward Bouresches.

Amid the carnage, Lieutenant Robertson blew his signal whistle to bring his two platoons forward. He then turned to locate his 3rd Platoon commander, Second Lieutenant John D. Bowling Jr., a twenty-three-year-old from Prince George's County, Maryland. Bowling was a 1916 graduate of the Maryland Agricultural College (later the University of Maryland). While in college, Bowling had served in the Cadet Corps, but he was also interested in science, serving as vice president of the Chemistry Club. After a year working as a commercial chemist for the Southern Railway, Bowling entered the Marine Corps in June 1917 and reported to the Rifle Range at Winthrop,

First Lieutenant James F. Robertson (*left*) with French soldiers in the woods near Le Thiolet a few days prior to the June 6 attack. (Marine Corps Archives, Quantico, VA)

Maryland, only a few miles from his home.[25] Almost immediately, Bowling was transferred to Quantico, where the brown-haired, blue-eyed lieutenant joined the fledgling 96th Company, 6th Marines, and completed a stint at the army's I Corps School. After a slow start, Bowling flourished as a Marine and received high marks in proficiency from his superior officers, who described him as "calm, even tempered and painstaking."[26] The chemist-turned-Marine now led his platoon forward but then seemed to disappear in the wheat. Robertson sent word down the line, asking, "Where is Johnny?" Suddenly, Bowling rose from the wheat, white-faced and with blood streaming from a bullet wound in the right shoulder. Despite shattered bones in his shoulder, he continued to advance on Bouresches.[27]

There was confusion among the officers of the 96th Company about the change from supporting the 3rd Battalion to attacking Bouresches. Second Lieutenant Cates, commanding the 4th Platoon, remembered, "We didn't know where we were going, if fact we didn't entirely understand our orders."[28] The company had covered another 100 yards when the German machine gun fire became so intense that the Marines went to ground in the wheat. It seemed impossible to cross the last few hundred yards to the town.

Private Harold I. Turney covered the first rush in safety, but then a shell burst just in front of the Marine. Jagged pieces of shrapnel tore into his groin and leg, leaving Turney bleeding and in agony.

Second Lieutenant Thomas R. "Tommy" Brailsford was killed in the first steps of the attack. He was a 1917 graduate of Texas A&M and a talented third baseman on both his college baseball team and the independent minor league team in Crockett, Texas. His body was not immediately recovered from the wheat field, leaving his friends and family with the hope that he was still alive. His wife placed requests in newspapers seeking information about his fate from any available source. They had been married shortly before he left Texas, destined for the 96th Company in Quantico, Virginia. Brailsford was officially listed as killed in action on July 29.[29]

With only three officers still in action and a seemingly impossible 300 yards to go, there was no doubt that if the Marines remained in the wheat field, the entire 96th Company would become casualties. The 2nd Platoon, commanded by Second Lieutenant Donald D. Page of the US Army, went to ground and tried to return fire, but to no avail. What remained of Page's and Bowling's platoons took refuge in a small ravine on the right. However, Cates's 4th Platoon continued the attack, advancing to within 200 yards of the town. "It is a wonderful thrill to be out there," Cates wrote home, "in front of a bunch of men that will follow you to your death."[30] The Germans renewed their fire at the sight of the charge, and Cates reported, "The bullets hitting the ground were as thick as raindrops."[31] A burst of machine gun fire caught Cates as he moved forward. A bullet smashed into the crown of his helmet, denting the steel and knocking Cates unconscious. The attack pressed on, leaving the fallen lieutenant behind.

Under the relentless fire, the 1st Platoon veered off to take cover in the ravine on the right, joining the remnants of the 2nd and 3rd Platoons that were not pinned down in the wheat field. However, Lieutenant Robertson continued to move with what remained of the 4th Platoon. The young lieutenant had been born in New Zealand, where he was a laborer and a farmer. He found his way to San Francisco in 1912 and enlisted as a private in the Marine Corps at the tender age of twenty-one. Marine Barracks Guam was Robertson's first post. He learned the ways of the Marine Corps under Captain Earl H. Ellis and achieved the rank of corporal and then sergeant within one year at Mare Island, California. With his quick rise in rank and a perfect disciplinary record, Robertson reenlisted in the Marine Corps in the fall of 1916 and became a recruiter. With the advent of war, Robertson was promoted to first lieutenant in August 1917 and became second in command of the 96th Company. Major Holcomb described Robertson as a "courageous and aggressive battle leader, and his men will follow him."[32]

Captain Duncan depended heavily on Robertson's leadership, and the two became great friends. Now, with Duncan killed during the first few minutes of the attack, Robertson led the survivors of the 4th Platoon into the town of Bouresches, where they established a foothold. The enemy light machine guns outside the town continued to fire, but the Marines started to encircle the guns. The Germans withdrew only when the Marines were within ten meters of their position, allowing Robertson to maneuver to the western edge of Bouresches. Of the 232 men who began the attack, only 26 Marines reached the town alive. Fifty-one Marines were killed or wounded in the assault, and the rest were scattered, leaderless, across the wheat fields.[33]

Captain Zane's 79th Company jumped off to the left of Duncan's men, following the last wave of the 96th Company. Among his men, Zane was known to be "calm as a cucumber." One of his lieutenants remembered, "I never saw the man excited, not [even] in the midst of fire."[34]

Second Lieutenant West's 3rd Platoon was assigned to protect the company's left flank. The platoon was to move across the rear of the 3rd Battalion's advance and then proceed to Belleau Wood. Once there, West and his Marines would turn and support Sibley's advance. However, West's men were angry as they moved forward. They had butchered a small calf the night before and had waited all day to cook the beef, having had nothing to eat but bread for the past five days. However, the new orders to attack meant leaving the uncooked meat behind and going into combat hungry. The Marines of the 3rd Platoon were not happy.[35]

West sent his lead squad, commanded by Corporal Alfred O. Halverson, into the wheat field in short rushes. West followed with the rest of his platoon. The ubiquitous German machine gun fire tore into the Marines, as did shrapnel from the shell bursts overhead. West's men passed over the dead and wounded of the 3rd Battalion. Those who were still alive called out for corpsmen and stretcher bearers, but the 3rd Platoon could do little to help. The lieutenant paused for a moment over a Marine who had been shot through both thighs. "Just a kid he was," recalled West, "crying hard." West made a tourniquet from his puttees and then moved on. When the lieutenant returned to the wounded Marine, he saw that "a shell had blown both his legs off and he was dead."[36]

Zane moved forward with his 1st and 4th Platoons, charging directly through the wheat fields toward Bouresches. The lead platoons encountered the same fire as the 96th Company. Private Harold T. Linnell was known as one of the bravest men in the company, having been awarded the Croix de Guerre in the trenches near Verdun in the spring. Machine gun bullets struck Linnell as he moved across the field, killing him instantly.

Corporal Raymond W. Boone was hit three times by German bullets and was sent to the rear. The bloody but infuriated Marine refused to leave the fight and returned to the field to carry the wounded to cover. He received the Distinguished Service Cross for his actions. When Boone returned home to Lake Elsinore, California, he bore the scars of battle, including bullet fragments embedded in his body, a bayonet scar across his upper lip, and a disfigured hand. When questioned about his service, he stated that he had done "no more than any Marine would have done."[37] Boone added, "You see, the joke was on the Germans, I am left handed and they got my right hand.[38]

First Lieutenant Murray led his 4th Platoon into the withering machine gun fire. The twenty-two-year-old had joined the Marine Corps only the previous year after graduating from Culver Military Academy. The native Pennsylvanian, known as "one of the most popular all around men in the school," had been president of the senior class and captain of the football team. Now engaged in his first real offensive combat, Murray and his command were pelted by a rain of machine gun bullets. Murray was hit in both arms and lay bleeding on the ground. Private Elbert E. Brooks, a twenty-four-year-old Marine from Memphis, Tennessee, placed his body in front of the lieutenant, shielding him from the intense fire while he attempted to bandage his wounds. Brooks was struck twice in the hip by German bullets. Murray was able to stagger to his feet and get to the rear, refusing any offer of assistance. Both men survived to receive the Navy Cross for their actions.[39] The Navy Cross was established by a 1919 act of Congress for heroism during World War I and after. The sailors and Marines who received the Distinguished Service Cross while serving with the army were awarded the Navy Cross for the same action.

First Lieutenant Erskine moved forward to lead the advance. Born in Columbia, Louisiana, Erskine was attending Louisiana State University when he was called to service as a sergeant bugler in the 1st Louisiana Infantry during the 1916 Mexican border intervention. He then returned to the university and graduated the following year. Erskine was determined to take part in the war as quickly as he could and enlisted in the Marine Corps in April 1917 at age nineteen. He was assigned to the 79th Company in Quantico. "He was a tall, thin, fine looking boy," remembered his company commander, while a fellow lieutenant remembered him as a "combination of spit and polish and combat leader."[40]

With the company attack now stalled, Erskine personally led the advance into the fields, only to be pinned down halfway to the town. The machine gun fire was relentless. "It just cut us to pieces," remembered Erskine. "It was murder."[41] He halted the Marines and ordered them to take cover in the wheat. Corporal Thomas A. Gragard "calmly rose and walked through the wheat to find a good position for his squad," but he was killed by the German fire. Private Oscar "Preacher" Rankin, Gragard's best friend, jumped up and, despite being known as a pious man, "swore as no parson has ever sworn."[42] Rankin gathered the remnants of the squad and headed through the wheat for Bouresches. Erskine kept the rest of the platoon in line, trying to hold the wheat field. In forty minutes, the fifty-eight-man platoon had been reduced to four men unhurt, including Erskine.[43]

Zane and his command group advanced with the assault waves. After moving a hundred yards, Marines began to fall. "I can safely say," wrote Private Hugo C. Meyer, "that no man crossed those fields and woods that day without praying." The captain halted with his headquarters group in the field behind a thorn patch. The bullets tore into the Marines, causing Private Meyer to remark, "All of us were as close to Mother Earth as possible and still they were hitting us." Meyer pushed his face into the thorns and dug a small hollow in the earth, but "even then a machine gun bullet scraped my helmet and hit the man on my right in the leg."[44] Determined to halt the German machine gun fire, Private John Flocken moved forward with his Chauchat light machine gun and was hit twice in the leg by enemy bullets. Flocken picked out the enemy gun and continued to crawl forward, dragging both his machine gun and his wounded leg for 200 yards. He then set up his gun and opened fire on the German position, silencing the enemy.[45]

Captain Zane's last reserve was Lieutenant Leonard's 2nd Platoon. Zane thought highly of the army lieutenant, writing later that he "cannot speak too highly of the courage, coolness, professional ability, and attractive personal qualities of this officer. Having him under my command was a great satisfaction and pleasure."[46] As Leonard's men waited to attack, they could see the men of the 96th Company being killed and wounded in the wheat field. Leonard passed the time by trying to roll a cigarette, but each time he filled the paper with tobacco and began to roll it, he ruined the cigarette, causing his men to smile to themselves. Finally, Leonard managed to complete his cigarette and smoked nervously as he waited. Stray machine gun bullets clipped the trees overhead, and leaves lazily drifted down on the prone Marines. Suddenly, shells struck their position, sending earth and rocks among the men. Sergeant Romeyn P. Benjamin looked around and found two Marines dead at his side. Lieutenant Leonard was still standing, smoking his cigarette. Benjamin remembered the light coming through the trees, creating "dancing shadows on the ground," as another Marine jumped up and moved to the rear, his hand pressing against a wound in his side. Leonard only smiled "and puffed hard on his cigarette," remembered Benjamin. "There was a tremendous noise and a continual hum of bullets. I could not think. I felt as though my stomach was melting in my body."[47] Lieutenant Leonard told his men, "We are going over and it's got to be done." He then shouted, "All right, 2nd Platoon, stick with me." In an instant, Leonard fired his pistol and shouted, "Come on men, for God's sake don't fail me now."[48]

The 2nd Platoon moved forward in a half-platoon column of twos, spaced as if they were on the drill field. A Marine in Corporal Hill's squad fell to the ground, hit in the chest, followed by another hit in the stomach. Both men called out, asking what they should do. Hill could only reply, "Get down and try to get back to the woods," before moving on.[49] Leading his men forward, Sergeant Benjamin "recovered [his] wits. I felt a strange calm difficult to describe."[50] He even laughed at the sight of his lieutenant, still smoking his homemade cigarette, walking calmly between the half-platoon columns.

Hill checked his platoon's front to make sure it was dressed evenly, "and it was." He was amazed at the calmness of his men. Corporal George P. Hunter, a veteran prewar Marine, moved forward with tobacco juice flowing from both sides of his mouth, mixing unnoticed into his black beard. As a German shell burst overhead and machine gun bullets whistled past, Corporal Lloyd E. Pike, the company wag, called out, "Say Hunter, do you think you'll be back in Washington for Thanksgiving dinner?"[51] There was no reply. Hunter would be wounded in the attack. Amid the mayhem, Sergeant Benjamin remembered how green the grass looked under the bright sunlight and how the machine gun bullets kicked up "little spurts of dust as they struck the ground."[52]

Halfway across the field, the German machine guns became even more deadly. At the edge of the next clover field, many of the Marines took cover on the ground. "I felt a tremendous blow and my left leg crumpled under me," remembered Corporal Glen Hill. "I tried to get up but fell over."[53] A bullet had smashed his kneecap and tore into his thigh. Hill was too weak to open his aid kit but was able to wrap the wound with his puttee, saving his life. A Marine to the left of Sergeant Benjamin took a round in the shoulder that exited through his side. As the sergeant moved to dress the wound, a bullet grazed Benjamin's left jaw, cutting his helmet strap. The force of the blow stunned Benjamin. Despite the blood streaming from his face, he was able to bind not only his own wound but also those of the Marines to his left.

Despite the heavy losses, Lieutenant Leonard continued to lead his men across the clover field, even as the machine gun bullets "were kicking up the dirt like rain." Leonard took cover behind a nearby tree. From that position, he could see that his platoon was attacking into the face of a triangular defensive position in the town, interspersed with machine guns. Sergeant John P. Martin lay nearby, scraping the earth with his bayonet, trying to create some cover in the open field. "It didn't take me long to make a pretty fair hole," Martin later recalled. After several moments, the German fire seemed to slacken. Lieutenant Leonard called out to Martin to pass the word "to advance by rushes from the left." Sergeant Martin left his makeshift hole and began to crawl to his left toward the next Marine in line. "Suddenly, I was seemingly struck quite a blow on my right heel," Martin later wrote, "and realized I was hit but managed to pass the word and then get back to my hole and report." Martin was out of the fight, with a machine gun bullet lodged in his hip, but was "greatly surprised by an entire absence of pain."[54]

On the left, Sergeant James McClelland maneuvered a small party of Marines to fire into the flank of the enemy position. The Marines were able to knock out a German machine gun, which opened a lane into the town. Leonard and McClelland led what remained of the platoon into the edge of Bouresches. A bullet hit the other Hill brother, Corporal Sidney Hill, in the left knee just as he reached the town. Lieutenant Leonard counted only eight of his fifty-six-man platoon still standing on the outskirts of Bouresches. Three bullet holes marked near misses in Leonard's blouse, but the lieutenant was not wounded.[55]

Other Marines from the 79th Company arrived in Bouresches, totaling twenty-two men under the command of Lieutenant Leonard and Gunnery Sergeant William J. Kirkpatrick. At least sixty-seven of the company's Marines were casualties, and the rest were pinned down in the fields. After seeing so many of their comrades killed and wounded, the Marines were anxious to close with the enemy. "If I knew an American who couldn't lick a German in a square fight any time any place," an angry Leonard wrote later, "I'd have the American locked up."[56] The small detachment moved down the main street, using a damaged wall as cover, until they reached the center of town, where they were hit by fire from a German machine gun emplaced in the steeple of a small church. Leonard led three of his men up the staircase, where they bayoneted the gun crew. He later remarked, "These Germans are no good when you have them going."[57] Although the group now had a foothold in the town, the odds were still in favor of the German defenders.[58]

Meanwhile, in the wheat field, the wounded and the dying struggled to find safety. Throughout the attack, a section of 37mm guns from the 6th Marines Headquarters Company, commanded by Lieutenant Clyde P. Matteson, had been firing on the Germans defending the town. Once the 37mm guns began to have an effect, suppressing the German machine guns, the Germans responded by shifting their fire from the American infantry to the guns themselves. Within minutes, Private Ronald Chisholm was hit by enemy fire, but he refused to leave his gun. As Private Alfred H. Harris worked his gun, a shell burst over him, sending jagged pieces of shrapnel into the Marine's position. Harris suffered fourteen wounds but refused to leave his gun until he was finally carried away.[59]

In the 96th Company's area of attack, Lieutenant Cates regained his senses and placed his damaged helmet back on his head. He looked around but could see only dead and wounded Marines. Cates then noticed a small band of Marines in the wheat who were still firing on the town with a French Chauchat machine gun. His first thought was to flee to the safety of the trees, but he fought the fear and focused on the battlefield. The lieutenant believed the Marine attack had been repulsed, but he discovered four Marines still alive and unhurt in a ravine to his right. Cates staggered across the field to join them, falling down several times. The men who had taken refuge in the ravine were from the 1st Platoon and were out of the fight. One of them was Sergeant Aloysius P. Sheridan, who poured wine from his canteen over Cates's head. The lieutenant cried out, "Don't pour that over my head, give me a drink of it."[60] Suitably refreshed, Cates picked up an abandoned French rifle and led his newfound command down the ravine toward Bouresches.

Ahead, Cates observed Lieutenant Robertson leading Marines into the western end of Bouresches and German soldiers running out. As the five Marines neared the town, they saw German soldiers assembling on its eastern edge. They opened fire on the group at a range of a hundred yards but somehow missed them. The Germans scattered for cover, carrying a heavy machine gun. Cates led his four men into the eastern edge of town, not knowing where the rest of the company was located. Cates moved cautiously into the center of town, looking for either friend or foe. He set up a machine gun position there under the command of Sergeant Earl F. Belfrey. Only a few Germans could be seen on the northern edge of town.[61]

Cates looked back across the wheat field and saw Robertson leaving Bouresches with the 4th Platoon. He shouted to his fellow lieutenant, but Robertson could not hear him. Cates then blew his whistle and succeeded in alerting Robertson to his presence. "Come on, let's go on and take the rest of that town," shouted Cates. "There's nobody in here right now." Robertson led the platoon back to town and turned command over to Cates. "I'll go back and get reinforcements," Robertson said. "You go in and clean the town out."[62] The orders were "a hell of a thing," Cates thought to himself as he watched Robertson depart, but he immediately took charge of Bouresches. The Germans still held houses throughout the town. "One town could not hold both parties," Private Miller later wrote, "so we started to move Heinie."[63]

Bouresches had only three streets—two leading east and west and one leading north—and all three joined in the center of town. Cates divided his command into three parts and dispatched Gunnery Sergeant Noyes V. Moore with eight men to clear the street to the west. Sergeant Earl Belfrey (who had been wounded in the wheat field) took the same number of Marines to clear the east. Cates himself took the rest of the Marines to attack north directly into German lines toward the railroad station. The three detachments began the task of securing the town, house by house.

The German defenders, men of the 2nd Battalion, 398th Regiment, 10th Division, held the town only as an outpost because the buildings lay in a ravine that was unsuitable for extended defense. The German main line of resistance centered on the hills beyond the town. Two companies, the 7th and 8th, were inside the town itself; two others with the 2nd Machine Gun Company held the railway embankment and could provide covering fire with six heavy machine guns. The Germans at the embankment took a heavy toll on the Marines attacking the village, but once the Marines descended into the town, they were safe from the machine gun fire. However, they still had to deal with the defenders within Bouresches.[64]

German machine guns raked the three streets of Bouresches. The machine gun in the church tower opened fire on the Marines, but as Cates later wrote, "the men soon silenced it."[65] Cates was halfway up the north street when another machine gun opened fire and tore into the Marines, cutting through the brim of Cates's helmet and clipping his ear. He quickly took cover against a stone wall when another round ripped into his shoulder, slicing his uniform and bending his lieutenant's bar but barely drawing any blood. Six of the Marines in the small party were killed or wounded. Cates drew his men back and divided them, sending half through the houses on the left side of the street and sending the other half forward on the right. Cates attempted to fire a rifle grenade at the German position, but the weapon exploded, burning his face and hand.

Eighteen-year-old Private Herbert D. Dunlavy was determined not to let the enemy stop the attack. He had been a popular student at Central High School and a gifted minor league baseball player in Houston, Texas, perhaps the best catcher in the city's history. Big-league baseball awaited the young Texan, but his athletic career was put on hold when he enlisted in the Marine Corps as soon as his classes ended in June 1917.[66]

Dunlavy crept from house to house until he got close to the German machine gun. Then he charged, shooting the German gunner in the leg, capturing the weapon, and turning it on his adversary. "Only a moment was it still," according to one account. "Then it began to crackle out its speeding death again—but this time the bullets were traveling toward the enemy."[67] Soon, however, the concussion from a shell burst killed Dunlavy, leaving no mark on his body. The private from Goose Creek, Texas, received the Navy Cross for his actions. Fellow Texan Private Johnnie Y. Matthews mourned the death of his friend, writing to Dunlavy's mother, "It is hard to give up these boys but they are going every day; one never knows when the time is coming."[68]

Bouresches town square after the battle. The town's church stands at the fork in the road. (Marine Corps Archives, Quantico, VA)

With the machine gun removed, Cates and his men were able to reach the north side of town. "It was a beautiful fight," Cates wrote later. "They ran like rabbits. . . . We finished a lot of them though—I killed my first German."[69] Private Alfred Earlson was wounded in the attack, but he continued to fight house to house against the German defenders. Private James W. Carter, who was also wounded, faced superior numbers of German soldiers and received the Navy Cross for his bravery. Sergeants Moore and Belfrey proved relentless as they moved through the houses, although the fighting was close and bloody. The redoubtable Sergeant Belfrey suffered a second, more serious wound and would die of his injuries in a field hospital two days later. A clerk from Chicago, Belfrey was survived by his wife, whom he had married in November before going overseas.

"It was the same old story," Private Miller wrote. "They would fire their guns until we were on top of them, then throw up their hands, shout 'Kamerad' and beg for mercy. But after you go through as far as that, you cease to be human and don't know what mercy is."[70] The desperate fight was extremely fierce, and the Marines took only one enemy prisoner. "It was a bad day for Fritz," Sergeant Sheridan wrote. "All we could see was blood."[71]

The battered remnants of the German 7th and 8th Companies, 398th Infantry, withdrew to the railroad embankment. There, the fearless Marines surrounded the machine gun positions and then approached within ten meters of the German gunners, who remained at their guns until the end.

Only twenty-one Marines remained standing at the end of the fight, but the town of Bouresches now belonged to the Marines of the 79th and 96th Companies. Twenty minutes later, the rest of the 96th Company's 2nd and 3rd Platoons arrived from the ravine, bolstering the number of Marines in town. In the aftermath, Robertson, Cates, and Belfrey were all awarded Navy Crosses for their leadership in taking the town. In total, six members of the 96th Company received Navy Crosses for that action.

At 8:30 p.m. Lieutenant Erskine still held his position in the wheat field with the remnants of the 79th Company's two platoons. Corporal Nelson crawled past his command post, bleeding heavily from a bullet wound through the nose. Erskine bandaged the corporal's face and then sent him back through the field to report to Captain Zane that he could advance no further under the German fire. The lieutenant was surprised to see the man return an hour later with a message. "I told the Captain what you said," he related, "and he said get going, goddammit." A message also arrived from Bouresches, informing Erskine that Lieutenant Robertson was in the town. Erskine moved forward with the four other survivors of the platoon, crawling slowly through the wheat. As the Marines neared the village, they were unsure who was in control of Bouresches.[72]

The survivors of the 79th Company moved into Bouresches, and Captain Zane took command of the town. When asked about the battle, Lieutenant Leonard simply replied, "I don't recall much of what happened. We spent much of our time hugging mother earth."[73] Only four Marines of his platoon were uninjured by the end of the day. Three more of Leonard's men returned to the town from German lines, wounded but bandaged. When questioned, they said they had been wounded in the attack and captured by the Germans as they withdrew. A veteran German sergeant had cared for their injuries and then sent them back, saying he "was tired of the war and didn't care whether he took any prisoners or not."[74]

In Bouresches, a German shell exploded near Captain Zane, killing one Marine outright and ripping the legs off one of the company's sergeants. Shrapnel from the same shell struck Zane in the thigh, while the concussion of the blast ruptured his left eardrum. He was evacuated and never returned to his cherished 79th Company. Zane's wounds healed well enough, but his deafness prevented him from returning to combat, so he became provost marshal for the port of Le Havre. He planned to return to the United States in October, but while awaiting transportation, Zane came down with Spanish influenza. His left ear also became abscessed, requiring two operations in a British base hospital. Zane telegraphed his family to inform them of his delayed departure, but he died in the hospital. After surviving the battlefield, Zane perished from an infection of the inner ear on October 24, 1918, perhaps one of the last Marines involved in the assault on Bouresches to die as a result of his wounds. Zane's father, Admiral Abraham Van Hoy Zane, also contracted influenza and died shortly after his son on January 2, 1919.[75]

From his headquarters, Holcomb witnessed the capture of Bouresches by the 79th and 96th Companies, but he was now concerned about his flanks. Captain Messersmith's 78th Company held the far right of the battalion and, indeed, of the entire 4th Marine Brigade. The lines of the army's 23rd Infantry extended from Messersmith's Marines to the east. The same was not true on the left of Holcomb's battalion, where there was a large gap between his battalion and Sibley's. A German counterattack in the area would have devastating consequences.

Holcomb dispatched his reserve company, the 80th, to fill the gap. Originally, the company had been ordered to support Sibley's advance, so the orders came at the right place and time. Captain Bailey M. Coffenberg was the least experienced of the 2nd Battalion's company commanders, having entered the Marine Corps in February 1917. The native New Yorker speedily reached the rank of captain in May 1917 and went to France in the fall of that year. Coffenberg took command of the 80th Company in March 1918.[76]

Coffenberg moved his men down the hillside, as the rest of the battalion advanced northward toward Belleau Wood. Out in the open, the 227 Marines of the 80th Company drew machine gun fire and airbursts from German artillery. Marines fell, but the company moved on. The Marines soon reached cover in the Bouresches–Lucy road. The road had been worn down into the earth and was now littered with wounded and dying Marines from previous assaults who had tried to use the roadside embankments for cover from the ever-present German machine guns.[77]

Major Sibley met the company as it entered the road and made a strong impression on the Marines. He had discarded his jacket and hat and had rolled his sleeves up above his elbows. He gave the order to attack into Belleau Wood but raged at the futility of it, shouting that he was "dam[n] mad about it" and wanted the Marines to know he did not agree with the order. One Marine described "the enraged Major, popping his fist into the palm of his hand, walking up and down the gully, yelling his explosive language." The men of the 80th Company, already shaken by the gore on the road, were further upset when Major Sibley shouted that he had been "ordered to send men to hell." Private Levi E. Hemrick, who witnessed the scene, later commented, "He was hard boiled, he was a man's man."[78]

Eventually, Sibley shouted, "Go!" and the company climbed out of the road and formed a line of attack. The men moved through the wheat, causing Private Hemrick to later write, "We were on our way to carry out an impossible assignment."[79] The 80th Company reached Belleau Wood without incident, but once again, command and control proved impossible. Half the company went into the woods, while the other half turned and attacked along the southern edge of the woods toward Bouresches.[80] The advancing Marines moved into the woods, the same area where Timmerman's Marines had passed earlier. The Marines pushed aside the underbrush until they came to a small clearing. With no sign of the enemy, the 80th Company moved into the clearing in small groups.

Once the first Marines had reached the clearing, the German machine guns opened fire, driving the Americans to the ground. Bullets raked the company line in a series of crossfire positions, killing and wounding Marines. Corporal John J. Ingalls was hit in the side by shell fragments and in the leg by a machine gun bullet, but he refused to be sent to the rear. Instead, the corporal helped other wounded Marines, including his closest friend. He refused to talk about his experiences for years afterward, with the exception of the rescue of his "buddy." Ingalls was awarded the Navy Cross for his bravery.[81]

Sergeant Grover C. O'Kelly, a former laborer from Birmingham, Alabama, led the remnants of his 2nd Platoon through the deadly clearing and up to a nest of rocks and boulders where the German defense line was located. The German gunners allowed the Marines to approach within thirty yards before opening fire. According to the survivors, "It was just a plain slaughter."[82] O'Kelly had the respect of his men, however. Private Hemrick called him the "most dedicated Christian Sergeant I ever met."[83] O'Kelly detected a machine gun position when he noticed the barrel of the gun protruding between two rocks. The German gunners could not be killed by rifle fire in their protected position, and the company had no hand grenades. The sergeant "would not or could not turn his back from the enemy," so he charged the machine gun with only his bayoneted rifle.[84] He got within a few yards of the gun before he was stitched by at least three bullets. One bullet struck O'Kelly over the eye, creasing his temple. The wounded sergeant passed the word back to his men to withdraw from his position, only twenty yards from the German gun. O'Kelly then crawled to a slight depression to await the next Marine assault. He could hear the enemy talking during the momentary quiet following the Marines' withdrawal.

Private Wellman H. Huey from Detroit, Michigan, lay beside the sergeant, insensible from his wounds. Unexpectedly, the dazed Huey jumped up and shouted, "For Gods sake don't shoot we're Marines," mistakenly believing that he had been hit by friendly fire. The Germans immediately riddled Huey's body with a burst of machine gun fire, and he fell dead across O'Kelly's back. The sergeant remained under the body of his comrade, going in and out of consciousness, until nightfall. As darkness approached, his platoon pulled back through the woods, leaving him for dead. He was "posthumously" decorated with the Navy Cross. In reality, O'Kelly was captured by the German machine gunners, who discovered the unconscious Marine when they pulled Huey off his back. In 1919 O'Kelly surprised his company when he returned from a prisoner of war camp.[85]

Private Huey's body lay untouched in the tangled undergrowth for several weeks until he was found by a surgeon searching for wounded Marines. The officer discovered a letter written to Huey's mother two days before his death. "Dear Mother," he wrote:

> I pray for your sake that this will never have to be sent to you, and I don't believe it ever will—but how do we know? Mother, if this is sent to you do not sorrow for me. . . . I send my love and a farewell kiss till we meet again. So be brave and cheerful as many other mothers are doing who have lost their dear ones for awhile. Goodbye for this time. I must get busy and think of other things. . . . Carry on, Wellman.[86]

The 77th Machine Gun Company and the remains of the 81st Machine Gun Company supported the attack by Sibley's and Holcomb's men. The machine guns at Triangle Farm were also ordered to support the attack of the army brigade to the right with an overhead barrage. The 81st Company was well led by Captain Allen M. Sumner Jr., a seasoned, Harvard-educated Marine. Born in the exclusive Back Bay district of Boston, Sumner was the son of a prominent family and had been educated abroad at an early age. He returned to attend a preparatory school in Connecticut, but Sumner longed for a life in the naval service. At the age of seventeen, he obtained a nomination to the US Naval Academy without his parents' knowledge. Once his father discovered the scheme, he forced Allen to turn down the nomination and attend Harvard instead. But the young man never forgot his dream. After graduating from the university in 1904, Sumner tried to find his niche in the world. He became a cattle rancher in New Mexico and then traveled around the world, from Europe to South America. Upon returning to the United States, Sumner took a position with the University Press in Cambridge.[87]

Still determined to follow his dream, Sumner finally entered the Marine Corps in 1907 as a second lieutenant. He served in various places, including Cuba, Annapolis, and Norfolk, and on the USS *Prairie* and USS *South Carolina*. After seven years of service, Sumner was forced to retire in 1914 to care for his invalid mother. He became a farmer in rural Tidewater Virginia. In March 1917 Sumner was recalled for three months' active duty to train new officers at Quantico. The lure of France was too much to resist, and Sumner shipped out with his unit, leaving behind his mother, his wife, and an eight-year-old daughter. Now, Sumner moved his gun crews forward behind Sibley's and Holcomb's infantry, but with the loss of the machine gun sections that had moved to Hill 142, the front was too large to be well covered.[88]

At 4th Brigade headquarters, Harbord waited anxiously as reports came in from the battlefield. He received no firm information about the success of the attack, only fragments of reports. Colonel Neville's headquarters received little news either. Two prisoners were brought to Harbord's headquarters, but they provided scant information to the general. At 6:38 p.m., believing the attack had been a success, he noted in the brigade log, "Our people have knocked hell out of them and they are running."[89]

The news filtering back to headquarters continued to be positive. A report dropped from a French reconnaissance aircraft indicated that the attack was progressing, and Lieutenant Timmerman's captured German platoon had passed Harbord at 7:12 p.m. Only when a 7:34 p.m. message arrived from Captain Tribot-Laspierre, the French liaison officer, did the brigade commander begin to learn the true nature of the combat taking place in the fields around Belleau Wood. After informing Harbord of Catlin's wound, Tribot-Laspierre's message concluded, "All was going alright when I left."[90] Shortly thereafter, news came of casualties in the wheat fields and in Belleau Wood itself. The mood at headquarters changed, and Harbord wanted more information from the front. His anger was focused on Lee, and at 8:55 p.m. Harbord sent him a blistering message. "I am not satisfied with the way you have conducted your engagement this afternoon. Your own regimental headquarters and this office have not had a word of report from you," Harbord wrote. "I want you to take charge and push this attack with vigor."[91]

In truth, the attack by Berry, Sibley, and Holcomb had been ground to a halt by the German defenders. Catlin and Berry were wounded, and half of Sibley's battalion had been swallowed in Belleau Wood. Although Holcomb's three companies had captured Bouresches, they could advance no farther. The company and platoon commanders struggled to locate and consolidate their units should the Germans counterattack. At his headquarters, Harbord had no way of knowing the true situation, except that the supposedly empty woods were actually full of Germans who had brought his attack to a halt. He ordered Lee, "Carry the attack through the woods, and send Sibley to take Bouresches. . . . I want reports from you every fifteen minutes."[92]

Lieutenant Colonel Lee knew he had little choice as night fell over Belleau Wood. Despite Harbord's order, the new commander of the 6th Marines directed his men to dig in and strengthen their positions. As night darkened the battlefield, Harbord achieved clarity about the events of the day. Finally, at 10:10 p.m., Harbord recognized the futility of continuing the attack and gave the order: "Consolidate positions attained. Make no further attempt to advance tonight."[93]

The heady success of the morning battle on Hill 142 was now overshadowed by the evening's casualty figures. Most of all, the strength of the German positions in the woods surprised everyone in the chain of command. According to French intelligence, they were not supposed to be there. Even more incredible, reports from front-line Marine units advising of the enemy's presence in Belleau Wood never reached brigade headquarters. For the moment, all of the 4th Marine Brigade's offensive operations were suspended. Hill 142 was secure, Sibley's battalion still held the southern end of Belleau Wood, and Holcomb's men had dug in at Bouresches. Lee still had Hughes's battalion in reserve should the front line need reinforcement from the inevitable German counterattacks.

June 6 was only the first day of the bloodbath at Belleau Wood. It would continue for almost a month. However, Harbord took the time on June 7 to send a curious shipment to Commandant Barnett in Washington. The package contained "the first Luger pistol carried by the first German officer captured by the brigade and a machine gun taken with the surviving member of its gun crew at the same time."[94] Both had been taken in the early-morning fighting on Hill 142 and represented the first war trophies earned at the Battle of Belleau Wood, constituting the first effort to memorialize the battle.

On June 26 it was announced that Belleau Wood was totally secure and in the hands of the 4th Marine Brigade. The brigade suffered 1,095 killed, missing, or died of wounds and 3,615 wounded during the twenty-six days in Belleau Wood, totaling 4,710 casualties, or approximately 180 casualties per day. Based on an authorized strength of 8,417 men, the brigade suffered 56 percent casualties in June 1918, although this number is somewhat skewed by replacements that joined the brigade in June. Correspondingly, the 2nd Division's army brigade lost 319 killed and 1,450 wounded in its fight on the Marines' right, culminating in the capture of Vaux on July 1, 1918.[95]

As in any battle, casualty figures can be deceiving. This is especially true of

Belleau Wood during the June 6 attacks. Marine companies went into battle with every man in line, including the headquarters platoon. Losses among those responsible for company administration made record keeping impossible. In addition, 2nd Division Administrative Memorandum 11 directed that all office records be kept to a minimum; any excess papers deemed not historical or not required by army regulations were to be destroyed. Most of the muster rolls and casualty lists compiled from these records were created after the battle ceased. On June 25, 1918, Captain George Shuler, the 5th Marines' adjutant, wrote of an early June casualty report: "It was impossible at the time this report was made out to make it complete as the regiment was on the firing line, without any office equipment whatever . . . the names, numbers, and companies of some 3600 men cannot be remembered and correct lists rendered under the circumstances we were in at the time."[96] However, Belleau Wood taught the 4th Brigade to make future attacks with the headquarters platoon in reserve.[97]

Any casualty figures for the early days of the battle must be viewed as approximate. With this in mind, the heaviest company losses occurred in the 67th Company on Hill 142, with 119 men lost, followed by the 49th Company with 109 casualties and the 20th Company with 108 killed and wounded in the wheat fields. Of the battalions engaged, Turrill's 1st Battalion, 5th Marines, suffered the highest casualty rate, with 333 Marines lost on Hill 142. Berry's 3rd Battalion, 5th Marines, lost 281 men attacking Belleau Wood; Sibley's 3rd Battalion, 6th Marines, suffered 199 casualties in Belleau Wood; and Holcomb's 2nd Battalion, 6th Marines, lost 132 men in the battle for Bouresches.

The June 6 losses among Marine officers were particularly devastating. Six were killed outright; twenty-four more were wounded, with four of those men dying from their wounds. There were 222 enlisted men killed in the attacks. Combined with 794 wounded, the casualty list for the enlisted ranks totaled at least 1,016. The official number of casualties for the day totaled 1,087 Marines, making it one of the bloodiest days in Marine Corps history. Prior to that date, all Marine casualties in all wars totaled approximately 700 men killed and wounded. In a single day in 1918, that total was eclipsed.

Many of the men who survived June 6 were killed or wounded in the following days while securing the woods. Newly arrived replacements also became casualties of the battle. The fighting became so furious that many of those who died on June 6 remained in the wheat and the woods until the battle ended twenty days later. Unlike in other areas, where the fallen could be properly buried, any action in the open wheat fields brought an immediate German reaction, even at night. The German dead received even less attention, resulting in an overwhelming stench that the Marines remembered long after the battle. After a month of decay, the remains of some Marines were never found.

On the evening of June 27, Chaplain Darche organized burial teams to locate and cover the remains in the fields just outside of the woods. The party succeeded in burying eleven men of the 47th and 51st Companies, but the ever-present German artillery halted any further work. Lieutenant Colonel Lee, commanding the 6th Marines, wrote on June 28, "There are about 50 more bodies at this point . . . it seems they were killed in the action of June 6th and the bodies are in such a state of decomposition that it is impossible to move them. It is suggested that chloride of lime be used on them, the ground being so hard as to prevent digging graves."[98]

Long after the battle, the echoes of June 6 continued to reverberate through the Marine Corps. Each Marine lost on June 6 caused a ripple across the Atlantic to his family. The severe losses among individual companies as well as higher battalion and brigade staff were compounded by the lengthy period of action. As a result, casualty reporting became very rudimentary. Company staff clerks were casualties themselves, meaning that incomplete lists of the killed and wounded were posted back to Marine Corps headquarters. The sheer number of men lost in combat overwhelmed the new Marines who were assigned to notify their families. By the end of September 1918, there were more than 4,000 Marine casualties, and each required three to four letters to parents and other relatives. Despite the overwhelming task, Commandant Barnett signed at least one personal letter to each family.[99]

One case was that of Private Arthur N. Fauble. He enlisted in the Marine Corps on May 30, 1917, at age twenty-five, leaving behind his trade as a stonemason in Akron, Ohio. He learned to be a Marine in the sands of Parris Island and was assigned to the 83rd Company at Quantico. In November 1917, while in France with his company, Fauble's luck turned bad. He was sick with the mumps for almost the entire month of March 1918. Then, in April, Fauble became one of the first casualties of the 6th Marines when he was overcome by an explosion of gas shells during the brigade's introduction to trench warfare. He was able to return to the company at the end of the month.[100]

Private Fauble was killed in the June 6 assault on Belleau Wood, and his body remained unburied until he was found on July 1. His family learned of his death that summer, and the grieving began. His mother and father, though divorced, agreed that his remains should be returned to Ohio. The tragedy deepened when Arthur's father passed away in 1919 before his son's body could be returned home. In 1921 Fauble's mother, Mrs. Samantha C. Seeley, sent a forlorn letter to the Marine Corps, stating, "I gave my son for his country and I think I should at least have the body. I can bury it in the same cemetery with his brothers and where I expect to be buried . . . please send the body of my son to me."[101] In 1922 work began to remove Arthur from his temporary grave in the Belleau Wood Cemetery; however, there was some question about the identity of the body in the grave. The Tablet of the Missing at the Aisne Marne Cemetery Chapel, adjacent to Belleau Wood, now honors Private Arthur Fauble, who is listed as missing in action on June 6, 1918.

For many of the Marines who were wounded on June 6, the road to recovery was a long one. The nature of the attacks by the 4th Marine Brigade meant that most of the wounded were left in exposed positions that were still covered by German fire. Some of the wounded were struck again and again by German bullets until they were dead. Others died in the fields before the stretcher bearers could be sent out after dark to recover them. Then the ambulances of the American Field Service scrambled to bring the wounded Marines to nearby hospitals. One of the ambulance drivers was forever impressed by the Marines' stoic courage. He recalled that "he never heard from them a word of complaint; fierce as these boys had been in the fight, they were gentle and patient under suffering."[102]

The agony continued for those Marines as they attempted to recover from their wounds in hospitals. Private Emery Bartlett, a twenty-three-year-old salesman from Salem, Oregon, suffered a massive head wound during the 20th Company's assault through the wheat fields on June 6. Somehow, he survived the initial trauma, but the injury rendered him unconscious. He lay out in the field until June 9, when litter parties found the young private and evacuated him to Base Hospital Number 2. After a preliminary examination, chief surgeon Joseph A. Blake pronounced the wound inoperable and spoke to the hospital's newly appointed Red Cross chaplain, the Reverend John S. Zelie, about Bartlett, noting that "there was nothing he could do" for him. Zelie had an eighteen-year-old son back home, and after watching the doctor trying to wake Bartlett, "it seemed to me one of the cases where I must do everything I could to find out and communicate with his family."[103] After examining his dog tags to learn the young man's name, the chaplain spoke to the comatose Marine repeatedly that day, but to no avail.

On returning to the hospital the following day, nurses informed Zelie that Bartlett had regained consciousness and flatly pronounced in a faint whisper that "he was doing just fine." Chaplain Zelie rushed to his bedside and held the private's arm. In a barely audible whisper, he told the chaplain his hometown and both his own name and his father's name. During the next few hours, the chaplain learned about Bartlett's family, particularly his father, Arthur. "It was most difficult for him to speak or for me to hear," Zelie later wrote, "but it was no less than a miracle that he should have regained consciousness to this extent." When he asked Bartlett if he wanted to send a message home, the wounded Marine's reply could not be understood. The chaplain then inquired if Bartlett wanted to send his family his love, and he received the quiet answer, "Yes, thank you doctor, I do." Zelie then asked, "Shall I send your love to your father?" Again, he heard the barely audible reply, "Yes, if you will." The chaplain questioned him about any other family members, specifically, brothers and sisters. Bartlett gave one final reply, "Yes," and asked the chaplain "to send his love to them too."[104]

Zelie then composed a lengthy letter to Bartlett's father. "He lies now a few feet from me in his bed, sleeping heavily and barely conscious at moments," he wrote. "I do not think it possible that he can recover and the doctors and nurses regard the end is near." Zelie continued, "My heart goes out to you and him for the great sacrifice you have each made for us all in his action. Nothing in the war has been finer than the action at the front of our Marines. They were swept away. And now, my dear sir, I want to send you these few lines, so little, about the one so dear to you."[105]

With the letter now completed, Zelie placed the pages in the dying Marine's hand and gently explained that the letter would be sent to his father. Bartlett "closed his hand and held to it and said, 'That is right.'" After amending the letter with the last words spoken by Private Emery Bartlett, the chaplain sealed the envelope. The next letter Zelie wrote to Arthur Bartlett informed him of the death of his son at 11:30 p.m. on June 12, 1918. "I do not think that he suffered greatly and I sometimes thought he did not suffer at all," Zelie wrote. "He was in a room with five other wounded men who were all conscious of him and deeply interested to know how he was doing from hour to hour and when it was over they felt it deeply."[106]

Private Bartlett was laid to rest on June 14 with both a French and an American honor guard. As it did for every American killed in action, the French government placed a wreath of palms on his grave, inscribed with the words "Hommage de Paris aux Défenseurs de la Patrie" (Paris honors the defenders of the nation). Private Bartlett now rests in the Suresnes American Battle Monuments Commission Cemetery near Paris. Those simple words constitute a fitting epitaph for every Marine who fought at Belleau Wood, for all have long since passed from this earth.

Belleau Wood Tour

Stop 12. Bouresches, 49°03'44.4"N 3°18'28.5"E

Continue on the road for 1.1 kilometers until you see a slight turnout on the right. Pause to orient yourself to the surrounding terrain. You are now in the area of the attack by Major Holcomb's 2nd Battalion, 6th Marines, coming down the hill to your right. Belleau Wood is still in front of you to your left. The dominating terrain beyond Bouresches is also visible. The main line of the German defense was on the high ground, and the enemy rained machine gun and artillery fire on the Marines' advance. The 79th Company broke into the town, passing over the ground here; the 96th Company attacked from the high ground to your right, where Captain Duncan was killed. Lieutenant Timmerman's platoon attacked from the edge of Belleau Wood, on the higher ground to the left rear of Bouresches. Proceed 750 meters to the town square, where you can park, walk, and examine.

8

Belleau Wood Conclusions
"America Became the Deciding Factor in the War"

ALTHOUGH A NATURAL RIVALRY EXISTED between the US Army and the US Marine Corps during World War I, the world's reaction to the Battle of Belleau Wood became an instant issue between the two services. The sanguine news from Belleau Wood captured the spirit of the American presence in the war, and the Allied press used this to great advantage in renewing the public's desire to win the war. The saga of the Marines' battle of June 6, 1918, captured the Allies' imagination at a critical moment. "It is certain that the morale of the lower grades of the French army is distinctly poor," General Pershing wrote to the secretary of war on June 21. "Both the French and British people are extremely tired of the war. . . . It is the American soldiers now in France on which they rely. It is the moral as well as material aid given by the American soldier that is making the continuation of the war possible."[1]

Inevitably, the attention that accompanied the Marines' involvement in combat brought both overt and covert criticism, particularly by the US Army. The army's reaction to the unsolicited publicity appeared almost immediately. The Marine-centric focus of the world media rankled army commanders, and they focused their anger on the Marine Brigade while attempting to correct the popular misconception that a single brigade of Marines had won the war by themselves.

On June 9, 1918, with most of Belleau Wood still in German hands, General Pershing visited General Foch at his headquarters and asked him about "his plans in case the German drive should endanger or even capture Paris." Foch replied that "they would fight to the last and that they counted on us to fight with them." Foch's words inspired Pershing to "jump up and shake hands with him right then and there. I told him he could count on us to the last."[2] Pershing then visited 2nd Division headquarters to congratulate the division and to deliver a personal message from Foch, conveying "his love and congratulations on their fine work of the past week."[3] Harbord issued a general order to the brigade, providing the Marines with the details of Pershing's visit and Foch's words.

Upon returning to headquarters, Pershing sent a telegram to General Bundy, citing the Marine Brigade's actions on June 6 and noting, "It was a magnificent example of American courage and dash." Instead of adding his own words of praise for the Marines, Bundy passed the message on to Harbord with the following endorsement: "The Division Commander takes this occasion to renew his expression of gratification over the fine conduct of all units of the Division during the past week."[4] At the end of the day, Pershing confided in his diary, "General Bundy disappoints me. He lacks the grasp. I shall relieve him at the first opportunity."[5]

As the battle for Belleau Wood thundered on during the month of June, newspapers around the world published headlines praising the Marines and carried exaggerated reports from the battlefield. On the same day as Pershing's visit, the *New York Times* published an article with the banner headline, "Marines Win Name of Devil Hounds." It quoted a German who regarded the Marines as the greatest fighting force on earth: "The American Marine come first, said the German, the Canadian Northwest Police is second and the Potsdam Guard is third." Also quoted was a Marine Corps bulletin that proclaimed, "in the past, the foe who encountered the prowess of the Marines received a mingled impression of wildcats and human cyclones and movements as quick as lightning . . . we Marines are not ashamed of our new special classification."[6] The name "Devil Dog" is synonymous with the Marines to this day.

In Washington, DC, the *Evening Star* ran a photograph of Pershing and Harbord on June 10 with the caption, "The Soldiers of the Sea have electrified both American and allies by the manner in which they plunged into the German line."[7] The *Seattle Daily Times* ran a cartoon of Harbord on June 13 with the headline, "Leads Victorious Marines."[8] In France, however, not every citizen focused on the Marines. The mayors of the small towns in the Meaux district, where the battle was fought, sent a resolution to General Bundy thanking the 2nd Division as a whole for saving their residents from the Germans.[9]

Army reaction to the unsolicited Marine publicity appeared almost immediately. Premier Clemenceau made a special visit to the 2nd Division on June 27, 1918, to pass on his good wishes and express his gratitude to the Marine Brigade. Unfortunately, the French premier never reached Harbord's headquarters; nor was he able to talk with any of the Marines under Harbord's command because no Marines had been invited to meet Clemenceau. General Bundy, however, had ordered the commanding officers of the 3rd Brigade and the 9th and 23rd Infantry Regiments to his headquarters, where they were introduced to and photographed with the French leader.

The *Washington Post* ran an article the following day with the headline, "Clemenceau Lauds American Troops, Congratulates Men Who Stopped the Hun Rush toward Paris."[10] On June 28 the *New York Times* reported that Clemenceau "came to felicitate the United States Army unit, which yesterday captured Belleau Wood," and it asserted that "Chateau Thierry is the most substantial military success of the American army to date."[11] When Pershing learned of the incident, Bundy tried to clarify his position by asking that Premier Clemenceau be informed of his own admiration for the fighting done by the Marines.[12]

Harbord did not discover the affront to the Marines until June 29, obtaining his information from newspaper accounts and a local news correspondent. He immediately sent a memorandum to General Pershing through 2nd Division headquarters, asking him to personally express "the regret of the brigade at not having had the honor of a visit from [Clemenceau], and its appreciation of the honor done it."[13] General Bundy endorsed the message, deflecting any criticism by explaining that the French premier had been "invited to visit the [4th] Brigade commander which the shortness of his stay prevented." Bundy also stated that the newspaper article might have mentioned the Marines if not for the censorship rules in place.[14]

The controversy surrounding Clemenceau's visit created lasting resentment among the Marines of the 4th Brigade. "No member of the Fourth Brigade knew of his visit until after it occurred and none of us were invited to be present," Harbord wrote in 1920. "I was quite indignant at the time and am not yet able to understand why, considering the close proximity to Division Headquarters, none of the Fourth Brigade were invited to meet the minister."[15]

On June 29 Major General Liggett visited Harbord's headquarters to discuss the Marine Brigade commander's concerns. Harbord complained bitterly about Clemenceau's visit and noted that Bundy's only excuse had been to claim that "his own stupidity . . . was at fault."[16] The Marine officers were furious over the slight and suspected Bundy of favoring his army brigade over the Marines. Foremost in the minds of the Marines was the lack of support after Belleau Wood was secure. Harbord's brigade remained in the woods despite repeated requests for relief. General Degoutte visited Liggett the same day and presented plans for the 26th American Division to finally replace the 2nd Division. Orders for the Marine withdrawal arrived the day after Bundy's 3rd Brigade attacked the small village of Vaux on July 1.

On July 11, 1918, the 2nd Division held an awards ceremony to present Distinguished Service Crosses to 121 Marines and soldiers as a result of their bravery at Belleau Wood and Vaux. Of that number, only thirty-three recipients were present to receive their decorations. Many had been killed in the battle, while others remained in hospitals recovering from their wounds. Some of the wounded never recovered and died of their injuries. Among those present were Noble and Timmerman of the 83rd Company, Feland and Turrill of the 5th Marines, Robertson of the 96th Company, and others who had participated in the June 6 attack. Sergeant Major John Quick, the recipient of two Medals of Honor, was honored for his resupply mission to Bouresches, as was white-haired Marine gunner Henry Hulburt, who had already received a Medal of Honor in Guam in 1898. Hulburt arrived sopping wet because he and his horse "Babe" had swum the Marne River to get to the ceremony. He noted that Babe "had difficulty making the last few yards so I left her back and finished a bit ahead of her. But here I am, on time."[17]

Despite attempts to avoid acknowledging the Marines in the 2nd Division, the importance of the Marine Corps' presence at Belleau Wood was not lost on the American public. Ironically, two days after French premier Clemenceau's visit, the *New York Times* published an article reflecting on the magnitude of the fight and identifying the Marines as "the famous fighting unit" in Belleau Wood. "As a demonstration of the efficiency and effectiveness of American troops, it is worth more than it is likely to receive," the paper noted. "Our Allies will rejoice, because if one or two of our battalions fight so famously the Germans will never be able to withstand the assaults of the Americans when they come to the field by divisions and divisions grow into armies." The reporter ended the article with this fateful sentence: "The enemy will remember Belleau Wood."[18]

With the end of the battle, popular public opinion in France was that the 4th Marine Brigade had been the only American unit in the fight. Little credit was given to the French army and the 2nd and 3rd American Divisions, despite their role in halting the Germans. The primary cause of this torrent of praise for the Marine Corps was the reported demise of Chicago war correspondent Floyd Gibbons in the wheat fields at Belleau Wood. His last story reached the American censor's office in Paris and was allowed to pass without change as a tribute to Gibbons. The unedited account identified the Marines by name. In less than twenty-four hours, the story of the Marines at Belleau Wood appeared on the front pages of newspapers around the world. Scarce mention was made of the army's 3rd Brigade, which lost a smaller number of casualties on the same front; the supporting 2nd Artillery Brigade; or other 2nd Division units. Gibbons actually survived the wounds he suffered on June 6 but lost an eye to a German machine gun bullet.

The first histories of the war tried to evaluate the United States' military contributions in general and the Marines' contributions in particular, but they could do little to change the narrative that had already been established.

Jennings C. Wise's 1920 history of the Second Battle of the Marne addressed the American contributions in June 1918. Wise was a published historian as well as a firsthand observer of the events, having been wounded while serving with the 80th Division in 1918. "The use of American troops at this critical hour, pitifully few as they were, was a trump card which was not to be recklessly played," he penned. "The proper play was to save them from a reverse and in every way possible to magnify their worth in the eyes of the enemy. This piece of French policy was complete successful." Wise noted that, "Justly entitled to high praise, their fighting powers were the subject of the wildest and most exaggerated reports which passed current everywhere." The French morale was restored, the German reaction was quite the opposite, and "the American public to a large extent believes them still."[19]

Although the price was high, the relentless Marine assaults on June 6 and beyond made a lasting impression on both the Allies and the enemy. "These attacks prove that the Americans, as far as their attack tactics and training in open terrain are concerned, are still novices of the lowest grade of the game." But Major Bischoff, whose German soldiers defended Belleau Wood, also noted that "the average man fights stubbornly and with valor," and "excellent training in the handling and firing of the rifle gives him a decided advantage."[20] The furious combat on June 6 and the ongoing battle for Belleau Wood proved that the United States was prepared to pay a steep price to achieve victory. For Germany, this evidence of American military power and commitment to the Allied cause proved that the war was now unwinnable. The same realization reverberated within the Allied ranks. David Lloyd George of Great Britain later wrote: "The fine performance of the Americans on June 6 was an omen of grim significance for the Germans."[21]

No matter what was written in the history books or the newspapers, the lasting impressions of June 6, 1918, were forever embedded in the memories of the combat-tested Marines, who knew what they had accomplished. Almost immediately, the Marines honored their past. On June 6, 1919, the 4th Brigade commemorated the first anniversary of the battle while serving as an occupation force in Germany. The actual circumstances of the Battle of Belleau Wood became Marine Corps legend as early as 1920.

Many of the Marine participants were asked to speak about their experiences in France before both local and national organizations. Brigadier General Neville addressed the Pennsylvania Commandery of the Military Order of Foreign Wars in January 1920 and claimed that it could be "universally conceded that the war was won or the Boche was stopped by the Help of God and a few marines." In the audience was Chaplain John J. Brady of the 5th Marines, who rose to comment on Neville's words. He quipped that the general had not brought up the name of God in his speech except to take it in vain several times. Brady then humorously concluded that the "work was done by Marines alone" and proceeded to talk about their exploits for the next hour.[22]

The Marine Corps publication *Recruiters' Bulletin* reported in January 1920 that a former Marine from New Albany, Indiana, with the last name of Wood had named his newborn son Belleau, in honor of the battle and his own wounding there.[23] The American public generally believed that Belleau Wood was the turning point of World War I and compared it to the Battle of Gettysburg in the Civil War. John Banderob, a Civil War veteran from Wisconsin, wrote that the accounts of the Marines at Belleau Wood "reminded him of the daring deeds performed by the Marine boys during the Civil War."[24] In 1920 two of the 75mm shell casings fired at Belleau Wood were accepted into the collections of the Smithsonian Institution.[25]

Most important, the significance of Belleau Wood was not lost on the Marines themselves, who still had many battles ahead of them. The hard fighting of June 1918 only solidified the Marine resolve. A letter written by Corporal Charles L. Dunn of the 6th Machine Gun Battalion to his mother on June 28, 1918, best sums up this attitude. He wrote simply but eloquently:

> Mama, don't ever get the idea that we will not win. We are going to win as sure as there is a God in Heaven. Of course, the price is awful, but it has to be paid and the men who are paying the price—Are they down hearted and glum? Not on your life! Never think that. I have heard jokes and laughter flying around when everybody had good reason to expect each minute to be the last. . . . Tons of love, Charlie.[26]

Entering into this perfect storm of US Army–Marine Corps turbulence over Belleau Wood was recurring pressure from Secretary of the Navy Daniels and Marine Commandant Barnett for a Marine Corps brigadier general to command the 4th Marine Brigade. Daniels wrote a letter to Secretary of War Baker on May 7, 1918, asking that a Marine Corps brigadier general be sent to France to replace Doyen, sending him first to a quiet sector and then allowing him to command the Marine Brigade when ready. Daniels also requested that a second Marine brigadier general be sent to Europe so that if there were a vacancy in the brigade, he would be ready to take command. The obvious choice was Brigadier General John Lejeune, a favorite of Daniels and a former assistant to Barnett.[27]

Lejeune believed his destiny lay in France, as did that of the Marine Corps. "The very depths of my soul were filled with an indescribable yearning,"

Lejeune confided in his memoirs, "for the opportunity for service overseas."[28] He believed the Marine Corps should send a full Marine division to France, accompanied by artillery, medical, engineers, signal corps, and all the other supporting units, allowing the Marines to demonstrate their full competence in modern warfare. Many officers fiercely endorsed Lejeune's idea, judging that the failure to support the war with the Marine Corps' full power reflected poorly on the organization. In addition, the contributions of only one brigade on the western front would be swallowed up by the massive army effort. However, Pershing blocked all efforts to expand the Marine presence in France. An opportunity arose for Daniels, Barnett, and Lejeune on May 7, when Doyen relinquished command of the 4th Marine Brigade. Major Douglas C. McDougal telephoned from headquarters with the news, causing Lejeune to depart immediately for the commandant's office. He informed Barnett that he knew of Doyen's imminent return to the United States and asked to replace him.

The commandant recalled his promise to send Lejeune overseas but, according to Lejeune, he "doubted whether I would want to go under the circumstances described in Pershing's telegram." Lejeune scanned the telegram himself and then leaped at the opportunity, stating, "I would be much nearer to the front in any part of France than I was at Quantico. . . . I felt sure I would be able to obtain a command at the front."[29] Barnett granted Lejeune fifteen days of leave, and on May 15 Lejeune received orders to prepare for overseas duty when his leave ended.[30]

Waiting at home was Laura Lejeune. "She faced the situation bravely and unselfishly," Lejeune remembered, "saying she would rather have me go than have me suffer the disappointment of not going, especially as she knew I would never get over it the rest of my life."[31] After a rousing send-off full of speeches and cheers, Lejeune left Quantico for the Brooklyn Navy Yard on May 22, where he would depart for France with four officers forming his staff and four enlisted men serving as orderlies.

The choice of Major Earl H. Ellis as one of Lejeune's four staff officers continued their close relationship. For many years, Ellis had repeatedly demonstrated his expertise as the leading Marine Corps staff officer, from his participation in advanced base theory and amphibious exercises at Culebra to his current work for Admiral Benson in the Office of the Chief of Naval Operations. There was no better choice to help Lejeune advance the cause of the Marine Corps in Europe. Once Lejeune reached France, Barnett ordered him to report to Pershing and accept whatever duty the general assigned him. Lejeune and his detachment came under US Army orders as soon as he reported to Pershing's headquarters.[32]

As Lejeune crossed the Atlantic Ocean to France, Doyen was making the same journey in the opposite direction. After landing in the United States, he wasted no time in visiting Secretary Daniels and requesting that a new medical board examine him, with the intent of returning to France. The secretary instantly rejected Doyen's request, arguing that any further action would stir up controversy with the army. He added, "You can't go back, as your relief has gone." Once Doyen realized that Lejeune had already been chosen to replace him, he abandoned his request, recognizing that further argument was useless. On May 29 Doyen wrote to Pershing, informing him of Daniels's decision, and opined, "I feel quite certain that it was rather a relief to him to have me at home . . . I have settled down to the inevitable." He also rejected any notion of serving under Lejeune, as "that would be too much of a blow to my pride."[33]

Just as Doyen was conferring with Daniels, Lejeune was attempting to gain entrance to Pershing's headquarters after landing in France on June 8. He soon learned that any noncombat American officer arriving in France could not leave the port areas until specific orders had arrived from AEF headquarters. Luckily, Lejeune reached some army friends in Paris who cut his orders overnight. Lejeune had had the foresight to bring a Cadillac automobile across the Atlantic with him, and the Marines were soon on their way to Paris. They first reported to US Navy headquarters and then went to the hospitals around Paris, where the Marines wounded at Belleau Wood were recovering. "Literally, we found battalions of wounded Marines," Lejeune remembered. "When they saw us in our Marine uniforms, [they] spontaneously began to sing the Marine's Hymn, and as we walked through the wards, its sound grew in volume as man after man took up the refrain until it made the welkin ring."[34]

Lejeune and his staff journeyed to Chaumont the following morning, which served as the "capital city" of the American Expeditionary Force. They checked into the Hotel de France just as evening fell. Lejeune entered the American headquarters building the following morning to report to Major General McAndrew. Their meeting started out less than cordial. McAndrew quickly read over Lejeune's orders and brusquely remarked, "The Marine Corps has no authority over you while you are on duty with the A.E.F. Your assignment to duty is entirely in the hands of General Pershing." Lejeune put the general at ease by responding, "I would not have it otherwise, even if it were in my power to do so." Lejeune then added that his real purpose for meeting with Pershing was to ask him to approve the formation of a full Marine division in France, "complete in all its parts."[35] He explained that the Marine Corps' expansion to over 30,000 men the previous year allowed for the creation of a second infantry brigade in Europe, along with artillery regiments and replacement battalions for the expected combat losses. Lejeune also explained that Congress was going to approve the further expansion of the Marine Corps to more than 76,000 men at any moment, guaranteeing the manpower to support a Marine division in France.

After listening intently to Lejeune's arguments, McAndrew relented, agreeing to arrange an interview with General Pershing within the next two days. Lejeune then visited with his friends at Chaumont and shared his views on the Marine division concept with various members of the AEF staff. At the same time, the army officers expressed their admiration for the ongoing battle by the 4th Marine Brigade at Belleau Wood. They disguised any irritation over the newspapers' tendency to sensationalize the Marines. Pershing arrived at Chaumont in the afternoon and invited Lejeune and McAndrew to join him for dinner that evening at the nearby château that served as his personal quarters.

The officers discussed no business over dinner, although when Pershing mentioned the Marines' ongoing fighting at Belleau Wood, he "express[ed] his deepest sorrow because of the heavy casualties they suffered," Lejeune recalled. "His voice broke and he showed deep emotion."[36] Members of the staff attempted to console the general about the inevitable realities of war, but Pershing excused himself at the end of the meal and returned to work. McAndrew and Lejeune retired to the library to smoke cigars and talk over the latest news from the United States. McAndrew then revealed that he had already briefed Pershing in a preliminary way and would follow up with further discussion of a possible Marine division as soon as possible.

Lejeune used the delay to visit the Army Staff College at Langres the following day and to call on his old friend from the Army War College, Major General Liggett, commanding the fledgling American I Corps at Neufchâteau. He informed the general of the plans for a Marine division in France and optimistically stated that "in certain respects [it] was an accomplished fact."[37] Lejeune's optimism seemed contagious, and Liggett immediately endorsed the concept and declared that he "would like nothing better than to command a corps composed of Marine divisions."[38]

The next morning, Lejeune met with McAndrew to hear about his meeting with Pershing. The chief of staff bluntly informed Lejeune that although the Marine concept had been discussed, Pershing "was noncommittal as to the decision reached." However, Lejeune confided in his memoirs, "It was apparent to me . . . that it was unfavorable."[39] He then asked to meet with Pershing himself, and an appointment was set for that afternoon. Lejeune knew that this would be his only chance to gain the general's approval, so he prepared his strongest talking points for the uphill battle ahead.

At the appointed time, Lejeune appeared in Pershing's office and set forth his best arguments for the Marine division concept. He mentioned the great desire of the Marine Corps to serve in France and be a larger part of the war, and he pointed out that without a full division, the Marines assigned to artillery and supporting units would have no opportunity to serve. Pershing listened to all the arguments put forth by Lejeune and then denied the request for the Marine division. He cited issues involving supply and replacements, but most of all, he said that a Marine division would work against his central concept of a standardized American army in France with all the parts working together. Lejeune tried to rebut these arguments, but he understood that Pershing's decision was final. "Seeing that it would be unavailing to say anything further," Lejeune remembered, "I thanked him for giving me the opportunity to lay the matter before him and left his office." McAndrew confirmed that he had known in advance what the general's decision would be, but he thought it best that Lejeune hear the pronouncement from Pershing himself. Lejeune asked if there was any prospect of a change in the future, and McAndrew replied, "No. It is final."[40]

On June 18, 1918, Pershing empathically stated, "Our land forces must be homogeneous in every respect. Units and personnel must be homogeneous in every respect. . . . While the Marines are splendid troops, their use as a separate division is inadvisable."[41] On June 29, 1918, Secretary of the Army March supported Pershing's position in a confidential cable, noting that it was "in harmony with the policy of the War Department." Then he carried the policy further by stating, "If you are called upon to send any troops from your forces to Italy or any other place, they will be selected from the Army and will not be chosen from the Marines."[42]

The denial of the Marine division concept severely affected Lejeune. All his future plans had been quashed, with no opportunity to alter the course of events. "I was depressed and disappointed, and could not bear to think of the effect of the news on the officers and men at home," he wrote. "However, I was comforted by the thought that I had done my best, and a man can do no more than that."[43] Lejeune was now a general without a command, and he asked to assume command of the 4th Marine Brigade when the current commander was promoted. The chief of staff brushed off that request as a possibility in the future, but first Lejeune must command an army brigade and learn the realities of war on the western front.

On June 18 Pershing issued orders for Lejeune to report to the 32nd Division for temporary duty as a brigade commander, but he and his staff were allowed to stop at 2nd Division headquarters on their way to the new assignment. The 32nd Division was composed of Michigan and Wisconsin National Guardsmen who were training in a quiet section of the western front in the Alsace region of France. Lejeune reported on July 5 and was assigned to command the 64th Brigade. He also visited III Corps headquarters, which was under the command of one of his friends, Major General Wright, "who greeted me like a long lost brother."[44]

Lejeune quickly came to admire the men of his brigade, calling them "great big fine looking fellows and look more like Marines than any of the other soldiers over here."[45] However, Lejeune's time with the 32nd Division proved to be short-lived, as Marine command assignments underwent significant changes. Harbord would soon be leading the 2nd Division, so command of the 4th Marine Brigade passed to Lejeune, who was still many miles away with the 32nd Division. Colonel Lee commanded the brigade while Harbord was on leave in Paris, and Major Holcomb took Lee's place as commander of the 6th Marines on July 13. On July 14 Lejeune received orders to report to his new command. Harbord received a telegram the same day assigning him to assume command of the 2nd Division once Lejeune had relieved him from brigade command. Although AEF headquarters issued orders for the V Corps commander to release Lejeune "at once," Lejeune could not leave the 32nd Division immediately.[46] Another telegram arrived two days later repeating the order and asking for confirmation of receipt, but Lejeune would not be able to depart until a replacement general arrived to take his place more than a week later. The 4th Marine Brigade would go into its next battle without his guidance.[47]

Belleau Wood Tour

Stop 13. Aisne Marne Cemetery, 49°04'45.7"N 3°17'31.3"E

Continue on the park road out of Belleau Wood and turn left onto the road to the town of Belleau. Turn left at the D 9 and then make an immediate left through the gates of the cemetery. The American Battle Monuments Commission maintains the cemetery, which is open to the public daily from 9:00 a.m. to 5:00 p.m., with the exception of December 25 and January 1. Buried here are 2,289 Marines, sailors, and soldiers who fell during the month-long battle for Belleau Wood, as well as casualties from other nearby battlefields in the summer of 1918. Also memorialized are 1,060 missing Americans in the Memorial Chapel. Be sure to explore some of the 42.5 acres of the cemetery, and sign in at the visitors' building to show respect for the fallen.

Take a few moments to walk among the rows of white crosses and look for the grave sites of many of the men mentioned in the narrative sections of this book. Thomas W. Ashley, Arthur N. Fauble, and Carl Williams are among those buried here or listed as missing in the Memorial Chapel.

Also buried here is Corporal Marion Maxey Collier of the 83rd Company, who died in the fighting on June 6. Collier, a former paving inspector in Houston, Texas, was orphaned and raised by his uncle, an 1884 graduate of the Naval Academy. In 1917, just short of his twenty-third birthday, Collier enlisted in the Marine Corps. The young Texan quickly adapted to military life and was appointed corporal only four months after his enlistment.[1] On June 25, 1918, Boyd T. Collier received the fateful telegram informing him that his brother had been killed in battle, just one year after his enlistment. Commandant Barnett asked the family to accept "my heartfelt sympathy in your great loss. Your brother nobly gave his life in service of his country."[2] The shock of Marion's death proved difficult for his two brothers and two sisters, but they wrote back to the commandant and asked for "our dear boys belongings," adding, "This poor fellow's death is an awful blow to us. While we are proud to be able to give this noble brother in the service of our wonderful country, it is a sad sad day for us."[3]

The lack of information was particularly upsetting to Collier's siblings. The exact date of Marion's death, the details of how he had died, and where he was buried proved elusive. The official correspondence initially stated that he had been killed between June 6 and 8. On September 2, 1918, a one-paragraph letter revealed his date of death as June 6 and stated that his remains had been buried in the ravine where he fell, near Belleau Wood. Despite letters to the 83rd Company's officers and the chaplain of the 6th Marines, the family received no more details from France. A death certificate dated May 31, 1919, revealed that Marion had been killed by multiple gunshot wounds and had been temporarily buried on June 9, 1918, but the family did not know exactly where his body rested. In 1921 the family informed the Marine Corps that it was their desire that Marion's body remain in France.

Even as late as 1920, the bodies of Americans killed in action were still being found at the rate of four to five a month. The remains of each American, whether Marine or soldier, were carefully exhumed and then reinterred in the nearest American cemetery. "The work of dis-interring the bodies is all done by Russians," wrote Leon G. Turovasy. "It must be a disagreeable job to say the least."[4] In August 1928 the bodies of a Marine, an American soldier, and a French poilu were discovered on the battlefield. The Marine was located on a path through the woods leading to an American flag—a path traveled by many thousands of visitors who had never noticed the body buried nearby.[5]

Former army private first class Ernest Stricker visited the cemetery here in 1928, walking among the rows of fallen just as you are now. Born in Switzerland, Stricker came to the United States in 1910 to settle as a famer in Stanfield, Oregon. He served in the 20th Engineers within a Forestry Company during the war and became an American citizen after his return home in 1919. He moved to Wisconsin to work in an automobile factory, but memories of the war still troubled his mind. Stricker eventually returned to France in February 1928, becoming an obviously distressed visitor to the Aisne Marne Cemetery. For a number of days, Stricker wandered through the cemetery, tearfully visiting the graves. Concerned cemetery attendants questioned Stricker, thinking he must have a relative buried there. But Stricker replied, "No, just buddies." Local citizens noticed the young man and whispered that he was a "shell shocked veteran who believed he was still back in 1918."[6] They invited him into their homes and tried to calm his nerves with cognac. On April 2 superintendent Adolph Kaess found Stricker's corpse lying next to the 2nd Division remembrance boulder by the American cemetery. A pistol lay by his side, and there was a bullet in his head. A note found on Stricker's body addressed to the American Legion Post No. 1 in Paris revealed his final thoughts:

As I was moving among the white crosses under which some of my truest friends are resting forever, a feeling came over me that I too can't go on anymore. . . . I can't go on comrades, I can't go on. It is my last wish to be buried under French soil among my comrades at arms as well as peace.

Your Comrade,

Ernest Stricker

He was laid to rest in the Belleau town cemetery on April 5, 1928, with full honors performed by a uniformed detachment from his American Legion Post in Paris. The final casualty of the battle could not be buried in the Aisne Marne Cemetery. Stricker had not perished during the war.

Consulting the cemetery's website may be helpful when planning your visit: www.abmc.gov/cemeteries-memorials/europe/aisne-marne-american -cemetery.

Stop 14. Belleau, 49°05'07.8"N 3°17'26.8"E

Return to the main gate of the cemetery and follow the street directly across from the gate. Park at the church on your right. As part of the July 1918 offensive eliminating the Marne salient, the 26th "Yankee" Division captured the town of Belleau, which was heavily damaged during the fighting. The veterans of the division rebuilt the church after the war. It is now one of the symbols of the American sacrifice of the First World War. As you go further into the town, note a stone water trough on the right; it was placed there to honor the Pennsylvania soldiers who fell during the battle. Proceed down the hill to the town hall, where the Musee de la Memoire de Belleau 1914–1918 offers displays of World War I uniforms and equipment. The infamous Devil Dog fountain is across the street in the private château area.

9

Grand Strategy
"Thanks to the Arrival of American Reinforcements, Time Was Working Not for Us but against Us"

GERMANY FACED A CRITICAL DECISION IN JUNE 1918. The series of hammer blows on the western front in the spring had been devastating to the Allied cause. The massive casualties and loss of ground proved near catastrophic to the morale of both the armies and the people of Great Britain and France. The latest attacks had pushed the battle line to within fifty miles of Paris, but it was now stalled along the Marne River. Of most concern to Quartermaster General Erich Ludendorff was the appearance of American divisions on the western front, despite the German admirals' assurances that their U-boats would keep the Americans from crossing the Atlantic. The German offensives had to proceed because failure to keep the initiative would only guarantee the arrival of more American forces, changing the balance of power on the western front. If Germany were unable to match the new Allied strength, it would mean certain defeat for the Central powers.

However, the large salient established on the Marne could not be held for long without a drastic improvement in German supply lines. The salient was sixty miles long and close to forty miles wide, meaning that the single railway line passing through Soissons was both insufficient and vulnerable. Without the means to support a long-term battle against the eventual Allied counterattack on any side of the salient, the only solution in the near term seemed to be first the capture of Reims and then the buildup of forces to strike in Belgium.

The loss of momentum caused by the French defense of the Marne salient was not lost on the German High Command. Chief of the General Staff Paul von Hindenburg summed up the battle on the Marne succinctly as "an imperfect and uncompleted task."[1] In truth, even though the Aisne offensive was now stalled, it had accomplished the German objective of drawing in the Allied reserves, including the new American divisions. Ludendorff could now focus on the original objective: a renewed attack on the British to cut them off from their English Channel supply line and take them out of the war. With so many French and American divisions in action on the Marne, the time was ripe to deal the British a deathblow before the Allied reserve could be reconstituted. Ironically, the ground gained at such a high cost in May and June proved to be an impediment to this plan.

As the French and Americans awaited a continuation of the attack along their defensive line of the Marne salient, the situation across the front and at German headquarters was much less stable than the Allies expected. For the Germans, the tactical situation on the ground was unsettled, primarily because logistics within the salient remained tenuous. They could support their forces by plundering captured towns for food, but all military supplies had to travel by rail or by less efficient animal or vehicle transport. Before any other consideration, Ludendorff first had to strengthen his hold on the ground gained by the May 27 offensive in the Marne salient.

The one railway line available was insufficient to support a defense against the expected Allied counterattack. Resources for the entire German 7th Army were dependent on the single railroad network running from the valley of the Aisne River near Soissons into the Vesle River valley. With this limited avenue of supply, the German forces desperately needed to widen the salient if they were to have any hope of holding their ground. The June 9 attack by the German 18th Army striking the town of Mery and the high ground beyond the Oisne River failed to widen the salient to the west. The fighting ended after two days of determined French counterattacks that pushed the Germans back to their starting point. The supply line remained tenuous, and additional local attacks against the French defenses on the Soissons side of the salient would not be worth the manpower expended.

General Ludendorff now pondered one of his most important decisions of the war: where to attack next? Faced by the inevitability of American reinforcements arriving in France in decisive numbers, continuing the offensive seemed to be his only option. However, Ludendorff was dealing from a position of strength. "Our troops remained masters of the situation both in attack and defense," he later wrote. "They proved themselves superior to the English and the French, even when their opponents were assisted by tanks."[2] Every offensive launched by the German army in 1918 proved successful, inflicting serious losses on the Allies, capturing key parts of the western front, and even threatening Paris.

Ludendorff initially attempted to divert Allied reserves to Italy, just as the victory at Caparetto had accomplished in 1917. On June 15 the Austro-Hungarian forces in Italy launched an offensive and achieved some initial success, but the Italian army halted the attack, with no loss of territory. Thus, no Allied reinforcements would be detached from France to support Italy. "This unsuccessful attack was extremely painful to me," Ludendorff wrote. "I could no longer hope that relief on the Western Front might be gained in Italy itself."[3] Faced with preparations for additional attacks in France, he ordered reinforcements from Italy, Bulgaria, and Turkey, but only four divisions of Austrian troops could be spared from Italy; they would not arrive in France for at least several months.

At the same time, German intelligence estimated that up to twenty American divisions were now in France, far more than Ludendorff had originally believed possible. These divisions would eventually negate the entire German force brought to the western front when Russia collapsed. With American reinforcements continually arriving in French and English ports, the Allies now outnumbered the German forces in France and would only continue to increase their advantage. For the moment, however, the German army could more than hold its own in combat with the Allies. In the coming weeks, however, that could change. The new American divisions might be inadequately trained, but they could occupy the quiet sectors of the front and free the veteran British and French divisions to meet any crisis that might occur. "This was of the greatest importance and helps to explain the influence exerted by the American contingent on the issue of the conflict," Ludendorff wrote in his memoirs. "It was for this reason that America became the deciding factor in the war."[4]

With both time and numbers against them, the German High Command had little choice but to force a decision on the western front. The German army had suffered serious losses since the start of the March offensives, but enough strength remained "to allow us to strike one more blow that should make the enemy ready for peace," Ludendorff later wrote. "There was no other way."[5] The initial choice for the location of the attack remained against the British in Flanders, following the success of the original German spring offensives. But this time, the Germans hoped to complete their goal of separating the British forces from their French allies and perhaps driving England out of the war. Most of the French reserves were long gone from the English sector, but the reconstituted Allied forces offset their losses in March and April. Ultimately, the logistical problems of transporting the required German forces from the salient proved too difficult to overcome, and the Flanders offensive was scrapped.

More inviting was the new salient driven into the Allies' lines in the May 27 attack. Most of the French reserves were on the Paris side of the salient, from Château-Thierry to Soissons, to protect the capital from capture, but the east side was believed to be relatively lightly defended. An attack could be made near Reims. If it was successful, the Germans could open the Marne salient to stable railroad supply, in addition to drawing more Allied reserves to the area. Then, with the Allies seriously weakened by dispatching their reserves to Reims, an offensive in Flanders could produce a decisive victory there in early August.

The capture of Reims, which had been bypassed earlier in favor of the attacks on the Paris road and Soissons, seemed to be the best option. At the same time, preparations for an eventual German attack in Belgium would proceed. Time was the primary issue. With every day that passed, more American forces arrived in France, despite the best efforts of the U-boat fleet. "We had to find some way of dealing with this situation," Hindenburg lamented. "Thanks to the arrival of American reinforcements," he later wrote, "time was working not for us but against us."[6] The Germans assembled forty-eight divisions, almost 1,000 aircraft, and 6,300 pieces of artillery to break open the French and American line. "If this was not an all-or-nothing effort," historian Dennis Showalter wrote, "it was as close as the German army could come."[7]

While the Germans pondered their next move, the Allies sought to regain the initiative on the western front. Rather than passively waiting for the next German offensive, Foch planned an attack of his own. The use of American manpower would be crucial. Walking a diplomatic tightrope, Foch placated the Americans' determination to fight under Allied control as soon as possible but to be commanded only by their own officers. Although Foch wanted to delay the assignment of an American sector on the western front, Pershing was already preparing for the formation of an American army, based on the creation of three corps.

While the formation of a corps system seemed simple on paper, the reality proved far more complex. On January 20, 1918, Major General Hunter Liggett took command of the fledgling I Corps, leading the new American divisions through their training areas and then to quiet sectors of the front, where they would acclimate to combat conditions. By mid-June, Pershing informed Liggett that the American I Corps would take over an active front on the Marne River. On June 18 Liggett established his headquarters at Château-Thierry, reporting to the French 6th Army in preparation for relief of the French III Corps. Six American combat-ready divisions, including the 2nd Division, constituted the I Corps, but they were interspaced with French divisions in different locations along the Marne front.

Almost immediately, Liggett faced problems in the 2nd Division. The men of the 4th Marine Brigade were angry over their long duty on the front without relief. Despite tremendous losses, the Marines were still holding the line of battle in Belleau Wood at the end of June and blaming their division commander, Major General Bundy, for their lengthy time in the front lines. Harbord and his Marines alleged that Bundy would not ask for relief until the 2nd Division's 3rd Army Brigade had captured the town of Vaux, enabling it to claim some of the credit for the month-long battle. The 3rd Brigade was composed entirely of soldiers, and although it had been holding the front line to the right of the Marine Brigade, it had provided only limited help in the fight for Belleau Wood. "We knew informally that if the Division Commander would ask it a division would relieve us," Harbord later wrote. "For some reason, he would not ask it."[8]

On June 10 Degoutte moved up to command the French 6th Army and was replaced by General Stanislas Naulin, who took over the XXI Corps and supervision of the 2nd Division, becoming Bundy's new senior officer. Bundy, Degoutte, and Naulin were aware of the problem with the Marines but did not pull the brigade from the line. The 3rd Division's 7th Infantry Regiment temporarily replaced one of the Marine regiments on June 15, while Bundy's 23rd Infantry of the 3rd Brigade extended the line to Bouresches, thus shortening the Marine Brigade's front. The French 167th Division took over more of the line on the opposite flank, relieving another Marine battalion. However, four decimated Marine battalions still remained in the hell of Belleau Wood.[9]

On June 19 AEF headquarters pressed Liggett to visit Bundy and arrange for the relief of the 2nd Division. Even Chief of Staff Preston Brown reported that "the 2nd Division was all in."[10] Liggett's staff rebuffed the pressure, with his approval. Colonel Pierpont L. Stackpole responded, pointing out that "the division was still under General Degoutte's command and when he thought the time had come for their relief it was his business to relieve it."[11]

Bundy reported to Liggett's headquarters on June 21. Colonel Stackpole wrote in his diary that Bundy "appeared vigorous and self-possessed and [had] no special complaint to make," and there was apparently no mention of relieving the 2nd Division. They visited the new XXI Corps commander the same day, and Stackpole noted that Naulin welcomed the Americans with open arms, expressing his satisfaction to be working with Liggett; he "spoke of us all as one family."[12] Three days later, Degoutte, Naulin, and Marshal Henri Philippe Petain, commander in chief of the French armed forces on the northeastern front, met with Liggett and informed him of the reorganization of the French III Corps, which would now be under his tactical control. The restructured corps consisted of two divisions, one American and one French. In fact, two American divisions would soon form the corps, along with the French 167th Division. More important, Liggett's new command would be responsible for holding the Belleau Wood front.

Liggett's first priority was emplacing the corps artillery, but he also ordered Bundy to request the relief of the 2nd Division. When Bundy failed to implement the order, Liggett visited the 2nd Division on June 26 to find out why. The generals had a confidential meeting, after which Liggett engaged Chief of Staff Brown in a "whispered conversation" concerning Bundy and the general condition of the division.[13] On the following day, Liggett went to 1st Division headquarters to assess the condition of the unit. At the same time, Liggett's I Corps continued to expand on paper, initially consisting of the 1st, 2nd, 26th, and 42nd Divisions on the front line; the 41st as a base and training division; and the 32nd, which served as a replacement division, for a total of 200,000 men. Although these numbers seem impressive, the American forces came under French control for training and combat, so Liggett's corps headquarters initially served as more of a staff than an actual combat command.

As the I, II, and III Corps grew and contracted, the 4th Marine Brigade still held its portion of the front at Belleau Wood, with no relief in sight. On July 2, 1918, the day after the 3rd Brigade's capture of Vaux, Brigadier General Harbord received orders to remove his 4th Marine Brigade from its hard-fought positions in Belleau Wood, pulling back to a reserve position to rest after more than thirty days of combat. Major General Clarence R. Edwards, commanding the 26th Division, arrived at a luncheon at Naulin's headquarters to plan the 2nd Division's relief. The lunch had been going well until Edwards's arrival. Known to be "bombastic and assertive," Edwards "butted in and spoiled the party," according to Stackpole. Naulin quickly sized up Edwards and became "coldly inattentive," assuming "an air of courteous frigidity of manner."[14]

Contributing to the day's discontent, Neville, commanding the 5th Marines, arrived at I Corps headquarters for the evening meal and complained repeatedly about Brown's orders and the Clemenceau incident. Adding even more fuel to the fire, orders arrived from Bundy directing that two companies of Marines be sent to Paris to participate in the Fourth of July parade. On July 4 the 26th Yankee Division arrived from its rest area, and the 52nd Brigade was assigned to replace the 5th and 6th Marines in Belleau Wood. To the Marines' delight, advance parties of the new brigade arrived to plan for the exchange of position, which meant that they were about to be relieved. The Independence Day news was an appropriate gift to the Marines, who were too exhausted to plan a special event to mark the day. Harbord accepted an invitation by General Schmidt, commanding the neighboring French division, to celebrate the occasion.[15]

The newly arrived men of the 26th Division were suitably impressed with the grizzled Marines and even referred to them as "famous." General Edwards was particularly concerned about the exchange of positions in Belleau Wood. "When the Fifty-second Brigade relieved the Marines in Belleau

Wood," remembered Edwards, "I walked around with fingers crossed and did a little private praying."[16] The exchange occurred without incident, but the "traditionally sinister character of Belleau Wood had a certain effect on the morale of the troops stationed there," noted the historian of the 26th Division. "The woods themselves were full of horror . . . a haunted place of dread." The new men were unprepared for the sight and smell of a month-old battlefield, and what the New Englanders witnessed when they moved into the Marines' fighting holes left a permanent impression. "Shapeless fragments of what once were men hung in the jagged branches of the trees, blown there by shells; stiffened shapes were found by the new troops, lying still unburied where they had fallen before German machine gun nests in the rocky hollows," recounted the historian. "A grisly odor of death hung in the summer air around the stone hunting lodge near the eastern skirt of the woods, and men there came to move and talk as when they know that ghosts are watching them."[17]

General Edwards was less than pleased with the conduct of the Marines, complaining to I Corps staff officers that "they were lazy and would not dig or get hot meals for themselves, though they could fight."[18] The entire process of relieving the 2nd Division proved overwhelming for Bundy, who was described as "somewhat over his head, if not off of it."[19] Both Bundy and Edwards provided less than stellar examples of leadership. When Liggett handed the relief orders to Edwards and Bundy, each of their chiefs of staff eagerly seized the orders out of their respective general's grasp so that they could implement the relief without confusion. Such behavior confirmed who actually ran both divisions.

Edwards carped about the dead Marines and Germans in the woods, but he was reluctant to assign his men to burial details. Edwards finally decided to ask Bundy for permission to bury the dead and told his aides, "Go see if any of the engineers will volunteer."[20] Bundy, "after hesitation," granted permission, but at least one corps staff officer believed that Edwards's intent was to denigrate the Marines, intending to criticize them for being "too lazy to bury their dead, and he had to do it for them."[21] Colonel George W. Bunnell, commanding the 26th Division's 101st Engineers, volunteered for the task, and the engineers spent two days "bury[ing] thousands of men."[22] The duty was so horrendous that the men wore gas masks to protect them from the smell of the rotting bodies.

Despite all the friction encountered in the structuring of the I Corps, Pershing was unwilling to slow the formation of an American army. The newest American corps, the III Corps, was formally organized on March 30, but only to exercise administrative control over the arriving American divisions. Major General William M. Wright, Pershing's roommate at West

Point, took command on June 17, but the III Corps was still being formed in the early days of July. The first four divisions assigned to Wright's command were scattered in quiet training sectors of the front, and his staff was ordered to report to Major General Robert L. Bullard's 1st Division at Beauvais on July 8. The next day, Pershing placed Bullard in command of the fledgling III Corps composed of the veteran American 1st and 2nd Divisions, establishing the corps at Château-Thierry.

With the gathering American strength now fully capable of making an impact on the war, Pershing visited General Foch on July 10 to renew discussions of his vision of establishing an American army and pulling together all the scattered American divisions serving on the western front. He proposed the creation of an American sector in the area around Château-Thierry, since most of the American divisions were already concentrated there. Foch countered by asking if Pershing intended to pull the six American divisions of the II Corps out of the British sector. Pershing firmly stated that he thought every division should be quickly withdrawn from Flanders but admitted that this "would be difficult . . . without causing some inconvenience to the British."[23] He asked Foch to approach Sir Douglas Haig, but the French general demurred, preferring that Pershing handle the matter himself.

Pershing then shifted the conversation back to the creation of a permanent American portion of the front. Foch suggested that instead of Château-Thierry, the quiet sector facing the Saint-Mihiel salient would be the best place for the Americans. Pershing responded that, with his forces "scattered all along the Western Front . . . assigned to no particular zone for future operations, we were postponing the day when the American Army would be able to render its greatest help to the Allied cause." Further, "We were dissipating our resources for lack of a plan. Instead of thinking of the future, even the immediate future, we were merely temporizing."[24] He then requested that Foch approve a proposed attack on the Saint-Mihiel salient as the American army's initial offensive. The formation of an American army remained central in the discussion, following an earlier tentative agreement between Pershing and General Petain. The American general also made it clear that the Americans were not content to simply hold the line at Saint-Mihiel. Pershing intended to attack the Germans as quickly as possible, as he considered trench combat unsustainable.

Foch readily agreed to the proposal. He reinforced his decision by exclaiming, "To-day, when there are a million Americans in France, I am going to be still more American than any of you. America must have her place in the war. America has the right to have her army organized as such."[25] They agreed that the six American divisions still in training would move to the Vosges area to support quiet sections of the front, relieving French and other

American units for service in areas of active battle. Pershing still pressed to undertake the initial stages of the formation of the American army in the Château-Thierry area, to which Foch agreed.

The French general also informed Pershing of a proposed attack in that area between July 20 and 31, with the American 1st and 2nd Divisions as crucial elements. If the July offensive proved indecisive, Foch would attack again in September to collapse the Marne salient. To Pershing's disappointment, Foch stated that unless the July attack succeeded, an American army could not be formed until after the September assault, or it might even have to be delayed until October. Foch then talked about the long-range preparations for a combined Allied offensive in 1919, which, at a minimum, must free northern France and much of Belgium and would perhaps take Germany out of the war.

Pershing understood the overall Allied strategy but was wary of the execution of Foch's plan. "The fact is that the tendency persisted on the part of the Allied governments to send expeditions here and there in pursuit of political aims," Pershing believed. "They were prone to lose sight of the fundamental fact that the real objective was the German army." He thought that all efforts should focus on the true mission, which was to defeat the enemy forces on the western front. Once that was accomplished, Pershing wrote, "the political and naval power of Germany would collapse."[26] These delays by the Allies were antithetical to Pershing's plan to win the war. Everything in Pershing's structuring of the American army for combat focused on the offensive, taking the initiative away from the Germans and breaking the stalemate on the western front. Ironically, the successful German offensives of 1918 brought large numbers of German soldiers out of their defensive trenches, where they were vulnerable to attack and destruction.

Pershing believed that the critical nature of the American contribution to the western front in July 1918 could not be overstated. By midmonth, Pershing's forces totaled the equivalent of fifty-two British or French divisions. On July 10 Americans held 12 percent of the western front, compared with 4 percent by the Belgians, 17 percent by the British, and 67 percent by the French. Within these forces, the combat-ready American divisions equaled the strength of thirty-four Allied divisions, and more American troops were on their way across the Atlantic. At the end of July the number of American forces in France would total 996,000 men. Without this dramatic influx of American manpower, Germany would have outnumbered the Allies on the western front by more than 144,000 men.[27]

Unknown to the commanders of the American divisions, Petain and Foch were preparing new plans for their July counterattack, even as more supplies were being sent to defend the front and assault units were preparing for another round of battle. The Allies knew that the Germans would attack, and they weighed their options to meet such an offensive. A preemptive attack would deal a dynamic but costly blow to German efforts. Instead, Petain ordered preparations for a swift counterattack once the predicted enemy offensive was halted. This had the potential to overwhelm the weakened German forces, which would necessarily be disorganized after their own assault. The planned assault extended all along the German line from Soissons to Reims, with a primary focus on the opposite side of the salient from the Germans' attack.

The lead counterattack would be carried out by General Charles E. M. Mangin's 10th Army, aimed just south of the town of Soissons. Mangin had a reputation in the French army for favoring *guerre à outrance,* or aggressive all-out war, earning him the nicknames the "Butcher" and the "Man Eater." He served with the French colonial troops for much of his career in French North and West Africa, Mali, and Tokin, suffering three wounds in these conflicts. As a result of these experiences, Mangin became the leading advocate of employing African soldiers on the western front. After fighting well at Verdun in 1916, Mangin suffered a great number of casualties for little gain in the Neville offensive the following year, tarnishing his reputation as a combat general and resulting in his removal from command of the 6th Army. Prime Minister Clemenceau and General Foch retuned Mangin to command the 10th Army in 1918, eager to take advantage of his tremendous aggressiveness for the Allied counterstroke.

In theory, the German defenders at Soissons would be at minimum strength, with their best units away fighting at Reims. Also favorable to the French was the proximity of the main German supply line on the Soissons–Château-Thierry road. If this road were threatened, the Germans would be compelled to shift their forces to hold the road, weakening the rest of the salient. If the 10th Army cut or even threatened this supply line, the salient would become untenable, forcing the Germans to withdraw to their original lines, giving up all their gains of late May and June. The initiative would belong to the Allies.

IO

July 16–17, 1918—Internal Battles and the Movement to Soissons
"We, the Lousy Infantry, SOL as Always"

ONE OF HARBORD'S FIRST TASKS after Belleau Wood was to dispel the rumor that he had been killed in the final days of the battle. His friends were quick to send notes of congratulations that he was still among the living. When Colonel Charles G. Dawes, a member of Pershing's staff, was asked about the rumor, he vehemently denied it, stating he had "just received a note from him and it wasn't postmarked *Hell!*"[1] Better news came for Harbord on July 4 in the form of a telegram from his wife, congratulating him on being promoted to the rank of major general. This was his first notice of the promotion, and although he was excited at the news, he refrained from celebration. "While anything my wife says is official enough for her husband," he confided in his diary, "one has to go through certain formalities before he can take over new rank and responsibilities, even with her say so."[2]

On the day after Pershing's July 11 meeting with Foch, Harbord received official notice of his promotion to major general. He attempted to keep the news quiet among the brigade, and in the evening he went to his rooms on the slope above Nantueil-sur-Marne to continue with his paperwork. His adjutant, Major Harry R. Lay, appeared at the door and informed him that someone had arrived and was waiting to see him. Harbord told Lay to show the man into headquarters, but the major insisted that Harbord come outside to meet the stranger. When Harbord reached the door, he was surprised to find the 5th and 6th Marines' regimental commanders and their staffs assembled outside, supported by the 6th Marines Band and several hundred other Marines who wished to congratulate their commander on his promotion. The band quickly struck up the Marine Hymn. As the notes to "From the Halls of Montezuma to the Shores of Tripoli" rang out, the assembled Marines broke into thunderous cheers. Colonel Neville, commanding the 5th Marines, and Lieutenant Colonel Lee, commanding the 6th Marines, presented Harbord with his new stars. The officers were then invited inside, where they celebrated for the rest of the evening. Harbord recalled in his diary, "We had what is usually had on such occasions in a land of vineyards."[3]

On July 12 Pershing visited 4th Marine Brigade headquarters at Nantueil-sur-Marne, where he shared a lunch with his former chief of staff. Fresh from the fighting at Belleau Wood, Harbord was full of anecdotes for Pershing, including the story of a lone Marine who had captured seventy-five prisoners by himself. Pershing remarked, "If he told such stories as that it was little wonder that he was popular with the Marines."[4]

Pershing informed Harbord that he was assigning him to command the 2nd Division, which greatly pleased the new major general. The two talked over the new brigadier general promotion list, which had recently arrived from the War Department. The results angered Pershing greatly. Many of the names proposed by the AEF commander had been rejected in favor of officers from the engineers and artillery.

More controversy occurred at dinner that evening, which was intended to be a celebration of the promotion of Malin Craig, the I Corps chief of staff, to brigadier general. Harbord attended the dinner, as did Colonel Malone, commander of the 23rd Infantry. Malone presented himself poorly, raising concern among the corps staff. "He is nervously wrought up, saying he scarcely had his clothes off from May 31 to date," Colonel Stackpole noted. Malone was "full of scorn of Marines, pride over his own regiment's achievements, and nervous because he had been jumped in promotions."[5]

Harbord wasted little time in asking Pershing for a short leave so that he could go to Paris and purchase the proper uniforms for his new command. It was granted immediately, but Harbord also needed permission from his superior, Major General Bundy, who still commanded the division. Bundy took his time with the request, perhaps miffed that Harbord would be taking his place. He let the request languish for twenty hours before granting Harbord permission to go to Paris for almost a week. Once he received approval, Harbord took off for the City of Lights accompanied by an orderly and his two Marine aides, Major Lay and First Lieutenant Robinson. Lee assumed command of the 4th Marine Brigade until Harbord's return.

Lay had a particular interest in defeating the Germans. A native of Washington, DC, he had studied at Princeton University but withdrew when he was commissioned a Marine second lieutenant in 1900, two days after his twenty-first birthday. Lay served in China, the Philippines, and Vera Cruz, as well as with the Great White Fleet; this was followed by service in the Adjutant General's Office at Marine Corps headquarters. Lay was also a White House aide at the end of President Theodore Roosevelt's term in 1908 and performed the same duty for President William H. Taft. In 1898 Lay's mother, a widow, married Count Gustav Adolf von Götzen, a noted German explorer and eventual governor of German East Africa who was then serving at the German embassy in Washington, DC. The couple moved to Berlin, where von Götzen died in 1910. Countess von Götzen was still living in Germany when the United States entered the war, separated from her son. "He is fighting his way to Berlin," a cousin related, "to get his mother out of that country."[6]

While Harbord shopped in Paris, the American command structure was undergoing a transformation for the new offensive. One of the first steps occurred when Major General Bullard took command of the American III Corps, with his headquarters at Meaux. However, Bullard's authority still existed primarily on paper. The 1st and 2nd Divisions formed the new American corps, still serving under General Degoutte's 6th Army command. Only the 1st American Division, now commanded by Major General Charles P. Summerall, remained under Bullard's tactical direction. The 2nd American Division, still serving in the second line of defense east of Château-Thierry, also reported organizationally to Bullard, but tactical leadership remained with Major General Liggett's American I Corps.

Despite the appearance of American command, the French still held tightly to the 1st and 2nd Divisions. Petain ordered both divisions to the Marne region, placing Bullard in actual command only after the organizational movement was completed. Both American divisions still formed a reserve attached to Degoutte's 6th Army but under the direct control of Petain. Together, these divisions formed a powerful weapon for Petain, equivalent to the strength of four French divisions. The 1st Division moved to Dammartin-en-Goele, while Bundy's 2nd Division remained in the Belleau Wood sector of the line.

All these bewildering organizational changes would be critical if it became necessary to meet the German offensive and then form the tip of the spear for the planned French counterattack. The French commanders were well aware of the date and time for the renewal of the German offensive. On July 15 the German attack would take place on the eastern, or Reims, side of the salient. While preparing to repulse the enemy divisions, Foch and Petain devised a masterful counteroffensive of their own. Once the Germans' initial attack was repelled, the Allies would assault the opposite sector of the salient at Soissons before the Germans could regroup their forces. Secrecy was a vital part of this plan. The Americans were not informed of the French intent, for fear of a breach of security. Pershing himself was informed only in a general way on the evening of July 13. At the same time, Petain needed to placate the Americans' desire to command their own units while planning the upcoming battle. Holding the two most experienced American divisions ready to lead the assault was an essential part of the French plan.[7]

At 7:00 p.m. on July 14, as Harbord was enjoying the Paris opera, the calm at 2nd Division headquarters in Champigny disappeared with the approach of a French staff officer bearing an order from General Degoutte. The order specified the immediate transfer of the 2nd Division to the French 10th Army, along with III Corps headquarters and Summerall's 1st Division. Not specified was the Americans' assignment as a focal part of the impending Allied counterattack, determined to eliminate the enemy salient driven toward Paris in the German offensive starting on May 27. The order stated that the 2nd Field Artillery Brigade must shift its position to Betz immediately, a fifteen-mile march to the north, and await further orders. At the same time, the division supply train was to move to Lizy-sur-Ourcq.[8]

The 2nd Division headquarters splintered under the weight of these orders. Chief of Staff Brown called I Corps headquarters and advised Colonel Stackpole of his concerns about the upcoming meeting with French 10th Army headquarters and the confusion of command between Bundy and Harbord. Adding to the bewilderment, Bullard called Stackpole and told him to inform Bundy that he would soon be assuming command of the fledgling American VI Corps, while Harbord took over the 2nd Division. Bullard also emphasized that Harbord must go alone to meet with the French the following day. Bundy told Stackpole that Harbord was still in Paris on leave and asked Stackpole to contact the new division commander directly at his hotel. After being informed of the changes in command, a somewhat ruffled Bundy quickly appeared at Major General Liggett's I Corps headquarters, awaiting the return of the corps commander. Stackpole wisely waited for Chief of Staff Craig to return and clear up the chain-of-command issues for Bundy before sending the message to Harbord.

Harbord was still in Paris, but he had been brought back to the realities of war when he visited three hospitals and spoke to wounded officers from Belleau Wood. "They seemed glad to see me, and none of them was too maimed to be cheerful," he wrote in his diary. "All were anxious to get back to the front."[9] At 5:00 p.m. Harbord went back to AEF headquarters, where the chief of staff, Major General James W. "Dad" McAndrew, informed him that he was to take command of the 2nd Division. McAndrew pointedly informed Harbord that although Pershing was reluctant to end his liberty in Paris, and although the decision of when to return to the front was Harbord's, it would be best if he was at division headquarters when the telegram notifying him of his appointment arrived. In that case, Harbord could personally relieve Bundy of his duties and direct him to report to AEF headquarters in Paris.

Harbord knew that his time in Paris would be cut short because of these new orders, so he went to dinner at the Inter-Allied Club to celebrate Bastille Day. To the accompaniment of a Greek tenor, champagne flowed freely, followed by speeches extolling the virtues of the "heroic Marine Brigade" and honoring the Marines as the "saviors of Paris." After hearing much more of this alcohol-flavored hyperbole, Harbord left the club and walked through the evening darkness across the Seine to his room at headquarters. A phone call at midnight from Chief of Staff Brown woke Harbord, informing him that division headquarters was aware of his new assignment and that "the sooner I joined them the better."[10]

Shortly after midnight on July 15, 1918, the Germans initiated their assault on Reims as expected, with the intent of surrounding the city by attacking both flanks of the French defenses. The German assault extended from Reims to the Marne River at Château-Thierry. Although the Germans achieved some initial success and took 14,000 prisoners, the first day's fighting proved disappointing. There would be no quick victory. Battle was renewed the following day, and the Germans hoped for a breakthrough, but to no avail. Learning from the previous battles of 1918, the French had made their second line of defense their primary line of resistance, allowing the main German artillery effort to be wasted on the intentionally weaker front trench line. Although fighting continued, prior knowledge of the enemy's plans sealed the victory for the Allied defenders.

Miles away, the Marines observed the flashes of artillery during the night, unaware that the German offensive signaled the secret redeployment of the 2nd Division. The immediate concern for the Americans was stabilizing their command structure. Craig returned to I Corps headquarters at midnight and informed a still anxious Stackpole that his role as intermediary was at an end. Harbord would arrive at his new command at 8:00 a.m., "and any further responsibility was assumed by him, with full approval of what I had done and said," a thankful Stackpole recorded in his diary.[11]

In Paris, Harbord woke his orderly, told him to have the car ready for an early departure, and then sent him to the Grand Hotel to alert Lay and Robinson to be ready to leave Paris at 5:30 a.m. After a few hours of sleep, Harbord and his party were on the road, heading back to the front. Their shopping was still undone, but they were confident that they would be returning to Paris in a couple of days after meeting with the French commanders. Unknown to Harbord, the rumble of artillery had already started, and muzzle flashes were lighting the sky before the break of dawn on July 15, revealing the German assault taking place beyond Château-Thierry. Ironically, the 2nd Division now had to move away from the fighting, rather than toward that part of the front.

After a quick trip across the countryside, Harbord arrived at 2nd Division headquarters but found that Bundy was still sleeping. He waited patiently until the general arose, then informed him of the change of command and passed along the order for Bundy to report to the chief of staff in Paris. Harbord was back in his car before 9:00 a.m., on his way to the conference at French 10th Army headquarters at Chamigny.

The meeting with French commander Mangin proved less than satisfactory. Harbord learned of the planned offensive at Soissons, but the timing was vague due to the uncertainty surrounding the ongoing German offensive. He returned to the 2nd Division to take command but found that Bundy still occupied division headquarters. The transition from Bundy to Harbord was less than cordial. The new commander fumed at the delay caused by this confusion, but he could do little while waiting for "little General Bundy to move his plunder out of my room, and get away."[12] The two generals had clashed on several occasions during the Battle of Belleau Wood over Bundy's slights toward the 4th Marine Brigade, and now "General Bundy stayed until after dinner the day of his relief, forgetting several times that he was no longer in command," Harbord confided to his diary. "I finally moved into the room just before bedtime."[13]

Bundy would eventually be assigned to command the VI Corps on July 26. Just as confusing was the transfer of the 2nd Division from Bullard's III Corps to the French 10th Army. Bullard and his staff moved on July 15 to be near the French army headquarters, but he was essentially a general without a command as the tactical control of his two divisions passed to French command. The 2nd Division changed command structure at least three times in as many days, but for the rank and file, there was no noticeable difference in their daily routine. Except for the senior leadership, most Marines and soldiers were oblivious to the rolling changes in the headquarters structure.

Command changes within the 2nd Division were more significant. Brigadier General Edward M. Lewis left his 3rd Infantry Brigade to command the 30th Division. He was replaced by Brigadier General Hanson E. "Cantigny" Ely, who came from the 28th Infantry, 1st Infantry Division. Ely had earned his nickname when he led his regiment in the first American offensive at Cantigny on May 28, 1918. Brigadier General Albert J. Bowley followed Brigadier General William Chamberlaine as the 2nd Artillery Brigade commander, after the latter departed to command the AEF Railway Artillery Reserve. Colonel Neville assumed command of the Marine Brigade, but because he was ill, Lieutenant Colonel Lee filled in until Neville's return from the hospital.

With combat imminent, all four senior commanders within the division were new appointees—Harbord as the new division commander, and Ely, Bowley, and Lee as the infantry and artillery brigade commanders. Both Marine regiments had new leadership as well. At best, each man had only weeks (in some cases, only days or even hours) to introduce himself to his new command and prepare to march. As expected, orders arrived from Degoutte at 8:30 p.m., which ended the day's suspense. The infantry and machine gun units had to be ready to board camions at 4:00 p.m. the following day, July 16, and proceed to an unidentified place near the French motor regulating area at Marcilly, where they would receive further instructions.[14]

With definite orders to march, Harbord and Brown woke early on July 16 to journey to French 10th Army headquarters. The 2nd Division spent much of the day preparing to move, but still the destination had yet to determined. Even the location to meet the French camions supporting the move was unknown. Nevertheless, the 1,149 officers and 24,085 men of the division prepared to move. Orders arrived at 10:30 a.m. for the six infantry battalion commanders and the Marine 6th Machine Gun Battalion to prepare to march immediately. The Marines packed with great anticipation and then waited; they were sure the orders meant their long-awaited trip to an idyllic rest camp or even Paris. However, additional orders from General Degoutte's 6th Army arrived at 3:00 p.m., initiating a frenzy of activity. Harbord had only an hour until the 4:00 p.m. departure time.[15]

The lead elements of the 5th Marines reached their loading point at 4:00 p.m., then waited patiently for three hours until they noticed the arrival of long columns of French camions operated by Vietnamese drivers. All hope of a rest area vanished immediately. "There before us on the road was an endless train of camions, as far as we could see," recalled Private Clarence L. Richmond of the 43rd Company. "The first effect was one of silence and then the storm broke forth. We knew they did not haul soldiers to the rear in camions."[16] Richmond had left the University of Tennessee in January 1918, at the age of twenty-one, to enlist in the Marine Corps and had entered combat at Belleau Wood as a replacement. He now "marched" toward his second battle since arriving in France on June 5.

The churning ranks of French trucks loaded with soldiers and Marines departed for the unknown in clouds of dust and gasoline fumes. The columns continued after nightfall, which proved to be "black as ink, and starless, and the truck carried no lights save a miserable oil lamp on each machine," wrote a Marine in Holcomb's battalion. "Accidents were frequent; occasionally a truck would be passed, thrown to the side of the road, with its nose in the ditch or up a tree." The drivers stopped for no one, and they passed artillery, ammunition wagons, and supply trucks with audacity; the camions took occasional daring detours into neighboring fields when traffic blocked the road ahead. The Marine passengers watched in horror as the drivers drank liberally from bottles of wine, supposedly to improve their night driving skills. As the drivers became increasingly intoxicated, the camions seemed to be "hopping all over the road when there was no apparent reason for

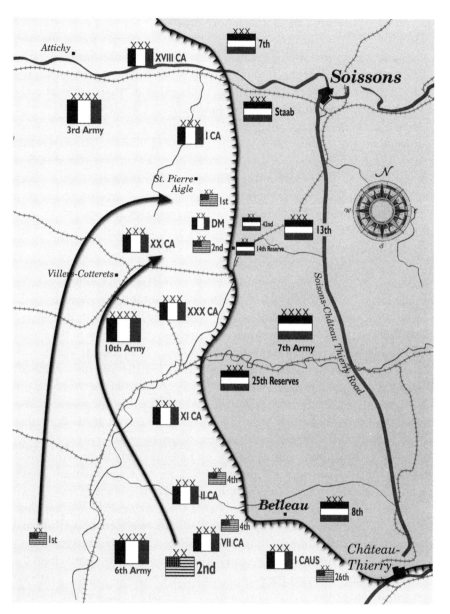

Map 12. Road to Soissons

it." The drivers placed the bottles under their seats between drinks, so the Marines decided to take action—the goal being self-preservation, along with other, less wholesome motives. The bottles found their way into the backs of the camions without the drivers' knowledge and were passed among the Marines, who enjoyed the libation but lamented that "there was not quite enough to go around the twenty four huskies with a single thirst."[17]

Before long, the drivers noticed that their precious wine was missing, resulting in an immediate tirade against the offending Marines. The Americans responded in kind and showed no remorse, given all the potholes they had endured. The absurd nature of the situation soon became apparent to both sides, causing the American Marines and Vietnamese drivers to burst into laughter, which led to the sharing of hidden cigarettes and sea stories. The monotony of the road soon returned, however, and the hours and miles blended into one another, seemingly without end.

After the infantry and machine gunners departed, Harbord saw little need to remain behind. With all the staff dispatched to monitor the movement north, Harbord left the Marne and traveled in his car with Chief of Staff Brown and his orderly to the new headquarters at Carrefour de Nemours in the Forest of Retz. Harbord then reported to General Pierre E. Berdoulat, commanding the French XX Corps, who welcomed him cordially into his command. Berdoulat was a tested veteran of war, having enlisted in the French army as a common soldier in 1879. He advanced in rank to corps command after graduating from the French Military College at St. Cyr in 1882. Berdoulat served with French colonial units and participated in several expeditions, including Senegal, Madagascar, Sudan, and Vietnam. He became the director of colonial troops at the Ministry of War in 1912 and then saw heavy combat in the early years of the war, including at the Somme.[18]

The American general later remembered the meeting as being "pleasant but casual," and before any business was discussed, the Frenchman "insisted that we have a bite of dinner." As the meal progressed, Harbord learned of his orders for the first time. The 2nd Division must be ready to attack on the morning of July 19, giving the division only thirty hours to prepare. Harbord was astounded by the orders. He realized that he had no idea where his division was located at that moment; nor did he have the ability to communicate with his command. The enormity of the task ahead was overwhelming, and Harbord's circle of command currently consisted of Brown and an orderly. Despite the quality of the food that night, the Americans quickly lost their appetite.[19]

The lack of information about his division presented the first obstacle for Harbord to surmount. "I knew nothing, except by rumor, of where they were to go, and nothing of where they would be at a given moment," he later recalled, "and was powerless to hurry or change conditions." The French corps commander and his staff essentially dictated the movement of the American division, and to prevent German knowledge of the attack, they refused to provide any further information—not even to the commander of the 2nd Division. "A division of twenty-eight thousand men, the size of a European army corps, had been completely removed from the control of its responsible commander, and deflected by marching or truck through France," Harbord wrote, "to [a] destination unknown to any of the authorities responsible for its supply, its safety, or its efficiency in the coming attack."[20] When Harbord questioned Berdoulat and his staff about the current location of his units, the French officers professed to have no knowledge of where the 2nd Division would halt for the evening or even where Harbord could send orders to reestablish communication with his division staff and brigade commanders.

While Harbord fumed, the 4th Brigade Marines suffered in the backs of their camions as the hours on the road passed at an agonizingly slow pace. With no springs to cushion the solid rubber wheels, the trucks seemed to strike every pothole. The Marines received so-called iron rations, consisting of hardtack and canned mutton. Small fires warmed the gelatinous breakfast, and cups of coffee warmed over the fires made the "monkey meat" somewhat more palatable. No real hot food was available because the field kitchens were located far to the rear, moving north from the Marne River.[21]

As dawn broke on July 17, Harbord and Brown wasted no time. Although the initial hurdle of composing the orders was complete, there was no one to issue them to, so Harbord and Brown departed in their automobile in search of every major unit in the division. They would deliver the attack orders and maps of the battlefield in person. The first good news came with the knowledge that Brigadier General Bowley's wandering artillery brigade was already emplaced in the Forest of Retz, having arrived on the evening of July 15. Bowley reported his position near Harbord's headquarters at Carrefour de Nemours, deep in the Forest of Retz between Villers Cotterets and Vivieres, but he had yet to examine the front where the attack would take place. The American artillery would be supported by the reserve French 69th Infantry Division's artillery regiment. Harbord was reassured by the knowledge that his men would have their own artillery support, but with the battle only hours away, he realized that, except for the artillery, "the whereabouts of not a single man was known to me."[22]

As the scattered Marine units arrived in the area, order began to emerge from chaos. French guides directed the seemingly endless streams of trucks to encampment sites concentrated around the newly established 4th Brigade headquarters. Both of the bleary-eyed regimental commanders soon reported to Major General Harbord, expecting to receive clarity after a night of little sleep and much uncertainty—the price of operational security. Under the early-morning light, Feland and Lee learned of the attack scheduled for the following morning at 4:45, now less than twenty-four hours away. Harbord then provided both commanders with their newly composed orders. He assigned Feland's 5th Marines the task of leading the assault, with Turrill's battalion entering the front line south of the Paris–Soissons road, crossing the forest, and then tying into the 23rd Infantry Regiment of the 2nd Division's 3rd Brigade. Major Ralph S. Keyser's 2nd Battalion, on the opposite side of the road, extended to the French 1st Moroccan Division. Major Shearer's 3rd Battalion formed the regimental reserve, positioned behind Turrill. Lee's 6th Marines, along with the army's 2nd Engineer Battalion, would serve as the division reserve, stationed in the Forest of Retz behind the 2nd Division's front; each battalion was posted on a road leading to the front.[23]

Major Keyser had joined the Marine Corps in 1905 and hailed from Virginia. He first saw sea duty on the battleship USS *Louisiana* in the Great White Fleet, standing for a promotion to first lieutenant. However, a physical examination in 1908 found Keyser unfit owing to a non-duty-related injury; this caused him to lose his seniority, and he was passed by twenty-seven other officers before being medically cleared in November. After he was promoted, Keyser performed expeditionary duty in the Philippines, Cuba, and Nicaragua. Keyser then served as an attaché at the American embassy in Tokyo for two years, beginning in 1912. However, he was most renowned in the Marine Corps for his marksmanship. He was a member, coach, and captain of the Marine Corps rifle team in 1911 and 1915.[24]

Like the Marines, the army's 3rd Brigade struggled to reconstitute its units after a long night without sleep on the camions. The 3rd Brigade was known informally as the Syracuse Brigade because its 9th and 23rd Infantry Regiments had been moved to the old state fairgrounds in Syracuse, New York, in 1917 to train and recruit up to war strength. Many local youths now belonged to both regiments, along with many Italian immigrants who worked in the mills of New England. Now far from upstate New York, the soldiers breakfasted on their iron rations while Brigadier General Ely and his regimental commanders drove off in their cars to find bivouac locations within the vast Forest of Retz, three to five miles away.[25]

At 4:00 p.m. Colonel Malone halted his 23rd Infantry inside the Forest of Retz. Second Lieutenant Marvin H. Taylor described it as a "dense forest of huge trees, whose branches intertwined formed an impenetrable canopy overhead." A native of Louisville, Kentucky, Taylor had entered the National Guard at age seventeen, was commissioned a second lieutenant in 1917, and was on his way to France in August of that year. Safe from observation by German aircraft, the regiment was ordered to "get all the rest and sleep possible, but it was not possible to sleep or even rest," Taylor noted. "Everyone sensed the impending movement and they were accordingly excited, unconsciously perhaps, but nevertheless, repose was futile. The endless stream of traffic along the road alone was enough to attract their attention to the exclusion of all else."[26] When Malone returned to his 23rd Infantry command post, orders arrived for his regiment to attack the following morning at 4:00 on the other side of the Forest of Retz. Colonel LaRoy S. Upton, commanding the nearby 9th Infantry, received the same orders. Both went immediately to Harbord's headquarters to learn more about the seemingly implausible directive.

In the midst of the confusion, Colonel Neville returned from a nine-day hospital stay. His appearance forced a complete reshuffling of the 4th Brigade's senior commanders. As a full colonel, Neville was now the ranking officer and assumed command of the brigade, allowing Lieutenant Colonel Feland to retain command of the 5th Marines and sending Lieutenant Colonel Lee back to command the 6th Marines, relieving Major Holcomb. Lieutenant Colonel Hiram I. Bearss remained the 6th Marines' executive officer, which allowed Holcomb to return to the 2nd Battalion. The major was pleased to be leading his old battalion into combat again.[27]

Such a shuffling of senior leadership would normally be difficult at best, but the changes in command were implemented effortlessly by the senior Marine officers. All were veterans of the month-long battle in Belleau Wood and had served together before the war, establishing implicit confidence in one another's abilities. The experienced regimental and battalion officers would now be tested by the difficult assignment facing the 4th Marine Brigade. Only hours remained before the attack the next morning. Simply locating the brigade's scattered units proved to be a challenge.

The responsibility of defending the targeted portion of the Marne salient belonged to the German 9th Army, which had taken over the sector at 8:00 a.m. on July 5. By July 10, the 9th Army was fully operational, with locked-in artillery support from the 18th Army on the right and the 7th Army on the left. The German 9th Army was divided into three corps, each named for its commander: Corps Francois, composed of the German 223rd, 211th, and 105th Divisions, defended the area at the northern end of the army line; Corps Staabs, with the 53rd Reserve, 241st, and 6th Divisions, defended the center; and Corps Watter, with the 42nd, 14th Reserve, and 115th Divisions, held the area just south of Soissons, directly in the path of the American 2nd Division. The 9th Army also held the Corps of Army Reserves with the 14th, 34th, and 47th Divisions, ready to support any threatened area of the front.[28]

News of problems on the western side of the Marne salient reached 9th Army headquarters, causing the chief of staff to inspect the 14th Reserve Division on July 17. Full reports of the deficiencies were made and discussed, including that the average strength in the companies was forty men and three light machine guns. The chief of staff acknowledged the difficulties facing Lieutenant General Robert Loeb but could do little to solve the problems. He assured the 14th Reserve Division commander that new units would replace his men shortly.[29]

The principal German defenders facing the 2nd Division were men from the veteran 14th Reserve Division, recruited primarily from Westphalia. American intelligence ranked the 14th Reserve Division as one of the finest German divisions and a first-class fighting unit. According to the intelligence summary, most of the men assigned to the division were young, between twenty and thirty years of age. The intelligence summary concluded, "It appears capable of serious effort."[30]

North of Vierzy, the experienced German 42nd Division extended the line near Soissons. Mobilized in Lorraine, which had been seized by Germany in 1870, many of the men were of French heritage. The division had suffered heavy losses in 1914, with one regiment reduced to fewer than 1,600 soldiers. Divided loyalties prompted the division's transfer to the Somme to engage British rather than French forces. The heavy fighting was costly. By late December, the 131st Regiment alone had lost more than 3,300 soldiers since the beginning of the war. Although acknowledging the division's "good composition, with a large percentage of men of the younger classes," Allied intelligence now rated the unit as third rate and effective only on defense.[31]

Corps Watter found it extremely difficult to gain intelligence about the French units it opposed. Its entire line of defense was in or facing the sprawling Forest of Retz, which blinded both ground and aerial observation. Gathering information from prisoners and monitoring French artillery activity were the only reliable methods of divining enemy intentions. The audio detectors indicated an increase in artillery after July 10, but it was still far behind the lines in a defensive posture. A better method would have been to withdraw a short distance for better fields of fire, but the Crown Prince's orders were to resume the attack at the end of July, so the forward positions were maintained. The best defensive solution for Corps Watter was to establish resistance based on extreme depth.

Across the lines, Neville's attack orders began to circulate through the 4th Marine Brigade. Second Lieutenant James H. Legendre, adjutant of the 2nd Battalion, 5th Marines, moved through each of the battalion's four companies camped near the woods, briefing them on the coming attack. He was

5th Marine Regiment
Soissons July 1918
Lt. Col. Logan Feland

Casualties during the battle drastically altered the battalion command structure.

Headquarters Company
Capt. Alphonse DeCarre

Supply Company
Maj. Bennett Puryear, Jr.

8th Machine Gun Company
Capt. John H. Fay

1st Battalion
Maj. Julius S. Turrill

17th Company (A)
Capt. Leroy P. Hunt

49th Company (B)
1st Lt. Walter T. H. Galliford

66th Company (C)
Capt. William L. Crabbe

67th Company (D)
Capt. Frank Whitehead

2nd Battalion
Maj. Ralph S. Keyser

18th Company (E)
Capt. Lester S. Wass

43rd Company (F)
Capt. Joseph D. Murray

51st Company (G)
Capt. William O. Corbin

55th Company (H)
1st Lt. Elliott D. Cooke

3rd Battalion
Maj. Maurice E. Shearer

16th Company (I)
Capt. Robert Yowell

20th Company (K)
Capt. Richard N. Platt

45th Company (L)
Capt. Thomas Quigley

47th Company (M)
Capt. Gaines Moseley

Chart 4. 5th Marine Regiment, Soissons

armed with his own notes and part of the French attack directive. Each company commander called his officers together to hear Legendre's briefing, not knowing that the attack was less than twenty-four hours away. "One does not know the precise day of the attack," Legendre ominously translated from the French orders. The officers of Captain Lester S. Wass's 18th Company seemed to be more impressed with the young lieutenant's grasp of the French language than with the orders, opining that he "spoke French like a native—sort of with his tonsils."[32]

An education at Princeton and Tulane had done nothing to cut Legendre's

Cajun accent, acquired in his hometown of New Orleans, Louisiana. He used it eloquently in translating the French document, much to the amusement of the gathered officers. His time at Tulane included managing the freshman track team and singing bass in the Glee Club; he was a member of the English Dramatic Association at Princeton. Legendre would receive the Distinguished Service Cross for rescuing two wounded Marines at Belleau Wood.[33]

Captain Wass lay on the ground, using his helmet as a pillow, as he listened to the Cajun. As Legendre briefed the group on the use of flares to signal movements on the battlefield, Wass interrupted the lieutenant. "We don't have caterpillars, green or any other color," he avowed, "and as a matter of fact, we don't even have Very lights." Legendre paused to scratch his head while he considered the question and then broke into a sheepish grin. "Well, we probably won't have any airplanes either," he countered, "so what's the difference."[34]

Of the three 2nd Division regiments designated to lead the attack in less than twelve hours, only the 9th Infantry began to march west immediately. Few if any men of the combat units had slept the previous night during their camion ride, and given the already late hour, they were facing a grueling night march if they expected to arrive in position before the scheduled time of the attack. The men were also hungry; even the tins of monkey meat and hardtack were long gone. Rations were just beginning to arrive, but the men had no time for a meal before their departure.

Instead of allowing his men to rest, Upton hastily but carefully arranged piles of instructions and maps to be distributed to them, down to the company level. He then drove to his regiment, which was already positioned in the forest, and "explained what we were going to do, and started them on their eight mile march through the woods."[35] First Lieutenant Ladislav T. Janda of Company M, 9th Infantry, recalled Upton's terse words: "Men, I know you and your men are tired but we've got a chance to break the line here, turn the German flank and make him retire. *We are going to do it.*"[36] The weary soldiers pulled on their packs and began to march.

First, the 9th Infantry moved to catch up with Malone's 23rd Infantry, camped one hour ahead on the road east. As the soldiers formed into their column of march, they wistfully observed the field kitchens preparing a dinner that they would never eat. Prompted by the arrival of Upton's men, Colonel Malone dispatched his three battalions into the forest behind the 9th Infantry, and the hungry soldiers left the smell of hot food behind them.[37] "It was black as pitch and raining, and there were two lines of vehicles of all sorts moving in the same direction in the road," recalled Lieutenant Taylor, "so the infantry was divided and started its march on either side of

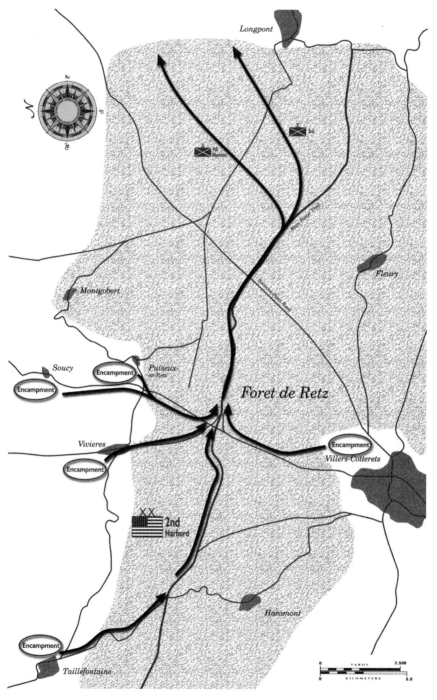

Map 13. Marines move to their jumping-off positions

the road. . . . We were either running, or standing, or slipping down in the mud—never marching."[38]

Darkness soon fell, deepening the gloom of the Forest of Retz. Observing the 9th and 23rd Infantry Regiments shift into motion, the 4th Brigade broke camp to follow the soldiers. Lieutenant Colonel Feland received the initial order to proceed with the 5th Marines to their attack positions for the morning assault, and he passed the order along to his battalion commanders at 6:00 p.m. They called their company commanders together to issue the order.

Major Keyser's 2nd Battalion received the order just three hours after Legendre's briefing. The shock rolled over the battalion like a tidal wave. "It hit us hard and cold, as though our belt buckles had turned to ice," remembered Elliot Cooke, commanding the 55th Company. "A nervous weakness took all of the spring out of my legs" and, having experienced "the smell of human dead in the Bois de Belleau, I had trouble in keeping my insides from crawling up my throat."[39] At 8:30 p.m. Keyser's battalion began to march deeper into the forest, following the main road east. Light disappeared in the tree canopy overhead, leaving the Marines feeling isolated from the rest of the world. Rain soon added to their misery, and with no moonlight filtering through the trees, darkness cloaked the Marine columns, concealing all the pitfalls in the road ahead.

Major Shearer's battalion was the last in line and farthest from the front, departing from camp at 9:00 p.m. The column stalled as Keyser's battalion moved into the road ahead of Shearer's men to catch up with Major Turrill's 1st Battalion at 5th Regiment headquarters. The limitations of the small, single-lane road were felt immediately. Progress proved very slow in the forest gloom.

Shearer's military service began during the Spanish-American War. He left high school to serve as a private with an Indiana artillery battery during the occupation of Puerto Rico. In 1901 he enlisted in the Marine Corps as a private, rising quickly in rank to second lieutenant in 1905. Shearer's career was varied; it included expeditionary duty in the Philippines, command of the Marine detachment on Midway Island in 1906 and of the Marine detachment on the USS *Arizona* in 1916, and numerous assignments to Marine Barracks on both coasts of the United States. In April 1917 he was transferred from Marine Corps headquarters to the recruitment depot at the Norfolk Navy Yard, followed by duty as an instructor at the fledgling Marine Corps Barracks in Quantico, Virginia. One day after his promotion to major, Shearer departed for France as commander of the 73rd Machine Gun Company, 6th Marines. In May 1918 he assumed command of the 1st Battalion, 6th Marines, and was considered one of the most competent battalion commanders in the brigade. Shearer received the honor of commanding the Marine detachment at the July 4, 1918, parade in Paris.[40]

Far from Paris, a mass of vehicles clogged the main road in the forest, forcing the Marines to one side. Large cannon moved forward slowly, towed by powerful tracked vehicles; teams of six or eight roan, black, and sorrel horses struggled with the French 75mm and 155mm artillery pieces. Mule-drawn field kitchens, caissons, and water wagons crept forward, interspersed with staff cars. Supply trucks filled the road, but much of the traffic consisted of the "never ending trains of heavy ammunition trucks, loaded, rumbling, and grinding, ever holding the center of the road." The vehicles that elicited the most curiosity among the Americans were the French tanks covered with "their weird camouflage in colors of green, red and brown." The noise of the vehicles announced their presence long before their arrival; they passed by with "rattle and crunch and groan and snort along, and no one argues with them in the matter of their right of way."[41]

Turrill's men took the road east and immediately ran into the mass of French trucks, wagons, tanks, and soldiers heading to their positions for the morning assault, making the road almost impassable. The traffic inched forward, forcing the Americans to find a way around it. "The road was packed with wheel traffic of all sorts and it was necessary to march in single file in the ditch on the right side of wood," Turrill later reported. "Even the ditch was blocked at various points by wagons or camions, which had slipped off the road. Rain with consequent slippery clay mud added difficulties."[42]

First Lieutenant Blake led his platoon of the 17th Company through the darkness, drenched by rain that was whipped by the wind into torrents of misery. The young lieutenant was a 1917 graduate of the University of California, where he had been one of the editors of the student newspaper the *Daily Californian* and a member of Phrontisterion, the history honor society. The promising historian had chosen the Marine Corps because, he wrote, "I didn't particularly like the thought of going in the Army, and the Marines seemed more interesting."[43] The current march proved to be one of the more "interesting" events of his long Marine Corps career. "I bumped my head into the rear of more horses than I thought existed," Blake recalled, "because you couldn't see your hand in front of your face."[44]

The Marines splashed forward in the ditch, only to find the way ahead blocked by an overturned truck or artillery caisson that had slipped off the road. The Marines snaked their way across the slowly moving lines of traffic into the ditch on the other side of the road—a crossing maneuver that had to be repeated whenever they encountered a similar blockage. All night the Marines plodded toward the front, aware that the minutes lost in the darkness meant that they might be unable to reach their attack positions in time for the barrage at 4:35 a.m.

Shearer's 3rd Battalion followed behind Keyser's, initially moving smoothly in a single file, surrounded on all sides and above by the limbs of the great trees of the forest. The first crisis occurred only an hour and a half into the march. A Marine in the last two squads of Captain Corbin's 51st Company, 2nd Battalion, paused to adjust his leggings, halting the entire column behind him. When the march resumed, the Marines hurried to catch up with the rest of the battalion, but they reached an intersection with no other Marines in sight and no guide left behind to lead them in the right direction. The two squads of the 51st Company came to a halt, not wanting to take a wrong turn. All the following columns of the battalion halted as well, stalling the march until the proper road could be ascertained.

The Marines were immediately struck by the formidable forest around them, filled with all the machines of war and the technology that supports them. "Majestic trees tower to a height of ninety feet above the moss covered floor of the forest," Private Fitch L. McCord of the 82nd Company wrote. "Small arms ammunition is piled along the road and under trees. There are rows upon rows of every caliber of shell, dumps of aerial bombs, hand grenades, and pyrotechnics."[45] Although raised in Paris, Illinois, McCord worked as a clerk in the American Car Company in St. Louis. He had attended the University of Illinois and served two years in the Illinois National Guard before enlisting in the Marine Corps.

The extent of the preparation for this major offensive impressed the Marines who had previously spent most of their time on the front line at Belleau Wood. They were, however, more interested in the French infantry camped among the trees. The French soldiers were equally curious about the Americans. Private McCord remembered the poilus "appraising us, smiling approvingly through wiry black beards and moustaches, as we plod along on the right side of the road."[46]

As the Marines trudged into the forest, the lead elements of Upton's 9th Infantry reached their attack positions at 9:00 p.m., only to find them ominously littered with dismembered horses and mules that had been torn to pieces by German shells. Upton had received no instructions from the French during the march, except for the location of guides to allow a smooth transition and the relief of French forces already in line, which proved to be incorrect. Upton gathered his officers and gave them their orders for the morning attack, only seven hours away. Each battalion then moved into its assault position, with the lead battalion ordered to relieve the French infantry ahead, clearing the zone of attack.

The American artillery supporting the soldiers and Marines was already positioned on a ridge just behind the town of Montgobert, having avoided the crowded road through the forest by leaving early. The problem was getting the reserve ammunition wagons onto the ridge, which was packed with artillery pieces in every open space. "On this crest the 75 mm. guns were practically hub to hub in one rank," First Lieutenant Pell W. Foster Jr. of Battery B, 12th Field Artillery, recalled, "with a line of 155 mm. immediately behind them."[47]

Of all the factors that combined to make the Marines' march one of absolute wretchedness, the worst was the rainfall, which soaked the packs and gear of every man, making them heavier by the minute. A few of the Marines fell by the wayside, unable to continue. The lack of food and sleep, combined with the rain and mud, began to sap the strength of the soldiers and Marines trudging through the forest.

Conditions worsened into the night as the column marched through the forest roads. "Each man was required to hold onto the belt of the man in front," recalled Cooke. "It gave the column a peculiar lockstep cadence, like prisoners marching to their cells. But we were headed for worse than that, and the going was awful tough."[48] There was no thought of a halt, as the Marines knew they must be in position by dawn to make their attack. Private Alfred H. Randall of the 18th Company remembered the march years later as a "heartbreaker, not a hike but a mad-house."[49] Those who lost their grip on the Marine in front of them soon reconnected with the column when the pick, shovel, or rifle they carried connected with the face of the man behind.

Sometimes, the Marines stood in the muddy ditch for long periods, waiting to overcome some obstacle in the darkness. The sounds of continual cursing rang out. At one point, Private Richmond of the 43rd Company called to his sergeant, saying he could go no further. He wrote after the war, "Not since I had been with the company, had we anything to compare with what we endured that night."[50] Like Richmond, Private Lewis Tintera, far from his home in North Dakota, was a recent replacement in the 43rd Company. The two Marines formed a friendship with Private Charles L. Fritz from Lancaster, Pennsylvania, an original member of the company. The three companions halted by the road to rest, intending to rejoin the company before the assault rumored to be taking place the following day. Tintera, formerly a fireman on the Pacific Railroad, fell asleep immediately with his feet in the ditch and his head squarely in the muddy road, risking serious injury from the machine gun carts passing by. Richmond and Fritz pulled Tintera to safety and then quickly fell asleep themselves. The seemingly endless column continued to pass through the mud without pause.

Soissons Tour

Stop 15. Oise Marne Cemetery: Cimetière Américain,
49°12'02.1"N 3°32'57.7"E

Leave the town of Belleau on the D 1390 and travel 5.1 kilometers to Epaux Bezu. Then take the D 87 (Place de l'Eglise, then Allee d'Amour) for 3.5 meters to the D 1. This road approximates the strategic 1918 road from Château-Thierry to Soissons. Turn left, and at 6.3 meters, exit at Rocourt-St. Martin (Rue de la Hottée du Diable). Follow the D 310 for 11.1 kilometers to Fere-en-Tardenois. Turn left on the D 967 into town, and after 350 meters, turn right on the D 2, which, after 2.7 kilometers, takes you directly to the cemetery.

The Oise Marne cemetery is your first stop in the Soissons battlefield tour. American casualties from the Soissons battle are buried here, as well as those from other battles in the summer of 1918. Viewing the 6,012 grave sites on the 36.5 acres of the cemetery will give you a sense of the significance of the July and August battles and the World War I generation's sacrifice, as well as the importance of preserving those values. The walls of the chapel memorialize the 241 missing casualties and hold the full-sized carved maps of the Oise Marne battlefields. Seek out the graves of the Marines who are mentioned in the narrative of this book.

The cemetery is open to the public daily from 9:00 a.m. to 5:00 p.m., except for December 25 and January 1. Enter the visitors' building to sign in and look at the World War I display. A staff member of the American Battle Monuments Commission is always on hand to answer questions. It is a good idea to consult the cemetery's website before visiting: www.abmc .gov/cemeteries-memorials/europe/oise-aisne-american-cemetery.

Stop 16. Courcy, 49°15'08.1"N 3°12'38.2"E

This route approximates the path of the 4th Marine Brigade and gives you an idea of what the Forest of Retz looked like in 1918.

Return 1.7 meters on the D 2 to Fere-en-Tardenois. There are several roundabouts in town, but remain on the D 2, indicated by signs for Soissons/ Villers Cotterets. You will cross the D 1 just after Grand-Rozy. Continue on the D 2 for 16.8 kilometers to St. Remy-Blancy.

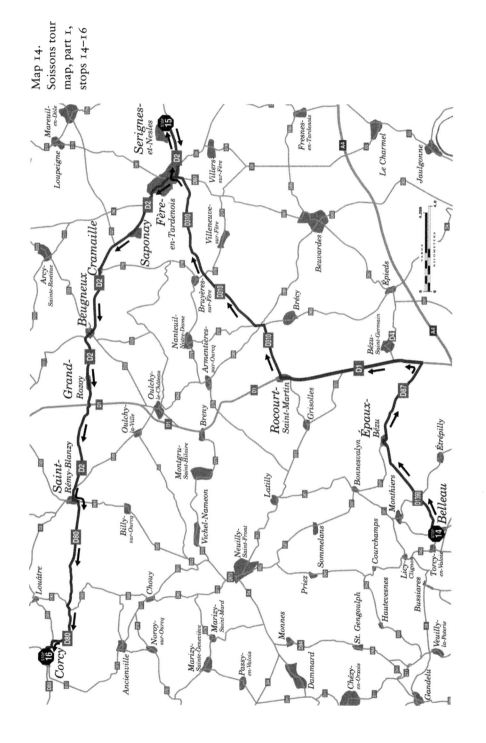

Map 14.
Soissons tour
map, part 1,
stops 14–16

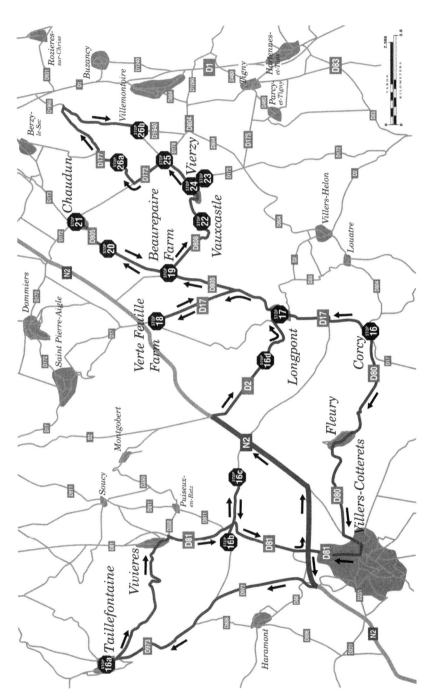

Map 15. Soissons tour map, part 2, stops 16–26

Pick up the D 80 to Courcy, 5.2 kilometers ahead.

Courcy is the dividing point of the Soissons staff ride. You have two options:

1. If you choose to go directly to the Soissons battlefield, proceed to Stop 17.
2. To take the optional tour, continue with Stops 16A–E. You will rejoin the staff ride at Longpont.

Stop 16A. *Taillefontaine, 49°18'46.7"N 3°02'41.0"E*

You are now entering the Forest of Retz, providing a good perspective of what the Marines encountered.

Continue for 19.6 kilometers on the D 80 to Villers Cotterets, and turn left on the D 231.

Turn right on the D 81 (Rue Lavoisier). In 2.9 kilometers, take the exit west on the N 2. (Go over the N 2 and then take the ramp on the highway.)

Proceed to the first exit for the D 973. Take the exit to Villers Cotterets, and then take the first exit at the roundabout to the D 973. Proceed 6.5 kilometers north to Taillefontaine.

You are now in the center of the 2nd Division's area on the morning of July 18, 1918. The French camions off-loaded soldiers and Marines after their midnight journey from Belleau Wood–Château-Thierry. After traveling 3.2 kilometers, you will be on the main east-west road taken by the 2nd Division; the Marines moved down the road toward you and then proceeded to your right. You will get a good feel for the density of the forest and the misery of the march on the night of July 18–19, 1918. You will pass Major General Harbord's 2nd Division headquarters a short distance to your right.

Warning: Do not detour down any of the nonpaved roads, as they often turn into dirt dead ends.

Continue on the D 273 to Taillefontaine.

Proceed on the D 973 (Rue de Compiegne) to the town, which is on your left. There is an intersection directly ahead, with a small memorial in the center where the roads converge. Park here.

There is a monument for American soldiers and airmen killed in the crash of a C-46 on May 23, 1945. This memorial, which few Americans visit, represents the French people's appreciation for the American sacrifice in both world wars. The town's monument to its own sacrifice is also in the park. The number of soldiers listed on this monument is a testament to the great losses suffered by many villages such as this one.

You can also view the Villemontaire from here and walk through the streets of this medieval town. The forest looms over the village, where most of the recently arrived Marines took shelter in 1918.

After a grueling day's travel, the camions bearing the 6th Machine Gun Battalion reached the area about one mile south of Taillefontaine at 3:00 p.m. The thankful men left the camions and moved into the Bois de la Taillefontaine, where they bivouacked for the night, concealed from German observation aircraft. They were dropped here without any awareness of what their next move would be.

Major General Bullard arrived here on July 15 and established his III Corps headquarters near that of General Mangin. Both his American 1st and 2nd Divisions were assigned to French tactical control, making him a general without a command. Harbord reported to Bullard here at around midnight on July 18–19, 1918, following his initial meeting with General Berdoulat, his immediate French commander. Harbord then attempted to make his way to his own headquarters, but Bullard stopped the exhausted general. "You may never find the spot," Bullard wisely noted, "and if you do, it is likely to be only a spot, not a headquarters. Stop here [at Bullard's headquarters] and give your orders."[1]

General Harbord and Chief of Staff Brown worked all night to compose the 2nd Division's attack order, using the III Corps' stenographers and mimeograph machine. Harbord and Brown departed after dawn in their staff car over the same road you just traveled, anxious to find the units of the division and distribute the freshly copied attack orders.

Stop 16B. Grenadier Guards, 49°16'57.8"N 3°06'53.2"E

Retrace your route back up the D 973, but bear left on Le Fond d'Essert for 4.9 kilometers to Viviers, where the road's name changes to Rue des Leups and then to La Croix d'Yseux. Turn right on the D 81.

After traveling 1.9 kilometers, turn left on Les Crapaudieres and park on the turnout. If you pass the road, you can easily proceed on the D 81, turn around, and come back to Les Crapaudieres.

The monument across the intersection commemorates British Sublieutenant George-Edward Cecil of the 2nd Battalion Grenadier Guards, who died in a bayonet charge during the 1914 battle. The remains of ninety-eight Grenadier Guards killed in the same engagement rest in a nearby cemetery on the D 81 on the far side of the ridge.

Warning: Parking is difficult in this area. Exercise caution when visiting the cemetery and monuments.

Stop 16C. *Lieutenant Henri de Chasseval,*
49°16′49.3″N 3°08′23.7″E

Continue on Les Crapaudieres for 1.9 kilometers. You will see a monument for Lieutenant Henri de Chasseval, a Frenchman killed by shell fire in the 1918 battle. The monument is inscribed: "Here is fallen for France, on June 12, 1918, Lieutenant Henri de Chasseval, of the 11th Dragoons, at the age of 25 years old."

Stop 16D. *General Mangin's Headquarters,*
49°16′51.4″N 3°08′33.8″E

Continue on the road for 210 meters and park in the parking area on your left. You are now traveling on one of the main east-west roads leading to the battlefield.

Here you will find the command post of General Mangin, where he directed the Battle of Soissons. There is a modern observation tower and a monument to the general, as well as several interpretive panels with photographs and maps to orient you to the battlefield, including some English-language text.

Stop 16E. *Captain Joost van Vollenhoven,*
49°16′33.1″N 3°11′46.9″E

Retrace your route and turn left on the D 81. In 2.3 kilometers, you will reach the N 2. Turn left on the ramp to Soissons. In 5.2 kilometers, use the roundabout to take the first exit onto the D 2. In 2.3 kilometers, stop at a monument to Captain Joost van Vollenhoven, a Dutch-born officer in the Régiment d'infanterie-chars de marine. Distinguished by his work in Indochina and French West and Equatorial Africa, he commanded a company in the attack on Parcy et Tigny on July 19, 1918, on the right flank of the 6th Marines. Vollenhoven received a head wound during the assault and died the following morning. The tribute on his tomb reads: "An officer of ancient valor and virtue, the incarnation of the most admirable and solid military qualities, mortally wounded just as he was electrifying his troops by his example, taking a stubbornly defended enemy position." The monument was damaged by the Germans during World War II but was restored in 1954.

Continue on the D 2. After 2.1 kilometers, turn left on the D 17. You will reach Longpont in 130 meters. Turn left on the Rue Saint-Louis. You will now rejoin the main portion of the tour.

Stop 17. Longpont, 49°16'22.8"N 3°13'12.8"E

Proceed north on the D 17 for 2.7 kilometers to Longpont. Turn left onto Rue de la Glaciere/D 2. In 120 meters, turn right on Rue St. Louis/D 17. In 91 meters, drive through the medieval gate and park in the town square. You will see the remains of a Cistercian abbey, founded in 1131. The German 28th Division captured the town on May 28, 1918, but a French counterattack retook Longpont two days later. On June 3 the Germans recaptured the town, only to be driven back again by French forces on July 13. Both the abbey and the town were severely damaged during the fighting. On July 18 this area was the jumping-off point for the French 38th Division on the right flank of the American 2nd Division, 1.6 kilometers north at your next stop.

11

July 18, 1918—Daybreak
"Revenge, Revenge"

THE INDIVIDUAL MARINES AND SOLDIERS trudging through the forest had no goal except to reach the line of departure on time. Their progress through the shadows brought Turrill's Marines to the 2nd Division's forward ammunition dump. Each rifleman drew an additional two bandoliers of rifle ammunition, for a total of four bandoliers, each of which contained 60 rounds; they also carried the standard 100 rounds in their "red" cartridge belts, totaling at least 340 rounds. The Marines were known to carry large amounts of ammunition into combat and were jokingly referred to as "Pershing's ammunition trains" or "walking ammunition trains," but they seldom ran out of munitions once they were in combat.[1]

In the lead was Captain William L. "Bill" Crabbe's 66th Company, which was the first to reach a barbed wire entanglement blocking the road. The French had stacked large piles of stones to form a dividing line between their lines and the German trenches only yards beyond. Turrill knew he was near the front line and deployed his four companies into the forest paths branching off north of the road. The presence of massed artillery batteries in the woods signaled Turrill's movement forward, bearing to the left. Crabbe's company then intermixed with a body of Moroccans on the left, separated from the main attack and now in the Marne zone of operations. Crabbe's 66th Company arrived in its positions, and the men were able to get a few minutes of needed sleep before waking to the sound of cannon fire.[2]

Crabbe was no stranger to battle, having enlisted in the Marine Corps in December 1913, leaving behind his job as a clerk in a distillery office. Less than four months later, he was fighting in the streets of Vera Cruz, Mexico, and went ashore in Haiti the following year, serving with the Gendarmerie d'Haiti. Crabbe rose rapidly in rank to corporal and then sergeant in 1916. Commandant Barnett selected Crabbe to become an officer in 1917 owing to his bravery in battle against the Haitian insurgents. Crabbe was immediately assigned to command the Marine Detachment for the American Legation in Nicaragua. He returned to Quantico just as rapidly and was assigned to the 66th Company in June; then he was on his way to France. Crabbe took command of the company in December of the same year.[3]

The veteran Captain Crabbe deployed his company in the forest in a skirmish formation, guiding the now-arriving 17th Company commanded by Captain Leroy P. Hunt. Hunt had also directed each of his Marines to pick up two bandoliers of ammunition from an unexpected heap beside the road. First commissioned a second lieutenant in 1917 direct from the University of California–Berkeley, Hunt had been a popular student and a member of the Skull and Keys Society. While the 66th Company extended from the road north, Hunt's 17th Company followed the line deeper into the woods. Turrill then called Hunt back for additional directives and ordered First Lieutenant Blake to take the company into the attack, as ordered. "Go ahead with the company," he directed the young lieutenant, "and deploy it and take off."[4]

As the companies broke into platoons and disappeared into the forest, Turrill gathered his battalion runners around him in the road and gave them orders for the pending attack. The orders were brief and easily understood. "We are in two waves," Turrill stated. "A barrage will lay for five minutes on Heine's firing line, and then roll on to the first objective. Tell the captains to follow the barrage."[5] Four of the runners disappeared, each man assigned to deliver the orders to one of the companies; two more were assigned to advance with the assault and then return to headquarters to inform the major when the two lead companies broke out of the woods.

The rest of the battalion was close behind. Captain Whitehead held the 67th Company in reserve behind the two lead companies, following Crabbe and Hunt in the attack. As the Marines neared the roadblock, the Germans detected the movement. They launched a single exploratory shell into the road, striking, by chance, a squad of Marines. In an instant, the company emptied the road, leaving only the shattered remains of the Marines hit by shrapnel. Whitehead moved his company deeper into the woods, deployed into skirmish lines.

Like many brigade company commanders, Whitehead was a former enlisted man, joining the Marines in 1908. A stint of duty at the naval prison in Portsmouth, New Hampshire, began his career, followed by expeditionary duty in Cuba, the Philippines, the American Legation in Beijing, the Dominican Republic, and sea duty aboard the USS *Helena* on the Asiatic Station. In 1917 Whitehead was one of the crack marksmen in the Marine Corps, serving as sergeant major of the 3rd Provisional Brigade based in Santo Domingo City. He quickly became an officer and arrived in France on New Year's Eve. Whitehead initially commanded Headquarters Company, 5th Marines, and took over the 67th Company in late June. He suffered shrapnel wounds in the last days of the struggle for Belleau Wood but was now leading his company in offensive combat for the first time.[6]

Turrill's last Marine unit, Captain Hamilton's 49th Company, arrived ten minutes later. Being the last to arrive, the company had the farthest to go, with only minutes before the barrage was set to begin. First Lieutenant Walter T. H. Galliford led the company's linkup with the French 1st Moroccan Division, establishing the far left of the battalion line as well as that of the entire 2nd Division. The proud 49th Company had suffered heavy losses at Belleau Wood and went into battle at Soissons with eight officers, only one of whom had been in place when the company overran Hill 142. Galliford had come over from the 17th Company on June 19 to lead the 49th, and First Lieutenant John W. Thomason Jr. was the most veteran of the new officers, having arrived on June 8. Three of the five second lieutenants were promoted directly from the company's enlisted ranks on July 13, including First Sergeant Robert E. Connor, who had arrived as a replacement on June 30. Gunnery Sergeant Arthur E. Lyng arrived on July 12 from a replacement battalion to serve as the company's first sergeant. The other companies in the regiment faced the same kind of turnover.[7]

Hamilton's men moved deeper in the forest, passing left of the 17th Company. With every step, they broke new ground through the trees, and the Marines felt distinctly alone. Only a few French infantrymen and a small number of trenches marked the front line as the Marines prepared to attack; nor were any of the promised guides present. The Americans had no time to confer with the French soldiers holding the line. Just minutes before the attack began, Turrill finally noticed Marines from the 2nd Battalion coming into the trees on his right. As the time for the attack approached, only the 66th Company was fully in line; the 17th and 67th Companies were still moving into position, and the 49th Company had plunged deeper into the woods, yet to connect with the Moroccans to the left of the American position.

Without warning, explosions shattered the silence promptly at 4:35 a.m. The Marines were so close to the concussion that some were knocked to the ground, and many of their watches stopped, never to work again. The Marines could see the impact of the shells as they struck the beech trees and ripped up whole sections of earth and foliage, sending them into the air. The violence of the barrage even impressed the veterans of Belleau Wood. The shells were "tearing the woods to chips right in front of us. Literally tearing it into chips," remembered Private Elton E. Mackin. "Great sections of beech trees came crushing down."[8] The Allied artillery shells continued to pass overhead, signaling that the time for the attack had arrived. German shells responded in kind to the barrage, striking into the treetops above the Marines, causing some casualties. Although not confident that the other Marine battalions were in place, Turrill had no choice but to order his men forward through the trees, following the barrage. The Marines turned and attacked to the east through the forest.[9]

Turrill's lack of confidence was well justified. After a seven-and-a-half-hour, all-night march through the pouring rain, Major Keyser's 2nd Battalion noticed that all the outgoing French traffic seemed to disappear behind them, making the march much easier but also indicating the proximity of the front line. Eventually, the rain ceased, lessening the torment of the thoroughly drenched column. The first hint of dawn also lifted the morale of the battalion members, who could barely see the way ahead but could now at least anticipate the end of complete darkness. Keyser reached the crossroads where the French guides were supposed to meet him, but like Turrill's battalion, he found no guides waiting to take them to their attack positions. Brigade commander Neville personally searched the surrounding woods for them, but to no avail. Several privates also hunted for the guides but returned with the same result as their commander.

Keyser followed Turrill's path forward toward the front line, as "we had maps and knew approximately [where to go], so we pushed on to the forward ammunition dump." The road led the battalion up a steep, muddy slope; they finally reached the ammunition dump just vacated by the 1st Battalion at 4:00 a.m. However, their attack positions were still about one kilometer away. The opening artillery bombardment was scheduled for 4:35 a.m., scarcely enough time to collect the needed ammunition and reach the front.

After a brief scramble, Keyser observed an approaching French officer followed by several of his enlisted men. Keyser mistook them for the guides, but the officer proved to be Lieutenant Colonel Imbert, commander of the French 48th Regiment, who was concerned by the Americans' absence as the time for the attack drew near. At 4:15 a.m. Imbert had left his headquarters to find the missing Marines, but he did not know where the Americans were supposed to deploy. Keyser entered into "a short and excited consultation with him over the map, we got approximately [to] where . . . our companies should go, and it was there they were taken by their French guides."[10]

With no time to spare, Keyser ordered his battalion forward. The headquarters officers ripped open the ammunition boxes and passed out two bandoliers of ammunition to each Marine as they passed in a double column, never breaking stride. Keyser placed a single French guide with each company to take them to their positions so they could at least attempt to reconnoiter the terrain ahead and develop a plan of attack. Once the required ammunition was loaded, the two lead companies of Captain Wass and Captain Murray disappeared into the forest. The French guides took Murray's Marines to an incorrect position north of the road into Turrill's zone of operations, while Wass correctly followed his guide south of the road to link up with the army brigade. Until more Marines arrived, Murray extended his company to the road, trying to link up with Wass covering the battalion's entire front south of the road, with little time to spare before the attack began.

Cooke's 55th Company halted on a hill half a mile from the front at 3:30 a.m. The men dropped their blankets and other unnecessary gear and made combat packs for the coming assault. The Marines were silent from that moment on, understanding what lay ahead of them. The company passed a bedraggled French machine gun detachment heading to the rear, happy to be leaving the front. Corporal Carl McCune noted the "bearded men, muddy from the trenches. . . . They appeared tired and glad to see the Marines." However, the terrain around the Americans changed noticeably as they approached the front. McCune understood the nearness of their line of departure. "Shell holes were everywhere, and the woods were thinning out," the corporal noted. "Two bandoliers of ammunition were issued and two grenades each."[11] McCune was from Gassaway, a small town in the West Virginia mountains. He left school in the eighth grade to work on the family farm and later left coal country for work in Akron, Ohio. In 1916 he was on his way to Port Royal, South Carolina, for basic training. McCune was an early member of the 55th Company, serving at the Rio Cauto sugar plantation in Cuba when war was declared.[12]

While the two companies of Marines ahead took their turn at the ammunition depot, Captain Corbin allowed his 51st Company to rest by the side of the road. That was where Lieutenant Cooke's men, bringing up the rear, found the 51st Company. Corbin had just returned to the battalion after being wounded at Belleau Wood and had taken command of the 51st Company on July 8. Cooke approached Corbin to ascertain the situation ahead but failed to learn much from him. "I couldn't find out what the new officer thought he was doing," Cooke observed, but both lead companies had already departed, so "I knew damn well my company had to be alongside Wass and Murray when the attack started."[13] The unexpected halt by the 51st Company broke the battalion into two pieces, potentially leaving Wass and Murray without help, with the attack only minutes away.

Captain Corbin had enlisted in the Marine Corps as a private in July 1900. After gaining experience in Panama in 1908, Nicaragua in 1912, and Vera Cruz in 1914, he rose in rank to a Marine gunner in April 1917 and a second lieutenant in June, in response to the need for officers to handle the wartime expansion of the Marine Corps. Corbin became a captain in November 1917 and was assigned to the 51st Company under the tutelage of Captain Williams. However, Williams was killed at Belleau Wood on June 11, and Corbin was wounded on the same day. Corbin returned from the hospital on July 8 and was commanding the company in combat for the first time.[14]

Cooke called forward his first platoon and moved his company past Corbin to catch up with the two companies ahead on the trail. They moved down the slope, where they met a staff officer at a road intersection. He directed them onto the path leading north and left them with the admonition, "Better hurry!" Cooke ordered the lieutenant commanding the lead platoon to move his Marines forward as quickly as possible, and Cooke took off ahead of the column to locate Wass and Murray. He soon ran into Major Keyser standing in the middle of the road, surrounded by ammunition boxes, ready to issue bandoliers "on the fly." Keyser called out to Cooke, telling him to rush his men into position but first to allow each man to take a single bandolier of ammunition as they passed the ammunition dump. According to Keyser, the attack position was just down the road, and the two lead companies were just ahead of Cooke. The lieutenant asked to look at the only map that had been provided to the battalion, to make sure he deployed his company correctly, but Keyser answered that Legendre still had the map. "But unless I catch Wass or Murray, I won't know where to go," Cooke replied. "Here," Keyser responded, shoving a French poilu forward, "This man will guide you."[15]

For the first time all night, Cooke felt confident of his bearings, thanks to his new guide, and lit up a celebratory cigarette. Keyser exploded at Cooke's nonchalance, saying angrily, "Listen Cooke, don't stand here all day. You have only ten minutes to make the front line before the barrage starts." The young lieutenant instantly realized that if he did not get his men into position before the artillery began, the advantage would go to the Germans, who would be waiting for the assault. Years later, he still remembered the look on Keyser's face as he gave the orders. "He had undergone a tough night too," recalled Cooke. "His lips were drained white by the strain of responsibilities."[16]

Without hesitation, Cooke took hold of the French guide and headed down the road, accompanied by the sound of their hobnailed boots striking the cobblestones as they ran. Cooke caught up to his lead platoon in five minutes but did not break stride, passing the word to the still soaked men, who also began to run. The French guide advised the Marines to proceed with caution, as they were near the front line, but Cooke knew that the artillery would begin in less than five minutes, followed by German counterbattery fire. If the company was caught out in the open during the exchange, massive casualties would result. At the last minute, the column rounded a bend in the road, finding the way ahead blocked by a cheval-de-frise and trenches going off to the right and left into the woods. Just then, explosions erupted around them, signaling the beginning of the Allied artillery bombardment.

The surrounding land changed before their eyes. "The cheval-de-frise actually bounced," Cooke recalled. "Cobblestones rattled like teeth in a cold shower. The whole landscape seemed to jump and settle, again and again, like a carpet being beaten with a stick."[17] The French guide leaped into a ditch beside the road and ran up the trench leading north, followed by the line of Marines. They all knew that only seconds remained before the German counterbattery fire began. As he watched his men go into the trench, Cooke saw a fountain of dirt explode across the road, followed by another explosion propelling stones and debris into the air. Two great trees rose up into the air, hung suspended for a moment, and then crashed to the ground. The familiar shriek of shrapnel cut through the sky, signaling the initial blast of the German guns.

Cooke's company hurriedly followed its French guide as the poilu took the column farther to the left, moving past Captain Murray's 43rd Company. This left Wass alone again on the south side of the road. Cooke's predicament worsened as he moved farther into the woods. He was unaware that he was ahead of Turrill's battalion, which was forming in the woods behind Murray with Crabbe's 66th Company directly behind Cooke's Marines. The thick woods and underbrush concealed the Marines from one another, which, combined with the mix-up of units and the lack of direction by the French guides, almost guaranteed friendly-fire casualties.

No time remained to reconnoiter the woods or for Keyser to unscramble his four companies. Corbin's 51st Company came last, completing its resupply at 4:30 a.m. and moving 300 yards down the forest road, where it was directed to the right of Wass's 18th Company. With no time remaining, Wass would have to attack by himself, with Corbin to follow. As the moment of the attack arrived, Keyser's 2nd Battalion was still hopelessly puzzled over its positions; it was unable to form completely for the attack south of the road, much less link up with the army regiment on its right. His lead companies commanded by Wass and Murray still lay on either side of the main road.

At 4:35 a.m. the massed Allied artillery opened fire from positions in back of the road. Included in the barrage were the cannon of the army's 2nd Field Artillery Brigade, 2nd Division. The American cannoneers arrived earlier than the infantry, taking forward positions during the night of July 16–17 and then firing positions as the infantry marched through the forest. The roar of the guns was overwhelming, sending wave after wave of shells into the German lines. The two batteries of the 3rd Battalion, 17th Field Artillery, fired 1,200 rounds during the barrage.[18]

Once the barrage started, Cooke's 55th Company broke into a double-time run to get to its positions in the woods. "Panting, stumbling, well-nigh exhausted; the men ran quickly through the counter barrage thrown over by the Germans," Corporal McCune remembered. "Men fell now and then, hit by shrapnel."[19] The Marines ran past the French infantry departing for the rear and then reached a barbed wire obstruction in the road ahead. A French soldier opened a gap in the obstacle to allow the Marines to move past the shell bursts and the fallen trees. They took cover in abandoned French fox-holes that were littered with equipment too heavy to carry away. The dog-tired Marines tried to get their breath amidst the mayhem. Keyser, who had followed Corbin's Marines, recalled, "Such a terrific bombardment I have never heard . . . these shells were passing over our heads and the noise of the explosions in our ears was terrific. It had a wonderful effect on the morale, however, as there was something about it that bucked everyone up."[20]

The excitement was short-lived, however, as German counterbattery fire struck the road within five minutes of the first Allied shelling. The Germans bracketed the road, striking flawlessly in the center of the path in the rear of Corbin's company and among Keyser's headquarters detachment. Within two minutes, twenty to thirty Marines were killed or wounded before they could seek cover.

The 51st Company quickly entered the dripping trees, chased by German shells. Corbin's company completed the 2nd Battalion's movement, led by their French guide. Corbin's men filled in south of the road to link up with the 9th Infantry on their right. German artillery fire continued to smash into the trees as the Marines moved forward, announcing that the American attack had been detected. Corbin reached his position but failed to link up with the American soldiers of the 3rd Brigade. The French guide did not know the exact position of the Americans on the right, and there was no time to search for them.[21]

In five minutes, the Allied barrage moved deeper into German lines. Hunger and fatigue were replaced by adrenaline. The lack of maps and proper reconnaissance and the fragmented deployments were forgotten. Both Marine battalions plunged ahead as the first light of dawn cast rays of sunlight into the gloom of the forest. Large trees filled the forest ahead as far the eye could see, giving the Germans deadly fields of fire. The battle would now become a point-blank affair, with both sides close enough to easily pick out their enemy. Bursts of German machine gun fire echoed through the woods, driving the Marines to cover. The German defense depended on interlocking machine gun fire, which momentarily fixed the Marines' advance. However, after a month at Belleau Wood, the Marines were expert at fighting in forests and knew how to deploy in short rushes using trees as cover. One unit drew the machine gun fire while another approached from a different direction. Once they were close enough, the Marines lobbed grenades into the German gun pits or simply rushed the machine guns with bayoneted rifles.

The 17th Company on the left flank first reached the German barbed

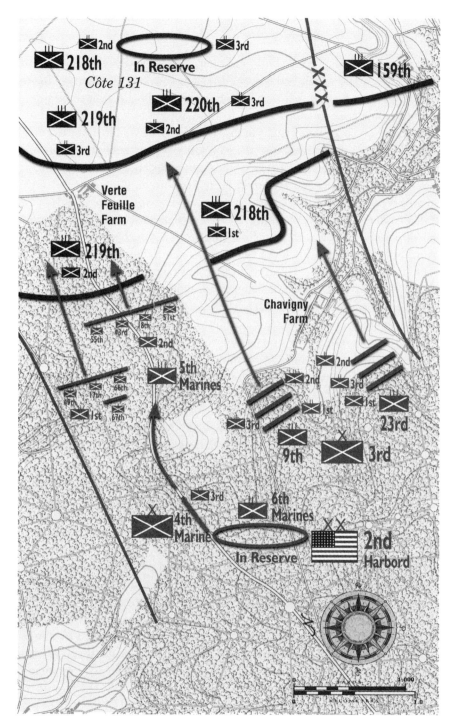

Map 16. Soissons, morning attack, July 18, 1918

wire stretched through the woods and then came under heavy machine gun fire and grenades, which brought the Marines to a stop. Lieutenant Blake noticed a gap in the wire directly in front of him and believed it to be a designated killing zone intended to lure Marines into it; then German machine guns could sweep anyone caught in the trap. As Blake watched, the opening seemed quiet, so he crawled into the gap. Once he was behind the wire entanglements, he had a perfect view of the German defenders on either side of him. "It was just like a picture you'd see in the London Illustrated Review," he observed. "The Germans were standing up heaving hand grenades and their machine guns were shooting."[22] He crawled back through the gap in the wire and returned with a machine gun section, which set up unnoticed, its field of fire directly down the German trenches. Once the American machine guns opened fire, the German position became untenable, and the survivors either surrendered or fled into the woods.

Battle in the close confines of the forest, interspersed with fallen trees and twisted strings of barbed wire, was defined by killing at short range, with the combatants only yards away from one another. The Germans were at first surprised by the attack and stunned by the unexpected barrage, but they put up a spirited defense until, one by one, their machines guns were silenced. The Marines were fearsome and, for the most part, refused to take prisoners among the surviving Germans, who raised their hands in surrender while their deadly machine guns still smoked. "Men are most dangerous in the heat of their first action, back of the barrage," recorded Private Mackin. "The letdown of the wait for zero hour, the relief of motion, and the thrill and feel of danger rob them for a time of reason, making them raving beasts. Gentle, decent fellows lose their heads and do heartless things . . . fellows who wanted to see the Fatherland again should not have stood up and pleaded so near the heated guns."[23]

An infuriating German machine gun held up the Moroccan advance on the left, causing the Marines to change direction to help their comrades. They charged forward by rushes through the trees until they could throw rifle grenades into the gun pit. Crabbe's men then rushed the machine gun but found only one young member of the crew still alive. He surrendered, but as the Marines led him back to safety, a Moroccan shot the German in the back with his pistol. Between six and eight Moroccans then crawled over to the corpse and began hacking at the body with their long knives. All the North Africans were wounded and eager to avenge their injuries. The Marines were momentarily shocked by the brutality of their allies but quickly resumed their attack deeper into the German position.[24]

Crabbe's 66th Company passed through Cooke's Marines, following the barrage as best they could. The Marines sloshed through the mud and scrambled over the fallen trees and broken limbs until they ran into the Germans' first line of defense. Crabbe's company quickly overran the first two machine guns they encountered, as the surprised gun crews desperately tried to activate their weapons. Normally, an Allied barrage would have gone on for hours or days, giving the defenders plenty of warning of an infantry attack, but the rolling barrage completely fooled the Germans.

The Marines surged ahead into the forest, emboldened by their quick success. The 66th Company soon struck the main German defense line, and staccato bursts of interlocking machine gun fire raked the woods. The short battle in the first line had alerted these German gunners, who were ready for the Marines this time. They allowed the Marines to get close before firing, intending to inflict maximum casualties. The Marines were experts in close fighting after their month-long experience at Belleau Wood, however, and individual Marines worked their way forward to take on the German machine guns at close range.

One of these veterans was Sergeant Matej Kocak, an old-time Marine who had enlisted in 1907. Born in Slovakia, he immigrated to the United States after a fierce quarrel with his parents. Kocak and his family settled in Pittsburgh and later moved to Binghamton, New York, where many Slovaks from his home village lived. In 1907 a recruiting poster's promise of a life of adventure led him to the Marine Corps, where the blue-eyed Kocak thrived. He was serving in the Dominican Republic when war was declared in 1917, but he soon returned to Quantico to become part of the 6th Marines.[25]

The initial blast of German fire took out half of Kocak's platoon, sending the survivors into the trees for cover. The Marines charged forward again, but they were pinned down by machine gun fire and could advance no further. Time was of the essence, as every moment the Germans delayed the American advance, the rolling barrage continued to forge ahead, leaving the Marines behind in the woods. They could not locate the deadly fire under the cover of the foliage, and the attack ground to a halt. Well aware of the consequences of delay, Kocak peered into the trees and detected the gray uniforms of German infantry. Knowing that these infantrymen must be providing security for the offending machine guns, Kocak ordered his men to stay under cover while he crawled forward alone to locate the German gun crews holding up their advance. As he crept forward, the German infantry protecting the machine guns poured heavy fire at the sergeant but missed with every shot. While the Germans continued to fire past him in the direction of the main Marine position, Kocak crawled around the right flank of the German trench undetected (the rain-soaked forest debris was too wet to crack under his weight), inching closer and closer to the German position until he was only a few yards away.

At that instant, the firing paused on both sides, leaving a ghostly silence across the battlefield. Still only a few feet from the German position, Kocak pulled himself over a fallen tree trunk, snapping a dry limb. The sound reverberated through the forest, alerting the Germans to his presence. One of them turned toward Kocak and locked eyes with him. With only seconds to spare, Kocak leaped up, sprinted the last few feet, and, before the German could react, bayoneted him in the throat. The man fell to the ground, coughing up blood, as Kocak swung his rifle butt and smashed the next German in the head, crushing his skull. He fought hand to hand with the remaining Germans. The struggle swung back and forth, each man grappling to kill his enemy, but after a few eerie seconds, the surviving Germans sprinted to the safety of the trees and disappeared into the forest.

Now that he was within the enemy's position, Kocak located the machine gun only thirty yards away when a brief flash of sunlight illuminated the weapon's blue metal barrel. Without pausing to think, he charged forward with his bayonet fixed, straight toward the gun pit. The German gunner saw the lone American approaching on the run and sent a hail of machine gun fire toward Kocak. A single round knocked his helmet to the ground, but somehow, the rest of the bullets missed. Kocak leaped into the gun pit, slashing and stabbing with his bayonet. He killed three Germans in the first few seconds of the fight, but the remaining six circled him, ready to exact revenge on the lone Marine. He jabbed with his bayonet, striking out in all directions. They would have taken Kocak down, no matter how fiercely he struck at them, but at that moment, the remaining Marines of his platoon leaped into the gun pit and charged the machine gun. With this reversal of fortunes, the Germans quickly surrendered and were taken to the rear by some wounded Marines.

At the same time, Sergeant Louis Cukela was also taking on the German machine guns holding up his platoon. Born on May 1, 1888, in Serbia, Cukela immigrated to the United States and settled in Minneapolis, Minnesota, where he worked as a cook. He first enlisted in the US Army in 1914 and was discharged in 1916 as a corporal. He then enlisted in the Marine Corps in January 1917, believing that the Marines would live up to their reputation as "First to Fight." He had a keen desire to fight (and kill) Germans after learning that his father had been imprisoned and shot by them. Cukela went into action murmuring, "Revenge, revenge," and he had a reputation as "a raving madman, possessed by such passions as could not be stayed."[26]

As the 66th Company's advance came to a halt against the main line of interlocking machine guns, Cukela crawled forward alone, despite the warnings of his Marines. Upon reaching the rear of the German machine gun, he charged into the gun pit with his bayoneted rifle, killing several of the crew. The remaining Germans fled into the forest. He then crept to another machine gun nest and tossed a German grenade into the pit, killing the crew and disabling the gun. Cukela was not done, however. He crawled to the next machine gun pit and threw another captured grenade into it, with the same results, but this time he also captured four Germans.[27]

Cukela's and Kocak's heroism would be rewarded later, but at the moment, the Germans still held the forest. The Marines continued their advance, pushing deeper into the woods. Still the Germans refused to yield, even though the Marines were now in the heart of the enemy's defense line. The battle devolved into a series of individual struggles between the Marines and the Germans. "It was hand to hand fighting around the trunks and bushes," one account noted, and "in the maze-like forest units became separated."[28]

Sergeant Kocak found himself alone in the woods, but he continued to move forward. He encountered a detachment of twenty-five Senegalese soldiers who had become separated from their command. Their officers had been killed, so Kocak immediately took command of the French troops, communicating only through "signs and gestures."[29] The now Allied force took two more machine guns, putting the German position out of action. Sergeants Cukela and Kocak were both awarded the Medal of Honor for their bravery in capturing the enemy position and leading the French colonial infantry.[30]

Just to the south of the two Marine companies, the two army regiments of Brigadier General Ely's 3rd Brigade struggled to get into position in time for the attack. They were out of sight of the Marines in the forest and had no time to link up with them. Colonel Upton's 9th Infantry was the only regiment in the 2nd Division to locate its attack position before dark. "We just got into place, [and] some one shoved a map into my hands," recalled First Lieutenant Janda of Company M, "but it was too dark to read it and I could not light a match." The orders that accompanied the map were equally murky. "All I knew was that we were to go 8 kilos. Whew, I thought, some distance to go thru an organized line with a bunch of men who hadn't had anything to eat for two days and also *no water.*"[31]

Unlike the Marines, the two army regiments would be attacking across open countryside, where visibility extended for several hundred yards; however, the soldiers had little time to contemplate the task ahead. By 4:30 a.m., the early light of daybreak provided their first look at the fields in front of them. The focus of the leading battalion was on the German defense line across the fields. An intense quiet permeated the battlefield, which gave the

2nd Division US Army
Soissons July 1918
Only Key Units Are Shown.

2nd Engineers Regiment

1st Battalion
Company A
Company B
Company C

2nd Battalion
Company D
Company E
Company F

4th Machine Gun Battalion
Company A
Company B

1st Field Signal Battalion

3rd Infantry Brigade

5th Machine Gun Battalion
Company A
Company B

9th Infantry Regiment

Headquarters Company

1st Battalion
Company A
Company B
Company C

2nd Battalion
Company E
Company F
Company G

3rd Battalion
Company I
Company L
Company M

23rd Infantry Regiment

Headquarters Company

1st Battalion
Company A
Company B
Company C

2nd Battalion
Company D
Company E
Company F

3rd Battalion
Company H
Company K
Company L

Chart 5. 2nd Division, Soissons,
July 1918

Americans some reassurance that the enemy was still unaware of their presence. One observer noted "the beauty of clear skies and bright sunlight. The tired men, crouching in readiness along the line from Longport into the woods near Montgobert, heard nothing but the beating of their own hearts and the songs of the sky larks."[32]

With H-hour only minutes away, Upton ordered his men into the attack alone, following the rolling barrage. "I began to think there would be no attack," he recalled, "but at 4:35 am, all broke loose for it seemed that a gun was barking every square yard of the woods behind us."[33] The quiet of the open fields burst into a continuous roar of shell fire as explosions rocked the German lines. "The song went to the blood of the men like wine," recorded an eyewitness, "and they stepped swiftly forward, erect and eager."[34] Lacking machine guns, mortars, and grenades, the soldiers attacked with only bayoneted rifles and light machine guns and the element of surprise.

The watchful German forward observers almost immediately pounded the American advance with artillery, slowing the battalion's three companies caught in the open fields. Each company changed its formation into squad columns to pick their way through the shell bursts and then charge into the German gun pits with bayoneted rifles. The men moved so quickly that they sometimes walked into their own rolling barrage. The impulsiveness of the attack worked for the soldiers, who pushed out into the open wheat fields and overwhelmed the surprised German defenders "with an impetuosity and dash that was irresistible."[35]

Major Arthur E. Bouton was at his best during the attack. The native of Trumansburg, New York, led the 9th Infantry, pressing his 2nd Battalion toward the German lines. Bouton had seen his share of conflict before the war, serving in the Philippines and on the Mexican border in 1916. After the capture of Vaux on July 1, German prisoners divulged that Bouton's battalion was known as the Red Devils, while the Marines were called the Black Snakes for Belleau Wood. Bouton wrote in a letter to his parents, "Together they admitted that we might become rather formidable adversaries after a time."[36]

A 1908 graduate of West Point, Bouton was a respected leader of the regiment. "He seemed to have but one wish, namely, to get into action, one desire for the appointed time to arrive," according to regimental chaplain Joseph A. McCafferty. "He went into battle with his coat off at the head of his battalion, a true soldier and true commander."[37] Losses mounted within the ranks of the 2nd Battalion. A shell fragment struck Bouton as he led his men against the German machine gun line, killing him instantly. The loss of their commander infuriated the battalion members, who carried the attack forward into the German machine gun pits, taking the guns along with twelve prisoners. Bouton left behind his fiancée, Blanche Holman, an instructor of English and literature at Elmira College. She eventually married in 1922 and died in 1972.

Captain Frank C. Foley led the 1st Battalion's Company A into the fray, following the rolling barrage by only fifty yards. Foley and Bouton, leading the 2nd Battalion, were close pals, a friendship that began when they were both second lieutenants at the 9th Infantry's training area in Syracuse, New York. Foley's company overran the first enemy line but was immediately struck by concentrated machine gun fire supported by "whiz bangs," the direct fire of a German artillery battery. "We could see the wheat being mowed down in front of us as if by unseen hands," the soldiers remembered. "The enemy artillery were making direct hits on our line."[38] Charging forward, the company took out the machine guns and then fought its way into the artillery battery, capturing seven guns, but at a heavy loss. At least 170 men were killed or wounded during the fight, leaving fewer than 80 men standing by the end of the day.[39]

The 3rd Battalion followed in support of Bouton's 2nd Battalion. Company I, 230 men strong, formed for the attack in a field of waist-high wheat. As the barrage opened, the company moved forward through the wheat field to the Germans' first line of defense, only 300 yards away. After a few moments of struggle, the German defenders broke for the rear, leaving behind only prisoners. The soldiers could now exact their revenge on the enemy, as each fleeting step increased the number of German dead and wounded. Captain Edward G. Ince pushed even deeper into the field but came under "grueling machine gun fire" for the next 1,000 yards of the advance. The German bullets took their toll, and with Ince out of action, Second Lieutenant Arnold M. "Mac" McInerny, the only officer left in the company, took command. The company pushed through the wheat, still soaked from the night's downpour, and succeeded in flanking several machine gun positions during the advance.[40]

Lieutenant McInerny was an All-Western tackle for the Notre Dame football team and "one of the biggest men who ever played on a Notre Dame team."[41] In the violent days of the flying wedge, "Big Mac" smashed "through opposing lines with deadly effectiveness; on the defense he broke through time and again and hurled the opposing players back for losses."[42] He was one of the first men from Notre Dame to receive an officer's commission and was one of at least ten players on the football team to enlist. McInerny was wounded in the next advance and died of his wounds the following day. Hall of Fame coach Knute Rockne, an assistant coach at Notre Dame during the 1915–1916 seasons, dedicated his 1925 book about winners to "Big Mac" McInerny.[43]

Marines on the recently captured road to Soissons, July 18, 1918. Verte Feuille Farm is in the background. (© Pierre PANSIER/ECPAD/Defense)

Following the barrage, which began "like a clap of thunder," Company M advanced from its position in a dirt roadbed just north of Chavigny Farm at the rate of 100 yards every two minutes.[44] The men noticed the German infantry sending up flares ahead, along their trenches, signaling for the German artillery to fire on the Americans. Soon, German shells began to burst in the American ranks, but they failed to slow the 9th Infantry. The first German prisoner they encountered was a sixteen-year-old who was bleeding profusely from a gunshot wound in the left ear. Efforts to calm the boy failed as he continued to shout, "Kamerad." He held his hands in the air long after his capture, evidently believing that he would be killed by the Americans.

The nearby 2nd Battalion, 9th Infantry, advanced deeper into the German rear areas until well-aimed machine gun fire raked Bouton's men from the gap on their left flank between the Marines and the 9th Infantry. Captain Corbin's 51st Company of the 2nd Battalion, 5th Marines, had yet to locate the 9th Infantry's advance. This allowed the Germans who were still in the forest to shoot at the soldiers from the flank and the rear, becoming more deadly as the soldiers advanced. Captain Roy W. Johnson's Company L moved forward from the second line of advance and filled in the gap, assisted by soldiers from the 1st Battalion. The 9th Infantry's axis of advance began to cut off the German defenders who were still opposing the 5th Marines in the Forest of Retz, forcing them to flee or surrender. Yard by yard, the soldiers advanced northeast, devastating the German defenders, who were now pressed from the front by the 5th Marines and cut off from retreat by the 9th Infantry. Upton reported at 5:40 a.m., "Everything went on the dot as far as we were concerned."[45]

The initial victory was not without cost, however. Upton waited for news at his headquarters, tucked into a small hollow at the edge of the forest. The promised detachment of French tanks arrived thirty minutes behind schedule, preventing them from going forward with the first waves of attack, but they pushed ahead to catch the infantry advance. With his regiment now moving forward, it was up to the three battalion commanders to follow the assault, leaving Upton to monitor their progress. "I could not stand the strain," Upton recalled, "so when everything was going all right, I went forward about a kilometer and witnessed a wonderful sight. Off to the right was the 23rd Infantry, while out in front was my regiment, and to our left a column of tanks going along the edge of the wood swatting every Boche machine gun that they could find."[46]

After an exhausting night march, the 3,000 soldiers of Malone's 23rd Infantry double-timed more than a mile to form on Upton's right, just along a road running north of the town of Chavigny and on rising ground extending south to the French 38th Division. The exhausted soldiers knew nothing about their surroundings and were unaware of any support for their impending attack. "I was completely at sea," Lieutenant Taylor recorded in his diary. "I had no idea where we were and did not even know the direction of the enemy. It was so wet and muddy that we could not even sit down for wet clammy clothing in the chill of that night would have been impossible."[47]

The soldiers moved past a house, where they received bandoliers of ammunition, and then took their attack position on a road in the forest. "We stepped into shell holes and mud almost to our waist," Taylor noted, "and moved through the dead bodies of French and Boche soldiers who had fallen there."[48] As the 23rd Infantry waited for dawn, the muffled sound of gasoline engines announced the arrival of the promised French tank support. Each tank was preceded by a French poilu armed with a flashlight to show the way forward, "then the lumbering mass of the tank itself would come creeping along, literally feeling its way."[49] A bundle of wood adorned the front of each tank, which could be dropped into a furrow or ditch to prevent stalling, and every so often, a tank in the column pulled a boat-shaped sled loaded with gasoline. The Americans normally would have exhibited curiosity at their first sight of tanks, but sheer fatigue muted this impulse.

The orders for the attack arrived late, at 4:30 a.m., only five minutes before the rolling artillery barrage began. At the same time, Malone placed his regimental headquarters just outside of Chavigny and deployed his three battalions in an attack formation in depth, with the 2nd Battalion leading the assault. The 2nd Battalion rushed into position just east of Chavigny on the backside of the hill, moving to the right of the ravine where the road passed north. Malone positioned the 1st Battalion half a mile behind the lead battalion, just behind the town and ready to follow. The 3rd Battalion lay half a mile behind the 1st Battalion, just on the edge of the forest. However, the units became somewhat separated in the darkness, and some remained in the forest waiting for orders to move. With only minutes remaining before the start of the attack, the 23rd Infantry waited fitfully with their supporting tanks until the artillery barrage exploded ar 4:35 a.m., as there was no sign of the supporting tanks and no word from the artillery.

The two regiments advanced side by side, driving ever deeper into the wheat fields. German fire still exposed the right flank of the 23rd Infantry's advance, as the soldiers had yet to meet up with the Marines, who were still battling in the forest. First Lieutenant Lambert A. Wood advanced his 9th Infantry machine gun company to meet the threat. A native son of Portland, Oregon, Wood would have graduated from Williams College in 1918, but he left during his junior year and joined the army in 1917. After being battle tested in June, the lieutenant believed that he commanded the best company in the regiment. He was justly proud of his men as they deployed in the fields with their fifty-pound Hotchkiss guns, defending the exposed flank. The simple task of preparing for combat proved exhausting, as the men had carried almost impossible loads through the forest that night. In addition to their machine guns and their individual packs, each man also hauled two boxes of ammunition.

The night march through the forest in the rain and mud had been daunting, and now the soldiers were leaving the open fields to enter the forest again, replacing fatigue with adrenaline. The company had confidence in Wood, who had proved on numerous occasions to be a fearless leader. Wood seemed to lead a charmed life, having escaped death on numerous occasions, even as men around him died. At one point during the battle, Wood quenched his thirst from a water barrel just as a shell struck the container, exploding in a spray of water and shell fragments. Wood was untouched. On July 11 Lieutenant Wood wrote to his parents in Oregon, "Love to all and write often, please. Don't worry, I am so busy I don't get time to get killed."[50]

As the Germans concentrated on their new peril, bullets rained through the trees over the Americans. "One machine gun squad would open up on an enemy position and be wiped out," recorded the company's survivors after the fight, "another squad taking their place. . . . Many were the Germans who were killed and wounded by the bullets from this company."[51] The fight then transitioned into hand-to-hand combat. The Americans suffered severely during the swirling melee. At least 50 percent of the company was killed or wounded, including the commander. Wood died behind a machine gun, holding a photograph of his girlfriend. His last words were to ask someone to tell his father that "he had willing[ly] given his all for the ideals that American soldiers were in France for."[52] Corporal Herbert E. Brown ably took command of the company, personally carrying ammunition boxes to replenish the beleaguered machine guns.

The 2nd Battalion of Malone's 23rd Infantry pushed forward into the fields next, followed by its supporting 1st Battalion. However, Company B could not be found. Colonel Malone soon located the missing company in the forest and strained his voice trying to direct the soldiers to their battalion, which was already engaged in the attack. Try as he might, he could not be heard over the crash of artillery, so he simply pointed to the avenue of advance leading to the ravine holding Chavigny Farm, Longmont, and the German lines beyond. Company B's first view of the ravine was a welcome one, as the forest had provided no line of sight to the battlefield. However, the mood quickly changed as the soldiers went deeper into the devastated ravine and were greeted by the effects of earlier battles. The village of Longmont lay in ruins, totally destroyed by artillery fire; rain-filled shell craters littered the valley, accompanied by the crumpled bodies of German and French soldiers, long dead but not buried.[53]

The soldiers also noticed the side hollows of the ravine littered with German equipment, including trench mortars and machine guns. The weapons were guarded only by the bodies of the Germans recently killed by artillery and the 2nd Battalion's advance. Wounded American soldiers also filtered back from the front line, encouraging the reserves with accounts of their surprise victory over the German defenders. Company B pulled out of the ravine, and the men were astonished by the wide plateau of wheat before them. The sounds of battle could be plainly heard, but much of the advance by the 9th Infantry and the 1st Battalion, 23rd Infantry, could not be seen in the waves of waist- and chest-high wheat. Only the silhouette of the French tanks could be detected. Company B was ordered to follow them across the plateau.

The soldiers of Company B better appreciated the French tanks once they encountered German machine gun fire, which came from positions hidden in the wheat. Lieutenant Taylor recalled, "A young lad who was standing near me was struck in the arm and the resulting sharp noise caused me to believe explosive bullets were being used, but I think more it was the impact of the bullet against the bone."[54] As if on cue, one of the tanks would pull out of line and drive the German machine gunners to ground with machine gun fire of its own, followed by a shell that sent fragments of the gun and its crew flying into the air. Despite their outstanding support, the soldiers were wary of the tanks' presence. "Of course the infantry was right [in] back of the tanks," Taylor observed, "and that is somewhat like standing [in] back of a target."[55] As the morning wore on, the soldiers felt the brilliant sun pressing down on the wheat fields, creating an irrepressible heat. As miserable as the rain had been the night before, the Americans' desire for water became intense as they drained their canteens much too quickly.

The heat also affected the French tankers. The crew of the Schneider tank ahead of Company B, 23rd Infantry, opened the back doors to allow better airflow inside the vehicle. The open hatch also revealed a bucket of water, which immediately caught the attention of the thirsty soldiers. "From time to time, man after man slipped out of the line," Taylor reported, "and stepped up and got a drink from the tank."[56] The soldiers never knew whether the French crew noticed the plunge in the bucket's water level, but they certainly appreciated the poilus' thoughtfulness for keeping a cup handy, bringing a small sliver of refinement to the battlefield.

The soldiers soon encountered isolated bands of the 1st Moroccan Division, which attached themselves to the Americans. Their first sight of the Moroccans was unforgettable. "They have straggly, stubby beards, you know, and they wear dilapidated turbans," recalled Taylor, "and instead of sending out a skirmish line . . . they just 'get the bunch together' and sling rifles over their backs, and draw out their huge knives, and trot out, and when they get tired they sit down and eat and drink and talk."[57]

The advance soon rolled over an abandoned French airfield. The soldiers discovered a hidden artillery position with cannon situated in the hangars and other structures, complete with underground bunkers for the crews. The Allied tanks and infantry quickly overran the abandoned artillery position, clearing the bunkers of any German stragglers. They were surprised to find evidence of the enemy's recent occupation, including an officer's table still set with a warm meal and a pot of coffee on the boil. The commander of the 1st Battalion, 23rd Infantry, Major Edmund Clivious Waddill III, paused to finish the meal, along with "the very excellent coffee that was bubbling merrily." Waddill had been a regular army officer before the war. Son of a federal judge in Richmond, Virginia, he graduated from the Virginia Military Institute in 1903 and entered the army two years later. He served two tours in the Philippines, saw service at Vera Cruz in 1914, and served as the army's inspector instructor for the state of Maryland in 1917. His battalion took many prisoners during its advance, many of whom surrendered from their bunkers, offering no resistance. Taylor noted, "We found boys of sixteen fighting in the Boche ranks beside men of forty."[58] Waddill would receive the Distinguished Service Cross, in part for his leadership that day.[59]

Having reached the 2nd Division's first and second intermediate lines of advance at 10:00 a.m., Upton now ordered his men to pivot to the southeast toward Vauxcastille and the town of Vierzy, while the Marines and Moroccans moved to their left. This maneuver allowed the French to take command of the 2nd Division's left flank, and both divisions would now push directly for the Soissons–Château-Thierry road.

Unfortunately, with the three American regiments scattered in the wheat fields after the morning attack, this pivot proved difficult at best. After an advance of several miles on a sixty-degree angle northeast, the 9th Regiment, the 23rd Regiment, and the 5th Marines now had to pivot to a line of attack thirty degrees southeast. In addition, communication with brigade and division commands had been lost; they were still mired in the morass of traffic in the Forest of Retz. Even runners could not cover the distance between the forest and the open fields. Only one message from the brigade reached Upton, and there were none from Harbord and 2nd Division headquarters. Units from all three regiments became hopelessly intermingled, moving southeast, for the most part, to the ravine past Beaurepaire Farm.

Soissons Tour

Stop 18. *Verte Feuille Farm,* 49°18'01.0"N 3°13'00.3"E

Leave Longpont through the spur of the Forest of Retz on the D 17. Pass the Chavigny ravine on your left, marking the 3rd Brigade's jump-off point. You are now driving in the 2nd Division's 3rd Brigade area. You can get a sense of the terrain faced by the two army regiments attacking here, from west to east.

Continue to follow the 9th and 23rd Infantry Regiments' advance on D 17, where the terrain starts to open up. At 1.5 kilometers, bear left on the D 17 as the D 805 branches off to the right. You are now at the location of the waist-high wheat field of 1918 and driving toward the area of the German 14th Reserve Division, the 2nd Division's first major opponent.

German defensive position overrun by the 4th Marine Brigade, Soissons, July 18, 1918. (© Pierre PANSIER/ECPAD/Defense)

At 1.7 kilometers, pull over at the small turnout before you reach the farmhouses ahead. You can now stand and see the entire battlefield before you. The 5th Marines attacked from your left and captured Verte Feuille Farm to your left. The army regiments, led by French tank battalions, did the same along the road you just traveled.

Take a moment to match your map with the ground to the east.

The Forest of Retz is to your left, and Verte Feuille Farm is 750 meters directly ahead on the D 17. The row of trees beyond the farm marks the road to Soissons, only 11 kilometers away, just as it did in 1918. Locate Beaurepaire Farm, the town of Chaudun, and the highest ground to the east; just beyond ran the main German supply road to Château-Thierry and the Marne salient. The 2nd Division's objective was the high ground on the horizon.

The Forest of Retz runs to the left of the D 17. The 9th and 23rd Infantry Regiments attacked across the wheat fields from the Chavigny ravine, led by the French St. Charmond tanks. The forest behind the farm is the area attacked by the 18th, 43rd, and 51st Companies of the 2nd Battalion, 5th Marines. The forest beyond the Soissons road is the battleground of the 1st Battalion, 5th Marines. This is the area where Sergeant Cukela and Sergeant Kocak fought; each of them received the Medal of Honor.

12

July 18, 1918—Morning Assault
"It Looks Like as If We've Got to Take on the Whole German Army by Ourselves"

AFTER ANNIHILATING THE GERMAN FRONT LINE in the Forest of Retz, Feland's 5th Marines continued its inexorable attack unabated, pushing deeper into the woods to take on any remaining German resistance. The northern flank of the 5th Marines still fought in the forest, intermingled with the 1st Moroccan Division. First Lieutenant Cooke wasted no time in organizing his company to resume the attack into the Germans' second line of defense. He sent two platoons forward, with another platoon following to take care of any bypassed German positions. As they advanced further into the forest, they continued to capture stray Germans who had fled when the Marines captured the initial trench line. The biggest problem was German snipers in tree platforms, who fired into the advancing Marines. Marines carrying the light Chauchat machine guns took no chances, peppering every large bunch of leaves in the trees. "Sometimes something fell out," Cooke reported, "and sometimes we drew a blank."[1]

Cooke's men advanced with heady excitement, enthused by the unexpected ease of the attack. The Marines captured a German artillery piece, a telephone communications station, and more prisoners. More important for the Marines was the liberation of hot coffee and bread from the German bunkers. This became the Americans' breakfast—after they made the Germans sample the food to make sure it was safe to eat. The 55th Company pierced the Germans' final line of defense and moved further into the trees with only small bursts of opposition, suffering no more than six casualties. However, the sounds of machine gun fire echoed through the woods across the road, indicating that Captain Wass or Captain Murray was running into trouble. Cooke could not shift over to flank the offending guns without losing contact with Turrill's 1st Battalion on the left. He went down the line to locate the company on his left flank, intending to send a platoon to help the battle to the right. He soon found Captain Crabbe advancing through the forest with the 66th Company and asked Crabbe if he had seen Major Turrill. "Search me," Crabbe jovially replied. "Haven't seen him or the rest of the battalion since last night." Cooke was surprised by that answer be-

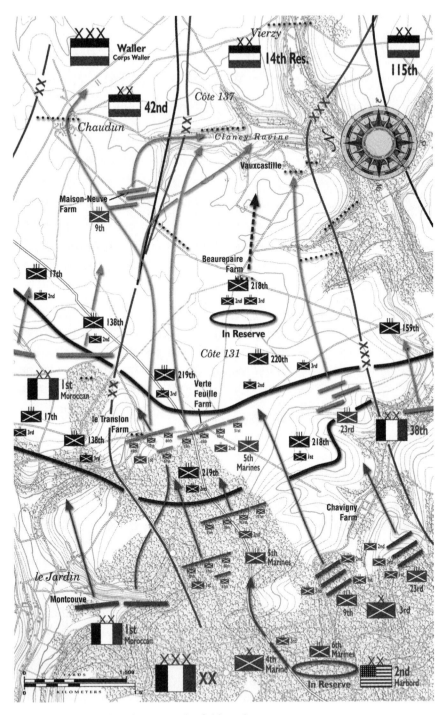

Map 17. Soissons, breakout into the fields, July 18, 1918, a.m.

cause it meant that Crabbe had attacked on his own, with no coordination with the rest of the battalion. "I was ordered to maintain liaison with your outfit," the captain explained. "When you came charging in on my right I thought it was time to go, and here I am." Crabbe then asked, "Where is the rest of *your* battalion?" Cooke realized, "Well, he had me there. Aside from the machine guns I had heard, I didn't have the faintest idea where Wass and Murray had gotten to."[2] Essentially, the two companies had fought together but had become separated from the rest of their battalions. Unknowingly, the two had forced a wedge deep into the German line with no coordination, other than to attack at the appointed time. They maintained cohesion with each other but lost the rest of their respective battalions.

As they left the woods, Cooke and Crabbe moved into terrain unlike that of the morning's forest battles. Wide, sweeping fields of wheat extended out to the horizon, where higher ground indicated the road from Château-Thierry to Soissons, about four miles away. The two officers examined the ground for the first time, noting that the almost level wheat fields were broken by the tree-lined road to Soissons extending out to their left and into the Moroccan zone of advance. The other prominent feature was the red tile roofs of the houses of Chaudon. Cooke and Crabbe, lacking maps, had not yet identified the village, which lay approximately two miles across the fields. No other American units could be seen, nor any Moroccans or Germans. The two officers realized they had broken through the German lines and were now somewhere in the enemy's rear area. The immediate question was what to do next.

Cooke remarked to Crabbe, "It looks like as if we've got to take on the whole German army by ourselves." "Fair enough," the Marine captain replied as he adjusted his belt. "You knock 'em down, and I'll count 'em." Cooke reviewed his brief notes from the attack order and knew that they had to pivot to the right on an eighty-six-degree heading. Now was as good a time as any for both companies to make the shift. Crabbe shrugged in agreement. Cooke was reassured by Crabbe's matter-of-fact attitude in the midst of the fight, noting, "Whether we fought Germans at eighty degrees or at a hundred and sixty was all the same to Captain Bill Crabb."[3]

Both officers then ran up and down their company formations, blowing their whistles and brandishing their arms to alert the Marines of the pivot to the right. The Marines made the shift, but not without some complaints about their commanders' wisdom. Cooke overheard one man say to his buddy, "Ain't that ignorant? If they wanted us to go in that direction, why didn't they say so in the first place?" Cooke then noticed two Italian American Marines pawing through a pile of German gear, evidently looking for souvenirs, and ordered them to join the advance. The two men turned out

Captured German artillery, July 18, 1918. The village of Chaudon is in the background. (© Pierre PANSIER/ECPAD/Defense)

to be soldiers from a patrol from the 9th Infantry. They explained that they were looking for German rifles to replace their own, which had been taken during the fighting in the woods. The soldiers had briefly been captured but managed to join the 55th Company in the confusion of the attack. "We looka for Marine and find plenty of Boche," they explained. "Da Boche, he took our gun. You catcha da Boche—we still no gotta gun!"[4] Though somewhat amused by their plight, Cooke was reassured that other units were on the field, and the Marines were not alone in the fight.

The Marines crossed the Soissons road without incident, but as they moved across the wheat fields, they found that the Germans still held the ground before them. As the Marines broke from the wheat, which offered some concealment, Crabbe's 66th Company almost walked into a German artillery position hidden in a slight ravine. Both sides, surprised to see the other, acted simultaneously. The Marines charged forward into the cannon, and the Germans wasted no time firing a volley of shells directly into the Americans' advance. The heat and concussion of the fire proved unforgettable to the Marines. "The belch of the cannon licked out like a hot breath," Cooke recalled. "I thought a couple of boilers had blown up in my face.

Water welled into my eyes, and my helmet jerked back against its chinstrap. The shells had screamed past before I could duck, but half blinded, I hit the deck anyhow."[5] The veteran Marines charged forward into the gun pits, reaching the cannon before the Germans could reload. The guns never fired another volley as the Americans burst into the ravine, taking prisoners and killing anyone who chose to resist.

They also took time to gather some souvenirs. One Marine held up an Iron Cross and exclaimed to Cooke, "I knew this was going to be my lucky day." Better news arrived as the Marines pushed past the ravine. Just approaching from over a slight rise were the 43rd and 18th Companies, led by Murray and Wass, who were obviously as pleased with the morning attack as Cooke and Crabbe were. "Murray was sauntering along in front of his troops; a half-amused, half cynical smile on his face," Cooke remembered, while Wass "walked with quick jaunty strides: not exactly hurrying, but like a man going somewhere on important business."[6]

Murray and Wass were two of the most extraordinary officers in a brigade of outstanding Marines. Both were from Massachusetts—Murray from Concord, and Wass from Gloucester. Individually, they were in their element in combat, but together, they were even more formidable in the swirling maelstrom of battle. Both had been attracted to a military career early in life. Wass was the major of his high school cadet battalion, and Murray became a member of the state militia while still in high school, serving as a private, corporal, and bugler in the 6th Massachusetts Infantry. Wass attended Dartmouth College for two years before selecting the Marine Corps as his profession, and Murray entered the Marine Corps as a private in 1906. Both attended the Marine Officers School at Parris Island in 1909, part of a class that included a future commandant of the Marine Corps, three of the first Marine aviators, and five general officers. After being commissioned second lieutenants, Murray was assigned to the USS *Dixie* on expeditionary duty in Panama and then duty at the naval prison in Boston, while Wass served at the Marine Barracks in Portsmouth, New Hampshire, close to his home. Both officers then embarked on expeditionary duty; Murray went to Cuba, and Wass spent the next three years in the Philippines, followed by a stint in Haiti.[7]

Both went ashore at Vera Cruz in 1914 as first lieutenants. Murray served as adjutant of the Marine Battalion in the initial landing. Both were at the center of the melee, and Wass lost two Marines who were shot next to him during the street fighting. Deployments to Haiti in 1915 and the Dominican Republic in 1916 continued their pattern of duty in foreign lands. However, Murray pulled ahead of Wass in rank, being promoted to first lieutenant in 1913 and captain on August 29, 1916, commanding the 43rd Company. Wass

French soldiers and 2nd Division Americans at Maison Neuve Farm, July 18, 1918. (© Pierre PANSIER/ECPAD/Defense)

was close behind, being promoted to captain of the 18th Company in 1917, with the rank dating from August 29, 1916, only twenty-two places behind Murray on the lineal list. When the 5th Marines left for France in June 1917, Wass and Murray were two of the most proficient officers in the regiment.[8]

What set Murray apart from any other Marine in the brigade was his choice of pet. While most companies had dogs or other domesticated mascots, Murray had a coatimundi that had been given to him by a Mexican girl during the occupation of Vera Cruz. He bonded with the coati—named "Jimmy"—and took the animal with him when he left Mexico. Jimmy, who was usually described around the Marine Corps as an anteater, possessed the intelligence and mischievousness of a hyperactive dog. Murray described him as a "raccoon, monkey and bear all in one, with a long rubber like nose." The bond between Jimmy and the 43rd Company became legend after a victorious encounter with a king trench rat earned Jimmy a wound stripe, and a tour of duty in Haiti earned him the respect of the 43rd Company, which adopted him as the company mascot.[9]

Even with all their combat experience, Murray and Wass witnessed something unique in the wheat fields before them. Six French tanks awaited the captains, the first they had ever seen on a battlefield. Cooke recalled: "They were funny looking things, clanking along with mechanical pugnacity. Their gun turrets, peering first to the right and then to the left, made me think of a nearsighted hunter looking for rabbits." The four companies now formed a united front, with the French tanks leading the advance across the wheat fields, deeper into the rear of the German defenses. Cooke recalled that the sweeping assault added to the Marines' confidence. "We felt capable of handling any Germans we might run into."[10]

The 1st and 3rd Battalions, 9th Infantry, also moved toward their next target, Maison Neuve Farm, which had to be captured to allow the soldiers to turn southeast without fear of a German strongpoint remaining on their flank. The farm on the left side of a nearby ravine proved particularly hazardous, bristling with machine guns positioned in the brick wall surrounding the farm buildings. The soldiers called out to the Marines that anyone crossing the road would be cut down by a machine gun positioned to rake the area. Company L ran into another camouflaged machine gun position and halted its advance until Corporal Nathan P. Sanders crawled forward on his own initiative and got close enough to kill the gunner and take four Germans prisoner, causing the other defenders to flee. Sanders then turned the weapon on the retreating Germans and opened the way to Maison Neuve Farm. Sanders received the Distinguished Service Cross for his actions, displaying "utter fearlessness and courage."[11]

The Germans dug in again at Maison Neuve Farm, this time with a battery of artillery positioned 100 yards to the northwest, firing directly on the American advance. The 9th Infantry stalled under this fire for almost an hour until two French Schneider tanks arrived unannounced but ready to take on the farm. The combined French and American forces soon rolled over the German defenders, and they began to mix with units of the 1st Moroccan Division, approaching from the north.[12]

Captain Hunt's 17th Company also burst out of the nearby trees, but out of sight of Crabbe's and Cooke's men and the soldiers of the 9th Infantry. Initially, Crabbe's 66th Company had attacked alongside the 17th Company, but in the confusion of the forest, they became separated. Crabbe focused on remaining in contact with Cooke's 55th Company, 2nd Battalion, on his right. Hunt kept his men on a more direct line through the woods, the 17th being on the far left of the five-company front line of Turrill's and Keyser's battalions. Hunt exited the woods on target with Transale Farm as planned, but in the low ground of the farm he could not see the two Marine companies to his right in the wheat fields. Hunt's primary concern then switched to the Moroccan division on his left, which began to crowd into the Marines' sector of the attack.

Hunt's men proceeded directly to their next objective, following the farm lane to its intersection with Crossroad 158 on the Soissons road. The battalion's orders indicated that this intersection was the far left of the 2nd Division's first intermediate objective line. Hunt's difficulty proved to be not the Germans but the Moroccan Division, whose soldiers advanced across the Marines' front into the 2nd Division's sector. The 17th Company reached the Soissons road with an open flank to the north. It encountered a forlorn army company of the 18th Regiment, 1st Division, attacking completely out of its own sector to the north. The wayward soldiers moved through the Moroccans and now rested on Hunt's intersection objective. Hunt informed the company commander of his mistake, but the army commander refused to believe the Marine and ordered his men to fortify their position.

Instead of digging in, Hunt bid adieu to the 1st Division soldiers and went looking for a fight. The Marines advanced deeper into the wheat fields ahead, but a few yards to the north, Hunt found that he could go no further until he eliminated the Germans in the village of Chaudon, beyond the 2nd Division's line of advance. Now that he was under German fire, the congested nature of his initial movement became a thing of the past. There were no other Allied forces nearby to assist him. The 1st Moroccan Division's zone supposedly lay on his left flank, and Moroccan units were visible in the fields behind his advance and even to the right. However, his only immediate reinforcements consisted of a feisty French lieutenant with twenty Moroccans who voluntarily attached themselves to Hunt's company, along with some Marines who had been separated from the 2nd Battalion during the attack through the forest.[13]

Hunt understood that he was the left flank company of the 2nd Division's zone, with his primary mission to eliminate the threat to the division's flank. Hunt shifted his company's advance toward the town, where the Germans fought back with a vengeance. The 17th Company captured the town within forty-five minutes, taking many prisoners and machine guns. At 9:00 a.m. Hunt turned his company away from Chaudon toward the road leading southeast, intent on reaching the final objective line extending north from Vierzy. He noticed that Marine units were still operating in the area and moved deeper into the Germans' rear. Hunt maneuvered his company to the east, past Maison Neuve Farm, until they reached the fields about 800 yards beyond the town of Chaudon. A German counterattack supported by concentrated machine gun fire halted the Marines' advance approximately on the second intermediate objective line. A German bullet struck Hunt in the shoulder, temporarily taking him out of the fight. As soon as a corpsman had treated the captain's wound, Hunt returned to his company to continue the attack. However, he soon collapsed from a combination of blood loss

French Schneider tank after the capture of Maison Neuve Farm. (© Pierre PANSIER/ECPAD/Defense)

and shock. Hunt was carried to the rear, and this time he did not return. An ambulance evacuated Hunt to a rear-area hospital, and the driver had a familiar face—Fred Duhring, a classmate from Berkeley.[14]

Adding to the confusion, the soldiers of the 9th and 23rd Infantry had now pushed far enough north to intersect with the Moroccans and the Marines. The 9th Infantry observed the advance of the 1st Moroccan Division, moving in a faultless arrangement of brigade columns into the American 2nd Division's zone of operations, as the soldiers battled the Germans at Maison Neuve Farm. In the confusion, the 5th Marines' companies broke out of the woods and joined the 9th Infantry's advance. At 10:30 a.m. Arthur Knott's Company M was relieved by the Moroccans and then moved to Maison Neuve Farm. An Algerian colonel soon arrived to take over the sector, so Knott rejoined the regiment to the southeast, in the ravine north of Vierzy.[15]

A combined attack by the 1st Battalion and Companies I and L from Captain Henry L. Worthington's 3rd Battalion, along with French tanks, took the farm. By now, the 9th Regiment's attack had evolved into an extraordinary assemblage of units elated by their breakthrough and moving across the fields in a northeasterly direction. "Companies, battalions, Regiments and even Divisions were mixed," recalled Captain Roy W. Johnson, "and the officers were kept busy during the advance and at the objective points, organizing the straying units into workable fighting units."[16] Company M fought side by side with the other companies of the 3rd Battalion, but for the initial phase of the attack, it advanced in a column of half platoons, following the 2nd Battalion as ordered. They encountered only German artillery fire during the first hours of the movement through the wheat, but after advancing half a mile, Company M caught up with the rolling barrage and the French tanks leading the assault. Now on the front line of the assault, the company broke into a single skirmish line to follow the attack further.

Typical of the implosion was the experience of Company K, 3rd Battalion, 9th Infantry, which fragmented into four separate platoon advances, each fighting on its own. The company commander moved with the 1st Platoon to the first objective line, independent of the rest of the company, and then advanced only 600 additional yards before halting. The platoon remained in position until noon of the following day, completely out of the fight. The 2nd Platoon advanced alone to a support position and awaited further orders, while the 3rd Platoon became disorganized almost immediately when a 9th Infantry battalion crossed its line of advance. The few men who still accompanied the lieutenant in command were ordered to join the nearest unit they could find and continue the attack until they finally arrived at Vauxcastille, where they tried to organize with other scattered units. Sergeant Bannon led the 4th Platoon, which became attached to a 9th Infantry unit after finding itself alone in the wheat fields. Most of Company K was eventually reunited in the evening and assumed a defensive role during the night.[17]

Despite the confusion in the wheat fields, small-unit commanders took the initiative and attacked German positions wherever they were found. Captain Johnson of Company F, 9th Infantry, waited patiently until enough Marines had joined his ranks to make an attack. Johnson's steadily growing force of soldiers and Marines was assisted by six French light tanks. Together, the multinational force made quick work of the German defenders, opening the way into the Vierzy ravine. A single French tank outflanked the German machine guns, moving down the eastern edge of the ravine and knocking out one position after another until the Germans broke for safety. Johnson's men stopped before entering Vierzy, and instead of attacking the village, they turned back to join the larger American force consisting of the 9th Infantry, 23rd Infantry, and 5th Marines coming together on the western edge of the ravine running north from Vierzy to Hill 137.[18] As the Marines broke into the open, a runner, Private Mackin, found the nearest lieutenant, asked him for the time, and informed him of his orders to go back to battalion headquarters. The officer provided the runner with the required information and then raised his hand in the direction of the open fields to the east, grimly remarking, "We'll be going in that direction."[19]

The combined Marine advance by Murray, Wass, and Cooke of Keyser's battalion, joined by Crabbe's 66th Company, broke easily across the wheat fields largely unopposed. The Marines climbed up a gradual slope onto a flat plain. From there, they noticed a cleared space in the middle of the fields that proved to be a crude forward airfield composed of two small ramshackle hangars and the remains of an airplane turned up on its nose. The view from the plateau was expansive but also somewhat puzzling. The company commanders knew that their final objective lay ahead on the road between Chaudon and Vierzy, as shown on their map, but the only two villages in sight were both on their left. Cooke believed the angle of advance was off center, judging from his visual sightings. "Say," he shouted to Captain Murray, who was leading the advance, "aren't we going too far to the right?" Murray checked his compass reading and disagreed. "We are on a course of eighty-six degrees," he offered. "At the next farm we change to one hundred and four."[20] The column pushed on, unaware that it was far off course. One of the unusual aspects of the battle in the wheat fields was the presence of "dimples," or small holes, in the wheat. Each man knew that every "dimple" signified an American, German, or French casualty lost in the swirling fight.[21]

The Marines were amazed to be joined by French tanks. Having never been exposed to such weapons before, they were uncertain how to coordinate their advance with the tanks. For the most part, they let the Frenchmen go ahead to break up the German defenses. In turn, the French tankers did not wait for the Americans, attacking on their own. Private Mackin of the 67th Company watched from the Paris road as a section of tanks pushed into the wheat before him, drawing fire from the German defenders. The slow-moving Schneider tanks proved easy targets for the gunners as they approached the Germans' second line of defense. "A tank or two or three would roll across the wheat field," Mackin remembered, "and a single tank would come to the top of a knoll and heiney hit him. And when he hit him he squatted and he began to smoke."[22] Teams of French tankers followed on foot to rescue the surviving crew as the tank burned, sending a pall of smoke over the battlefield. The scene was repeated again and again during the advance.

The four-company advance continued across the wheat fields to the southeast, guided by Captain Murray's compass. The Marines encountered no German resistance, but the further they proceeded, the more convinced Cooke became that they were off course. Before he could voice his concerns, the Marines ran directly into the 9th Infantry's line of battle and merged with the soldiers taking cover in the roadbed. This mixture of units indicated that someone had deviated from their axis of advance, but determining the offender proved problematic. The 9th Infantry was in position before the large ravine that extended north of the town of Vierzy, which was strongly held by the Germans. The Marines hardly paused among the infantry, led onward by Captain Murray and his questionable compass. Though Cooke was an army officer, he had been commanding a Marine platoon for more than a month; he knew the ways of Marines and, in particular, he knew Murray's thoughts. "He was a Marine and Marines have seagoing habits," Cooke wrote later. "Give one of them a compass bearing and he will follow that little steel needle 'til elephants roost in trees."[23] Murray took the Marines through the army formation and beyond, dead set on attaining the objective given to him by Turrill that morning in the dark forest. Now, in the open fields before the Vierzy ravine, the four determined companies of Marines continued to advance deeper into German lines.

The 9th Infantry soldiers sprang spontaneously from their positions along the road and joined the Marines, not waiting for orders from their officers. The Marine officers tried to send them back to the road, but the soldiers would not be denied: "No damn Marines were going to pass the 9th Infantry."[24] Despite the best efforts of their respective officers, the soldiers and the Marines became hopelessly intermixed within thirty seconds, bound together by the irresistible tide of the Marine advance and Murray's compass. The column moved forward to the edge of the ravine, ready to engage the Germans. The whistling of shells passing overhead and bursting in the ravine finally checked the advance, bringing the soldiers and Marines to a grinding halt. The Allied artillery pounded the German defenses in the expansive ravine, with the shells "barely scraping over our helmets." The Americans drew back from the explosions, watching intently as the barrage tore into the valley, reminding some of the men of the preset explosions in rock quarries at home. Cooke was pleased with the barrage, knowing that "as long as the shelling lasted, Murray couldn't follow that compass of his."[25]

The officers of the mixed battalions took advantage of the halt to attempt to restore organization within their ranks. Cooke found that the right half of his 55th Company was easily restored, "but the left was rapidly turning into a madhouse."[26] There, the artillery had yet to strike the German strongpoint in a farmhouse, which was now supported by more defenders at the end of the ravine. A combined force of Crabbe's 66th Company, the left half of the 55th Company, and an estimated battalion of the 9th Infantry took on the Germans, led by a brace of French tanks. A force of Moroccans sprang unannounced from the wheat fields, adding power to the attack. Casualties accumulated, primarily from the German machine

Wounded prisoners escorted out of the wheat fields. (© Pierre PANSIER/ECPAD/ Defense)

guns' indirect fire over the ravine. The Marines paused as a group of French tanks worked their way around the ravine to the north and then attacked the Germans on the east side of the gorge.

The combined force of Marines, soldiers, and Moroccans then fought their way across the ravine, capturing many German prisoners, while the French tanks overcame the German machine gun positions. With the Germans now cleared from the gorge, Murray, Crabbe, and Wass positioned their men on the lip of the ravine. The Marines were impressed by the French tanks' success in cleaning out the detestable machine guns. "To[o] high praise cannot be given to the work of the tanks," Major Keyser reported. "The way they assisted the advance and kept liaison with the troops was remarkable."[27]

An angry army major who was attempting to organize the disparate units in the attack stood face-to-face with Cooke and shouted, "Pull your go' damn Marines out of here! Get over on the left where you belong and protect my flank." Bullets rang around both men, ending the discussion. Cooke's men, mixed in the 9th Infantry, were attacking in line of battle from the Maison Neuve farmhouse to the ravine, which meant that pointing them in a new direction would be a difficult maneuver under fire. He stood up so the Marines could see him, blowing his whistle and waving his hand in circles above his head. The 55th Company Marines moved to join Cooke, but he soon saw that other men who did not belong to his command were following them. Cooke was surprised to see soldiers and Marines appearing from every direction, as well as a squad of Moroccans.[28] The army major grew angrier. "Hey, you're getting some of my men. . . . Stop it," he shrieked. "You're breaking up my formation." The major tried to chase his soldiers back into line, but they seemed determined to attack rather than to wait for their own commander.

Cooke wasted no time in separating the group of men gathered around him, which had grown to at least 125. One of the last to join him was army second lieutenant Fred H. Becker, commanding one of Wass's 18th Company platoons. "What happened to Crabb?" Cooke asked the lieutenant, who replied with a laugh and a shake of his head. "He had enough of us, when he saw some of his own battalion attacking that town over there; he pulled out and went with them."[29]

Before Cooke could move his men, the army major reappeared, taking Cooke by the arm and pulling him along as he said, "All officers this way. We've taken the intermediate objective, and I've called an officers meeting at eight fifteen. We can get your men sorted out there." Cooke had no intention of attending such a meeting, knowing full well the power and accuracy of German artillery in targeting such gatherings. He moved to the left, in the opposite direction. Cooke reached the road leading to Maison Neuve Farm, now adorned with an abandoned French tank. He knew he could support the major's flank from there and perhaps rejoin Crabbe's Marines, already in the ravine. He could also see Marines among the red-roofed houses of Chaudon to the north.

As Cooke continued to ponder the situation, a new threat arrived, this time from the air. A gaggle of German fighter planes appeared overhead, circling the Marines and making the sky come "alive with airplanes." The Germans weaved above the Marines until two of the aircraft swooped down low enough for Cooke to see one of the pilot's eyes through his goggles as he leaned out of the cockpit. The pilot's audacity proved too much for the lieutenant, who "brought my thumb to my nose and wiggled four derisive fingers." Cooke's gesture of defiance brought an immediate reaction from the German. "Look out!" Cooke's runner warned. "You made him mad." The pilot quickly turned his aircraft and began a strafing run directly at the Marines' position. A second pass followed, after which the German circled over Cooke's men one last time, hurling a small bomb as a parting gift.

Immediately after the airplane's departure, several of the lieutenant's men took issue with the impudent gesture that had set off the attack from above.

FT-17 tank overturned after attacking a German position. (© Pierre PANSIER/ ECPAD/Defense)

"You shouldn't have done that, Mr. Cooke," one man retorted. "We got enough guys to fight on the ground without you go picking 'em out of the air." Another Marine spoke up as well, asking, "What kind of game are you playing, anyhow?" First Lieutenant Gilder D. Jackson of the 43rd Company arrived in time to add to Cooke's discomfiture. "Captain Wass sent me across to see what was on the left flank," he said. "What shall I tell him you are doing—trying to join the flying corps?" Cooke could only respond, "Aw, pipe down," ending the exchange.

Second Lieutenant Taylor's Company B, 23rd Infantry, also joined the fight across the lower end of the ravine. The men watched as the French tanks split up; one moved to eliminate the German machine guns dug in at Château Vauxcastille, flanking the American advance across the ravine, while the rest turned north, attempting to move around the end of the ravine. The Germans in Vauxcastille were silenced, while the main tank detachment flanked the German defenses on the eastern edge of the ravine. A shell struck one of the tanks, flipping the vehicle on its side. As the Americans approached, a fiery blast rocked the tank, sending plumes of black smoke into the air. Although this was a spectacle for the Americans, the surviving French tankers seemed to regard the loss as inevitable, with "gestures of resignation as though that were the end expected and attached themselves to others of the rumbling monsters."[30]

The 9th Infantry's machine gun company was still in the fight but stalled along the ravine. Hunger added to the men's misery, as they had had no food for more than twenty-four hours. Then good fortune revealed itself when an abandoned German bunker offered up an entire barrel of sauerkraut, which was devoured "with bare hands, dirt and all."[31] However, the lower portion of the ravine extending north from Vierzy stopped the company, just as it had all the other American units in the attack. A coordinated effort by the fragmented American and French units was required to avoid being beaten in detail, but the confused nature of the fight and the unknown terrain ahead rendered such an attack impossible. Germans occupied the base of the ravine itself, while hidden interlocking machine gun nests were located in the crest on the far side of the gully, 300 yards away.

The loss of their captain had fragmented the company's leadership. The valiant Corporal Brown had been promoted to company first sergeant in May but then busted down to private only three weeks later. Brown now had something to prove, and the ravine seemed like a good place to do so. He led the remnants of the machine gun company and decided to take on the enemy position almost by himself. "We had to play the old Indian game, hiding behind poles and trees," Brown wrote home. "Three of my friends and myself crawled down into the ravine and up the other side so we could get to the machine gunners from the rear."[32] Miraculously, the four soldiers were able to get close to the Germans undetected. Their initial focus was the one concealed German machine gun that was inflicting the most damage on the Americans and pinning their company down across the ravine. Brown soon located the deadly weapon and silently maneuvered to the position's flank. He charged the gun crew, which fled when confronted by the murderous corporal. Brown then turned the weapon around and enfiladed the German lines.

The Germans first replied with a vengeance, and the four soldiers found themselves "in a bad way," Brown explained in his letter. "If the boches had put up any kind of a scrap they would have gotten us before we could have made our way back." Just then, the rest of the company attacked across the ravine, and the German line disintegrated under the unexpected fire. Most of the Germans surrendered, but Brown later casually admitted to his family, "That was one time I was lucky."[33]

Meanwhile, Major Speer was still leading his 1st Battalion, 9th Infantry, despite being wounded while overrunning a German artillery battery. Ignoring the rain of German artillery and machine gun fire, Speer took off alone to reconnoiter the left flank of the German position. Finding weakness, he brought up his battalion and attacked across the ravine. The soldiers took the far ridge of the ravine and, like Brown, turned an enfilading fire on the Germans, forcing them to withdraw. Speer was not yet satisfied with the progress of the attack and prepared another drive into the wheat fields ahead. His men then realized that the major could no longer walk, having been wounded a second time in the latest attack. Speer ordered his men forward, while he stayed behind to await help from the rear.[34]

First Lieutenant Janda led his platoon from Company M, 9th Infantry, to the outskirts of Vierzy. Separated from the rest of the company, Janda's thirty-five men quickly became the focus of the town's German defenders. Janda later described his predicament: "Machine guns cross firing from the front, enemy machine guns catching us from the right rear, Richthofen's flying circus bombing us and a counterattack by 100 Dutchmen coming toward us." The lieutenant gave no thought to withdrawing, as he and his men had reached their first objective line, and "that was our place to stay." The soldiers waited until the Germans had come close and then "opened just as fast as we could," repulsing the attack. "Everything worked out," remembered Janda, "except I got hit." He remained with his men for several more hours before walking to the rear, escorted by his runner, who "waggled the stump of a forefinger," which was still attached by a piece of flesh cradled in the palm of his hand.[35]

At noon, the German resistance was finally overcome by the fragmented attacks, allowing the 5th Marines and the 9th and 23rd Infantry Regiments to reorganize in the cover of the ravine, reforming units and replacing fallen commanders. Captain Alvin Colburn assumed command of the 2nd Battalion, 9th Infantry. Once the companies of the 3rd Battalion came together, they discovered that only three officers remained after the morning battles; all the rest were casualties. Captain Worthington still commanded the battalion, assisted by two first lieutenants.[36]

Major Waddill, commanding the 1st Battalion, 23rd Infantry, made his headquarters in one of the German dugouts in the ravine and took stock of his four companies as they reached his position. As the soldiers and Marines regrouped, their most immediate concern was water. "Water was the greatest necessity; the day had been terribly hot, and as we lay on the ground in the cruel rays of the sun our thirst was enormous," Lieutenant Taylor recalled. "We stripped our own dead and all of the German dead, and prisoners of their canteens, but it became increasingly difficult to prevent the men from filling their canteens from little pools of stagnant water."[37]

The remnants of the German 14th Reserve Division took advantage of the lull in the battle as well, believing that the Americans must be advancing their artillery and would need several hours before they could resume the attack. They reorganized their forces into a defense in depth to withstand the next assault, dividing their front between two brigades: the German 27th Reserve Brigade, 47th Reserve Division, took control in the north sector with the German 40th Fusiliers Regiment and 219th Regiment, while the 94th Reserve Brigade, 14th Reserve Division, commanded the southern portion of the line using the 16th Reserve Regiment and 218th Regiment. Each of the battered regiments from the morning's battle was cobbled together with the recently arrived regiments from the reserve. That the German commanders were able to utilize so many different units from various brigades and divisions within two hours and remain effective was a testament to the skill of the German soldiers. Even the extra staff officers were sent to round up stragglers and bring them back into the ranks.

Every pause by the Americans allowed more German reinforcements to arrive. The offensive spirit was not lost on the soldiers and Marines, but the initiative to continue the fight devolved into the hands of small-unit commanders such as Cooke and Jackson of the 55th Company. Without maps, they could not know that the ravine they faced extended south into a larger canyon-sized space that held the town of Vierzy, which was still held by the Germans. The depth of the valley hid the town from the two lieutenants, causing them to misidentify the villages they could actually see. Although Murray, who was nearby, placed the two advancing battalions of the 5th Marines correctly, Cooke and Jackson had their doubts, mistaking the town of Chaudon for Vierzy.

They incorrectly identified their next objective as being in the fields between Le Croix de Fer and Chaudon, instead of the actual target between Chaudon and Vierzy. The two lieutenants faced a momentous decision as Captains Murray and Wass and the rest of the Marine advance rapidly disappeared to the west. "They must be off course," thought Cooke. "Something must be done." The two lieutenants paused for a moment, considering the safer option of following the rest of the advance or the riskier choice of striking out on their own. "I saw the thought coming up from the depths of Jackson's eyes," Cooke remembered, "like a swimmer rising to the surface of a pool . . . we would go between those two towns and take the division objective ourselves . . . [and] when the generals got through decorating us, there wouldn't be enough medals left to go around."

Spurred by the thought of proving themselves right and everyone else wrong, the two lieutenants raced toward their rendezvous with destiny. "Come on," Cooke gave the fateful order. "Let's go!" Sixty to seventy men rose to their feet and began to move north through the wheat fields, distancing themselves from the rest of the battalion moving east. Cooke's Marines, soldiers, and Moroccans moved easily through the wheat, encountering no opposition. They did not know that Hunt's 17th Company had cleared Chaudon earlier in the morning, but the Germans who had been driven from the town were still in the area. They also unknowingly ventured beyond the 2nd Division's zone of operations.

As the Marines advanced to the left of the town, they reached the crest of a small knoll. Cooke was shocked to see a cluster of Germans retreating from Chaudon on the backside of the hill. Both sides were surprised by the presence of their enemy, only yards away. "For a split second there was a pause," Cooke remembered, "a test of morale, each side waiting to see what the other would do." In that moment, Cooke's instincts took over, and he led his men in a charge toward the Germans. Most of the enemy ran back into the fields, but a few of them charged up the hill, led by an officer who was a "big husky with black stubbled chin and crazy eyes." The German ran at Cooke with a fixed bayonet. The two men locked eyes, seconds away from a mortal brawl. Carrying only a sidearm, and unable to fire his weapon, Cooke believed that his time had come, but a nearby Marine bayoneted the German in midstride, helped by the deadly Moroccans. The rest of the Germans were killed as well. As the Marine cleaned his bayonet, he chastised Cooke. "Lucky I came along today, instead of staying back like you wanted me to!" The lieutenant had no time to thank the Marine, as one the Moroccans began to kick the body of the fallen German officer. Cooke was sickened by the abuse of the dead and warned the Africans to stay away from the corpse.

Cooke then led his men across the road between the villages and paused at an old trench line, overlooking a field that dropped off into another ravine after 1,000 yards. "Well, we are here," he shouted out to Jackson. "This must be the division objective!" As the men spread into the trench, the eerie silence caused some concern. The detachment was all alone; there were no Allied forces nearby and no German defenders either. If this was the division's objective, no one seemed to care but Cooke and his men. He scouted the empty field before him, noting some ineffective machine gun fire from the ravine. Cooke sat down in the trench and wrote a message to Major Keyser, informing him of their conquest, stating, "The Marines have captured Vierzy." He dispatched a runner to deliver the message. As he rested in the trench, an entire Moroccan battalion entered from the right, reinforcing Cooke's small band. In fact, the Americans were far into the 1st Moroccan Division's sector, and the Moroccans were probably wondering why Cooke was there.

Keyser arrived soon thereafter, walking along the parapet of the trench, oblivious to the German machine gun bullets popping overhead and the

An American and two French soldiers examine a German defensive position.
(© Pierre PANSIER/ECPAD/Defense)

warnings to take cover. His first reaction was to ascertain whether the young lieutenant "had gotten shell shocked or was just plain nuts." Cooke asked, "If we are not in the right place, then where are we?" indicating the two villages on the right and left. The major did not know for sure, but he was certain that Cooke was totally wrong.

Final evidence arrived when a body of men crossed the front of Cooke's line. Both officers walked forward to learn the identity of the unit, and the commanding officer confirmed that the 18th Regiment of the American 1st Division had arrived. "The major [Keyser] let me down easy," Cooke recollected later, "better than I deserved." Keyser allowed the detachment to remain in place, and he departed to ascertain the positions of his other three companies, telling Cooke, "I'll send for you if I need you." The demoralized lieutenant found an old dugout in the trench line, where he promptly went to sleep, "feeling pretty small." This was Cooke's first rest in two days.[38]

Nearby, Private Mackin, a member of Captain Whitehead's 67th Company, reached a German trench in his journey through the wheat fields, following the path created by tank treads crushing the wheat. The battered helmets, canteens, and other debris of war indicated that the French had originally used the trench as a futile defense when the German offensive began. The Germans had then taken it over as a line of defense, leaving behind many personal items when they departed. The furrow was now a refuge for wounded men and sulkers who were avoiding the battle in the fields to the east. A wounded Marine rested against the trench wall, having been bandaged by a departed corpsman. A Senegalese soldier was dying nearby, "slowly without complaint," according to Mackin. "His great hands gripping round his upper thigh, against the groin. His eyes were patient, docile, making no appeal. Rich heavy blood crept stealthily across his big black fingers." Further up the trench, several Marines were gathered around one of their friends lying on the trench floor, protected from the dirt by a single blanket. Mackin immediately noticed the somber mood of the men. Their companion, who had been wounded in the stomach by a sniper, had no hope of recovery. But the Marines were determined that he would not die alone, showing "a tenderness and gentleness beyond all expectation." Mackin noted, "When soldiers show an honest worried grief for anyone to see, its source is in their hearts. They have no ready word for what they feel."[39]

The men placed a folded blouse under the stricken man's head and kept talking to him, offering a few words of futile encouragement. "The wounded man rested easily, with little movement. A gray band of paleness rimmed his thin-lipped mouth and one could note the vise-like set of jaw and watch the nostrils quiver as he fought against the shock and pain for breath," Mackin recalled many years later. The man suddenly vomited blood, "gasping and choking and tried to smile." He then asked for water, causing Mackin to step in. He warned the men that giving water to someone with a stomach wound would prove fatal. The Marines paused, evaluating the stranger and noting Mackin's runner's armband. Silence deadened the trench for a moment, and then the wounded man called for water again, this time in an impassioned whisper that caused his friends to reach for their canteens. Mackin ordered them to stop, and instantly he saw the muzzle of a Colt .45 pistol pointed directly at him, accompanied by the admonition, "He drinks, Buck, see?" For a split second, Mackin feared for his own life, and he said no more as the men poured water into the wounded Marine's mouth. The man tried to smile but then retched up the water, mixed with blood. He died under the mournful gaze of his comrades. Mackin backed away from the group, leaving them to their sorrow.[40]

———

In only four hours, the attack had reached the designated first objective and was now paused at midday along the second objective. The final objective line, the vital Soissons–Château-Thierry road, was only a mile away. The rapid advance of the infantry outpaced even that of the supporting artillery. By 8:45 a.m., the cannon paused their fire and immediately began to move into the open fields. At 1:00 p.m. the advance reached the ruins of Verte Feuille Farm and went into a battery formation, allowing the 12th and 17th Field Artillery Regiments to better support a further breakthrough.[41]

The 2nd Division reserves consisted of the 6th Marines, the 2nd Engineer Battalion, and the 4th and 5th Machine Gun Battalions. Confusion during the night march prevented the engineers, the 4th Machine Gun Battalion, and two companies of the 5th Machine Gun Battalion from reaching their designated positions in the forest. Colonel William A. Mitchell later reported that the column was "so much confused by the various cross roads and illegible signs that they camped after midnight in the woods about a mile from their proper camp."[42]

Worse still was the situation of the 5th Machine Gun Battalion. After being unloaded from the camions on the morning of July 17, the battalion's machine guns were left behind to await further transportation. Upon reporting to 9th Infantry headquarters to locate the infantry battalions they were supposed to support, the battalion discovered that no one had any idea where those units were. The machine gunners then labored to reach 2nd Division headquarters; from there, they were sent to join the 3rd Brigade, already on the march. While the soldiers were marching back and forth through the forest, their machine guns were picked up by trucks but dumped somewhere short of 2nd Division headquarters. At least four ration trucks were dispatched to pick up the guns and deliver them to the 5th Machine Gun Battalion, but only after disposing of their rations. After finally locating the machine guns, the trucks got stuck in the morass of mud and traffic, unable to move at all.[43]

The army reserve moved again at 5:30 a.m. and arrived at their proper location by 9:30 a.m., still within the Forest of Retz. While on the march, the 5th Machine Gun Battalion received orders from Chief of Staff Brown to join the 5th Marines, as two companies of its 6th Machine Gun Battalion had been forced to attack without their guns, which had yet to arrive. Unfortunately, the army gunners faced the same situation as their Marine comrades: no machine guns. The situation was rectified by the swift arrival of the 4th Battalion's machine guns, allowing the battalion to march to the front an hour later. Colonel Mitchell received orders from Brown at 10:28 a.m. to move the entire force to Verte Feuille Farm and await further orders.

The engineers immediately began to clear the road, removing fallen trees and filling in shell holes.

The issue now became the danger of proceeding deeper into German territory without protection on either flank. The French units to the north and south had not kept up with the American advance, thus leaving their flanks vulnerable to attack. The heavy losses suffered during the morning battle also worried Harbord, as a German counterattack seemed inevitable. Further attack could prove disastrous, obviating the morning's gains. However, the 2nd Division reserves had yet to be committed to the fight. Until additional orders arrived, regimental commanders Upton, Malone, and Feland kept their men under cover, waiting for the French on either flank to push far enough forward to protect the jump-off to the last objective. Across the battlefield, every minute of delay allowed the Germans to reorganize their beaten units and add reinforcements of their own to the battlefield.

At the other end of the chain of command, Major General Harbord remained mired in the forest, practically motionless in his automobile amid the crush of men, tanks, trucks, horses, and myriad of other support elements of the assault. He struggled all morning with command and control of his division, receiving little or no information from his forward units. Unfortunately, his choice of a headquarters location proved fatal to any attempt to influence the assault after the initial attack. Cut off from higher command, battalion and company commanders were forced to make decisions in the absence of leadership from above.

Brigadier General Ely struggled all morning to maintain contact with his attacking 3rd Brigade. At 8:30 a.m. he left his headquarters at Fonds Douchards, far from the battle line, and traveled by automobile through the mile and a half of stalled traffic along the forest roads, eventually reaching Chavigny Farm just before 10:00 a.m. He expected to find Malone there with the headquarters of the 23rd Infantry, but instead, Ely learned that both Malone and Upton were at Beaurepaire Farm. He also mistakenly believed that the 5th Marines were held up at Verte Feuille Farm. Ely proceeded to Beaurepaire Farm by way of Longpont, arriving at 12:30 p.m. After meeting with his regimental commanders, Ely decided to report the morning's fight to Harbord and get further orders. While on his way to division headquarters, a staff officer met his car in the roadway and delivered a message from Harbord, who was asking for information about the battle. This was the first communication between Harbord and Ely since the attack started at 4:45 a.m.

Unknown to the 2nd Division's brigade and battalion commanders leading the advance, General Berdoulat had issued orders to resume the attack at 11:00 a.m. He assigned Harbord's 2nd Division the task of cutting the main German supply line—the road from Soissons to Château-Thierry—

and establishing a strong defensive position on the road between the Bois de Concrois and Hartennes. Harbord would tie in with the 1st Moroccan Division at the Villemontoire woods and with the French XXX Corps on the right at Hartennes. Harbord knew the assignment would be difficult, as the Germans would fight hard to hold their supply line. Before making the attack, Harbord first had to find out where his two infantry brigades were located and whether they were in any kind of shape to push forward toward the Soissons road. Accordingly, he got in his automobile and drove toward the front to meet with his commanders.[44]

As Ely continued to fight through the tangle of vehicles, he met Harbord's vehicle moving toward the front, though still deep in the forest. The two conferred long enough for Ely to inform his division commander of the current state of affairs. Harbord ordered a renewal of the attack, but it was now set for 6:00 p.m. Berdoulat's order contained erroneous intelligence that two French cavalry divisions were past the positions occupied by Ely's and Neville's men. The order indicated that French infantry were already beyond the Americans on both flanks, demonstrating that the 2nd Division was significantly behind the Allied advance. Berdoulat also mistakenly believed that the Americans had to catch up with the French forces before the overall XX Corps movement forward could continue. In fact, his orders implied that "the attack would be nothing more than a march forward."[45]

Troubled by this news, Ely turned his car around and began to make his way back through the forest roads to the front. Preparations for the attack began immediately, although the 3rd Brigade commander knew only too well that the attack order was based on false intelligence. "The French were behind us on both flanks and the cavalry behind our center," he reported, recognizing immediately that his two army regiments and the supporting 5th Marines must be reorganized if the attack were to have any chance of success. Due to the urgency of the attack order, Ely sent orders to his commanders via motorcycle, as well as by couriers on horseback.

The 2nd Division artillery moved forward to Beaurepaire Farm at 3:00 p.m., while other batteries unlimbered their guns in the open fields just short of the captured German artillery position. Several of the German cannon were still operational, with plentiful ammunition piled nearby. Army gunners quickly turned the enemy cannon to the west and added their fire to the barrage unleashed on the German high ground. The entire 12th Field Artillery's gun line soon ran along the ravine just east of the farm buildings.[46]

Ely finally arrived at 3rd Brigade headquarters at Beaurepaire Farm at 4:00 p.m. He discovered that the mounted courier had arrived only fifteen minutes before him, while the motorcyclist had never appeared at all. Another frustrating thirty minutes elapsed before the regimental commanders were located, along with the French tank commander who would support the attack. Ely then ordered Malone's 23rd Infantry to attack Vierzy no later than 6:00 p.m. As per Harbord's orders, he borrowed Turrill's 1st Battalion, 5th Marines, and the 6th Machine Gun Battalion from Neville's 4th Marine Brigade to support Malone. He directed Colonel Upton's 9th Infantry to advance on Malone's left, moving across the ravine north of Vierzy and then into the wheat fields beyond.[47]

Upton advanced his headquarters at noon to Beaurepaire Farm, where he reorganized his regiment for another attack after taking all three of the day's objectives. The farm and its surroundings proved to be a scene of utter desolation. The house and barns had been destroyed by the French in 1914 to keep them from the German advance. Wounded and dying men from the nearby fields and ravines now gathered there, their suffering intensified by the lack of water to ease their thirst. Upton, exhausted by little sleep and the excitement of the morning's battle, finally lay down to rest until Ely arrived to give the order for another attack.

When the regimental commanders were informed that the attack would resume at 6:00 p.m., they protested, emphatically stating the impossibility of having their men ready in time. In addition, the French commander reported that his tank battalion would not arrive until 7:00 p.m. Ely refused to relent over the timing of the attack, despite the protests by Upton and Malone. "It was imperative that the attack be made as soon as possible," he later reported, "and the order was given."[48] Ely instructed them to make their attacks as soon as possible, but no later than 6:00 p.m. The French tank commander received similar orders, but he was told that the Americans would attack without him if his tanks were not in place at the appointed time.

Upton understood that his men were close to their breaking point. The lack of sleep and continual marches, followed by the fierce morning battle, had pushed the regiment to exhaustion. "As the men had no water or food all day," he recollected, "I knew that to make the attack start, I would have to start it in person."[49] Upton left to join his regiment in the ravine north of Vierzy, while Malone immediately dispatched runners to Majors Edmund C. Waddill and d'Alery Fechet, alerting them to prepare to attack. He also included Turrill's battalion in his attack order, but he had no idea where to locate the Marines. Assistance also came from 2nd Division headquarters, which set up a center of operations at Verte Feuille Farm, where the 2nd Engineers and 4th and 5th Machine Gun Battalions remained in reserve. The 4th Battalion was motorized, loaded on Ford trucks that had made slow progress in the mass of vehicles on the forest roads. The battalion reached the farm in midmorning, spending the night alongside the road after becoming deadlocked in traffic.

Just as Malone did not know the location of his Marine support, the 5th Marines knew little of the army regiments on their right. As the Marines' advance slowed around the town of Vierzy, Turrill maintained his headquarters on the Soissons road, east of Verte Feuille Farm. At 5:15 p.m. he received orders from Ely's adjutant to renew the attack on Vierzy, but with no explanation of the army's planning. Turrill understood that he must attack alone, independent of army command. At the time, he had only his 1st Battalion headquarters detachment and the 5th Marines' reserves consisting of two companies from Major Shearer's 3rd Battalion, the 16th Company led by Captain Robert Yowell, Captain Richard N. Platt's 20th Company, and a segment of the 49th Company that had become separated from the rest of the company and was now attached to the reserves.

Turrill guided his command carefully through the wheat fields below Maison Neuve Farm and turned south toward Beaurepaire Farm, avoiding the areas where the German artillery spotters could directly observe the Marines. A 9th Infantry runner from Colonel Upton reached the column on the move, requesting that Turrill unite with his command for the attack. The messenger was actually looking for Keyser's battalion but found Turrill instead. "In view of my orders," Turrill later reported, "[I] did not do so."[50] The runner departed, never realizing he had reached the wrong Marine battalion.

Shortly after Turrill's departure, Lieutenant Colonel Feland received another order at 6:00 p.m., informing him of the 9th Infantry's attack and requesting Marine support to secure the army regiment's left flank. With the last of the 5th Marines' reserves heading for Vierzy to support the 23rd Infantry's attack, Feland had no more men to send forward to the 9th Infantry. However, Major Keyser's 2nd Battalion was in a perfect position in the ravine leading north of Vierzy, on the army's left flank. Feland dispatched a runner to Keyser with the proper order, but given the distance to the battalion, there was insufficient time to deliver the message before the attack began.[51]

Soissons Tour

Stop 19. Beaurepaire Farm, 49°17'50.9"N 3°14'24.9"E

Reverse your direction on the D 17, using the farm road intersection. Continue on the D 17 for 1.8 kilometers and turn left on the D 805. Drive 1.8 kilometers to Beaurepaire Farm. Pull over at the intersection of the D 805 and D 808 away from the farm buildings, which are private property. You can see that although the view from Verte Feuille Farm looked flat, there are rolling swales that provided cover for the German artillery in this area. Using your map, note that the 5th Marines' advance continued to Beaurepaire Farm, which the Marines captured. Compare the rolling nature of the terrain here with the Belleau Wood terrain and the attacks there. This was also the hospital area for the Marines and soldiers wounded during the July 18 fighting.

Stop 20. Maison Neuve Farm, 49°18'42.1"N 3°15'11.6"E

Continue on the D 805 to the farm buildings, which were heavily damaged during the fighting on July 18.

As you can see from your map, the 5th Marines' attack shifted north and into the zone of the 1st Moroccan Division. German resistance continued to be haphazard but was focused on Maison Neuve Farm. A combined attack of French tanks, supported by Algerians, and the 9th Infantry's 1st Battalion and Companies I and L from Captain Henry L. Worthington's 3rd Battalion took the farm on the morning of July 18.

Stop 21. Chaudon, 49°19'08.9"N 3°15'57.1"E

Continue 1.1 kilometers on the D 805 to Chaudon. Pause on the approaches to the town so that you can appreciate the difficult terrain facing Captain Leroy P. Hunt's 17th Company of Marines, along with men from the 1st Moroccan Division. Park at the town square in the center of town.

The Marines had no maps to guide them across the sea of wheat fields. Hunt's Marines attacked toward the German line of heavier resistance as reinforcements began to arrive. Once they took the town, their original orders directed them to pivot south and return to their own zone. By now, the

Captured German machine gun positions in the wheat fields. Note the faint line of trees on the horizon, marking the Soissons road. The solid stand of trees on the left horizon is the Forest of Retz. (© Pierre PANSIER/ECPAD/Defense)

battle lines were a mixture of soldiers, Marines, and Moroccans. The 5th Marines would now go south and join the 3rd Army Brigade in capturing the ravine north of Vierzy.

Stop 22. Vauxcastille, 49°17′27.7″N 3°15′24.0″E

Return on the D 805 to Beaurepaire Farm. Turn left onto the D 808, traveling 1.4 kilometers on the road leading to Vauxcastille. *Pause at the intersection, remembering that the château is private property.*

You are now at the location of the 3rd Army Brigade's toughest battle. The soldiers managed to take the area, but only after a severe fight that weakened them for the next task—the capture of Vierzy, just ahead. This is the area where the 6th Marines and 6th Machine Gun Battalion arrived on the afternoon of July 18, still in reserve.

13

July 18, 1918—Evening Assault
"Rage Carried Us over Those Last Few Yards to the Boche"

As COLONEL UPTON hurriedly prepared his attack on the northern end of the line, Colonel Malone organized his own 23rd Regiment's assault centered on Vierzy. He reached Vauxcastille at 6:35 p.m. and found his 1st and 2nd Battalions beginning their advance, having received their orders five minutes before his arrival. Malone met with Major Edmund C. Waddill, leading the 1st Battalion, and then moved across the ravine to confer with the French tank commander about providing support for the advance. As the two officers conversed, Malone observed his lead battalions appearing over the hill before him, advancing to the right of the Vierzy ravine. He also noticed the 9th Infantry in the distance, moving to his north.

Ahead of the 23rd Infantry's advance was Turrill's Marine battalion. Within five minutes of halting in the Vierzy ravine, Turrill was surprised to see Captain John H. Fay's 8th Machine Gun Company arrive as well. Fay had initially received orders to join the morning attack, with two platoons assigned to Keyser and another to Turrill, but unfortunately, the company had no heavy weapons. The Marine machine gunners belonged to the 5th Marine Regiment, independent of any battalion in the regiment. They normally supported the infantry but were not to be used as infantry. Unfortunately, their machine guns had traveled with the supply train during the move from the Marne, with the hope that they would arrive before the battle began. The long-awaited machine guns and ammunition finally arrived at 6:00 p.m., and Chief of Staff Brown immediately ordered the 8th Machine Gun Company to participate in the evening's assault. As the machine gunners advanced into the wheat fields, Colonel Neville joined them, issuing additional orders and moving the company to the 3rd Brigade's attack. Shortly thereafter, Fay received his third set of orders, this time directly from division commander Harbord, sending him to Beaurepaire Farm. An hour later, yet another order arrived from Harbord: "Take the town of Vierzy."[1]

Fay moved his men down the ravine past Vauxcastille and found Major Turrill in the road ahead with the same mission. Thankful to locate the Marine battalion, Fay informed Turrill of his specific orders to support the assault on Vierzy. Fay felt no compulsion to place himself under Turrill's command, deciding that Harbord's orders took precedence. In fact, Fay later reported that Turrill and his men "went forward with me" to Vierzy.[2] Despite Fay's independence, Turrill's command now consisted of his own headquarters detachment, the 8th Machine Gun Company, and the two companies of Shearer's 3rd Battalion. Without explicit orders of his own, Turrill had little choice but to make the attack with no additional support and no coordination with the units of the army's 3rd Brigade, which were supposedly nearby.

Turrill stood in the road with his staff, discussing their options. They had no knowledge of the enemy's defenses and were unsure of the location of the 3rd Brigade. Renewed German resistance indicated that the capture of Vierzy would prove costly. German snipers added to Turrill's difficulties, making the conversation more challenging as rounds hummed near the group of officers. Until he could properly assess the situation, Turrill ordered his men to shelter in the roadside ditches. He dispatched two squads of Marines to the ridgeline north of Vierzy to suppress the German snipers. Until the infantry reached the edge of the ravine, the snipers hidden in the town continued to fire at all available targets, attempting to pick off any Marine who showed himself. Captain Yowell's 16th Company arrived next. Turrill allowed Yowell's men fifteen minutes to rest before deploying to the south side of the road leading into Vierzy.[3]

Turrill and Captain Hamilton, now attached to battalion headquarters, pored over a map of the area and sent a runner to the nearest infantry company to dispatch a platoon or more to clear the town and unite the battalion in Vierzy. At 8:00 p.m. Turrill's headquarters group turned from their discussion to watch the approach of a staff car in a cloud of dust, announcing the arrival of the 3rd Brigade commander with a blast of the horn. Brigadier General Ely jumped from the car, searched for an officer among the nearby Marines, and ordered them to inform their battalion commander that he wished to see him. Ely was in a foul mood, now that he knew the intelligence for his attack could not have been more wrong.

The French divisions on each flank were behind the 2nd Division, not ahead of it, and the two French cavalry divisions were actually in the center of the 2nd Division, not ahead of it as he had originally been informed. The 1st Moroccan Division on the left lagged behind the 5th Marines' advance by 1.25 miles, while the German stronghold on the grounds of the Vierzy château had halted the French 38th Infantry on the right. This meant that Ely's attackers moved alone into a German defense that was positioned to fire on the Americans from three sides. Success now rested on the 5th Marines' ability to coordinate their attack with those of the 9th and 23rd Infantry Regiments to protect their flanks, which seemed almost impossible. Turrill's composite battalion in the Vierzy ravine was far from the two remaining battalions of the 5th Marines, located in the ravine north of town.[4]

Unaware of the tension at 3rd Brigade headquarters, Turrill dutifully walked the fifty yards to where Ely waited, protected from the German snipers by a bend in the road. Ely first asked Turrill to repeat his orders. Turrill informed him that he had been ordered to "support the 3rd Brigade." Ely first noted the time and then unleashed a blast of acrimony on the battalion commander, shouting, "Major, just where in hell are you and where in hell do you think you are?" The extended tongue-lashing surprised Turrill. "His excitement and anger gave me the impression that there had been some miscarriage of plans," Turrill reported, "and that the person responsible therefor had not as yet been ascertained."[5]

As Turrill started to reply, the army officer cut him off, interjecting, "Held up, hell, you were supposed to have captured that town! . . . Go get that—." But before Ely could finish, Turrill anticipated the order to take Vierzy, stating, "But sir, I've sent for help from the companies. I've got to have some men." Looking around, the army officer observed the forty men of the battalion headquarters and shouted, "Men? Men? Jesus! You want men? What's the matter with all of these around you in the ditches here—are they boy scouts?" Ely ordered Turrill to take Vierzy and then "keep going" until he reached the town of Hartennes on the Paris road, reporting when the Marines had reached their new objective.[6] The major knew that the order meant driving almost four miles into the German defenses on a front of 1,600 yards, with darkness only hours away. Ely's 23rd Infantry received the same orders, but the Marines were directed to attack even if the army regiment failed to do so. Turrill protested, pointing out his casualties and noting that the men remaining were staff officers, clerks, orderlies, and runners. Ely refused to relent. His agitation morphed into a sound that the nearby Marines described as a "silken purr." He spoke softly, but loud enough for them to hear. "But they are Marines, aren't they?" Then he quietly demanded, "God dammit, take the town."[7] He reiterated, "I don't give a damn if you only got twenty of them, they are Marines, my dear major, and I'm ordering you to take the town." Turrill could only answer, "Aye, aye, sir."[8]

Turrill characteristically went into combat with a cigarette in his mouth, which his Marines used like a weather vane to gauge his temper. After the general departed, Turrill turned to his men, with his cigarette swiveled at an angle that meant business. One of the runners recalled that "he looked like a dirty old hawk" while he delivered orders for the assault. Many of the Marines carried only sidearms, but they formed a ragged skirmish line, knowing they had only a few moments to prepare to assault Vierzy. Turrill devised a three-pronged attack to capture the town. Despite the order to attack at once, Turrill ordered Captain Platt's 20th Company, reinforced by a platoon from the 45th Company, and the 1st Battalion headquarters group to hit the town head-on using the road into the ravine. At the same time, Captain Yowell's 16th Company would sweep the edge of the ravine to the south as Fay's machine gun company moved to the high ground on the north side.[9]

With the shrill blast of a whistle, the Marines went on the attack, scattering through the back lots of the town and entering the first houses they came to, with the headquarters men picking up German rifles as they went. The Marines carried the attack forward, dodging through the streets and buildings of Vierzy led by Turrill and Hamilton. Both officers set an example for their men, staying with the lead elements of their detachment. The Germans refused to back away, and according to one Marine, "All hell broke loose."[10] Second Lieutenant John A. Gustafson recalled, "There were lots of machine guns working on us, also a few snipers."[11] The Marines lost a few men as they charged across the open ground, eventually taking positions in the extreme western buildings of Vierzy, where they were protected from the German machine gunners. The attack then became a close-in brawl, as the Marines cleared each house and building one by one.

The Americans soon located the most destructive German fire. It was coming from the tower of the town church, which dominated the streets of Vierzy. Additional machine gun fire erupted from a nearby factory. German mortar shells pounded the houses, killing and wounding both Marines and Germans. Watching the battle with professional interest from the high ground above the town, the Marines in the infantry companies later remarked, "Even the damn dog robbers can charge, when they hafta."[12]

The Marines from headquarters continued to move forward house by house, using the cover of the buildings to protect them from the machine guns in the steeple. "You take a curve in the street, you take advantage of it and duck over there to walk to that side of the building," Private Mackin recalled. "When you come to another curve you ducked across." As the Marines worked their way deeper into the town, the risks increased. Mackin watched as Private Glayron E. Hill sprinted across the main street, only to be taken down by the Germans positioned in the church. "They stitched him right across both legs upon the knees about half way up the thighs," Mackin recalled. "I never saw him again."[13] Hill died of his wounds on July 28.[14]

Private Mackin obtained a German rifle from the brick factory and then ran forward, following a sergeant around the corner of the building. The two Marines had gotten no more than twenty feet when German rounds struck the sergeant. "You could just hear them go thump, thump, thump, right into him," Mackin remembered. "He threw up his hands [and] fell

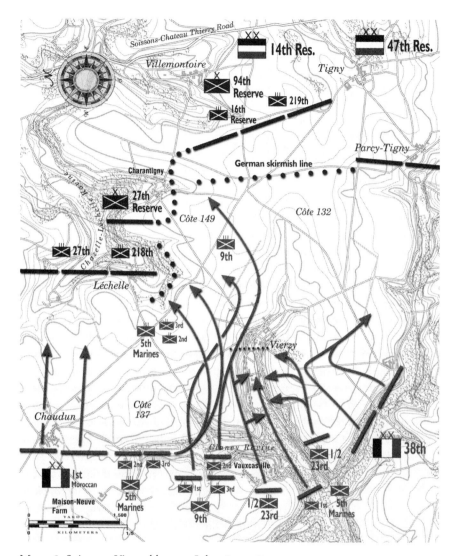

Map 18. Soissons, Vierzy blowup, July 18, 1918, p.m.

backwards into my arms. I went back and dragged him backwards on his heels and around the corner of the building. He was dead as far as I knew." As he was dragging the sergeant, Mackin noticed Private Ruben W. Salisbury running through a garden and saw a shell explode at his feet and toss him into the air, "tumbling like a rag." Mackin helped carry the stunned Marine to safety, where he proved to be unhurt except for the shock of the detonation, which left him "twitching horribly, his eyes rolling up and showing white."[15]

The advances soon struck the Germans' key defensive position—a factory building surrounded by a brick wall. The Marines broke into the factory yard, only to be confronted by a mass of German soldiers ready to surrender to the astonished Americans. The prisoners now outnumbered the guards, causing the Marines to worry that they would be unable to secure their captives. A search of the factory revealed more Germans, some of whom still offered resistance. The Marines found a young German soldier standing over a machine gun with his hands raised and calling out, "Kamerad, Kamerad." Before the Marines could answer, the German dropped his hands and pressed his thumbs on the gun, shooting at the Marines. The Americans shot him before he could get off more than a few rounds, leaving his lifeless body draped over the gun and the Marines momentarily puzzled by the suicidal act.

Turrill's men collected prisoners from all over Vierzy until the village was secure. Mackin and two other Marines gathered the surviving Germans into the main street of the town, forming the fifty to sixty men into a column five abreast. The three Marines were wary of their captives, who could have easily overpowered them. The prisoners acted with surprising arrogance. One German officer stepped out of the formation and called out to Mackin, "Hi buddy, I'm from Chicago. I was over here and got hooked into the God damn thing. Glad to see ya. I wanna give you some cigarettes." Fearing some trickery, Mackin brandished his bayoneted rifle and replied, "Stay back, Heinny." The German persisted and said, "Oh hell, don't take yourself seriously," and he walked up to the private. Mackin backed off, calling out, "Stay back, God damn ya, stay back or I will kill you." The German continued to move toward the private, holding out a pack of cigarettes. This time, Mackin knew the German was too close and he sensed danger, yet he allowed the prisoner to get within two feet of him. In that instant, Mackin knew he had to end the confrontation. "I swung a butt stroke right up to the side of his jaw," he recalled. "He must have gone through the air I bet six feet before his shoulders hit the deck. He was just a trembling wreck. Some of his men dragged him in. We didn't have any more trouble."[16]

Turrill's Marines sighted elements of the tardy 23rd Infantry on the high ground south of Vierzy, complemented by a unit of Moroccans and more infantrymen on the north side as well. They joined the attack on the upper border of town, but by then, almost all of Vierzy was secure, only an hour after the assault had begun. German machine guns positioned in the terraces on the north side of the ravine took a toll on the infantrymen as they crossed into the open fields, but the soldiers never paused, sprinting down the slope of the ravine and into the protection of the houses below. They fought house to house, eliminating any remaining German snipers. The sol-

Postwar view of Vierzy, looking east toward Tigny. Note the factory with the large smokestack and the château on the hill at the marker on the right. (US Army Heritage and Education Center, Carlisle, PA)

diers and Moroccans passed through Marine lines and began clearing more houses as well as the caves within the ravine. The soldiers then commenced the "arduous climb up to the opposite slope." Lieutenant Taylor noted, "There were fences and walls enclosing the grounds of each house and they were still intact. The destruction of war had apparently skipped that little town, for some unaccountable reason." The structure of the town made any attempt at a formation impossible, forcing the 23rd Infantry to struggle up the slope "in groups made up of all outfits, infantrymen, Moroccans, in a strange hodgepodge."[17]

Upon reaching the crest of the ravine, Taylor and his men found a German machine gun position hidden in defilade in the midst of a shrub border. The gunner was slumped over his weapon, his finger still on the trigger, ready to fire. A bullet hole marred his forehead, and a bayonet had torn open his throat. The bodies of the rest of the crew were found in the cellar of a nearby house. That machine gun had wreaked havoc on the Americans' advance over the open field, and now revenge belonged to them. "I never thought

I would reach a point where I would glory in death," Taylor remembered, "but the sight of that fellow positively caused a thrill of exaltation to sweep over me, and tired as I was, I laughed out loud." The rest of the platoon joined him in "a grim short laugh that boded no good for any other Boche we met up with that day."[18]

Once on the high ground, the advance continued into the fields beyond. The 23rd Infantry moved into the fields past town, while the Marines concentrated on the ridge just beyond the town cemetery. Turrill's men remained in defilade, safe from the German artillery striking from the ridge. After taking his prisoners to the rear, Mackin returned to the front line, which was now up on the ridge just past Vierzy, nicknamed Buzacot Hill. Turrill pulled the three-pronged assault into one unit, which he deployed up the eastern slope of the Vierzy ravine. Just ahead was a battalion of the 23rd Infantry commanded by Major Fechets.[19]

German shell fire soon located the Marines, but most of the shells passed over the ridge and fell into the town below. The shells tore through the cemetery just behind the Marines' position, ripping up the tombstones and exposing the bones and coffins of the dead. One of the shells actually tore into the crest of the hill, blowing Second Lieutenant John M. McClellan up in the air "like a spread eagle right through the air and down."[20] The shell burst tore off most of the officer's clothing and a substantial portion of his flesh, hurling his lifeless body into the wall of the cemetery. McClellan served as the 5th Marines' intelligence officer and was known for his "genial, cheerful disposition." The news of his death deeply affected the entire regiment, as he was "well known and liked by all who came in contact with him."[21]

The shells passing over the cemetery ripped into Vierzy, striking men of the 23rd Infantry as they neared the church. "Houses began to tumble, causing clouds of thick dust and smoke," recalled Taylor, who believed the shells were short rounds from the American artillery barrage meant for the Germans. The advance continued, however, and when it reached the open ground on the edge of Vierzy, the 23rd Infantry was a mixed-up collection of soldiers from every unit in the regiment. A rain of machine gun bullets announced that the soldiers were again in contact with the Germans, but this time, the enemy was not retreating. Major Waddill, commanding the 1st Battalion, led the soldiers into the open field ahead, braving intense fire. The soldiers reached a sunken road and then halted, unable to move forward. Casualties mounted, including an orderly who was struck while lying flat on the ground. The bullet exited through his chest, leaving a huge, gaping wound.

With the attack stalled, the 5th Marines and the 23rd Infantry dug in on the crest of the hill outside of Vierzy, facing the 800 yards of open fields before Tigny. A lucky few carried entrenching tools, and others borrowed shovels from the dead, but most just dug with their helmets and implements from their mess kits. As they labored, they watched German reserves pour into town, entering the buildings and taking positions on both sides of Tigny. The influx of new troops gave the Americans pause, as they knew from experience the signs of a German counterattack. Captain Fay positioned six machine guns on the east side of Vierzy, with another six facing the northeast and protecting the left flank of the town.[22]

Arriving in the middle of Vierzy was a full battery of French 75mm guns, intent on moving up the road and taking firing positions on the ridge. Major Turrill sent a runner to halt the battery and inform it of the impending German counterattack. The French artillerymen quickly unlimbered their guns and assumed firing positions in defilade behind the Marines. Four French officers gathered around a map laid out on the ground, preparing for their first mission. Without warning, a German shell burst directly on the map, killing all four men and leaving only a few scraps of paper on the ground. The Marines watching the scene below were speechless at the accuracy of the German artillery and saddened at the loss of the French officers, who died without warning. A German observation plane droned above, directing the German fire.[23]

Sounds of laughter broke out from Private Eugene Clevenger, who could not contain himself, grasping his sides and releasing peals of hysterical laughter at the sight of the dead artillerymen. Given all the death they had experienced since dawn, the Marines were shocked at his inexplicable behavior, but the laughter became infectious, and others joined in without understanding the humor of such a tragic situation. "For Christ sake, Gene, what is there to laugh about?" Private Mackin asked. "What's so funny?" Clevenger replied, "Oh gee, I bet those bastards were surprised."[24] His reaction to the absurdity of death on the battlefield reflected the impact of combat on the Marines, who knew that any one of them could die the same way as the Frenchmen.

The French artillery soon took its revenge, firing at the rate of three rounds per minute on the Germans flooding into Tigny until the potential counterattack was broken into pieces. The Germans searched for cover in the town and the surrounding fields while their machine guns continued to fire at the American positions, with most of the shots passing harmlessly overhead. "The bullets made noises like angry hornets *zeep*ing overhead," remembered Mackin, "or popping like champagne corks near our ears when they were close."[25]

While the fighting continued in Vierzy, Colonel Upton arrived at 9th Infantry headquarters at 6:00 p.m., thirty minutes after the time for the initial attack.

He immediately called all his commanders together and informed them of the new attack order. The regiment must move in thirty minutes in a column of two battalions forming the front line, followed by the second two battalions. The 2nd Battalion, 5th Marines, would be the lead left battalion, and the 2nd Battalion, 9th Infantry, would lead on the right. The 1st Battalion would follow the Marines, and the 3rd Battalion, 9th Infantry, would follow the infantry's 2nd Battalion. Major L. W. T. Waller's reserve 6th Machine Gun Battalion broke apart to support the assault; the 15th Company moved forward in support of the 9th Infantry's advance, as did the 23rd Company with Keyser's battalion of Marines. Captain Alvin Colburn asked whether tank support was available, but Upton knew nothing about any support from the French. The three army battalion commanders issued orders to their subordinates and then formed their men in the cover of the ravine, waiting for the time to attack.[26]

Major Keyser received orders from Ely's adjutant at his headquarters at Verte Feuille Farm. He was directed to join the planned attack, scheduled to jump off at 5:30 p.m., and position his battalion between the 1st Moroccan Division and the 9th Infantry, protecting both the American and French flanks by attacking the edge of the wide plateau at Lechelle, marking the northern limit of the 2nd Division's sector. Keyser quickly moved back to the Vierzy ravine, where Captains Wass, Murray, and Corbin were still waiting for orders. Each full-strength company normally numbered 250 Marines, but after the losses from the morning, Keyser could scrape together only 250 men from all three companies to make the assault. He dispatched a runner to Cooke's 55th Company with orders to leave his distant trench and rejoin the battalion, yet he knew the company would not arrive in time. Even so, time seemed to drag as the Marines waited in the ravine for the order to move forward.[27]

Far to the left, the remnants of the 55th Company remained in their position in the old trench line near Chaudon, as their company commander caught up on his sleep. At last, Lieutenant Jackson shook Lieutenant Cooke awake by the shoulder, forcing him to regain consciousness. "For Pete's sake, wake up," Jackson insisted. "There is something funny going on around here." As Cooke rubbed his eyes, Jackson continued, "We've been ditched. There is not another cockeyed soul left on the battlefield but us."[28] The two officers then scanned the empty fields around them with alarm. The 18th Infantry, 1st Army Division, was no longer in sight, having moved to the east, as had the Moroccan battalion, continuing the attack. Even the soldiers and Moroccans who had attached themselves to the 55th Company had disappeared, leaving Cooke in command of about sixty Marines.

Cooke's men were isolated from the rest of their battalion. To make matters worse, the Marines were hungry, having had no rations in more than twenty-four hours. Major Keyser's last order had been to remain in place until needed, and so they did. At last Cooke noticed a lone Marine emerge from the low ground to the south, looking about with obvious confusion. The lieutenant waved to the man, who immediately ran for the trench line. He proved to be the runner from Keyser with orders for Cooke to rejoin the battalion, which was moving forward at 7:00 p.m. The men of the company left their position with renewed energy, anticipating a meal once they had rejoined their battalion. Cooke's runner spoke hopefully of a good evening meal of "slum," a tasty stew made from whatever meats and vegetables were on hand, to which Cooke replied, "Slum, hell! I am going to buy you the biggest steak in France. Two inches thick and covered in mushrooms."[29]

As Colonel Upton continuously moved up and down the battle line, he ran into the lone reinforcement sent by Chief of Staff Brown to join the assault: the two combat platoons of Captain Roy Hilton's Company B, 4th Machine Gun Battalion. Hilton formally reported that his men were there to support the attack. "Very well," Upton replied, "there is my regiment, we attack in about ten minutes, make your dispositions."[30] Hilton understood that Upton's regiment had no other heavy machine guns to aid in the assault, and he also knew that his two platoons were inadequate to support a regimental attack over unfamiliar ground. He divided his command, sending one platoon to the left of the regiment and one to the right. Hilton could do little more.

The machine gunners noticed with horror two large gatherings of wounded soldiers and Marines in the ravine, numbering at least a hundred men. Hilton observed, to his dismay, that these men were receiving no medical treatment, including some who were bleeding to death. He dispatched a runner to the nearest first-aid post at Beaurepaire Farm. The man soon returned, bearing a message that the aid station was currently overwhelmed with casualties and would send help to the ravine as soon as possible. Hilton and his men could do nothing to assist the wounded as they scrambled forward to join the 9th Infantry in the field ahead.[31]

At 7:15 p.m. Colonel Upton arrived at Keyser's headquarters at the north end of the ravine to make certain the Marine battalion understood its attack orders, which had it proceeding in a southeasterly direction. After Upton ended the meeting, Keyser had only fifteen minutes to prepare his battalion with final instructions and move the men into position for the 7:30 jump-off time. Keyser also grimly informed his officers that there would be no tank or artillery support. Keyser's Marines led the advance on the left, while the 2nd Battalion, 9th Infantry, did the same on the right.

At precisely 7:30 p.m. Colonel Upton ordered the attack into the wheat fields to the east. Noticeably absent was any artillery support to suppress the

German fire. The soldiers and Marines advanced alone. Captain Colburn's 2nd Battalion, 9th Infantry, climbed out of the ravine and formed the right flank of the assault. Once they were out of the Vierzy ravine, Keyser quickly placed his three companies in two lines on a 550-yard front. Most of the 250 Marines were in the lead line, deployed with five-step intervals between them. The remaining Marines were in combat teams behind them. Keyser was comforted by the sight of the 9th Infantry to his right, but ominously, he saw no sign of the Moroccans in the fields on his left.

Having not seen the target terrain until now, Upton could not know that the edges of the spacious field ahead were broken by several ravines, providing perfect cover for the German defenders. The fingers of three large ravines jutted out toward the American advance, marked by the villages of Lechelle, Charantigy, and Villemontoire. Each of the ravines naturally fragmented the attack into channeled crossfire and allowed the Germans to move freely from point to point, including forays by flanking machine gun fire into the fields of wheat.[32]

As Keyser's Marines and Colburn's soldiers moved into the open field, the Marines advanced toward the Lechelle ravine, as did Captain Charles E. Speer's 1st Battalion, aligning toward Shearer's Marines on the left. Speer hailed from Catonsville, Maryland. He began his military career as a corporal with the 5th Regiment, Maryland National Guard, serving on the Mexican border in 1916. By the end of the year, he had been accepted as a second lieutenant in the regular army and was promoted to captain in August 1917. Speer temporarily lost his eyesight after being gassed at Belleau Wood on June 13, but he recovered in time to command his battalion for the movement to Soissons. Unknown to Speer, his brother Talbott fought with the 1st Division, only miles away to the north.[33]

Upton led his two right battalions through the sugar-beet fields toward the Germans' Charantigny and Villemontoire positions. Colburn maintained his advance, with Captain Henry L. Worthington's 3rd Battalion following in a second wave. The Marines and soldiers surged across the fields but halted when sixteen French tanks arrived to lead the attack. A German reconnaissance aircraft suddenly appeared from the rear, flying at an extremely low level parallel to the American advance, and dropped several signals flares over the Marines and soldiers. The combat veterans below knew what this meant: German artillery would soon follow.[34]

After passing Hill 137, a storm of artillery and machine gun fire rained down on the Americans. After about 600 yards, machine gun fire stopped the soldiers' advance, causing Keyser to halt his battalion to protect its flank. After the 9th Infantry cleared its front, the advance resumed, moving forward more than half a mile. The united column moved steadily until it came abreast of the Lechelle woods on high ground to the north. The French tank commander asked Colburn to halt until his tanks could pass the infantry and lead the attack. Captain Colburn sent a runner to Colonel Upton for orders, and when the runner returned, he reported that Upton refused to stop the attack. He instructed Colburn to push forward. On hearing the American reply, the French commander hotfooted it back to his tanks. A second runner then arrived, with orders to continue the advance until it met hard opposition; then the slow-moving tanks could move through the infantry into the open ground ahead.

The German defenders in the woods and ravines ahead allowed the Americans to proceed until they reached what would become a killing ground dominated by the deadly combination of German artillery and machine guns. When the 5th Marines and 9th Infantry reached a point from which they could not easily escape, machine gun fire ripped into the American flank, forcing Keyser to veer his battalion away from Upton's main line of advance to face the German fire. Murray's 43rd Company on the left took on a German machine gun strongpoint, assisted by Wass and the 18th Company in the center of the attack. This fire caused a fracture, as half the Marines in the 18th Company split off to cover their flank. The army reserve line also split: Worthington's 3rd Battalion followed Colburn's advance, while Speer's 1st Battalion trailed the Marines toward the wooded slope. The Marines, soldiers, and French tanks moved together in a direct attack on the Lechelle woods and ravine, while Upton continued east with the second detachment of tanks and his 2nd and 3rd Battalions.

The two-battalion 9th Infantry advance persisted for another half mile, until it arrived at a crossroads before a larger hill and woods. The German fire reached a crescendo of shell bursts and bullets. Upton halted the column to allow the tanks to move forward, but the pause gave the Germans time to focus on the Americans. Captain Colburn took a machine gun bullet through the shoulder and was knocked to the ground; he managed to reach the safety of a recently unearthed shell hole. Two of the French tanks rolled up, took position on either side of the hole, "and opened up on the Germans with everything they had," but they also drew fire from the Germans, much to the discomfiture of Colburn himself.[35]

Keyser's advance faced the same opposition. The experienced German machine gunners were difficult to locate in the high wheat. "It seemed impossible for us to go through another attack that day," the 18th Company historians later recorded, "but that is what we did . . . men dropped like flies."[36] The Germans initially defended an old 1914 trench system in the wheat field, stopping the Marine advance. Wass went forward, personally directing the elimination of enemy strongpoints. As the Marines engaged the

Front-line triage station, July 18, 1918. Note that there are German, French, and American wounded. (© Pierre PANSIER/ECPAD/Defense)

Germans, six French tanks appeared amidst the shell bursts, advancing at three miles per hour and moving further into the wheat field. The supporting tanks were a welcome sight for the Marines, but the German barrage bracketing them was not. An observation aircraft flew overhead, chasing the tanks with shell bursts, adjusting to every move they made. The shells caused shrapnel to fall over the Marines' battle lines, resulting in severe casualties.

With the arrival of the tanks, and as the machine guns on his left went silent, Keyser renewed his attack. His men cautiously searched for the Germans on their left but could find no sign of the offending machine guns in the wheat; nor did they draw any enemy fire from that direction. The Marines believed the Germans had departed, so they moved deeper into the wheat fields. It was readily apparent that this attack faced much different opposition than the morning assault and was about to become far more lethal. The joint leadership of Murray, commanding the remnants of his 43rd Company, and Wass, leading half of the 18th Company, carried the Marines forward, supported by Corbin's 51st Company. The Marines still maintained their two-wave formation.

Sadly for the Marines, the German machine gunners were expert at their craft. They hid in the wheat, waiting quietly until the Americans had moved past them before changing position and opening a deadly fire on the rear of the attacking column. The second line of Marines halted its advance in the wheat to face the attackers, leaving the first line still advancing and fragmenting the attack. After ten minutes, the few Marines not committed were called forward to support this skirmish line, leaving no one to continue the attack. The machine guns raked the Marines, pinning them to the ground.

The German artillery proved to be deadly accurate, pounding Keyser's battalion with airbursts of shrapnel raining down on the Marines. Four of the six supporting tanks were shattered by the shell fire, along with their crews. Plumes of black oily smoke wafted into the sky, representing a shroud of death for the Frenchmen. The two surviving tanks forced their way to the rear of the Marines' attack, only to be followed by six more French tanks retreating along the same path as the first group. Then, instead of moving through the Marine formation that was still under fire, the column crossed in front of Keyser's battalion, unobserved by the spotter aircraft, and turned west, miraculously reaching safety without losing a tank.

Keyser's three companies now fought alone. Captain Speer's 1st Battalion followed the Marines for a time but peeled off to try to bridge the gap between the Marines and Upton's two battalions at the southeast corner of the Lechelle ravine. A band of 18th Company Marines attached themselves to Speer's movement, perhaps judging that an attack to the right was better than remaining in their field of sugar beets. During the attack, Speer was wounded for a second time that day, severely enough for him to order his soldiers to leave him in the field and continue their attack without him. The remnants of the battalion somehow obtained a foothold in the woods but could not drive the Germans any further, ending all hope of uniting the attacking columns. Speer was awarded the Distinguished Service Cross for his bravery on July 18.[37]

Keyser's only hope for assistance was Cooke's wayward 55th Company. He understood that Cooke was supposed to join the attack, but the company had yet to appear on the field. Without any immediate sign of support, Captain Wass, in typical style, positioned himself in front of his company to lead the attack. In the midst of the melee, Wass was mortally wounded by shrapnel, although some men swore their captain was killed by a burst of machine gun fire. The shock of this loss swept over the 18th Company, but there was no time to mourn their fallen captain. The shelling continued unabated.[38]

Captain Murray fought beside Wass's men, but the depleted Marine companies suffered too many losses from the Germans' forward line of defense.

There were simply too few Marines left to effectively assault the main German line of resistance, which still lay ahead. A round struck Murray in the head, denting his helmet before ricocheting off into the fields. Blood poured down his face, but Murray was not critically injured. If not "for the old tin hat that I had on," Murray recalled later, "I would probably have settled my accounts and cashed in, but it happened that the old hat just got a little dent and saved me from sudden death."[39] The bloodied captain walked back to the rear, guarding four German prisoners.

The large amount of ground to cover, combined with a veteran German defense over open ground, proved unmanageable for the Marine and army battalions. Consequently, the widening split between Colburn's and Keyser's lead battalions may have precipitated the fatal error in the attack. The Marines and Speer's 1st Battalion pivoted to their left to attack the flanking fire from the wooded high ground of the Lechelle woods without properly communicating this movement to Upton. The other two army battalions continued to advance in a southeasterly direction, directly toward the high ground of the Château-Thierry road, more than a mile away at Villemontoire.

As Upton's forlorn two-battalion attack advanced 200 yards toward the Charantigny ravine, the German machine gunners positioned in the Villemontoire ravine took a heavy toll, causing Captain Worthington's reserve 3rd Battalion to move forward and join the lead battalion, creating one long line of attack. That movement left Upton with no reserves in support ten minutes after the attack began, with both columns of advance now flanked by German machine gun fire. Worthington was killed early in the attack, leaving the battalion with only two uninjured officers. First Lieutenant George A. Davis of Company L took over command of the battalion. After the loss of Captain Ince and Lieutenant McInerny, Sergeant Leonard Snyder led Company I, followed by Sergeant William D. Brown after Snyder became a casualty. Brown was the fourth commander of the company that day and would survive to lead it for the rest of the battle.[40]

Upton correctly perceived that the German flanking fire from the Lechelle woods also prevented his attack from proceeding any further toward the Château-Thierry road. He positioned himself on the left of his line in an attempt to coordinate the advance, but as he soon realized, "It was impossible to locate anyone."[41] He knew Keyser's battalion remained locked in a struggle for the unseen ravines, but he hoped it would be able to open the way forward to the east by driving the Germans from the woods. He requested runners from each of the Marine companies, but only two men arrived at his headquarters, both of them wounded. Upton also knew that the Germans' defenses were in the 1st Moroccan Division's sector; that division should have cleared the area to allow him to advance further east, but there was no sign of the French colonial troops. With retreat not an option, Upton, Keyser, and the three army battalion commanders had little choice but to remain pinned down until darkness ended the fighting.

As the 9th Infantry and Keyser's Marines initially pushed through the wheat fields, the commander of the 5th Marines, Lieutenant Colonel Feland, learned that he now commanded only his regimental staff and ten Marines from Shearer's 3rd Battalion. The entire regiment had been committed to battle under army command. At 9:00 p.m. Colonel Neville informed Feland that Ely had doled out Turrill's battalion and the regimental machine gun company to the 23rd Infantry, while Keyser's battalion now served with the 9th Infantry. Shearer's 3rd Battalion already reinforced Turrill and Keyser, effectively leaving Feland with no command responsibility on the battlefield. He spent the evening at 4th Brigade headquarters at Vauxcastille, listening to the sounds of battle in the fields ahead.[42]

While the artillery and machine guns pounded the Marines' advance, Cooke's 55th Company approached the battlefield. The battalion runner led them back to Maison Neuve Farm and then into the ravine below, the scene of the battle fought by Crabbe's 66th Company that morning. The floor of the ravine was like a charnel house, filled with the bodies of both Americans and Germans, reflecting the ferocity of the battle. The effect on the Marines was instantaneous. All thoughts of food were driven away by the "sweetish stink of dead flesh" from the corpses, which had assumed various shapes in death. "Some were sprawled at full length," Cooke noticed, while "others lay huddled in queer, pain racked postures." The runner arrived at the entrance of a deserted cave and promptly announced, "This is where the major was when I left him." Cooke was at a loss as to what to do next. His futile morning foray was a reminder of the consequences of misplaced initiative, but Cooke knew that, judging from the sound of battle ahead, he had to locate Major Keyser as soon as possible.[43]

As he pondered the situation, a Marine appeared at the eastern lip of the gully and promptly fell down into the ravine. The man was badly wounded; there was a great yawning hole in his chest that bled with every breath he took, and blood ran from his mouth as well. He would probably die soon, regardless of efforts to bandage his wounds. Cooke stepped forward to interrogate the Marine, hoping to ascertain the location of the battalion, although "it seemed the lowest form of cruelty to make that boy talk." In between gasps of breath, the wounded man was able to speak, telling Cooke about the battalion's attack in support of the army's advance at Vierzy. That information sent the Marines up to the crest of the ravine, where the evening assault unfolded before them. They could see the army's advance to the right and were able to pick out the Marines on the left, attacking the ravine at the town of Lechelle.[44]

As the Marines watched the fighting, they noticed with dismay the presence of German helmets above the wheat, moving into the gap between the two American forces. Of even more concern was the sight of heavy machine guns being hauled into position behind a slight dirt embankment formed by an underground railroad tunnel extending north out of Vierzy. The Germans worked their way, unnoticed, into the rear of the Marines' assault and would soon send a devastating fire onto the Marines' line of battle. However, the Germans were oblivious to the presence of Cooke's men, now behind them. "It was up to us," Cooke thought. "We had to get those guns." It now became a question of who would act first—the Germans setting up their machine guns, or the 55th Company taking them out. "There wasn't any time to give orders," Cooke knew. "I couldn't even yell or blow a whistle without attracting the attention of the Boche machine gunners. We just started down the slope, a ragged straggling line of men, but with cold murder in our hearts."[45]

The Marines moved forward, watching with fascination as the hated German machine gunners fed lengthy belts of ammunition into the guns and then snapped back the firing mechanisms. Cooke and his men were still more than a hundred yards away, and they were concerned that the Germans would detect their presence and turn the machine guns on them. They watched anxiously as the gunners took their place on the gun sleds and adjusted their sights, only seconds away from opening fire on the Marines attacking the high ground near Lechelle. "The running feet, the swish of legs through the tall wheat," and "the sobs of fury from our panting ranks" alerted one of the Germans, who turned and saw the Marines sprinting toward him. "With bulging eyes of terror," he signaled with his arms to warn the other machine gun teams. The Germans frantically tried to turn their guns toward the new threat approaching from their rear.

The difference between life and death was only a matter of seconds as the Marines sprinted to close on the enemy before they could open fire. They got within seventy-five yards and then only fifty yards, close enough to see that one of the machine guns had been turned on them. Bullets raked the Marines, cutting down several of them just short of the German position. "A crescendoing roar of bullets bored into us, cut us down, almost stopped us," Cooke recalled, "but not quite . . . rage carried us over those last few yards to the Boche." Within seconds, the Marines were engaged in hand-to-hand combat with the machine gunners, killing the Germans without mercy. Cooke wrote after the war, "We didn't leave much that was recognizable."[46]

Once the fight was over, the remaining Marines collapsed on the railroad embankment, physically spent. The men of the 55th Company had saved their comrades on the hillside, but at the moment, they were focused on assisting their wounded and mourning their dead. Cooke immediately noticed that his runner was missing. A quick search of the battlefield found "Whitey" lying in the wheat; bullets from a German machine gun had torn open his midsection, leaving only a gory mass of flesh. The Marine was still conscious, but it was obvious that he would not survive his injury. "Hello, Mr. Cooke," he muttered. "I'll trade you my Iron Cross for a cigarette." At first, the lieutenant refused because of the man's wound, but Whitey replied, "I don't smoke with my stomach. My lungs are alright." Cooke had to steady his trembling hands to light the cigarette and place it in the stricken man's mouth. Just then, a bloodied runner from the 18th Company appeared, seeking the company commander. Too weak to stand on his own, he was held up by men of the 55th Company as he delivered his message to Cooke: Captain Wass had been hit in the back by a machine gun bullet and was out of action.

Cooke knew that there were more machine guns hidden in the wheat, but he had to take his remaining men and support the 18th Company in the assault on the high ground ahead. A quick glance over the railroad parapet revealed a storm of artillery pounding the Marine battalion, "like the sound of a dozen blacksmiths rhythmically pounding an anvil. Wham, wham, wham, and again, wham, wham, wham." He took one last look at his fallen runner and then moved forward into the storm of shells bursting in the ground ahead. As Cooke departed, Whitey called out, "When you get out, eat that big steak for me, will you?" referring to his earlier conversation with the lieutenant. With tears in his eyes, Cooke pushed into the fields filled with dead and wounded Marines. Some of the injured were able to stagger to the rear, others begged for help, and some of them just lifted their heads, watched the Marines go by, and then laid back in stillness.

Cooke noticed two wayward tanks heading his way, accompanied by an array of shell bursts. The Marines gave the tanks a wide berth and watched as a shell ripped one of them open; the two crewmen ran from the tank, followed by the flames of an erupting fire. The last tank made its way safely past the Marines in the midst of a storm of explosions, making a stark impression on Cooke. "The other animated pillbox waddled hurriedly past us," he noted, "rattling its way to safety, but with a fringe of bursting shells close to its stern."[47]

Cooke recognized the injured Captain Murray stumbling to the rear, blinded by the blood running down his face and unable to hear Cooke's attempts to communicate. The sight of such a superb leader in that helpless state left Cooke in shock, and he wondered whether he would ever follow

Murray's compass again. Cooke now knew that at least two of the 2nd Battalion's four company commanders were wounded, and he pushed forward into the crushing shell bursts, eager to join the advance. He preferred the front line of any assault to the horrendous sights around him.

Soon thereafter, Cooke arrived at the rear line of the battalion, hugging the ground between an abandoned trench and the road leading toward the crest of the hill. Miraculously, he also reached the far side of the barrage after running into the Marines' second assault line. Cooke recognized Second Lieutenant Fred H. Becker pushing his 18th Company platoon forward to join the first line of the attack. He shouted out to Becker, who smiled and waved in acknowledgment. Becker, known by his football nickname "Slats," was a 1916 All American tackle for the University of Iowa, the first Iowa football player to achieve that honor.[48] Becker took one step toward Cooke and then disappeared in an explosion. The blast knocked Cooke to the ground and left him with a wound in his stomach. "A long, prolonged icicle drove deep in my side" was how he described the pain. "The ice melted into molten fire which spread slowly up one side of my body." He carefully got to his feet and immediately saw Becker's lifeless body. A piece of shrapnel had ripped into his neck, severing his jugular vein. "The boy I had come to France with, bunked, eaten and played with, was gone," he observed. "Hardly enough of his body remained for a decent burial."[49]

One of his last letters home arrived in late July, wherein "Slats" confided to his parents while recovering after his first wound at Belleau Wood, "Everyone wants to get in on the action, and all feel slighted when not in combat when there is important fighting to be done."[50] On August 3, 1918, the fallen army lieutenant's family in Waterloo, Iowa, had their worst fears realized when official word of his death arrived. A letter arrived addressed to Becker's mother, sent by a Marine officer, that expressed an ultimate tribute to her son. "He was loved and respected by his men, and they would follow him anywhere," the officer wrote, "He had the admiration of all the Marine officers. We were glad and proud to have him as one of us."[51]

Becker's body was first buried with other Americans on the field where he fell, marked by an upturned rifle, his identity tag attached with a piece of wood. He was later moved to a larger cemetery with other American graves, "hurriedly dug, each with a wooden cross, or a rifle and a helmet as a headpiece."[52] His remains were recovered and returned to his home in Waterloo, Iowa, in 1921. More than 5,000 people turned out for his funeral, including many Iowa students, members of the 1916 Iowa football team, and brothers from Becker's Kappa Sigma fraternity.[53]

The Marines paused in the wake of the explosion, awaiting orders. Although he was in severe pain, Cooke refused to let his men down. He motioned to the front 200 yards away and simply ordered, "Come on." Shells were still exploding around them as the German spotters shortened the range, but the Marines kept going, reaching the front line quickly. They found that the leading assault wave had halted short of the road but only a hundred yards from the crest of the Lechelle ravine. They could go no further. The German barrage savaged the Marines' advance; machine gun and rifle fire swept the road only yards away, blocking the Marines' path. Cooke saw no other officers in the line, which was in disorder.

Some Marines tried to crawl forward, while others took cover behind any available shelter in an attempt to survive the enemy fire. Cooke knew that a counterattack would certainly overrun the Marines, and it could occur at any moment, as darkness was beginning to cloak the battlefield. "Get back in the trench," Cooke shouted, pointing down the hill. At first, the Marines remained motionless, for they had been taught never to give up ground. Many refused the order until they recognized Cooke. "He's all right," a Marine spoke up, "it's Mr. Cooke." The men withdrew to the relative safety of the trench, pulling in as many of the wounded and dead as they could.

Safely established in the trench, Cooke heard a voice call out, "Who gave that order to fall back?" He turned to see an angry First Lieutenant Percy D. Cornell striding up the ditch. When Cornell realized that it had been Cooke, he ended his inquiry with a simple, "Oh." When asked whether there were any other officers who were unhurt in the three companies, Cornell replied, "How many do you see?" Cooke knew his wounds would soon put him out of action, and he had to pass his command to the senior officer, even if that was Cornell. Cornell reported that Keyser had been seen nearby, but a quick search failed to find the major. "He crawled forward to reconnoiter just before the barrage came down," a Marine reported. "He must be either killed or captured by now."[54]

To make matters worse, a runner arrived from Ely, bearing an order that Cooke described as "dripping with vitriol." The commander of the 3rd Brigade informed the Marines that the 9th Infantry's flank was completely open and his soldiers were taking fire from the enemy at Lechelle woods. Ely wanted "to know where we were and what the this-and-that we thought we were doing." Essentially, he "wanted us to get on the job and do something about it." The runner had been authorized to take the senior Marine officer to the correct position so there would be no mistake. "The hell you pipe," Cooke replied. "Go back and tell your Colonel we never heard of Lechelle Woods. And he'd better look out for his own flank. Both ours are open and if anyone needs protection, it's us. But we're gonna take this hill and unless you want to stay for the fireworks, you better beat it." Even as he chased the army runner away, Cooke knew that he was done. He turned command over to Cornell and was helped to the rear. "It was a bitter feeling to have to give up," he observed as he went back down the hill. "So many of my pals had stayed to the finish," he mourned. "On my way back to the ravine I saw them in the fields, their bodies stiff and inert but still facing the enemy."[55]

Unknown to Cooke, Keyser was still alive, but he was pinned down by machine gun fire in between the two lines of Marines. First, he tried to get back to the second line of advance but was driven to shelter in a wagon rut with both his battalion runners. They attempted to get back to the battalion, but the bullets ranging overhead made it impossible. As the shadows fell over the battlefield, they crawled to a shallow ditch that led them back to the scattered Marines still in advance of the trench-line position that Cornell commanded. As Keyser moved among the Marines, he noticed they had exhausted their supply of grenades during the daylong fight. Absent tank support, it would be too costly to try to take out the machine guns in the darkness without grenades. In addition, Keyser had received no word from the 18th Company, which he believed had advanced with the army, and he no idea of its position.[56] Reaching the same conclusion as Cooke, Keyser ordered the Marines to take cover in the trench line. He then moved to the remaining Marines in the forward line and pulled them back as well. He dispatched runners to Feland at regimental headquarters, advising him of his position and adding, "I shall remain here holding [the] line until further orders. My whole battalion is utterly exhausted, having had no hot food or drink for 60 hours."[57]

The impossibility of coordinating the attack came to Upton as he crossed the fields under German artillery fire. Six runners followed the colonel, but a shell burst killed one man and took the foot off another. The headquarters group paused while the wounded soldier was bandaged and then ran forward again. Following the sound of machine gun fire to locate his forward units, Upton pressed ahead through the wheat fields, where he found the wounded being cared for by their comrades. Upton ordered the uninjured soldiers to leave the wounded and join his column. He then proceeded to his farthest units on the right, discovering that they were being held up by German machine guns in the wheat field. With darkness approaching, Upton knew he had to halt the attack. All three of his battalion commanders had been killed or wounded, and only 300 men remained of the 2nd and 3rd Battalions on the right, now commanded by young first lieutenants. No word came from the left flank. He knew nothing about the status of either his 1st Battalion or Keyser's Marine battalion.

The only 2nd Division units that were not in the fight were Colonel William Mitchell's 2nd Engineer Battalion and most of the 4th and 5th Machine Gun Battalions, which finally received their guns at 6:00 p.m. Chief of Staff

Brown ordered Mitchell to enter the ravine east of Vauxcastille and serve as the 2nd Division reserve, explaining that Mitchell might have to use his "own judgment after arriving there because messages were not being properly delivered to their destination."[58] At 9:20 p.m. Mitchell learned of the fall of Vierzy and ordered his regiment forward. Half of the 4th Machine Gun Battalion never moved forward, despite orders from General Bowley to join the attack; the battalion claimed it received "later orders" to remain in place until nightfall. Casualties were heavy. The two platoons of the 4th Machine Gun Battalion that supported Upton's attack lost the equivalent of three squads killed and wounded, which forced the survivors to leave their machine guns on the field during the night. The 5th Machine Gun Battalion bravely entered the wheat fields with two companies each assigned to the 9th and 23rd Infantry Regiments. The machine gunners made a valiant effort to establish contact with their assigned infantry battalions, but with little success.[59]

Under the cover of darkness, Upton finally resigned himself to the attack's failure. The orders for his 9th Infantry to halt at nightfall and entrench in a line 100 yards from the edge of the German wheat field simply confirmed what the soldiers had already wisely decided to do: dig in and wait for daylight. Battalions and companies remained intermixed. Contact was established with the 23rd Infantry on the right at Hill 132, but there was still no sign of the Moroccans on the left. Both battalions of the 2nd Engineer Regiment appeared as well. The engineers moved through the murky wheat fields in platoon columns until they reached the forward line of the infantry regiments, helping them dig in for the night and broadening the trenches toward Hill 132. Major Brown's 1st Battalion dug in with the 23rd Infantry, while the 2nd Battalion supported the 9th Infantry.

The four companies of the Marine 6th Machine Gun Battalion also reflected the fragmented nature of the evening attack. The reserve battalion came forward at the end of the fight to help stabilize the front. The 15th Company remained with the 9th Infantry, facing Charantigny, while the 23rd Company supported the 23rd Infantry east of Vierzy. The 77th Company found its way to back to Vierzy after the 9th Infantry's attack, and the 81st Company dug in, in reserve, at Beaurepaire Farm.[60]

The best news was the arrival of food. Colonel Mitchell ordered the engineer field kitchens to set up in the Vierzy ravines to the rear. Three trucks reached Vierzy as well, filled with lifesaving entrenching tools. With Mitchell now on the battlefield, Ely left to report the results of the day to division headquarters. Mitchell took over command of the 3rd Brigade until Ely's return at 2:20 a.m. More of the absent machine gun companies arrived in the darkness, and they were deployed to cover the ground to the east in support of the infantry line.[61]

Upton dug his own "grave like" foxhole, scattered straw over the dirt floor, and then covered himself with straw to serve as a blanket. Still, sleep eluded the colonel as a stream of messages arrived from brigade headquarters. The messages finally ended at 1:35 a.m. when a runner from Ely arrived, ordering Upton to report to headquarters for a meeting at 1:30 a.m. The tired colonel assured the runner that by the time he walked the two and a half miles to headquarters, the meeting would be long over. No more messages arrived that night. Upton ordered an officer to share his foxhole for warmth. The two shivered until dawn, finally sleeping from sheer exhaustion.[62] Rest also proved difficult for the Marines who were trying to sleep in their forward positions. "The night was cool and clear, the stars shining," recalled Corporal McCune. "Wounded Marines lay groaning in the fields because there were not enough stretchers to care for all."[63]

At the same time, General Fayolle, commanding the French Group of Armies of the Reserve, issued new orders after evaluating the successes of the day. The 10th Army made the largest advances on July 18, with the XX Corps led by the American 2nd Division at Vierzy. However, the Allied line angled back on both flanks from Harbord's farthest advance. The 1st Moroccan Division and the 1st American Division pushed past Chaudon and Ploisy to the north, while the French XXX and XI Corps captured Villers le Petit and Chouy, respectively. The French 6th Army also made smaller gains on its front to the south, including Courchamps, Licy-Clignon, Torcy, and Belleau. However, the most credit belonged to the XX Corps, which captured 10,000 of the 12,000 Germans taken prisoner during the assault.[64]

Despite the victories of the day, General Mangin only partially accomplished his initial objectives for July 18. The primary objective had yet to be achieved—that is, cutting the Soissons–Château-Thierry road by taking the high ground between Hartennes and Villemontoire. At 8:00 p.m. he ordered a renewal of the attack the following morning at 4:00. The II Cavalry Corps would now lead the attack, in the hope that the mounted force could break through the shattered German lines and race to the high ground. However, the potential folly of such an attack, even against broken lines, caused Mangin to caution the II Cavalry Corps to send its forces into the attack "separately and, especially by small units." At the same time, the surviving tank units received the same orders that had been so successful in breaking the German lines earlier that day. "Infantry divisions will employ the tank units at their disposal," read the XX Corps' plan of attack, "using the heavy tanks first, insofar as possible, and employing the light tanks only in case of necessity."[65] Just as on the morning of July 18, no prior artillery preparation would be employed. Instead, rolling barrages would cover the advance and, it was hoped, preserve the element of surprise.

Even as these orders were being written at 10:00 p.m., Major General Harbord transferred his 2nd Division headquarters from Verte Feuille Farm to Beaurepaire Farm, just over a mile from the 2nd Division's front lines. By doing so, he eliminated the frustrations he had experienced during the day when trying to communicate with his commanders; however, his new vantage point also gave him a firsthand view of the rigors of battle. Beaurepaire Farm became a prominent medical and supply collecting point for the 2nd Division due to the nearby Verte Feuille Farm, which marked the main road through the Forest of Retz between Soissons and Villers Cotterets. A constant stream of couriers, ammunition supply parties, and Marines and soldiers passed by.

The most unnerving sights and sounds, however, came from the aid station established there, which even the veteran Harbord labeled "a very distressing scene." The rapid advance and resulting traffic jam prevented the 2nd Division's medical support from reaching the battlefield. The wounded who had assembled at the aid station went without treatment all day and into the night. The constant trickle of injured grew to a throng that filled the farmyard and spilled into the nearby fields. Evacuation proved impossible; ambulances simply could not reach the front. The cruelest difficulty was the lack of water to quench the thirst of the Marines and soldiers who had fought all day in the open fields under the hot sun. Random German aircraft added to the misery by droning overhead, disturbing the sleep of the men below. "There were wounded Germans, Americans and dark skinned Moroccans side by side on the ground, blood over everything," Harbord recalled, "clothes cut away, some men dead, and a ceaseless stream of traffic still pouring to the front with ammunition and supplies for the fighting."[66]

Not yet aware of the orders being prepared for a renewal of the attack, Harbord paused at his headquarters at Beaurepaire Farm to reflect on the day, describing it as a "hectic one for a new Division Commander," but then he focused on the issues his division would face the following morning.[67] He refused to sleep and attempted to prepare his command for battle, which was a difficult task, considering his lack of knowledge of the terrain ahead or the friendly units on his flanks. The 2nd Division's line of communications was immediately broken, given its length and the rapidity of the advance that day. As a result, little knowledge of the battle's progress reached division headquarters.

At 2:00 a.m. a courier arrived at Beaurepaire Farm with orders from XX Corps headquarters to renew the attack at 4:00 a.m., only two hours away. Harbord felt less comfortable about the order when the courier expressed astonishment at the advanced position of the 2nd Division, which differed from the understanding at corps headquarters. Regardless of the disconnect, the order to attack stood. Where the Americans were situated made little difference. The road ahead on the high ground must be cut before the Germans recognized their difficulty and prepared their defense accordingly.

Harbord and Chief of Staff Brown quickly drew up four-paragraph Field Order 16, translating the XX Corps directive. At 3:00 a.m. Harbord published the order, which simply established the known German line of defense and the 2nd Division's objective: capture a line running from the town of Hartennes et Taux to Bois d'Hartennes and finally to Bois de Concrois. Once this line was taken, the 2nd Division would own two miles of the crucial road to Château-Thierry.

To support the attack, Harbord advanced the division's skirmish line into the wheat fields east of Vierzy, to a line running north and south just over half a mile east of the town. The division artillery was already in place. The 12th Artillery Regiment had moved forward to Beaurepaire Farm the previous afternoon, shortening the range to the German defenders; other batteries unlimbered their guns in the open fields, just short of the captured German artillery position. Several German cannon were still operational, with plenty of ammunition piled nearby. Army gunners quickly turned the enemy cannon to the west and added their fire to the barrage to be unleashed on the German high ground.[68]

At the same time, Harbord knew that the remaining units at his disposal were inadequate for the mission ahead. Three full infantry regiments had made the attack the previous day and suffered heavy casualties while accomplishing the breakthrough. Now Harbord had little choice as he selected the units to participate in the attack. Every infantry unit under his command had fought hard that day, except for the XX Corps' reserve, the 6th Marines.[69]

Having witnessed the large number of German prisoners being escorted to the rear and the massive enemy casualties in the fields as they moved forward, the officers and men of the 6th Marines were "in high spirits at the brilliant success of the drive and were eager to take their part in the advance," according to their regimental history.[70] The stragglers who had fallen out during the night march rejoined the regiment in groups of ones and twos, and by 11:00 a.m., the regiment was close to full strength. The men of the 6th Marines were now ready to take part in the battle, though up to that point, their only brush with combat involved being strafed by German aircraft while resting in their reserve position.

Although the main effort would fall to the 6th Marines, it would be supported by the 2nd Engineer Battalion fighting as infantry, the division's 4th

Machine Gun Battalion, and the four companies of the Marine Brigade's 6th Machine Gun Battalion. The entire "force [was] regarded by me as inadequate to the task," Harbord reported, "but no other was available."[71] In fact, much of the planned support failed to materialize. Colonel Mitchell, commanding the 2nd Engineer Battalion, protested that his men were already committed to holding the 2nd Division's line and could not be spared. Mitchell's 2nd Battalion defended the 9th Infantry's lines, tenuous after the losses of the night before, while the 1st Battalion backed up the 23rd Infantry in front of Vierzy. Brown refused to change the orders, so Mitchell gave the job to the 1st Battalion, choosing to keep his 2nd Battalion with the 9th Infantry. The army's 4th and 5th Machine Gun Battalions also fell away from the attack, as they were required to support the 9th and 23rd Infantry positions.[72]

Harbord recognized that these four designated Marine battalions and another battalion of engineers were inadequate to take the high ground ahead. The previous evening's failed attack over the same ground had involved nine infantry battalions, aided by the critical element of surprise, which was no longer in play. The attackers had managed to capture the Vierzy ravine, but the fields from the high ground at Lechelle to Charantigny to the fields before Tigny had thwarted the 2nd Division's evening movement with little trouble. In addition, the Germans had used the entire night to bring up reserves, position artillery, and build a proper line of defense.

The only additional support Harbord could count on was a promised detachment of twenty-eight French tanks to attack with the Marines and engineers, along with two regiments of the French 6th Cavalry Division, which had been ordered to fight dismounted on the Americans' right flank. Despite their orders, both the French commanders and the division and brigade commanders protested the use of cavalry in the attack, stating that they "preferred not to be used in actual fighting unless a gap occurred in the line."[73]

Most important, virtually every soldier and Marine who was still in the fight had had no food or water for the past twenty-four hours, except for what could be scavenged from nearby farms. However, "sensible" food arrived for a few lucky soldiers of the 23rd Infantry, still posted in the fields outside of Vierzy. Some of their field kitchens were able to get rations through to the front. Canned tomatoes, applesauce, "corn willy," and coffee constituted the feast, which was much appreciated by the thirsty and hungry soldiers. Everyone else went hungry.[74]

Despite an inadequate attacking force, the difficult terrain, the short time to plan, the lack of support on each flank, and the exhaustion of his command, Harbord knew the attack must proceed, no matter the difficulties. The only thing he could do to alter the order was to delay the timing of the attack. Given the late arrival of the French corps' missive, Harbord recognized the impossibility of crafting an assault in an hour. He therefore delayed the jump-off time to 7:00 a.m., although this meant losing the advantage of the partial concealment of dawn. This gave the Marine staff officers a few more hours to prepare, and most of the Marines were able to get a few precious hours of sleep, much needed after spending the last two nights traveling by camion and marching in the rain. Despite the fighting ability demonstrated by the 6th Marines, the 6th Machine Gun Battalion, and the army's 4th and 5th Machine Gun Battalions and 2nd Engineers at Belleau Wood, Harbord knew that their losses suffered in July would likely be as high as those in June.[75]

The 2nd Field Artillery Brigade also received orders to support the attack. German aircraft had bombed the guns of the 3rd Battalion, 17th Field Artillery Regiment, during the night but inflicted only one casualty among the massed weapons. As daylight approached, they deployed forward again, with Battery E moving to Beaurepaire Farm and Battery F moving to Vauxcastille.[76]

At 4:30 a.m. the men of the 6th Marines were awakened from their bivouac in the ravine near Beaurepaire Farm, and at 5:00 a.m. they received orders to move to the front lines. They were ordered to leave behind everything except their weapons and ammunition. The Marines gave a last wistful look at their "clean clothes and blankets" and began "a stiff march" forward into the Vierzy ravine at 6:00 a.m., reaching their attack positions thirty minutes later.[77] Major Holcomb's 2nd Battalion led the march, followed by Hughes's 1st Battalion and then Sibley's 3rd Battalion. The regiment's 2,800 Marines silently filed down the ravine and then marched to the railway station, where they found Lieutenant Colonel Lee at his headquarters, awaiting the column.[78]

Daybreak signaled the return of German aircraft, which quickly established air superiority over the battlefield. Soldiers of the 9th Infantry recalled that "flock after flock of Bosche planes flew over, giving the Bosche artillery exact range of our position" and giving notice that any further advance would be targeted by shell fire.[79] German aircraft soon identified the 6th Marines' movement and called in artillery on the Marines marching along the roads. Shells struck around the column, as the German air superiority proved decisive. Aircraft added their own bombs to the shelling, inflicting casualties before the Marines got near the front line.[80]

Soissons Tour

Stop 23. Vierzy Railroad Station, 49°17'27.7"N 3°16'40.0"E

Continue on the D 808, bearing right at the intersection, and proceed into the town of Vierzy. D 808 becomes the Rue du Vieux Chateau. At 2.0 kilometers, turn right, following the D 808. Carefully cross the railroad tracks and park at the railroad station. The modern track is on the same ground as in 1918, and the battle scars are still visible on the original station. The station became headquarters for the 4th Brigade, and it was where Colonel Lee briefed his battalion commanders before dawn on July 19.

Carefully look down the tracks toward the town, where you can see the tunnel used by both the Germans and the Americans as a hospital. Many Germans were captured here, and the tunnel was blocked during the war so they could not escape from the other end.

Notice the steep ravines that held the caves where many Germans were captured. The 23rd Infantry and the 5th Marines arrived and fought to take the town of Vierzy, which was accomplished by midafternoon.

The D 808 now turns into the D 174. Proceed on the D 174, stopping in 559 meters at the town hall parking area. You can walk down the main street and get an idea of the house-to-house fighting that took place on July 18. The factory building across the tracks was the site of fierce German resistance and eventual surrender. You can easily imagine the fighting that unfolded here, with army units on both sides of Vierzy battling their way down the ravine. Note the château on the high ground south of town, which was also the scene of heavy fighting.

Stop 24. Vierzy Cemetery, 49°17'15.8"N 3°17'23.3"E

Continue on the D 174 for 550 meters; it now becomes the D 172. There is a small parking area at the entrance to the cemetery. Park here and get out to examine the terrain, which perfectly illustrates the peculiar nature of the battlefield. You cannot see the flat plains around the town; nor can you be seen.

This terrain was heavily contested by the 5th Marines and was a jumping-off point for the 23rd Infantry's evening attack on July 18. On the following morning, the 6th Marines and 6th Machine Gun Battalion staged their attack from the end of this ravine.

German artillery rained shells on the town on the evening on July 18 with deadly accuracy, thanks to German aircraft spotters. Some of the approximately 800 German prisoners became casualties, along with the soldiers and Marines. These captive Germans posed a threat should they decide to rush the Americans and continue the fight. Major Lay, the 4th Brigade's adjutant, pulled six Marines from their line companies and had them escort the Germans to the rear. "He was zealous, cool and courageous," Lay's Navy Cross citation read. "He was an inspiration to the men."[1]

The deadly artillery continued to inflict many casualties and led to many narrow escapes. While Lay was conferring with another Marine officer, a deadly whistle signaled the approach of a 150mm shell. The shell exploded only ten feet away, giving the Marines no time to take cover. Five officers and seven men were killed instantly, and ten more were wounded. The blast propelled Lay into the doorway of a nearby building, but miraculously, he escaped death.[2]

14

July 19, 1918—Attack of the 6th Marines
"We Threw Away the Hope of Life, and Yelling at the Top of Our Voices, We Struck Their Line"

THE MEN OF THE 5TH MARINES, still holding in the fields before Lechelle, awoke at 4:00 a.m. to the pall of a general haze surrounding them. They "stood to" and withdrew to the woods near the Vierzy ravine, "worn out, clothes torn, and covered with mud."[1] Hot food arrived from the company field kitchens, carried by four recently acquired German prisoners. The Marines rested and took advantage of the rare opportunity to observe the division artillery in the ravine, positioned wheel to wheel to support the 6th Marines' attack. Additional guns arrived, taking less comfortable positions in the open fields nearby. Wagons filled with ammunition delivered shells to the anxious batteries, then departed to take on new loads. Another distraction arrived in the form of a wounded French aviator floating down in a parachute after a losing encounter with a German fighter plane. German aircraft still ruled the skies over the battlefield.

Lieutenant Colonel Lee concentrated the 6th Marines at the Vierzy railway station at 6:40 a.m. The attack force now consisted of his three infantry battalions, along with the regimental 73rd Machine Gun Company and the 81st Machine Gun Company from the 6th Machine Gun Battalion. Veteran Marine officers of long standing, battle hardened from a month in Belleau Wood, commanded each of the battalions. Major Hughes led the 1st Battalion, Major Holcomb commanded the 2nd Battalion, and Major Sibley headed the 3rd Battalion.

Among the 6th Marines, Lee was considered a "rough specimen" and an "uneducated man." It was reputed that "at one time [he] had been a fireman" on a railroad. His lack of education and coarse demeanor presented difficulties for many of the college-educated officers under his command. "He drank his share of liquor in battle or any old damn time," remembered First Lieutenant Worton of the 78th Company. "He handled things in a

6th Marine Regiment
Soissons July 1918
Lt. Col. Harry Lee
Casualties during the battle drastically altered the battalion command structure.

Headquarters Company
1st Lt. Wesley W. Walker

Supply Company
Maj. Henry N. Manney, Jr.

8th Machine Gun Company
Capt. Roy C. Swink

1st Battalion
Maj. John A. Hughes

74th Company (A)
1st Lt. Frederick W. Clarke, Jr.

75th Company (B)
1st Lt. Frederick C. Wheeler

76th Company (C)
1st Lt. Macon C. Overton

95th Company (D)
Capt. John Kerns

2nd Battalion
Maj. Thomas Holcomb

78th Company (E)
Capt. Robert E. Messersmith

79th Company (F)
1st Lt. Carlton S. Wallace

80th Company (G)
Capt. Egbert T. Lloyd

96th Company (H)
Capt. Wethered Woodword

3rd Battalion
Maj. Berton W. Sibley

82nd Company (I)
1st Lt. Frederick I. Hicks

83rd Company (K)
Capt. Alfred H. Noble

84th Company (L)
Capt. Frederick W. Karstaedt

97th Company (M)
Capt. Robert W. Voeth

Chart 6. 6th Marine Regiment, Soissons, July 1918

rough way," particularly with regard to his battalion commanders. Lee's command style especially irritated Holcomb and Sibley, who both considered themselves comparative scholars. "They didn't like this rough fellow," Worton recalled, "coming down there and telling them off."[2] Major Hughes was much more accepting of Lee's rough-and-tumble spirit.

Holcomb had commanded the regiment while Lee led the 4th Brigade, awaiting Colonel Neville's return from the hospital. When the regiment moved to Soissons, Holcomb had been offered the position of executive officer of the regiment under Lee, which was appropriate to his rank. However,

Holcomb preferred to remain with his battalion through the battle, after which he would return to the regimental position.[3]

The attacks by the 5th Marines and the 9th Infantry had ended in darkness the night before, leaving only a few hours before the launch of the morning attack. Lee therefore had no real chance to properly reconnoiter the battlefield ahead. Nor could he establish contact with the Moroccans to the north and the French to the south to ensure that the attack would be a combined one, with both flanks secure. The same fog of war affected the entire chain of command, extending from the French army commander to the corps commander. No one in either headquarters was fully aware of the actual position of the American 2nd Division.

Harbord had few options in the early-morning hours of July 19. The attack order had been given in the hope that the corps reserve, the 6th Marines, would be able to repeat the success of the previous day. The German control of the air over the battlefield, combined with the lack of accurate intelligence from the ground, pushed Lee's reinforced Marine regiment into the heart of the German defenses protecting the Soissons–Château-Thierry road, now teeming with newly arrived units that were ordered to hold the line at all costs. The costly attack by the 9th Infantry and the 5th Marines the previous evening demonstrated the ferocity of the German defense. The 6th Marines, moving into the same ground, had no reason to expect anything other than an even stronger effort by its opponents.

Even more troubling, the American 1st Division and the 1st Moroccan Division on the left had not kept up with Harbord's advance, nor had the French division on the right. The German artillery could now center on the American attack across the wheat fields, perfectly guided by both aircraft wireless and forward observers. In designing the attack that morning, Lee intended for the two lead battalions to advance together, presenting a united front against the German defenses ahead of them. No one in the regiment had seen the terrain ahead, except from a distance; nor was there time to learn from the battered Marine and army commanders still in line from the evening assault.

The success of the 2nd Division's morning attacks on July 18 had captured the attention of German commanders. Although their makeshift defensive line had succeeded in stopping the Americans, it proved difficult to locate individual units once they were committed to the fight. At 1:35 a.m. the German 2nd Battalion, 110th Grenadier Regiment, was finally recognized as being on the front lines at La Raperie, ending an argument about its remaining in reserve. The battalion commander reported during the night that the forces holding the center of the division's line were inadequate to meet the anticipated morning assault. The fragments of the German 16th

Reserve, 53rd Reserve, and 159th Infantry Regiments defending the area from La Raperie to Parcy-Tigny had been badly cut up in the previous day's fight. Battalions of the German 110th Grenadier Regiment held both flanks of these units, but the weakened center would require additional support to hold back the expected American infantry and the French tanks.

After early-morning aircraft reconnaissance alerted the Germans to the coming assault, the two grenadier battalions received orders at 7:00 a.m. to extend their flanks across the center of the position, taking up the division's core defensive positions and allowing the remnants of the three regiments to go into reserve. The commanders of the German 27th and 94th Brigades also instructed their front-line units to send patrols ahead of the main line of resistance, eliminating any Allied surprises.[4]

Unknown to the front-line 6th Marine commanders who had planned and executed the assault, the farther the Marines advanced into the open fields, the farther they entered a killing zone where both flanks were held by German defenders. On Holcomb's left, Germans still held Charantigny; on Hughes's right, German defenders occupied the ravine and the town of Parcy-Tigny. Combined with the defenses on the high ground directly ahead, extending from Tigny to Villemontoire, the 6th Marines were attacking into a three-sided killing zone on a flat plain of wheat fields offering little or no cover. They also faced a much different German defense than they had the day before. Massive German artillery reserves were now positioned to command the fields where the 6th Marines would advance. The hills from Tigny to Hill 160 were laced with three full battalions of artillery, supported by three more sections of guns. Behind these cannon were four more battalions capable of longer-range fire. Another battalion covered the northern flank at Villemontoire, while two more battalions held the southern flank at Hartennes. A total of 148 cannon covered the two-mile front of the reconstituted German line on the morning of July 19, with more nearby in support.[5]

At 7:00 a.m., after a brief war council with his battalion commanders, Lee led the march through the town of Vierzy, heading for the German lines. The first objective was only 875 yards away, but almost two miles of open fields stretched ahead of them before they would reach the high ground beyond the Soissons–Château-Thierry road. As Lee's men began their march, the sound of shells ripping through the sky overhead announced the start of the American and French artillery barrage to support the attack. The Marines passed a line of French I Groupment tanks on the town's main street. "The French crews were deathly pale," remembered Private James Hatcher, "and although some of our men tried to cheer them a bit as we passed, they only stared vacantly."[6]

After passing through the village ravine, the three battalions of the 6th

Marines marched up the old sunken road leading east to the wheat fields. Then they separated, taking positions in preparation for their attack. Holcomb and Hughes posted their men in attack formations, with Sibley following in reserve. The Marines were still protected from German sight by the edge of the ravine leading east from Vierzy, but they could not see the terrain that lay ahead. At least fair weather greeted the Marines' advance across the waist-high wheat glistening in the morning sun. The sight of 2,450 Marines spread across the virtually flat fields proved memorable to all who observed the attack. Holcomb's battalion alone extended almost 550 yards across three-foot-high wheat, with 328 yards between the last wave of the first two companies and the front line of the two following behind.

Sibley's 3rd Battalion emerged from the cover of the sunken road, allowing Hughes's battalion to move forward but still remaining in defilade on the slope exiting Vierzy, forming a reserve behind the two lead battalions. Sibley's Marines used the time to banter with one another, telling stories to overcome their nervousness as they waited. A single German artillery round passed overhead, exploding on the back slope of their position. There was little doubt what lay ahead. The Marines knew that the round established the range of the German artillery, and the enemy knew the Marines were coming.

Many Marines were able to peer over the horizon and watch their own shells "ploughing the Boche front line to bits, and destroying many of our enemy," recalled Second Lieutenant Joseph C. Grayson of the 78th Company. He then noticed that the shelling suddenly shifted to only a few yards from the American line ahead. The Marines knew the time for the attack had arrived. Grayson watched as the Marines silently and individually "bade goodbye to 'Her' whom he left in the States." Every man then "gripped his rifle harder, and over the top we went," Grayson remembered. Soon "a yell went up that let the Boche know that we were attacking again, and that they had only a few short hours to live unless they yelled Kamerad and yelled it quickly."[7]

As the two lead battalions of the 6th Marines left the shelter of the Vierzy ravine between 8:00 and 8:20 a.m., the fire from the German artillery pounded Sibley's battalion, which was still under the slope leading out of town. The 84th Company took several casualties before it could even fire a shot. Second Lieutenant Perkinson was one of the first wounded, struck by a machine gun bullet after only fifty yards. The round smashed the bones in his wrist before striking his hip and causing a horrible contusion near his groin. Perkinson realized he was hit "when he felt his wrist give way, and noticed his bloodstained uniform."[8] He was bandaged right away and sent to the rear, walking two painful miles before reaching a hospital for treatment. By the end of the day, all seven of the 84th Company's officers would be hit.

Holcomb and Hughes then approached the 3rd Brigade skirmish line about half a mile east of Vierzy, which was held by elements of the 9th and 23rd Infantry Regiments. They paused to link up with their French tank support, preparing to follow the tanks into the fields ahead. Captain de Blic, commanding the thirty-five French tanks, believed the attack would begin at 7:00 a.m.; he was unaware of the change of time by the Americans. He took his tanks forward at the designated hour but found that the Marine infantry was still waiting for an attack at 8:00 a.m.

The confusion caused a delay of several minutes as the tanks moved forward to lead the 6th Marines across the wheat fields. While the Marines waited, Second Lieutenant John W. Overton of the 80th Company called over to 1st Lieutenant Charlton S. Wallace , commanding the nearby 79th Company, and asked him to make sure his "Skull and Crossbones" pin was sent home to his mother should he fall in battle. Overton was a graduate of Yale University and a "bonesman" of its secret society. He was also a famed college athlete, running the mile in four minutes, sixteen seconds.[9]

The 6th Marines advanced again, following the French tanks at 8:35 a.m. The four lines of the 2nd Battalion advanced "as straight as a die," recalled Major Robert L. Denig, executive officer of the battalion. "Their advance over the open flat plain with their bayonets shining in the bright sunlight was a picture I shall never forget."[10] Lee reported fifteen minutes later, "The attack [is] moving nicely with only four casualties from shell and shrapnel."[11] Despite Lee's optimism, a series of concealed circumstances combined to threaten the attack's success. The distance from the covered ground where the 6th Marines began their movement to the front line of the 3rd Brigade had not been accounted for in the planning; nor had the planners factored in the minutes spent waiting for tank support, as the vehicles moved at a maximum speed of five miles per hour. The time required to get past the front-line positions resulted in the loss of artillery support by the 15th Field Artillery Regiment, which began to fire as soon as the Marines entered the wheat fields and ended as the Marines moved past the American front line, just when Lee was most dependent on the covering fire. The lack of time to conduct an effective barrage also prevented an adequate reconnaissance of the terrain ahead. The regiment, battalion, and company officers had little opportunity to adjust their lines as they continued the assault.[12]

The final hindrance for the 6th Marines was perhaps the most important. Once again, the 1st Moroccan Division, tasked with the mission of protecting the Marines' left flank, failed to advance, as did the 38th Division on the right. This combination of dire news meant that the 2,450 Marines and French tankers were attacking without coordinated artillery support, air support, or support on either flank; moving across open wheat fields with little or no cover; and facing a German defense that was alert and expecting the attack.

Lee was aware of few, if any, of these concerns, but even if he had known, there was nothing he could have done about them. He could only focus on getting his regiment to the Soissons road. Lee established his headquarters on the road to Cabane, just behind the town cemetery. He was especially concerned with the capture of a German major and nine other prisoners from a machine gun detachment taken near Tigny. Lee interrogated the major, who had lived in New York City prior to the war and responded in perfect English. He informed Lee that the German forces defending the fields had been significantly reinforced during the night and were awaiting a new attack by the Americans. This vital intelligence alarmed Lee, who directed that the prisoners be taken back to Neville for his consideration. But before the column had moved a hundred yards on the road back to Vierzy, a large German shell exploded in the midst of the group, killing everyone, including the guard. Neville never received the intelligence, as the momentum of the attack moved forward to the wheat fields to the east.[13]

The Marines of Hughes's battalion advanced toward the cover of a sunken road, just ahead of the 23rd Infantry's advance positions. There they waited for the supporting French tanks to move into position, all the while being subjected to accurate German artillery fire. After what seemed like an eternity, the tanks finally arrived, allowing Hughes to order his lead companies to attack. They followed fifty yards behind the tanks—eight large Schneider and four light FT-17 tanks. The Marines had little time to communicate with the tank crews to coordinate their attack as the tanks lumbered ahead into the open fields.

German artillery immediately fired at the tanks but scored no hits. The tanks moved into the wheat fields, and the Marines followed at a respectful distance, wary of the tanks' ability to draw German fire. The larger vehicles' top speed was just over four miles an hour, but their cruising speed proved to be an agonizingly slow one to two and a half miles per hour, forcing the Marines to maintain the same pace. All their training mandated a rapid advance to clear the killing zone, pushing the attack into the German lines with as few casualties as possible. Instead, the slow Allied advance allowed the German artillery to punish the Marines with a heavy barrage, bracketing both tanks and men.[14]

The veteran German machine gunners at first offered only docile resistance, waiting patiently until the Americans had moved well past the 23rd Infantry's front line. Once the Marines were completely within the killing zone, they would be unable to withdraw easily. At 9:50 a.m. Lee reported,

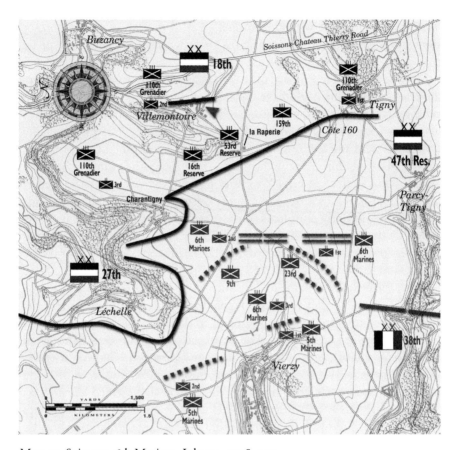

Map 19. Soissons, 6th Marines, July 19, 1918, a.m.

"We are advancing nicely. Think Tigny ours. Tanks are doing fine work. The enemy are retiring. Things are going well. Casualties normal."[15] At the same time, Sibley advanced to support the apparent success of the lead battalions, with two companies in attack waves and two in support. Sibley sent the 84th Company to cover Hughes's left flank and the 82nd and 83rd Companies to assist Holcomb's right. The 97th Company went forward in reserve of the 84th Company. All three battalions of the 6th Marines were now committed to the assault, leaving the 6th Machine Gun Battalion as Lee's only reserve should the attack falter.

Shortly before 10:00 a.m. the Germans opened fire with full force on the Marines, using artillery, machine guns, and rifles. As the German machine gunners joined the storm of shells striking both battalions in their advance past the 23rd Infantry, Holcomb and Hughes diverged, drifting in opposite directions but both of them moving toward a severe threat from flanking machine gun fire. The wheat fields offered little cover from the storm of shot and shell that washed over the open formations. Although the tanks were unharmed, casualties mounted in Hughes's battalion.

The German 1st Battalion, 110th Grenadier Regiment, added to the artillery barrage with rifle and machine gun fire 650 yards in front of the trenches, bringing the attack to a halt. "The Boche start firing at once with one pounders, machine guns, and seventy sevens," recalled Private Vivian D. Corbly of the 74th Company. "The tanks receive most of the shells at first but as we gain on them in the heavy wheat field, we are the target."[16] The tanks would turn back toward the Marines and lead them forward, repeating the maneuver to get the Americans closer to the German grenadiers.[17]

Hughes's Marines took heavy fire on their exposed flank. The German machine guns primarily punished First Lieutenant Macon C. Overton's 76th Company, which suffered heavy casualties when two captured French tanks appeared from the low ground near Parcy-Tigny. Hughes ordered Second Lieutenant Walter S. Fant Jr. and the fifty-eight Marines of his platoon to maneuver through the wheat and attack the tanks from their flank. Getting into position with little or no cover cost Fant two-thirds of his Marines. The lieutenant and two of his men finally reached the tanks; at such short range, the tanks' weapons could not deploy to hit the Marines. However, all three Marines were out of ammunition, making the contest almost equal. Not to be denied, Fant and his Marines broke into the vehicles with their trench knives, engaging in hand-to-hand combat with the crews until all the Germans were killed. All three Marines were seriously wounded in the fight, and Fant was later decorated with the Silver Star.[18]

After eliminating the tanks, Hughes's men advanced toward Tigny but were stopped when a hidden German machine gun cut into their right flank, driving the Marines to cover. The German machine gunners patiently waited until the entire battalion had passed before firing, allowing them to take perfect shots at the entire Marine formation. Second Lieutenant Scott M. Johnston and Corporal William H. Faga of the 76th Company charged the gunners and captured the deadly machine gun; Johnston was severely wounded in the head and chest. The lieutenant refused to leave his men until he was ordered to the rear by Overton. Both Johnston and Faga received the Navy Cross for their bravery. Johnston died of his wounds on August 15.[19]

Hughes's advance approached close enough for the German cannon to target the French tanks. At 10:30 a.m. the first tank exploded after being hit by a shell, and for the next thirty minutes, more suffered the same fate. German riflemen and machine gunners raked the Marines, who continued to rush forward. The German grenadier battalion kept pummeling the Marines, expending 30,000 light machine gun rounds in two hours, until it finally ran out of ammunition at 11:20 a.m. Hughes's battalion fragmented into small groups of Marines that still pushed forward. "The struggle thro [*sic*] the wheat came near making us 'all in.' . . . We are ordered down many times, but get up again and go forward," Private Corbly wrote. "The entire line never wavered but went forward, regardless of the gaps made in it."[20]

At 11:45 a.m. the battalion came within fifty yards of the German lines but could advance no farther. The Germans were contemptuous of the Marines' tactics, estimating that the Americans had lost at least half their initial strength and positing that some Marines got close only "because of the reckless employment, again and again, of new waves of infantrymen, who suffered the heaviest losses possible."[21] The 1st Battalion took refuge in a narrow, sunken road running in a generally north-south direction and awaited further orders.

The 2nd Engineer Regiment waited along the 3rd Brigade's line as the Marines passed over them into the wheat and sugar-beet fields ahead. The engineers and the Marines had formed a bond at Belleau Wood, based on mutual respect earned in battle. "Being in combat with the Marines, cutting wire and going over with them earned our battalion many honors," Private First Class Ralph Williams recalled, "and they adopted us, which is very unusual for Marines to do."[22] Where the Marines went, the soldiers went too, even into the cauldron of fire in the wheat fields. They also had the somber knowledge of what awaited them after watching the 6th Marines disappear into the wheat.

Colonel William A. Mitchell gave the word for his 1st Battalion, 2nd Engineers, to follow Hughes's Marines in support of their attack. "We received orders to advance and join the front line," Private Williams recalled, "and took off on the run . . . it was a terrible experience, but not a man quit." The 2nd Engineers kept up their momentum and passed the beleaguered 6th Marines' lines without realizing it, until Williams noticed two Marines down in a foxhole. The two surprised Marines shouted, "Where in the hell do you think you are going?" When the soldiers replied that they were searching for the Marines' front line, the men in the foxhole informed them that they had passed it thirty yards back and advised them to drop back and "dig in."[23]

Williams and his comrades took the Marines' advice, trying to avoid the sweeping fire of the German machine guns, which were cutting wide paths through the wheat in search of the Americans hidden within. A friend dug a hole about three feet to the right of Williams, calling out that unless he dug deeper, the young private would get a bullet in his butt. Williams called back, "Yeah, buddy, better keep your head down." Williams then noticed "the funniest expression came across his face, which seemed to elongate three inches. Then blood was trickling down his face." A German bullet had smashed across his helmet and passed through his skull, killing the soldier instantly.

Major Holcomb's battalion on the left flank faced the same unrelenting fire, causing his two lead companies to stall. Captain Messersmith, commanding the 78th Company, was one of the regiment's longest-serving officers, having been the third officer to join the 6th Marines at Quantico. He was known as "a tough hombre"—a true compliment in a unit of similarly tough Marines.[24] Messersmith was justly proud of his impressive-looking company, as seventy-two men of the original company were over six feet tall. The company mascot was a bulldog named Dixie, a gift to the first sergeant by his girlfriend at Quantico. The Marines smuggled Dixie to France and trained her so that the dog was allowed to accompany the men to the front lines.

Both the 78th Company and the 79th Company, commanded by First Lieutenant Carleton S. Wallace Jr., were smothered by crossfire from machine guns in front of them and on their left flank, as well as artillery from above. "For the time it lasted, this was one of the bloodiest battles the Seventy-Eighth Company was ever in," recorded the company's postwar history. "Those of us who were not hit dug 'foxholes' in the beet field, and held our position through a day of extreme peril and hardship."[25] A shell fragment took Messersmith out of the fight, and the company's leadership fragmented as officers and noncommissioned officers were killed and wounded one by one. Four second lieutenants, two gunnery sergeants, and six sergeants were wounded by the end of the day. Command of the company fell to First Lieutenant Amos R. Shinkle, aided by Second Lieutenant James P. Adams and Sergeant Elmer L. Sutherland, acting as first sergeant. Lieutenant Shinkle commanded the remains of the company for the rest of the battle. He was a former enlisted Marine, having left his job as a Pennsylvania carpenter to enter the Marine Corps in 1913. He served in Vera Cruz in 1914 but spent much of his enlisted duty as a part-time carpenter at the Marine Barracks in Washington, DC, and was rewarded by a lengthy tour on the presidential yacht USS *Mayflower*. When the war began, Shinkle had just been promoted to corporal, but in the rush to staff officers for the 6th Marines, he was promoted to second lieutenant in July 1917.[26]

First Lieutenant Wallace's 79th Company endured the same misery as Shinkle's Marines. Wallace had been a star long-distance runner at the University of Minnesota and was one of three students recommended by the university president for a Marine Corps commission in 1917. On March 29, 1917, he was elected captain of the university track team, and on May 17 he reported to Parris Island as a second lieutenant. Wallace had just returned to his company after being hospitalized for a wound suffered in April. He now

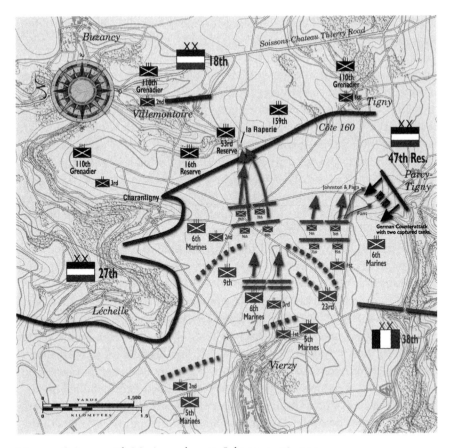

Map 20. Soissons, 6th Marines advance, July 19, 1918, a.m.

moved through the wheat and sugar-beet fields amidst a torrent of machine gun fire and shrapnel. A piece of jagged metal ripped into Wallace's knee, knocking him to the ground. His men were carrying him to the rear on a stretcher when a German fighter strafed the Marines, missing everyone, but putting several holes in the stretcher. Wallace was out of action again less than two weeks after being released from the hospital after his first wound.[27]

The time now came for Holcomb's reserve companies to take the lead. Captain Woodworth's 96th Company moved out of the second line onto the left flank of the battalion to deal with the threat of enfilading fire. Captain Egbert T. Lloyd did the same with the 80th Company, moving to the left and forming the left flank company of the entire regiment. Lloyd was relatively new to the company, having taken command in mid-June, and he was known for carrying a cane into battle. This, among other peculiarities, made the Marines wonder whether he had come to the company directly from an office job. Sergeant Don V. Paradis remembered Lloyd leading the attack: "I could see him in the first wave formation swinging that cane and urging his men forward."[28]

The Marine companies never faltered in their advance, despite the killing fire from three sides. Gaps appeared in the waves of platoons, created by sudden explosions of shell fire or the sweep of a German machine gun. Each individual company's first mission was to catch up to the French tanks. The Marines then had to slow their progress to match the tanks' plodding speed. This frustrated the Marines, who knew that each moment in the open meant more casualties. Once they caught up with the armor, the French tanks became the focus of the German fire. Many of the tanks were put out of action within minutes, bursting into flames as their gasoline tanks exploded. German aircraft also plunged down from above, strafing the Marines with deadly machine gun fire.

The French tanks and the 80th and 96th Companies struck the German trench line at about the same time, causing panic among the cobbled-together elements of the German 16th, 53rd, 220th, and 159th Reserve Regiments, which broke for the rear or attempted to surrender. A mass of sixty Germans popped up from the wheat in front of the 80th Company, intent on surrendering, but their own machine gunners opened fire on both the Marines and the Germans. In the resulting exchange of fire, the surviving Germans ran back to the safety of the Villemontoire ravine. The 80th Company charged through a sugar-beet field after the retreating foe, which disappeared north of the road into the 1st Moroccan Division's zone of operation.

Private Carl Brannen saw Second Lieutenant John W. Overton walking backward toward the German lines, carrying a cane in his left hand and a pistol in his right. Overton shouted something at the Marines, but no one could hear his words with the shell bursts exploding over the company. They all knew what he meant, however: move forward in the attack. Overton was killed shortly thereafter, but his Skulls and Bones pin was recovered and sent home.[29]

The 80th and 96th Companies moved forward to follow the assault on the left flank, losing men with every pass of machine gun fire and every artillery explosion. The gaps in the ranks were quickly filled, but the losses mounted with every step. "A shell hit close to Captain Woodworth and Second Lieutenant Robertson and wounded both of them," Second Lieutenant Clifton Cates of the 96th Company wrote in a letter home. Woodworth pulled himself from the ground, wiping blood from his face. Despite his wounds, the captain smiled and signaled to Cates to lead the company forward.[30]

"On we went," Cates continued. "Soon Lieut. Duane was shot through the leg with a bullet. Next Lieut. Fritz was shot through the hand. That left me the only officer in the company . . . a shell hit right at me and cut a slit in my breeches about four inches across the knee. It gave me a slight wound."[31] The 96th Company took heavy casualties as it closed on the German line. Woodworth reported back to Holcomb on his way to the rear. "His head all tied up, coat torn in rags, left arm helpless, thigh cut up, and in general he was a mass of blood," Major Denig, the battalion's executive officer, wrote in his diary, "but his eyes were sparkling and he was full of pep and ginger."[32]

Cates chased after the Germans below the sugar-beet factory in La Raperie, and they "jumped out and ran like wild deer. Up to that time, the men had kept perfect formation but when the Boche commenced running the men swarmed after them shooting as they ran. The men yelled like a bunch of cow boys as they chased them. It was too funny for words."[33]

Cates's orderly, Private Robert M. Rhodes, became separated from the lieutenant and suddenly found himself alone in the firestorm sweeping the sugar-beet field. Rhodes had enlisted in March and joined the 96th Company in late June as a replacement; he now faced his first real combat, four months and one day after joining the Marine Corps. The former coal miner from Swanton, Maryland, took shelter in a shell hole occupied only by an abandoned German machine gun. Despite the solitary nature of his position, Rhodes joined in the fight, intending to turn the weapon back on the Germans. In his search for ammunition, he found five abandoned German machine guns in a nearby shell crater, each loaded with a belt of ammunition, ready to fire. Rhodes unleashed a barrage of fire on the guns' former owners. The target-rich fields ahead allowed no time to reload, so Rhodes expended each belt of 250 rounds and then moved on to the next weapon and repeated the process. The firepower generated by Rhodes drew the attention of the Germans throughout the day. They assumed the shell crater was an American strongpoint and sent an observation aircraft to discover the source of the deadly rounds, but Rhodes drove off the intruder with a few well-aimed bursts from one of his weapons.[34]

Captain Lloyd, commanding the 80th Company, chased the enemy soldiers running for cover in the Villemontoire ravine north of La Raperie's sugar-beet factory and into the narrow valley leading to town. Holcomb received word from Egbert that, as of 11:00 a.m., he occupied Villemontoire, several hundred yards from the battalion's left flank occupied by Cates's 96th Company. The advance of the two companies broke the Germans' main line of resistance and scattered elements of six German regiments, in addition to Pioneers and *Minenwerfer* crews. "Everybody and everything drifted back through the ravine and to Villemontoire," proclaimed the war diary of the German 3rd Battalion, 216th Infantry. Rumors swept through the panicked ranks that "hostile black colonial troops" were in pursuit of the routed German forces. The terror spread to the artillery, causing the gunners of the German 8th Battery, 269th Artillery Battalion, to abandon their cannon.

A combination of the panic on their right, the approaching French tanks, and a lethal high-explosive barrage laced with gas in the ravine behind them caused the German 2nd Battalion, 110th Grenadiers, to pull back over the hill to the Soissons–Château-Thierry road and beyond, widening the gap in the German lines. Lloyd and his exhausted Marines, the conquerors of Villemontoire, filled their canteens from the town fountain and prepared to hold their position. All the supporting tanks had disappeared, however, pulling back after a well-placed artillery shell blew apart the lead tank on the road near La Raperie. The retreat of the tanks eliminated any chance of continuing the assault, even though the survivors of the 80th Company were only 300 yards from the Soissons–Château-Thierry road.[35]

The attack on Villemontoire and the sugar-beet factory started a panic in the German lines, and more men joined the routed artillerymen. "Our own infantry was retreating in droves," the German 14th Division's war diary recorded. "Mounted officers were able to stop part of them."[36] Not knowing that only a small number of Marines were present in the town, Corps Watter headquarters pulled back the left flank of the German 42nd Division, while elements of the German 14th Reserve Division held defensive positions on the ridge northeast of Charantigny, preventing any further Marine movement down the ravine past Villemontoire.

With their line now secure, the Germans counterattacked with their newly arrived reserves, dispatching two regiments of the 46th Reserve Division and elements of the German 20th Division to retake the lost guns and drive the Americans out of town. The 214th Infantry Regiment of the 46th Reserve Division was ordered to move immediately to retake Villemontoire, and all units were admonished that "the enemy must be prevented at all costs from gaining ground towards the east and across the highway."[37] The Marines' lodgment in the town proved dangerous for the German front, but Lloyd hoped his few men could sustain their position even without reinforcements. As long as they maintained an aggressive front, the enemy would not realize how few Marines were in the town.[38]

As a result of the two days of battle, ten German regiments from five different divisions now defended the German 14th Division's front, with another division on the way, indicating the importance of defending the Soissons–Château-Thierry road. Despite all odds, the handful of Marines not only held their ground but advanced. The Germans reported "some elements descended toward the road."[39]

Villemontoire town square after the battle, summer 1918. (© Pierre PANSIER/ECPAD/Defense)

Meanwhile, the rest of Holcomb's battalion had no idea of the 80th Company's exploits. They were being cut to pieces with every minute they advanced, until "we had nothing left with which to continue the attack."[40] Almost every battalion officer and noncommissioned officer was killed or wounded, with entire platoons annihilated. "The attack just died out," remembered Major Denig, who followed Holcomb with the battalion headquarters detachment. Unable to proceed, the survivors took shelter in the wheat, searching for even the smallest element of protection from the relentless shell fragments and sweeps of German machine guns. The Marines discovered a line of unfinished German trenches, which proved to be a stroke of luck for the battalion; the men took sanctuary in the small depressions of hollowed-out dirt. At least 70 percent of the battalion was out of action. By the end of the day, only six company officers remained unharmed, while nineteen had been killed or wounded. Lieutenant Cates took command of the 96th Company, as all the other officers were out of action. Cates and First Sergeant Maurice E. Barnett advanced the company another several hundred yards. Although wounded, Cates took a position in the slight cover

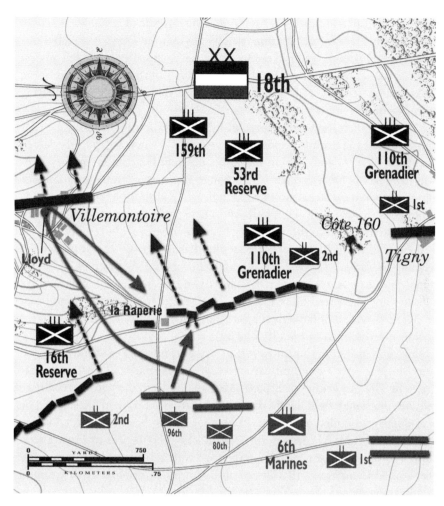

Map 21. Soissons, 80th and 96th Companies attack, July 19, 1918

provided by a rock pile and an abandoned German trench near the Vierzy–La Raperie road. In only two hours, the 96th Company had lost twenty-six Marines killed and fifty-six wounded.[41]

Holcomb and his headquarters detachment sprinted for cover close to La Raperie's factory, hurdling into the wheat and then disappearing into whatever cover might offer a respite from the sweep of machine gun fire. Denig "gathered speed, made a record jump and landed in a fox hole."[42] Holcomb leaped into the same hole, which immediately became the impromptu battalion headquarters. Holcomb looked toward the German lines, while Denig leaned back against the dirt, facing his commander. Denig still carried his entrenching tool and quickly started deepening his side of the hole. Holcomb critiqued his spade work, offering friendly advice until Denig passed him the shovel and Holcomb resumed the work himself, while Denig offered advice. Spent shrapnel rained down on the two Marines during the entire process, striking their helmets, their field glasses, and the men themselves but causing no real wounds.

Holcomb's first concern was securing the battalion's defensive line, not knowing that the 80th Company's advance had opened a gap in the left of the enemy line. At some point during his digging, Holcomb requested support from Major Sibley's reserve battalion to secure that left flank. A familiar figure appeared walking through the wheat, apparently impervious to the explosions around him. Holcomb and Denig quickly recognized Captain Lloyd, who reported to them carrying his distinctive cane; he reminded those in the makeshift headquarters of a shepherd as he walked across the wheat, seeming to lead a "charmed life as stuff was bursting all around him."[43] He stated that he was holding trenches far beyond the sugar mill with only six Marines and requested more men to defend the place. When he found that no Marines were available to support him, Lloyd sadly walked back to his position, determined to hold it anyway.

Holcomb also communicated with Cates, who held a position with sixteen Marines only a hundred yards to their left behind a pile of rocks near the mill. The physical appearance of the young lieutenant from Tennessee reflected the tough fight across the fields; his trousers were in tatters, and he was slightly wounded in the knee. Cates refused to be evacuated, choosing to remain with his Marines in the trench. The early benefit of French tank support proved to be a disadvantage for Holcomb's battalion. When the crews abandoned tanks that were still operational, opportunistic German infantrymen turned the weapons on the Marines.[44]

On the 6th Marines' right, Hughes gathered his remaining men to make another rush to take Tigny. A rolling barrage from the 2nd Artillery Brigade was requested to support the attack, but the artillerymen were under attack themselves. "We changed our gun positions so frequently that there was no time for camouflage," remembered army private Frank Hodson, a gunner with Battery F, 15th Field Artillery. "So guns and men stood exposed to the enemy's fire from German airplanes. One day about sixteen of these planes in battle formation flew over us and for an hour or so made life Hell by dropping bombs wherever they could count the most."[45] The army gun crews worked tirelessly to support the 6th Marines' attack, even using captured German artillery and ammunition. At the same time, they enjoyed a number of German luxuries, including electric lighting, brass beds, and fine china found in underground bunkers.[46]

With both lead battalions and the engineers stalled in the wheat and sugar-beet fields, 6th Regiment commander Lee ordered Sibley's battalion to join the attack. "With the earsplitting crashes of bursting shells and the calls of the wounded ringing in our ears, we lay close to the ground awaiting the order that would commit us to the attack," recalled Private Hatcher. "In a few minutes a second order was called down the line, 'over you go.'"[47] The 36 officers and 850 Marines of Sibley's 3rd Battalion pressed forward into the tempest of machine gun fire to fill the gap between Holcomb and Hughes. Lee knew that the center of the line was unsupported and vulnerable, so he expected Sibley to link his lead battalions. At 9:50 a.m. Sibley detached his two lead companies to fill the gap between Holcomb and Hughes, followed by his second line at a distance of 1,000 yards. Both lead companies of the 3rd Battalion swept into the battle twenty minutes after the initial advance.

However, Sibley could see that his men would be unable to fill the hole entirely. Just as Lee had divided the regiment, Sibley had little choice but to go into battle the same way. He sent the 83rd Company to support Holcomb, while the 84th Company veered to the right to come in on Hughes's left. As the two companies crested the low rise before them, they were greeted with a panoramic view of the wheat fields stretching out to the rolling hills on the horizon. "A lazy breeze gently moved the wheat, which spread like a golden blanket across the smooth plain before us," Private Hatcher recalled. "Heat waves shimmered along the horizon to the right and left while a mile and a half to the front, covered with green trees, rolling hills rose from the plain."[48] Among those distant hills lay the vital German supply line, the road linking Soissons and Château-Thierry. As Sibley entered the killing fields, he noticed gaps still remaining between Holcomb and Hughes. Recognizing that his battalion could not cover all the ground ahead, Sibley brought up his 82nd and 97th Companies, the last 6th Marine infantry companies in reserve. They now joined the other ten already engaged.

At 10:10 a.m. Sibley executed the mission of his two follow-on companies: to attempt to cover the vulnerable ground between Holcomb and Hughes. Lieutenant Hicks took his 82nd Company to the left of Holcomb's battalion to secure that flank, while Captain Voeth's 97th Company joined Captain Karstaedt's 84th Company, advancing to the right near Hughes's battalion. Sibley then ordered Karstaedt and Captain Noble's 83rd Company to move forward and form a line "to fill any gap that may occur between 1st and 2nd Battalions," maintaining contact with each other as they did so.[49] The same wheat fields that looked so spectacular from a distance were already an absolute hell for the two battalions of the 6th Marines.

For those Marines who were still able to dig in, burrowing into the earth proved more difficult than expected. The ground was solid as a rock, but each man managed to scratch out enough dirt to provide cover from the machine gun fire; however, the shells and aircraft still sought their targets in the wheat and sugar-beet fields. Although some units succeeded in pushing forward another half mile or so, both Holcomb and Hughes ordered a halt at 10:30 a.m., acknowledging that their Marines could go no further without adding most of command to the already long list of killed and wounded. The Marines who were still on their feet took shelter in an unfinished line located in the middle of the fields, built by the Germans but never completed. Only Sibley's reinforcements could continue the advance, but the 6th Marines had no more men to call on. The leading French tanks had been the first unit to break, with survivors of the shattered wreckage abandoning their vehicles after advancing only 1,000 yards. The German fire concentrated on knocking out the tanks, which became death traps for the crews.

With his last two companies disappearing into the wheat, Sibley could now evaluate his position. The objective of the Soissons–Château-Thierry road was still more than a mile away. With the depletion of the regiment's reserve, the attack was running out of options. As he watched his battalion depart, Sibley knew the firestorm ahead would require more Marines to punch through the German lines. Sibley gathered his Headquarters Company and two nearby machine gun platoons from the 6th Machine Gun Battalion and made ready to join the attack.[50]

The amount of activity at Sibley's headquarters soon drew the attention of low-flying German artillery observers. The movement of runners bearing dispatches to company and regimental headquarters was unmistakable, and the German aircraft unleashed a barrage of high-explosive shells into the ravine, smashing directly into the Marines gathered there. The Headquarters Company and machine gun platoons suffered heavy casualties, including most of the battalion intelligence detachment and several machine guns.

The 2nd Battalion, 12th Field Artillery, was ordered to follow up the attack by moving onto the open plain. The battalion limbered up and moved to the narrow road between Vauxcastille and Vierzy. German observation aircraft soon discovered the mass of artillery and wagons at a standstill in the defile and called in an artillery barrage mixed with gas shells. Recognizing the impossibility of their mission, the soldiers turned their artillery and caissons to the rear with great difficulty but eventually made their way back to the Beaurepaire ravine, where they rejoined the rest of the regiment, which was pounding Tigny and the Bois d'Hartennes with high-explosive shells.[51]

Despite the ferocious German artillery fire, Sibley's 3rd Battalion pushed through the wheat. It was supported by the 15th, 77th, and 81st Companies of the 6th Machine Gun Battalion; single platoons from the 73rd Machine Gun Company, which was the regimental gun company of the 6th Marines;

6th Machine Gun Battalion
Soissons July 1918
Maj. L. W. T. Waller

Casualties during the battle drastically altered the battalion command structure.

15th Machine Gun Company
Capt. Matthew H. Kingman

23rd Company
1st Lt. William B. Croka

77th Company
Capt. Augustus B. Hale

81st Company
Capt. Alan M. Sumner

Chart 7. 6th Machine Gun Battalion, Soissons

and the Stokes mortar and 37mm gun platoons from Headquarters Company, 6th Marines. Except for Turrill's battalion holding Vierzy, almost every available Marine was now engaged in the attack.

At 10:30 a.m. Noble's 83rd Company reached the remains of Holcomb's Marines, while Voeth's 97th Company did the same with Hughes's battalion. Hicks's 82nd Company joined Holcomb's battalion at 11:00 a.m. but could do little to facilitate the advance, as direct fire from German artillery pummeled the wheat field and machine guns on both flanks raked the Marines' positions. Hicks had only just returned to the company on July 12 after spending a month recovering from a June 6 shell burst that rendered him unconscious. Hicks took command of the company as its senior officer, but the unlucky lieutenant was severely wounded by a German shell burst in the nearby field. First Lieutenant Kortright Church took over the company.

Church, a native of Washington, DC, and a noted athlete excelling in football, basketball, and water polo, attended Phillips-Exeter Academy and then Yale University, graduating in 1912. He studied law at George Washington University and was admitted to the District of Columbia bar, the Supreme Court, and the Court of Appeals. Church worked for munitions manufacturers, including the Winchester Arms Company, until April 1917, when he joined the Army Ambulance Corps. Like many young men of the time, he sought a more active role in the war and requested a transfer to the Marine Corps.[52] Church enrolled as a second lieutenant on August 2, 1917, and was assigned to the fledgling Marine Officers Training Camp at Quantico, Virginia. He was then assigned to the 1st Replacement Battalion, arriving in France in February 1918. Church joined the 82nd Company on June 9 at Belleau Wood, where he saw his first combat in France. When he took over its command from Hicks, he found he could do little to advance his beleaguered Marines.

The rain of shells and bullets forced the Marines to dig in, allowing little opportunity to return fire. Reports back from the company commanders indicated that they had already suffered 60 percent casualties in only sixty minutes of combat. Sibley also noted that the American artillery was silent under the onslaught. Each company fought alone, as contact between them was almost impossible due to snipers, shell bursts, and machine gun fire. Sibley went forward into the wheat, pushing his headquarters closer to the front line to direct his Marines.

In the center of the attack, Karstaedt's 208 Marines of the 84th Company shook off the German fire, refusing to admit defeat. Captain Karstaedt was an old-time enlisted Marine, born in 1878 of German parents. He entered the Marine Corps in 1900 at the age of twenty-one and rose to the rank of sergeant major of the 2nd Battalion, 5th Marines, in 1917. He became a captain in December 1917 in the push to find competent officers to lead the 4th Marine Brigade. Karstaedt took over the 84th Company in March of the following year and was wounded the same month in the company's first duty in the trenches near Verdun. His Marines were veterans now, and they knew exactly what they faced. They also knew that "one must not surrender his thoughts to the horrors about him. That was the spirit of the regiment. Every man did his best by word and by example to cheer his companions."[53]

The storm of German fire soon engulfed the company, with most of the early casualties lost to artillery fire. Private Jonas Johnson disappeared in a "burst of flame, a rush of smoke and dust, and it seemed small pieces of a human body flung far into the air."[54] He is memorialized in the chapel at the Aisne Marne American Cemetery.

Sergeant Russell S. Rankin took command of his platoon after its lieutenant was wounded, leading his Marines into the wheat fields and overrunning a German strongpoint that was delaying the attack. A shell detonated in front of Rankin, ripping the membrane and muscle from his face and leaving it hanging on his chest, attached by only a small strip of skin. Despite the pain, Rankin pressed the remnants of his face onto his head and stumbled to the rear. He recovered from his wounds and returned to duty after the war. Rankin received the Silver Star for his bravery.[55]

Despite its losses, the 84th Company continued to advance, pushing forward in broken platoon lines but never stopping. Marines moved up to fill the gaps left by the fallen. "The shells seemed to come in one solid, scream-

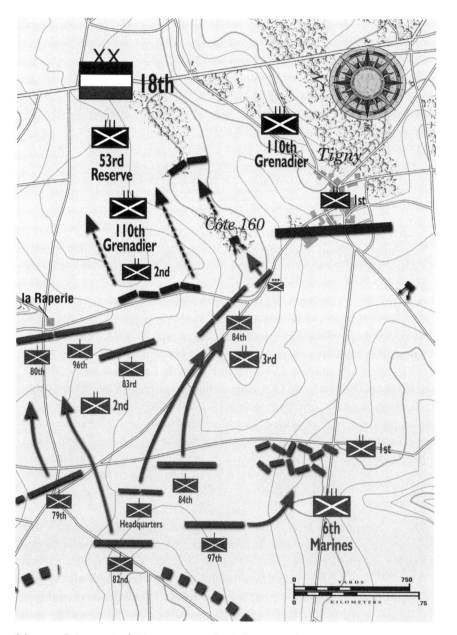

Map 22. Soissons, 84th Company attacks, July 19, 1918

ing, rushing stream," Private Hatcher remembered. "The ground seemed alive with bursting geysers of smoke and dust. Heavy clods and rocks continually rained down upon us and littered the ground."[56]

The shelling was so intense that the Marines' eyes and throats burned from the smoke of the explosions. The 84th Company soon passed the Marines of Hughes's battalion, who were also caught in the barrage. A wounded Marine staggered into their formation, doubled over in pain from a stomach wound. He pitifully called for a hospital apprentice, but there was little chance of him getting to the rear for help. The blood gushing from his stomach wound had already discolored his uniform and created pools of soaked earth under his feet as he paused every few steps and fell to his knees. The vivid memory of this dying Marine remained with the men of the 84th Company, even in the midst of the innumerable horrific sights they witnessed.[57]

The 84th Company followed an old farm trail, which shielded it from some of the German fire; the men of the company were targeted less by the flanking fire that struck the Marines on both sides of their advance. However, the path directed them, as if by fate, to Hill 160, the key to the German positions defending the Soissons–Château-Thierry road just yards away. The hill not only commanded the entire plateau of wheat and sugar-beet fields where the 6th Marines now struggled but also outflanked the German line in Tigny to the south and Villemontoire to the north. Best of all, the vital Soissons–Château-Thierry road lay just beyond the hill, only a rifle shot away.

Although the 84th Company had yet to realize the tactical and strategic opportunity the trail provided, the Marines knew the time had come to repay the enemy for all their fallen comrades in the fields behind them. Their only means of attack was a frontal assault against the German machine guns on the hill. First Lieutenants Edward D. Kalbfleisch and Mark A. Smith, Second Lieutenant Lloyd E. Battles, and Gunnery Sergeant George Gregory were all wounded as the company attacked up the long slope.[58]

The advance swept forward, close enough to allow the enemy to lower their artillery pieces and fire directly at the Marines. The shells ripped through the 84th Company. One passed so close to the head of one Marine that he was almost knocked down by the shock wave. The round hit the ground near another Marine, who was peppered with small pieces of shrapnel but was saved from a fatal wound by the bulk of his "Chau Chau" light machine gun, which deflected most of the shrapnel. The Germans shifted their fire, raining shells on the Marines behind the 84th Company who had gone to ground in the sweeping fields stretching back to Vierzy. Orders came to pause the assault and dig in, taking advantage of the cover. However, German machine gun and rifle fire continued to cut the wheat stalks around the Marines as they scraped the ground with their entrenching tools.

Directly ahead of them was a German machine gun position based on the higher ground of Hill 160 and partially covered by a small group of trees. The Marines' present position was untenable. The ground could not be held, and it was vulnerable to counterattack. The only options remaining were to withdraw or move forward. Captain Karstaedt ordered a continuation of the attack, discarding any notion of retreat. The 84th Company had come too far to fall back now. Before the remnants of the company could make further progress in the dirt, orders came along the line, "Up and at 'em."

As the Marines rose up from the wheat, they looked to their left and right, hoping to see someone who would support them in the attack. They saw only empty fields on both flanks. The 84th Company was alone, but it was nearer its objective than any other 6th Marines unit. Without hesitation, the remaining Marines charged toward the slight elevation ahead, covered with trees and filled with German machine gunners of the 1st Battalion, 110th Grenadiers, and a *Minenwerfer* detachment that destroyed at least two French tanks and dispatched more mortar rounds into the Marines' advance.

The remnants of the 84th Company ran toward a lower patch of ground that extended directly into the tree line, ostensibly offering a bit of cover. As the Marines sprinted to the trees, they were struck by machine guns from their front, left, and right at such close range that the streams of bullets could hardly miss. The veteran German gunners had allowed Captain Karstaedt's Marines to enter the killing zone and were now exacting a heavy toll. The captain led the attack himself until a bullet struck him in the back of the head, appearing to blow open his skull. Of the seven officers who began the attack, only two were still unhurt: Second Lieutenant Ansel Jay Van Housen and First Lieutenant Horatio P. "Hap" Mason III.

Van Housen had left his job as a mail-room clerk at an Eglin, Illinois, publishing house to become an original member of the 84th Company, formed at Quantico in August 1917. He picked up a quick promotion to corporal two months later, reached the rank of sergeant in December, and was promoted to second lieutenant only five days before the attack. Mason was a more experienced officer. A native of Hampton, Virginia, he entered the Marine Corps in 1917 direct from the Virginia Military Institute. Hap spent nine months with the Virginia National Guard, serving on the Mexican border in 1916, and he was a veteran of Belleau Wood, where he was slightly wounded on June 6, 1918. Mason saw Karstaedt go down and knew the momentum of the attack would stall. The Marines were "going down like ten pins," and survival seemed impossible on the shallow slope.[59] Without hesitation, Hap ran ahead of the company and gestured for the Marines to resume the charge. A German bullet struck him in the right shoulder, almost knocking him to his knees. For a split second, the Marines' assault seemed to be in peril as their new commander went down, but Mason quickly shifted his pistol to his left hand and waved the company forward. The Marines responded immediately, rushing to the crest of Hill 160. Private Hatcher observed the blue flash of a machine gun and then picked out the gunners' helmets just yards away. "Making sure of my aim, I fired," Hatcher recalled, "his head gave a sudden jerk then he slumped forward over the gun."[60]

The Marines staggered under the fire of the Germans around them, but they knew their only chance was to close quickly with the enemy and fight at close range, where the German advantage was nullified. "We threw away the hope of life, and yelling at the top of our voices, we struck their line," Private Hatcher recorded, and "although we were hopelessly outnumbered, the fury of our rush overran their machine guns."[61] Hatcher entered the tree line only to find the barrel of a machine gun pointing directly at him through a small thicket of bushes. He fired under the muzzle and then jumped over the brush with his bayoneted rifle, only to find the gun abandoned and the crew disappearing through the trees. Similar short encounters killed or captured the Germans who stood and fought, while the rest ran for safety.

Despite his wounds, Hap Mason led the forty remaining Marines in a sprint up the hill. The Marines devastated the German defenders on the front of Hill 160, capturing twenty-six men, four machine guns, a trench mortar, and a gas projector. Incredibly, Mason and his men had survived the shells and bullets of the wheat fields and now held a key position in the center of the German line of defense. Just ahead of them on the backside of the hill was the Soissons–Château-Thierry road, less than 1,000 yards away. However, by advancing only 100 yards to the hillcrest, they could actually direct fire on the road. The 6th Marines' objective lay within their grasp, but it would be gained at a heavy cost. Mason and his men, however, had no idea of the importance of their position, nor the location of the road ahead.[62]

With the hill now in hand, a quick look about revealed many dead Germans and some prisoners but very few Marines. Hatcher only saw eight to ten Marines near him, but they continued to advance, pushing deeper into the trees until they reached the forward crest of Hill 160, where the trees ended. Ahead in the open ground lay a cluster of German dugouts, with fresh footprints leading to the entrances. Beyond the dugouts was another group of trees and then the vital road to Soissons, a section of which was now in sight.

The Marines ventured into the open ground in the saddle of Hill 160, ordering the Germans in the dugouts to come out and surrender. The men inside were silent, even under the threat of grenades. A sudden shot rang out, and a Marine watching from the safety of the woods died, shot through the head. The focus on the dugouts had allowed a sniper to take a shot at the

Tigny-Villemontoire road   Vierzy Château   Tour sans toit   Meaux-Soissons highway

Postwar view looking back from Hill 160 toward Vierzy, illustrating the open terrain traversed by the 6th Marines. The car on the road is traveling from Villemontoire to Tigny. (US Army Heritage and Education Center, Carlisle, PA)

Marines; this was followed by machine gun fire. The dusting of bullets in the dirt around the Marines in the clearing reawakened them to the danger of being out in the open, and they all fell back into the trees. The exhausted Marines found shelter in German bunkers built within the tree line and assessed their situation. Mason and his few men were far from the nearest Marine position and essentially surrounded by German forces on the hill. Instead of worrying about their position, many of the exhausted Marines went to sleep.

Foremost in their minds was that Mason, Van Housen, and their forty Marines stood only 400 yards north of Tigny, which could now be outflanked and open Hughes's advance. Mason could also dominate the German defenders to the north, allowing Holcomb to advance. Without more men, however, Mason could do none of these things, and he sent a runner back to battalion headquarters begging for reinforcements. The runner reached Sibley just before noon, after he had committed Voeth's 97th Company, leaving him with only the battered Headquarters Company and two platoons of machine gunners.

Sibley knew that Mason's position was a crucial one, but he also con-

Postwar view of Tigny from Hill 160. The flanking position of Hill 160 relative to the German positions in town caused the withdrawal of the 1st Battalion, 110th Grenadiers. The 2nd Division boulder is indicated by the far-right marker. (US Army Heritage and Education Center, Carlisle, PA)

sidered his situation barely tenable. Word from Hughes indicated that his entire battalion had been reduced to a hundred Marines holding in a road-bed 1,000 yards short of Tigny. His 97th Company and the rest of the 84th Company on that flank were reportedly "almost all casualties" as well.[63] Though contemplating sending more Marines to Mason, Sibley believed that just holding the line in the wheat field would be difficult. Nevertheless, he dispatched his last Marines to Mason, cobbled together from the Headquarters Company, commanded by First Lieutenant Wesley W. Walker, and a platoon of Captain Roy C. Swink's 73rd Machine Gun Company.

The alert German 1st Battalion, 110th Grenadier Regiment, observed the 84th Company's capture of Hill 160 and also noticed that the German 218th Reserve Infantry, which was supposed to be defending the area, "was nowhere to be found."[64] The French 38th Division was pressing on Parcy-Tigny on the Germans' left flank. Fearing envelopment by the Allied forces and almost out of ammunition, the Germans pulled back to the southeast, linking up with the right flank of the German 115th Division but leaving Tigny and Parcy-Tigny unoccupied.

With a gap in the center of the German position, the vital road was now open, but the Marines on Hill 160 were too few to exploit their break-through, and Hughes's battalion was dispersed in the wheat fields with heavy losses. The French tanks were long gone, destroyed or abandoned by their crews. The German 46th Reserve Division, along with remnants of the battered German 218th and 53rd Reserve Regiments, was ordered to move into the gap, defending a line running down the Soissons–Château-Thierry road to Taux, across the road from Mason's company on Hill 160. All spare staff officers went into the fields to gather up the demoralized stragglers and return them to the front in composite combat groups.[65]

As the Marines' attack stalled, the guns of the 2nd Artillery Brigade attempted to suppress the German fire and pound the Soissons–Château-Thierry road. Messages sent back from the front asked for heavy fire on Tigny and Parcy-Tigny.[66]

With the arrival of the 97th Company and the 1st Battalion, 2nd Engineers, Hughes once again ordered his men forward in a last attempt to capture Tigny, unaware of the events on the hill to his left. Artillery support arrived in the form of a rolling barrage from the 2nd Field Artillery Brigade, crashing into the wheat field only twenty-five yards from the Marines' front line. The first shells burst among the engineers' foxholes, just in front of the Marines. "How many of us came through it," recalled Private Williams, "we will never know."[67] As the shells advanced toward Tigny, a corresponding German barrage struck the engineers. After a few minutes, the German shells crept back toward Vierzy to prevent more Americans from participating in the attack. The Germans had no way of knowing that no more reinforcements would be joining the 1st Battalion.

The Hotchkiss machine guns of Captain Sumner's 81st Machine Gun Company drew the most German fire. Sumner ordered his men to remain under cover until the attack began. Sumner, however, was standing in the field where his men could see him as they prepared for the assault, waiting for the order to advance. A wave of thirty German aircraft swept over the Marines, machine-gunning the wheat and dropping small bombs as they passed at low altitude. An explosion from a bomb or an artillery shell sent metal fragments into Sumner's stomach and crushed one leg. A Navy corpsman was immediately at the captain's side, but to no avail. Sumner bled to death in the summer wheat and was buried where he fell.[68]

Major L. W. T. Waller Jr., cousin to Sumner's wife Mary, wrote a letter of condolence to her and the family. "His death was painless, and he was unconscious from the moment he was hit," Waller wrote. "It is useless to tell

you how sorry I am. I simply can't express it. . . . Allen did not die in vain—
he left his mark, a shining example to all of the officers of the battalion . . .
to make them better able to lead to the ultimate victory which is sure to be
ours."[69]

As the German barrage traveled further into the wheat, the Marines once
again charged over the foxholes of the engineers. The soldiers were amazed
as they watched the Marines run forward, singing their battle songs: "From
the Halls of Montezuma," "Around Her Neck, She Wore a Yellow Ribbon," and "Hinky Dinky Parlez Vous."[70] However, casualties mounted as
the movement continued. Again, the 81st Company took heavy casualties,
losing 57 out of 119 Marines engaged. First Lieutenant Jack S. Hart led the
company after Sumner was killed, and two more officers were wounded
while leading their men forward. A new replacement officer, Second Lieutenant James P. Schwerin, advanced his section of thirty-eight Marines in the
morning, but only twelve men reached the 1st Battalion's right flank to set
up their two remaining machine guns, with only two boxes of ammunition
for each gun.[71]

The 74th Company quickly ran into an overwhelming crescendo of German machine gun fire, striking the Marines from the front and from both
flanks. The Marines were close enough to see the Germans firing from the
windows in the houses of Tigny, raking the company relentlessly. "It seemed
impossible to make a further advance," First Lieutenant Frederick W. Clarke
Jr. reported, "and I gave orders to dig in."[72] Clarke linked up with Overton's
76th Company on the right, setting up a line of defense to shelter his men as
much as possible. He also dispatched a runner to Hughes to inform him of
the situation in his front. The German artillery and machine gun fire never
ceased, and snipers added to the threat, as any Marine movement drew fire.
Clarke was recommended for the Distinguished Service Cross for advancing
his company forward despite heavy losses, leading his Marines "until it was
impossible to advance another foot." He then held his position under heavy
fire, defending his piece of the wheat field with machine guns obtained from
the abandoned French tanks.[73]

Captain Robert "Bert" Voeth's 97th Company from Sibley's 3rd Battalion
moved with the 81st Company. Born and raised in Kansas, Voeth left the
coalfields of his hometown of Pittsburg (appropriately named after the more
famous Pennsylvania steel town) and went to the University of Kansas in
1900. He studied in the Schools of Arts for two years and then transferred to
the School of Medicine. After four years, Voeth left the university without a
degree and returned to Pittsburg, where he took an office job with the local
coal company. After several years of unfulfilling work, Voeth left Kansas
and was appointed a Marine Corps second lieutenant, graduating fifth in

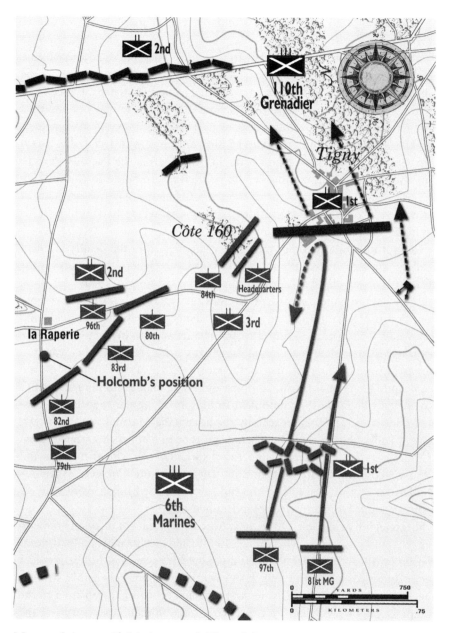

Map 23. Soissons, 6th Marines attack Tigny, July 19, 1918

his 1909 class of fifty-five officer candidates. He eventually earned a degree in zoology in 1926.[74]

Voeth's first duty was in Cuba, followed by assignment to the Marine officers' school as an instructor in 1911. He saw combat in Nicaragua the following year, after which he was promoted to first lieutenant. Expeditionary duty continued, and Voeth participated in landings in Culebra and then Vera Cruz in 1914. The exotic clime of East Asia was next on his itinerary, and he served in the Philippines and China until war was declared in 1917. The demand for veteran officers brought Voeth across the Pacific Ocean to Quantico, and during the journey home he was promoted to captain. On arrival, Voeth took command of the 97th Company. The wheat fields of Kansas were a long way from those of Soissons, where he would lead his company smartly in the attack.[75]

The 97th Company took immediate casualties from the deadly German artillery, directed from both aircraft and ominous balloon observers on the horizon. The effects of the shelling proved devastating to Voeth's Marines, but they kept moving forward. With rifles carried at high port, they entered the inferno of wheat and sugar beets as shells plowed into the fields and threw earth into the air around them. The lines were broken only by the bodies of men at their feet, requiring short detours to avoid the dead and wounded from the first advance of the morning. The 97th Company moved on, despite the cries for help, stopping only long enough to plunge a man's bayoneted rifle into the ground next to him, marking the spot for the hospital corpsmen. The images seen by the advancing Marines were unforgettable. "Those killed cleanly by machine guns or rifle bullets lay stretched out as though in natural sleep or sometimes sprawled out with their arms and legs twisted in awkward or grotesque angles," wrote Corporal Havelock D. Nelson. "Others caught by the full fury of a shell burst, were scarcely distinguishable from a heap of bloodstained rags."[76]

Shrapnel inflicted some of the most horrific wounds. "I distinctly remember one man passing by with the left half of his face torn away," Corporal Nelson recalled, "so that there was a gaping hole where his lower jaw had been. As he passed to the rear, his eyes stared incomprehensibly straight ahead."[77] That man was Private Archie L. Lake, who had returned to the company only a week before the attack. Lake miraculously survived the journey to Vierzy and then to a hospital, where he died of his wounds. Unfortunately, it took a while for his family to receive confirmation of his death. They were informed that he was in a hospital on August 29, 1918, and had lost his memory as a result of his wounds. No further information on his whereabouts was received until March 5, 1919, when a cablegram confirmed that Lake had died and was buried in the fields of Soissons. The nightmare for the family continued, as they clung to the hope that the initial hospital report had been correct and that Archie was alive. In 1920 a friend posted articles in American newspapers across the country, pleading for information about Lake. The family sent letters to all the army hospitals as well, to no avail. A cross stands today in the Oise Marne Cemetery with Lake's name and date of death: July 19, 1918.[78]

The Marines of the 97th Company pushed over the 74th Company's position, taking casualties as they went. Lieutenant Clarke's men pulled several of the wounded to safety and bandaged their wounds as best they could. An artillery barrage bracketed the 97th Company as it plowed further into the wheat field. "Without exaggeration, shells simply rained down on us," Corporal Nelson remembered. "Every ten square yards of ground within the area covered by the company appeared to be sprouting geysers of dirt and smoke. The din was terrific, as the waves of concussion came so rapidly that the pressure on our eardrums seemed continuous." Nelson looked left and right to make sure his squad maintained proper intervals and noticed that "everybody moved along with hunched shoulders, heads down, as though forcing our way through a bad wind storm."[79]

A shell fragment entered the left shoulder of Private Frank Collier, ending his time in the battle. Collier made it back to the aid station, where he was evacuated to Base Hospital 24, but he succumbed to infection on July 29, 1918. The accurate German artillery fire rained down on the 97th Company Marines. High-explosive shells killed Privates George L. Langell and Frank L. Colwell instantly, and Private Guy De Lamaten Hoxie became the first man killed from his hometown of Ottawa, Illinois.[80]

Voeth noticed a German sniper located in a clump of trees and called out, "Go get that sniper." Three Marines ran forward to take him out, and the German hit Private Kerlin "Bab" Lehman in the head, killing him instantly. His closest friend, Private James A. Flynn, reported that the Marine died with "a smile . . . on his lips." Flynn later sent Lehman's Bible home to his mother with a letter expressing his sorrow at the death of his friend. "Bab as everyone knew him, was only a boy. But he did a man's work. He was like a brother to me," Flynn wrote, "and I feel his loss keenly."[81] Lehman's death delivered a deadly warning for the Marines to keep under cover. Son of a druggist from Chicago, Lehman was only seventeen—one of the youngest Marines in the brigade. His body was not recovered in the wheat field that night.[82]

Private Francis Probert became another casualty as the company swept forward. Probert and Private Benjamin R. Roberts had made a pact that should either one be killed, the survivor would write a letter home providing the particulars of his death. Roberts fulfilled his obligation to Probert's mother after the battle. "Frank died like man," Roberts penned. "Machine guns were sweeping the fields. It was one of these that got him. Your Frank died in my arms as I was preparing first aid, only a few seconds after being hit. His grave is marked by two crossed bayonets. . . . The kind French will never let the grave die. It shall always be green."[83]

A shell struck in the midst of the company headquarters group, wounding several men, but the Marines were encouraged to see Captain Voeth emerge from the smoke unscathed. He sprinted to a better vantage point and calmly swept the ground ahead with his binoculars. Voeth ordered his 1st Platoon to deploy to the road on his right, covering the exposed right flank from the Germans in Parcy-Tigny. He then led the remains of his company directly toward Tigny. Another shell burst nearby, and a steel fragment ripped into Voeth's left leg. The wound was not life threatening but was enough to take him out of the fight.[84]

The 97th Company paused at a dirt road that provided momentary protection from the shelling, expecting that the advance had gone far enough. Instead, Gunnery Sergeant Morris C. "Rich" Richardson climbed up on the embankment and emitted a high-pitched scream from his whistle, signaling "Forward."[85] The already exhausted Marines jumped over the embankment, formed a skirmish line, and continued the attack. They passed a machine gun crew of the 81st Company that had found its way past the front lines and was now set up to fire overhead as the Marines advanced.

The German shelling resumed, taking out even more Marines, until there were only about 50 of the original 180 remaining. Richardson continued to lead the men forward, with the deadly cracking of machine gun bullets adding to the din. "It was like a hideous nightmare which could only end in death," thought Corporal Nelson, "when we were suddenly on the edge of wheat." Tigny lay only 300 yards away, across a sugar-beet field that offered no cover. At that moment, Richardson crumpled in a heap, disappearing into the cloud of a shell burst. The entire Marine line went down as well; a minute passed, with no movement among the Marines. Everyone thought the gunnery sergeant was dead, but suddenly, Richardson jumped to his feet unhurt. He had "a strange wild expression in his eyes, the whites of which, along with his teeth, gleamed with startling whiteness against his smoke blacken[ed] face." His men were awestruck—first, that he was still alive, but also that he "waved his cane overhead like a sword, bellowing, 'Come on, boys, we are going to take that town!'" The Marines pressed forward. Most of them were certain that no one would survive the charge across the field, but they would not allow their gunnery sergeant to go forward alone.

Just as the Marines emerged from the edge of the wheat and into the sugar-beet field, Second Lieutenant Donovan Wilmot appeared from nowhere, ordering the Marines to crawl fifty yards back into the wheat field and dig in. Donovan was a newly minted officer; he had been a corporal in the 84th Company and had joined the 97th Company only three days before. The men pulled back and learned that their captain was back at the sunken farm lane, wounded in the leg. They also learned that they were the only unhurt Marines left in the company. What the 97th Company did not know was Tigny was only lightly defended by snipers left behind during the earlier German withdrawal. After all of the sacrifice of the 6th Marines on July 19, the village was theirs for the asking.

The body of a lone Marine in the sugar-beet field marked the 6th Marines' farthest advance toward Tigny. A sniper's bullet struck the man in the forehead, killing him instantly. He was a new replacement in the 97th Company, joining the unit shortly before the attack. His name was unknown to the fifty men who entered the field with him.

Far back from the action, a message arrived at Sibley's headquarters at 12:45 p.m. from Lieutenant Colonel Lee, requesting information about the progress of the attack. "Has the town of Tigny been taken by our troops?" he asked. "If you don't know find out. If you are stopped, dig in."[86] Sibley quickly prepared a field message to his battalion addressed to "All Companies. Hold the line you now have," he ordered, "dig in—get in touch with Co.s on your right and left. Reinforcements coming."[87] He then informed Lee that Tigny was still in German hands, and his 84th Company had reported German soldiers gathering for a counterattack. Sibley also informed Lee of his decision to have the battalion entrench, effectively halting the attack. Ammunition was running low, and Sibley admitted that he had no one to carry more to the front. The hard-won opportunities to break the German lines at Villemontoire, Hill 160, and Tigny were now lost.

Unable to advance or withdraw, the Marines of Holcomb's, Sibley's, and Hughes's battalions could do nothing but dig in, attempting to protect themselves from the ever-present machine gun fire and shell bursts expertly targeted by the German forward observers. Corporal Nelson remembered that "the degree of hardness of the ground was slightly less than concrete."[88] Only by using his bayonet to chip away at the dirt two inches at a time was Nelson able to dig a suitable hole, using the clumps of dirt as a parapet.

Even the effort of scratching at the soil inches at a time drew fire, and the relentless heat of the day pressed down on the Marines. They shook their canteens dry for every drop of water to quench their thirst and cared for the wounded who could not be evacuated. Few dared to leave their holes to search for water, and those who did and survived the challenge returned shell-shocked and with empty canteens. Parched and suffering from the heat, the Marines held on, waiting for relief. "This afternoon was a hard grind," recalled Private Corbly, "doing nothing but wonder which shell had my name on it."[89]

The German artillery dominated the wheat and sugar-beet fields, expending so much ammunition that replenishing shells became a serious problem for the gunners. All the batteries of Corps Watter were resupplied with two days' ammunition on the night of July 17–18, but the American advance captured all the ammunition of the German 14th Reserve Division on the morning of July 18. The Germans resorted to transporting shells from the nearest depot, almost twenty-five miles from the battlefield. A truck caravan was assembled from the German corps and army headquarters, but the stream of vehicles could not keep up with the number of shells pounding the Americans. Each battery's supply of shells was depleted but never completely expended.[90]

The reality of the 6th Marines' dilemma became apparent to the battalion commanders, who were pinned down with the rest of their men. The information rippled back to Lieutenant Colonel Lee in Vierzy, who informed division commander Harbord of the dire predicament facing his regiment. Should the Germans counterattack across the fields, the possibility of the 6th Marines being overrun became a major concern, and Harbord abandoned any thoughts of taking the high ground behind Tigny. At 3:45 p.m. Harbord ordered the regiment to hold in place, no matter the consequences. Lee echoed the order to his battalion commanders and to the commander of the 1st Battalion, 2nd Engineers. "The Division Commander directs us to dig in and hold our present line at all costs. No further advance will be made at the present," Lee wrote. "He congratulates the command on its gallant conduct in the face of severe casualties."[91] Lee never called on the relatively fresh engineer battalions to advance in support of the Marines. The soldiers remained in their trenches, being bombed and strafed by German aircraft for most of the day.

At 3:00 p.m. Captain Lloyd could hold his isolated position no longer. As casualties mounted and ammunition dwindled, he withdrew the remnants of his company from Villemontoire and rejoined the rest of Holcomb's battalion. Holcomb simply could not support the 80th Company with what was left of his battalion, and no additional reinforcements could be expected. The covered ravine offered a potential avenue deep into the German positions and was much more secure than the wheat fields, but Lee's decision to halt the attack obviated any advantage gained by the 80th Company. Word of the capture of the town reached General Berdoulat, who mistakenly ordered the 11th Tirailleurs Regiment of the French 58th Division reserve to march toward Villemontoire "due to the significant advance of the 2nd USID" but not to engage unless ordered to attack by XX Corps command.[92]

Despite every effort to conceal their positions, casualties mounted with every passing minute, especially among the company officers, who had to stand clear to effectively command their men and presented easy targets for the Germans. Hughes's 1st Battalion lost three officers killed and eight wounded, while Holcomb's 2nd Battalion took heavier losses, losing all but three company officers killed or wounded. Sibley's 3rd Battalion suffered at least 39 percent officer casualties, despite coming into the fight from the reserve. A quick account of his battalion revealed that only sixteen of thirty-six officers remained, while only 385 of the 850 enlisted Marines remained unhurt, a 45 percent loss in only three hours. Both the 84th and 97th Companies reported only fifty men in each company who were still able to fight, and seven officers combined. The 6th Marines' Headquarters Company was reduced to only four officers and thirty men.[93]

The heat of the day added to the misery of the surviving Marines pinned down in the open fields. Food was just as scarce as water. Any endeavor to dispatch details to the rear to refill canteens proved suicidal for anyone making the attempt. Six fortunate Marines from the 74th Company came up with the idea of searching an abandoned tank for supplies. They were rewarded with enough food for a meal for each man, along with some water to relieve their thirst.[94]

Lieutenant Mason and the Marines on Hill 160 still held their ground and began to explore the woods around their positions, which were honeycombed with bunkers and gun pits. Several of the larger positions contained tunnels that were thirty yards deep. In one of these underground rooms, Private Hatcher came upon five Germans resting, their rifles leaning against the wall just out of reach. Hatcher covered them with his pistol and called for help from a friend in a nearby tunnel. The Germans attempted to rush Hatcher while he was alone, but he showed them that he meant business with the pistol, and his prisoners were soon being escorted to the rear. They confirmed the disappointing news that the Germans still held Tigny, whose pinned-down Marine attackers were the closest help to the 84th Company's position.

Mason and his men watched carefully for a German counterattack, but only a testing patrol attempted to press the Marines' position; it was driven off without fanfare. German snipers were the immediate threat, picking off individuals from the 84th Company, which could not afford to lose any more men. German aircraft flew low overhead, but the Marines refused to fire at them, reluctant to give away their positions. The hill was quiet, in contrast to the fields below. Only a few shell bursts and single gunshots broke the silence.

The whine of an incoming round often proved lethally accurate. "We heard the sound of a bullet sing close by and a young sergeant, who had only recently joined us, clasped his hand over his heart," Private Hatcher recorded. "For a moment, he straightened out and looked appealingly toward us. Then his eyes turned glassy and he collapsed. Not a word passed his lips but that one glance from his dying eyes had told us as much."[95] Sergeant Ellis M. Miles from Spokane, Washington, now rests in the Oise Marne Cemetery. Only thirty-five Marines remained unhurt on Hill 160.

As the afternoon dragged on, the men tried to pass the time without calling attention to themselves. Some cleaned their rifles, others checked their gas masks, and each company attempted to determine the status of every man in the command. An accurate count proved impossible, and the result was generally the same in each unit: "Some killed, some wounded, some missing."[96] Despite their best attempts to maximize their shelter, casualties continued to mount during the afternoon. Private Corbly vividly recalled the shock from the storm of bullets and shells, writing, "For no time during the next seventeen hours did I expect to leave that field except in pieces. The water shortage made it terrible."[97] German snipers were especially vigilant, picking off any Marine who moved away from cover. The 6th Marines had entered the battle that morning with almost 2,800 men, making the assault with approximately 2,450 Marines and 350 men in reserve. Losses during the day totaled 1,300 Marines killed or wounded, or just over half of the regiment.[98]

The men of the army's 23rd Infantry remained in the foxholes they had hastily dug the previous evening, unable to support the 6th Marines in front of them. They soon observed eighteen German aircraft passing low overhead, so close to the ground that the soldiers could easily pick out the black crosses on the wings and the individual pilots. The memorable scene turned bleak as the Germans initiated strafing runs at the helpless Americans in their holes below. After the initial shock, they realized that the aircraft were having difficulty firing straight down into the dugouts, so only a few men were wounded. The soldiers fired back, hitting one of the aircraft with a lucky shot and causing the German to crash nearby, to the cheers of the Americans.[99]

For the men of the 6th Marines still holding their ground in the wheat field, the long afternoon seemed like an eternity. They occupied a series of holes two feet deep and a yard wide, with three Marines to a hole. Two men could sleep while one kept watch. German aircraft, artillery, machine gun, and rifle fire relentlessly pounded their positions. At least three more tanks were set ablaze during the afternoon, while flames and smoke from the town of Charantigny rose into the fetid air, combining with the black, burning gasoline plumes from the tanks and forming funeral pyres for the fallen French tank crews and American Marines. The cries of the wounded and dying resonated through the fields, but no one could risk moving into the open to help them. "Throughout the day you could hear men calling for help in the wheat and beet fields," Major Denig recalled. "Their cries would get weaker and die out."[100]

Medical support proved almost impossible, as the regimental corpsmen became targets as soon as they attempted to tend to the wounded. The 82nd Company's Pharmacist Mate Second Class John H. Balch refused to be stopped by the German fire. Astounded Marines watched him tend one wounded man after another, often running to the site of a new detonation before anyone else could get there. Time and again, over the course of sixteen hours, Balch repeated his miracle work for five separate companies of Sibley's and Hughes's battalions. Those who witnessed such courage described him as "omnipresent." They fully expected him to be struck by German fire at any time, but Balch survived the day and night unharmed. He received the Medal of Honor for his actions. "The risk of life that he took was beyond that of his comrades," Major Sibley wrote, "and the services rendered were greater than could be expected of one man."[101] Ambulances arrived at 1:00 p.m. to remove the long-suffering wounded from the Vierzy ravine and transport them to the rear for medical care. Having no compassion for the Allied wounded, German artillery pounded the roads used by the ambulances.[102]

Seemingly unnoticed, Major Turrill's 1st Battalion, 5th Marines, and the 45th Company from Major Shearer's 3rd Battalion formed the last reserve of the 4th Marine Brigade. They remained under cover near the town cemetery all day, and Neville never called on them to join the 6th Marines. Nor were the army's 4th and 5th Machine Gun Battalions or the 2nd Battalion of the 2nd Engineers sent to join the battle. Even so, Turrill's battalion suffered many casualties during the day without firing a shot. German aircraft directed accurate artillery fire, punctuated by strafing runs and hand grenades tossed from the air. At 5:00 p.m. the battalion was finally withdrawn to a large cave in Vierzy.[103]

The combined German airpower, artillery, machine guns, and infantry fire made communication between the scattered units impossible and any movement on the plain lethal. The commander of the army's 5th Machine Gun Battalion related after the battle that his "companies were all past Vierzy but were unable to locate their respective battalions as liaison between units of the same regiment were difficult to maintain because of the rapidity of the advance . . . the troops went forward so fast and became so intermingled that no one had definite information as to where any particular unit was."[104]

In the heat of two days of battle, the commander of the 2nd Division, Major General Harbord, had yet to fully comprehend the losses suffered. Official reports of casualties were imperfect at best, but based on the information at hand, of the 24,085 men in the ranks on July 17, only 22,403 were ready for duty on the afternoon of July 19. This reported loss of 286 men on the first day of combat and 1,396 men on the morning of July 19 was significant, but it underestimated the actual number of casualties, which would eventually total 154 officers and 3,788 enlisted men killed or wounded. Harbord knew that the bulk of these losses had occurred in his front-line battalions, and any further attacks would cripple his command.[105]

No hope of French reinforcement existed, although a French brigade of the 6th Dragoons held the gap connecting the 2nd Division with the 38th Division on the right. The brigade commander informed Harbord that the cavalry was not to be disturbed, as he "preferred" his dragoons "not to be used in actual fighting unless a gap appeared in the line." The cavalrymen would hold the ground they had gained over the past two days, but the commander emphatically reported, "I desire to insist most strongly that they should not be called upon for further offensive effort."[106]

Recognizing the futility of continuing the advance, Harbord penned a report to General Mangin, admitting that the 2nd Division was completely exhausted. He boldly cited the problems overcome by the 2nd Division since the overnight camion run from the south and the night march through the Forest of Retz, which resulted in the uncertain morning assault on July 18. The final blow came when he informed his French commander that the majority of the command had been "without food or water for the last twenty four hours." The report ended by affirming that "this condition . . . exists as a result of no fault of anyone connected to this division, and the further prosecution of the offensive in our front [should] be done by divisions in the second line, passing through our present position."[107]

General Mangin had little choice but to relieve the Americans, dispatching orders at 6:00 p.m. for the French 58th Division to pass through the 2nd Division's lines, allowing Harbord's men to withdraw. However, the 2nd Division artillery brigade would remain in place to support the French reinforcements. At 10:00 p.m. the men of the 6th Marines were told to be ready to withdraw at 11:00 p.m. Their main opponent of the past two days was also leaving the battlefield. At 5:00 p.m. the decimated German 14th Reserve Division was ordered to leave the battlefield and move across Aisne River, leaving the newly arrived German 20th Division to take over the center of Corps Watter. All the German units previously attached to the sector departed as well, but the newly arrived regiment of the German 46th Division remained in place, as did the 14th Reserve Division's artillery batteries. The German High Command was relieved by the day's results all along the threatened front. The Germans considered the behavior of their soldiers "outstanding . . . which deserves all the more credit, since most of the units participating had for a long time been employed on a difficult part of the front or had very few days of rest behind them."[108] Almost every German unit had been understrength when the battle began but still fought tenaciously on July 19.[109]

The 2nd Division's withdrawal from the front lines began at midnight and continued through the early-morning hours. A steady stream of American soldiers and Marines moved past division headquarters to concentrate in the woods to the east of Verte Feuille Farm, which, for many, had been their starting point on the morning of July 18.

At 1:00 a.m. the 6th Marines moved in single file with five-yard intervals between each man, respecting the accuracy of the German artillery. They walked through the fields where they had fought the day before, now covered by darkness. The night march provided an eerie experience. "Flares lit up the sky now and then; occasionally a shell whizzed by and exploded," Corporal McCune of the 55th Company recalled. "At intervals the sharp staccato rasp of a Maxim gun cut the air; to die quickly . . . wrecked machine gun emplacements and empty cartridge shells were scattered about."[110]

As darkness fell on the battlefield, Private Rhodes moved from his shell hole to locate Cates and the rest of the 96th Company. Unable to find his comrades, he came across a French officer positioning his poilus in the sugar-beet field. The Frenchman asked the Marine to stay in his position overnight to repel any attacks by the Germans. Rhodes obliged, returning to his machine guns to await dawn and a return to his company.[111]

The men of the 74th Company paused in Vierzy to drink from the town's wells and fill their canteens with precious water. After a day pinned down under the blazing July sun, the Marines quenched their thirst with delight, causing Private Corbly to remark, "Oh Lord, how good it tasted."[112] Only thirty-eight men and two officers left the wheat field unharmed, as the company had suffered more than a hundred casualties.

At 4:00 a.m. General Prioux, commanding the French 58th Division, arrived at 2nd Division headquarters, where Major General Harbord greeted him. Prioux then officially relieved the 2nd Division. The French poilus took over the front lines before the break of dawn, allowing the exhausted soldiers and Marines to fall back to the Forest of Retz to regroup. Harbord made a special effort to ensure that every wounded American was taken back to safety before leaving the battlefield. A forward evacuation station was established at the aid station at Beaurepaire Farm, where trucks and ambulances from the division's supply train made repeated trips, despite

German shell fire and gas attacks. The heroic drivers gave their gas masks to the wounded, risking their own exposure to the poisonous fumes.

The 6th Marines went into bivouac in the forest near Verte Feuille Farm, which had been badly battered by artillery from both sides. Many of the trees had been shattered by shell fire and shrapnel, but the men were grateful for the safety they provided, far from the deadly wheat fields of the day before. However, a strong wind blew through the forest, causing some of the immense tree limbs to fall down on the sleeping Marines, adding to the already long list of wounded. The lack of sleep for the past two nights, the march in the pouring rain, the brutal attack of the day before, and now a seemingly random act of nature "added greatly to the mental and physical exhaustion of the troops," according to the regimental history written shortly after the war.[113] The survivors must have felt that safety was simply something they would never find at Soissons.

The 4th Marine Brigade also took stock of its losses in the aftermath of the battle. Each company commander carefully accounted for every Marine lost, whether wounded or killed in action. Verification was difficult. Although the survivors were questioned about each man missing from the company ranks, this failed to account for everyone. As the casualties were tallied, individual Marines reflected on their own experiences on July 19. Processing their emotions was a complex and personal experience, but a common theme was pride in themselves and their lost comrades. "There are no words in the English language that can adequately describe that famous advance," Lieutenant Grayson recorded in a history of Holcomb's battalion. "It surpassed imagination. Even the charge of the Light Brigade at Balaclava was puny in comparison." When the 4th Marine Brigade left the battlefield for rest and recuperation, most of the men were more than happy to depart. They "never again saw the battle front at Soissons," the battalion historian recorded, "and I will leave it to the reader whether they had done their bit."[114]

Major General Harbord and Chief of Staff Brown stood silently by the roadside in the gray light of dawn, watching in amazement at the soldierly bearing of the depleted ranks of the 2nd Division. "Battalions of only a couple of hundred men, companies of twenty-five or thirty," Harbord later wrote. They had "no doubt in their minds as to their ability to whip the Germans. Their whole independent attitude, the very swagger of their march, the snatches of conversations we could hear as they swung past, proclaimed them a victorious division."[115]

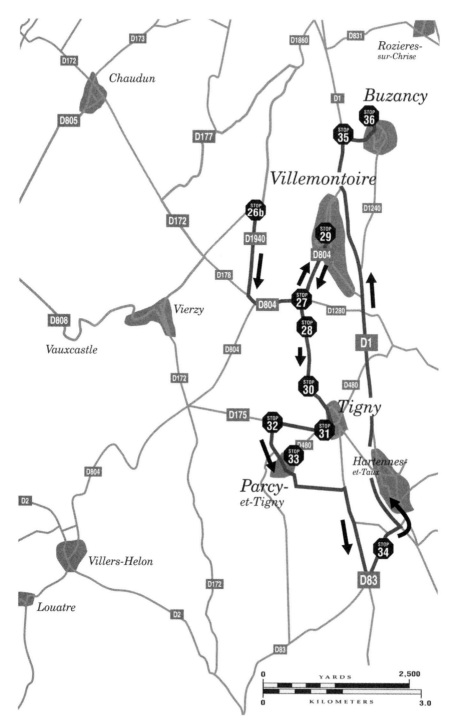

Map 24. Soissons tour map, part 3, stops 26–36

Soissons Tour

Stop 25. 2nd Division Boulder, 49°17'54.3"N 3°17'50.9"E

Leave Vierzy, proceed 900 meters, and turn left on the D 804. Drive 2 kilometers to the intersection with the D 178 and turn left on the D 178. Drive 1.2 kilometers to one of the 2nd Division markers placed by veterans after the war ended. Turn into the D 172 and pull off by the 2nd Division boulder on your left. You have now reached the left flank of the 2nd Division, having driven the width of the American positions.

Look down the D 172 in the direction you were traveling. You are standing in the gap between the Marine and army attack. Observe the tree line on the right side of the road and the field on the left. You can now see the attack area and the location of the 5th Marines' furthest advance on the evening of July 18. An old trench line ran from this intersection into the open field.

The 5th Marines attacked over the trench across the road and toward the German positions in the tree line on the right. This time, the Marines faced veteran German reinforcements who had prepared their positions during the afternoon as the 2nd Division paused. Interlocking machine gun fire combined with artillery and air support brought the American advance to a standstill. The Marines fell back to the 1914 trench line under the cover of darkness. Major Thomas Holcomb's battalion attacked on the following day across the fields to your right, supported by the 15th Company, 6th Machine Gun Battalion.

Note that the objective of the high ground ahead had not been reached, and German reserves were arriving to close the gap in their lines. On your map, locate Tigny and the D 1 on the high ground, which is still the main artery from Soissons and Château-Thierry.

Look to the south. You have a perfect view of the ground for the July 19 attack by the 6th Marines. The flanking fire from Charantigny and Villemontoire caused the Marines to face north and stalled the attack in the fields before you.

Stop 26. German Grenadier Positions,
49°18'24.6"N 3°17'24.5"E

The railroad tunnel from Vierzy exits in the low ground a short distance beyond the village. Continue on the D 172 through the assault area and turn right on the D 177 at 1.2 kilometers. Turn right and proceed 850 meters to the village of Lechelle. Pause here. You are now within the defenses of the German 40th Fusilier Regiment. You can see that the village is in a protected ravine, giving the fusiliers natural defensive positions.

Turn left on Rue Marie Therese Aubert and proceed 1 kilometer. Take a slight right on La Foulerie. Proceed 2.9 kilometers and turn right on the D 1860. In 1.9 kilometers you will arrive at Charantigny. Pause here. You are now in the lines of the 3rd Battalion, 110th Grenadier Regiment, opposing the 9th Infantry. Again, the ravine sheltered the Germans from the American attack.

Stop 27. La Raperie, 49°17′36.2″N 3°19′34.3″E

Leave Charantigny on the D 1940. In 1 kilometer you will reach the D 178. Turn left and drive 1.3 kilometers. Park near the monument at the intersection with the D 804. A traditional French sugar-beet mill stood in the southeast corner of the intersection. After suffering heavy casualties while driving the German defenders from this location, Holcomb's battalion could go no further. Holcomb went to ground a few yards into the field across the road from where you are standing. The remnants of the 96th Company, led by Lieutenant Cates, took shelter in a shallow roadbed about twenty yards into the field to the east, where he penned his famous message, "I will hold."

Here also stands a monument to the French 67th Regiment, which was raised primarily from the Soissons area. This monument is another reminder that the battle continued to rage after the 2nd Division's withdrawal. The 2nd Battalion of the 67th Regiment recaptured Villemontoire on July 25, 1918, after repulsing six German attempts to retake the town. The original monument was destroyed by the Germans in 1940 but was replaced after World War II.

Stop 28. British Cemetery, 49°17′30.5″N 3°19′32.2″E

Go back on the D 804 and take a quick left onto the unnamed road. Drive 170 meters and park at the British Cemetery.

You are now on the Germans' main line of defense on July 19 and at the center of the storm for Holcomb's 2nd Battalion, 6th Marines. Soissons is just over six miles to the north, and the vital highway to Château-Thierry is less than a mile to the east.

This spot provides an invaluable view of the battlefield from the German side. Looking back across the open ground, you can see the excellent fields of fire for the German machine guns and artillery. This area was held by the remnants of many units destroyed in the previous day's fighting.

The British Cemetery is also a reminder of the sacrifice of the Allied forces that continued to battle over this ground after the 2nd Division's withdrawal. The cemetery holds the graves of more than 600 men of the 15th Scottish and 34th Divisions, who died July 23–August 2, 1918, while finally taking the Soissons road.

Stop 29. Villemontoire, 49°18'00.76"N 3°20'00.93"E

Return to your car and drive back to the intersection with D 804. Turn right on the D 804 and then quickly turn left at the 67th Regiment's monument, heading toward Villemontoire. In 1 kilometer, bear right on the Rue du 67 Eme and park at the town's monument to the fallen of World War I.

As the unnerved Germans left, Captain Egbert T. Lloyd led six of his men of the 84th Company into the village at 11:00 a.m. on July 18. The Marines quenched their thirst from the town well and awaited reinforcements that would never come. Lloyd withdrew his men as the inevitable German counterattack approached.

Sergeant John O. Stover was one of the Marines of the 80th Company attacking across the sugar-beet fields on July 19. The oldest of nine children raised by their mother on a farm in North Lebanon Township, Pennsylvania, Stover enlisted in the Marine Corps in 1911. He served in the Philippines, followed by recruiting tours and service at Marine Corps headquarters in Washington, DC. Stover was on recruiting duty in Chicago when war was declared, and he immediately requested to be transferred overseas with his old company, now part of the 6th Marines. Stover was ready to cross the Atlantic with the regiment when he contracted measles and had to stay behind in Quantico. Unwilling to be denied his place in the fight, Stover took a reduction in rank to corporal to join the 1st Replacement Battalion. He visited his mother one last time at Christmas 1917 before shipping out to France. He regained his rank in France and joined the 80th Company in the middle of the battle in Belleau Wood. A shell fragment killed Stover as he led his Marines into the attack. His body was lost in the aftermath, and back in Lebanon, Pennsylvania, his mother, paralyzed by a stroke in May, received word of her son's death in August. The entire community went into mourning and formed the John O. Stover Society to support the war effort. Mrs. Stover exacted a promise from the Marine Corps that the body of her oldest son would be brought home after the war. The promise was fulfilled in 1921. Today, Sergeant Stover rests at the Ebenezer Cemetery in his hometown.[1]

Stop 30. *6th Marines' High-Water Mark,*
49°16'58.4"N 3°19'37.8"E

Leave Villemontoire on the Rue Jacques Moquet and proceed for 1.1 kilometers to the junction with the D 1. This modern road follows the path of the 1918 road from Soissons to Château-Thierry, the 2nd Division's final objective and the 6th Marines' target on July 19. You can now judge how close the Marines came to achieving their goal. Without maps, it is doubtful that the company and platoon leaders knew how close they were to victory.

Turn right, proceed 190 meters, and then turn right on the D 1280. Drive 1.3 kilometers and turn left on the Rue de Villemontoire. Proceed 1.2 kilometers, driving past the British Cemetery to the high ground at the first large bend in the road. Look to the west across the wheat fields. You are now standing on Hill 160, the high point of the 6th Marines' advance. From here, you can easily understand the difficulty of the 6th Marines' advance as you look back toward Vierzy, which is hidden in the low ground. To your right is Villemontoire, and to your left is the town of Tigny.

The determined remnants of the 84th Company advanced to this spot, following the farm lane across the road, and reached the wheat fields before you. Turn and face the crest of Hill 160 across the road. The Germans defending the hill had a perfect vantage point, targeting the Marines with their machine guns and *Minenwerfers* flanking Holcomb's advance to the north and Hughes's to the south. You can easily calculate the odds of any Marine's safe arrival at this point.

First Lieutenant Horatio P. Mason Jr. led the advance, the only uninjured officer out of the seven who had started the attack. Mason led the final charge across the ground where you now stand, taking the remnants of the 84th Company into the German gun pits. Mason was wounded in the charge, but the Marines took the hill with bayonets, pistols, and fists, driving the enemy back to the Soissons–Château-Thierry road. Mason and his men now held the key to the battlefield, and the Germans holding Villemontoire and Tigny were now flanked themselves. Mason dispatched runners to inform Lee of his position, requesting reinforcements to hold the hill. With every unit already committed, Lee had no Marines to send to Hill 160 except for his own Headquarters Company, commanded by First Lieutenant Wesley W. Walker. The company went forward to join Mason, but they were too few to exploit the breakthrough.

One of the Marines participating in the attack was Corporal William M. Barnett of Oswego, New York. The grandson of Irish immigrants, "Willie" was a relative newcomer to the 84th Company, having joined the unit in June 1918 as a replacement in the battle for Belleau Wood. Barnett had left his job as an assistant master mechanic with a steel company to enlist in the Marine Corps. The twenty-six-year-old was killed instantly by a German sniper in the wheat fields. His body was never recovered, as his comrades were relieved by French soldiers during the night. He is listed among the missing in the chapel at the Aisne Marne Cemetery in France, but his family placed a remembrance stone at St. Paul's Cemetery in his hometown.[2]

This stop is also the perfect occasion to look back across the open ground from the vantage point of the German defenders. The sight of two battalions of Marines in perfect formation must have looked imposing at first, but the artillery and machine gun fire turned the Marines' orderly lines into turmoil. The Germans' initial focus was Turrill's advance on Tigny to their left and Holcomb's attack on the right, allowing the 84th Company to approach Hill 160 between the battalions in relative order. The Germans soon changed their focus, however, to the Marine company coming directly at them with no intention of stopping. When Mason led his final charge up the slope before you, many of the Germans ran rather than face the Marines' bayonets.

Stop 31. 2nd Division Marker, Tigny, 49°16′39.4″N 3°19′51.3″E

Continue on the Rue de Villemontoire for 700 meters to the center of Tigny, and turn right on the Rue de la Forge. Drive 280 meters until you reach a fork in the road with a small park. Here, there is another 2nd Division marker. Park and walk a short distance on the D 175 (the right fork) to get the best view. Major Hughes's 1st Battalion, 6th Marines, and two platoons of the 77th Machine Gun Company attacked using this road as their southern flank and extended into the fields north. Hughes's Marines halted at the distant rise ahead on the D 175. You can see the lone tree on the right side of the road, marking the farthest point of their advance. Look to your right and identify Hill 160. It is easy to evaluate the importance of the dominating terrain held by the Germans. As you can see, the attack across the wheat fields had little chance of success, unlike the attack the previous day. The German reserves were fully in place on July 19, ready with massed artillery.

Reinforcements arrived in the form of the 97th Company of Sibley's battalion, supported by the 81st Company of the 6th Machine Gun Battalion. They advanced directly toward your position, using the wheat fields on the right side of the road. Return to the 2nd Division marker and look back up the Rue de la Forge. The boulder where you now stand marks the farthest advance by the 97th Company. The large house directly down the road, about a hundred yards away, marks the 1918 limits of the town. The Marines entered the then-open ground but were called back, unaware of their lost opportunity. The capture of Hill 160 forced the Germans to evacuate the town, leaving behind only snipers to hinder the Marines' advance. No further attempt was made to capture the town.

One of the 97th Company's casualties was twenty-one-year-old Corporal John T. Ring of Kernersville, North Carolina. He graduated with honors from Trinity College (later renamed Duke University) in 1916. "His genial sunny disposition, his strong personality, and his keen intellect made him a general favorite."[3] He enlisted in January 1918 and arrived in France in May of that year. Soissons was Ring's first battle. Just before the company began its advance, Ring made a pact with his best friend, Private J. Grant Frye from Missouri, that if one of them fell in combat, the survivor would contact his parents. They both prepared two-part letters, with the opening pages written and addressed by themselves and the second part left blank to be filled in by the survivor. They exchanged the letters and then advanced side by side into the wheat. Ring was struck by a high-explosive shell and killed instantly, while his friend Frye was only an arm's length away. Unable to stop and tend to his friend's body, Frye mentally marked the location, hoping he would be able to return. He later learned that Ring had been buried "with decent rites of burial" by other Marines during the night.[4]

Ring's remains were initially listed as being in a marked grave in the American Parcy-Tigny cemetery, but when all the remains were moved in 1919 to the larger Ploissy military cemetery nearby, Ring's grave site was listed as unknown. His father wrote to the army quartermaster, asking for the location of his son's body and the return of his personal belongings. "We have never yet had any information from your department as to having located our son's body," he wrote. "We will thank you to let us know if you have located his grave, and oblige."[5] After waiting for several months, he wrote again, with the same request. It turned out that there was no record of Ring's burial, as his grave had mistakenly been marked as unknown. A 1920 cemetery audit finally resolved the issue, and Ring's grave was properly identified. Mr. Ring then requested that his son's body be returned to North Carolina.

Ring's body was exhumed one last time in 1921 and returned home to Kernersville, where he rests today. More than 1,000 people attended the memorial service at the Methodist Episcopal church in town. The service began with the hymn "Abide with Me," sung by a choir made up of Ring's friends, followed by tributes from officials from Trinity College, his fraternity brothers, and his college roommate. Most important was the address given by Grant Frye of the 97th Company, who had been with Ring when he died.[6] Ring's father established a scholarship at Trinity College in his son's name.

He erected a large monument and bronze tablet to mark John's grave in the family plot in Mount Gur Cemetery, and they still stand over his grave today.

Stop 32. *Hughes's Advance, 49°16'43.4"N 3°18'59.2"E*

Leave Tigny on the D 175 (right fork in the road) and proceed 1 kilometer to the lone tree on the right. Park your vehicle carefully, as there is only a small turnout here.

You are now on the farthest point reached by Major Hughes's 1st Battalion, 6th Marines. Take a moment to reorient yourself to the terrain. The D 175 continues to Vierzy, and it is 2.5 kilometers to Colonel Lee's headquarters at the town cemetery. The road branching off to the left leads to Parcy-Tigny, held by the Germans on the morning of July 19. Now locate Hill 160, marked by the trees to the left of Tigny.

Hughes's Marines advanced toward Tigny using the D 175 as their right flank, extending into the fields on the rising ground to the north. They advanced to this point with heavy casualties and took sanctuary in the sunken road marked by the tree in front of you. The depth of the dirt road seems inadequate to offer protection from the German machine guns, but it was a welcome sanctuary for the Marines who had survived to this point. They remained here for most of the day, subjected to artillery fire and the strafing of German aircraft. The ground extending back to Vierzy would have been littered with the morning's dead and wounded.

It is easy to see why the battalion could advance no further, due to the flanking fire from Parcy-Tigny. The foray by the captured French tanks and the counterattack by Lieutenant Fant's platoon of the 76th Company took place in the field on the south side of the road looking back toward Vierzy. This is also the place where Lieutenant Schwerin set up two of the 81st Machine Gun Company's Hotchkiss machine guns to cover the advance.

Shell fire was particularly deadly for the machine gunners during the advance. One of the bursts killed Private Frederick C. "Freddie" Hinds, who had been a Marine for just five months. The twenty-six-year-old blue-eyed, brown-haired Marine from Dutton, Montana, was initially buried in the nearby field. Either his remains were moved but never identified during the first mass reburial or they still remain in the field. Hinds is listed among the missing in the chapel of the Aisne Marne Cemetery, but there is no other indicator of his sacrifice. In 1920 and again the following year, the family requested the return of his body to the United States. When informed of his missing status, Johanna Hinds, his adopted mother, asked only that she be sent an American flag in remembrance of her son. The army quickly complied with her request. In 1931 Mrs. Hinds declined to go to France as part of the Gold Star Mothers' pilgrimage. The following year, the army quartermaster wrote to her, encouraging her to make the trip. "While it is regretted to advise that the remains of your son have not been located and you will understand no grave can be shown you as that of your son," Captain A. D. Hughes wrote, "there is a more than even chance that his remains have been recovered and lacking means of identification, have been interred in the Aisne Marne American Cemetery in France under a cross inscribed: 'Here Lies an American Soldier Known but to God.'"[7] Mrs. Hines again declined the invitation.

You can judge for yourself how close the attack came to success. Had the reserve of the 6th Marines and 6th Machine Gun Battalion gone forward on July 18 to follow up the attack by the 5th Marines and 3rd Army Brigade, perhaps the Soissons–Château-Thierry road could have been breached. However, the German High Command knew that the road was in easy range of the French and American artillery and would inevitably fall into Allied hands. The Germans also knew their position was now untenable and ordered a withdrawal from the Marne salient immediately.

15

Aftermath
"How Many Hopes, Cherished during the Last Few Months, Had Probably Collapsed at One Blow!"

By July 21, 1918, the German attack from Reims to Château-Thierry had not only stalled; the entire Marne salient was now untenable and had to be evacuated to prevent a disaster of colossal proportions. The attackers became defenders, fighting for time to allow the Germans to withdraw. Hindenburg sadly wrote, "We seemed to have very little left of all we had striven for."[1]

Foch's perfectively timed offensive on the morning of July 18, led by the 1st Moroccan Division and the American 1st and 2nd Divisions, reverberated far beyond the wheat and sugar-beet fields southwest of Soissons. The Allied offensive drove the surprised defenders back toward the single railroad supplying the entire German force inside the salient and within artillery range of the vital Soissons–Château-Thierry road. Should that supply line be severed, catastrophe loomed for the approximately thirty German divisions within the salient. Although Hindenburg was able to stabilize and hold the Allies at bay for the moment, he was forced to withdraw from Château-Thierry. The pronouncement was a momentous one. "We must evacuate the salient and say goodbye to the Marne," Hindenburg later wrote. "It was a grievous decision, not from the purely military standpoint but from that of professional pride."[2] Many of the forces preparing to attack the British were now needed on the Marne front to prevent a disaster during the withdrawal.

With that decision, the end of World War I was in sight. The growing American reinforcements ensured that Foch would retain and carry the initiative on the western front, to which the Germans had little reply. "How many hopes, cherished during the last few months, had probably collapsed at one blow!" Hindenburg pronounced in his memoirs. "How many calculations had been scattered to the winds!"[3] General Foch, commander of the Allied military effort, presented his own interpretation. "Victory had been passed to the Allied banners," he wrote, "thanks to the rapid and sustained development of the operations following the German offensive of July 15."[4]

344

A series of Allied attacks in the coming months would drive the Germans back toward their own borders and bring the war to an end on November 11, 1918.

The cessation of hostilities only underscored the significance of the battles to the Marine Corps. June 6, 1918, proved to be a watershed for the Marine Corps. The Battle of Belleau Wood changed forever both how the Marines thought about themselves and how the nation viewed the Marine Corps as an organization. Before World War I, the Marine Corps had played important but small roles in each of the nation's conflicts. The Marine Corps' virtual absence from the largest American conflict, the Civil War of 1861–1865, demonstrated to the leadership that more had to be done to improve the Corps' role in future conflicts.

The importance of the Marines' participation in the Spanish-American War, the Boxer Rebellion, and the Philippine Insurrection laid the foundation for the Marine Corps' significant participation in World War I. The success of the Marines in France, starting on June 6, 1918, prepared the Corps to assume a major role in America's future on the world stage. At the same time, Marines felt differently about themselves. They knew they had helped change the course of history. Future commandant Shepherd of the 55th Company wrote home on June 9, 1918: "You probably read at the time what the Marines did. We surely made a name for ourselves and helped up the reputation of the Marine Corps. . . . I tell you the Marines covered themselves with glory. . . . Since then the Marines have been keeping up their good work, but I don't think there are many left now."[5]

The bravery of individual Marines left lasting impressions around the world, bringing hope to the Allied nations that hungered for good news issuing from a conflict that had caused so much suffering. An astonishing ninety-four Army Distinguished Service Crosses were awarded to Marines for actions on June 6 alone, with corresponding Navy Crosses to follow. From living rooms in the United States to the pubs of London and bistros of Paris, people of all the Allied nations, and Americans in particular, rejoiced at the newspaper accounts of the Marines' bravery and sacrifice.

With the end of the battle, popular opinion in France pronounced that the men of the 4th Marine Brigade were the only Americans in the fight. Little credit was given to the French army or to the 3rd American Division. Thanks to the dispatches of Floyd Gibbons and other newspapermen, this flawed impression resonated around the world. Scarce mention was made of the army's 3rd Brigade, which suffered significant casualties on the same front, or the supporting artillery brigade and other 2nd Division units.

General Foch himself, as representative of the Allied war leaders both military and civilian, supported this interpretation. The good news from

Belleau Wood captured the American spirit and was used extensively by the Allied press to great advantage in renewing the public's desire to win the war.

The battle had an immediate material effect on the Marine Corps. On July 1, 1918, the Naval Appropriations Act passed both houses of Congress. It raised the wartime strength of the Marine Corps to 75,500 men. Almost every point pressed by Marine Commandant Barnett and Quartermaster Brigadier General Charles L. McCawley in February was contained in the legislation, including the establishment of a new logistics reserve, additional clerks for headquarters, and additional land for Marine training bases. Certainly, the fighting at Belleau Wood vindicated Barnett's impassioned call for more Marines.[6]

In turn, the French understood the importance of the Marines' sacrifice at Belleau Wood and their contribution to Allied morale. On June 30, 1918, General Degoutte recognized the Marines with 6th Army Order 6930/2, changing the name of Belleau Wood to honor the 4th Brigade. The order read, "In view of the splendid conduct of the 4th Brigade of the 2nd U.S. Division . . . in all official papers, the Bois de Belleau shall be named *Bois de la Brigade de Marine.*"[7] However, a corresponding movement began almost immediately to change the name to Bois de la Brigade des Americains. The *Washington Post* felt the need to report that although the Marines were constantly mentioned in the news, other units had also fought well in the battle. The article mentioned Harbord but proclaimed, "Bundy led the Marines."[8]

News of the official renaming reached American shores very quickly. On July 5, 1918, the *New York Times* printed an article under the headline "French Generals Proud of Our Men." The reporter quoted an unnamed French general: "I am particularly delighted to have American troops under my command. They have fought splendidly, and as a mark of our appreciation Belleau Wood will be henceforth called the Wood of the Americans in all Army orders." The anonymous general could only be Degoutte, who commanded the 6th Army during the Belleau Wood fighting. The article also quoted the unnamed French corps commander in charge of the 2nd Division's sector: "Monday's affair at Vaux was an even harder job than Belleau," the commander stated. "Not only was the village crammed with machine guns, but the wood behind it was full of machine guns, minenwerfer, and artillery . . . it was one of the most brilliant little operations one could describe."[9] Interestingly, the 3rd Brigade's capture of Vaux was accomplished on the evening of July 1, with the loss of 328 men killed and wounded, compared with almost 5,000 casualties during the month-long battle at Belleau Wood.[10]

Many newspapers adopted the "American" rather than the "Marine" interpretation. The *New York Times* reported on July 12, 1918, that the woods would be named after the Marine Brigade, despite referring to the unit only as "American troops." The newspaper also noted a "Paris Dispatch" reporting that the French general commanding in the Belleau Wood area had announced that the new name would be "Bois des Americans."[11] On July 11 the *Detroit Free Press* printed an article that discussed the Battle of Belleau Wood as "injun fighting" and praised the attack on Vaux as a model in military efficiency. The reporter who wrote glowingly of the army's capture of Vaux made no mention of any Marines.[12]

Assistant Secretary of the Navy Franklin D. Roosevelt was in France on an inspection trip at the time and quickly uncovered the slight to the Marines. He wrote to the secretary of the navy, "I have later learned that there was some mean piece of hocus pocus by some narrow minded Army officer in this connection." Roosevelt actually made a special trip to the front and visited Degoutte's headquarters, where he asked the general about his recognition of the Marines. "Degoutte, as he told me with his own lips, announced the change in a general order to his entire army, in which among other things he gave especial praise to the Marine Brigade for their work in Belleau Wood," Roosevelt wrote in his journal. "Somewhere down the line, whether it was in the Corps headquarters or in the Division headquarters, or perhaps even back at American General Headquarters, a public announcement was made that the French had changed the name of the wood to Bois des Americaines."[13] Roosevelt wanted to get the mistake on the record, as "jealous individuals" might work to prevent the 4th Marine Brigade from gaining proper recognition in future operations.

Roosevelt made certain that the 4th Marine Brigade received credit for both Belleau Wood and Soissons. On August 7, 1918, he said in an interview that, from "the look on the faces of those Marines whom I inspected at Nancy . . . they have earned the right today to be placed among the keenest and the most efficient of all the troops on the Western Front." He then related an anecdote about a Marine wounded at Soissons who was being treated in a British hospital. When asked if he was an American, the wounded man said, "Hell, no! I'm a Marine!"[14] On August 10, 1918, Roosevelt dispatched a cable to the secretary of the navy, stating, "This wood has been renamed Bois De La Brigade de Marines."[15]

In a personal letter to Secretary Daniels three days later, Roosevelt wrote, "Those Marines are simply magnificent . . . they certainly do need more Marines over here."[16] He also took the time to personally inspect the Marine Brigade and prepared a special order that would please every Marine in the command. Roosevelt authorized all Marines to wear the Marine Corps emblem on their shirt collars, thus distinguishing themselves and their Corps to every person they encountered.[17]

The French promptly reaffirmed the proper name of the woods. *L'Illustration* printed an article on August 31, 1918, entitled "The American Brigade of Marines at Bois de Belleau," which confirmed the new Marine-specific name and commented, "Like all 'troupes d'elite' with a long war-like tradition, they have a strong esprit de corps and a pride in their uniform. 'If you wish action,' say they in their recruiting poster, 'join the Marines.'" The article ended with a plea for Frenchmen to recognize members of the Marine Brigade. It advised readers, if an American wore on his collar an emblem with the "world crossed by an anchor and surmounted by an eagle you should give that soldier a particularly respectful and sympathetic look; he belongs to an heroic brigade, he is a Marine."[18]

Another newspaper recounted the story of a wounded French cavalryman being treated at an American field hospital. The young officer was very curious about the American troops fighting to the left of his unit. He had been astounded and greatly impressed when, in one jump, the Americans mounted French horses that had lost their riders and galloped into the American lines. "I believe they are your soldiers from Montezuma," he said. "At least, when they advanced this morning, they were singing 'From the halls of Montezuma to the shores of Tripoli.'"[19]

The tide also turned in American newspapers. The Navy Department released a detailed letter written from Belleau Wood to Commandant Barnett that provided comprehensive information about the exploits of the 4th Marine Brigade. The *New York Tribune* used this letter for an article on August 11, proclaiming, "Brigade of 'Sea Soldiers' More than Upheld Fighting Traditions of Their Corps."[20] The letter provided details of the capture of Bouresches and named many prominent Marines of the June 6 battle for the first time, including Holcomb, Berry, Sibley, Robertson, Dunlavy, and others. Harbord himself became one of the most well-known generals in the American Expeditionary Force. This fame generated any number of lurid descriptions of Harbord and his command. One unnamed literary wit described the "unrelaxing throat-hold [that] swept the dachshund spew from Château Thierry and beyond."[21]

The *Chicago Tribune* printed an article concerning a one-man show at the Orchestra Hall titled "Paris, 1918." Much of the performance consisted of an exhibition of wartime photographs of the city narrated by a "Mr. Newman," but the discourse reached an exciting crescendo when the Paris Fourth of July parade was discussed. "Listen," said Mr. Newman, "and you will hear the crowd shout, Vive les Marines! whereupon the battling Leathernecks swing into view with their spirited step, every one of them a page from the purple testament of Belleau Wood."[22] Newman's description of the exploits of the Marines elicited a rousing cheer from the crowd, which openly displayed its pride in the soldiers of the sea. As controversy between the army and the Marines boiled, the rank and file of the Marine Brigade knew little about the ongoing battles being waged in the newspapers. They did know about the significance of the battle at Belleau Wood in real time.

Interestingly, the program for Harbord's promotion on July 11, 1918, contained a poem titled "Bois de Belleau," written by Second Lieutenant Bradford Perin. The verses are poignant and reveal the 4th Marine Brigade's attitude only days after the battle:

> Little Bois Bleu,
> Come blow your horn!
> Your oaks are splintered
> and thrown over and torn.
> Even your name, Bois Bleu, is unmade,
> Now you are called: Bois Marine Brigade.
>
> What's in a name, in some there's naught,
> But your name, Bois Bleu, was dearly bought.
> We gave our blood
> We gave you our aid
> Come blow your horn,
> Bois Marine Brigade!

The opposite was true of Soissons. The two days of intense combat gave the Marines little time to reflect on the significance of their actions there. Withdrawn under the cover of darkness, the brigade never saw the battlefield again, and their lasting impressions consisted of suffering heavy casualties and failing to reach the Soissons–Château-Thierry road. The French 158th Division also failed to take the road, despite occupying the forward positions left to it by the 6th Marines. The American 1st Division reached the road near Buzancy on July 21 after five days of combat and was relieved by the 15th Scottish Division, which carried the attack into Buzancy and secured the road on July 28.

The struggle for Belleau Wood lasted from June 1 through July 9, 1918, thirty-nine days of combat. During that time, the Marine Brigade suffered 4,598 casualties. In only two days of combat at Soissons, 2,015 men were killed, wounded, or captured. The ferocity of these two battles resulted in the loss of 6,613 men in less than two months. With an authorized strength of 8,417 men, the 4th Marine Brigade's devastation was severe. Wounded Marines who returned to duty and replacements that arrived during and after Belleau Wood helped balance the losses, but each company remained depleted on July 20. Despite its casualties, the Marine Brigade was unbroken. Battle awaited the Marines in September at Saint-Mihiel.[23]

Harbord believed the entire division had come together during the Soissons battle and was now a truly unified command rather than individual Marine and army brigades with their own identities. However, Harbord's leadership of the 2nd Division was short-lived. On July 27 Pershing ordered Harbord to his headquarters for a meeting. "All through the journey," wrote Harbord, "my mind was full of conjecture as to what could be the subject of the conference."[24] Late in the evening he was ushered into Pershing's headquarters, where, "with true Pershing directness he at once went to the point." Harbord would be reassigned to the Services of Supply, where he was desperately needed. On July 29 Harbord bade farewell to the 2nd Division. The parting proved difficult. "It is unnecessary to say that I regretted very bitterly that the General thought it was necessary to bring me back here," Harbord later penned to a comrade. "I owe so much to him, however, and so much to the cause that I accepted it as necessary."[25] Brigadier General Lejeune would soon assume command of the 2nd Division.

The French continued to laud the Marines' actions at Belleau Wood, with citations for the 4th Marine Brigade, 5th Marines, 6th Marines, and 6th Machine Gun Battalion in the French army orders of October 22, 1918. Based on these and other citations, the honor of the *Fourragère* in the colors of the Croix de Guerre was bestowed on the 5th Marines, 6th Marines, and 6th Machine Gun Battalion. Although the 6th Machine Gun Battalion has ceased to exist, both Marine regiments still proudly display their honor to this day.

In September, Barnett and Bundy exchanged personal letters that ended some of the animosity in the army-Marine controversy. "I shall never cease to congratulate myself on my good fortune in having the Marine Brigade as part of the 2nd Division," Bundy wrote to the commandant. "It was an honor to command them."[26] Still, a feeling of ill will became prevalent among the officers of the 4th Marine Brigade. Captain Edwin N. McClellan wrote in November 1918, "There is no question but that the Marines, as far as the American Army is concerned, are not to be given a further place in the sun."[27] Most of the friction was caused by the continued widespread belief in America that the Marines had saved Paris, a belief that was shared by the French people. The sight of a Marine in France would inevitably invoke cries of "Vive la Marine" and "Belleau Wood." The American forces would accumulate many accomplishments during the rest of 1918 that far overshadowed Belleau Wood in a tactical and strategic sense. Still, the Marines' iconic battle continued to be a source of irritation for American army commanders.

The end of the war did not end the controversy. In fact, emotions intensified on both sides. On May 25, 1919, a special correspondent for the *New York Times* revealed the depth of the army's frustration when he penned an article with the incendiary title "Stories of the War that Didn't Happen, Even the Marines Themselves Admit They Received an Oversupply of Credit." Edwin L. James led off with the story of the Marines at Belleau Wood, stating, "It may be interesting to run over two or three oft-repeated mistakes." James implied that the wartime censors permitted Marine units to be mentioned at the start of the battle but then disallowed the naming of specific units, which led to the "impression in the United States, it appears, that about all the fighting around Chateau Thierry was done by marines, although as a matter of fact, the marines comprised one brigade of one of six divisions which participated in the fighting." The article continued with scathing attacks on the Marine legends of Belleau Wood. According to James, before the capture of Vaux on July 1, all the war correspondents were informed that the attack would be carried out not by the Marines but by the 9th and 23rd Regiments. Unfortunately, once their accounts of the fighting were submitted to the army censor, all mention of the 3rd Brigade's regiments was deleted, only adding to the army's aggravation. The article continued by disparaging the "soiled and dirty" Marines in the Fourth of July parade in Paris. It even claimed that the "Retreat? Hell no!" comment attributed to Captain Williams should take "its place in fiction."[28]

The men of the 2nd Division also continued to experience strong feelings of resentment after the war. Brigadier General Malone, who commanded the 2nd Division's 23rd Infantry at Belleau Wood, complained to General Harbord when the Marine Corps asked for 10,000 selected Marines to serve in France with a pay increase. He wrote on June 13, 1919, "Once more the Marines see an opportunity. With the advantage of being able to select their men individually and being able to fix a special pay rate for their troops in France the comparison between the Marines and other troops serving 'On the Rhine' will be very much to the advantage of the Marines." He concluded by stating that the Marines were "a bunch of adventurers, illiterates and drunkards who will leave nothing to be desired when it comes to making comparisons."[29]

Despite the comments of officers like Malone, the passage of time made the Battle of Belleau Wood even more iconic to the American people and the Marine Corps. A correspondent for the *Washington Post* visited Belleau Wood in 1919 and wrote an article titled "Relics Strew Marines' Woods." The two-paragraph piece was filled with graphic images: "Days after the fighting has eased, human fragments, helmets, gas masks, cartridge belts, toilet articles, letters, postal cards, canteens, loaves of bread, rifles, wrecked machine guns, first aid packages, raincoats, German officers helmets, bayonets, swords, [and] trench knives" can be seen, the reporter wrote, "a hundred and one things to emphasize the fierceness of the strife."[30]

The paper battle over Belleau Wood continued to rage in the United States as well. On April 19, 1919, the *Literary Magazine,* the *New York Times,* and the Associated Press ran a story titled "Doughboys, and Not Marines, Won at Chateau Thierry." Two days later, Commandant Barnett dispatched personal letters to each publisher to dispute the article. "I at first decided not to say anything in reference to the matter," he wrote. "However, I have been appealed to by so many people who are interested in the Marines, that I wish to make just one statement to your paper." The commandant simply asked each publication to print General Pershing's reports and cablegrams relating to the Marine Brigade at Belleau Wood that mentioned Château-Thierry as a sector.

On April 23, 1919, the *New York Times* reported that Commandant Barnett was challenging accounts by unnamed army officers that disputed the presence of Marines at Château-Thierry. Technically, there were no Marines in the town itself, but they were definitely present at the overall Battle of Château-Thierry, of which Belleau Wood was a component. To prove his point, Barnett released for the first time the full extent of the casualties suffered by the 4th Marine Brigade in June 1918, totaling 126 officers and 5,073 men killed or wounded. The article closed by pointing out that General Pershing himself had presented Distinguished Service Crosses to Marines for their valor at Château-Thierry. The *Literary Digest* replied to Barnett, agreeing that although the use of the name Château-Thierry created much confusion, "We think no one has questioned the great work of the Marines along the entire front which you credit to them."[31]

In San Francisco, Barnett himself made a definitive statement regarding the army's claims. "There has been some little controversy as to the use of the name Chateau Thierry," he wrote, and "as a matter of fact, the marines were not in the town of Chateau Thierry, but were fighting in and around Belleau Wood, which was in the Chateau Thierry sector and practically within sight of the town."[32] On April 24 Barnett sent another round of letters to several publications, including the *Denver Post.* He enlisted Harbord in this effort, writing to him the same day and noting that the article originated from the "Watch on the Rhine" newsletter published by the 3rd Division. "The Marines need no defense in the eyes of those who are in a position to know what they accomplished in France," Barnett wrote. "However, in the minds of thousands of readers in the United States, articles such as this are bound to create an erroneous impression . . . I thought it only proper to let you know of the attempt being made to belittle the Brigade's achievements."[33] Barnett ended the letter by asking for Harbord's help refuting the rising tide of army opinion. The controversy became white hot in early May, after Secretary of the Navy Daniels forwarded Barnett's letter to Acting Secretary of the Army Crowell for comment. Crowell replied that the issue had been sent to Pershing, and he sent Daniels a copy of General Orders 4 and 41, which defined the extent of major operations.

With so much controversy over Belleau Wood, the Marine Corps acted quickly to document the history of the 4th Marine Brigade, as well as to preserve it for the purpose of recruiting future Marines. The 4th Brigade's chief of staff, Major Charles D. Barrett, recognized the significance of the battle for the Marine Corps and suggested that a relief map be created on the same scale as the famous map of Gettysburg. Barrett understood that a map of Belleau Wood would generate a connection with the American public. In fact, while on the voyage home in 1919, Barrett mentioned to Captain Lemuel Shepherd, "I think we ought to make a map of Belleau Woods because it is of great historical significance to the Marine Corps, it's the greatest battle the Marine Corps has ever participated in."[34]

As the 4th Brigade disbanded in Quantico on August 13, 1919, Major Barrett received permission to carry out the surveys necessary to construct the relief map. Engineering and survey equipment were quickly obtained from the Marine Corps schools, and in less than two weeks, battle veterans Captain Shepherd, Captain Samuel C. Cumming, and First Lieutenant Lothar R. Long accompanied Barrett to France, along with a detachment consisting of an aide to the commandant, an officer from Public Works, five officers from the officers' training camp, and fifty-one enlisted men, including a corpsman and a pay clerk. Shepherd later remembered, "I'd been gone over two years and only had time to have a weekend with my parents. We went right back to France."[35] The map detachment sailed from New York on a battered freighter making only twelve knots per hour.

The project proved to be so popular that it was expanded, with the goal of plotting all the Marine battlefields in France. The follow-up surveying party was dispatched to France in 1920 with the mission of creating extremely detailed maps of the Marine battlefields at a scale of 1/1,200 feet, or one inch of map equaling 100 feet of actual terrain. The two teams needed twenty weeks to complete the task, surveying 259 square kilometers. Every shell hole, trench, tree, fence, road, and path were documented.

The survey teams found that the condition of the battlefield had changed little from its 1918 appearance. Signs of the fierce fighting were still evident. In fact, members of the map detachment found themselves performing the duties of casualty recovery as they located the bodies of both Marines and Germans in the fields and woods, just where they had fallen in June 1918.

One survey party led by Shepherd discovered the remains of a Marine and a German soldier together in a well, still wearing their uniforms. "Whether they were fighting and fell into the well, I don't know," he later remembered, "but we recovered their remains and buried them in the cemetery."[36]

After members of the detachment completed their surveys and topographical maps, they returned to headquarters with the results. Barrett combined the individual Belleau Wood maps to create one unified fifteen-foot map. An enlisted man drew color sketches of each house on the map.[37] The total cost of the project was estimated to be at least $14,000, which was approved by the secretary of the navy in April 1920.[38]

The Marine Corps Officers School in Quantico was then ordered to construct three-dimensional maps of each battle. The maps were transformed into huge models crafted in plaster and painstakingly painted, costing another $3,500. Five officers oversaw the work of twenty-two enlisted men and a civilian carpenter with expertise in drafting, molding, painting, and carpentry. Just as in the survey maps, every feature of the ground was represented: woods, orchards, and individual houses in every village; fields differentiated by type of crop; roads and fences. Warrant Officer Gustav Broadstrum reproduced the buildings in clay and hand-painted each one individually. The work took a year to complete at Quantico, and the intention was to use the maps to educate the public about the exploits of the 4th Marine Brigade.[39]

In 1922 the map of Belleau Wood, the first one completed, was offered to the Smithsonian Institution. The Marine Corps touted these grand displays as "of the greatest value, not only as works of art, but also as reproductions of battle areas which can never again be reproduced accurately, owing to the fact that they have been thoroughly restored." The Belleau Wood map was massive, measuring sixteen square feet; it was divided into 140 individual map squares. The Smithsonian accepted the huge relief map as part of the American legacy and proudly displayed it in Washington, DC. Lejeune also used the map as a recruiting tool, stationing an enlisted man who had lost an arm during the battle with the map; the Marine, who had "all of the official reports of the battle," was there to answer all questions and explain the exhibit.[40]

The follow-on maps were offered to institutions across the country, including the Chicago Historical Society, Brooklyn Institute of Arts and Science, and Memorial Hall in Philadelphia. Many refused the offer because of space limitations and the cost of the glass cases required for each exhibit. First Lieutenant Lemuel A. Haslup, in command of the Cleveland recruiting station, wrote to Marine Corps headquarters explaining that Mr. Marshall Rea, director of the Cleveland Museum of Natural History, had refused the map due to a lack of exhibit space. "I used every possible means at my command to persuade Mr. Rea to accept same," Haslup wrote, "but his decision on the matter could not be changed."[41] After World War II, the Smithsonian's Belleau Wood map was returned to Quantico to become part of the newly established Marine Corps Museum. However, it was put into storage and then disappeared, lost to the pages of history.

The Marine Corps also acted quickly to produce an accurate history of its participation in the war. On November 26, 1919, Major Edwin N. Mc-Clellan wrote, "It is absolutely essential that the Marine Corps publish a tentative history in order to keep the public and the Naval Service personnel straight as to the facts." Marines across the country were being questioned about their role in France and lacked an accurate source. The US Army had already published *The War with Germany, a Statistical Summary*, which would soon be reprinted in a second edition with additional data. On the same day, McClellan forwarded a copy of his succinct manuscript to Commandant Barnett, who quickly approved the book for publication.

In early 1920 *The United States Marine Corps in the World War* was published at ten cents per copy. It provided 103 pages of facts and statistical data on every aspect of the Marines' wartime service. Paper bound and with twenty-seven chapters of fully indexed data, this publication provided every Marine with dates, numbers, and names related to all the prominent 4th Marine Brigade battles. Additional chapters documented Marines' service on battleships and cruisers; in aviation units, headquarters departments, and recruiting stations; and as rifle instructors. Importantly, only basic analysis and interpretation were presented.

McClellan also produced a series of articles on the 4th Marine Brigade that appeared in the *Marine Corps Gazette*, again with the caveat that it was "yet too early for any Historical Division to place its stamp of approval on a composition purporting to be a close analysis of an event occurring during the war."[42] As with his earlier work, McClellan declined to make any controversial judgments about the war, preferring to limit the articles "to the statement of facts secured in a mechanical fashion from official operation reports, field orders, general orders, orders, war diaries, etc., . . . in none of the published articles under its name will opinions, conclusions, or criticisms be expressed." He defused the inevitable controversies with the army by stating that even the Marine reports were "inconclusive if there exists a conflicting report of another organization."[43] The basic Marine Corps position on every aspect of the war would be established, regardless of the views of any other service.

However, the Marine commanders themselves honestly examined the Belleau Wood battle from a purely professional military point of view.

Following the war, there was some quiet discussion within the Marine Corps over the necessity of the June 6 attack and the capture of Belleau Wood, the town of Bouresches, and Hill 142. With hindsight, they recognized that subsequent Allied attacks would have caused an evacuation of these positions no matter who held the lines just north of the Marne. Indeed, the month-long battle by the 2nd Division and the 4th Marine Brigade was meant to outflank the German positions on the Paris road. Certainly, the cost in lives to take these positions was overwhelming, considering that the terrain was not critical in a strategic sense. The June 6 attack and the costly assaults on Belleau Wood for the remainder of the month constituted further questions.

Harbord reflected on the attack, stating, "That question did not have to be decided by us. We undertook the capture of those places in response to orders of the 6th French Army, with which, however, I was in strong sympathy." He concluded by saying, "I do not think that the necessity of those operations there will be questioned by anybody, except perhaps, someone jealous of the gallant achievements of the organizations that fought there."[44]

Harbord, commander of the 4th Marine Brigade, described the Marines' role in a 1919 letter reviewing Colonel Catlin's book *With the Help of God and a Few Marines*. "No one who knows the incomparable United States Marine, his splendid élan, his dash, and his traditions can read this account . . . without a swelling in the heart and a tear in the eye," Harbord wrote. "The story of the gallantry of the Marines at Bois de Belleau and Bouresches reads like a romance of the First Empire."[45]

When questioned about this matter in 1920, Harbord replied, "I do not feel called upon to undertake to write anything as to the necessity about the capture. . . . I believe that they [orders] were absolutely necessary and that the stand made there by the Marine Brigade saved a further advance on Paris."[46] Stopping the Germans was certainly imperative to Allied success, and Harbord believed should not be forgotten as a monumental event in the fearful days of late May and early June 1918.

On July 4, 1920, a ceremony expressed French sentiment about the United States without commenting on the battles themselves. A procession of 20,000 French children walked to a reviewing stand in the Tuileries Gardens, where they honored US Ambassador Wallace. They represented the 22,000 French war orphans who had been adopted in the United States. A small girl whose father had been killed at Verdun walked up to Wallace and made a speech for all to hear. "Mr. Ambassador, I am a little Paris girl. I was 7 years old when my father was killed in the war," she stated:

My brothers and I cried a lot, but my mother didn't see us cry, because she was in mourning. Then one day mother began to smile again and she told us that on the other side of the big sea, there were a lot of little boys and little girls who were going to help us. . . . Mother says that in speaking to you it is the same as if we spoke to all the children and big people in America. So, Mr. Ambassador, we say that we like you very much and we will always love you.

Wallace picked her up in his arms and kissed her to end the emotional ceremony.[47]

Although there were more French outpourings of appreciation for the Americans' contribution, the legacy of the battle continued to reverberate in the United States as the years passed. In 1922 a committee of Marine officers was formed to raise funds to commission a portrait of Harbord to be presented to the Army and Navy Club in Washington, DC, where it would join the many portraits of American military leaders already on display. Harbord said, "I take it as an honor which means more to me than any other I could ever hope for."[48] The battlefield itself became a tourist attraction for those visiting the western front. During the summer of 1922 more than 10,000 visitors toured the battlefield, anxious to walk the fields around Belleau Wood.

Brigadier General George Richards captured the Marine Corps' attitude about the 4th Marine Brigade in an address to the officers in training at Quantico in 1922. Richards was an old-time Marine who had lost his arm during the Boxer Rebellion; he now served at Marine Corps headquarters. As the Marines from France returned to the United States, there was some discussion about why the 4th Brigade had performed so well. One veteran attributed that success to the united efforts of all Marines for the past thirty years. Richards told the young officers assembled before him, "The 4th Brigade . . . was not the fruit of thirty years of effort, not by any means. It was the work of 146 years. Back I would go to the very beginnings. Back to those men whose names are now almost forgotten, men who for years have lain in their graves. They laid the foundations upon which our building began." He then spoke to the Marines who had returned from France. "Your deeds in France must be told and retold to one another and you must gather and regather that their memory be preserved."[49] Richards assured his audience of Marines that the history and traditions of the Marine Corps were central to the core of every Marine and must be protected and maintained.

Groups of Marine veterans formed their own organizations, such as the Veterans of Belleau Wood (US Marine Brigade) in New York City. In 1923 this group set up a circus, complete with sideshows, that ran for eight nights in a National Guard armory on Broadway. Lejeune, now commandant of the Marine Corps, opened this extravaganza on March 17, followed by Lieutenant General Bullard on army night, Admiral Plunkett on navy night, and undisclosed speakers on fraternal and National Guard nights. General admission was only $1, but a box holding six people could be reserved for one night for $20. The proceeds from the event were to be used "for a memorial clubhouse for Marine and ex-Marines."[50] The price of admission also guaranteed a chance to win an Overland automobile and $1 million in circus money to be spent at the sideshows.

On June 6, 1923, Belleau Wood Day was celebrated across the United States, primarily consisting of activities generated by Marine Corps veterans and Marine Corps recruiting stations. In Quantico, 3,000 visiting Shriners boarded charter boats and two navy craft and were transported to the base dock. Once ashore, the assemblage was divided into smaller groups and escorted to lunch in the various mess halls on the base. After their meal, the Shriners viewed a field demonstration by Marines on the parade deck, featuring all their current weapons. The 200-man base band also serenaded the conventioneers with music throughout the day.[51]

At the celebrations in Washington, the Marine Band played a new march, "Belleau Wood," on June 6 in honor of Major General Harbord. The massed bands of the US Army, US Navy, and US Marine Corps performed a number of patriotic tunes, including "Semper Fidelis" and "Stars and Stripes Forever," but "Belleau Wood" seemed to be the favorite, being intertwined with the Marine Hymn. Mrs. James C. Frazer, president of the Belleau Wood Memorial Association, carried a copy of the song directly to France, where a French band played it during the French celebration on June 24.[52]

French General Henri Gouraud also visited Quantico in 1923. His French 4th Army included the 4th Marine Brigade in the later months of 1918, and the general retained a fondness for American Marines. Gouraud left Washington aboard the presidential yacht *Mayflower,* accompanied by Secretary of the Navy Daniels, Commandant Lejeune, and several other generals and admirals. The group paused at Mount Vernon to lay a wreath at the tomb of George Washington and then reached the dock at Quantico, where they were met by a number of Marine aircraft flying overhead and General Smedley D. Butler ashore. Lunch was served in a quiet grove where electric fans were positioned in the trees, ensuring a gentle breeze. The highlight of the visit was a review of the 5th Marines, 6th Marines, and 10th Marines. The Marines remembered the one-armed French general by the glint in his eyes, his left-handed salute, and his good hand's steady grip on a nearby rail during most of the review.[53]

As General Gouraud walked past the regimental colors to end the ceremony, he paused for several moments. As each Marine color-bearer dipped his regimental flag, the French general leaned forward and kissed the battle streamers hanging from it. That simple act forever impressed the Marines who witnessed it, as well as those who heard the story later. Gouraud also toured the barracks where Captain Wass's 18th Company had been quartered before going to France in 1917. Above many of the individual bunks were small white labels bearing the names of the Marines who had slept there during training and were later killed in France. The impression left on General Gourand was profound. He wrote to General Butler, noting that the event was "the best day I have spent until now on America soil, I congratulate you very sincerely for leading such a wonderful corps."[54]

A 1923 article in *Leatherneck Magazine* again summarized the evolving sentiments of the Marine Corps toward Belleau Wood:

> Where is the Marine who can recall the events of June 1918, without experiencing a rush of feeling? Recollection of those days of strife stirs all that is best in us; pride in the manhood of America, pride in the Achievement of our Corps, pride in the possession of our noble traditions. May we not hope that this pride may be translated into determination, determination to be men, determination to keep bright the reputation won for us, determination to abide by and live up to the traditions built up in every time of national emergency.[55]

This same feeling is present in the men and women of the modern Marine Corps.

Belleau Wood became a touchstone for the Marine Corps, with each succeeding generation of Marines inculcating the lore of 1918. In the last year of World War II, *Marine Corps Gazette* devoted an article to the heroes of Belleau Wood, quoting Pershing: "The Gettysburg of this war has now been fought."[56] The large numbers of 4th Brigade casualties were cited, perhaps to prepare the Marines of 1945 for their approaching battles with Japan.

While the Marine Corps inculcated Belleau Wood into its ethos, the greater American struggle over the history of the battle continued unabated through the 1920s. In 1926 Lieutenant Colonel Thomas J. Dickson, US Army (retired), wrote an article in the *Washington Post* that faulted the teaching of the history of World War I, remarking that many of the new textbooks contained critical errors, including the Marines' participation at Belleau Wood. On December 27, 1926, Marine Corps commandant Lejeune deemed the issue important enough to respond with a three-page letter to Dickson. He first disputed the army officer's statement contradicting the fact that the Battle of Belleau Wood halted the German advance on Paris. Lejeune proved his point by quoting General Pershing's final report of 1919, which stated that the 2nd Division deployed on the Paris road on June 1, "where it stopped the German advance on Paris." Lejeune then corrected Dickson's attribution of other units in addition to the 4th Marine Brigade, which included the 7th Infantry, the 26th Division, and "French Divisions." The commandant also addressed the familiar Château-Thierry argument by citing General Headquarters orders designating the Belleau Wood engagement as part of the Château-Thierry sector. The Marine general finished his letter with rigid logic. "In studying the history of the Civil War battle of Gettysburg," Lejeune wrote, "I find that several of the army corps on both sides did not enter the city of Gettysburg during the progress of the battle; yet, nevertheless, all of them participated in the battle of Gettysburg."[57]

In 1930 the Marine Corps League, a Marines-only veterans organization founded in the wake of World War I, dispatched national vice commandant Maurice A. Illch to France. His stated purpose was to purchase a small plot of land on the battlefield and erect a suitable monument to the Marines of Belleau Wood. A growing memorial fund established by the veterans had grown to several thousand dollars to ensure preservation of the battlefield. Illch chose a location in the center of Lucy-le-Bocage. He reported, "This spot is passed by every sightseeing bus going to Belleau Wood. They all stop while the guide explains that here the first American troops, which included the Marines, actually got started on their way to battle."[58]

With the site selected, Illch visited the American embassy, which sent him to a young army lieutenant who headed the American Battle Monuments Commission. The lieutenant informed Illch that no monument could be placed without the commission's approval. If the monument was approved, the commission would then work with the French government to take all the steps necessary to erect the monument. Importantly, one of the regulations stipulated that "no battlefield memorial will be erected to any unit smaller than a Division, unless in the opinion of the commission, its services were of such a distinguished character as to warrant a separate memorial."[59] The monument was never built.

The army-Marine tension continued to simmer even into World War II, with ramifications on many of the command decisions regarding the Marine Corps' role in the Pacific. The 1944 relief of army general Ralph Smith during the Battle of Saipan by Marine general Holland M. Smith, who served at Belleau Wood on the 4th Brigade staff, was fraught with implications from 1918. Indeed, the seeds of the 1950 apology issued by President Harry Truman, a World War I army artillery officer, to commandant of the Marine

Corps Cates, the hero of Bouresches, had been planted at Belleau Wood. Truman's words, asserting that the Marine Corps had a "propaganda machine that is almost equal to Stalin's," reiterated the army complaint that first surfaced after Belleau Wood.

The protection of the interpretation on the battlefield proved necessary, as evidenced by a visit in 1949 by Colonel Robert D. Heinl, who found little or no mention of the Marines anywhere. As a Marine Corps historian, he was outraged. "As an individual officer, I wrote a letter to the Commandant of the Marine Corps, yes, sir," he later remembered, "and put the Army on report, and said that I felt it was a disgrace to the Marine Corps that this condition existed."[60] The matter also upset Cates, but he could do little because he was involved in the crisis over the unification of the armed services at the time.

The issue of maintaining the battlefield continued when 5th Marines veteran Lemuel Shepherd became commandant and revisited Belleau Wood during a NATO meeting. He immediately noticed there were no markers for the Marine Brigade, not even a sign that identified the place as the Bois de Brigade de la Marine. Shepherd blamed the army-led American Battle Monuments Commission for the oversight and was determined to correct the omission. He visited the 5th Marines in Korea during his next trip and informed the regimental commander, Colonel Tommy Tompkins, of the problem. Shepherd told the officers at headquarters, "There's nothing to show that Belleau Wood was captured by the Marines. Of course, I know it. You know it, but fifty years from now when my grandchildren visit Belleau Wood they will not know the Marines captured it from the Germans in W.W. I."[61]

Within a month, the regiment sent a check for $1,500 to start a fund to erect a Marine monument; officers of the 6th Marines added to the fund. Felix de Weldon, sculptor of the Marine War Memorial in Arlington, Virginia, was commissioned to create a monument to the Marines at Belleau Wood. The resulting bronze bas-relief was mounted on a black granite slab and unveiled in November 1955, a month before Shepherd retired.

Curiously, Soissons has become an almost forgotten battlefield. There are no monuments to the Marines' sacrifice on July 18–19. Details of the battle were not well understood in 1918 and have become even more obscure with the passage of time. Perhaps that is because even the Marines who fought there never fully understood the true nature of their fight, including the lost opportunities of Villemontoire, Hill 160, and Tigny. Few Marines knew then, and none know now, of the valor of Lieutenant Lloyd and his handful of 80th Company Marines in Villemontoire, holding battalions of German infantry at bay for much of July 19, waiting for reinforcements that would never come.

More Marines saw the capture of Hill 160 by Mason's men of the 84th Company, reinforced by the Headquarters Company, 6th Marines. This key ground was given up in the early-morning hours of July 20, 1918, when the French soldiers refused to occupy such an exposed position far ahead of the rest of their line. Rumors of the evacuation of Tigny ahead of the 97th Company circulated around the Marine Brigade after the battle but were dismissed as unbelievable. The town was reoccupied by the Germans during the evening hours, exposing another opportunity lost. Only through German sources are these critical actions revealed for the first time, incredible as each episode might seem. The tide of battle can turn with the actions of a few indomitable men such as these Marines.

The violence at Soissons during July 18–19 matched the violence at Belleau Wood on June 6, 1918. Those three days, with all their intricate maneuverings, offer an illuminating, multilayered look at the Marines of World War I and their lasting legacy.

16

Final Conclusions
One Battle Remembered,
One Battle Forgotten

A DETAILED STUDY of the 4th Marine Brigade's crucial days of combat on
June 1–6 and July 18–19, 1918, reveals much about the American forces'
contribution on the western front. Ironically, although the 2nd Division's
battle at Soissons was arguably the Marines' most decisive strategic contribution to the war, it remains obscure, comparable to the capture of Blanc
Mont and the November 1, 1918, breakthrough in the Argonne. Although
the 4th Marine Brigade was only one of many American and Allied brigades,
chance determined that it would play a crucial role in the two battles fated
to change the course of World War I. At Belleau Wood, the Marines did not
stop the German offensive by themselves; fierce fighting by French forces
accomplished that. But the Marines demonstrated to the world the American willingness to fight, to take serious casualties, and still remain combat
effective.

Deserved or undeserved, the Marines took the stage at a critical moment
in history, as both Allies and enemies questioned whether the Americans
could turn the war in favor of the Allies. News of the 1st Division's offensive
at Cantigny and the 3rd Division's defense of Château-Thierry attracted
widespread attention, but the last dispatch of war correspondent Floyd Gibbons about the 4th Brigade captured the world's imagination, rejuvenating
the morale of exhausted Allied nations while deflating the Germans' will
to fight. The headlines proudly bestowed the honor of the battle on the
Marines, while overlooking the contributions of the French and American
soldiers who fought alongside them. The word "Marine" meant victory to
the Allied cause.

Interestingly, the June 6 attack at Belleau Wood was a poorly executed
brigade-level operation. Only the valor of the individual Marine companies
led to success at Hill 142, Belleau Wood, and Bouresches, although they paid
a very heavy price for that ground. In fact, Belleau Wood was of little strategic value and limited tactical worth to both sides. The real victory at Belleau
Wood was one of morale, which in June 1918 meant more than almost any
battlefield victory. All the heavy losses from the Germans' spring offensives

pushed the Allies to the limit, exhausting their resources after so many years of war with no decisive resolution.

Conversely, the July 18–19 attacks by the American 1st and 2nd Divisions at Soissons were of vital strategic value in shifting the advantage to the Allies. The Belleau Wood battle has been the subject of many books and articles and receives annual publicity on Memorial Day weekend, but Soissons has been forgotten, with only a handful of books even scratch the surface of events there. Only a few miles separate the two, but in terms of understanding, the distance is equivalent to the length of the Grand Canyon. In a strict military sense, at a strategic level, Soissons was far more significant than Belleau Wood. The assault undertaken by the French XX Corps, led by the penetration of the 2nd Division, forced the Germans to withdraw from the entire Marne salient. Other French and American attacks along the salient forced the issue as well, but the location of the XX Corps' assault gave the Germans no choice but to withdraw to avoid catastrophe. From that moment until the end of the war, the Allies retained the initiative on the western front, ending in the German defeat on November 11, 1918.

That sacrifice—breaking open the German defensive lines at Soissons—caused the abandonment of the German pocket of Aisne-Marne, signaling a seismic shift of power to the Allied forces that lasted until the end of the war. The realignment of German forces from other parts of the front assisted the crushing French and British offensives that followed. General John J. Pershing wrote, "We snatched the initiative from the Germans almost in an instant. They made no more formidable attacks, but from that moment on until the end of the war they were on the defensive. The magnificent conduct of our 1st and 2nd Divisions and the Moroccan Division marked the turning of the tide."[1] General Foch believed that, "After four months on the defensive, imposed on us by the enemies' numerical superiority, a victorious counter offensive had once more placed in our hands the initiative of operations and the power to direct the progress of events in this long vast war."[2]

Ludendorff maintained, "The attempt to make the nations of the Entente inclined for peace before the arrival of the American reinforcements by means of German victories had failed. The energy of the army had not sufficed to deal the enemy a decisive blow before the Americans were on the spot with considerable force. It was quite clear to me that our general situation had thus become very serious."[3]

Modern historians of the First World War have been slow to recognize the critical importance of the Soissons offensive, with only a handful of academic histories acknowledging the attack on July 18–19 as a turning point in the war. "The Second Marne's near anonymity in the literature is especially unfortunate," maintains Michael S. Neiberg, "because it marks the point when the fortunes of war turned for good in favor of the Allies."[4] Rolfe L. Hillman can be commended for his work on the American 1st and 2nd Divisions at Soissons, resulting in his collaboration with Douglas V. Johnson on the only book specifically devoted to the American participation in the battle. Their preface succinctly states, "This book is written to tell the tale of a forgotten battle."[5]

Far below the rarefied air of contemporary and modern strategic and historical equilibrium, controversies erupted within the confines of the 2nd Division after the battle, much as they did after Belleau Wood. The major contention raging after Soissons focused on who captured Vierzy—the army's 3rd Brigade or the 4th Marine Brigade. An investigation was initiated, and evidence was collected in support of arguments on both sides, but the issue quickly dissipated once Lejeune took command of the division. Lieutenant Colonel Lee's own assessment of his 4th Marine Brigade's performance focused on the disparity between the success of July 18 and the tragedy of July 19. In an interview just after the end of the war, Lee partially held the French units on each flank responsible for both the lack of further success and the large number of casualties suffered by the Marines. He flatly stated that he had been "promised that the French would cooperate but they [did not] advance . . . we had to look after our own flanks."[6]

The ferocity of the German defense on July 19 remained the primary recollection among those who fought at Soissons. The explosions of artillery, the staccato burst of machine guns, and the roar of strafing German aircraft were forever imprinted on the memories of those who struggled through the wheat. Even in the midst of horrific losses, the 4th Brigade was proud of its accomplishments during the two days of battle. Most of all, the sacrifice made by the 6th Marines in the face of overwhelming firepower would never be forgotten. "There was not another battalion on the entire Western Front that could have the terrible punishment that those two Marine battalions were enduring, and still advance," recorded Second Lieutenant Joseph C. Grayson in his history of the 2nd Battalion, 6th Marines. "Truly, it was wonderful."[7]

A close examination of the 4th Marine Brigade in the summer of 1918 also illuminates the evolution of tactical innovations, including the use of aircraft in ground support operations in both attack and defense, the implementation of tanks and artillery, and much more. The successes and failures of the 4th Marine Brigade, one of four American brigades participating in the French XX Corps' attack on July 18–19, 1918, are an indication of the evolving technical proficiency of one of the most experienced American units in the war.

The modern conception of protracted trench warfare as the primary experience of American soldiers and Marines, reinforced by the obligatory trench exhibits in American museums, has also been proven inaccurate. The Americans trained in classic trenches, but in June, July, and August they fought in offensive operations in more open warfare. Unlike the epic battles of the Somme and Verdun, warfare in 1918 was much different from previous years. The successful German offensives of 1918 opened up the western front to the equally successful Allied counterattacks that ended the war. Innovative tactical methods of breaking trench lines, supported by technological innovations and reinforced by massive American forces, proved decisive in 1918.

Soissons illustrates the changing patterns at play on the western front. The use of French tanks and aviation units for observation and ground attacks proved crucial to the American successes of July 18 as well as the losses of July 19. Intertwined were issues involving French command relationships, the introduction of replacements, changes in division and brigade command due to the rapidly arriving American forces that demanded veteran leadership, and many other factors that provide an accurate glimpse of the American way of war in the summer of 1918. The commitment of the American Expeditionary Force into combat as quickly as possible during the crisis months of 1918 proved decisive, but at a heavy human cost.

The Americans had little time to become acclimated to combat in 1918. Once the Allies seized the opportunity to end the war in 1918, American forces were committed to offensive combat. The constant Allied pressure through the summer and fall resulted in an American army slogging through the hell of the Argonne and suffering horrific casualties. These men, along with Allied forces involved in offensives of their own, brought an end to four years of war on November 11, 1918. The casualties endured by the 2nd Division at Belleau Wood and Soissons delivered a strong message to both sides that the United States was willing to suffer such losses to achieve a victorious end to the war.

Casualties could be justified by the American leadership at strategic levels of the military. However, the impact was significantly different for the soldiers and Marines who fought in these battles. Processing their emotions became a complex individual experience for the Marines, but a common theme was the solemn remembrance of their own sacrifices and those of their lost comrades. The loss of life by the 4th Marine Brigade is perhaps best summed up by these words spoken at a memorial service for Lieutenant Tom Ashley: "From the date of his death will, we believe, be reckoned the beginning of the end of this great struggle for all that human civilization has learned to hold dear."[8] For those who survived the battle, the mental and physical scars of the brutal fighting would never be forgotten. "God, it was sure enough Hell," one Marine wrote home. "A Chaplain told me that he has been preaching about Hell for 12 years now but he never knew what it was until now."[9]

The officers and men who witnessed the battles firsthand believed they changed history. Army lieutenant Henry Leonard of the 79th Company wrote that his runner would "carry my messages twice through awful fire, and die with a fire and beauty in his face that was never there before." Leonard went on to praise his platoon:

> I have lived with them through days when death was too close for comfort. And I have seen them die. I have censored hundreds of their home letters. I have been with them when they were keyed to the highest tension, and when they were relaxed in utter weariness . . . I have had the great honor to have been a part of the army of devoted men who are making this world better to live in.[10]

Leonard would return to the United States and become an instructor at Camp Sherman, only to die of influenza in December 1918. Although Leonard was an army officer, the Marine Corps claimed the honor of conducting his funeral, a request that his father granted. His widow gave birth to a daughter eight months after his death.

Private Leo Freel of the 95th Company wrote to his mother about the lasting effect of Belleau Wood on himself and his fellow Marines. "I know it has made a bigger, cleaner, stronger man out of me and Dode too. No one can look his maker in the face for eighteen days without being purified by the Celestial fire," he wrote. "It is like casting your soul into the furnace—the gold returns more precious."[11] Private Dunham, one of the Marines who took Hill 160 at Soissons, treasured most of all the memories of the Marines he served with. Celebrating his hundredth birthday in 1995, Dunham admitted, "Every time I look at the picture of my company and all of those young men, I cry because I'm just about the only one left alive."[12]

Even today, Belleau Wood continues to be a symbol of the meaning of World War I to the United States, while Soissons remains in comparative obscurity. In truth, both battles must be interpreted together to better understand the American sacrifices and contributions during World War I. Even the July 19 cauldron at Soissons became a source of uplifting pride for the Marines who fought there.

Decisive or not, battles always come with a human cost. The Marines' sacrifice in June and July 1918 was balanced by the significance of those days. For the rest of their lives, each Marine felt justly proud of his role in the fighting in the summer of 1918. "Like Job of old, we were tested," wrote Private Hemrick, "and like Job, we never gave up. We were U.S. Marines."[13]

Soissons Tour

Stop 33. *French Cemetery,* 49°16'19.7"N 3°19'17.5"E

Leave the D 175 and proceed south on the Rue de la Saviere for 1.1 kilometers. You will enter Parcy-Tigny, in the French zone of operations. Turn left on the Rue de Clocher, proceed 240 meters, and stop at the stone marker on the right side of the road. This memorial to the 1st Regiment Infanterie Colonial de Marrocans marks the furthest point of its advance on July 19, 1918. The stone points out where Joost van Vollenhoven, a captain with the regiment and the former governor-general of French West Africa, was killed during the attack.

This is a perfect place to examine the 6th Marines' attack from the southern flank. The Germans held the town until the evening of July 19 and could easily enfilade the Marine advance. This killing fire became more effective with every step taken toward Tigny.

Stop 34. *German Cemetery,* 49°15'52.2"N 3°20'56.5"E

Return to Parcy-Tigny on the Rue de Clocher for 170 meters. Turn left on the Rue de Clocher at the center of town, where it becomes the D 480. Proceed 500 meters, turn left at the intersection, and drive 1.2 kilometers. Turn right on the Rue du Jeu d'Arc. Drive 850 meters and turn left onto the D 83. Drive 650 meters and stop at the gate of the German Cemetery. Here rest 4,256 Germans who died in the July 1918 battles, which speaks to the ferocity of the fighting here.

Stop 35. *American 1st Division Monument,*
49°18'49.8"N 3°20'12.4"E

Continue 450 meters on the D 83, passing under the modern D 1. Turn left immediately after the tunnel, on the ramp leading to the D 1 toward Soissons. Proceed 5.7 kilometers on the D 1, then turn right onto the D 1240 to Buzancy. As you leave the D 1, you will see the memorial to the American 1st Infantry Division, with bronze plaques commemorating the division's 2,213 killed in the July 1918 attack. This area marks the pinnacle of the American advance that cut the road on July 21, 1918. Just after the turn, there is a pull-off where you can park and walk back to the monument.

Stop 36. 15th Scottish Division Cemetery, 49°18'52.4"N 3°20'30.7"E

Proceed on the D 1240 for 850 meters to Buzancy. Turn left on the Rue de la Montagne and proceed 300 meters, where the roads ends. Stop at the British Cemetery, which is on your right. On July 28, 1918, the 15th Scottish Division launched an attack to capture Buzancy. Companies of Gordon Highlanders, Seaforth Highlanders, Black Watch (Royal Highlanders), and other Scottish units captured the village after ninety minutes of desperate house-to-house fighting using demolitions and a flamethrower. They found themselves alone because the French supporting units had been held up by an enemy strongpoint south of Buzancy. The Highlanders were forced to withdraw following heavy German counterattacks, after holding the town for only six hours. Here lie 264 of the dead from that battle and others that took place from July 23 to August 5, 1918.

This action illustrates the tenacity of the German defense of this area, long after the withdrawal of the American Marines and soldiers of the 1st and 2nd Divisions. Note the monument on the left wall of the cemetery. This was erected by the French 17th Division to mark the furthest point reached by the Highlanders' assault on July 28. The inscription reads: "Here the noble thistle of Scotland will flourish forever amongst the roses of France."

The Germans ended the battle here with a general withdrawal during the night of August 1–2, signaling their successful withdrawal from the Marne salient. French units recaptured Soissons the same day.

Retrace your route to the D 1 to return to Château-Thierry.

Appendix
Tables of Organization:
Allied and German Units

2nd Division
Belleau Wood June 1918
Maj. Gen. Omar Bundy

Only Key Units Are Shown.

3rd Brigade Army
Brig. Gen. Edward M. Lewis

9th Infantry Regiment	5th Machine Gun Battalion	23rd Infantry Regiment
Col. Leroy S. Upton	Maj. Harry T. Lewis	Col. Paul B. Malone

4th Brigade (Marine)
Brig. Gen. James G. Harbord

5th Marine Regiment	6th Machine Gun Battalion (Marine)	6th Marine Regiment
Col. Wendell C. Neville	Maj. Edward B. Cole	Col. Albertus W. Catlin

2nd Artillery Brigade
Brig. Gen. William E. Chamberlaine

12th Artillery Regiment	15th Artillery Regiment	17th Artillery Regiment
Col. Manus McCloskey	Col. John R. Davis	Col. Alfred J. Bowley

Divisional Troops Army

2nd Engineer Regiment
Col. James F. McIndoe
4th Machine Gun Battalion
Maj. Edmund L. Zane

2nd Division
Soissons July 1918
Maj. Gen. James G. Harbord

Only Key Units Are Shown.

3rd Brigade Army
Brig. Gen. H. E. Ely

9th Infantry Regiment	5th Machine Gun Battalion	23rd Infantry Regiment
Col. Leroy S. Upton	Maj. Harry T. Lewis	Col. Paul B. Malone

4th Brigade (Marine)
Col. Wendell C. Neville

5th Marine Regiment	6th Machine Gun Battalion (Marine)	6th Marine Regiment
Lt. Col. Logan Feland	Maj. L. W. T. Waller, Jr.	Lt. Col. Harry Lee

2nd Artillery Brigade
Brig. Gen. Albert J. Bowley

12th Artillery Regiment	15th Artillery Regiment	17th Artillery Regiment
Col. Manus McCloskey	Col. John R. Davis	Col. John R. Kelly

Divisional Troops Army

2nd Engineer Regiment
Lt. Col. Cary H. Brown
4th Machine Gun Battalion
Maj. Edmund L. Zane

Chart 8. 2nd Division, Belleau Wood, June 1918, and Soissons, July 1918

Allied Units
Belleau Wood
June 1918

The French method of defending the German attacks at Belleau Wood did not employ divisions or even regiments in their entirety, but primarily depended on piecemeal deployment on the battlefield. French units were fed into the line as they arrived, fighting separately from the rest of their home regiment or division.

This method of combat divided regiments and battalions by miles of terrain and eventually resulted in the relief of the 6th Army commander. Until then, the French fought by "groupments," led by their unit commanders—gathering together many disparate units to halt the German advance.

Only French units fighting alongside the American 2nd Division are listed:

6th Army
Gen. Denis Auguste Duchene

21st Army Corps
Gen. Jean-Marie Degoutte

43rd Division
Gen. Camille Michel
Into Reserve, June 5
133rd Regiment
356th Regiment

164th Division
Gen. Leon Gaucher
Relieved by 2nd Division (American), June 4
152nd Regiment
158th Regiment

167th Division
Gen. Schmidt
Relieved 43rd Division, June 5
116th Regiment
170th Regiment
174th Regiment
409th Regiment (One Battalion)

2nd Division (American)
Maj. Gen. Omar Bundy
Assumed Responsibility for Front Line, June 4-5

Attached
Darlange Brigade (Dismounted Cavalry)
4th Hussars
8th Dragoons
12th Madagascar Battalion
1st Battalion de Chausser
31st Battalion de Chausser
43rd Battalion de Chausser
59th Battalion de Chausser

Chart 9. Allied Units, Belleau Wood, June 1918

German Army
Belleau Wood
June 1918

Each German infantry division at this time of the war was composed of a division headquarters, a brigade headquarters, and three infantry regiments composed of three battalions, one artillery regiment of three battalions, and supporting units.

Each infantry battalion was composed of four infantry companies and a machine gun company. Each field artillery regiment was composed of three battalions of three batteries each.

German infantry division strength was 8,407 infantrymen, 1,363 artillerymen that, with attached troops, totaled 11,643 men, or half the size of an American infantry division. It is correct to consider a German infantry division to be somewhat equal to an American infantry brigade, and an American infantry division to be twice the size of a German infantry division.

For simplicity, only these units and supporting artillery detachments that fought in the 4th Marine Brigade are listed. The 36th Infantry Division, 197th Infantry Division, 201st Infantry Division, and 231st Infantry Division also belong to Corps Conta but fought on other areas of the line.

IV Reserve Corps (Corps Conta)

10th Infantry Division
20th Infantry Brigade

6th Grenadier Regiment

398th Grenadier Regiment

2nd Battalion
56th Regiment

47th Infantry Regiment

56th Artillery Regiment

11th Foot Artillery

28th Infantry Division
55th Infantry Brigade

40th Fusilier Regiment

110th Grenadier Regiment

109th Body Grenadier Regiment

14th Field Artillery Regiment

55th Foot Artillery Battalion

197th Infantry Division
210th Infantry Brigade

273rd Reserve Infantry Regiment

28th Ersatz Infantry Regiment

7th Saxon Jäger Regiment

261st Field Artillery Regiment

237th Infantry Division
244th Infantry Brigade

460th Infantry Regiment

462nd Infantry Regiment

461st Infantry Regiment

83rd Field Artillery Regiment

3rd Battalion, 23rd Foot Artillery

Chart 10. German Army, Belleau Wood, June 1918

Allied Units
Soissons
July 1918
10th Army

In addition to the units listed below, two British and two French colonial divisions formed the Army reserve. All units are French unless otherwise noted.

10th Army Tanks
Lt. Col. Chederville

Army Reserve
1st Battalion Light Tanks
3 Companies of 15 Tanks
Maj. Goubernard

2nd Battalion Light Tanks
3 Companies of 10 to 15 Tanks
Maj. Wattel

3rd Battalion Light Tanks
2 Companies of about 10 Tanks, 1 Company of about 5 Tanks
Maj. Peraldi

1st Army Corps
(on Left)

11th Division

72nd Division

153rd Division
III Groupment: Schneider Tanks
3 Battalions with 3 Batteries
Maj. Refebvre

11th Army Corps
(on Right)

5th Division

41st Division

128th Division

Chart 11. Allied Units, Soissons, July 1918

German Army
Soissons
July 1918

Brigade organization is not generally shown, as most reinforcing units were committed individually to 14th Division command.

Army Group German Crown Prince
9th Army
XIII Corps: Corps Watter

42nd Division
This division was in position from Chaudon to Missy.
65th Infantry Brigade
131st Regiment
17th Infantry Regiment
138th Regiment

14th Reserve Division/47th Reserve Division (Combined)
This division was in position at Vauxcastille and Vierzy.
27th and 94th Reserve Brigades
16th Reserve Regiment
53rd Reserve Regiment/218th Reserve Regiment (Combined)
159th Regiment/219th Reserve Regiment (Combined)
219th Reserve Regiment
220th Reserve Regiment

7th Army

115th Division
34th Regiment
This unit was on the right and connected to the 14th Division on July 18, 1918.
40th Regiment
This unit was in the center.
171st Regiment
This unit was on the left.

Chart 12. German Army, Soissons, July 1918

NOTES

Abbreviations

AEF	American Expeditionary Force
NARA	National Archives and Records Administration, Washington, DC
NARA II	National Archives and Records Administration II, College Park, MD
RG	Record Group

Introduction

1. Albert E. Powis, "A Leatherneck in France, 1917–1919," *Military Images Magazine* 3, 2 (September–October 1981): 11.

2. Frederic M. Wise, *A Marine Tells It to You* (New York: J. H. Sears, 1929), 157.

3. Wise, *A Marine Tells It to You,* 158.

4. Joseph D. Murray, Manuscript History of the 43rd Company, 13, Ben Fuller Papers, Marine Corps Archives, Marine Corps History Division, Marine Corps University, Quantico, VA.

5. Virginia Military Institute, *Bomb,* 1917; "Twenty-Seven Men of Class of 1917 Graduated on May 2," *Cadet,* May 21, 1917, 7.

6. Murray, Manuscript History of 43rd Company.

7. Wise, *A Marine Tells It to You,* 158–159.

8. Murray, Manuscript History of 43rd Company.

9. Murray, Manuscript History of 43rd Company.

10. United States War Department, Office of the Adjutant General, *Tables of Organization, United States Army, 1917* (Washington, DC: Government Printing Office, 1917), 4–6; United States War Department, Office of the Adjutant General, *Tables of Organization and Equipment, United States Army, 1918* (Washington, DC: Government Printing Office, 1918), table 1, Infantry Division; table 3, Infantry Brigade; table 4, Infantry Regiment; table 5, Headquarters Company, Infantry Regiment.

11. US War Department, *Tables of Organization and Equipment, US Army, 1918,* table 7, Rifle Company, February 26, 1918; 74th Company Muster Roll, August 1917, Records Relating to Marine Participation in World War I, RG 127, Records of the United States Marine Corps, NARA.

12. Edwin N. McClellan, *The United States Marine Corps in the World War* (Washington, DC: Government Printing Office, 1920), 11–12, 21; US War Department, *Tables of Organization and Equipment, US Army, 1918,* table 4, Infantry Brigade.

13. McClellan, *United States Marine Corps in the World War,* 9–10, 15.

14. William A. Worton, Oral History Transcript, 52–53, Oral History Program,

Marine Corps History Division, Quantico, VA. Unless otherwise noted, all oral histories cited are from the Marine Corps Oral History Program.

15. Worton, Oral History Transcript, 22.

16. Report of the Major General Commandant of the United States Marine Corps, in United States Navy, *Annual Report of the Secretary of the Navy* (Washington, DC: Government Printing Office, 1917), 836.

17. Pershing to Adjutant General, War Department, August 31, 1917, paragraph 14, Cablegrams Exchanged between General Headquarters, American Expeditionary Force, and the War Department, RG 120, Records of the AEF, NARA II.

18. McCain to Pershing, cablegram 184-R, September 17, 1917, 6th Regiment Organization file, Records Relating to Marine Participation in World War I. Brigadier General McCain was the great-uncle of Senator John McCain.

19. General Headquarters to March, AEF cablegram 1968-Z, September 23, 1918, Cablegrams Exchanged between General Headquarters, American Expeditionary Force, and the War Department.

20. 4th Marine Brigade file, Records of Marines in France, Records Relating to Marine Participation in World War I.

21. Oliver Lyman Spaulding and John Womack Wright, *The Second Division, American Expeditionary Force in France, 1917–1919* (1937; reprint, Nashville, TN: Battery Press, 1989), 6–7, 13–15; McClellan, *United States Marine Corps in the World War,* 29–33.

22. John J. Pershing to General Barnett, November 10, 1917, Records Relating to Marine Participation in World War I.

23. Cablegram from Adjutant General to Commandant of the Marine Corps, January 16, 1918, 6th Marine files, Records Relating to Marine Participation in World War I.

24. Worton, Oral History Transcript, 20.

25. Worton, Oral History Transcript, 20.

26. William McB. Sellers and George B. Clark, eds., World War I Memoirs of Lieutenant Colonel James *McBrayer Sellers, USMC* (Pike, NH: Brass Hat, 1997), 43, 44.

27. McClellan, *United States Marine Corps in the World War,* 33; Peter F. Owen, *To the Limit of Endurance: A Battalion of Marines in the Great War* (College Station: Texas A&M University Press, 2007), 212; George B. Clark, ed., *History of the First Battalion, 5th Marines, June 1917–August 1919* (Pike, NH: Brass Hat, 2002), 7.

28. Emil H. Gehrke, 82nd Company Muster Roll, April 1918, Marine Corps *Muster Rolls, RG 127,* Records of the United States Marine Corps, NARA.

29. "First Marine Killed by Enemy in France," *Recruiters' Bulletin* 4, 8 (June 1918): 30.

30. "Arbor Vitae Boy Slain in France," *New North* (Rhinelander, WI), April 18, 1918, 1.

31. John J. Pershing to Charles A. Doyen, April 29, 1918, Charles A. Doyen Papers, Marine Corps Archives; Secretary of the Army to Secretary of the Navy, May 1, 1918, Records Relating to Marine Participation in World War I.

32. Endorsement of Recommendation of Charles A. Doyen Promotion to Major General, May 1, 1918, Commander of American Expeditionary Force, Doyen Papers.

33. "Marines at Belleau Wood," undated statement, George Barnett Papers, Marine Corps Archives.

34. McClellan, *United States Marine Corps in the World War,* 39.

35. James G. Harbord, *The American Army in France: 1917–1919* (Cranbury, NJ: Scholars Bookshelf, 2006), 264–265.

36. Julian Smith, Oral History Transcript, 98.

37. Smith, Oral History Transcript, 283.

38. Albertus W. Catlin, *With the Help of God and a Few Marines* (Garden City, NY: Doubleday, Page, 1919), xiii.

39. Frederick Palmer, "Pershing's Generals," *Colliers Magazine,* April 19, 1919, James G. Harbord Papers, Library of Congress, Manuscript Division, Washington, DC.

40. American Battle Monuments Commission, *2nd Division Summary of Operations in the World War* (Washington, DC: Government Printing Office, 1944), 14.

41. Holger H. Hedwig, *The First World War: Germany and Austria-Hungary, 1914–1918* (London: Arnold, 1997), 414–416.

42. Robert B. Asprey, *The German High Command at War* (New York: William Morrow, 1991), 414–418.

1. *May 31–June 1, 1918—Movement to the Marne*

1. Havelock D. Nelson, "Paris Metz Road," *Leatherneck Magazine* 23, 1 (January 1940): 10.

2. Eldon L. Freel diary, entry for June 5, 1918, Eldon L. Freel Papers, Collection MS 114, State Historical Society of Iowa, Des Moines.

3. Robert E. Messersmith, "Operations of Company E, 78th Company, 6th Regiment Marines, 2nd Division at Belleau Woods, June 1–13, 1918," 5, Advanced Infantry Course, 1928–1929, World War I Personal Experience Monographs, Donovan Research Library, Maneuver Center of Excellence Libraries, Fort Benning, GA.

4. Gerald B. Clark to "Folks," June 18, 1918, Gerald B. Clark Papers, Marine Corps Archives, Marine Corps History Division, Marine Corps University, Quantico, VA; Field Orders 3, May 30, 1918, 8:00 a.m., in Clyburn Otto Mattfeldt, comp., *Records of the Second Division (Regular),* 10 vols. (Washington, DC: US Army War College Historical Section, 1924–1928), vol. 1.

5. Onnie J. Cordes and Janice D. Cordes, eds., "The Immortal Division," 8, Onnie J. and Janice D. Cordes Papers, Marine Corps Archives.

6. George B. Clark, ed., *His Time in Hell: A Texas Marine in France. The World War I Memoir of Warren R. Jackson* (Novato, CA: Presidio Press, 2001), 97.

7. Clark, *His Time in Hell,* 97.

8. Albert E. Powis, "A Leatherneck in France, 1917–1919," *Military Images Magazine* 3, 2 (September–October 1981): 12.

9. Stephen Brown and Carl H. Geores, "55th Co. Marines in World War I," undated newspaper article, 5th Marines file, Records Relating to Marine Participation in World War I, RG 127, Records of the United States Marine Corps, NARA.

10. Elliot D. Cooke, *Americans versus Germans: The First AEF in Action* (New York: Penguin Books, 1942), 85. This work republished Cooke's *Infantry Journal* articles "We Can Take It" (July–August 1937) and "We Attack" (November–December 1937).

11. Brown and Geores, "55th Co. Marines in World War I."

12. Brown and Geores, "55th Co. Marines in World War I."

13. J. D. Wilmeth, "Bois de la Brigade de Marine," *Marine Corps Gazette* 23, 1 (March 1939): 27–28. Wilmeth based his article on the Fort Benning Infantry School Papers of Raymond E. Knapp, Henry Larsen, and Robert E. Messersmith. Only Knapp belonged to the 47th Company.

14. Craig Hamilton and Louise Corbin, eds., *Echoes from over There: By the Men of the Army and Marine Corps Who Fought in France* (New York: Soldiers' Publishing Company, 1919), 4.

15. Cooke, *Americans versus Germans,* 89.

16. Powis, "Leatherneck in France," 12.

17. Powis, "Leatherneck in France," 13.

18. Don V. Paradis memoir, Don V. Paradis Papers, Marine Corps Archives; field message from Commanding General, 4th Brigade, to Commanding General, 2nd Division, June 1, 1918, in United States Army Center for Military History, *U.S. Army in the World War, 1917–1919,* 17 vols. (1948; reprint, Washington, DC: United States Army Center for Military History, 1988–1992), 4:79–80.

19. John J. Pershing to Secretary of War and Chief of Staff, cable 1235-S, June 3, 1918, James Harbord Papers, Library of Congress, Manuscript Division, Washington, DC.

Belleau Wood Tour: Stops 1–3

1. Robert E. Messersmith, "Operations of Company E, 78th Company, 6th Regiment Marines, 2nd Division at Belleau Woods, June 1–13, 1918," 7, Advanced Infantry Course, 1928–1929, World War I Personal Experience Monographs, Donovan Research Library, Maneuver Center of Excellence Libraries, Fort Benning, GA.

2. Chester Lancaster, "A Short Biography," Chester Lancaster Papers, Marine Corps Archives, Marine Corps History Division, Marine Corps University, Quantico, VA.

3. Clifton B. Cates to Mother and Sister, June 10, 1918, Clifton B. Cates Papers, Marine Corps Archives.

4. Craig Hamilton and Louise Corbin, eds., *Echoes from over There: By the Men of the Army and Marine Corps Who Fought in France* (New York: Soldiers' Publishing Company, 1919), 14.

5. Glen G. Hill to G. M. Neufeld, December 28, 1979, Glen G. Hill Papers, Marine Corps Archives.

6. Hill to Neufeld, December 28, 1979.

7. Battery C, 17th Field Artillery Report, n.d., 17th Field Artillery Reports of Operations, Chateau-Thierry and Soissons, June–July 1918, Records of the 2nd Division, Records of Combat Divisions, RG 120, Records of the AEF, NARA II.

2. *June 3, 1918—Digging In*

1. Message from 23rd Infantry to 2nd Division, 4:06 p.m., June 3, 1918, in Clyburn Otto Mattfeldt, comp., *Records of the Second Division (Regular)*, 10 vols. (Washington, DC: US Army War College Historical Section, 1924–1928), vol. 4.

2. Adjutant General's Office, *Official Army Register for 1914* (Washington, DC: Government Printing Office, 1914), 286; George W. Cullum, *Biographical Register of the Officers and Graduates of the U.S. Military Academy at West Point, N.Y., from Its Establishment in 1802*, 7 vols. (Chicago: R. R. Donnelly & Sons, Lakeside Press, 1930), 4:570, 5:513, 6A:690, 7:375.

3. Society of the Fifth Division, *The Official History of the Fifth Division, U.S.A.* (New York: Wynkoop Hallenbeck Crawford, 1919), 29–30.

4. Field messages from Harbord to Neville, 1:45 p.m. and 3:08 p.m., June 3, 1918, in *Records of the Second Division*, vol. 4.

5. Field message from Harbord to Catlin, 3:20 p.m., June 3, 1918, in *Records of the Second Division*, vol. 4.

6. Field message from Commanding Officer, 5th Marines, to Commanding Officer, 4th Brigade, 1:30 p.m., June 3, 1918, in *Records of the Second Division*, vol. 4; field message from Captain Kingman to Major Cole, 6th Machine Gun Battalion, 4:25 p.m., June 3, 1918, ibid., vol. 5.

7. Field message from Captain Williams to Commander, 2nd Battalion, 5th Marines, 2:15 p.m., June 3, 1918, in *Records of the Second Division*, vol. 5.

8. "They're Human," *Washington Times*, November 10, 1921, George K. Shuler Papers, Marine Corps Archives, Marine Corps History Division, Marine Corps University, Quantico, VA.

9. Lloyd W. Williams, Biographical File, Reference Branch, Marine Corps History Division; Lloyd W. Williams Papers, Marine Corps Archives; Lloyd W. Williams Alumni File, Special Collections, Carol M. Newman Library, Virginia Tech, Blacksburg, VA.

10. "Controversy over Legend Clarified by Marine Captain," *Quantico Sentry*, June 13, 1936, 1.

11. Field message, 3:10 p.m., June 3, 1918, Frederic M. Wise Papers, Marine Corps Archives.

12. Logan Feland, "Retreat, Hell," *Marine Corps Gazette* 6, 3 (September 1921): 290.

13. Field message from Commanding Officer, 4th Brigade, to Colonel Catlin, 4:00 p.m., June 3, 1918, in *Records of the Second Division*, vol. 4.

14. Berton W. Sibley, letter, December 20, 1926, Correspondence with Former Division Officers, RG 117, American Battle Monuments Commission, NARA II.

15. Field message from Major Edward B. Cole to 4th Brigade Commander, June 3, 1918, in *Records of the Second Division*, vol. 4.

16. United States Naval Academy, *Lucky Bag* [yearbook] (Annapolis, MD, 1915), 67.

17. Field message from Cole to Brigade Commander, June 3, 1918, in *Records of the Second Division*, vol. 4; report of a conversation between Colonel Brown and General Harbord, June 3, 1918, ibid.

18. Arthur Clifford, letter, June 20, 1918, Arthur Clifford Papers, Marine Corps Archives.

19. Howard Fletcher Davidson diary, entry for June 3, 1918, transcribed by Ed Davidson, Delaware County, NY, Genealogy and History Site, http://www.dcny hisotry.org/diaryfletcherdavidson.html.

20. Field message from 4th Brigade Commander to Commander, 5th Marines, 3:08 p.m., June 3, 1918, in *Records of the Second Division*, vol. 5.

21. Order 72/PC, XXI Army Corps, 4:00 p.m., June 3, 1918, in United States Army Center for Military History, *U.S. Army in the World War, 1917–1919,* 17 vols. (1948; reprint, Washington, DC: United States Army Center for Military History, 1988–1992), 4:115.

22. Field message from Commander, 5th Marines, to Commander, 2nd Battalion, 5th Marines, 5:30 p.m., June 3, 1918, in *Records of the Second Division*, vol. 5.

23. Field message from "Murray" to Commander, 5th Marines, 6:35 p.m., June 3, 1918, in *Records of the Second Division*, vol. 5.

24. Log, 12th Madagascar Battalion, June 3, 1918, Memoire des Hommes, Ministere des Armees, Republique Francais, memoiredeshommes.sga.defense.gouv.fr/en/.

25. Malone to Bundy, message 46, 6:30 p.m., June 3, 1918, in *Records of the Second Division*, vol. 4.

26. Logs, 152nd Infantry Regiment and 158th Regiment, June 3, 1918, Memoire des Hommes.

27. Stephen Brown and Carl H. Geores, "55th Co. Marines in World War I," undated newspaper article, 5th Marines file, Records Relating to Marine Participation in World War I, RG 127, Records of the United States Marine Corps, NARA.

28. Lemuel C. Shepherd, Student Record, Virginia Military Institute Archives, Lexington, VA.

29. Lemuel C. Shepherd to Mother, April 18, 1918, RG 66, Virginia War History Commission 1915–1931, Library of Virginia, Richmond.

30. Lemuel C. Shepherd, Oral History Transcript, 326, Marine Corps Oral History Program, Marine Corps History Division, Marine Corps University, Quantico, VA.

31. Shepherd to Mother, June 9, 1918, Library of Virginia.

32. War diary, 197th Division, June 3, 1918, in Gustav J. Braun and Trevor W. Swett, comps., *Translations: War Diaries of German Units Opposed to the Second Division (Regular) 1918,* 5 vols. (Washington, DC: Second Division Historical Section, Army War College, 1930–1932), vol. 4.

33. Brown and Geores, "55th Co. Marines in World War I."

34. Robert W. Blake, Oral History Interview, 1968, Marine Corps Oral History Program.

35. Undated message, 1st Battalion, 461st Infantry, in *War Diaries of German Units*, vol. 4.

36. Report of Activities of the 3rd Battalion, 460th Regiment, 237th Division, June 3, 1918, in *War Diaries of German Units*, vol. 4.

37. War diary, 237th Division, June 3, 1918, in *War Diaries of German Units*, vol. 4.

38. Log, 1st Chasseur Battalion, June 3, 1918.

39. Log, 1st Chasseur Battalion, May 31–June 3, 1918.

40. Log, 133rd Regiment, June 3, 1918, Memoire des Hommes; annex, 273rd Infantry, June 3, 1918, in *War Diaries of German Units*, vol. 4.

41. War diary, 237th Division, June 3, 1918.

42. Report of Activities of the 3rd Battalion, 460th Regiment, 237th Division, June 3, 1918.

43. War diary, 3rd Battalion, 460th Regiment, 237th Division, June 3, 1918, in *War Diaries of German Units*, vol. 4.

44. Dispatches, 7:20 p.m. and 10:50 p.m., June 3, 1918, war diary annex, 3rd Battalion, 460th Regiment, 237th Division, in *War Diaries of German Units*, vol. 4.

45. War diary, 237th Division, June 3, 1918.

46. War diary, 237th Division, June 3, 1918.

47. Log, 1st Chasseur Battalion, June 3, 1918, Memoire des Hommes. A Calvaire is a religious shrine placed on French roadsides in memory of the crucifixion of Jesus Christ on Calvary Hill.

48. War diary, 237th Division, June 3, 1918.

49. Combat report, 7th Company, 28th Ersatz Regiment, in *War Diaries of German Units*, vol. 4; log, 1st Chasseur Battalion, June 3, 1918.

50. War diary, 197th Division, June 3, 1918; Division Order 2, 197th Division, 10:46 p.m., June 3, 1918, in *War Diaries of German Units*, vol. 4.

51. Messages from Colonel Malone to General Bundy, 7:50 p.m. and 8:35 p.m., June 3, 1918, in *Records of the Second Division*, vol. 4.

52. Field Order 7, 8:00 p.m., June 3, 1918, in *U.S. Army in the World War*, 4:119.

53. Field message from 1st Battalion, 6th Marines, to 6th Marine Headquarters, 7:50 a.m., June 4, 1918, in *U.S. Army in the World War*, 4:124; field message from Colonel Malone to Headquarters, 3rd Brigade, 2:55 a.m., June 4, 1918, ibid.

54. War diary, June 3, 1918, 2nd Battalion, 462nd Regiment, in *War Diaries of German Units*, vol. 4.

55. War diary, 237th Division, June 3, 1918.

56. "Shelled out 'Y' Man Hunts for Wounded," *San Francisco Chronicle*, July 21, 1918, 7.

57. "Courageous Y.M.C.A. Worker," *Saskatoon Daily Star*, June 28, 1918, 12; "Private Citizen Gets French Croix de Guerre," *Iron County (UT) Record*, May 30, 1919, 1.

58. *Our Navy: The Standard Publication of the U.S. Navy*, vol. 13 (New York: Our Navy Publishing Company, 1919), 13; "Pastor of San Rafael Cited for Bravery," *San Francisco Chronicle*, September 9, 1918, 7.

59. Frank Whitehead, "Aisne Defensive," Correspondence with Former Division Officers.

60. Field message from 82nd Company to Battalion Commander, 6th Marines, 8:20 p.m., June 3, 1918, in *Records of the Second Division*, vol. 5.

61. Field message from 1st Battalion Commander to 6th Marine Commander, 9:40 p.m., June 3, 1918, in *Records of the Second Division*, vol. 5.

62. Memorandum report, 2nd Battalion, 5th Marines, June 19, 1918, in *Records of the Second Division*, vol. 7; field message from Commanding Officer, 2nd Battalion, 23rd Infantry, 12:10 a.m., June 3, 1918, in *U.S. Army in the World War*, 4:107.

63. War diary, 4th Marine Brigade, June 3, 1918, in *Records of the Second Division*, vol. 4.

64. John T. Miller, "Why I Hate a German," in *What Our "Boys" Did over There: By "Themselves,"* ed. Henry L. Fox (New York: Allied Overseas Veterans, 1918), 119. The date of this incident is not fixed.

65. Miller, "Why I Hate a German," 119.

66. Annex 1106, 1st Army Corps, Command Post, June 3, 1918, in Ministère de la Guerre, État-Major de l'Armée, Service Historique, *Les Armées Françaises dans la Grande Guerre* (Paris: Service Historique de la Défense, 1929–1934), book VI, vol. 2, 252–253.

67. Annex 1093, 6th Army to Army Group North, 8:40 p.m., June 3, 1918, in *Les Armées Françaises dans la Grande Guerre*, book VI, vol. 2, 235.

68. 6th Army Journal, June 3, 1918, Memoire des Hommes.

69. Order 73, XXI Corps, 7:15 p.m., June 3, 1918, in *U.S. Army in the World War*, 4:118–119.

70. Journal, 21st Corps Medical Corps, June 3–4, 1918, Memoire des Hommes.

71. Annex 1103, VI Army Headquarters, June 3, 1918, in *Les Armées Françaises dans la Grande Guerre*, book VI, vol. 2, 250.

72. Annex 1105, Operations Order 3208, VI Army Headquarters, June 3, 1918, in *Les Armées Françaises dans la Grande Guerre,* book VI, vol. 2, 252.

73. War diary, 2nd Division, June 3, 1918, in *Records of the Second Division*, vol. 4.

74. Field message from 4th Brigade Commander to 2nd Battalion, 6th Marines, Commander, 9:45 p.m., June 3, 19198, in *Records of the Second Division*, vol. 5.

75. Annex 1112, 38th Army Corps, 0745 hours, June 3, 1918, in *Les Armées Françaises dans la Grande Guerre*, book VI, vol. 2, 259.

76. Annex 1092, Group of Armies of the North (GAN), 2045 hours, June 3, 1918, in *Les Armées Françaises dans la Grande Guerre*, book VI, vol. 2, 234–235.

77. Annex 1094, Group of Armies of the Reserve (GAR), General Staff, 2nd Bureau Headquarters, June 3, 1918, in *Les Armées Françaises dans la Grande Guerre*, book VI, vol. 2, 236–240.

78. Annex 1095, GAR, June 3, 1918, in *Les Armées Françaises dans la Grande Guerre*, book VI, vol. 2, 240.

79. John J. Pershing to Secretary of War and Chief of Staff, cable 1235-S, June 3, 1918, James G. Harbord Papers, Library of Congress, Manuscript Division, Washington, DC.

80. Erich Ludendorff, *Ludendorff's Own Story, August 1914–November 1918: The Great War from the Siege of Liège to the Signing of the Armistice as Viewed from the Grand Headquarters of the German Army* (New York: Harper, 1919), 269.

81. Corps order, June 4, 1918; telephone message, June 3, 1918, 4th Reserve Corps, in *War Diaries of German Units*, vol. 1.

3. *June 4, 1918—First Contact*

1. J. E. Rendinell and George Pattullo, *One Man's War: The Diary of a Leatherneck* (Whitefish, MT: Kessinger Publishing, 2010), 95.

2. Kemper Frey Cowing, comp., *"Dear Folks at Home—": The Glorious Story of the United States Marines in France as Told by Their Letters from the Battlefield*, ed. Courtney R. Cooper (Boston: Houghton Mifflin, 1919), 140–141.

3. Cowing, *"Dear Folks at Home,"* 141.

4. Field message from 1st Battalion, 6th Marines, to 6th Marine Headquarters, 7:50 a.m., June 4, 1918, in Clyburn Otto Mattfeldt, comp., *Records of the Second Division (Regular)*, 10 vols. (Washington, DC: US Army War College Historical Section, 1924–1928), vol. 7; field message from Colonel Malone to Headquarters, 3rd Brigade, 2:55 a.m., June 4, 1918, in United States Army Center for Military History, *U.S. Army in the World War, 1917–1919*, 17 vols. (1948; reprint, Washington, DC: United States Army Center for Military History, 1988–1992), 4:124.

5. Order 445-30.1, Relief of French Units by American Troops, 4:00 p.m., June 3, 1918, in *U.S. Army in the World War*, 4:115.

6. Rendinell and Pattullo, *One Man's War*, 95.

7. Rendinell and Pattullo, *One Man's War*, 95; Berton W. Sibley, *History of the Third Battalion, Sixth Regiment, U.S. Marines* (Hillsdale, MI: Akers, MacRitchie & Hurlbut, 1919), 13.

8. Berton W. Sibley, letter, December 20, 1926, Correspondence with Former Division Officers, RG 117, American Battle Monuments Commission, NARA II.

9. Field message from Colonel Neville to Captain Wass, 18th Company, 8:36 a.m., June 4, 1918, in *U.S. Army in the World War*, 4:124; Keller E. Rockey, letter, December 16, 1926, Correspondence with Former Division Officers.

10. Onnie J. Cordes and Janice D. Cordes, eds., "The Immortal Division," 8, Onnie J. and Janice D. Cordes Papers, Marine Corps Archives, Marine Corps History Division, Marine Corps University, Quantico, VA.

11. Cordes and Cordes, "Immortal Divison," 142.

12. Albert E. Powis, "A Leatherneck in France, 1917–1919," *Military Images Magazine* 3, 2 (September–October 1981): 12. The 66th Company muster rolls for June 1918 document Carpenter's wound and the death of Davis and four other Marines on the same date.

13. Unidentified newspaper clipping in the possession of Don Butler of Bowling Green, KY, who allowed that item and others to be used for this book.

14. George B. Clark, ed., *History of the Fifth Regiment Marines (May 1917–December 31, 1918)* (Pike, NH: Brass Hat, 1995), 10.

15. James G. Harbord, *The American Army in France: 1917–1919* (Cranbury, NJ: Scholars Bookshelf, 2006), 288; Fielding S. Robinson, Alumni File, Virginia Military Institute Archives, Lexington, VA.

16. Field Order 202.32.1, 2nd Artillery Brigade, June 4, 1918, in *U.S. Army in the World War,* 4:127.

17. Report of operations, 2nd Battalion, 5th Marines, June 4, 1918, in *Records of the Second Division,* vol. 7.

18. Stephen Brown and Carl H. Geores, "55th Co. Marines in World War I," undated newspaper article, Records Relating to Marine Participation in World War I, RG 127, Records of the United States Marine Corps, NARA.

19. Memorandum for Major Edwin N. McClellan, Army personnel attached to Marines, n.d., Records Relating to Marine Participation in World War I.

20. Frederic M. Wise, *A Marine Tells It to You* (New York: J. H. Sears, 1929), 201.

21. Craig Hamilton and Louise Corbin, eds., *Echoes from over There: By the Men of the Army and Marine Corps Who Fought in France* (New York: Soldiers' Publishing Company, 1919), 4.

22. Hamilton and Corbin, *Echoes from over There,* 4.

23. Hamilton and Corbin, *Echoes from over There,* 4.

24. Memorandum for McClellan, Army personnel attached to the Marines, n.d.

25. William B. Moore, "The Bloody Angle of the AEF," *American Legion Weekly* 4, 8 (February 24, 1922): 16.

26. Memorandum for McClellan, Army personnel attached to Marines, n.d.

27. James R. Nilo, "The Babe," *Marine Corps Gazette* 55, 11 (November 1971): 27–28.

28. Cowing, *"Dear Folks at Home,"* 98–99.

29. Lemuel C. Shepherd, Oral History Transcript, 330, Marine Corps Oral History Program, Marine Corps History Division, Marine Corps University, Quantico, VA.

30. Moore, "Bloody Angle of the AEF," 17.

31. Charles Dunbeck, ed., *History of the Second Battalion, 5th Regiment, U.S. Marines, June 1st–January 1st 1919* (n.p., n.d.), 8; Shepherd, Oral History Transcript, 328.

32. Preliminary Report of Two Prisoners, June 5, 1918, in *Records of the Second Division,* vol. 9.

33. Eldon Freel diary, entry for June 4, 1918, Eldon Freel Papers, State Historical Society of Iowa, Des Moines.

34. George B. Clark, ed., *His Time in Hell: A Texas Marine in France. The World War I Memoir of Warren R. Jackson* (Novato, CA: Presidio Press, 2001), 95.

35. Freel diary, entry for June 4, 1918.

36. John A. West, letter, January 17, 1979, Belleau Wood Geographical File, Reference Branch, Marine Corps History Division, Marine Corps University,

Quantico, VA; Robert E. Messersmith, "Operations of Company E, 78th Company, 6th Regiment Marines, 2nd Division at Belleau Woods, June 1–13, 1918," 11, Advanced Infantry Course, 1928–1929, World War I Personal Experience Monographs, Donovan Research Library, Maneuver Center of Excellence Libraries, Fort Benning, GA; Henry L. Larsen, "The Battle of Belleau Woods," 11, Advanced Infantry Course, 1924–1925, ibid.

37. John J. Pershing diary, entry for June 4, 1918, John J. Pershing Papers, Library of Congress, Manuscript Division, Washington, DC.

38. "Tales Told by Overseas Marines," *Recruiters' Bulletin* 4, 12 (October 1918): 30.

39. Don V. Paradis, Oral History Transcript, 1973, 38, Marine Corps Oral History Program.

40. Paradis, Oral History Transcript, 39.

41. Paradis, Oral History Transcript, 39.

42. Paradis, Oral History Transcript, 40.

43. Paradis, Oral History Transcript, 40.

44. Paradis, Oral History Transcript, 41.

45. Bailey M. Coffenberg, letter, April 18, 1930, Correspondence with Former Division Officers.

46. Glen G. Hill to G. M. Neufeld, December 28, 1979, Glen G. Hill Papers, Marine Corps Archives.

47. French 21st Corps, memorandum 1933/3, June 4, 1918, in *U.S. Army in the World War,* 4:131.

48. War diary, 4th Marine Brigade, June 4, 1918, in *U.S. Army in the World War,* 4:135.

49. Havelock D. Nelson, "Paris Metz Road," *Leatherneck Magazine* 23, 1 (January 1940): 18.

50. Memorandum for McClellan, Army personnel attached to Marines, n.d.

51. Annex 1133, Army Group North Headquarters, 1100 hours, June 4, 1918, in Ministère de la Guerre, Etat-Major de l'Armée, Service Historique, *Les Armées Françaises dans la Grande Guerre* (Paris: Service Historique de la Défense, 1929–1934), book VI, vol. 2, 284.

4. *June 5–6, 1918*

1. Eldon Freel diary, entry for June 5, 1918, Eldon Freel Papers, State Historical Society of Iowa, Des Moines.

2. French XXI Corps, General Operations Order, 3:00 p.m., June 5, 1918, in United States Army Center for Military History, *U.S. Army in the World War, 1917–1919,* 17 vols. (1948; reprint, Washington, DC: United States Army Center for Military History, 1988–1992), 4:141–142.

3. Memorandum, Commanding General, 2nd Division, to Commanding General, 4th Brigade, 4:53 p.m., June 5, 1918, in *U.S. Army in the World War,* 4:141–142, 145.

4. Henry Hoge, "Account of Belleau Wood," World War I Veterans Service Data, New York State Archives, Albany, NY; 4th Brigade, Record of Conversation, Harbord and Brown, 3:00 p.m., June 5, 1918, in Clyburn Otto Mattfeldt, comp., *Records of the Second Division (Regular),* 10 vols. (Washington, DC: US Army War College Historical Section, 1924–1928), vol. 4.

5. Field Order 1, 4th Marine Brigade, 10:25 p.m., June 5, 1918, in *Records of the Second Division,* vol. 4; field order, Catlin to Sibley, 9:00 p.m., June 5, 1918, ibid., vol. 5; report of operations, 2nd Battalion, 5th Marines, June 5, 1918, ibid., vol. 7.

6. J. E. Rendinell and George Pattullo, *One Man's War: The Diary of a Leatherneck* (Whitefish, MT: Kessinger Publishing, 2010), 97.

7. Gerald C. Thomas, Oral History Transcript, 1966, 30, Marine Corps Oral History Program, Marine Corps History Division, Marine Corps University, Quantico, VA.

8. John A. Hughes, Biographical File, Reference Branch, Marine Corps History Division; "Fighting Colonel to Address Vets," *Cleveland (OH) Plain Dealer,* May 23, 1927, 4.

9. Thomas, Oral History Transcript, 31.

10. Thomas, Oral History Transcript, 31.

11. Thomas, Oral History Transcript, 33; field message, June 6, 1918, in *U.S. Army in the World War,* 6:353.

12. Jonas Platt, "Holding Back the Marines," *Ladies' Home Journal* 36, 9 (September 1919): 37.

13. Platt, "Holding Back the Marines," 37.

14. Platt, "Holding Back the Marines," 37.

15. Service record, synopsis, Logan Feland Papers, Marine Corps Archives, Marine Corps History Division; Robert B. Asprey, *At Belleau Wood* (New York: G. P. Putnam's, 1965), 148; Platt, "Holding Back the Marines," 114.

16. Platt, "Holding Back the Marines," 114.

17. Onnie J. Cordes and Janice D. Cordes, eds., "The Immortal Division," 8, Onnie J. and Janice D. Cordes Papers, Marine Corps Archives.

18. Pell W. Foster, *A Short History of Battery "B," 12th Field Artillery, Second Division in the World War* (New York: Evening Post Printing Office, 1921), 10.

19. Combat reports of Second Lieutenant Bezon, 1st Platoon, 9th Company, 3rd Battalion, 460th Regiment, 237th Division, June 14, 1918, in Gustav J. Braun and Trevor W. Swett, comps., *Translations: War Diaries of German Units Opposed to the Second Division (Regular) 1918,* 5 vols. (Washington, DC: Second Division Historical Section, Army War College, 1930–1932), vol. 4.

20. *Americans Defending Democracy: Our Soldiers' Own Stories* (New York: World War Stories, 1919), 87.

21. Elton E. Mackin, *Suddenly We Didn't Want to Die: Memoirs of a World War I Marine* (Novato, CA: Presidio Press, 1996), 17.

22. Jonathan Porter Ashley, *An Ashley Genealogy* (Deerfield, MA, 1924), 17.

23. Kemper Frey Cowing, comp., *"Dear Folks at Home—": The Glorious Story*

of the United States Marines in France as Told by Their Letters from the Battlefield, ed. Courtney R. Cooper (Boston: Houghton Mifflin, 1919), 125–126.

24. Field message, 1st Battalion to Commanding Officer, 5th Marines, June 5, 1918, in *Records of the Second Division*, vol. 5; George W. Hamilton, Biographical File, Reference Branch, Marine Corps History Division.

25. Unit Historian, *The History of the 1st Battalion, 5th Marines, 1917–1919* (Germany: privately printed, 1919), 11.

26. Edwin N. McClellan diary, entry for November 22, 1918, Edwin N. McClellan Papers, Marine Corps Archives; "Croix de Guerre Marine Succeeds Major Yates as Recruiting Officer," *Buffalo (NY) Evening News*, August 2, 1919, 13.

27. Combat reports of Second Lieutenant Bezon, June 14, 1918.

28. Mackin, *Suddenly We Didn't Want to Die*, 18.

29. Cowing, *"Dear Folks at Home,"* 126.

30. Charles A. Ketcham, ed., "In Memoriam, Lt. Thomas Williams Ashley, USMC," *Marines Magazine* 6, 9 (September 1921): 13.

31. Cowing, *"Dear Folks at Home,"* 126.

32. Combat reports of Second Lieutenant Bezon, June 14, 1918.

33. Report of Sergeant Becker, June 7, 1918, in *War Diaries of German Units*, vol. 4.

34. Platt, "Holding Back the Marines," 114.

35. Cowing, *"Dear Folks at Home,"* 126.

36. Reports on the deaths of officers, 5th Marines, October 6, 1918, 4th Brigade, Records Relating to Marine Participation in World War I, RG 127, Records of the United States Marine Corps, NARA.

37. Harry R. Stringer, ed., *Heroes All! A Compendium of the Names and Official Citations of the Soldiers and Citizens of the United States and of Her Allies Who Were Decorated by the American Government for Exceptional Heroism and Conspicuous Service above and beyond the Call of Duty in the War with Germany, 1917–1919* (Washington, DC: Fassett, 1919), 316; Platt, "Holding Back the Marines," 114.

38. Report of casualties, 5th Marines, Records Relating to Marine Participation in World War I.

39. Dispatch, 3rd Battalion, 460th Infantry, 7:30 a.m., June 6, 1918; combat reports of Second Lieutenant Bezon, June 14, 1918; war diary of the 3rd Battalion, 462nd Infantry, June 1–16, 1918, in *War Diaries of German Units*, vol. 4; Stringer, *Heroes All!* 231.

40. Platt, "Holding Back the Marines," 114.

41. Combat report of 3rd Battalion, 462nd Infantry, June 5–10, 1918, in *War Diaries of German Units*, vol. 4.

42. "Heroes of Belleau Come Back Smiling," *Recruiters' Bulletin* 4, 11 (September 1918): 5–6.

43. Platt, "Holding Back the Marines," 114.

44. Memorandum from Julius Turrill to Naval Board of Awards, March 2, 1920, Office of the Commandant, General Correspondence, RG 127, Records of the United States Marine Corps, NARA.

45. "Heroes of Belleau Come Back Smiling," 5.

46. Cowing, *"Dear Folks at Home,"* 127.

47. War diary, 2nd Battalion, 462nd Infantry, June 6, 1918, in *War Diaries of German Units,* vol. 4; combat report, June 9, 1918, ibid.; Belleau Wood Manuscript History, Records Relating to Marine Participation in World War I.

48. Platt, "Holding Back the Marines," 114.

49. Cowing, *"Dear Folks at Home,"* 127, 127–128.

50. "Heroes of Belleau Come Back Smiling," 6.

51. Platt, "Holding Back the Marines," 114.

52. "DAV Leader Was Hero of World War I," *DAV Service Monthly,* March 9, 1948, Personnel N–S Folder, Records Relating to Marine Participation in World War I.

53. Platt, "Holding Back the Marines," 116.

54. Recommendation for awards, 15th Machine Gun Company, June 18, 1918, Records Relating to Marine Participation in World War I.

55. General Orders 40, 2nd Division, Publication of Commendation, July 5, 1918, Logan Feland Papers, Marine Corps Archives. Feland would receive the Distinguished Service Cross for his bravery on June 6, 1918, and for other actions at Belleau Wood.

56. *Americans Defending Democracy,* 174; General Orders 40, July 5, 1918.

57. Albert E. Powis, "A Leatherneck in France, 1917–1919," *Military Images Magazine* 3, 2 (September–October 1981): 12.

58. Powis, "Leatherneck in France," 12.

59. John H. Fay, Biographical File, Reference Branch, Marine Corps History Division.

60. William R. Matthews, "Memoir of Belleau Wood," Robert Asprey Papers, Marine Corps Archives.

61. Roswell Winans, Biographical File, Reference Branch, Marine Corps History Division; "On the Heels of the Hun," *Recruiters' Bulletin* 1, 1 (November 1918): 34.

62. Cordes and Cordes, "The Immortal Division," 9.

63. General Orders 40, July 5, 1918.

64. Robert W. Blake, Oral History Transcript, 11, Marine Corps Oral History Program.

65. Second Lieutenant Koch, report of the 10th Company, 460th Infantry, covering the combat period from June 2–6, 1918; Second Lieutenant Weitkunat, report of the 11th Company, 460th Infantry, covering the combat period from June 2 to June 6, 1918, June 7, 1918, in *War Diaries of German Units,* vol. 4.

66. Ashley, *Ashley Genealogy,* 17–18.

67. Cordes and Cordes, "The Immortal Division," 10.

68. Cordes and Cordes, "The Immortal Division," 10.

69. "Information Regarding Lt. Thos W. Ashley," Thomas W. Ashley, Alumni Biographical File, Amherst College Archives and Special Collections, Amherst, MA.

70. Keller E. Rockey to Charles H. Ashley, November 2, 1920, Ashley Alumni File; Elliot D. Cooke, *Americans versus Germans: The First AEF in Action* (New York: Penguin Books, 1942), 104.

71. Report of the 10th Company, 460th Infantry, n.d., and report of the 11th

Company, 460th Infantry, June 7, 1918, in *War Diaries of German Units*, vol. 4; Lt. Col. J. Turrill, interview, December 11, 1918, Records Relating to Marine Participation in World War I.

72. Benjamin S. Berry to Edwin N. McClellan, May 8, 1920, Records Relating to Marine Participation in World War I.

73. Report of 11th Company, 460th Infantry, June 7, 1918.

74. Edward Hope to Father, June 16, 1918, History and Museums Branch, Miscellaneous Records of the Adjutant and Inspectors Department, RG 127, Records of the United States Marine Corps, NARA.

75. Lieutenant Colonel John Magruder, 2nd Division field notes, April 4, 1919, Records Relating to Marine Participation in World War I; field message from Berry to Feland, 7:20 a.m., June 6, 1918, in *Records of the Second Division*, vol. 5; Stringer, *Heroes All!* 197.

76. Peter Conachy, undated letter, Correspondence with Former Division Officers, RG 117, American Battle Monuments Commission, NARA II.

77. Cordes and Cordes, "The Immortal Division," 10.

78. War diary, 273rd Reserve Infantry, June 6, 1918, in *War Diaries of German Units*, vol. 4.

79. Field message from K. E. Rockey, 5:37 a.m., June 6, 1918, in *Records of the Second Division*, vol. 5; Stringer, *Heroes All!* 202–203.

80. "Old Timers Keep Alive Sacred Traditions of the U.S. Marines," *Providence (RI) News*, November 10, 1923, Henry Hulbert, Biographical File, Reference Branch, Marine Corps History Division.

81. Daniel A. Hunter, Biographical File, Reference Branch, Marine Corps History Division.

82. Muster rolls, 67th Company and 49th Company, 5th Marines, June 1918, Marine Corps Muster Rolls, RG 127, Records of the United States Marine Corps, NARA.

83. Platt, "Holding Back the Marines," 116.

84. Russell A. Warner, "Outline of Experience," 2nd Engineers, 2nd Division, World War I Veterans Survey, Army Heritage and Education Center, Carlisle PA.

85. Field message from Logan Feland, situation 7:00 a.m. to present, June 6, 1918, Records Relating to Marine Participation in World War I; Hoge, "Account of Belleau Wood."

86. Stringer, *Heroes All!* 231, 160.

87. Cowing, *"Dear Folks at Home,"* 128; combat reports of Second Lieutenant Bezon, June 14, 1918.

88. Stringer, *Heroes All!* 20.

89. Memorandum from Major General Commandant to the Adjutant General of the Army, March 19, 1923, Office of the Commandant, General Correspondence.

90. Platt, "Holding Back the Marines," 116; Stringer, *Heroes All!* 231.

91. Reports on deaths of officers, 5th Marines, October 6, 1918.

92. Lemuel Shepherd to Dr. Elizabeth R. Carmichael, April 6, 1981, Vernon L. Somers, Alumni File, Virginia Military Institute Archives, Lexington, VA.

Belleau Wood Tour: Stops 4–8

1. Craig Hamilton and Louise Corbin, eds., *Echoes from over There: By the Men of the Army and Marine Corps Who Fought in France* (New York: Soldiers' Publishing Company, 1919), 4.

2. Memorandum for Major Edwin N. McClellan, 55th Company, Army personnel attached to Marines, June 1918, Records Relating to Marine Participation in World War I, RG 127, Records of the United States Marine Corps, NARA.

3. Frank Whitehead, "The Aisne Defensive," Correspondence with Former Division Officers, RG 117, American Battle Monuments Commission, NARA II.

4. Havelock D. Nelson, "Paris Metz Road," *Leatherneck Magazine* 23, 1 (January 1940): 12.

5. Nelson, "Paris Metz Road," 12.

5. *June 6, 1918—Berry's 3rd Battalion, 5th Marines*

1. Supplement to Order 81, June 6, 1918, in United States Army Center for Military History, *U.S. Army in the World War, 1917–1919*, 17 vols. (1948; reprint, Washington, DC: United States Army Center for Military History, 1988–1992), 6:359; Harbord to McClellan, August 3, 1920, Edwin N. McClellan Papers, Marine Corps Archives, Marine Corps History Division, Marine Corps University, Quantico, VA. There is no record of the time of Degoutte's message to the division.

2. Telephone message from 21st Army Corps to 2nd Division Headquarters, June 3, 1918; aero plane observer message, 1:35 p.m., June 2, 1918; message from Lt. Nouvelon forwarded to General Bundy, 8:25 a.m., June 5, 1918, all in Clyburn Otto Mattfeldt, comp., *Records of the Second Division (Regular)*, 10 vols. (Washington, DC: US Army War College Historical Section, 1924–1928), vol. 4.

3. Message from 2nd Bureau, 21st Corps, to 2nd Division, 2:00 p.m., June 6, 1918, in *Records of the Second Division*, vol. 4.

4. Harbord to General George Richards, July 23, 1928, Records Relating to Marine Participation in World War I, RG 127, Records of the United States Marine Corps, NARA.

5. Harbord to Richards, July 23, 1928.

6. Field Order 3, 2nd Field Artillery Brigade, 2:00 p.m., June 6, 1918, in *U.S. Army in the World War*, 4:363.

7. Operations report, 2nd Division, June 5, 1918, in *U.S. Army in the World War*, 4:146.

8. Summary of intelligence, 2nd Division, June 5, 1918, in *Records of the Second Division*, vol. 9.

9. Field Order 2, 4th Marine Brigade, 2:05 p.m., June 6, 1918, in *Records of the Second Division*, vol. 2.

10. Albertus W. Catlin, *With the Help of God and a Few Marines* (Garden City, NY: Doubleday, Page, 1919), 110.

11. Memorandum from Headquarters, 6th Regiment, to Battalion Commanders,

June 6, 1918, Miscellaneous Memorandums, Records Relating to Marine Participation in World War I.

12. J. D. Wilmeth, "Bois de la Brigade de Marine," *Marine Corps Gazette* 23, 1 (March 1939): 27.

13. Floyd Gibbons, *And They Thought We Wouldn't Fight* (New York: George H. Doran, 1918), 307–308.

14. Thomas H. Miles Jr., Alumni Record, Seely G. Mudd Manuscript Library, Princeton University, Princeton, NJ.

15. Reports on the deaths of officers, 5th Marines, October 6, 1918, Records Relating to Marine Participation in World War I; Harry R. Stringer, ed., *Heroes All! A Compendium of the Names and Official Citations of the Soldiers and Citizens of the United States and of Her Allies Who Were Decorated by the American Government for Exceptional Heroism and Conspicuous Service above and beyond the Call of Duty in the War with Germany, 1917–1919* (Washington, DC: Fassett, 1919), 170, 161, 227; field message from 4th Marine Brigade Headquarters, 2:15 a.m., June 7, 1918, in *Records of the Second Division*, vol. 5; field message to Colonel Neville, 5th Marines, June 6, 1918, ibid.; muster rolls, 45th Company, 5th Marines, Marine Corps Muster Rolls, RG 127, Records of the United States Marine Corps, NARA.

16. Merwin H. Silverthorn, Oral History Transcript, 43, Marine Corps Oral History Program, Marine Corps History Division, Marine Corps University, Quantico, VA; University of Minnesota, *Gopher* [yearbook] (Minneapolis: University of Minnesota, 1920), 204.

17. Major Josef Bischoff, biographical summary, estate auction ID 8016, lot 113, July 2017, antique auction, Hamburg, Germany, https://veryimportantlot.com/en/lot/view/preussen-nachlass-des-major-josef-bischoff-komm-8016.

18. Kemper Frey Cowing, comp., *"Dear Folks at Home—": The Glorious Story of the United States Marines in France as Told by Their Letters from the Battlefield*, ed. Courtney R. Cooper (Boston: Houghton Mifflin, 1919), 118.

19. Cowing, *"Dear Folks at Home,"* 119.

20. Stringer, *Heroes All!* 147; University of Minnesota, *Gopher,* 217.

21. Silverthorn, Oral History Transcript, 46.

22. Carl B. Mills, "My First Impressions as a Marine Recruit," Carl B. Mills Papers, Marine Corps Archives.

23. Mills, "My First Impressions as a Marine Recruit."

24. "Tales Told by Overseas Marines," *Recruiters' Bulletin* 4, 12 (October 1918): 32.

25. "Hun Called Dirty Fighters," *Minneapolis Journal,* August 25, 1918, General News and City section.

26. Silverthorn, Oral History Transcript, 49.

27. Press telegram from Lieutenant von Hollander, 237th Infantry Division, n.d., in Gustav J. Braun and Trevor W. Swett, comps., *Translations: War Diaries of German Units Opposed to the Second Division (Regular) 1918,* 5 vols. (Washington, DC: Second Division Historical Section, Army War College, 1930–1932), vol. 4.

28. Raymond E. Knapp, "Operations of the 3rd Battalion, 5th Regiment, U.S.

Marines in Belleau Wood, June 5–28, 1918," 11, Company Officers Course, 1924–1925, World War I Personal Experience Monographs, Donovan Research Library, Maneuver Center of Excellence Libraries, Fort Benning, GA.

29. Arthur Clifford to Mabel, June 20, 1918, Arthur Clifford Papers, Marine Corps Archives.

30. Wilmeth, "Bois de la Brigade de Marine," 28.

31. Gibbons, *And They Thought We Wouldn't Fight,* 309.

32. Gerald B. Clark to "Folks," June 18, 1918, Gerald B. Clark Papers, Marine Corps Archives.

33. Knapp, "Operations of the 3rd Battalion," 9.

34. Clark to "Folks," June 18, 1918.

35. Victor M. Landreth to "Lou," June 7, 1918, Victor M. Landreth Papers, Marine Corps Archives.

36. Wilmeth, "Bois de la Brigade de Marine," 28.

37. Wilmeth, "Bois de la Brigade de Marine," 28.

38. Landreth to "Lou," June 7, 1918.

39. Clark to "Folks," June 18, 1918.

40. Clark to "Folks," July 12, 1918, Clark Papers.

41. Stringer, *Heroes All!* 265.

42. Knapp, "Operations of the 3rd Battalion," 11.

43. Wilmeth, "Bois de la Brigade de Marine," 28.

44. Landreth to "Lou," June 7, 1918.

45. Berry to McClellan, May 8, 1920, Records Relating to Marine Participation in World War I.

46. "Lieutenant Synnott Is Killed at Belleau Wood," *Passaic (NJ) Daily News,* July 11, 1918, 1.

47. "J. F. Singleton Listed among Dead in France," *New York Times,* July 12, 1918, 6.

48. "Funeral of Lieutenant Synott," *Montclair (NJ) Times,* September 10, 1921, 16; "American Flier Wounded," *New York Herald,* July 8, 1918, 3; "Navy Cross for Dead Hero," *Montclair (NJ) Times,* December 25, 1920, 7.

49. "Former Esky Boy Is Real Trench Hero," *Escanaba (MI) Morning Press,* July 12, 1918, 1, Adrian J. Michels Papers, Marine Corps Archives.

50. "Passaic Man with Marines Believed Killed in Action," *Passaic (NJ) Daily News,* July 8, 1918, 1.

51. "Friends Wearing the Gold Star," *Escanaba (MI) Morning Press,* July 17, 1918, 2.

52. "Twenty Years Later," *Escanaba (MI) Morning Press,* July 13, 1938, 4.

53. Major F. A. Barker to Mrs. Elsie M. Michels, October 5, 1920, Adrian J. Michels, Official Military Personnel File, RG 92, National Personnel Records Center, St. Louis, MO.

54. Elsie Michels to Marine Headquarters, April 15, 1922, Michels, Official Military Personnel File.

55. Michels, Official Military Personnel File; "Nine More Badger Mothers, Widows Go to France," *La Crosse (WI) Tribune and Leader Press,* May 24, 1932, 14.

56. James L. Clark, biographical sketch, James L. Clark Papers, Belleau Wood Detachment, Marine Corps League, Columbus, OH.

57. Clark biographical sketch.

58. Field message from Berry to Neville, 6:10 p.m., June 6, 1918, in *Records of the Second Division,* vol. 5.

59. Gibbons, *And They Thought We Wouldn't Fight,* 311.

60. Berry to McClellan, May 8, 1920.

61. Gibbons, *And They Thought We Wouldn't Fight,* 319.

Belleau Wood Tour: Stops 9 and 10

1. Press telegram, 237th Infantry Division, n.d., in Gustav J. Braun and Trevor W. Swett, comps., *Translations: War Diaries of German Units Opposed to the Second Division (Regular) 1918,* 5 vols. (Washington, DC: Second Division Historical Section, Army War College, 1930–1932), vol. 4.

2. Merwin H. Silverthorn, Oral History Transcript, 49, Marine Corps Oral History Program, Marine Corps History Division, Marine Corps University, Quantico, VA.

6. June 6, 1918—Sibley's 3rd Battalion, 6th Marines

1. David Bellamy diary, entry for December 30, 1917, David Bellamy Papers, Marine Corps Archives, Marine Corps History Division, Marine Corps University, Quantico, VA.

2. Alfred H. Noble, interview by Lloyd E. Tatem, 1968, Oral History Transcript, 7, Marine Corps Oral History Program, Marine Corps History Division; Norwich University, *Reveille* 35, 9 (June 1900): 127–129.

3. Albertus W. Catlin, *With the Help of God and a Few Marines* (Garden City, NY: Doubleday, Page, 1919), 109.

4. Berton W. Sibley, *History of the Third Battalion, Sixth Regiment, U.S. Marines* (Hillsdale, MI: Akers, MacRitchie & Hurlbut, 1919), 18; Kemper Frey Cowing, comp., *"Dear Folks at Home—": The Glorious Story of the United States Marines in France as Told by Their Letters from the Battlefield,* ed. Courtney R. Cooper (Boston: Houghton Mifflin, 1919), 238; "Brief History of the Sixth Marine Regiment," 11, Bernard A. Schwebke Papers, Marine Corps Archives.

5. History of the 237th Division, June 4, 1918, RG 120, Records of the AEF, NARA II.

6. Dwight F. Smith, record of war service, Norwich University, Archives and Special Collections, Northfield, VT; Norwich University, *War Whoop* [yearbook] (Northfield, VT, 1908); William A. Ellis, *Norwich University, 1819–1911: Her History, Her Graduates, Her Roll of Honor* (Montpelier, VT: Capital City Press, 1911), 433.

7. Cowing, *"Dear Folks at Home,"* 238; Sergeant David M. Vincent to Lou, July 1, 1918, original in possession of Dale Niesen.

8. [Dana Lovejoy], "That's How It Feels to Be Shot," *Marines Magazine* 4, 7

(July 1919): 43. The author of the article is identified only as a gunnery sergeant of the 6th Marines. Only two 6th Marine gunnery sergeants were wounded on June 6: Dana C. Lovejoy and Morris C. Richardson. Richardson was wounded by gas, and Lovejoy was wounded by a gunshot in the left buttock, which identifies him as the author.

9. Lovejoy, "That's How It Feels to Be Shot," 43; muster roll, 82nd Company, June 1918, microfilm, Reference Branch, Marine Corps History Division.

10. "Tales Told by Overseas Marines," *Recruiters' Bulletin* 4, 12 (October 1918): 33.

11. "Tales Told by Overseas Marines," 33.

12. Memorandum/report, 3rd Battalion, 6th Marines, June 18, 1918, in Clyburn Otto Mattfeldt, comp., *Records of the Second Division (Regular)*, 10 vols. (Washington, DC: US Army War College Historical Section, 1924–1928), vol. 7; war diary, 2nd Battalion, 461st Infantry, in Gustav J. Braun and Trevor W. Swett, comps., *Translations: War Diaries of German Units Opposed to the Second Division (Regular) 1918*, 5 vols. (Washington, DC: Second Division Historical Section, Army War College, 1930–1932), vol. 4.

13. Catlin, *With the Help of God*, 115.

14. Catlin, *With the Help of God*, 118.

15. Memorandum from Wendell C. Neville to Adjutant General, US Army, November 6, 1918, Office of the Commandant, General Correspondence, RG 127, Records of the United States Marine Corps, NARA.

16. John H. Clifford, "The Wounding of General Catlin," *Marines Magazine* 4, 7 (July 1919): 20.

17. John L. Tunnell, "Belleau Wood," Belleau Wood Geographical File, Reference Branch, Marine Corps History Division.

18. "Arizona Hero Home from over There," *Bisbee (AZ) Daily Review*, November 10, 1918, 5.

19. "Tales Told by Overseas Marines," 33.

20. Harry R. Stringer, ed., *Heroes All! A Compendium of the Names and Official Citations of the Soldiers and Citizens of the United States and of Her Allies Who Were Decorated by the American Government for Exceptional Heroism and Conspicuous Service above and beyond the Call of Duty in the War with Germany, 1917–1919* (Washington, DC: Fassett, 1919), 103.

21. George Henry Nettleton and Lottie Genevieve Bishop, *Yale in the World War*, 2 vols. (New Haven, CT: Yale University Press, 1925), 1:335–336.

22. Raymond Savageau, ed., *History of the Class of 1919, Sheffield Scientific School, Yale University* (New Haven, CT: Class Book Committee, 1919), 1:224.

23. Nettleton and Bishop, *Yale in the World War*, 336.

24. Nettleton and Bishop, *Yale in the World War*, 336.

25. Noble, Oral History Transcript, 23.

26. Louis F. Timmerman Jr., interview, April 23–24, 1964, 5, Robert Asprey Papers, Marine Corps Archives.

27. "Writes of Brilliant Attack of U.S. Marines," *St. Louis Post Dispatch*, August 14, 1918, 3.

28. Timmerman interview, 8.

29. Noble, Oral History Transcript, 22.

30. Timmerman interview, 4.

31. Richard W. Murphy, student record, Virginia Military Institute Archives, Lexington, VA.

32. "Pamona Boy, 19, Wins French War Cross, *Los Angeles Herald*, October 4, 1918, 10; George B. Clark, ed., *Decorated Marines of the Fourth Brigade in World War I* (Jefferson, NC: McFarland, 2007), 126.

33. Timmerman interview, 4.

34. "Tribute to Richard W. Murphy," *Tuscaloosa (AL) News*, June 18, 1918, 4.

35. Murphy Family Scrapbook, in personal possession of Richard Kimbrough and Grace Neighbors.

36. "A Hero Every Day, Brave Deeds of Men in American Fighting Service," *Evening News* (Harrisburg, PA), September 23, 1918, 6.

37. Yolanda Rodriguez, "Marine History Pays a Visit in Dress Blues," *Los Angeles Times,* February 17, 1990, B-1.

38. Byron Scarbrough, ed., *They Called Us Devil Dogs* (Morrisville, NC: LuLu, 2005), 74.

39. "His Death Confirmed," *Carolina Mountaineer and Waynesville (NC) Courier,* May 8, 1919, 1. Private Graham is listed as missing on the June 1918 muster roll for the 83rd Company but was captured by the Germans on June 6.

40. "His Death Confirmed."

41. Information provided by Jean Blake, Greensboro, NC, and Virginia Szenas, St. Petersburg, FL. Both are nieces of Private Williams. Carl Williams, Burial Case Files, box 5234, RG 92, Records of the Office of Quartermaster General, Cemeterial Division, National Personnel Records Center, St. Louis, MO; "Morrison to Get Right into the Race," *News and Observer* (Raleigh, NC), December 15, 1918, 2; "Memorial Service," *Carolina Mountaineer and Waynesville (NC) Courier,* May 15, 1919, 2.

42. "Private Wayne C. Colahan and Private Jules A. Martin, Affidavits, January 1919, and Related Notes," Personal Folders, American Prisoner of War Reports, June 3, 1938, box 54, Records of the United States Marine Corps; "Obituary," Eugene S. Schrautemeier, *St. Louis Post and Dispatch,* September 25, 1921, 67.

43. Louis F. Timmerman Jr., Alumni Record, Seely G. Mudd Manuscript Library, Princeton University, Princeton, NJ.

44. Timmerman interview, 9.

45. Morris D. Moore, Marine Corps Muster Rolls, Records of the United States Marine Corps.

46. "Germans Fire on Own Men; Get P.B. Man," *Weekly Citizen Democrat* (Pine Bluff, MO), September 12, 1918, 2.

47. Scarbrough, *They Called Us Devil Dogs,* 79.

48. Scarbrough, *They Called Us Devil Dogs,* 81.

49. Timmerman interview, 9.

50. Timmerman interview, 9.

51. Scarbrough, *They Called Us Devil Dogs,* 85.

52. "2 St. Louisans with Marine Are Killed," *St. Louis Post Dispatch,* June 26, 1918.

53. "Writes of Brilliant Attack of U.S. Marines."

54. "St. Louis Captain Missing and Two Marines Killed," *St. Louis Post Dispatch,* June 26, 1918.

55. Scarbrough, *They Called Us Devil Dogs,* 84.

56. Timmerman interview, 9.

57. Scarbrough, *They Called Us Devil Dogs,* 79.

58. Scarbrough, *They Called Us Devil Dogs,* 87.

59. "A Hero Every Day, Brave Deeds of Men in American Fighting Service," *Evening News* (Harrisburg, PA), September 7, 1918, 6.

60. "Edward and Louis Steinmetz Give up Their Lives in Great World War," *Butler County Democrat* (Hamilton, OH), September 19, 1918, 4.

61. Frederick W. Karstaedt, Biographical File, Reference Branch, Marine Corps Archives.

62. "Wounded Marine Lived Here," *Baltimore Sun,* April 27, 1918, 9.

63. "Marine 'Devil Dog' Recalls World War I Battle in France," undated newspaper clipping, Belleau Wood Geographical File, Reference Branch, Marine Corps Archives.

64. J. E. Rendinell and George Pattullo, *One Man's War: The Diary of a Leatherneck* (Whitefish, MT: Kessinger Publishing, 2010), 99. Captain Voeth is confirmed as commanding the 97th Company by Major General Louis R. Jones, interview by Thomas E. Donnelly, 1970, Oral History Transcript, 16, Marine Corps Oral History Program; memorandum report, 3rd Battalion, 6th Marines, June 18, 1918, in *Records of the Second Division,* vol. 7.

65. C. Boyd Maynard, Alumni File, Washington State University, Manuscripts, Archives, and Special Collections, Pullman, WA.

66. "Wounded Sergeant Saw Maynard Fall," *Pullman (WA) Herald,* December 13, 1918, 1.

67. "Wounded Sergeant Saw Maynard Fall."

68. "Body of Pullman Hero in Last Resting Place," *Pullman (WA) Herald,* July 1, 1921, 8.

69. "Pullman Man Dies a Decorated Hero," undated newspaper clipping, History of the American Legion Post 52, 1918–1938, Maynard File, Washington State University, Pullman.

70. Havelock D. Nelson, "Lucy Le Bocage," *Leatherneck Magazine* 23, 2 (February 1940): 19.

71. Nelson, "Lucy Le Bocage," 16.

72. Nelson, "Lucy Le Bocage," 19; William T. Scanlon, *God Have Mercy on Us: A Story of 1918* (Boston: Houghton Mifflin, 1929), 15; memorandum report, 3rd Battalion, 6th Marines, June 18, 1918.

73. Scanlon, *God Have Mercy on Us,* 17–18.

74. Leon D. Huffstater, Service Record Book, Official Military Personnel Files, RG 92, National Personnel Records Center, St. Louis, MO.

75. L. W. T. Waller, "Machine Guns of the 4th Brigade," L. W. T. Waller Papers, Marine Corps Archives.

76. T. J. Curtis and L. R. Long, *History of the Sixth Machine Gun Battalion, Fourth Brigade, U.S. Marines, Second Division, and Its Participation in the Great War* (Neuwied-on-the-Rhine, Germany: n.p., 1919), 15; Army Personnel Attached to Marines, Records Relating to Marine Participation in World War I, Records of the United States Marine Corps.

77. Harold D. Campbell, records of war service, Norwich University, Archives and Special Collections, Northfield, VT.

78. Letter to *Waterbury Record,* August 1, 1917, Harold D. Campbell, Alumni Records, Campbell University, Wiggins Memorial Library, Buies Creek, NC.

79. Letter to *Waterbury Record,* August 1, 1917.

80. Biographical file, Harold D. Campbell Papers, Marine Corps Archives.

81. Pell W. Foster, *A Short History of Battery "B," 12th Field Artillery, Second Division in the World War* (New York: Evening Post Printing Office, 1921), 10.

82. Roland McDonald, interview by Gunnery Sergeant Richard Albright, March 10, 1967, Oral History Transcript, 19, Marine Corps Oral History Program.

7. *June 6, 1918—Evening*

1. Clifton B. Cates, interview, June 25, 1923, 2, Robert Asprey Papers, Marine Corps Archives, Marine Corps History Division, Marine Corps University, Quantico, VA.

2. Cates interview, 2.

3. Graves B. Erskine, interview by Benis M. Frank, 1975, Oral History Transcript, 17, Marine Corps Oral History Program, Marine Corps History Division.

4. Captain Lucien H. Vandoren, "Statement in Regard to Operation of the Second Battalion, 6th Marines, 5–6 June 1918," and Thomas Holcomb, "Statement, 24 April 1919," Records Relating to Marine Participation in World War I, RG 127, Records of the United States Marine Corps, NARA.

5. Joseph C. Grayson, "A Record of the Operations of the Second Battalion, Sixth Regiment Marines," Records Relating to Marine Participation in World War I; "History of the Sixth Marines," 11, Bernard A. Schwebke Papers, Marine Corps Archives; James F. Robertson, chronological data, June 1918, Official Military Personnel Files, RG 92, National Personnel Records Center, St. Louis, MO.

6. Erskine, Oral History Transcript, 36.

7. Randolph T. Zane, Biographical File, Reference Branch, Marine Corps History Division.

8. William A. Worton, Oral History Transcript, 42, Marine Corps Oral History Program.

9. "How Lieutenant Leonard Did His Part at Bouresches," newspaper clipping, Wallace M. Leonard Jr., Alumni Biographical Files, Amherst College, Archives and Special Collections, Amherst, MA.

10. John P. Martin, letter, July 8, 1918, John P. Martin Papers, Marine Corps Archives.

11. Romeyn P. Benjamin, "June, 1918," *Marines Magazine* 4, 4 (July 1919): 6.

12. Wallace M. Leonard Jr. file, Records Relating to Marine Participation in World War I; Martin letter, July 8, 1918.

13. Glen G. Hill to G. M. Neufeld, December 28, 1979, Belleau Wood Geographical File, Reference Branch, Marine Corps History Division.

14. Hill to Neufeld, December 28, 1979.

15. Donald F. Duncan, Biographical File, Reference Branch, Marine Corps History Division; Willard I. Morrey, ed., *The History of the 96th Company, 6th Marine Regiment in World War I* (Quantico, VA: US Marine Corps, 1967), 21.

16. Morrey, *History of the 96th Company*, 22.

17. Aloysius P. Sheridan, letter, August 14, 1918, Asprey Papers.

18. Kemper Frey Cowing, comp., *"Dear Folks at Home— ": The Glorious Story of the United States Marines in France as Told by Their Letters from the Battlefield*, ed. Courtney R. Cooper (Boston: Houghton Mifflin, 1919), 103.

19. Henry L. Fox, ed., *What Our "Boys" Did over There: By "Themselves"* (New York: Allied Overseas Veterans, 1918), 120.

20. George B. Lockhart, Alumni File, Virginia Military Institute Archives, Lexington, VA.

21. Sheridan letter, August 14, 1918; "St. Joseph Young Men Show Valor," *Catholic Tribune* (St. Joseph, MO), July 20, 1918, 5.

22. Hill to Neufeld, December 28, 1979; Cowing, *"Dear Folks at Home,"* 101.

23. Sheridan letter, August 14, 1918; George C. Strott, *The Medical Department of the United States Navy with the Army and Marine Corps in France in World War I: Its Functions and Employment* (Washington, DC: Bureau of Medicine and Surgery, US Navy Department, 1947), 106.

24. Fox, *What Our "Boys" Did over There*, 120–121.

25. John D. Bowling, Alumni File, University of Maryland Archives, College Park, MD; Stuart S. Janney and Karl Singewald, *Maryland in the World War, 1917–1919: Military and Naval Service Records*, 2 vols. (Baltimore: Maryland War Records Commission, 1933), 1:198.

26. John D. Bowling Jr., Service Record Book, Official Military Personnel Files.

27. Cowing, *"Dear Folks at Home,"* 103.

28. Cates interview.

29. "Wife of Officer Missing in Action Wants Information," *Eagle* (Bryan, TX), July 2, 1918, 1.

30. Cates to Mother and Sister, June 10, 1918, Clifton B. Cates Papers, Marine Corps Archives.

31. Cates to Mother, June 14, 1918, Cates Papers.

32. James F. Robertson, Service Record Book, Official Military Personnel Files.

33. Robertson, Service Record Book; war diary, 2nd Battalion, 398th Infantry, Source C, June 6, 1918, in Gustav J. Braun and Trevor W. Swett, comps., *Translations: War Diaries of German Units Opposed to the Second Division (Regular) 1918*, 5 vols. (Washington, DC: Second Division Historical Section, Army War College, 1930–1932), vol. 4.

34. Zane, Biographical File; Erskine, Oral History Transcript, 36.

35. John A. West, letter, January 17, 1979, 4, Belleau Wood Geographical File, Reference Branch; report, 2nd Battalion, 6th Marines, June 19, 1918, in Clyburn Otto Mattfeldt, comp., *Records of the Second Division (Regular),* 10 vols. (Washington, DC: US Army War College Historical Section, 1924–1928), vol. 7.

36. West letter, January 17, 1979, 5.

37. "Fighting Marine Home with Medals and Scars," *Elsinore (CA) Press,* August 1, 1919.

38. "They Got Wrong Arm," *El Paso (TX) Herald,* August 5, 1919, 12; General Orders 40, July 5, 1918, Logan Feland Papers, Marine Corps Archives.

39. Charles I. Murray, Biographical File, Reference Branch; Culver Military Academy, *Roll Call* (Chicago: Rogers, 1917), 111; Harry R. Stringer, ed., *Heroes All! A Compendium of the Names and Official Citations of the Soldiers and Citizens of the United States and of Her Allies Who Were Decorated by the American Government for Exceptional Heroism and Conspicuous Service above and beyond the Call of Duty in the War with Germany, 1917–1919* (Washington, DC: Fassett, 1919), 200.

40. Worton, Oral History Transcript, 15; Robert C. Kilmartin, interview by Benis M. Frank, 1979, Oral History Transcript, 10, Marine Corps Oral History Program.

41. Erskine, Oral History Transcript, 31; Graves B. Erskine, Service Record Book, Official Military Personnel Files.

42. Graves B. Erskine to Major X. H. Price, December 9, 1918, Correspondence with Former Division Officers, RG 117, American Battle Monuments Commission, NARA II.

43. Graves B. Erskine to Robert Asprey, January 12, 1961, Graves B. Erskine Papers, Marine Corps Archives.

44. "Tales Told by Overseas Marines," *Recruiters' Bulletin* 4, 12 (October 1918): 30.

45. General Orders 29, 40, Records Relating to Marine Participation in World War I.

46. Captain R. T. Zane, undated letter, Army Personnel Attached to Marines, Records Relating to Marine Participation in World War I.

47. Benjamin, "June, 1918," 6.

48. Martin letter, July 8, 1918.

49. Hill to Neufeld, December 28, 1979.

50. Benjamin, "June, 1918," 6.

51. Hill to Neufeld, December 28, 1979.

52. Benjamin, "June, 1918," 6.

53. Hill to Neufeld, December 28, 1979.

54. Martin letter, July 8, 1918.

55. Wallace M. Leonard to Father, n.d., Leonard Alumni Biographical File. In a letter to Sergeant John P. Martin in March 1919, Leonard's father claimed that only four members of the platoon reached the village with his son. W. M. Leonard to Sergeant Martin, March 1919, Martin Papers.

56. "How Lieutenant Leonard Did His Part at Bouresches," newspaper clipping, Leonard Alumni Biographical File.

57. "How Lieutenant Leonard Did His Part at Bouresches."

58. "Wounded Belleau Wood Heroes," *Recruiters' Bulletin* 1, 2 (December 1918): 39; General Orders 40, 39, Records Relating to Marine Participation in World War I.

59. Clyde P. Matteson, memorandum, April 7, 1930, Correspondence with Former Division Officers; George Pattullo, *Hellwood* (New York: US Marine Corps Mobilization Bureau, 1918), 20; General Orders 26, 40, Records Relating to Marine Participation in World War I.

60. Cates interview; Cates to Mother and Sister, June 10, 1918, 4.

61. Cates to Mother and Sister, June 10, 1918, 4; Clifton B. Cates, personal observations, 2, Cates Papers.

62. Cates interview, 4; Cates letters, June 10 and 17, 1918, Cates Papers.

63. John T. Miller, "Why I Hate a German," in *What Our "Boys" Did over There: By "Themselves,"* ed. Henry L. Fox (New York: Allied Overseas Veterans, 1918), 121.

64. Combat report, 398th Regiment, June 3, 1918, in *War Diaries of German Units,* vol. 1; war diary, 2nd Battalion, 398th Infantry, June 6, 1918.

65. Cates, personal observations, 2. Both the 79th and 96th Companies claim credit for destroying the machine gun in the church tower, and both claim to have been the first Marines to enter the town. These claims are impossible to prove, and based on the available evidence, they arrived within seconds of each other. Marines from both companies fought side by side in the swirling melee, irrespective of company.

66. "Herbert Dunlavy Was a Promising Athlete," *Houston Post,* July 4, 1918, 8.

67. "A Hero Every Day, Brave Deeds of Men in American Fighting Service," *New Castle (PA) Herald,* August 26, 1918, 4.

68. "Tells Story of Houston Boys' Deaths," *Houston Post,* September 4, 1918.

69. Cates letter, June 10, 1918, Cates Papers; Cates interview. In the letter, Cates claims he was shot at after taking the town.

70. Miller, "Why I Hate a German," 121.

71. Sheridan letter, August 14, 1918.

72. Graves B. Erskine, letter, December 9, 1926, Correspondence with Former Division Officers; Erskine, Oral History Transcript, 37.

73. Leonard, Alumni Biographical File.

74. Leonard, Alumni Biographical File. The dispute over whether the 79th or 96th Company arrived in Bouresches first caused lasting bitterness. Over the years, the 96th Company has received the lion's share of recognition for capturing the town, while the 79th Company's role in the attack has yet to be acknowledged. Lieutenant Leonard's father wrote in 1919, "I am rather tired of 'Lieut. Robertson took Bouresches with twenty men.'" Leonard to Martin, March 1919.

75. "Son-in-Law of Gov. Stephens Was Hero," *Los Angeles Times,* November 24, 1918, 26; Major Randolph T. Zane, US Navy Burial Records, 1898–1932, Records of the Bureau of Medicine and Surgery, RG 52, Department of the Navy, NARA; "Major Zane Died of Wounds, Not Influenza," *Sacramento (CA) Bee,* November 11, 1918.

76. Lt. Col. Holcomb, interview, December 12, 1918, Records Relating to Marine Participation in World War I.

77. Report, 2nd Battalion, 6th Marines, June 19, 1918, in *Records of the Second Division,* vol. 7.

78. Levi E. Hemrick, *Once a Marine* (New York: Carlton Press, 1968), 107.

79. Hemrick, *Once a Marine,* 107.

80. Bailey M. Coffenberg, letter, April 19, 1930, Correspondence with Former Division Officers.

81. "Cite Maquoketa Boy for Bravery," *Quad-City Times* (Davenport, IA), September 1, 1919, 2; Stringer, *Heroes All!* 205.

82. Don V. Paradis to Thomas Holcomb, December 1937, Don V. Paradis Papers, Marine Corps Archives.

83. Hemrick, *Once a Marine,* 109.

84. Hemrick, *Once a Marine,* 110.

85. Paradis to Holcomb, December 1937. The date of this action is sometimes given as June 7–8. Primary sources, including the postwar company history and Coffenberg's 1930 letter, establish that the attack occurred on June 6, with a follow-up attack the next morning.

86. "Detroit Boy Slain in Action Had Premonition of Death," *Detroit (MI) Free Press,* August 6, 1918, 16.

87. Allen Sumner, Alumni Files, Class of 1904, Harvard University Archives, Pusey Library, Cambridge, MA.

88. Sumner, Alumni Files.

89. Diary of the 4th Brigade, June 6, 1918, Records Relating to Marine Participation in World War I.

90. Field message from Captain Laspierre to 4th Brigade Headquarters, 7:34 p.m., June 6, 1918, in *Records of the Second Division,* vol. 4.

91. Field message from Commanding General, 4th Brigade, to Lt. Col. Lee, 8:55 p.m., June 6, 1918, in *Records of the Second Division,* vol. 4.

92. Diary of the 4th Brigade, June 6, 1918.

93. Interview with Colonel Harry Lee, December 12, 1919, Records Relating to Marine Participation in World War I.

94. Lee interview; memorandum from Headquarters, 4th Brigade, Marine Corps, concerning letter from James G. Harbord to George Barnett, June 7, 1918, Records Relating to Marine Participation in World War I.

95. Edwin N. McClellan, *The United States Marine Corps in the World War* (Washington, DC: Government Printing Office, 1920), 65. The casualties cited by McClellan span May 31–July 9, 1918, the entire time the Marine Brigade participated in the Aisne defensive–Château-Thierry campaign, which included days with little or no combat. The percentages given are approximate, pending more definitive research.

96. Memorandum from Captain George K. Shuler, Headquarters, 5th Marines, June 25, 1918, Records Relating to Marine Participation in World War I.

97. Administrative Memorandum 11, Headquarters, 2nd Division, May 8, 1918, Records Relating to Marine Participation in World War I; "Casualties for the

Fourth Brigade, June 1 to 10 July 1918, Inclusive," History and Museums Branch, Miscellaneous Records, Adjutant and Inspectors Files, RG 127, Records of the United States Marine Corps, NARA.

98. Lieutenant Colonel Harry Lee to Colonel Wendell Neville, June 29, 1918, Army Personnel Attached to Marines, Records Relating to Marine Participation in World War I.

99. George Barnett to John W. Maxey, September 25, 1918, Marion M. Collier, Service Record Book, Official Military Personnel Files.

100. Arthur N. Fauble, Service Record Book, Official Military Personnel Files.

101. Mrs. S. C. Seeley, letter, May 19, 1921, Fauble Service Record Book.

102. George Preston Barton and Emma Welles Barton, comps., *War Service Record and Memorial of Lester Clement Barton, Thyrza Barton Dean, William Sidney Barton, Raymond Welles Barton* (Rochester, NY: E. R. Andrews, 1922), 4; Frank H. Potter, *The Potter Record* (n.p., 1921), 30.

103. Emery A. Bartlett file, Oregon War Records, World War I, Oregon State Archives, Salem, OR. The following paragraphs are drawn from Private Bartlett's file, including the letters written by Chaplain Zelie on June 10 and 13, 1918. The papers incorrectly identify the date of his wounding as June 7. The booklet contained in the file, *In Memoriam, Private Emery Augustus Bartlett 1895–1918, a Hero of Belleau Wood* (n.p., n.d.), codifies the account.

104. Bartlett file.

105. Bartlett file.

106. The letters sent to Arthur Bartlett were first mailed to Grinnell, Iowa, which Emery identified as his hometown. When the letters arrived, the town telegraphed them directly to his father, who was living in Salem, Oregon. Private Bartlett considered Iowa his home, despite the family's move to Oregon in 1910.

8. *Belleau Wood Conclusions*

1. John J. Pershing to Secretary of War, cable 1342-S, June 21, 1918, James G. Harbord Papers, Library of Congress, Manuscript Division, Washington, DC.

2. John J. Pershing diary, entry for June 9, 1918, John J. Pershing Papers, Library of Congress.

3. General Orders 12, Headquarters, 4th Marine Brigade, June 9, 1918, Harbord Papers.

4. Telegram from John J. Pershing to Omar Bundy, June 9, 1918, Harbord Papers.

5. Pershing diary, June 9, 1918.

6. "Marines Win Name of Devil Hounds," *New York Times,* June 9, 1918.

7. "Commands the Marines on the Marne," *Evening Star* (Washington, DC), June 10, 1918, 4.

8. "Leads Victorious Marines," *Daily Times* (Seattle, WA), June 13, 1918.

9. Oliver Lyman Spaulding and John Womack Wright, *The Second Division, American Expeditionary Force in France, 1917–1919* (1937; reprint, Nashville, TN: Battery Press, 1989), 71; Edwin N. McClellan, "A Brief History of the Fourth

Brigade of Marines," *Marine Corps Gazette* 5, 4 (December 1919): 350; G. Leegol, Mayor of Meaux, to Omar Bundy, June 26, 1918, Harbord Papers.

10. "Clemenceau Lauds American Troops," *Washington Post,* June 28, 1918. 1.

11. "Clemenceau Congratulates Belleau Wood Victors on a Neat Job Done in a Way 'Peculiarly American,'" *New York Times,* June 28, 1918, 1.

12. Edwin N. McClellan, "The Battle of Belleau Wood," *Marine Corps Gazette* 5, 4 (December 1920): 400.

13. Memorandum from Harbord to John J. Pershing, June 29, 1918, Office of the Commandant, General Correspondence, RG 127, Records of the United States Marine Corps, NARA.

14. McClellan, "Battle of Belleau Wood," 400.

15. James G. Harbord to Edwin N. McClellan, August 3, 1920, Edwin N. Mc-Clellan Papers, Marine Corps Archives, Marine Corps History Division, Marine Corps University, Quantico, VA.

16. Robert H. Ferrell, ed., *In the Company of Generals: The World War I Diary of Pierpont L. Stackpole* (Columbia: University of Missouri Press, 2009), 90.

17. "Won D.S.C. and Swam River on Horse to Get It," *New York Herald,* July 11, 1918.

18. "Belleau Wood," *New York Times,* June 29, 1918, 10.

19. Jennings C. Wise, *The Turn of the Tide: American Operations at Cantigny, Chateau Thierry, and the Second Battle of the Marne* (New York: H. Holt, 1920), 92.

20. Dispatch from Major Bischoff, 461st Infantry Regiment, June 12, 1918, in Gustav J. Braun and Trevor W. Swett, comps., *Translations: War Diaries of German Units Opposed to the Second Division (Regular) 1918,* 5 vols. (Washington, DC: Second Division Historical Section, Army War College, 1930–1932), vol. 4.

21. David L. George, *War Memoirs of David Lloyd George,* vol. 6 (London: Ivor, Nicholson & Watson, 1936), 89.

22. A. W. Grant to Edwin N. McClellan, January 19, 1920, McClellan Papers.

23. "U.S. Recruiting Service," *Recruiters' Bulletin* 6, 1 (January 1920).

24. "U.S. Recruiting Service."

25. Manus Benjamin to Edwin N. McClellan, January 18, 1920, McClellan Papers.

26. Charles L. Dunn to Mother, June 28, 1918, Charles L. Dunn Papers, Marine Corps Archives.

27. Secretary of the Navy to Secretary of the Army, May 7, 1918, Records Relating to Marine Participation in World War I, RG 127, NARA.

28. John A. Lejeune, *The Reminiscences of a Marine* (Philadelphia: Dorrance, 1930), 247.

29. Lejeune, *Reminiscences of a Marine,* 248.

30. General Orders 5, 4th Marine Brigade, May 7, 1918; memorandum from Commandant Marine Corps to Doyen, May 23, 1918, Charles A. Doyen, Service Record Book, Official Military Personnel Files, RG 92, National Personnel Records Center, St. Louis, MO; memoranda from Major General Commandant to Brigadier General John A. Lejeune, May 7 and 15, 1918, John A. Lejeune, Service Record Book, ibid.

31. Lejeune, *Reminiscences of a Marine*, 248.

32. Memorandum from Barnett to Lejeune, May 22, 1918, Lejeune, Service Record Book.

33. Brigadier General Charles A. Doyen to General John J. Pershing, May 29, 1918, Charles A. Doyen Papers, Marine Corps Archives.

34. Lejeune, *Reminiscences of a Marine*, 254.

35. Lejeune, *Reminiscences of a Marine*, 256.

36. Lejeune, *Reminiscences of a Marine*, 258.

37. Ferrell, *In the Company of Generals*, 85.

38. Lejeune, *Reminiscences of a Marine*, 259.

39. Lejeune, *Reminiscences of a Marine*, 259.

40. Lejeune, *Reminiscences of a Marine*, 259.

41. Pershing to the Chief of Staff and the Secretary of War, cable 1331-S, June 19, 1918, Cablegrams Exchanged between General Headquarters, American Expeditionary Force, and the War Department, RG 120, Records of the AEF, NARA II; March to Pershing, cable 1561-R, June 19, 1918, Harbord Papers.

42. McCain to Pershing, cable 1561-R, June 20, 1918, Records of the AEF.

43. Lejeune, *Reminiscences of a Marine*, 261.

44. John A. Lejeune to Laura Lejeune, June 22, 1918, John A. Lejeune Papers, Marine Corps Archives.

45. John A. Lejeune to Eugenia Lejeune, June 22, 1918, Lejeune Papers.

46. Telegram from GHQ AEF to Commanding Officer, 5th Corps, 5:45 p.m., July 14, 1918, Lejeune, Service Record Book.

47. Special Order 169, July 18, 1918, and Special Order 180, July 19, 1918, GHQ AEF, Lejeune, Service Record Book; General Orders 63, 32nd Division, July 5, 1918, ibid.; Wisconsin and Michigan War History Commissions, *The 32nd Division in the World War, 1917–1918* (Milwaukee: Wisconsin Print Co., 1920).

Belleau Wood Tour: Stops 13 and 14

1. Marion M. Collier, Official Military Personnel Files, National Personnel Records Center, St. Louis, MO.

2. George Barnett to Boyd T. Collier, June 25, 1918, Collier, Official Military Personnel Files.

3. Boyd T. Collier to Commandant Marine Corps, June 28, 1918, Collier, Official Military Personnel Files.

4. Leon G. Turovasy to Edwin McClellan, June 28, 1920, Edwin N. McClellan Papers, Marine Corps Archives, Marine Corps History Division, Marine Corps University, Quantico, VA.

5. "2 U.S. Soldiers' Bodies Found in Belleau Wood," *Washington Post*, August 21, 1928, 2.

6. "U.S. Veteran Kills Self by Graves of Comrades," *Washington Post*, April 3, 1928, 1.

9. Grand Strategy

1. Paul von Hindenburg, *Out of My Life* (London: Cassell, 1920), 370.

2. Erich Ludendorff, *Ludendorff's Own Story, August 1914–November 1918: The Great War from the Siege of Liège to the Signing of the Armistice as Viewed from the Grand Headquarters of the German Army* (New York: Harper, 1919), 2:269.

3. Ludendorff, *Ludendorff's Own Story,* 2:274.

4. Ludendorff, *Ludendorff's Own Story,* 2:276.

5. Ludendorff, *Ludendorff's Own Story,* 2:278.

6. Ludendorff, *Ludendorff's Own Story,* 2:372, 374.

7. Dennis Showalter, *Instrument of War: The German Army 1914–18* (London: Osprey Publishing, 2016), 265.

8. James G. Harbord, *Leaves from a War Diary* (New York: Dodd, Mead, 1931), 307.

9. Oliver Lyman Spaulding and John Womack Wright, *The Second Division, American Expeditionary Force in France, 1917–1919* (1937; reprint, Nashville, TN: Battery Press, 1989), 63.

10. Robert H. Ferrell, ed., *In the Company of Generals: The World War I Diary of Pierpont L. Stackpole* (Columbia: University of Missouri Press, 2009), 86.

11. Ferrell, *In the Company of Generals,* 86.

12. Ferrell, *In the Company of Generals,* 87.

13. Ferrell, *In the Company of Generals,* 88.

14. Ferrell, *In the Company of Generals,* 91.

15. Ferrell, *In the Company of Generals,* 91; Harbord, *Leaves from a War Diary,* 307–308; field message from Commanding Officer, 6th Regiment, to Commander, 1st Battalion, 2:05 p.m., July 4, 1918, in Clyburn Otto Mattfeldt, comp., *Records of the Second Division (Regular),* 10 vols. (Washington, DC: US Army War College Historical Section, 1924–1928), vol. 5.

16. Harry A. Benwell, *History of the Yankee Division* (Boston: Cornhill, 1919), 102.

17. Emerson G. Taylor, *New England in France, 1917–1919: A History of the Twenty-Sixth Division, U.S.A.* (Boston: Houghton Mifflin, 1920), 164.

18. Ferrell, *In the Company of Generals,* 94.

19. Ferrell, *In the Company of Generals,* 94.

20. Taylor, *New England in France,* 164.

21. Ferrell, *In the Company of Generals,* 94.

22. Taylor, *New England in France,* 164.

23. John J. Pershing, *My Experiences in the First World War,* vol. 2 (New York: Frederick A. Stokes, 1931), 143.

24. Pershing, *My Experiences in the First World War,* 144.

25. Pershing, *My Experiences in the First World War,* 144.

26. Pershing, *My Experiences in the First World War,* 149.

27. Leonard P. Ayres, *The War with Germany: A Statistical Summary* (Washington, DC: Government Printing Office, 1919), 15.

10. *July 16–17, 1918—Internal Battles and the Movement to Soissons*

1. James G. Harbord, *Leaves from a War Diary* (New York: Dodd, Mead, 1931), 309.

2. Harbord, *Leaves from a War Diary*, 309.

3. Harbord, *Leaves from a War Diary*, 310.

4. John J. Pershing, *My Experiences in the First World War*, vol. 2 (New York: Frederick A. Stokes, 1931), 148.

5. Robert H. Ferrell, ed., *In the Company of Generals: The World War I Diary of Pierpont L. Stackpole* (Columbia: University of Missouri Press, 2009), 96.

6. "Maj. Lay Safe, Dispatch Says," *Washington Post*, August 3, 1918, 2; "Marriage of Count Von Goetzen and Mrs. Stanley Lay," *Evening Star* (Washington, DC), January 4, 1898, 8.

7. Order 1282, French Group of Armies of the Reserve, July 12, 1918, in United States Army Center for Military History, *U.S. Army in the World War*, 17 vols. (1948; reprint, Washington, DC: United States Army Center for Military History, 1988–1992), 5:237–238.

8. Order 1506, Group of Armies of the Reserve, July 14, 1918, in *U.S. Army in the World War*, 5:240–241.

9. Harbord, *Leaves from a War Diary*, 313.

10. Harbord, *Leaves from a War Diary*, 314.

11. Ferrell, *In the Company of Generals*, 99.

12. Harbord, *Leaves from a War Diary*, 315.

13. Harbord, *Leaves from a War Diary*, 315.

14. Journal of operations, 2nd Division, July 15, 1918, in Clyburn Otto Mattfeldt, comp., *Records of the Second Division (Regular)*, 10 vols. (Washington, DC: US Army War College Historical Section, 1924–1928), vol. 6.

15. War diary, 2nd Division, July 17, 1918, in *Records of the Second Division*, vol. 6.

16. Episode 6, "Long Tiring March Begins," in Robin Richmond, ed., *The War Diary of Clarence Richmond*, http://wavefront.com/~rrichmon/wardiary/diary6.htm, accessed November 9, 1998.

17. Neal D. Van Haften, "The Attack and Capture of Bouresches, June 6, 1918," Records Relating to Marine Participation in World War I, RG 127, Records of the United States Marine Corps, NARA.

18. Pierre E. Berdoulat, dossier, LH/185/55, Archives Nationales, France, http://www.culture.gouv.fr/Wave/savimage/leonore/LH015/PG/FRDAFAN83_OL0185055v025.htm.

19. Harbord, *Leaves from a War Diary*, 317–318.

20. Harbord, *Leaves from a War Diary*, 318.

21. Statement of Major R. S. Keyser, US Marines, December 7, 1918, Correspondence with Former Division Officers, RG 117, American Battle Monuments Commission, NARA II; "Memoir," Alfred H. Randall Papers, Marine Corps Archives,

Marine Corps History Division, Marine Corps University, Quantico, VA; Soissons manuscript, n.d., Records Relating to Marine Participation in World War I.

22. Harbord, *Leaves from a War Diary*, 320; Special Orders 224, French XX Army Corps, July 15, 1918, and Operations Order 227, XX Corps, July 16, 1918, in *U.S. Army in the World War*, 5:289, 291.

23. Draft history of the 4th Brigade, n.d., Records Relating to Marine Participation in World War I.

24. "Major Keyser Hero, Advanced on Lineal List," *Bee* (Danville, VA), February 28, 1923, 1. Keyser's place in the lineal list was corrected in 1923 by an act of Congress.

25. "Tompkins Men Fight Gallantly on Marne Front," *Ithaca (NY) Journal*, June 13, 1918, 3.

26. Lieutenant Marvin H. Taylor diary, entry for July 24, 1918, in Oliver Lyman Spaulding and John Womack Wright, *The Second Division, American Expeditionary Force in France, 1917–1919* (1937; reprint, Nashville, TN: Battery Press, 1989), 263–264.

27. The role of Lieutenant Colonel Bearss in the command structure of the 6th Marines remains murky. The July 1918 regimental muster roll lists Bearss as executive officer until July 21, but George B. Clark's editing of Asa Smith's biography (*His Road to Glory: The Life and Times of "Hiking Hiram" Bearss* [Pike, NH: Brass Hat, 2000]) locates Bearss in Paris for much of July, returning to the regiment on July 18.

28. Order 6023, Headquarters, Army Group German Crown Prince, July 3, 1918, and FOP message, 9th Army to Army Group Crown Prince, July 5, 1918, in Gustav J. Braun and Trevor W. Swett, comps., *Translations: War Diaries of German Units Opposed to the Second Division (Regular) 1918,* 5 vols. (Washington, DC: Second Division Historical Section, Army War College, 1930–1932), vol. 5.

29. War diary, 14th Reserve Division, July 1918, in *War Diaries of German Units*, vol. 5.

30. Intelligence Section, General Staff, American Expeditionary Force, *Histories of Two Hundred and Fifty-One Divisions of the German Army Which Participated in the World War, 1914–1918* (Washington, DC: Government Printing Office, 1919), 243.

31. AEF, *Histories of Two Hundred and Fifty-One Divisions of the German Army*, 452.

32. Elliot D. Cooke, "We Attack," *Infantry Journal* 44 (November 1937): 483.

33. *Jambalaya*, Tulane University Yearbook, 1910, 46; *The Princeton University Bric-a-Brac* (Philadelphia: E. A. Wright Bank Note Company, 1913), 14, 56, 69; *The Princeton University Bric-a-Brac* (Philadelphia: E. A. Wright Bank Note Company, 1917), 81. One of the Marines Legendre saved was Colonel Catlin.

34. Cooke, "We Attack," 483.

35. LaRoy S. Upton, "Notes of a Regimental Commander on Recent Fighting in Chateau Thierry District, circa July 1918," Records of the 2nd Division, Records of Combat Divisions, RG 120, Records of the AEF, NARA II.

36. Landislav T. Janda, letter, December 18, 1919, 9th Infantry, 2nd Division, World War I Veterans Survey, US Army Heritage and Education Center, Carlisle, PA.

37. LaRoy S. Upton, comments, January 3, 1927, Correspondence with Former Division Officers.

38. "Tells of Yanks Crossing the Marne," *Courier Journal* (Louisville, KY), August 24, 1918, 6.

39. Cooke, "We Attack," 484.

40. "First Word of Major Schearer Is Received," *Indianapolis News*, March 12, 1918, 2; "Officer of Heroic U.S. Marines Here on Visit with Parents," *Indianapolis News*, August 29, 1919, 2; Maurice E. Shearer, Marine Corps Muster Rolls, 1901, 1905, 1916–1918, RG 127, Records of the United States Marine Corps, NARA. Although the spelling of Shearer's last name varies in some accounts, it is listed as "Shearer" in Marine Corps muster rolls.

41. Fitch L. McCord, memoir, in Spaulding and Wright, *Second Division*, 257.

42. Report on operations, 1st Battalion, 5th Regiment of Marines, July 16–20, 1918, in *Records of the Second Division*.

43. Robert W. Blake, *From Belleau Wood to Bougainville: The Oral History of Major General Robert L. Blake USMC and the Travel Journal of Rosselet Wallace Blake* (Bloomington, IN: Author House, 2004), 10.

44. Robert W. Blake, Oral History Transcript, 12, Marine Corps Oral History Program, Marine Corps History Division, Marine Corps University, Quantico, VA.

45. McCord memoir, 256.

46. McCord memoir, 256; Soissons manuscript, n.d.

47. Pell W. Foster, *A Short History of Battery "B," 12th Field Artillery, Second Division in the World War* (New York: Evening Post Printing Office, 1921), 17.

48. Cooke, "We Attack," 486.

49. "Memoir," Randall Papers.

50. Episode 6, "Long Tiring March Begins."

Soissons Tour: Stops 15–17

1. Robert E. Bullard, *Personalities and Reminiscences of the War* (New York: Doubleday, Page, 1925), 217.

11. *July 18, 1918—Daybreak*

1. Elton E. Mackin, oral history interview by Carl D. Klopfenstein, June 29, 1973, Rutherford B. Hayes Museum and Library, Fremont, OH.

2. Draft history, 1st Battalion, 5th Marines, Records Relating to Marine Participation in World War I, RG 127, Records of the United States Marine Corps, NARA.

3. "Louisville Soldier Is Promoted for Bravery," *Courier Journal* (Louisville, KY), March 7, 1917, 2.

4. Robert W. Blake, Oral History Transcript, 12, Marine Corps Oral History Program, Marine Corps History Division, Marine Corps University, Quantico, VA.

5. Elton E. Mackin, *Suddenly We Didn't Want to Die: Memoirs of a World War I Marine* (Novato, CA: Presidio Press, 1996), 91.

6. "Captain Frank Whitehead a Veteran Leatherneck," *Boston Globe,* February 16, 1919, 14.

7. Muster rolls, 49th Company, June–July 1918, Marine Corps Muster Rolls, RG 127, Records of the United States Marine Corps, NARA.

8. Mackin, *Suddenly We Didn't Want to Die,* 91.

9. Interview with Lieutenant Colonel Julius. S. Turrill, December 11, 1918, Records Relating to Marine Participation in World War I.

10. Statement of Major Ralph S. Keyser, US Marines, December 7, 1918, Correspondence with Former Division Officers, RG 117, American Battle Monuments Commission, NARA II; journal of the 48th Infantry Regiment, July 16–19, 1918, 18, JMO 26N637/4, Memoire des Hommes, Ministere des Armees, Republique Francais.

11. Sergeant Carl McCune diary, 55th Company, entry for July 18, 1918, in Oliver Lyman Spaulding and John Womack Wright, *The Second Division, American Expeditionary Force in France, 1917–1919* (1937; reprint, Nashville, TN: Battery Press, 1989), 261. July 1918 muster rolls for the 55th Company indicate that McCune's rank was corporal. He became a sergeant in October of that year. The name on his gravestone is Carl, but he also spelled it Karl.

12. Carl McCune, Census of 1900 and 1910; State of Ohio, *The Official Roster of Ohio Soldiers, Sailors, and Marines in the World War, 1917–18* (Columbus, OH: F. J. Heer, 1926), 442; muster rolls, 55th Company, July 1918, Marine Corps Muster Rolls.

13. Elliot D. Cooke, "We Attack," *Infantry Journal* 44 (November 1937): 486.

14. William O. Corbin, 1900, 1908, 1912, 1914, 1917, and 1918, Marine Corps Muster Rolls.

15. Cooke, "We Attack," 487.

16. Cooke, "We Attack," 487.

17. Cooke, "We Attack," 487.

18. Report of Battery C, 17th Field Artillery, n.d., 17th Field Artillery Reports of Operations, Chateau-Thierry and Soissons, June–July 1918, Records of the 2nd Division, Records of Combat Divisions, RG 120, Records of the AEF, NARA II.

19. McCune diary, July 18, 1918, 261.

20. Keyser statement, December 7, 1918.

21. Commanding Officer, 2nd Battalion, 5th Marines, report of attack of July 18, 1918, in Spaulding and Wright, *Second Division.*

22. Blake, Oral History Transcript, 19.

23. Mackin, *Suddenly We Didn't Want to Die,* 92.

24. Albert E. Powis, "A Leatherneck in France, 1917–1919," *Military Images Magazine* 3, 2 (September–October 1981): 13.

25. "Naming a Street for City Hero Is Considered," *Binghamton (NY) City Press,* October 2, 1943, 13.

26. William A. Depuy, "He Was a Corporal Once," *Evening Public Ledger* (Philadelphia), August 16, 1921, 8.

27. Louis Cukela, Medal of Honor citation, in Harry R. Stringer, ed., *Heroes All! A Compendium of the Names and Official Citations of the Soldiers and Citizens of the*

United States and of Her Allies Who Were Decorated by the American Government for Exceptional Heroism and Conspicuous Service above and beyond the Call of Duty in the War with Germany, 1917–1919 (Washington, DC: Fassett, 1919), 18; "Native Austrian Cause of Emperor's Grief," *Huntington (IN) Herald,* November 4, 1918, 10.

28. Theodore Roosevelt and John W. Thomason Jr., "Heroes of the Service," *News Tribune* (Waco, TX), September 4, 1927.

29. Roosevelt and Thomason, "Heroes of the Service."

30. Stringer, *Heroes All!* 21.

31. Ladislav T. Janda to "Folks," December 18, 1918, World War I Veterans Survey, US Army Heritage and Education Center, Carlisle, PA.

32. "Summary of Operations, 2nd Division," 12, Records of the 2nd Division.

33. Upton, "Notes of a Regimental Commander," 6, Records of the 2nd Division.

34. "A Brief History of the Second Battalion," 12, Records Relating to Marine Participation in World War I.

35. "Summary of Operations, 2nd Division," 12.

36. "Honor Cross and Promotion Asked for Major Bouton," *Ithaca (NY) Journal,* August 10, 1918, 5.

37. Joseph A. McCafferty to E. P. Bouton, November 19, 1918, in United States Military Academy Association of Graduates, *Fiftieth Annual Report of the Association of Graduates of the United States Military Academy, 19 June 1919* (Saginaw, MI: Seeman & Peters, 1919), 57.

38. Peter W. Kegerreis, "Who's Who and Why, a Brief History of Company A, 9th Infantry," World War I Veterans Survey.

39. Frank J. Franek, "Fighting Companies of the Fighting Ninth, How Each Helped to Win the War," August 9, 1919, World War I Veterans Survey.

40. Operation report, Headquarters Company, 9th Infantry, August 14, 1918, in Clyburn Otto Mattfeldt, comp., *Records of the Second Division (Regular),* 10 vols. (Washington, DC: US Army War College Historical Section, 1924–1928), vol. 7.

41. "The 1915 Season," *Notre Dame Scholastic* 49 (December 11, 1915): 220.

42. "The Monogram Men," *Notre Dame Scholastic* 50 (December 9, 1916): 183–184.

43. Knute Rockne, *The Four Winners—the Head—the Hands—the Foot—and the Ball* (New York: Devin Adair, 1925), 2.

44. Report, Company L, 9th Infantry, operations Chateau Thierry, May 31–July 18, 1918, in *Records of the Second Division,* vol. 7.

45. Field message from Colonel Upton to Brigadier General Ely, 5:40 a.m., July 18, 1918, in *Records of the Second Division,* vol. 4; Roy F. Johnson to American Battle Monuments Commission, December 3, 1928, Correspondence with Former Division Officers.

46. Upton, "Notes of a Regimental Commander."

47. Taylor diary, entry for July 24, 1918, in Spaulding and Wright, *Second Division,* 264.

48. "Tells of Yanks Crossing Marne," *Courier Journal* (Louisville, KY), August 24, 1918, 6.

49. Taylor diary, 264.

50. *Letters of Lambert A. Wood, First Lieutenant, U.S.A. from "Somewhere in France" to His Parents Dr. and Mrs. W. L. Wood, Portland, Oregon* (Portland, OR: Louis H. Strickland, 1919), 74; "Lieutenant Wood Killed in Action in Marne Battle," *Oregon Daily Journal* (Portland), August 5, 1918, 1.

51. *Letters of Lambert A. Wood,* foreword.

52. Franek, "Fighting Companies of the Fighting Ninth."

53. Taylor diary, 264.

54. Taylor diary, 264.

55. "Tells of Yanks Crossing Marne," 6.

56. "Tells of Yanks Crossing Marne," 6.

57. "Tells of Yanks Crossing Marne," 6.

58. "Tells of Yanks Crossing Marne," 6.

59. Edmund C. Waddill, Alumni File, Virginia Military Institute Archives, Lexington, VA.

12. *July 18, 1918—Morning Assault*

1. Elliot D. Cooke, "We Attack," *Infantry Journal,* November–December 1937, 448.

2. Cooke, "We Attack," 489.

3. Cooke, "We Attack," 489.

4. Cooke, "We Attack," 489.

5. Cooke, "We Attack," 489.

6. Cooke, "We Attack," 489.

7. Lester D. Wass, Biographical Files, Reference Branch, Marine Corps History Division, Marine Corps University, Quantico, VA.

8. "Capt Lester S. Wass of Marine Corps Killed," *Boston Globe,* August 20, 1918, 2; "Capt Lester S. Wass Killed in France," *Boston Globe,* August 21, 1918, 6.

9. "Maj Murray Takes Charge of Local Marine Corps Recruiting Office," *Boston Globe,* August 19, 1919, 14; "Jimmy—The Anteater," *Recruiters' Bulletin* 3, 12 (October 1917): 13.

10. Cooke, "We Attack," 490.

11. Nathan P. Sanders, citation, Distinguished Service Cross, General Orders 117, War Department, 1918, in Office of the Adjutant General of the Army, *American Decorations (1862–1926)* (Washington, DC: Government Printing Office, 1927), 541.

12. Report of Company L, 9th Infantry, operations Chateau-Thierry, May 31–July 18, 1918, in Clyburn Otto Mattfeldt, comp., *Records of the Second Division (Regular),* 10 vols. (Washington, DC: US Army War College Historical Section, 1924–1928), vol. 7.

13. Leroy P. Hunt, "Statement Concerning the Capture of the Town of Chaudon, 2 July 1919," in *Records of the Second Division,* vol. 7.

14. "Some Washington Men Who Fought at Chateau Thierry," *Washington Herald,* October 27, 1918, 10.

15. Arthur R. Knott to American Battle Monuments Commission, July 26, 1924, Correspondence with Former Division Officers, RG 117, American Battle Monuments Commission, NARA II.

16. Roy F. Johnson to American Battle Monuments Commission, December 3, 1928, Correspondence with Former Division Officers; George A. Davis to American Battle Monuments Commission, December 3, 1928, ibid.

17. Company K, 23rd Infantry, report of operations, July 18, 19, 22, 1918, in *Records of the Second Division,* vol. 7.

18. Johnson to American Battle Monuments Commission, December 3, 1928; Alvin Colburn, letter, December 1928, Correspondence with Former Division Officers.

19. Elton E. Mackin, oral history interview by Carl D. Klopfenstein, June 29, 1973, Rutherford B. Hayes Museum and Library, Fremont, OH.

20. Cooke, "We Attack," 28.

21. Theodore Roosevelt and John W. Thomason Jr., "Heroes of the Service," *News Tribune* (Waco, TX), September 4, 1927, 23.

22. Mackin, oral history interview.

23. Cooke, "We Attack," 28.

24. Cooke, "We Attack," 28.

25. Cooke, "We Attack," 28.

26. Cooke, "We Attack," 28.

27. Major Ralph S. Keyser, report of attack, July 1918, in *Records of the Second Division,* vol. 7.

28. Cooke, "We Attack," 28; Sergeant Carl McCune diary, 55th Company, entry for July 18, 1918, in Oliver Lyman Spaulding and John Womack Wright, *The Second Division, American Expeditionary Force in France, 1917–1919* (1937; reprint, Nashville, TN: Battery Press, 1989), 261–262.

29. Cooke, "We Attack," 28.

30. Taylor diary, in Spaulding and Wright, *Second Division,* 266.

31. "War Veteran, 20, Cited," *Baltimore Sun,* March 7, 1919, 8.

32. "War Veteran, 20, Cited."

33. "War Veteran, 20, Cited."

34. Stuart S. Janney and Karl Singewald, *Maryland in the World War, 1917–1919: Military and Naval Service Records,* 2 vols. (Baltimore: Maryland War Records Commission, 1933), 2:1969–1970.

35. Ladislav T. Janda to "Folks," December 18, 1918, World War I Veterans Survey, US Army Heritage and Education Center, Carlisle, PA.

36. Report of Company L, 9th Infantry, operations Chateau-Thierry, May 31–July 18, 1918.

37. Taylor diary, 266.

38. Cooke, "We Attack," 33.

39. Elton E. Mackin, *Suddenly We Didn't Want to Die: Memoirs of a World War I Marine* (Novato, CA: Presidio Press, 1996), 102.

40. Mackin, *Suddenly We Didn't Want to Die,* 104.

41. Report of Battery C, 17th Field Artillery, n.d., 17th Field Artillery reports of operations, Chateau-Thierry and Soissons, June–July 1918, Records of the 2nd Division, Records of Combat Divisions, RG 120, Records of the AEF, NARA II.

42. Report of operations, July 16–21 inclusive, 1918, 2nd Engineer Battalion, World War I, Organization Records, 2nd Engineers, July 25, 1918, box 1152, RG 391, Records of U.S. Regular Army Mobile Units, NARA.

43. Brief report of the 5th Machine Gun Battalion in the Chateau-Thierry sector, May 31–August 2, 1918, Records of the 2nd Division.

44. Field Orders 23, French XX Army Corps, 11:00 a.m., July 18, 1918, in United Stated Army Center for Military History, *U.S. Army in the World War, 1917– 1919,* 17 vols. (1948; reprint, Washington, DC: United States Army Center for Military History, 1988–1992), 5:296.

45. Report of operations, 3rd Brigade, July 15–21, 1918, in *Records of the Second Division,* vol. 6.

46. Pell W. Foster, *A Short History of Battery "B," 12th Field Artillery, Second Division in the World War* (New York: Evening Post Printing Office, 1921), 18.

47. Brigadier General Hanson E. Ely, Headquarters, 3rd Brigade, 2nd Division, first endorsement, July 27, 1918, in *Records of the Second Division,* vol. 5.

48. Report of operations, 3rd Brigade, July 15–21, 1918.

49. Upton, "Notes of a Regimental Commander," Records of the 2nd Division.

50. 1st Battalion, 5th Marines, report of operations, July 16–20, 1918, Records Relating to Marine Participation in World War I, RG 127, Records of the United States Marine Corps, NARA.

51. Memorandum from Commanding Officer, 5th Marines, to Commanding General, 3rd Brigade, July 25, 1918, Records Relating to Marine Participation in World War I.

13. *July 18, 1918—Evening Assault*

1. John H. Fay, report of operations of the 8th Machine Gun Company, July 21, 1918, Records Relating to Marine Participation in World War I, RG 127, Records of the United States Marine Corps, NARA.

2. Fay, Report of operations of the 8th Machine Gun Company.

3. Robert Yowell, statement concerning the capture of Vierzy, July 18, 1918, Records Relating to Marine Participation in World War I.

4. Report of action of the 3rd Brigade, July 15–21, 1918, and report of operations of the 3rd Brigade, July 17–21, 1918, in Clyburn Otto Mattfeldt, comp., *Records of the Second Division (Regular),* 10 vols. (Washington, DC: US Army War College Historical Section, 1924–1928), vol. 6.

5. Julius S. Turrill, report of operations of the 1st Battalion, 5th Marines, July 1918, Records Relating to Marine Participation in World War I.

6. Turrill, report of operations of the 1st Battalion; Elton E. Mackin, oral history interview by Carl D. Klopfenstein, June 29, 1973, Rutherford B. Hayes Museum and Library, Fremont, OH.

7. Mackin, oral history interview.

8. Elton E. Mackin, *Suddenly We Didn't Want to Die: Memoirs of a World War I Marine* (Novato, CA: Presidio Press, 1996), 109–110.

9. Yowell, statement concerning the capture of Vierzy.

10. Mackin, *Suddenly We Didn't Want to Die,* 111.

11. John A. Gustafson, statement concerning the capture of Vierzy, July 18, 1918, Records Relating to Marine Participation in World War I.

12. Gustafson, statement concerning the capture of Vierzy; Mackin, *Suddenly We Didn't Want to Die,* 11. The derogatory term "dog robber" refers to headquarters enlisted men but evolved to include Marine staff officers.

13. Mackin, oral history interview.

14. Muster rolls, 67th Company, July 1918, Marine Corps Muster Rolls, RG 127, Records of the United States Marine Corps, NARA.

15. Mackin, oral history interview.

16. Mackin, oral history interview.

17. Taylor diary, in Oliver Lyman Spaulding and John Womack Wright, *The Second Division, American Expeditionary Force in France, 1917–1919* (1937; reprint, Nashville, TN: Battery Press, 1989), 267.

18. Taylor diary, 267.

19. Turrill, report of operations of the 1st Battalion; K. W. Harding, statement concerning the capture of Vierzy, July 18, 1918, Records Relating to Marine Participation in World War I.

20. Mackin, oral history interview.

21. Officer casualties roster, June–July 1918, Records Relating to Marine Participation in World War I.

22. Fay, report of operations of the 8th Machine Gun Company.

23. Mackin, oral history interview.

24. Mackin, oral history interview.

25. Mackin, *Suddenly We Didn't Want to Die,* 116.

26. T. J. Curtis and L. R. Long, *History of the Sixth Machine Gun Battalion, Fourth Brigade, U.S. Marines, Second Division, and Its Participation in the Great War* (Neuwied-on-the-Rhine, Germany, 1919), 26.

27. Commanding General, 3rd Brigade, to Commanding Officer, 5th Marines, report of operations, second endorsement of memorandum, July 27, 1918, Records Relating to Marine Participation in World War I; statement of Major Ralph L. Keyser, December 1918, 5th Marines, Records of the 2nd Division, Records of Combat Divisions, RG 120, Records of the AEF, NARA II.

28. Elliot D. Cooke, "We Attack," *Infantry Journal,* January–February 1938, 43.

29. Cooke, "We Attack," 43.

30. Roy C. Hilton to American Battle Monuments Commission, n.d., Correspondence with Former Division Officers, RG 117, American Battle Monuments Commission, NARA II.

31. Hilton to American Battle Monuments Commission.

32. Keyser, report of attack, July 1918, in *Records of the Second Division,* vol. 7.

33. "Wounded in Action on the Western Front," *Evening Sun* (Baltimore), July 10, 1918, 14; "Capt. Speer Was Gassed," *Baltimore Sun*, June 20, 1918, 16.

34. Alvin Colburn to American Battle Monuments Commission, December 1924, Correspondence with Former Division Officers.

35. Colburn to American Battle Monuments Commission; Keyser statement, December 1918.

36. Harry B. Field and Henry G. James, *Over the Top with the 18th Company, 5th Marines: A History* (1919; reprint, Rodenbach, Germany: n.p., n.d.), 22.

37. "Capt. C. E. Speer Is Awarded D.S.C.," *Baltimore Sun*, April 8, 1923, 10.

38. Field and James, *Over the Top with the 18th Company*, 22.

39. "Maj Murray Takes Charge of Marine Corps Recruiting Office," *Boston Globe*, August 19, 1919, 14.

40. Operation report of Company I, 9th Infantry, in the Soissons sector, July 29, 1918, and operation report of Company L, 9th Infantry, in Chateau-Thierry, May 31–July 18, 1918, in *Records of the Second Division*, vol. 7. The identification of Sergeant Snyder is based on transport rolls. Further research is necessary for definitive identification.

41. Commanding General, 3rd Brigade, to Commanding Officer, 5th Marines, report of operations, July 27, 1918.

42. Memorandum from Logan Feland, July 25, 1918, Records Relating to Marine Participation in World War I.

43. Cooke, "We Attack," 44.

44. Cooke, "We Attack," 44.

45. Cooke, "We Attack," 45.

46. Cooke, "We Attack," 45.

47. Cooke, "We Attack," 46.

48. Mike Chapman, *Triumph and Tragedy: The Inspiring Stories of Iowa Football Legends, Fred Becker, Jack Trice, Nile Kinnick, and Johnny Bright* (Newton, IA: Culture House Books, 2010), 16.

49. Cooke, "We Attack," 45; Captain DeWitt Peck, 18th Company, report of officer casualties, June–July 1918, Records of the 5th Marine Regiment, Records Relating to Marine Participation in World War I.

50. Lieut. Fred Becker Is Recovering from Wounds in Battle," *Waterloo (IA) Courier*, July 21, 1918, 4.

51. "Lieut. Becker Calm in Face of Death, Writes His Captain," *Waterloo (IA) Courier*, March 6, 1919, 14.

52. "Grave of Famous Iowa Athlete Found in France," *Davenport (IA) Quad-City Times*, August 4, 1919, 2.

53. "Eight Iowans among Killed and Wounded," *Marshalltown (IA) Evening Times-Republican*, August 8, 1918, 1; "Chateau Thierry Hero's Body Is Here for Funeral," *Waterloo (IA) Courier*, May 13, 1921, 8.

54. Cooke, "We Attack," 46.

55. Cooke, "We Attack," 47.

56. Keyser, report of attack, July 1918.

57. Field message from Commanding Officer, 2nd Battalion, to Commanding Officer, 5th Marines, 10:00 p.m., July 18, 1918, in *Records of the Second Division,* vol. 5.

58. Report of operations, 2nd Regiment of Engineers, July 25, 1918, Records of the 2nd Division.

59. Report of operations, 5th Machine Gun Battalion, July 21, 1918, Records of the 2nd Division.

60. Curtis and Long, *History of the Sixth Machine Gun Battalion,* 26–27.

61. Curtis and Long, *History of the Sixth Machine Gun Battalion,* 26–27.

62. Upton, "Notes of a Regimental Commander," Records of the 2nd Division.

63. McCune diary, entry for July 18, 1918, in Spaulding and Wright, *Second Division,* 262.

64. Instructions for 10th and 6th Armies, July 18, 1918, French Group of Armies of the Reserve, in United States Army Center for Military History, *U.S. Army in the World War, 1917–1919,* 17 vols. (1948; reprint, Washington, DC: United States Army Center for Military History, 1988–1992), 5:249–250.

65. Plan of attack, Order 201-32.7, C.P. French XX Corps, July 18, 1918, in *U.S. Army in the World War,* 5:280–281, 299; 10th Army, journal of operations, situation on the morning of July 18 through 8:00 p.m., in *Records of the Second Division,* vol. 6.

66. James G. Harbord, *Leaves from a War Diary* (New York: Dodd, Mead, 1931), 327.

67. Harbord, *Leaves from a War Diary,* 327.

68. Pell W. Foster, *A Short History of Battery "B," 12th Field Artillery, Second Division in the World War* (New York: Evening Post Printing Office, 1921), 18.

69. French 10th Army, Order 301, 8:00 p.m., July 18, 1918, in *U.S. Army in the World War,* 5:280–281; 2nd Division, journal of operations, July 19, 1918, in *Records of the Second Division,* vol. 6.

70. "A Brief History of the 6th Regiment, USMC," circa 1919, Records Relating to Marine Participation in World War I.

71. Report from Commanding General, 2nd Division, to Commanding General, XX Army Corps, July 19, 1918, *Records of the Second Division,* vol. 6.

72. William A. Mitchell, *The Official History of the Second Engineer Regiment and Second Engineer Train in the World War* (San Antonio, TX: San Antonio Printing Company, 1920), 34.

73. Report from Commanding General, 2nd Division, to Commanding General, XX Army Corps, July 19, 1918, in *U.S. Army in the World War,* 5:336.

74. Taylor diary, 267.

75. Headquarters, 2nd Division, Field Order 16, 3:00 a.m., July 19, 1918, Records of the 2nd Division.

76. Battery C, 17th Field Artillery, report of operations, n.d., Chateau-Thierry and Soissons, June–July 1918, Records of the 2nd Division.

77. Battery C, 17th Field Artillery, report of operations.

78. Report, advance of the 2nd Battalion, 6th Marines, July 19, 1918, in *Records of the Second Division,* vol. 6.

79. Company L, 9th Infantry, operation report, Chateau-Thierry, May 31–July 18, 1918, in *Records of the Second Division*, vol. 7.

80. Report of operations, 2nd Division, July 17–21, 1918, in *Records of the Second Division*, vol. 6.

Soissons Tour: Stops 23 and 24

1. Harry R. Stringer, ed., *The Navy Book of Distinguished Service: An Official Compendium of the Names and Citations of the Men of the United States Navy, Marine Corps, Army, and Foreign Governments Who Were Decorated by the Navy Department, for Extraordinary Service above and beyond the Call of Duty in the World War* (Washington, DC: Fassett, 1921), 165.

2. "Big 159-Pound Shell Misses Maj. Harry Lay," *Evening Star* (Washington, DC), July 27, 1918, 2.

14. *July 19, 1918—Attack of the 6th Marines*

1. McCune diary, entry for July 18, 1918, in Oliver Lyman Spaulding and John Womack Wright, *The Second Division, American Expeditionary Force in France, 1917–1919* (1937; reprint, Nashville, TN: Battery Press, 1989), 262.

2. William A. Worton, Oral History Transcript, 46, Marine Corps Oral History Program, Marine Corps History Division, Marine Corps University, Quantico, VA.

3. Field message from Commanding Officer, 6th Regiment, to Commanding Officer, 4th Brigade, 6:40 a.m., July 19, 1918, in Clyburn Otto Mattfeldt, comp., *Records of the Second Division (Regular),* 10 vols. (Washington, DC: US Army War College Historical Section, 1924–1928), vol. 5.

4. War diary, 14th Reserve Division, July 19, 1918, in Gustav J. Braun and Trevor W. Swett, comps., *Translations: War Diaries of German Units Opposed to the Second Division (Regular) 1918,* 5 vols. (Washington, DC: Second Division Historical Section, Army War College, 1930–1932), vol. 5.

5. Map, Redistribution of the Artillery on 18 July 1918, Situation on the Evening of 18 July, Reemployment during the Night of 18 July, in *War Diaries of German Units*, vol. 5; General Staff, War Office, Great Britain, *The German Army Handbook of 1918* (Yorkshire, UK: Front Line Books, 2008), 67–69.

6. James E. Hatcher, memoir, James E. Hatcher Papers, Marine Corps Archives, Marine Corps History Division, Marine Corps University, Quantico, VA; Joseph C. Grayson, "A Record of the Operations of the 2nd Battalion, Sixth Regiment, Marines," Records Relating to Marine Participation in World War I, RG 127, Records of the United States Marine Corps, NARA.

7. Grayson, "Record of Operations of the 2nd Battalion, Sixth Regiment."

8. Mrs. Dennee Perkinson to James R. Anderson, September 29, 1918, Allan C. Perkinson, Alumni File, Virginia Military Institute Archives, Lexington, VA.

9. Grayson, "Record of Operations of the 2nd Battalion, Sixth Regiment";

war journal, 501st Tank Regiment, Memoire des Hommes, Ministere des Armees, Republique Francais.

10. Robert L. Denig diary, entry for July 19, 1918, Robert L. Denig Papers, Marine Corps Archives.

11. Field message from Commanding Officer, 6th Regiment, to Commanding Officer, 4th Brigade, 8:45 a.m., July 19, 1918, in *Records of the Second Division*, vol. 5.

12. Memorandum from Lieutenant Colonel J. R. Davis to 15th Field Artillery, July 19, 1918, in *Records of the Second Division*, vol. 5.

13. Harry Lee to Major X. A. Price, January 13, 1927, Correspondence with Former Division Officers, RG 117, American Battle Monuments Commission, NARA II.

14. "A Brief History of the 6th Regiment," circa 1919, RG 127, Records of the United States Marine Corps, NARA.

15. Field message from Commanding Officer, 6th Regiment, to Commanding Officer, 2nd Division, 9:50 a.m., July 19, 1918, in *Records of the Second Division*, vol. 5.

16. Carl W. Smith and William J. Mosher, "History of the Seventy Fourth Company," 7, Records Relating to Marine Participation in World War I.

17. War diary, 1st Battalion, 110th Grenadiers, July 19, 1918, in *War Diaries of German Units,* vol. 5.

18. Memorandum from Company Commander, 76th Company, to Commanding Officer, 1st Battalion, 6th Marines, recommendations for Medals of Honor and Distinguished Service Cross, July 23, 1918, original in possession of Emmett Fox, Dallas, TX.

19. Frederic C. Wheeler to American Battle Monuments Commission, December 21, 1918, Correspondence with Former Division Officers. The tank is sometimes identified as German, but no German tank units participated in the July 19 action. The tanks were identified with French markings and were abandoned by French tankers early in the 1st Battalion's attack or in the sector of the French 38th Division. George B. Clark, ed., *A List of Officers of the 4th Marine Brigade* (Pike, NH: Brass Hat, n.d.), 25, 28; Harry R. Stringer, ed., *Heroes All! A Compendium of the Names and Official Citations of the Soldiers and Citizens of the United States and of Her Allies Who Were Decorated by the American Government for Exceptional Heroism and Conspicuous Service above and beyond the Call of Duty in the War with Germany, 1917–1919* (Washington, DC: Fassett, 1919), 142, 212.

20. Smith and Mosher, "History of the Seventy Fourth Company," 7.

21. Smith and Mosher, "History of the Seventy Fourth Company," 7.

22. Ralph L. Williams, 2nd Engineer Regiment, 2nd Division, World War I Veterans Survey, US Army Heritage and Education Center, Carlisle, PA.

23. Ralph L. Williams, *The Luck of a Buck* (Madison, WI: Fitchburg Press, 1985), 141–142; field message from Commanding Officer, 2nd Engineers, to Chief of Staff, 2nd Division Headquarters, July 19, 1918, in *Records of the Second Division*, vol. 4.

24. Worton, Oral History Transcript, 42.

25. George H. Donaldson and Willoughby Jenkins, *Seventy-Eighth Company of*

Marines, Sixth Marines, Second Division, Army of Occupation (Neuwied, Germany: n.p., 1919), 4.

26. Muster rolls, 78th Company, July 1918, Marine Corps Muster Rolls, RG 127, Records of the United States Marine Corps, NARA.

27. "Carleton Wallace Returns from the War," *Star Tribune* (Minneapolis, MN), December 20, 1918, 10.

28. Peter F Owen, ed., *The World War Memoirs of Don V. Paradis, Gunnery Sergeant, USMC* (Morrisville, NC: Lulu.com, 2010), 73.

29. Clifton B. Cates, description of the attack of the 2nd Battalion, 6th Marines, July 19,1918, Correspondence with Former Division Officers; Carl Brannen, memoir, 19, Carl Brannen Papers, Marine Corps Archives.

30. George H. Seldes, "Between Battles with Our Fighting Men in France," *Atlanta Constitution*, October 6, 1918, 4.

31. Clifton B. Cates to Mother and Sister, August 1, 1918, Clifton B. Cates Papers, Marine Corps Archives.

32. Denig diary, July 19, 1918.

33. Cates to Mother and Sister, August 1, 1918; field message from 2nd Battalion, 110th Regiment, to Headquarters, 110th Regiment, 1:00 a.m., July 19, 1918, in *War Diaries of German Units,* vol. 5.

34. Seldes, "Between Battles with Our Fighting Men," 4.

35. War diary, 14th Reserve Division, July 19, 1918; combat report, 102nd Artillery Commander, July 18–19, 1918, in *War Diaries of German Units,* vol. 5.

36. War diary, 14th Reserve Division, July 19, 1918.

37. Division order, 14th Reserve Division, 2:25 p.m., July 19, 1918, in *War Diaries of German Units,* vol. 5.

38. Robert L. Denig to American Battle Monuments Commission, July 10, 1930, Correspondence with Former Division Officers; war diary, 7th Army, July 19, 1918; XIII Corps order, 11:15 a.m., July 19, 1918, and Corps Watter, combat report, July 19, 1918, in *War Diaries of German Units,* vol. 5.

39. War diary, 94th Reserve Brigade, July 19, 1918, in *War Diaries of German Units,* vol. 5.

40. Lucian H. Van Dorn, "A Brief History of the 2nd Battalion, 6th Regiment, U.S. Marine Corps over the Period of July 13–25, 1918," Records of the 2nd Division, Records of Combat Divisions, RG 120, Records of the AEF, NARA II.

41. History of the 96th Company, 6th Marine Regiment in World War I, 1967, Records Relating to Marine Participation in World War I.

42. Denig diary, July 19, 1918; war diary, 14th Reserve Division, July 19, 1918; report by the Commanding General, 14th Reserve Division, covering the events during the French attack of July 18, 1918, in *War Diaries of German Units,* vol. 5.

43. Denig diary, July 19, 1918.

44. History of the 80th Company, 2nd Battalion, 6th Marines, Records Relating to Marine Participation in World War I.

45. Frank Hodson diary, F Battery, 15th Field Artillery, entry for July 19, 1918, in Spaulding and Wright, *Second Division,* 260.

46. Amos N. Wilder, *Armageddon Revisited* (New Haven, CT: Yale University Press, 1994), 123.

47. Hatcher memoir.

48. Hatcher memoir.

49. Field message from Major Sibley to Captain Noble, 10:10 a.m., July 19, 1918, and field message from Major Sibley to Captain Karstaedt, 10:10 a.m., July 19, 1918, in David E. Bellamy, "Military History of 3rd Battalion, 6th Marines, Marine Corps, A.E.F., June 1 to August 10, 1918," entries for July 16–25, 1918, Records of the 2nd Division.

50. Field messages from Sibley to Noble and Karstaedt, July 19, 1918.

51. Pell W. Foster, *A Short History of Battery "B," 12th Field Artillery, Second Division in the World War* (New York: Evening Post Printing Office, 1921), 19.

52. John C. Proctor, Edwin M. Williams, and Frank P. Black, eds., *Washington—Past and Present: A History,* vol. 5 (New York: Lewis Historical Publishing, 1930–1932), 888.

53. Hatcher memoir.

54. Hatcher memoir.

55. Hatcher memoir; Jane Blakeney, *Heroes: U.S. Marine Corps, 1861–1955; Armed Forces Awards, Flags* (Washington, DC: Guthrie Lithograph, 1957), 151.

56. Hatcher memoir.

57. Hatcher memoir.

58. Muster rolls, 84th Company, June 1917–July 1918, Marine Corps Muster Rolls.

59. Muster rolls, 84th Company, June 1917–July 1918; Hatcher memoir; Ansel Jay Van Housen, Census of 1910. The 1910 census recorded Van Housen's occupation and is the last verifiable indicator of his work experience.

60. Hatcher memoir.

61. Hatcher memoir.

62. Report of Major Sibley, in Bellamy, "Military History of 3rd Battalion, 6th Marines."

63. Report of Sibley; field message from Major Sibley to Lieutenant Colonel Lee, circa 11:00 a.m., July 19, 1918, in *Records of the Second Division,* vol. 4.

64. War diary, 1st Battalion, 110th Grenadiers, July 19, 1918, in *War Diaries of German Units,* vol. 5.

65. War diary, 94th Reserve Brigade, July 19, 1918; war journal, 38th Division, July 19, 1918, in *War Diaries of German Units,* vol. 5.

66. Field message from Captain Stacey Knopf, 1st Battalion, 12th Field Artillery, to General Bowley, 12:30 p.m., July 19, 1918; field message from Commanding Officer, 12th Field Artillery, to Commanding Officer, 2nd Division, 12:30 p.m., July 19, 1918; field message from Artillery Commander, 2nd Field Artillery Brigade, to Commanding Officer, 2nd Division, 12:50 p.m., July 19, 1918, all in *Records of the Second Division,* vol. 5.

67. Williams, *Luck of a Buck,* 142.

68. Mrs. Maud B. Denig to Mrs. Mary R. J. Sumner, November 24, 1918, Allen Sumner, Alumni Files, Harvard University Archives, Pusey Library, Cambridge, MA.

69. "If Either of Us Should Fall, Write Mother," *Ogden (UT) Standard*, November 29, 1918, 9.

70. Williams, *Luck of a Buck*, 142.

71. Howard Fletcher Davidson diary, entry for July 19, 1918, Delaware County, NY, Genealogy and History Site.

72. Synopsis of the attack on Tigny by the 74th Company, 1st Battalion, 6th Regiment, USMC, Records Relating to Marine Participation in World War I.

73. Joseph R. Anderson, *Virginia Military Institute, World War Record* (Richmond, VA: Richmond Press, 1920), 319.

74. Robert W. Voeth, Service Record Book, Official Military Personnel Files, National Personnel Records Center, St. Louis, MO.

75. Voeth, Service Record Book.

76. Havelock D. Nelson, "In Action, Another True Tale of the 97th Company in Action," *Leatherneck Magazine* 23, 6 (June 1940): 13.

77. Nelson, "In Action," 13.

78. Archie Lake, 97th Company, 6th Marines, July 1918, Marine Corps Muster Rolls; "Seeks Trace of Wounded Hero, Lost 20 Months," *Chicago Tribune*, May 1, 1920, 17.

79. Nelson, "In Action," 15.

80. Frank Collier, 97th Company, 6th Marines, July 1918, Marine Corps Muster Rolls. Collier is buried in Oak Ridge Cemetery, Springfield, IL. Affidavits of service were compiled by members of the 97th Company, 6th Regiment, 3rd Battalion, 6th Marines, for Private George L. Langell, sent to his mother, Emma B. McCombs; Private Guy D. Hoxie, sent to his mother and father, Joseph B. Hoxie; Private Frank L. Colwell, sent to his father and mother, Cora Colwell. Lists and Casualties, 1919, Records Relating to Marine Participation in World War I. Langell is buried at the Oise Marne American Cemetery in France. Hoxie and Colwell were returned home in 1921; both were buried in their hometown cemeteries with markers in their honor.

81. Kemper Frey Cowing, comp., *"Dear Folks at Home—": The Glorious Story of the United States Marines in France as Told by Their Letters from the Battlefield*, ed. Courtney R. Cooper (Boston: Houghton Mifflin, 1919), 263.

82. Affidavit of service for Private Kerlin L. Lehman, compiled by members of the 97th Company, 6th Regiment, and sent to his mother, Ida M. Lehman. Lists and Casualties, 1919, Records Relating to Marine Participation in World War I.

83. "If Either of Us Should Fall, Write Mother," 9.

84. "Saw Hanbery in a Base Hospital," *Sun* (Pittsburg, KS), August 27, 1918, 1.

85. "Saw Hanbery in a Base Hospital," 1.

86. Field message from Lieutenant Colonel Lee to Major Sibley, 12:15 p.m., July 19, 1918, in *Records of the Second Division*, vol. 4; Bellamy, "Military History of 3rd Battalion, 6th Marines."

87. Field message from Major Sibley to Lieutenant Colonel Lee, circa 12:45 p.m., July 19, 1918, in *Records of the Second Division*, vol. 4.

88. Nelson, "In Action," 15.

89. Smith and Mosher, "History of the Seventy Fourth Company."

90. Corps Watter, ammunition situation of Corps Watter during the engagements of July 18–24 and July 26, 1918, in *War Diaries of German Units,* vol. 5.

91. Field Message 10 from Commanding Officer, 6th Regiment, to Commanding Officers 1st, 2nd, 3rd Battalion Headquarters Company, 2nd Engineers, July 19, 1918, in *Records of the Second Division*, vol. 5.

92. War journal, 58th Infantry Division, July 19, 1918, in *War Diaries of German Units,* vol. 5; Denig to American Battle Monuments Commission, July 10, 1918.

93. Field message from Major Sibley to Lieutenant Colonel Lee, 6:00 p.m., July 19, 1918, in *Records of the Second Division*, vol. 5; Bellamy, "Military History of 3rd Battalion, 6th Marines."

94. "Brief History of the 6th Regiment."

95. Hatcher memoir.

96. Smith and Mosher, "History of the Seventy Fourth Company."

97. Smith and Mosher, "History of the Seventy Fourth Company."

98. "Brief History of the 6th Regiment."

99. Taylor diary, in Spaulding and Wright, *Second Division*, 268.

100. Denig diary, July 19, 1918; Smith and Mosher, "History of the Seventy Fourth Company."

101. Commanding Officer, 3rd Battalion, to Commanding Officer, 6th Regiment, recommendation for award of the Medal of Honor to John C. Balch, July 22, 1918, Office of the Commandant, General Correspondence, RG 127, Records of the United States Marine Corps, NARA.

102. McCune diary, July 18, 1918, 262.

103. Thomas Quigley to American Battle Monuments Commission, November 19, 1926, Correspondence with Former Division Officers.

104. Brief report of the 5th Machine Gun Battalion in the Chateau-Thierry sector, May 31–August 2, 1918, Records of the 2nd Division.

105. Spaulding and Wright, *Second Division*, 132; "War Diary of the Second Division, 17, 18, 19 July 1918," in *Records of the Second Division*, vol. 5.

106. "Report, 19 July 1918, Commanding General 2nd Division to Commanding General 20th Army Corps," in *Records of the Second Division*, vol. 5.

107. "Report, 19 July 1918, Commanding General 2nd Division to Commanding General 20th Army Corps."

108. War diary, Army Group German Crown Prince, July 18, 1918, in *War Diaries of German Units,* vol. 5.

109. Army Order Ia 1049, Source D, 1:30 p.m., July 19, 1918; Corps Order 19, HQ XIII, section Ia, no. 239, noon, July 19, 1918; Corps Order to 14th Reserve Division and 20th Division, 3:55 p.m., July 19, 1918, all in *War Diaries of German Units,* vol. 5.

110. McCune diary, July 18, 1918, 262.

111. Seldes, "Between Battles with Our Fighting Men," 4.

112. Smith and Mosher, "History of the Seventy Fourth Company."

113. "Brief History of the 6th Regiment."

114. Grayson, "Record of Operations of the 2nd Battalion, Sixth Regiment."

115. James G. Harbord, *Leaves from a War Diary* (New York: Dodd, Mead, 1931), 329–330.

Soissons Tour: Stops 25–32

1. "Sergeant Stover's Body to Be Brought Home," *Lebanon (PA) Daily News,* August 9, 1918, 1; "The Washington Cornet Band," *Evening Report* (Lebanon, PA), May 27, 1921, 10; "Philadelphia Homes Hit by War Loss, Guard Units Suffer Most," *Philadelphia Inquirer,* August 10, 1918, 2.

2. William Michael Barnett, World War I Veterans' Service Data and Photographs, series A0412, New York State Education Department, Division of Archives and History, New York State Archives, Albany; muster rolls, 84th Company, 6th Marines, June–July 1918, Marine Corps Muster Rolls, RG 127, Records of the United States Marine Corps, NARA; listing for William M. Barnett, Aisne Marne Cemetery, American Battle Monuments Commission.

3. "Funeral Services for Corporal John Ring," *Western Sentinel* (Winston-Salem, NC), May 17, 1921, 1.

4. "Letter Received from Comrade of John Ring," *Twin City Sentinel* (Winston-Salem, NC), August 17, 1918, 8.

5. S. G. Ring to Graves Registration Service, Paris, France, December 9, 1919, John T. Ring, World War I Burial Files, RG 92, National Personnel Records Center, St. Louis, MO; "Kernersville," *Winston-Salem (NC) Journal,* August 15, 1918, 10.

6. "Funeral Services for Corporal John Ring."

7. Captain A. D. Hughes to Mrs. Johanna Hinds, March 5, 1932, Frederick C. Hinds, World War I Burial Files.

15. *Aftermath*

1. Dennis Showalter, *Instrument of War: The German Army 1914–18* (London: Osprey Publishing, 2016), 378.

2. Showalter, *Instrument of War,* 383.

3. Showalter, *Instrument of War,* 386.

4. T. Bentley Mott, trans., *The Memoirs of Marshal Foch* (London: William Heinemann, 1931), 455.

5. Shepherd to mother, June 9, 1918, RG 66, Virginia War History Commission 1915–1931, Library of Virginia, Richmond.

6. Public Act 182, July 1, 1918, in *Hearings before the Committee on Naval Affairs of the House of Representatives on Estimates Submitted by the Secretary of the Navy, 65th Congress* (Washington, DC: Government Printing Office, 1918).

7. Edwin N. McClellan, *The United States Marine Corps in the World War* (Washington, DC: Government Printing Office, 1920), 42.

8. "Huns in France Face Noted American Generals," *Washington Post,* June 11, 1918, 1.

9. "French Generals Proud of Our Men," *New York Times,* July 5, 1918, 3.

10. Oliver Lyman Spaulding and John Womack Wright, *The Second Division, American Expeditionary Force in France, 1917–1919* (1937; reprint, Nashville, TN: Battery Press, 1989), 78.

11. "Americans Stop Raid," *New York Times,* July 12, 1918, 3.

12. "Allies Praise Battle Worth of Americans," *Detroit Free Press,* July 11, 1918, 9.

13. Franklin D. Roosevelt, personal journal, 1918, 21, Franklin D. Roosevelt Papers, Franklin D. Roosevelt Presidential Library, Hyde Park, NY.

14. Typescript of interview, Franklin D. Roosevelt, Inspections and Reports, Records Relating to Marine Participation in World War I, RG 127, Records of the United States Marine Corps, NARA.

15. Memorandum, August 10, 1918, George Barnett Papers, Marine Corps Archives, Marine Corps History Division, Marine Corps University, Quantico, VA.

16. Franklin D. Roosevelt to Josephus Daniels, August 13, 1918, Roosevelt Presidential Library.

17. Appendix C, "The Assistant Secretary's Tour of Inspection of U.S. Naval Activities in Europe, United States Navy," in *Annual Report of the Secretary of the Navy for the Fiscal Year 1918* (Washington, DC: Government Printing Office, 1919).

18. "The American Brigade of Marines at Bois de Belleau," *L'Illustration,* August 31, 1918, Harbord Papers.

19. "New Stories of the American Soldiers Abroad," *Tuscaloosa (AL) News,* September 15, 1918, 7.

20. "Marines Calmly Shaved after Belleau Battle," *New York Tribune,* August 11, 1918, 3.

21. "Promotion from the Ranks," undated newspaper article, Harbord Papers.

22. "Newman the Gadder, at Orchestra Hall on Paris, 1918," *Chicago Tribune,* October 10, 1918, 15.

23. McClellan, *Unites States Marine Corps in World War I,* 65. Official Marine casualty totals vary, depending on the source. The numbers used here are low compared with other figures.

24. James G. Harbord, *Leaves from a War Diary* (New York: Dodd, Mead, 1931), 342.

25. Harbord to General McCoy, September 25, 1918, Harbord Papers.

26. Omar Bundy to George Barnett, September 15, 1918, Barnett Papers.

27. Edwin N. McClellan diary, entry for November 14, 1918, Edwin N. McClellan Papers, Marine Corps Archives.

28. "Stories of the War that Didn't Happen, Even the Marines Themselves Admit They Received an Oversupply of Credit," *New York Times,* May 25, 1919, 3.

29. Memorandum from Paul B. Malone to James G. Harbord, June 13, 1919, entry 6, Records of the 2nd Division, Records of Combat Divisions, RG 120, Records of the AEF, NARA II.

30. "Relics Strew Marines' Woods," *Washington Post,* August 25, 1919, 16.

31. Allan Updegraff to Major General Commandant, April 24, 1919, Records Relating to Marine Participation in World War I.

32. "Marines at Belleau Wood," undated statement, Barnett Papers; "5,199

Marines Lost in Belleau Wood Area; General Barnett Discloses Casualties of the Brigade in the Action North of Chateau Thierry," *New York Times,* April 23, 1919, 3.

33. George Barnett to James G. Harbord, April 24, 1919, Records Relating to Marine Participation in World War I.

34. Lemuel C. Shepherd, Oral History Transcript, 19–20, Marine Corps Oral History Program, Marine Corps History Division, Marine Corps University, Quantico, VA.

35. Shepherd, Oral History Transcript, 20.

36. Shepherd, Oral History Transcript, 24.

37. Shepherd, Oral History Transcript, 22.

38. Memorandum, April 29, 1920, Marine Corps Infantry School, Quantico, VA, and memorandum from Charles D. Barrett to Major General Commandant, April 23, 1920, Office of the Commandant, General Correspondence, RG 127, Records of the United States Marine Corps, NARA.

39. Charles D. Barrett to Edwin N. McClellan, December 15, 1920, McClellan Papers; memorandum from Commanding Officer, France Map Detachment, to Commanding Officer, Topographical Department, Marine Corps School, Quantico, VA, December 16, 1920, Office of the Commandant, General Correspondence.

40. John A. Lejeune to Superintendent, Memorial Hall, Philadelphia, June 22, 1922, Office of the Commandant, General Correspondence.

41. L. A. Haslup to Recruiting Section, Headquarters, U.S. Marine Corps, June 7, 1922, Office of the Commandant, General Correspondence; Shepherd, Oral History Transcript, 22.

42. Edwin N. McClellan, "A Brief History of the Fourth Brigade of Marines," *Marine Corps Gazette* 5, 4 (December 1919): 342.

43. McClellan, "Brief History of the Fourth Brigade," 342.

44. McClellan, "Brief History of the Fourth Brigade," 342.

45. Harbord to Doubleday, Page and Company, May 8, 1919, Harbord Papers.

46. James G. Harbord to Edwin N. McClellan, April 8, 1920, McClellan Papers.

47. "Paris War Orphans Parade and Cheer," *New York Times,* July 4, 1920, 13.

48. "Portrait of General Harbord to Be Painted," *Leatherneck Magazine* 5, 51 (October 21, 1922): 1; "Many Travelers Visit Belleau Wood," *Leatherneck Magazine* 12 (October 7, 1922): 4.

49. George Richards, "Don't Give up the Ship," *Marine Corps Gazette* 7, 1 (March 1922): 62.

50. J. W. Hughes to Smedley D. Butler, March 12, 1923, Smedley D. Butler Papers, Marine Corps Archives.

51. "Quantico Entertains 3,000 Shriners on Belleau Wood Day," *Leatherneck Magazine* 6, 23 (June 9, 1923): 2.

52. "Belleau Wood Day Celebrated Widely," *Leatherneck Magazine* 6, 23 (June 9, 1923): 4; "Writes New March Called Belleau Wood," *Leatherneck Magazine* 6, 18 (May 5, 1923): 1.

53. "General Gouraud Reviews Marines," *Leatherneck Magazine* 6, 28 (July 14, 1923): 1.

54. General J. H. Gouraud to Smedley Butler, July 10, 1923, Butler Papers.

55. "Belleau Wood," *Leatherneck Magazine* 6, 23 (June 9, 1923): 8.

56. "Belleau Wood, Retreat Hell, We Just Got Here," *Marine Corps Gazette* 29, 1 (January 1945): 27.

57. John A. Lejeune to Thomas J. Dickson, December 27, 1926, Office of the Commandant, General Correspondence.

58. Frank X. Lambert, "The Marine Corps League News," *Leatherneck*, November 1930, 25.

59. Lambert, "Marine Corps League News," 25.

60. Shepherd, Oral History Transcript, 12.

61. Shepherd, Oral History Transcript, 30.

16. *Final Conclusions*

1. John J. Pershing, *My Experiences in the First World War,* vol. 2 (New York: Frederick A. Stokes, 1931), 161.

2. T. Bentley Mott, trans., *The Memoirs of Marshal Foch* (London: William Heinemann, 1931), 424.

3. Erich Ludendorff, *Ludendorff's Own Story, August 1914–November 1918: The Great War from the Siege of Liège to the Signing of the Armistice as Viewed from the Grand Headquarters of the German Army* (New York: Harper, 1919), 323.

4. Michael S. Neiberg, *The Second Battle of the Marne* (Bloomington: Indiana University Press, 2008), 190.

5. Douglas V. Johnson II and Rolfe L. Hillman Jr., *Soissons, 1918* (College Station: Texas A&M Press, 1999), xv.

6. Interview with Colonel Harry Lee, December 12, 1919, Records Relating to Marine Participation in World War I, RG 127, Records of the United States Marine Corps, NARA.

7. Joseph C. Grayson, "A Record of the Operations of the 2nd Battalion, Sixth Regiment, Marines," Records Relating to Marine Participation in World War I.

8. Thomas Williams Ashley, memorial, September 1, 1918, Thomas W. Ashley, Alumni Biographical File, Amherst College Archives and Special Collections, Amherst, MA.

9. Harold D. Campbell to E. E. Campbell, June 25, 1918, published in *Waterbury Record,* July 17, 1918, Harold D. Campbell Papers, Marine Corps Archives, Marine Corps History Division, Marine Corps University, Quantico, VA.

10. Henry M. Leonard to Alice Shumway, October 27, 1918, Wallace M. Leonard, Alumni Biographical File, Amherst College Archives and Special Collections.

11. Eldon L. Freel to Mother, June 18, 1918, Eldon Freel Papers, State Historical Society of Iowa, Des Moines.

12. "Veteran Celebrates 100 Years," *Quad-City Times* (Davenport, IA), January 25, 1995, 1.

13. Levi E. Hemrick, *Once a Marine* (New York: Carlton Press, 1968), 106.

BIBLIOGRAPHY

Archival Sources

Amherst College Archives and Special Collections, Amherst, MA
    Thomas W. Ashley Alumni Biographical File.
    Wallace M. Leonard Jr. Alumni Biographical File.
Belleau Wood Detachment, Marine Corps League, Columbus, OH
    James L. Clark Papers.
Campbell University, Wiggins Memorial Library, Buies Creek, NC
    Harold D. Campbell Alumni Records.
The Citadel Archives and Museum, Charleston, SC
    Davis A. Holladay, Records of the Alumni Association.
Delaware County, NY, Genealogy and History Site
    Howard Fletcher Davidson Diary. https://www.dcnyhistory.org/diaryfletcherda vidson.html.
Franklin D. Roosevelt Presidential Library, Hyde Park, NY
    Franklin D. Roosevelt Papers.
Harvard University Archives, Pusey Library, Cambridge, MA
    Allen Sumner Alumni Files, Class of 1904.
Library of Congress, Manuscript Division, Washington, DC
    James G. Harbord Papers.
    John J. Pershing Papers.
Library of Virginia, Richmond, VA
    Record Group 66. Virginia War History Commission 1915–1931:
    Lemuel Shepherd letters.
Marine Corps History Division, Marine Corps University, Quantico, VA
    Marine Corps Archives:
        Robert Asprey Papers.
        George Barnett Papers.
        David Bellamy Papers.
        Carl Brannen Papers.
        Smedley D. Butler Papers.
        Harold D. Campbell Papers.
        Clifton B. Cates Papers.
        Gerald B. Clark Papers.
        Arthur Clifford Papers.
        Onnie J. and Janice D. Cordes Papers.
        Robert L. Denig Papers.
        Charles A. Doyen Papers.
        Charles L. Dunn Papers.

Graves B. Erskine Papers.
Logan Feland Papers.
William J. Flaherty, Newspaper Files.
Ben Fuller Papers.
James E. Hatcher Papers.
Glen G. Hill Papers.
John A. Hughes Papers.
Chester Lancaster Papers.
Victor M. Landreth Papers.
John A. Lejeune Papers.
John P. Martin Papers.
William R. Matthews Papers.
Edwin N. McClellan Papers.
Adrian J. Michels Papers.
Carl B. Mills Papers.
James Nilo Papers.
Don V. Paradis Papers.
Alfred H. Randall Papers.
Bernard A. Schwebke Papers.
George K. Shuler Papers.
L. W. T. Waller Papers.
Lloyd W. Williams Papers.
Frederic M. Wise Papers.
Marine Corps Oral History Program:
Robert W. Blake.
Graves B. Erskine.
John Groff.
Louis R. Jones.
Robert C. Kilmartin.
Roland McDonald.
Alfred H. Noble.
Don V. Paradis.
William M. Rogers.
Lemuel C. Shepherd.
Merwin H. Silverthorn.
Julian C. Smith.
Gerald C. Thomas.
William A. Worton.
Reference Branch—Belleau Wood Geographical File:
Glen G. Hill to G. M. Neufeld. Letter, December 28, 1979.
"Marine 'Devil Dog' Recalls World War I Battle in France." Undated newspaper clipping.
John L. Tunnell. "Belleau Wood."
John A. West. Letter, January 17, 1979.

Reference Branch—Biographical Files:
  Donald F. Duncan.
  John H. Fay.
  George W. Hamilton.
  Thomas Holcomb.
  John A. Hughes.
  Henry Hulbert.
  Daniel A. Hunter
  Frederick W. Karstaedt.
  Charles I. Murray.
  Julius S. Turrill.
  Lester D. Wass.
  Lloyd W. Williams.
  Roswell Winans.
  Randolph T. Zane.
Reference Branch—Microfilm:
  82nd Company, June 1918.
Memoire des Hommes, Ministere des Armees, Republique Francais (memoiredes hommes.sga.defense.gouv.fr/en/)
  1st Chasseur Battalion.
  6th Army Journal.
  12th Madagascar Battalion.
  21st Medical Corps.
  48th Infantry Regiment.
  133rd Infantry Regiment.
  152nd Infantry Regiment.
  158th Infantry Regiment.
Miami University and Western College Archives, Oxford, OH
  Walter W. Rogers. *Recensio* [yearbook], graduating class of 1914.
National Archives and Record Administration, Washington, DC
  Bureau of the Census:
  Census Records, 1900–1919. Accessed at Ancestry.com.
  1900 United States Federal Census [online database]. Provo, UT: Ancestry.com Operations, 2004. Original data: Bureau of the Census. *Twelfth Census of the United States, 1900.* Washington, DC: Government Printing Office, 1900.
Record Group 52. Records of the Bureau of Medicine and Surgery, 1812–1975:
  U.S. Navy Burial Records, 1898–1932.
Record Group 127. Records of the United States Marine Corps:
  Adjutant and Inspectors Department, Register of Deaths, World War I.
History and Museums Branch, Miscellaneous Records of the Adjutant and Inspectors Department, 1919–1932, Casualties for the Fourth Brigade, June 1 to 10 July 1918, Inclusive.
  Marine Corps Muster Rolls, 1893–1958.
  Office of the Commandant, General Correspondence, 1913–1938.

Records Relating to Marine Participation in World War I, 1916–1945.
Record Group 391. Records of U.S. Regular Army Mobile Units.
National Archives and Records Administration II, College Park, MD
Record Group 117. American Battle Monuments Commission:
Correspondence with Former Division Officers, 1st and 2nd Divisions:
Bailey M. Coffenberg.
Alvin Colburn.
Peter Conachy.
George A. Davis.
Robert L. Denig.
Roy C. Hilton.
Roy F. Johnson.
Ralph S. Keyser.
Arthur R. Knott.
Thomas Quigley.
Keller E. Rockey.
Berton W. Sibley.
Frederic C. Wheeler.
Frank Whitehead.
Record Group 120. Records of the American Expeditionary Force (World War I):
Cablegrams Exchanged between General Headquarters, American Expeditionary
Force, and the War Department, 1917–1918.
Organizational Records of the American Expeditionary Force:
6th Machine Gun Battalion.
Records of Combat Divisions, 1913–1939:
Records of the 2nd Division.
National Personnel Records Center, St. Louis, MO
Record Group 92. Records of the Office of Quartermaster General, 1774–1985,
Correspondence, Reports, Telegrams, Applications, and Other Papers Relating to
Burials of Service Personnel, 1915–1939, World War I Burial Files:
Marion M. Collier.
Arthur N. Fauble.
Frederick C. Hinds.
John T. Ring.
Carl Williams.
Official Military Personnel Files, 1905–1998:
James N. Allen.
Albert P. Baston.
John D. Bowling Jr.
Marion M. Collier.
Louis De Roode.
Charles A. Doyen.
Graves B. Erskine.
Arthur N. Fauble.

Leon D. Huffstater.
John A. Hughes.
John A. Lejeune.
Bernard C. McEntee.
Adrian J. Michels.
Luther W. Pilcher.
James F. Robertson.
Vernon L. Somers.
Robert W. Voeth.
Carl F. Winn.
New York State Archives, Albany, NY
 Henry Hoge. World War I Veterans Service Data.
Norwich University, Record of War Service, Archives and Special Collections, North-
 field, VT
 Harold D. Campbell.
 Raymond E. Knapp.
 Clinton I. Smallman.
 Dwight F. Smith.
Oregon State Archives, Salem, OR
 Emery A. Bartlett File. Oregon War Records. World War I.
Princeton University, Seely G. Mudd Manuscript Library, Princeton, NJ
 Thomas H. Miles Jr. Alumni Record.
 Louis F. Timmerman Jr. Alumni Record.
Private Collections
 Don Butler. Newspaper Collection.
 Richard Kimbrough and Grace Neighbors. Richard W. Murphy Family Scrapbook.
 C. Starry Kirkham. Orlando C. Crowther Letters.
 Dale Niesen. David M. Vincent Letters.
 Macon C. Overton Jr. Macon C. Overton Papers.
 Robin Richmond. Episode 6, "Long Tiring March Begins." In *The War Diary
 of Clarence Richmond,* ed. Robin Richmond. http://wavefront.com/~rrichmon
 /wardiary/diary6.htm. Accessed November 9, 1998.
Rutherford B. Hayes Museum and Library, Fremont, OH
 Elton E. Mackin. Oral history interview by Carl D. Klopfenstein, June 29, 1973.
State Historical Society of Iowa, Des Moines, IA
 Eldon Freel Papers.
University of Maryland Archives, College Park, MD
 John D. Bowling Jr. Alumni File.
US Army Heritage and Education Center, Carlisle, PA
 World War I Veterans Survey, 2nd Division:
 Frank J. Franek, 9th Infantry.
 Ladislav T. Janda, 9th Infantry.
 Peter W. Kegerreis, 9th Infantry.
 Russell A. Warner, 2nd Engineers.

Virginia Military Institute Archives, Lexington, VA
  George B. Lockhart Alumni File.
  Richard W. Murphy Student Record.
  Allan C. Perkinson Alumni File.
  Fielding S. Robinson Alumni File.
  Lemuel C. Shepherd Student Record.
  Vernon L. Somers Alumni File.
  Edmund C. Waddill Alumni File.
Virginia Tech, Carol M. Newman Library Special Collections, Blacksburg, VA
  Lloyd W. Williams Alumni File.
Washington State University, Manuscripts, Archives, and Special Collections, Pullman, WA
  C. Boyd Maynard Alumni File.
World War I Personal Experience Monographs, Donovan Research Library, Maneuver Center of Excellence Libraries, Fort Benning, GA
  Raymond E. Knapp. "Operations of the 3rd Battalion, 5th Regiment, U.S. Marines in Belleau Wood, June 5–28, 1918." Company Officers Course, 1924–1925.
  Henry L. Larsen. "The Battle of Belleau Woods." Advanced Infantry Course, 1924–1925.
  Robert E. Messersmith. "Operations of Company E, 78th Company, 6th Regiment Marines, 2nd Division at Belleau
  Woods, June 1–13, 1918." Advanced Infantry Course, 1928–1929.

Books and Articles

Adjutant General's Office. *Official Army Register for 1914.* Washington, DC: Government Printing Office, 1914.
American Battle Monuments Commission. *2nd Division Summary of Operations in the World War.* Washington, DC: Government Printing Office, 1944.
Americans Defending Democracy: Our Soldiers' Own Stories. New York: World War Stories, 1919.
Anderson, Joseph R. *Virginia Military Institute, World War Record.* Richmond, VA: Richmond Press, 1920.
Annual Report of the Secretary of the Navy for the Fiscal Year 1918. Washington, DC: Government Printing Office, 1919.
Ashley, Jonathan Porter. *An Ashley Genealogy.* Deerfield, MA, 1924.
Asprey, Robert B. *At Belleau Wood.* New York: G. P. Putnam's, 1965.
———. *The German High Command at War.* New York: William Morrow, 1991.
Ayres, Leonard P. *The War with Germany: A Statistical Summary.* Washington, DC: Government Printing Office, 1919.
Barde, Robert E. *The History of Marine Corps Competitive Marksmanship.* Washington, DC: Government Printing Office, 1961.
Barton, George Preston, and Emma Welles Barton, comps. *War Service Record and Memorial of Lester Clement Barton, Thyrza Barton Dean, William Sidney Barton, Raymond Welles Barton.* Rochester, NY: E. R. Andrews, 1922.

"Belleau Wood." *Leatherneck Magazine* 6, 23 (June 9, 1923).

"Belleau Wood Day Celebrated Widely." *Leatherneck Magazine* 6, 23 (June 9, 1923).

"Belleau Wood, Retreat Hell, We Just Got Here." *Marine Corps Gazette* 29, 1 (January 1945).

Benjamin, Romeyn P. "June, 1918." *Marines Magazine* 4, 4 (July 1919).

Benwell, Harry A. *History of the Yankee Division.* Boston: Cornhill, 1919.

Bevilacqua, Alan. "From Exile to Hero, Henry Hulbert." *Leatherneck Magazine,* January 1999.

Blake, Robert W. *Bayonets and Bougainvilleas.* Bloomington, IN: 1stBooks Library, 2001.

———. *From Belleau to Bougainville: The Oral History of Major General Robert L. Blake USMC and the Travel Journal of Rosselet Wallace Blake.* Bloomington, IN: Author House, 2004.

Blakeney, Jane. *Heroes: U.S. Marine Corps, 1861–1955; Armed Forces Awards, Flags.* Washington, DC: Guthrie Lithograph, 1957.

Braun, Gustav J., and Trevor W. Swett, comps. *Translations: War Diaries of German Units Opposed to the Second Division (Regular) 1918.* 5 vols. Washington, DC: Second Division Historical Section, Army War College, 1930–1932.

Bullard, Robert E. *Personalities and Reminiscences of the War.* New York: Doubleday, Page, 1925.

Catlin, Albertus W. *With the Help of God and a Few Marines.* Garden City, NY: Doubleday, Page, 1919.

Clark, George B., ed. *Decorated Marines of the Fourth Brigade in World War I.* Jefferson, NC: McFarland, 2007.

———. *His Time in Hell: A Texas Marine in France. The World War I Memoir of Warren R. Jackson.* Novato, CA: Presidio Press, 2001.

———. *History of the Fifth Regiment Marines (May 1917–December 31, 1918).* Pike, NH: Brass Hat, 1995.

———. *History of the First Battalion, 5th Marines, June 1917–August 1919.* Pike, NH: Brass Hat, 2002.

———. *The History of the Third Battalion, 5th Marines, 1917–1918.* Pike, NH: Brass Hat, 1996.

———. *A List of Officers of the 4th Marine Brigade.* Pike, NH: Brass Hat, n.d.

———. *We Can Take It and We Attack.* Pike, NH: Brass Hat, 1994.

Clifford, John H. "The Wounding of General Catlin." *Marines Magazine* 4, 7 (July 1919).

Cooke, Elliot D. *Americans versus Germans: The First AEF in Action.* New York: Penguin Books, 1942. Republished from Cooke's *Infantry Journal* articles "We Can Take It" (July–August 1937) and "We Attack" (November–December 1937).

———. "We Attack." *Infantry Journal,* November–December 1937.

———. "We Can Take It." *Infantry Journal,* July–August 1937.

Cowing, Kemper Frey, comp. *"Dear Folks at Home—": The Glorious Story of the United States Marines in France as Told by Their Letters from the Battlefield.* Edited by Courtney R. Cooper. Boston: Houghton Mifflin, 1919.

Crowell, Benedict. *America's Munitions, 1917–1918*. Washington, DC: Government Printing Office, 1919.

Cullum, George W. *Biographical Register of the Officers and Graduates of the U.S. Military Academy at West Point, N.Y., from Its Establishment in 1802*. 7 vols. Chicago: R. R. Donnelly & Sons, Lakeside Press, 1930.

Culver Military Academy. *Roll Call*. Chicago: Rogers, 1907, 1917.

Curtis, T. J., and L. R. Long. *History of the Sixth Machine Gun Battalion, Fourth Brigade, U.S. Marines, Second Division, and Its Participation in the Great War*. Neuwied-on-the-Rhine, Germany, n.p., 1919.

Donaldson, George H., and Willoughby Jenkins. *Seventy-Eighth Company, Sixth Marines, Second Division, Army of Occupation*. Neuwied, Germany: n.p., 1919.

Dunbeck, Charles, ed. *History of the Second Battalion, 5th Regiment, U.S. Marines, June 1st–January 1st 1919*. N.p., n.d.

Ellis, William A. *Norwich University, 1819–1911: Her History, Her Graduates, Her Roll of Honor*. Montpelier, VT: Capital City Press, 1911.

Feland, Logan. "Retreat, Hell." *Marine Corps Gazette* 6, 3 (September 1921).

Ferrell, Robert H., ed. *In the Company of Generals: The World War I Diary of Pierpont L. Stackpole*. Columbia: University of Missouri Press, 2009.

Field, Harry B., and Henry G. James. *Over the Top with the 18th Company, 5th Marines: A History*. 1919. Reprint, Rodenbach, Germany: n.p., n.d.

"First Marine Killed in Enemy in France." *Recruiters' Bulletin* 4, 8 (June 1918).

Foster, Pell W. *A Short History of Battery "B," 12th Field Artillery, Second Division in the World War*. New York: Evening Post Printing Office, 1921.

Fox, Henry L., ed. *What Our "Boys" Did over There: By "Themselves."* New York: Allied Overseas Veterans, 1918.

"General Gouraud Reviews Marines." *Leatherneck Magazine* 6, 28 (July 14, 1923).

General Staff, War Office, Great Britain. *The German Army Handbook of 1918*. Yorkshire, UK: Front Line Books, 2008.

George, David L. *War Memoirs of David Lloyd George*. Vol. 6. London: Ivor, Nicholson & Watson, 1936.

Gibbons, Floyd. *And They Thought We Wouldn't Fight*. New York: George H. Doran, 1918.

Gulberg, Martin. *A War Diary: Into This Story Is Woven an Experience of Two Years' Service in the World War with the 75th Company 6th Regiment United States Marines*. Reprint, Pike, NH: Brass Hat, 1993.

Hamilton, Craig, and Louise Corbin, eds. *Echoes from over There: By the Men of the Army and Marine Corps Who Fought in France*. New York: Soldiers' Publishing Company, 1919.

Harbord, James G. *The American Army in France: 1917–1919*. Cranbury, NJ: Scholars Bookshelf, 2006.

———. *Leaves from a War Diary*. New York: Dodd, Mead, 1931.

Hearings before the Committee on Naval Affairs of the House of Representatives on Estimates Submitted by the Secretary of the Navy, 65th Congress. Washington, DC: Government Printing Office, 1918.

Hedwig, Holger H. *The First World War: Germany and Austria-Hungary, 1914–1918*. London: Arnold, 1997.

Hemrick, Levi E. *Once a Marine*. New York: Carlton Press, 1968.

"Heroes of Belleau Come Back Smiling." *Recruiters' Bulletin* 4, 11 (September 1918).

Herron, Frank. "Private Eugene Lee." *Leatherneck Magazine* 87, 1 (January 2004).

In Memoriam, Private Emery Augustus Bartlett 1895–1918, a Hero of Belleau Wood. N.p., n.d.

Intelligence Section, General Staff, American Expeditionary Force. *Histories of Two Hundred and Fifty-One Divisions of the German Army Which Participated in the World War, 1914–1918*. Washington, DC: Government Printing Office, 1919.

Janney, Stuart S., and Karl Singewald. *Maryland in the World War, 1917–1919: Military and Naval Service Records*. 2 vols. Baltimore: Maryland War Records Commission, 1933.

"Jimmy—The Anteater." *Recruiters' Bulletin* 3, 12 (October 1917).

Johnson, Douglas V., II, and Rolfe L. Hillman Jr. *Soissons, 1918*. College Station: Texas A&M Press, 1999.

Ketcham, Charles A., ed. "In Memoriam, Lt. Thomas Williams Ashley, USMC." *Marines Magazine* 6, 9 (September 1921).

Lambert, Frank X. "The Marine Corps League News." *Leatherneck,* November 1930.

Lejeune, John A. *The Reminiscences of a Marine*. Philadelphia: Dorrance, 1930.

Letters of Lambert A. Wood, First Lieutenant, U.S.A. from "Somewhere in France" to His Parents Dr. and Mrs. W. L. Wood, Portland, Oregon. Portland, OR: Louis H. Strickland, 1919.

Liggett, Hunter. *A.E.F.: Ten Years Ago in France*. New York: Dodd, Mead, 1928.

———. *Commanding an American Army*. Boston: Houghton Mifflin, 1925.

[Lovejoy, Dana]. "That's How It Feels to Be Shot." *Marines Magazine* 4, 7 (July 1919).

Ludendorff, Erich. *Ludendorff's Own Story, August 1914–November 1918: The Great War from the Siege of Liège to the Signing of the Armistice as Viewed from the Grand Headquarters of the German Army*. New York: Harper, 1919.

Mackin, Elton E. *Suddenly We Didn't Want to Die: Memoirs of a World War I Marine*. Novato, CA: Presidio Press, 1996.

"Many Travelers Visit Belleau Wood." *Leatherneck Magazine* 12 (October 7, 1922).

Mattfeldt, Clyburn Otto, comp. *Records of the Second Division (Regular)*. 10 vols. Washington, DC: US Army War College Historical Section, 1924–1928.

McClellan, Edwin N. "The Battle of Belleau Wood." *Marine Corps Gazette* 5, 4 (December 1920).

———. "A Brief History of the Fourth Brigade of Marines." *Marine Corps Gazette* 5, 4 (December 1919).

———. *The United States Marine Corps in the World War*. Washington, DC: Government Printing Office, 1920.

Mead, Frederick S., ed. *Harvard's Military Record in the World War*. Boston: Harvard Alumni Association, 1921.

Ministère de la Guerre, Etat-Major de l'Armée, Service Historique. *Les Armées Françaises dans la Grande Guerre.* Paris: Service Historique de la Défense, 1929–1934.

Mitchell, William A. *The Official History of the Second Engineer Regiment and Second Engineer Train in the World War.* San Antonio TX, San Antonio Printing Company, 1920.

"The Monogram Men." *Notre Dame Scholastic* 50 (December 9, 1916).

Moore, William B. "The Bloody Angle of the AEF." *American Legion Weekly* 4, 8 (February 24, 1922).

Morrey, Willard I., ed. *The History of the 96th Company, 6th Marine Regiment in World War I.* Quantico, VA: US Marine Corps, 1967.

Mott, T. Bentley, trans. *The Memoirs of Marshal Foch.* London: William Heinemann, 1931.

Neiberg, Michael S. *The Second Battle of the Marne.* Bloomington: Indiana University Press, 2008.

Nelson, Havelock D. "In Action, Another True Tale of the 97th Company in Action." *Leatherneck Magazine* 23, 6 (June 1940).

———. "Lucy Le Bocage." *Leatherneck Magazine* 23, 2 (February 1940).

———. "Paris Metz Road." *Leatherneck Magazine* 23, 1 (January 1940).

Nettleton, George Henry, and Lottie Genevieve Bishop. *Yale in the World War.* 2 vols. New Haven, CT: Yale University Press, 1925.

Nilo, James R. "The Babe." *Marine Corps Gazette* 55, 11 (November 1971).

"The 1915 Football Season." *Notre Dame Scholastic* 49 (December 11, 1915).

Norwich University. *War Whoop* [yearbook]. Northfield, VT, 1908, 1917.

Office of the Adjutant General of the Army. *American Decorations (1862–1926).* Washington, DC: Government Printing Office, 1927.

"On the Heels of the Hun." *Recruiters' Bulletin* 1, 1 (November 1918).

Our Navy: The Standard Publication of the U.S. Navy. New York: Our Navy Publishing Company, 1919.

Owen, Peter F. *To the Limit of Endurance: A Battalion of Marines in the Great War.* College Station: Texas A&M University Press, 2007.

———, ed. *The World War Memoirs of Don V. Paradis, Gunnery Sergeant, USMC.* Morrisville, NC: Lulu.com, 2010.

Palmer, Frederick. "Pershing's Generals." *Colliers Magazine,* April 19, 1919.

Pattullo, George. *Hellwood.* New York: US Marine Corps Mobilization Bureau, 1918.

Pershing, John J. *My Experiences in the First World War.* Vol. 2. New York: Frederick A. Stokes, 1931.

Platt, Jonas. "Holding Back the Marines." *Ladies' Home Journal* 36, 9 (September 1919).

"Portrait of General Harbord to Be Painted." *Leatherneck Magazine* 5, 51 (October 21, 1922).

Potter, Frank H. *The Potter Record.* N.p., 1921.

Powis, Albert E. "A Leatherneck in France, 1917–1919." *Military Images Magazine* 3, 2 (September–October 1981).

Proctor, John C., Edwin M. Williams, and Frank P. Black, eds. *Washington—Past and Present: A History.* Vol. 5. New York: Lewis Historical Publishing, 1930–1932.

"Quantico Entertains 3,000 Shriners on Belleau Wood Day." *Leatherneck Magazine* 6, 23 (June 9, 1923).

Rendinell, J. E., and George Pattullo. *One Man's War: The Diary of a Leatherneck.* Whitefish, MT: Kessinger Publishing, 2010.

Richards, George. "Don't Give up the Ship." *Marine Corps Gazette* 7, 1 (March 1922).

Rockne, Knute. *The Four Winners—the Head—the Hands—the Foot—and the Ball.* New York: Devin Adair, 1925.

Savageau, Raymond, ed. *History of the Class of 1919, Sheffield Scientific School, Yale University.* New Haven, CT: Class Book Committee, 1919.

Scanlon, William T. *God Have Mercy on Us: A Story of 1918.* Boston: Houghton Mifflin, 1929.

Scarbrough, Byron, ed. *They Called Us Devil Dogs.* Morrisville, NC: LuLu, 2005.

Sellers, William McB., and George B. Clark, eds. *World War I Memoirs of Lieutenant Colonel James McBrayer Sellers, USMC.* Pike, NH: Brass Hat, 1997.

Showalter, Dennis. *Instrument of War: The German Army 1914–18.* London: Osprey Publishing, 2016.

Sibley, Berton W. *History of the Third Battalion, Sixth Regiment, U.S. Marines.* Hillsdale, MI: Akers, MacRitchie & Hurlbut, 1919.

Society of the Fifth Division. *The Official History of the Fifth Division, U.S.A.* New York: Wynkoop Hallenbeck Crawford, 1919.

Spaulding, Oliver Lyman, and John Womack Wright. *The Second Division, American Expeditionary Force in France, 1917–1919.* 1937. Reprint, Nashville, TN: Battery Press, 1989.

State of Ohio. *The Official Roster of Ohio Soldiers, Sailors, and Marines in the World War, 1917–18.* Columbus, OH: F. J. Heer, 1926.

Stringer, Harry R., ed. *Heroes All! A Compendium of the Names and Official Citations of the Soldiers and Citizens of the United States and of Her Allies Who Were Decorated by the American Government for Exceptional Heroism and Conspicuous Service above and beyond the Call of Duty in the War with Germany, 1917–1919.* Washington, DC: Fassett, 1919.

———. *The Navy Book of Distinguished Service: An Official Compendium of the Names and Citations of the Men of the United States Navy, Marine Corps, Army, and Foreign Governments Who Were Decorated by the Navy Department, for Extraordinary Service above and beyond the Call of Duty in the World War.* Washington, DC: Fassett, 1921.

Strott, George C. *The Medical Department of the United States Navy with the Army and Marine Corps in France in World War I: Its Functions and Employment.* Washington, DC: Bureau of Medicine and Surgery, US Navy Department, 1947.

"Tales Told by Overseas Marines." *Recruiters' Bulletin* 4, 12 (October 1918).

Taylor, Emerson G. *New England in France, 1917–1919: A History of the Twenty-Sixth Division, U.S.A.* Boston: Houghton Mifflin, 1920.

———. *United States Army in the World War, 1917–1919: Reports of the Commander-in-Chief, Staff Sections and Services.* 17 vols. Washington, DC: Government Printing Office, 1988–1992.

United States Army Center for Military History. *Order of Battle of the United States Land Forces in the World War: American Expeditionary Forces.* 2 vols. Washington, DC: Government Printing Office, 1988.

———. *U.S. Army in the World War, 1917–1919.* 17 vols. 1948. Reprint, Washington, DC: United States Army Center for Military History, 1988–1992.

United States Military Academy Association of Graduates. *Fiftieth Annual Report of the Association of Graduates of the United States Military Academy, 19 June 1919.* Saginaw, MI: Seeman & Peters, 1919.

United States Naval Academy. *Lucky Bag* [yearbook]. Annapolis, MD, 1915.

United States Navy. *Annual Report of the Secretary of the Navy.* Washington, DC: Government Printing Office, 1917.

United States War Department, Office of the Adjutant General. *Tables of Organization, United States Army, 1917.* Washington, DC: Government Printing Office, 1917.

———. *Tables of Organization and Equipment, United States Army, 1918.* Washington, DC: Government Printing Office, 1918.

Unit Historian. *The History of the 1st Battalion, 5th Marines, 1917–1919.* Germany: Privately printed, 1919.

University of Minnesota. *Gopher* [yearbook]. Minneapolis: University of Minnesota, 1920.

Virginia Military Institute. *The Bomb.* Lexington: Virginia Military Institute, 1917.

Von Hindenburg, Paul. *Out of My Life.* London: Cassell, 1920.

Wilder, Amos N. *Armageddon Revisited.* New Haven, CT: Yale University Press, 1994.

Williams, Ralph L. *The Luck of a Buck.* Madison, WI: Fitchburg Press, 1985.

Wilmeth, J. D. "Bois de la Brigade de Marine." *Marine Corps Gazette* 23, 1 (March 1939).

Wisconsin and Michigan War History Commissions. *The 32nd Division in the World War, 1917–1918.* Milwaukee: Wisconsin Print Co., 1920.

Wise, Frederic M. *A Marine Tells It to You.* New York: J. H. Sears, 1929.

Wise, Jennings C. *The Turn of the Tide: American Operations at Cantigny, Chateau Thierry, and the Second Battle of the Marne.* New York: H. Holt, 1920.

"Wounded Belleau Wood Heroes." *Recruiters' Bulletin* 1, 2 (December 1918).

"Writes New March Called Belleau Wood." *Leatherneck Magazine* 6, 18 (May 5, 1923).

Zaloga, Steven J. *French Light Tanks of World War I.* New York: Osprey Publishing, 2010.

Newspapers

Akron (OH) Evening Times. "Cuyahoga Falls Boy is Killed in France," June 26, 1918.

Atlanta Constitution. George H. Seldes, "Between Battles with Our Fighting Men in France," October 6, 1918.

Baltimore Sun. "Wounded Marine Lived Here," April 27, 1918; "Capt. Speer Was Gassed," June 20, 1918; "War Veteran, 20, Cited," March 7, 1919.

Bee (Danville, VA). "Major Keyser Hero, Advanced on Lineal List," February 28, 1923.

Binghamton (NY) City Press. "Naming a Street for City Hero Is Considered," October 2, 1943.

Bisbee (AZ) Daily Review. "Arizona Hero Home from over There," November 10, 1918.

Boston Globe. "Capt Lester S. Wass Killed in France," August 20, 1918; "Capt Lester S. Wass of Marine Corps Killed," August 21, 1918; "Captain Frank Whitehead a Veteran Leatherneck," February 16, 1919; "Maj Murray Takes Charge of Local Marine Corps Recruiting Office," August 19, 1919.

Buffalo (NY) Evening News. "Croix de Guerre Marine Succeeds Major Yates as Recruiting Officer," August 2, 1919.

Butler County Democrat (Hamilton, OH). "Edward and Louis Steinmetz Give up Their Lives in Great World War," September 19, 1918.

Carolina Mountaineer and Waynesville (NC) Courier. "His Death Confirmed," May 8, 1919; "Memorial Service," May 15, 1919.

Catholic Tribune (St. Joseph, MO). "Young Men Show Valor," July 20, 1918.

Chicago Tribune. "Newman the Gadder, at Orchestra Hall on Paris, 1918," October 10, 1918.

Courier Journal (Louisville, KY). "Louisville Soldier Is Promoted for Bravery," March 7, 1917; "Tells of Yanks Crossing the Marne," August 24, 1918.

Daily Times (Seattle, WA). "Leads Victorious Marines," June 13, 1918.

Detroit Free Press. "Allies Praise Battle Worth of Americans," July 11, 1918; "Detroit Boy Slain in Action Had Premonition of Death," August 6, 1918.

Eagle (Bryan, TX). "Wife of Officer Missing in Action Wants Information," July 2, 1918.

El Paso (TX) Herald. "They Got Wrong Arm," August 5, 1919.

Elsinore (CA) Press. "Fighting Marine Home with Medals and Scars," August 1, 1919.

Escanaba (MI) Morning Press. "Former Esky Boy Is Real Trench Hero," July 12, 1918; "Friends Wearing the Gold Star," July 17, 1918; "Twenty Years Later," July 13, 1938.

Evening News (Harrisburg, PA). "A Hero Every Day, Brave Deeds of Men in American Fighting Service," September 23, 1918.

Evening Public Ledger (Philadelphia). "He Was a Corporal Once," August 16, 1921.

Evening Report (Lebanon, PA). "The Washington Cornet Band," May 27, 1921.

Evening Star (Washington, DC). ; "Commands the Marines on the Marne," June 10, 1918; "Big 159-Pound Shell Misses Maj. Harry Lay," July 27, 1918.

Evening Sun (Baltimore). "Wounded in Action on the Western Front," July 10, 1918.

Houston Post. "Herbert Dunlavy Was a Promising Athlete," July 4, 1918; "Tells Story of Houston Boys' Deaths," September 4, 1918.

Huntington (IN) Herald. "Native Austrian Cause of Emperors Grief," November 4, 1918.

Indianapolis News. "First Word of Major Schearer Is Received," March 12, 1918; "Officer of Heroic U.S. Marines Here on Visit with Parents," August 29, 191.

Iron County Record (Cedar City, UT). "Private Citizen Gets French Croix de Guerre," May 30, 1919.

Ithaca (NY) Journal. "Honor Cross and Promotion Asked for Major Bouton," August 10, 1918; "Tompkins Men Fight Gallantly on Marne Front," June 13, 1918.

La Crosse (WI) Tribune and Leader Press. "Nine More Badger Mothers, Widows Go to France," May 24, 1932.

Lancaster (OH) Eagle-Gazette. "Base Ball," June 13, 1918.

Lebanon (PA) Daily News. "Sergeant Stover's Body to Be Brought Home," August 9, 1918.

Los Angeles Herald. "Pamona Boy, 19, Wins French War Cross," October 4, 1918, 10.

Los Angeles Times. "Son-in-Law of Gov. Stephens Was Hero," November 24, 1918; Yolanda Rodriguez, "Marine History Pays a Visit in Dress Blues," February 17, 1990.

Minneapolis Journal. "Hun Called Dirty Fighters," August 25, 1918, General News and City section.

Montclair (NJ) Times. "Navy Cross for Dead Hero," December 25, 1920; "Funeral of Lieutenant Synott," September 10, 1921.

New Castle (PA) Herald. "A Hero Every Day, Brave Deeds of Men in American Fighting Service," August 26, 1918.

New North (Rhinelander, WI). "Arbor Vitae Boy Slain in France," April 18, 1918.

News and Observer (Raleigh, NC). "Morrison to Get Right into the Race," December 15, 1918.

News Tribune (Waco, TX). "Theodore Roosevelt and John W. Thomason, Jr. Heroes of the Service," September 4, 1927.

New York Herald. "American Flier Wounded," July 8, 1918; "Won D.S.C. and Swam River on Horse to Get It," July 11, 1918.

New York Times. "Marines Win Name of Devil Hounds," June 8, 1918; "Clemenceau Congratulates Belleau Wood Victors on a Neat Job Done in a Way 'Peculiarly American,'" June 28, 1918; "Belleau Wood," June 29, 1918; "French Generals Proud of Our Men," July 5, 1918; "J. F. Singleton Listed among Dead in France," July 7, 1918; "American Stop Raid," July 12, 1918; "Father Brady Back, a Hero of Marines," March 3, 1919; "5,199 Marines Lost in Belleau Wood Area; General Barnett Discloses Casualties of the Brigade in the Action North of Chateau Thierry," April 23, 1919; "Paris War Orphans Parade and Cheer," July 4, 1920.

New York Tribune. "Marines Calmly Shaved after Belleau Battle," August 11, 1918.

Norwich Record (Northfield, VT). "Late Col. Sibley, '00," Served in Two Wars," April 28, 1944.

Ogden (UT) Standard. "If Either of Us Should Fall, Write Mother," November 29, 1918.

Oregon Daily Journal (Portland). "Lieutenant Wood Killed in Action in Marne Battle," August 5, 1918.

Passaic (NJ) Daily News. "Passaic Man with Marines Believed Killed in Action," July 8, 1918; "Lieutenant Synnott Is Killed at Belleau Wood," July 11, 1918.

Philadelphia Inquirer. "Philadelphia Homes Hit by War Loss, Guard Units Suffer Most," August 10, 1918.

Pullman (WA) Herald. "Wounded Sergeant Saw Maynard Fall," December 13, 1918; "Body of Pullman Hero in Last Resting Place," July 1, 1921.

Quad-City Times (Davenport, IA). "Cite Maquoketa Boy for Bravery, September 1, 1919; "Veteran Celebrates 100 Years," January 25, 1995.

Quantico (VA) Sentry. "Controversy over Legend Clarified by Marine Captain," June 13, 1936.

Reveille (Norwich University, Northfield, VT). "Commencement Week," June 1900.

Sacramento Bee. "Major Zane Died of Wounds, Not Influenza," November 16, 1918.

San Francisco Chronicle. "Shelled out 'Y' Man Hunts for Wounded," July 21, 1918; "Pastor of San Rafael Cited for Bravery," September 9, 1918.

Saskatoon (SK) Daily Star. "Courageous Y.M.C.A. Worker," June 28, 1918.

Star Tribune (Minneapolis). "Carleton Wallace Returns from the War," December 20, 1918.

St. Louis Post Dispatch. "St. Louis Captain Missing and Two Marines Killed," June 26, 1918; "2 St. Louisans with Marines Are Killed," June 26, 1918; "Writes of Brilliant Attack of U.S. Marines," August 14, 1918; obituary of Eugene S. Schrautemeier, September 25, 1921.

Sun (Pittsburg, KS). "Saw Hanbery in a Base Hospital," August 27, 1918.

Tuscaloosa (AL) News. "Tribute to Richard W. Murphy," June 18, 1918; "New Stories of the American Soldiers Abroad," September 15, 1918.

Twin City Sentinel (Winston-Salem, NC). "Letter Received from Comrade of John Ring," August 17, 1918.

Washington Herald. "Some Washington Men Who Fought at Chateau Thierry," October 27, 1918.

Washington Post. "Huns in France Face Noted American Generals," June 11, 1918; "Clemenceau Lauds American Troops," June 28, 1918; "Maj. Lay Safe, Dispatch Says," August 3, 1918; "Relics Strew Marines' Woods," August 25, 1919; "U.S. Veteran Kills Self by Graves of Comrades," April 3, 1928; "2 U.S. Soldiers' Bodies Found in Belleau Wood," August 21, 1928.

Washington Star. "Commands the Marines on the Marne," June 10, 1918.

Weekly Citizen Democrat (Poplar Bluff, MO). "Germans Fire on Own Men; Get P.B. Man," September 12, 1918.

Western Sentinel (Winston-Salem, NC). "Funeral Services for Corporal John Ring," May 17, 1921.

Winston-Salem (NC) Journal. "Kernersville," August 15, 1918.

INDEX

1st Moroccan Division, *continued*
  gains at Soissons on July 18, 285–286
  impact of Soissons on the outcome of
    World War I and, 344
  morning assault at Soissons on July 18,
    237, 241, 243, 246, 253, 258, 261
I US Corps, 168, 177, 179, 186, 187, 188
2nd American Infantry Division
  Allied grand strategy in mid-1918 and,
    182
  American I Corps and, 177, 179
  American III Corps and, 181
  Army-Marine controversy over Belleau
    Wood and, 351
  assignment to the French Group of Armies
    of the Reserve, 13
  assignment to the French X Corps, 10
  changes in the Allied command structure
    prior to Soissons and, 186, 187,
    188–189
  command changes within prior to
    Soissons, 189–190
  creation and organizational structure of, 8
  first combat casualties in France, 10–11
  Germany's Operation Blücher and, 13
  James Harbord assigned command of,
    170, 185, 187–189
  James Harbord's reassignment from,
    350–351
  John Lejeune as commander, 350–351
  movement to the Marne, May 31–June 1,
    15–20
  See also 4th Marine Brigade; 9th Infantry
    Regiment, 2nd Division; 23rd Infantry
    Regiment, 2nd Division
2nd American Infantry Division (Belleau
    Wood)
  actions on June 3, 25–29, 36–38, 39, 42
  actions on June 4, 45–58
  attack by the 3rd Battalion, 5th Marines
    on June 6, 88–103
  attack by the 3rd Battalion, 6th Marines
    on June 6, 107–131, 132, 135–136
  casualty figures, 154
  Clemenceau controversy and, 161–162
  fight for Hill 142 on June 5–6, 59–83
  Pershing's response to the battle and,
    160–161
  relief from combat, 177–180
  See also Belleau Wood, Battle of
2nd American Infantry Division (Soissons)
  5th Marines and (*see* 5th Marine
    Regiment)

  6th Marines and (*see* 6th Marine
    Regiment)
  attack orders for July 18, 194
  attack orders for July 19, 287
  casualty figures, 329, 330, 331–332, 349
  change of division headquarters to
    Beaurepaire Farm on July 18, 286–287
  condition at the end of July 18, 284–286
  controversy over who captured Vierzy, 367
  daybreak assault of the 9th and 23rd
    Infantry Regiments on July 18,
    223–232, 234
  evening assault of the 9th and 23rd
    Infantry Regiments on July 18,
    264–265, 268–275, 277, 278–279
  headquarters at Taillefontaine, 207
  impact of Soissons on the outcome of
    World War I, 344
  marker at Tigny, 340–342
  morning assault of the 9th and 23rd
    Infantry Regiments on July 18, 241,
    243–248, 249, 250–251, 256–260, 261,
    262
  movement to jumping-off positions,
    198–203
  movement to Soissons, 190–195
  organization at Soissons, 224
  preparation for the July 19 assault, 287–290
  reserve units, 256–257, 259, 284–285, 331
  significance of the battle, 366–367, 368
  treatment of the injured from July 18,
    286–287
  units in reserve, 256–257
  withdrawal from the front lines on July
    19, 332, 333–334
  See also Soissons, Battle of
2nd American Infantry Division boulder
  at Le Thiolet, 22–23
  at Lucy-le-Bocage, 23–24
  at Soissons, 336
2nd Battalion, 2nd Engineer Regiment, 2nd
    Division
  at Belleau Wood, 82
  division reserves at Soissons, 194, 256,
    259, 284–285
  preparation for attack at Soissons on July
    19, 288, 289
  in reserve at Soissons on July 19, 331
2nd Battalion, 5th Marine Regiment, 2
2nd Battalion, 5th Marine Regiment (Belleau
    Wood)
  actions on June 3, 26, 29, 30, 31, 36, 37, 41
  actions on June 4, 47, 49–53, 57, 58